START-TO-FINISH
VISUAL BASIC 2005

Start-to-Finish Visual Basic 2005

Learn Visual Basic 2005 as You Design and Develop a Complete Application

Tim Patrick

✦✦ Addison-Wesley

Upper Saddle River, NJ • Boston • Indianapolis • San Francisco
New York • Toronto • Montreal • London • Munich • Paris • Madrid
Capetown • Sydney • Tokyo • Singapore • Mexico City

Many of the designations used by manufacturers and sellers to distinguish their products are claimed as trademarks. Where those designations appear in this book, and the publisher was aware of a trademark claim, the designations have been printed with initial capital letters or in all capitals.

The author and publisher have taken care in the preparation of this book, but make no expressed or implied warranty of any kind and assume no responsibility for errors or omissions. No liability is assumed for incidental or consequential damages in connection with or arising out of the use of the information or programs contained herein.

The publisher offers excellent discounts on this book when ordered in quantity for bulk purchases or special sales, which may include electronic versions and/or custom covers and content particular to your business, training goals, marketing focus, and branding interests. For more information, please contact:

U.S. Corporate and Government Sales
(800) 382-3419
corpsales@pearsontechgroup.com

For sales outside the United States, please contact:

International Sales
international@pearsoned.com

Safari BOOKS ONLINE ENABLED

This Book Is Safari Enabled

The Safari® Enabled icon on the cover of your favorite technology book means the book is available through Safari Bookshelf. When you buy this book, you get free access to the online edition for 45 days. Safari Bookshelf is an electronic reference library that lets you easily search thousands of technical books, find code samples, download chapters, and access technical information whenever and wherever you need it.

To gain 45-day Safari Enabled access to this book:

Go to http://www.awprofessional.com/safarienabled

Complete the brief registration form

Enter the coupon code **QWCR-PYSD-XF79-XYDG-PGTY**

If you have difficulty registering on Safari Bookshelf or accessing the online edition, please e-mail customer-service@safaribooksonline.com.

Visit us on the Web: www.awprofessional.com

Library of Congress Cataloging-in-Publication Data:

Patrick, Tim, 1966-
  Start-to-finish Visual Basic 2005 : learn Visual Basic 2005 as you design and develop a complete application / Tim Patrick. -- 1st ed.
     p. cm.   12-12-06
  ISBN 0-321-39800-9 (pbk. : alk. paper) 1. BASIC (Computer program language) 2. Microsoft Visual BASIC. 3. Application software--Development. 4. Microsoft .NET. I. Title.

  QA76.73.B3P25436 2006
  005.13'3—dc22

                              2006026655

ISBN 0-321-39800-9
Text printed in the United States on recycled paper at *R.R. Donnelley in Crawfordsville, IN.*
First printing, November 2006

To Maki, my lovely wife

CONTENTS

PREFACE

Welcome to *Start-to-Finish Visual Basic 2005*! I know you're going to enjoy it; I've read it five times already. You're probably anxious to get to Chapter 1, but I recommend you read this preface to make sure you paid for the right book.

Who Is Reading This Book?

Writing a book is a lot like writing a Visual Basic application. Well, except for the parts about finding a publisher and working with an editor. And then there's that pesky rule about correct spelling. Come to think of it, they're really quite different. But in one way, books and programs are similar: They are both written to meet the needs of the user. When writing software applications, the user's needs drive the organization and features of the final program. When writing a book, like the one you're looking at now, the needs of the user—that's you, the reader—drive the organization and features of the final text.

So it was with you in mind that I set out to write this book. Oh, there's the fame and the prestige, but it's really about you. You, the person who seeks to understand Visual Basic and the .NET Framework on which it is built. When I thought about you and your needs, I came up with these ideas:

- *You might know how to program, but maybe not.* In the programming world, there are four types of people: (1) those who already program joyfully; (2) those who don't program, but will learn it and love it; (3) those who don't program, but will learn it and struggle; and (4) those who should return this book immediately to the bookstore. If you are in one of the first three groups, this book is definitely for you. I believe that anyone who can break down a task into its basic step-by-step instructions can successfully program in Visual Basic. If you are unsure about your ability to quantify tasks in this way, you might want to start out with a book on basic programming concepts. One example is Dan Appleman's *How Computer Programming Works* (Apress, 2000).

■ *You might know how to program in Visual Basic or .NET, but maybe not.* And that's OK, because this book will teach you. Most of the chapters introduce important topics in Visual Basic and .NET development, like object-oriented programming concepts, or using the different types of variables available to you, or interacting with a database. If you already know how to use Visual Basic 6 or earlier, that's great, but it's not a prerequisite.

■ *You want to write programs.* Most programming books teach you to write code in ten-line increments. At least that's what's scattered throughout their pages. I've put some of those "code snippets" in this book. But I spend my days writing real programs, not ten-line sample programs. If you want to write whole programs, you should learn using whole programs. And so I also put a program in my book—*a whole program.* Over the next several hundred pages, I will develop a real program—a database for a small library—and you will write it with me.

I put all of these ideas into 25 easy-to-read chapters and had Addison-Wesley glue the pages together for your convenience. When you reach the index, you will have learned how to write complete programs in Visual Basic and .NET. It will be a programming adventure, so let's get started!

What's in This Book?

Since we are going to be spending a lot of time together, you probably want to know something about me. Well, my name is Tim Patrick, and I live just up the street from the big Microsoft campus. I've been writing programs for nearly 25 years. I spend my days writing custom database-oriented Visual Basic applications for small- to medium-sized businesses. And I'm not alone. Most Visual Basic developers write business-level software. If that's what you do, or plan to do, then you're in great company.

As you move through the pages of this book, you will read about the major .NET and Visual Basic activities that drive the development of business-level and general consumer applications. If you plan to do some other type of programming, such as games development, this book will be somewhat helpful, but I don't talk about advanced or specialized features such as interactive 3-D models or geometric transformations.

Each chapter discusses a major programming topic and then follows it up with a practical implementation of that topic: the creation of the Library database program. I don't show every line of code in the book; if I did, the book would weigh 53 pounds and cost $254.38, plus tax. To get every line of source code, you'll have to download the accompanying source code from the book's web site (www.awprofessional.com/titles/0321398009). The code and the book's text are united in one purpose: to train you in the skilled use of Visual Basic on the .NET platform, so that you can develop the highest-quality applications possible. The text and the source code both include valuable resources that you can use every day in your programming life.

What's in the Software Download?

You're going to like the download. It contains all the source code for the Library database project. What's cool is that when you install the source code examples, they become part of Visual Studio. Once installed, you can create a new chapter-specific project right from the **File ➤ New Project** menu in Visual Studio. Appendix A, "Installing the Software," has all of the download and installation details.

The project code was written using Visual Basic 2005 Professional Edition. Some portions may not be compatible with earlier .NET versions of the language. None of it is compatible with Visual Basic 6.0 or earlier, so don't even bother trying. The source code will work with any edition of Visual Basic 2005, including the Express Edition.

The source code also uses SQL Server 2005 for its database storage. You can use any edition of SQL Server 2005, including the Express Edition. Chapter 4, "Designing the Database," introduces databases and SQL Server 2005. If you will be using the database in an IT department-controlled network environment, you may need to talk with your IT department representative about installing the sample database. The SQL code I use is pretty vanilla, so it should work on previous versions of SQL Server, and it could be easily adjusted to work with Oracle, DB2, Microsoft Access, or other common database engines.

You can use the downloadable source code for your own projects, but please give credit where credit is due. There is a license agreement associated with the code (see Appendix B, "Software License Agreement"), so please don't go selling the software as your own work. Just to be on the safe side, I've added a few hard-to-find bugs. Just kidding! No, I'm not!

ACKNOWLEDGMENTS

The development of *Start-to-Finish Visual Basic 2005* has been a labor of love for me, and I am blessed to have had so many others go through the labor with me. Joan Murray was my Addison-Wesley editor for this project. She, along with Curt Johnson, Chris Zahn, and Jessica D'Amico, are really like a team of obstetricians. They take an author who is going through a labor of words, and deliver up a living and breathing book. Their skill and their bedside manner in this project have meant a lot to me.

Several other authors and programmers took time out of their day jobs to review each chapter of the book and point out its deficiencies, which were numerous before their arrival. I especially wish to thank Glenn Berry, Alex Bierhaus, Harry Chen, Ken Getz, Lowell Mauer, and Dan Sullivan for their superb comments.

Many thanks to Joe Binder, Jay Roxe, Prasadi de Silva, and Eric Knox, all members of the Visual Basic team at Microsoft. Each of them fielded a relentless onslaught of questions about esoteric Visual Basic and .NET features, and provided answers filled with knowledge, patience, and grace.

My agent, Claudette Moore, always deserves her own paragraph in any computer book I write. Not only does she do a great job at all of the normal agency things, but also she shares personally in the joys and sorrows of the authors under her charge. Thank you for another fun year in books.

To Maki, my wife, and to Spencer, my son, I give a special wave of thanks. If you've ever spent time with an author, then you know how cranky they can get. But Maki and Spencer combat crankiness with care and love, and it works. The words "thank you" seem so inadequate when I owe both of them so much. Thanks be to God because he provided such a tremendous family to me.

ABOUT THE AUTHOR

Tim Patrick is a software architect and developer with nearly 25 years of experience in designing and building custom software solutions. As a Microsoft Certified Solution Developer, he spends his days gainfully employed in writing Visual Basic 2005 applications. Tim is the author of *The Visual Basic Style Guide* and *The Visual Basic .NET Style Guide*, and co-author of *Visual Basic 2005 in a Nutshell* and *Visual Basic 2005 Cookbook*.

CHAPTER 1

INTRODUCING .NET

Welcome to .NET! I might as well have said, "Welcome to the Solar System," because like the solar system, .NET is huge. And it's complex. And it's filled with black holes and other things that don't always make sense. Yet it (.NET, not the universe) turns out to be a fantastic system in which to develop software applications.

The .NET Framework was not developed in a vacuum (unlike the universe); Microsoft designed it and its related development languages—especially C# and Visual Basic—to address various issues that plagued Windows software developers and users. To fully understand why .NET was necessary, we need to take a short trip down computer memory lane.

Before .NET

Practical general-purpose computers have been around since the mid-twentieth century. However, they were inaccessible to most people because (a) they cost millions of dollars, (b) they consumed gobs of electricity, (c) maintenance and programming could only be done by highly-trained specialists, and (d) they tended to clash with the living room furniture.

Fast forward about 30 years. IBM comes out with the "personal" computer. These "desktop" computers represented a great advance in technology, but only a minority of people ever used them. They continued to be expensive (thousands of dollars), and maintenance and programming still required significant investments in training. IBM PCs also looked hideous around the living room furniture.

Then came the Apple Macintosh. With its sleek design and its user-friendly functionality, it introduced the joy of computing to the masses. And while programming it was not always straightforward, it did give nice results. It's no wonder that Bill Gates decided to copy—oops, I mean improve upon—its functionality.

Microsoft Windows 1.0 brought a greater level of usability to the IBM/Intel computing platform. But it wasn't a free ride for programmers. MS-DOS development was hard enough without the addition of the "message pumps" and the hundreds of Application Programming Interface (API) calls needed by Windows programs. Visual Basic 1.0, introduced in 1991, greatly simplified the development process, but with the advent of 32-bit systems, ActiveX and COM components, and the Web, even VB programmers soon felt overwhelmed.

Throughout the 1990s, the situation only seemed to worsen. Microsoft saw increased competition in the form of the Java language and the Linux operating system. Hackers were exploiting buffer overruns and other security issues present in the Windows platform. Users experienced myriad computer problems stemming from conflicting standards, competing data integration technologies, registry bloat, and "DLL hell." In frustration, an Excel user's group set fire to the entire Microsoft campus in Redmond.

Well, it didn't get that bad. But Microsoft did see that it needed to address the overall software development and usability issues on its beloved Windows platform. Its solution came in the form of the .NET Framework.

Back to Introducing .NET

When Microsoft announced its plans for .NET, it surprised many developers, especially Visual Basic developers, who saw it as a giant step backward for "Rapid Application Development." But the release of the .NET Framework version 1.0 in 2002 did bring many needed benefits.

- *.NET introduced a unified programming environment.* All .NET-enabled languages compile to "Microsoft Intermediate Language" before being assembled into platform-specific machine code. Visual Basic and C# are language wrappers around this common .NET "language." Because all .NET-enabled compilers speak the same underlying language, they no longer suffer from the many data and language conflicts inherent in other component-based systems such as COM. The .NET version of Visual Studio also unified the standard user interface that lets programmers craft source code.

- *.NET committed developers to object-oriented technologies.* Not only does .NET fully embrace the object-oriented programming paradigm, *everything* in .NET is contained in an object: all data values, all source code blocks, and the plumbing for all user-initiated events. Everything appears in the context of an object.
- *.NET simplified Windows programming.* Programming in Visual Basic before .NET was easy enough, until it came time to interact with one of the API libraries, something that happened a lot in professional programming. With .NET, most of these APIs are replaced with a hierarchy of objects providing access to many commonly needed Windows features. Because the hierarchy is extensible, other vendors can add new functionality without disrupting the existing framework.
- *.NET enhanced security.* Users and administrators can now establish security rules for different .NET features to limit malicious programs from doing their damage. .NET's "managed" environment also resolved buffer overrun issues and memory leaks through features such as strong data typing and garbage collection.
- *.NET enhanced developer productivity through standards.* The .NET Framework is built upon and uses many new and existing standards, such as XML and SOAP. This enhances data interchange not only on the Windows platform, but also in interactions with other platforms and systems.
- *.NET enhanced Web-based development.* Until .NET, a lot of Web-based development was done using scripting languages. .NET brings the power of compiled, desktop development to the Internet.
- *.NET simplified the deployment of applications.* If .NET is installed on a system, releasing a program is as simple as copying its EXE file to the target system (although an install program is much more user-friendly). Features such as side-by-side deployment, ClickOnce deployment (new in 2005), and an end to file version conflicts and "DLL hell" (the presence of multiple versions of the same DLL on a system, or the inability to remove a version of a DLL) make desktop and Web-based deployments a snap.

If you didn't understand some of the terms used in this section, that's all right. You will encounter them again, with explanations, in later chapters.

The .NET Object

To fully understand software development in .NET, you must understand what an **object** is. (If you are familiar with object-oriented programming—OOP—then you can probably skip down to the next section, although you will miss some really great content.) Although some of this section's information will also appear in Chapter 8, "Classes and Inheritance," it is so important to the discussion of .NET that a portion appears here as well.

Objects and Data

From a programming standpoint, a computer performs four basic tasks:

1. It stores *data* in the computer's memory area.
2. It supports processing of this *data* through basic operations, including addition and subtraction, Boolean algebra, and text string manipulation.
3. It allows the user to interact with the *data* stored in memory.
4. It provides a way to bring the *data* in and out of memory, through input and output devices such as keyboards and printers, and through long-term storage media, such as hard drives.

The core of these four activities is **data**. Computers exist to manipulate data. Operating systems provide the basic foundation for these activities, but it is software applications that make these features—the ability to manipulate data—real and meaningful to the user. High-level programming languages are the primary tools used to develop these applications, each of which uses some general methods to make data manipulation features available to the programmer. Back in the good old days of assembly language development, if you knew the memory address of a piece of data, you could access and manipulate it directly. In early flavors of BASIC and in most other "procedural" languages, data was accessed through **variables**.

As languages grew in complexity and purpose, so did their view of data. In the LISP (short for "List Processing" or "Lots of Irritating Silly Parentheses") language, any data value exists within a larger *list* or *set* of data. But in .NET languages, data is viewed through the *object*.

Objects are collections of data values and associated source code. Whereas in older BASIC dialects, each data element was more or less independent through its named variable, related data values in OOP languages can be grouped into objects. Objects often include source code designed to manipulate the data values of that object.

Objects generally represent some *thing*, often a thing that has a real-world counterpart, whether physical or conceptual. For instance, your code may include a *House* object that has data **fields** or **properties** for the address, the exterior paint color, and the number of people living in the house. Associated source code could manage that data; a *Paint* **method** could alter the color value used for the exterior paint.

The data and code elements within an object are called **members**. Some members are hidden inside the object and can be accessed only by the object's source code. Other members are more public; any code in your application can use them, not just that subset of application code found inside the object. Consider a television as an object (see Figure 1-1).

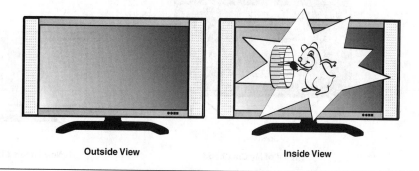

Outside View   **Inside View**

Figure 1-1 A TV: It's an object, not just objectionable.

The public members of a TV are generally easy to use: the power button, channel selector, volume control, and so on. They are the conduits through which the user controls the data values of the TV (its video and audio output). There are also hidden members inside of the TV; you could use these members to impact the picture and sound quality, although this would be a bad idea for most users. You don't want me messing with the internal members of your TV set, trust me. In the same way, an object doesn't want code outside of the object to mess with its internal members *except through the public members.* I don't care how a TV works internally, as long as I can get pictures and sound out of it by using the controls that are exposed (power, channel, volume).

Objects and Interfaces

The public members of an object represent its **interface**. If code outside of the object wants to manipulate the data belonging to that object, it uses the members of the interface. It doesn't have to figure out the hidden members or how they work, and that's good. It's especially good if those internal members ever change for any reason, which happens more often then you think. Consider how the internals of TVs have changed just in the last 30 years. Here's a drawing of the TV my family had when I was a kid. Compare it with modern flat-screen TVs available today (see Figure 1-2).

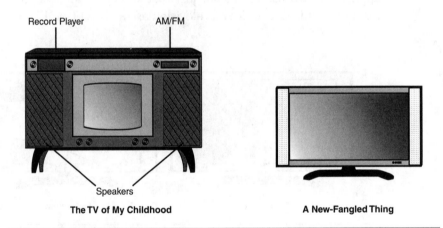

Figure 1-2 Are those really TVs?

My family's TV was cool. It had an AM/FM stereophonic hi-fi radio, a turntable that could play 33-1/3, 45, *and* 78 RPM records, and a large 19-inch display with vivid black-and-white crystal-clear display. You could hide two kids behind it when playing hide and seek. And my friend who had the same model said that you could draw these really cool permanent lines on the screen with a magnet. Who cares that the speaker panels looked like vertical shag carpet? Who cares that the unit took up 30 percent of the floor space in the room? Who cares that you could cook sausages on top of it from the heat generated by the vacuum tubes? It was more than a TV; it was an *entertainment center.*

Now compare it to the wimpy little flat screen job on its right. If you look closely, you find that the interface to the TV hasn't really changed much in three decades. There are still controls for power, volume, and channel selection (although Horizontal Hold and Vertical Hold are gone, sniff). What has changed is the internal configuration. Gone are the humming vacuum tubes, all replaced with efficient transistors and solid-state components. But it doesn't really make much difference to the TV viewer, because the public interface remains the same.

Objects in OOP development work in the same way. As long as the public interface remains the same, the object's actual code and internal data storage system—also known as the object's **implementation**—can change with no impact to the overall application.

Objects and Instances

The interface and implementation of an object really only represent its design; these are the parts created through the source code. They exist even before the program is compiled and installed on the user's computer. In fact, at this level, objects really aren't even known as objects. In most languages (including Visual Basic), the word **class** indicates the implementation of an object's interface.

Once your application is installed on a computer and starts up, the code creates **instances** of the class to store actual data in memory. These instances are the true objects of OOP development. Depending on how your code is written, a single class implementation might create just one or hundreds of objects in memory at the same time.

In .NET, all of your code and data values appear inside of objects. Pretty much everything you see in a running program is an object: Windows forms are objects; a list box control on that form is an object; and a single item in that list box is an object.

The Parts of the .NET Framework

So now you know all about objects, and you are probably thinking it's time to toss this book into the pile and start programming. But there are a few more parts of the .NET Framework still to discuss. These parts show up *ad nauseum* in the .NET documentation, and they each have a three-letter acronym (TLA), or thereabouts.

The Common Language Runtime

At the center of the .NET Framework is the **Common Language Runtime** (CLR), so named not because it is *common* or ordinary, but because all .NET-enabled languages share it in *common*. Everything you do in a .NET program is *managed* by the CLR. When you create a variable, thank the CLR and its data *management* system. When you say good-bye to a piece of data, thank the CLR and how it *manages* the release of data through its garbage collection system. Did you notice how the word "manage" keeps showing up in those sentences? My editor sure did. But "manage" is the *mot juste*, because that is what the CLR does. In fact, software written for the .NET Framework is called **managed code**. Any code that falls outside of the CLR's control, including COM (ActiveX) components used by your .NET application, is known as **unmanaged code**.

The CLR is a lot like Los Angeles International Airport. If you have ever been to LAX, you know that there is a whole lot of activity going on. Airplanes arrive and depart each minute. Cars by the thousands enter and leave the two-level roadway and the central parking structures. People and pickpockets move constantly between the eight main terminals and the massive international terminal. There's a lot happening, but so much of it is managed. Planes cannot take off or land without approval from the control tower. Access points and gates manage the roadways and parking garages. Friendly, courteous security personnel manage the flow of passengers and pickpockets into and out of the secure areas of the terminals.

The control and management structures in place at LAX ensure an orderly and secure flow of people between its planes and the city of Los Angeles. The control and management structures of the CLR ensure an orderly and secure flow of data between .NET code and the rest of the computer or connected network.

You'd probably like to know the secret of how the CLR is able to process programs written in any .NET language, including Visual Basic, C#, and Fortran. So would Microsoft's competitors. Actually, they do know, because there is no secret. All .NET-enabled languages convert (that is, "compile") your source code into **Microsoft Intermediate Language** (or **MSIL**, pronounced "missile," and more commonly abbreviated as just **IL**).

For those of you familiar with assembly language, it looks a lot like that. For those of you not familiar with assembly language, it looks a lot like gibberish. For example, here is some Visual Basic source code for a **console application** (a non-Windows text-based program, like the old MS-DOS programs) that simply outputs "Hello, World!" from a code procedure called "Main."

```
Module Module1
    Sub Main()
        Console.WriteLine("Hello, World!")
    End Sub
End Module
```

That's the whole .NET program. When the Visual Basic compiler converts it to IL, the "Main" procedure looks like this (slightly modified to fit on this page).

```
.method public static void  Main() cil managed
{
  .entrypoint
  .custom instance void [mscorlib]System.
    STAThreadAttribute::.ctor() = ( 01 00 00 00 )
  // Code size       11 (0xb)
  .maxstack  8
  IL_0000:  ldstr     "Hello, World!"
  IL_0005:  call
    void [mscorlib]System.Console::WriteLine(string)
  IL_000a:  ret
} // end of method Module1::Main
```

Yes, it is gibberish. But that's okay, because it fulfills the International Computer Book Association's requirement that every Chapter 1 include a "Hello, World" code sample. Also, the CLR understands it, and that's what really counts in .NET. As long as you can get your code into IL, .NET will process it. The Visual Basic compiler just happens to generate IL for you. Other .NET language compilers, including C#, target IL as well. You can even write your own IL code, but you're probably reading the wrong book for that. Just to put your mind at ease, this will be the last bit of IL you will see in this book.

The Common Language Specification

Languages that claim to support .NET cannot just say so for any old reason. They truly have to be compatible with .NET and its workings. This is done through the **Common Language Specification** (CLS). The CLS defines a minimum set of features that a language must implement before it is considered to be .NET-compliant, or more accurately, CLS-compliant.

A language can go way beyond that minimum if it wants, and .NET includes many additional features upon which language-specific features may be built. A language that only implements the minimum CLS-specified features may not be able to fully interact with components from languages that exceed the minimum specification. Visual Basic is, of course, CLS-compliant, and in fact goes way beyond that minimum.

The Common Type System

Because the CLR is controlling your source code anyway, Microsoft thought it would be good to have it control the source code's data as well. The .NET Framework does this through its **Common Type System** (CTS), which defines all of the core data types and data mechanisms used in .NET programs. This includes all numeric, string, and Boolean value types. It also defines the **object**, the core data storage unit in .NET.

The CTS divides all data objects into two buckets. The first bucket, called **values types**, stores actual data right in the bucket. If you have a 32-bit integer value, it gets put right in the value type bucket, ready for your immediate use. The other bucket contains **reference types**. When you look in this bucket, you see a map that tells you where to find the actual data somewhere else in the computer's memory. It seems like value types are easier to use, and they are, but they come with a few restrictions not imposed on reference types.

Programs and components written using the CTS standard can exchange data with each other without any hindrances or limitations. (There are a few .NET data types that fall outside of the "core" CTS types, but you only need to avoid them when you want to specifically interact with components that can only use the core CTS types.)

When you write your applications in Visual Basic, most of your code will appear in **classes**. Classes are reference types that include both data values and associated code. The data values included in a class are most often the core CTS data types, but they can also contain objects that you design elsewhere in your application. Visual Basic also includes

structures, the weaker yet quicker younger brother of classes. Structures implement value types, and also include both data and code.

Classes and structures are just two of the data/code types available in Visual Basic. **Interfaces** are class and structure skeletons; they include design details of what should appear in a related class or structure, but don't include any actual implementation or working code. **Delegates** define a single procedure (but not its implementation), and are used to support **events**, those actions (initiated by the user, by the operating system, or by your code) that tell your code, "Get to work now!" **Sea otters** are aquatic mammals that are curiously related to the weasel, and like to eat sea urchins. **Modules** are blocks of code and data, but unlike classes and structures, you can't create independent objects from them. **Enumerations** group a set of related integer values, generally for use as a list of choices.

In .NET parlance, all of these terms (class, structure, interface, delegate, module, and enumeration, but not sea otter) are known collectively as **types**. You probably already knew that .NET had some confusing elements in it; you wouldn't have bought a book about it if it was easy. But despite all of the complex technology, it is this simple word "type" that causes the most confusion. You will likely experience some angst throughout this book each time you read it. The problem: It's too general. Not only does it refer to these core elements of the Common Type System, but it is also used when talking about just the Visual Basic-specific value types (more often called the Visual Basic "data types"). The nickname for structures is "user-defined types," yet another confusing use of "type." Programmers who used Visual Basic before its .NET incarnation also remember "Type" as the language statement used to create user-defined types. Arrrgh! Microsoft should have used some word other than "types" for the world of classes, interfaces, enumerations, and so on. "Bananas" would have been a better choice because it is only sometimes used to discuss software. But "type" *is* the word, so you better get used to seeing it. I will try to include as much context as possible when using the word throughout this volume.

The members of a type usually consist of simple data fields and code procedures, but you can also include other types as members. That is, a class can include a **nested** class if it needs to. Only certain types support nesting (see Chapter 8 for details). I also talk about **access levels** in that chapter. Each member has an access level that says what code can use that member. There are five access levels, ranging from **Public** (anybody and their brother can use the member) to **Private** (you have to be inside the type to even know it's there).

Chapter 6, "Data and Data Types," discusses the .NET type system in greater detail, including the information you crave on classes, structures, and other bananas.

.NET Class Libraries

Computers are actually quite stupid. While I can count all the way to 17, a computer tops out at 1; it only knows the digits 0 and 1. The CPU includes a set of simple operators used to manipulate the digits 0 and 1, and a few more operators that compare 1s and 0s in complex ways. The computer's last great trick is its ability to move 0s and 1s into and out of memory, but whoop-dee-doo. Sure it does these things at nearly the speed of light, but can it calculate π to three million decimal places?

Well, actually it can. Computers don't know anything about the letters of the alphabet, and they really only can handle the digits 0 and 1, yet here I am using a computer to write an award-winning book. It is the ability to combine the simple one-bit data values and operators into increasingly complex *libraries* of functionality that make useful computers possible.[1]

The .NET Framework is built upon decades of increasingly complex functionality. When you install the .NET Framework, the CLR and its associated type system represent the core of the framework. By itself, the framework includes all of the basic functionality needed to let you add 2 and 2 together and correctly get 4. And as a business application developer, you spend a lot of time doing just that. But what if you want to do something more complex, something that you know some other programmer has already done, like sorting a list of names or drawing a colored circle on a form? To get that answer, go to the **class libraries**, the .NET Class Libraries. These libraries, installed with the Framework, include a lot of pre-written (increasingly complex) functionality that you don't have to write from scratch.

There are two class libraries in .NET: the **Base Class Library** (BCL) and the **Framework Class Library** (FCL). The BCL is smaller, and contains the most essential features that a program just couldn't do without. It includes only those classes that are an absolute must for supporting applications on the framework if Microsoft were, say, to port the framework to Linux.

---

[1] If you want to read a truly fascinating book on how complex software and hardware operations are formed from the most basic uses of 0 and 1, read Charles Petzold's book *Code: The Hidden Language of Computer Hardware and Software* (Microsoft Press, 1999).

The FCL is larger, and includes everything else Microsoft thought you would want to have in your programs, but was not absolutely essential to have in the BCL. Don't even ask how many classes there are in the FCL; you don't want to know. I bet that Microsoft doesn't even really know the full number. I am convinced that those wacky pranksters at Microsoft have included "gag" classes in the FCL, but they are so deeply buried that few programmers ever encounter them.

With thousands (yes, thousands!) of classes, enumerations, interfaces, and other types included in the BCL and FCL, you would think that it would be hard to find just the class you need. But it's not that difficult, at least not overwhelmingly difficult. The .NET Framework includes a feature called **namespaces**. All types in .NET appear in a hierarchy—a tree-like structure—with just a few minimal entries at the root. Each **node** in the hierarchy is a namespace. You uniquely identify any class or other type in the libraries by naming all of the namespaces, from the root down to the local namespace that contains the class, separating each node with a period (.).

Unlike most hierarchies that have all branches starting from a single root node, the .NET namespace hierarchy has multiple root nodes. The largest root namespace is named **System**. It includes many classes, but it also includes several next-tier hierarchy nodes (namespaces). Because the framework includes features for both Windows-based and Web-based application development, there are namespaces that contain the Windows-specific and Web-specific development features. These namespaces appear just within the *System* namespace, and are called **Windows** and **Web**. All code related to on-screen Forms in the *Windows* namespaces appears in the **Forms** namespace, and within this namespace is the actual class that implements a form, named **Form**. Figure 1-3 presents an image of this namespace subset.

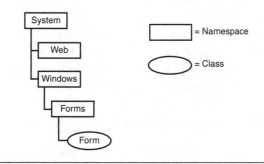

Figure 1-3 A hierarchy of namespaces and classes

In Visual Basic, you identify a class by qualifying it with all of its namespaces, starting from its root namespace. The *Form* class has the following fully qualified name:

```
System.Windows.Forms.Form
```

All classes and types exist somewhere in the hierarchy, although not every class descends from *System*. Many of the supporting features specific to Visual Basic appear in the *Microsoft.VisualBasic* namespace, which has "Microsoft" as its root node instead of "System." When you create new projects in Visual Basic, the name of the project is, by default, a new top-level node in the hierarchy. If you create a new Windows application, the default "Form1" form has the following fully qualified name:

```
WindowsApplication1.Form1
```

This new application's namespace is not just a second-class appendage hanging off of the *System* namespace. It is fully integrated into the full .NET namespace hierarchy; the *WindowsApplication1* namespace is a root node, just like the *System* and *Microsoft* root nodes. Visual Basic includes features that let you alter the default namespace for your application, or place one of the application's classes in a specific namespace. You can even place your application's classes in the *System* namespace branch. Changing *WindowsApplication1* to *System.MySuperApp* moves *Form1* to:

```
System.MySuperApp.Form1
```

If your application is actually a component or library destined for use in programs, your app's classes will appear in the namespace you specify when the other program loads your component into its application area. Your code will look like it is part of the Microsoft-supplied namespaces. Is that cool or what?

Although you can add your classes to the *System* namespace, you will incur the wrath of other .NET programmers. The *System* namespace is supposed to be for "system" (read: Microsoft-supplied) features, and that's it. Also, there's a chance that two vendors might use the same namespace path. So, to avoid potential namespace conflicts *and* dirty looks from other programmers, you should name your application's classes as:

```
CompanyName.ApplicationName.ClassName
```

A single class or other type cannot be split across multiple name-spaces, even within the same hierarchy branch. However, two classes or types may share a common name in different namespaces, even within the same branch.

All classes of the BCL and FCL appear intermingled throughout the entire namespace hierarchy. This means that you cannot necessarily tell whether a particular class is from the BCL or the FCL. Frankly, it doesn't really matter; your code won't care which library a class comes from, as long as it is available for use on the user's workstation.

Assemblies and Manifests

An **assembly** is a "unit of deployment" for the parts of a .NET application or library. In 99.9% of cases, an assembly is simply a .NET executable file (an "exe" file) or a .NET library of classes and other types (a "dll" file). It is possible to split an assembly between multiple files, but usually it is one file for one assembly.

What makes an ordinary *exe* or *dll* file an assembly is the presence of a **manifest**. For single-file assemblies, the manifest appears right in the file; it can also appear in a file of its own. The manifest is a chunk of data that lists important details about the assembly, including its name, version information, default culture, information on referencing external assemblies and types, and a list of all the files contained in the assembly. The CLR will not recognize an assembly without its manifest, so don't lose it.

Assemblies can include an optional **strong name**. This helps to ensure the integrity and authenticity of an assembly through a digital signature attached to the manifest. The strong name uses public key cryptography to guarantee that the assembly is unique and has not been tampered with. Visual Studio and the .NET Framework include tools that let you add a strong name to an assembly.

When you deploy your application, you will normally place all assembly files, configuration files, and any related files specific to your application in the application's install directory, just like in the old Jurassic days before .NET. Shared assemblies designed to be used by more than one application on a single machine can be stored in the **global assembly cache** (GAC). All assemblies placed in the GAC must have strong names. Some systems may only allow the system administrator to add assemblies to the GAC.

Metadata and Attributes

Assemblies are brought to you by the letter "m." In addition to *manifests* and type *members*, assemblies also contain **metadata**. The application code and data elements stored in an assembly parallel the code and data items found in the related Visual Basic source code; for each type and member in your source code, there is associated executable code in the deployed assembly. This makes sense, and is not much of a change from pre-.NET deployments. What is different is that the Visual Basic compiler now attaches additional information—metadata—to each type and member in the assembly. This metadata documents the name of the associated content, information about required data types, information on class inheritance for the element, and security permissions required before the element can be used by the user or other software.

Your Visual Basic source code can enhance the metadata for any element of your assembly through **attributes**. The metadata generated by an attribute is more than just some ID number. Attributes implement full .NET classes, with their own data values and associated logic. Any .NET code that knows how to process attributes can examine the attributes for a type or member and take action as needed. This includes Visual Studio, the Visual Basic compiler, and your own custom applications.

How's this for a mundane example: The .NET Framework includes an attribute named *ObsoleteAttribute*. This attribute lets you mark types or members of your assembly as obsolete or no longer supported. (Visual Studio uses this attribute to display a warning whenever you attempt to use an out-of-date BCL or FCL feature.) To use the attribute, add it to a member of your application using angle brackets.

```
Class MyClassWithOldMembers
    <ObsoleteAttribute> Sub DoSomeWork()
    End Sub
End Class
```

This code defines a single class (*MyClassWithOldMembers*) with a single member procedure (*DoSomeWork*), a procedure that clearly does some work. The procedure is tagged with the *ObsoleteAttribute* attribute. By custom, all attribute names end in the word "Attribute." You can leave off this portion of the word if you wish, as long as the resulting word does not conflict with any Visual Basic language keywords.

```
Class MyClassWithOldMembers
    <Obsolete> Sub DoSomeWork()
    End Sub
End Class
```

When you compile the class and store it in an assembly, the *<ObsoleteAttribute>* attribute is stored as part of *DoSomeWork's* definition. You can now write a separate Visual Basic application that scans an assembly and outputs the name and status of every type and member it finds. When that analysis program encounters the obsolete member, it would detect *ObsoleteAttribute* in the metadata, and output the status:

```
DoSomeWork Procedure: Obsolete, don't use it!
```

Most attributes are designed with a specific purpose in mind. Some attributes instruct Visual Studio to display the members of a class in specific ways. You've probably already played with the form-editing features of Visual Studio to design a simple Windows desktop application. When you add a control (such as a button or a list box) to a form and select that control, Visual Studio lets you edit details of that control through the Properties panel area (see Figure 1-4).

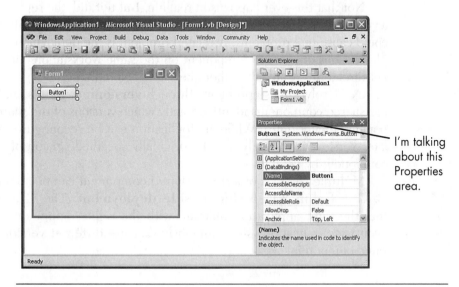

Figure 1-4 The Properties panel in Visual Studio

The Button control is implemented as a class, and many of its class members appear in the Properties panel, but not all of them. When the Button class was designed, attributes were added to its members that tell Visual Studio which members should appear in the Properties panel, and which should not. Visual Studio dutifully examines these attributes, and displays the requested properties only.

Versioning

Like you, my applications are perfect from their initial release, and I never have a reason to modify them or add additional features. But there are software development organizations—including one large company that, so as not to cause embarrassment, I will refer to only by its initial letter of "M"—that feel the need to "one-up" their competition by coming out with "improved" versions of their previously released software offerings. Let's say that "M" happened to have a popular word processor that includes version 1.0 of a spell-check component. "M" also happens to sell an email tool that depends specifically on version 1.0 of that same shared component. If, in a show of competitive machismo, "M" releases an update to the word processor *and* the spell-check component (now version 2.0), what happens to the email tool's spell-checking ability?

Not that this ever happens in real life. But if it did, the replacement of a vital shared component with a newer but somewhat incompatible version could cause real problems. A related problem is the deployment of multiple versions of a single component on the same workstation, all in different directories. Can any of them be safely deleted?

.NET solves these problems through **versioning**. All assemblies that use shared components identify exactly which versions of the shared components they require. While an application can be reconfigured to use a later version, it will only use the originally specified version of a shared component by default.

Multiple versions of a single shared component can be added to the GAC, a feature called **side-by-side deployment**. The CLR ensures that the right application links up with the right component. You can even run applications simultaneously that use different versions of the same component.

From Source Code to EXE

Now you know pretty much everything there is to know about .NET except for that pesky programming thing. Before delving into some actual code, let's take a little snack break and examine the lifetime of an application, from start to finish (see Figure 1-5).

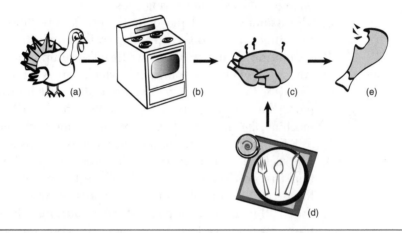

Figure 1-5 The real Visual Basic development process

So here's what happens, step by step:

1. You, as the programmer, are responsible for preparing the basic ingredients *(a)* of the application. For Visual Basic programs, this means creating one or more source code files with a ".vb" extension. Your ingredients may also include other support files, such as resource files (text and graphic files, often used for multi-language support).

2. Your application is cooked by the Visual Basic compiler *(b)*. The result is an assembly, complete with a manifest and metadata. The output is actually semi-compiled IL and includes ready-to-execute versions of the original source code's types and members, including all member and type names. All this content can be

"decompiled" (returned back to full IL, although not to full Visual Basic) using a tool named *ildasm.exe* (the Microsoft Intermediate Language Disassembler), which is included with the .NET Framework. Because you probably don't want just anyone disassembling your application and looking at the code, Microsoft (and other third parties) also supplies an **obfuscator**, which sufficiently scrambles the content of your code to make it just difficult enough to discourage prying eyes.

3. The assembly *(c)* is deployed to the user's workstation. There are a few different methods used to deploy the application, including (1) generating a standard Windows Installer setup package, (2) generating a **ClickOnce** deployment, which is new with version 2.0 of .NET, or (3) performing an **xcopy** install, which involves nothing more than copying the EXE assembly itself to the destination machine. No matter which deployment method you choose, the .NET runtime *(d)* must also be installed on the user's workstation.

4. The user eats—I mean runs—the program *(e)*. The CLR does a final **just-in-time** (JIT) compile of the IL assembly, to prepare it for use on the local platform. It then presents the application to the user, and manages all aspects of the application while it runs. The user experiences a level of joy and satisfaction rarely encountered when using other software applications.

As with the preparation of a Thanksgiving meal, the actual development process is somewhat more involved than just reading a paragraph (or a recipe book) about it. But it's not so difficult that it can't be put in a book, a book like this one.

What About Visual Studio and Visual Basic?

Wait a minute, what about Visual Studio? That last section didn't even mention it. And it didn't need to, because *you do not need to use Visual Studio to develop, compile, deploy, or run Visual Basic applications.* The entire .NET Framework—including the Visual Basic compiler—is available for free from Microsoft's web site; download it and use it to develop and deploy applications that are every bit as powerful and complex as, well, Visual Studio.

The July 1983 issue of *Datamation* magazine includes a letter from manly reader Ed Post entitled, "Real Programmers Don't Use Pascal."[2] I highly recommend that you read this article, as it will help you quickly separate the real programmers from the "quiche eaters." And when you do, run away as fast as you can from the real programmers. Oh sure, they can reconstruct your source code from the obfuscated .NET assembly, but they will be useless on a team project using Visual Studio.

A "real programmer" could code any .NET application using Notepad, and it would run. Actually, they would use *emacs* or *vi* instead of Notepad (because Windows does not include a keypunch interface), but the results would be the same. They would growl as you blissfully type away in Visual Studio's elegant, well-designed, and fully customizable and extensible user interface. They would gripe and bare their cheese-cracker-with-peanut-butter-encrusted teeth at you while you use the IntelliSense and AutoCompletion features built into the Visual Studio code editor. They would consume another slice of quiche-shaped cold pizza while you drag-and-drop both Windows and web-based user interfaces.

Yes, the real programmer could generate full applications with just a text (or hex) editor and a .NET compiler, but you would get the glory, because you would be done in a fraction of the time it would take the FORTRAN lover to eek out his code.

Visual Studio 2005

Because this is a book on Visual Basic development and not on Visual Studio usage, I won't be delving too much into Visual Studio's features or its user interface elements. It is a great application, and its tight integration with the .NET Framework makes it the best tool for developing applications with .NET. But as the real programmer would tell you, it is really just a glorified text editor. Visual Studio hides a lot of the complexity of .NET code, and its automatic generation of the code needed to build your application's user interface is a must-have. Most of its features exist to simplify the process of adding code to your application.

Although I will not be including a 20-page review of Visual Studio right here, you will find images of Visual Studio throughout the text, placed so as to advance your understanding of the topics under discussion in each

---

[2.] *Datamation*, Volume 29, Number 7, July 1983, pp. 263–265. I also found the text of the article on the Internet by doing a search on the title. A similar version of the text, with only minor editorial changes, also exists under the name "Real Programmers Don't Write Pascal."

chapter. When you start up Visual Studio for the first time, it displays the Start Page. (The screenshots in this book are taken from the Professional Edition of Visual Studio 2005.)

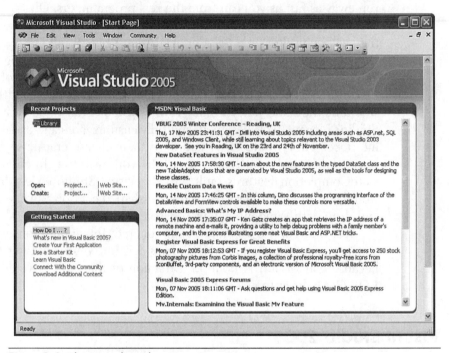

Figure 1-6 The Visual Studio "Start Page"

Visual Studio 2005 is the third major release of the product since .NET's initial introduction in 2002. Each release (in 2002, 2003, and 2005) corresponded to a related release of the .NET Framework (versions 1.0, 1.1, and 2.0, respectively) and of the .NET implementation of Visual Basic. The 2003 release was a relatively minor update to Visual Basic and the Framework, but the 2005 release is major. It is packed with new usability features, and comes in five delicious flavors.

- *Visual Studio 2005 Express Edition.* This entry-level product is geared toward the home hobbyist and weekend programmer who wants to learn .NET and one of its core programming languages, but won't be snuggling up to it on a daily basis. Visual Studio 2005 Express Edition is actually multiple Express Edition language products bundled together, including Visual Basic 2005 Express Edition (although Visual Basic 2005 Express Edition is also provided separately). Microsoft's goal is to introduce as many people as possible to the joys of .NET programming, so it offers the Express Edition at no cost. The package includes a simplified Visual-Studio-like user interface, but it does impose a few restrictions on your program-crafting ability. You can still edit the source code directly and craft applications of any complexity, but the Express UI won't always assist you with this. For instance, you cannot develop web applications with the Express product unless you install the separate Visual Web Developer product. Also, Express doesn't include much support for deployment; applications designed with the Express Edition are generally expected to be used on your own workstation only.

- *Visual Studio 2005 Standard Edition.* Visual Studio's Standard Edition is just like the Express Edition, with a few extras thrown in, such as documentation on how to use the BCL and FCL (amazing), and deployment support through the ClickOnce deployment feature. It also includes support for mobile devices, such as cell phones and PDAs.

- *Visual Studio 2005 Professional Edition.* This is the minimum level required by programmers who will develop applications on a daily basis for money. It's the version that I use, and it includes all of the "power" features needed by a single programmer for both desktop and web-based development. The straightjacketed Express user interface is out, replaced by the full Visual Studio "mighty" Integrated Development Environment (IDE). But wait, there's more. You also get SQL Server 2005 Developer Edition. All instructions in this book that relate to using the development environment refer to the Professional Edition. But if you are following along using the Express or Standard Editions, you will be just fine because the interfaces are quite similar.

- *Visual Studio 2005 Tools for the Microsoft Office System.* This "TOS" version is the Professional Edition, but all support for mobile devices is removed, replaced by special components that target the Microsoft Office suite.

- *Visual Studio 2005 Team System.* The *crème de la crème* of the Visual Studio product line is Team System. It includes features needed by development teams that work on projects together, features such as project management tools and source code control. *Visual Studio 2005 Team Foundation Server*, a separate product, can be installed on a shared server, and enhances the features of the Team System package.

Microsoft is pushing its new version of SQL Server—SQL Server 2005—this time around. An Express Edition is available for entry-level programmers; a Developer's Edition is included in the Visual Studio 2005 Professional Edition and beyond. A special "Everywhere" edition targets mobile platforms. Of course, there's the complete SQL Server product available for full-scale deployments. Microsoft continues to support Microsoft Access, but it is encouraging the use of SQL Server for even small projects due to its tighter integration with .NET (starting with the 2005 release).

Beyond the database support, Visual Studio 2005 has been endowed with several new usability and feature enhancements.

- *Edit and Continue.* This blast from the past was in Visual Basic since version 1.0, but it has been conspicuously absent since the first .NET release in 2002. Edit and Continue allows you to modify Visual Basic source code while actively running and debugging the application within Visual Studio, and continue running the modified application without a restart. The programmers at "M" have surely given their blood, sweat, and tears to this feature, so use it well.
- *Enhanced compile-time warnings and errors.* Visual Studio always flagged invalid statements in your code, but it now flags warnings on code that will compile, and may give unexpected results when executed. Figure 1-7 shows a warning for a declared variable that has yet to be used in code.

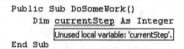

Figure 1-7 Fair warning

When actual syntax errors appear in code, Visual Studio now makes recommendations on how to fix them (in many cases), and will fix them for you at the click of a mouse button. In Figure 1-8, clicking on the "Insert the missing 'Next'" line in the *Error Correction* window will add in the missing "Next" keyword. If that small red circle and the black arrow to its right look familiar, that's because they're from the Smart Tags feature found in Microsoft Office products.

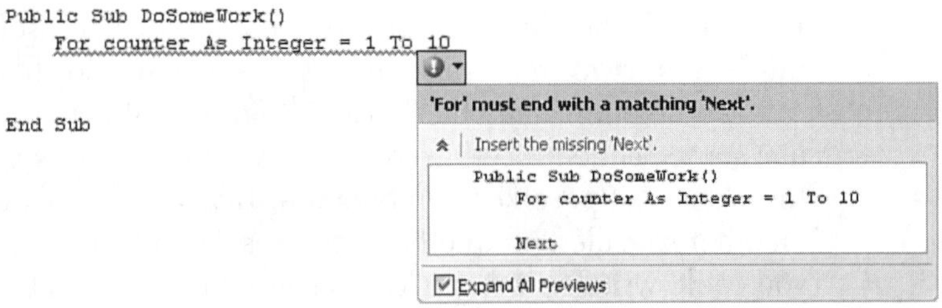

```
Public Sub DoSomeWork()
    For counter As Integer = 1 To 10

End Sub
```

'For' must end with a matching 'Next'.

    Insert the missing 'Next'.

```
Public Sub DoSomeWork()
    For counter As Integer = 1 To 10

    Next
```

☑ Expand All Previews

Figure 1-8 Easy error correction

- *ClickOnce Deployments.* This new method of distributing .NET applications imposes fewer requirements on the installing user. For instance, a ClickOnce deployment does not require administrator-level security to install and use the application. Of course, some features may be disabled if the user lacks sufficient privileges.
- *Code Snippets, Project and Item Templates, and Starter Kits.* These features make it easier to integrate pre-written code into your new projects. The Code Snippets feature lets you save a hierarchy of short code blocks for quick insertion into your source code. They include fill-in-the-blank areas if you need them. If you install the source code supplied with this book, you will have a chance to try out Project Templates and Code Snippets, as the samples use those technologies.
- *Generics.* Both the .NET Framework and Visual Basic include support for **generics**, a new feature discussed in Chapter 16, "Generics." Generics allow you to enforce the use of specific data types on classes that would otherwise impose no such restrictions.
- *Operator Overloading.* Visual Basic adds new support for over-loaded operators. This feature lets you assign special meanings to standard language operators, such as the addition operator (+). Instead of adding just numbers together, you develop code to add your own complex classes together; you define what "adding" means for your class.
- *My.* That's right: just "My." *My* is a new Visual Basic feature that provides simple and centralized access to FCL features that would normally be spread throughout that class library. You can read more about it in the very next chapter.

Despite all of these great new features, Microsoft still refuses to implement the most requested Visual Studio feature, "Procedure AutoCompletion," in which Visual Studio would create the entire content of a source code procedure based on your entry of its name and the use of the Control+Space key combination. Instead, they fritter away their time on other so-called productivity features. With Procedure AutoCompletion, you could write entire applications in minutes. Until that feature becomes available, you and I will have to continue writing software, crafting the quality code that users have come to expect from our fingers.

Summary

Over fifteen years ago, Visual Basic transformed the Windows development landscape, with its drag-and-drop programming model and its glitzy event-driven development structure. But Windows has changed a lot since those days of Windows 3.x. As Windows has changed, Visual Basic has changed right along with it. Visual Basic 2005, through its association with the .NET Framework, provides access to the programming tools needed to develop quality applications for the Windows desktop, the Internet, and the next generation of mobile devices.

And Microsoft is not halting this progress with the 2005 release. The next version of Visual Basic, code-named "Orcas," promises to include even more advanced features that will take full advantage of Windows Vista and its .NET Framework 3.0 (formerly named *WinFX*) programming interface.

The Project

Welcome to the Project section, the part of each chapter where you have an opportunity to get "hands on" with Visual Studio 2005 and Visual Basic. Development of the Library project, the main project focus of this book, formally begins in Chapter 3, "Introducing the Project," but there's still project work to do in the meantime. In this chapter, I'll introduce you to the sample source code provided with this book, and we'll take a stab at using it.

Because most Project sections, including this one, will involve Visual Studio, make sure you have it installed and ready to use. Also, because each Project section is designed for you to use interactively with the supplied source code, I will assume that you have downloaded and installed the source code (see Appendix A, "Installing the Software," for instructions), and are viewing the source code with one eye while you read this section with the other. I will print sections of the source code in the book, but with tens of thousands of source code lines in the Library project, I will not be able to print every line here. You will certainly get a lot out of each Project section by simply reading them, but you will get even more if you have access to the full source code.

In this chapter's project, we'll load a sample program into Visual Studio and run it. There are two ways to do this. The first way is just to open the existing project directly from the installation directory. Browse to the directory where you installed this book's source code, open the "Chapter 1" subdirectory, and double-click the *Chapter1.vbproj* file. This will open the project directly in Visual Studio, ready to use.

The second way is to use the chapter-specific project templates to create new projects in Visual Studio. The Setup program for this book's source code modified your installation of Visual Studio, adding new entries in the *New Project* dialog window. Each of these new "project templates" can be used as the starting point for a new Visual Basic project. To load the Chapter 1 sample program using the template, start Visual Studio. The Start Page will appear, as shown way back in Figure 1-6. From the **File** menu, select **New Project** to display the **New Project** dialog box (see Figure 1-9).

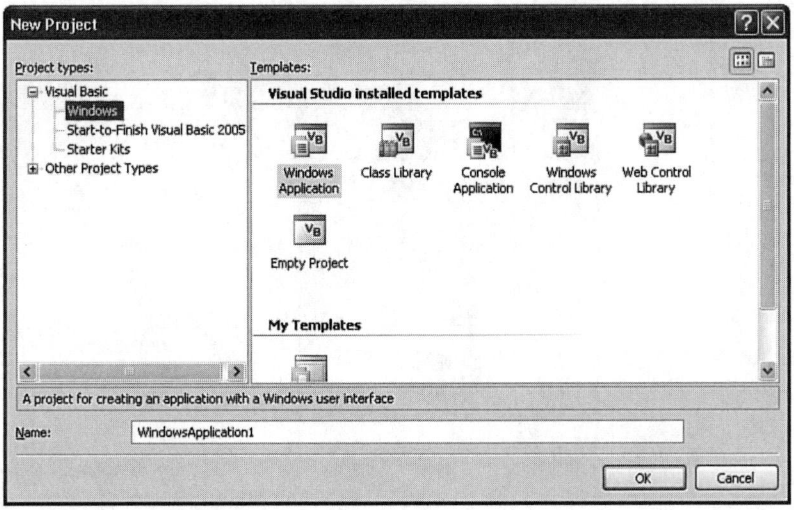

Figure 1-9 The New Project dialog box—so many choices

Your **New Project** dialog box may differ slightly depending on the features you chose to install with Visual Studio. The available projects are grouped by the description in the **Project types** field. For instance, Figure 1-9 shows the various default project types you can create in Visual Basic, including *Windows Applications* (standard desktop applications for the Windows platform, *Class Libraries* (a DLL of class-defined features), and *Console Applications* (command-line text-based applications). To create a new application, first select the project type, select the **Template** to use, and finally enter the name of the new project in the **Name** field. Clicking the **OK** button creates a new project.

To use the sample Chapter 1 project, select the *Start-to-Finish Visual Basic 2005* entry within the *Visual Basic* project type, and then select *Chapter 1 Sample* from the **Template** field (see Figure 1-10). Finally, click **OK** to create the new sample project.

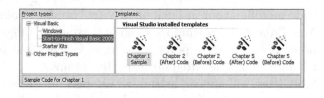

Figure 1-10 Selecting the Chapter 1 Sample project

Once the project loads, access the program's main form by double-clicking on the *Form1.vb* file in the **Solution Explorer** (see Figure 1-11).

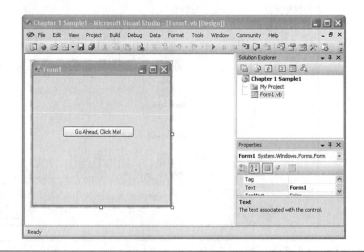

Figure 1-11 The main form of the sample application

This default presentation of Visual Studio Professional Edition includes three editing components: (1) the main editing area, where the view of "Form1" appears; (2) the **Solution Explorer** panel, which provides access to all files included in the project; and (3) the **Properties** panel, which lets you edit various aspects of the currently selected item in the main editor area or elsewhere in the user interface.

The sample project is pretty basic. It includes one form with a single action button. Clicking this button in the running application displays a simple message. Run the project by pressing the F5 key. When the main form appears, clicking on the **Go Ahead, Click Me** button to display the message in Figure 1-12 (goal, sweet goal).

Figure 1-12 Hello again, world!

So, how about all of that complex code I had to write to develop this multifaceted application? It's all there for the viewing. From the **Solution Explorer** panel, right-click on the *Form1.vb* entry, and select **View Code** from the shortcut menu. (As with most source code samples presented in this book, I have had to slightly adjust the code so that it displays properly on the printed page. Generally, this involves splitting a long logical line into two or more shorter ones.)

```
Public Class Form1
    Private Sub Button1_Click(ByVal sender As System.Object, _
        ByVal e As System.EventArgs) Handles Button1.Click
        MsgBox("Hello, World!")
    End Sub
End Class
```

We'll get into the intricacies of such code in later chapters, but here is the gist.

- The main form, **Form1**, is represented in code by a class, named *Form1*.
- The form includes a command button named **Button1** that exposes a *Click* event. This event is handled by the *Button1_Click* procedure, a member of the *Form1* class.
- The "event handler," *Button1_Click*, includes a single statement, a "MsgBox" statement. This statement does the heavy lifting by presenting the ever-friendly message box to the world.

That's all of the code that I wrote for *Form1.vb*. It sure seems pretty short for all the work it does. There has to be more code hiding somewhere. And sure enough, there are actually half-a-dozen or so more files included in the project. Visual Studio hides these by default, since it manages some or all of the content in these files on your behalf. To view the files, click on the **Show All Files** button (the second toolbar button from the left in the **Solution Explorer** panel). Look at all those files! To see the additional files associated with *Form1*, expand it by clicking on the plus sign to its left (see Figure 1-13).

Figure 1-13 Viewing hidden files through the Solution Explorer

Double-click on the *Form1.Designer.vb* entry to see the code that Visual Studio automatically wrote for this form. (Dramatic pause.) Wow! Look at all of that scary code. Actually, it's not that bad. By the end of this book, you will have a firm grasp on all of it. Here in Chapter 1, it's not really necessary to comprehend it all, but there are a few interesting lines to note.

I'm including line numbers to make it easier to find the matching code in Visual Studio. If you want to view line numbers in Visual Studio (Professional Edition instructions listed here):

1. Select the **Tools ➤ Options** menu item to display Visual Studio's options.
2. Select **Text Editor ➤ Basic ➤ Editor** from the tree-view to the left. If the **Show all settings** field is checked, the last component in the tree-view will be **General**, not **Editor**.
3. Select (check) the **Line Numbers** field on the right.
4. Click **OK** to apply the changes.

If you're new to Visual Basic or .NET programming, don't worry now if all this code doesn't make sense; it will all become clear as you pass through the pages of this book.

```
 1   <Global.Microsoft.VisualBasic.CompilerServices. _
        DesignerGenerated()> _
 2   Partial Public Class Form1

20   <System.Diagnostics.DebuggerNonUserCode()> _
21   Protected Overloads Overrides Sub Dispose _
        (ByVal disposing As Boolean)
```

These lines show *attributes* in action. These two attributes (*DesignerGenerated* and *DebuggerNonUserCode*) are somewhat like the *Obsolete* attribute discussed earlier, in that they provide some informational identity to the related code. *DesignerGenerated* modifies the entire section of *Form1*'s code, while *DebuggerNonUserCode* only modifies the *Dispose* member. For clarity, both attributes include their full namespace paths. The *Global* keyword at the beginning of the *DesignerGenerated* attribute is actually a Visual Basic keyword that says, "Start at the very tippy-top of the namespace hierarchy; this is not a relative path."

```
 2   Partial Public Class Form1
```

Did you see the word *Partial* right there on line 2? I know I did. Hey, wait a minute; "Public Class Form1" also appeared in the *Form1.vb* file, but without the *Partial* keyword. Visual Basic 2005 includes a new feature that lets you divide a single class (*Form1* in this case) among multiple source code files by including the *Partial* keyword with at least one of the parts. Pretty cool, eh? It allows Visual Studio to add complex initialization code for your form (as found in this *Form1.Designer.vb* file) without it bothering your main source code file (*Form1.vb*).

```
3   Inherits System.Windows.Forms.Form
```

The *Inherits* keyword defines the inheritance relationship between this new *Form1* class and the previously written *System.Windows.Forms. Form* class. *Form* is the "base" class, while *Form1* is the "derived" class; *Form1* inherits all of the functionality of the *Form* class, including its initial look and feel. I'll discuss these class relationships in more detail in Chapter 8.

```
44   Friend WithEvents Button1 As System.Windows.Forms.Button
```

Line 44 defines the **Go Ahead, Click Me** button that appears in the center of the form. All controls that appear on your form are separate instances of classes. (*Friend* is a declaration statement described in the next chapter.) The *WithEvents* keyword indicates that this instance of the *Button* class will respond to events, such as a user clicking on it with the mouse. This line doesn't actually create an instance of the *Button* class; that happens back on line 22.

```
22   Me.Button1 = New System.Windows.Forms.Button
```

The *New* keyword creates new instances of classes. In this case, that new instance is assigned to the *Button1* class member defined on line 44. At this moment, *Button1* is a default instance of the *Button* class; it doesn't have any of its custom settings, such as its size and position, or the **Go Ahead, Click Me** display text. All of that is set in lines 27 to 31.

```
27   Me.Button1.Location = New System.Drawing.Point(64, 104)
28   Me.Button1.Name = "Button1"
29   Me.Button1.Size = New System.Drawing.Size(152, 23)
30   Me.Button1.TabIndex = 0
31   Me.Button1.Text = "Go Ahead, Click Me!"
```

Finally, the button is "glued" onto the form on line 38.

```
38   Me.Controls.Add(Me.Button1)
```

This adds the *Button1* instance to the list of *Controls* managed by *Form1*. The *Me* keyword used throughout this code refers to the *Form1* class itself, so *Me.Button1* refers to the *Button1* class member specifically in the current *Form1* class.

Most of the code in this file appears in the *InitializeComponent* member procedure.

```
21   Private Sub InitializeComponent()
        . . .
43   End Sub
```

When Visual Basic creates an instance of *Form1* to display on the screen, it calls the *InitializeComponent* procedure to do the work of adding the controls to the form. Actually, Visual Basic calls the form's **constructor**, which in turn calls *InitializeComponent*. Constructors are special class members that perform any needed initialization on a class instance. They are called automatically by .NET each time a class instance is created. In Visual Basic, all constructors use the name **New**, as with the following code:

```
Friend Class ClassWithConstructor
    Public Sub New()
        ' ----- All initialization code goes here.
    End Sub
End Class
```

I'll talk much more about constructors in Chapter 8, but for now, locate the constructor in the code for *Form1*. (Very long pause.) What? There is no constructor? So, if there isn't a constructor, how is the *InitializeComponent* member ever called?

That's what I'd like to know. Actually, when the Visual Basic compiler generates the IL code for *Form1*, it adds a constructor silently, a constructor that calls *InitializeComponent*. How about that! Why didn't Microsoft simply include the constructor's code right in the source code? It's a

simplicity-for-the-programmer thing. They needed to have a default constructor that would call *InitializeComponent*, but they didn't want a conflict to arise if you added your own default constructor in the non-Designer
file. So they hid all of the code until it came time to actually compile the
form. Clearly, it's all rather hush-hush, so let's move on.

Well, that's pretty much the entire code, at least the part that matters
to us now. Although we will rarely, if ever, examine the Visual Studio-
generated code for the forms in the Library project, it's good to see what's
going on behind the scenes. If you were a Visual Basic 6 programmer, you
probably looked at the source code for your forms through Notepad at one
time or another. If you did, you noticed that the form and all of its controls
were defined with a hierarchy of special commands, and not with actual
Visual Basic code. In .NET, that's all changed; the form and all of its controls are created with ordinary Visual Basic code, so you can access it all
and see what is really going on.

Now, turn to Chapter 2, "Introducing Visual Basic," where I delve into
the Visual Basic language itself.

INTRODUCING VISUAL BASIC

It was a dark and stormy night. Hector gazed wearily through his bloodshot eyes, through the black-rimmed corrective lenses, and through the haze of the fluorescent overhead lights at the phosphor-enriched display. Had it really been four months since he started the six-month project? Did his boss really threaten to fire him after seeing his progress? It seemed like all of those MS-DOS programs he had written for the company over the years meant nothing. Why did he promise to port the company's main internal system to Windows? In a moment of despair, tears streamed down his cheeks, diluting his last remaining can of Jolt Cola.

8:00 a.m. A loud thump on Hector's desk brings him suddenly out of his slumber, the drool still trickling out of the corner of his mouth. What's that? What's that box on his desk? "V-i-s-u-a-l B-a-s-i-c?" A note on the box says to rewrite his code in "this." Desperate to try anything, Hector installs the three floppy disks on his 386 powerhouse.

Six weeks later, Hector has completed the project, ahead of schedule, feature-complete, and with the accolades of his boss and department. And it's all due to Visual Basic. But VB didn't just improve his programming life. Overall, he's happier, has kicked the caffeine habit, is able to bench press 300 pounds, no longer walks with a limp, has increased libido, and has whiter teeth. "Thank you, Visual Basic 1.0!"

The History of the Visual Basic Revolution

It's possible that I got a few of the details wrong in Hector's life. But for many business developers, Visual Basic 1.0 was a breath of fresh air. It's not that they could do more with Visual Basic; programs written in C were more powerful and had greater flexibility. But business programmers didn't always need that flexibility back in the transition from MS-DOS. They just wanted to manage data, and they didn't want to worry about how to present every little pixel on the screen. Visual Basic provided the tools to write applications quickly and with much less effort than that required by other Windows development tools and languages.

Visual Basic's simplicity was embraced by developers everywhere, but the honeymoon quickly wore off. Given the speed at which programs of reasonable quality could be cranked out with Visual Basic, programmers and businesses began demanding more. And Microsoft provided. Visual Basic 2.0 and 3.0 were released in quick succession in 1992 and 1993, each providing enhanced database integration and additional visual development features. Version 4.0, released in 1996, introduced 32-bit programming to the language, and support for the already-popular Windows 95 platform. Two more quick releases—Visual Basic 5.0 in 1997 and Visual Basic 6.0 in 1998—added even more features and complexity to the otherwise "basic" language, features supporting some but not all object-oriented programming (OOP) techniques, ActiveX control development, and web-based logic coding. Microsoft had even integrated the core Visual Basic engine—christened Visual Basic for Applications, or VBA—into its suite of Office products, proclaiming it as the new official macro language, and making the engine available to any third party that wanted to do the same.

Seven years after its initial introduction, Visual Basic had taken the programming world by storm. Millions of developers were using the language, including in-house developers at Fortune 500 companies, writing applications that supported core business functions. VB still retained some of the flavor of the original BASIC language—a "beginner's" programming language developed by John Kemeny and Thomas Kurtz at Dartmouth College back in 1963. This caused no end of snickering from C and C++ developers and other cola addicts. But VB programmers could see a powerful future for their language of choice.

Then the unthinkable happened. Microsoft announced that it would no longer enhance the core Visual Basic engine. Instead, it would rewrite and re-implement Visual Basic using its soon-to-be-released .NET development platform. Yes, Visual Basic would be endowed with all the power promised for Microsoft's new C- and Java-like language, C#. But for many hard-core VB developers, it was wrong, just wrong. Words were exchanged. Petitions were crafted. Letters to the editor sounded the call to the Visual Basic faithful, urging them to never write a single line of Visual Basic .NET code, ever. In frustration, a Visual Basic user's group set fire to the entire Microsoft campus in Redmond.

Well, that didn't happen. In fact, nothing bad happened at all. Visual Basic .NET turned out to be a software *wunderkind*, providing power and features that far surpassed anything available in Visual Basic 6.0. Its initial release in 2002 was proof of that. Visual Basic .NET 2002 was powerful, but it was also a little hard to use, at least compared with version 6.0, and especially when compared with the original 1.0 product. Visual Basic .NET 2003, released just a year later (obviously), was a relatively minor update with not much in the way of new or easier functionality.

Visual Basic 2005, the latest VB offering from Microsoft, marks a return to the simpler days of Visual Basic development, days of harmony and peace between "newbies" and their general-purpose programming language. Not only has Microsoft removed the term ".NET" from the product name, it has removed some of the barriers that kept entry-level programmers from approaching the language. Pre-.NET features, such as Edit and Continue and the display of forms through the simple use of the form's name, have once again found their way into the language and into the hearts of software engineers. Visual Basic still retains all of the power it gained with .NET, but with true improvements in usability. It's like when they add a label to your toothpaste that says, "New package, same great regular flavor!" except that Visual Basic's flavor is improved, too. Visual Basic is once again accessible to first-time developers.

Since the 2005 release, Microsoft hasn't just been sitting on their laurels, as painful as that would be. They are hard at work on the next release of Visual Basic, code-named "Orcas," with its support for the .NET Framework 3.0 (formerly named *WinFX*) and Windows Vista. That release will also introduce new language syntax to support LINQ (Language Integrated Query), the ability to use SQL-like syntax to manipulate in-memory collections of objects.

Visual Basic from the Inside Out

As a general-purpose development language, Visual Basic includes gobs of features that allow you to develop just about any type of application supported by Microsoft Windows platform. As such, all of its features could never be covered in a concise, 20- or 30-page chapter, and I won't try. What I will do in this chapter is introduce you to the basics of the language, and its core features.[1] Features not covered in this chapter are discussed

---

[1.] This book introduces Visual Basic features using a tutorial approach. If you are also looking for a good reference work that discusses each feature of the Visual Basic language in gory detail, rush out to your bookstore and buy *Visual Basic 2005 in a Nutshell*, a book I co-wrote and revised for Visual Basic 2005. (O'Reilly Media, 2005)

throughout the rest of the book. It has to be that way, because I don't want you to finish this chapter, and then say to yourself, "That Tim Patrick is so amazing. I learned all I needed to know about Visual Basic in one chapter; I didn't even have to read the rest of the book." My publisher would not be amused.

In the remainder of this chapter, I will take the "from the inside out" approach, starting the discussion with the core concepts of logic and data, and adding layer after layer of Visual Basic functionality as you turn the pages.

The Basics of Logic and Data

Lest you forget it, let me remind you again: Computers are not really very smart. They only know how to do the simplest of tasks. If you want them to do anything remotely complex, you have to give precise, step-by-step instructions down to moving individual bits of data—only 1s and 0s, remember—around in memory. Fortunately, most of the code you would ever need at that low level has already been written for you, and incorporated into the Windows operating system and the .NET Framework. Microsoft- and third-party-supplied code libraries give you a lot of pre-written functionality that's available for use in your own programs. And that's good, because you would rather be hurtled into space on a giant bungee cord than have to write business applications at the **machine code** level all day long.

Even though you have all of this great pre-written code in your arsenal, you still have to tell the computer precisely what you want it to do, in fine detail, or it won't do it. And that's where **high-level languages** like Visual Basic come in. They provide the grammar you need to communicate with the computer. For any given tasks that the computer needs to perform, your job as a programmer is to determine the individual steps to accomplish that task—the **logic**—and translate those steps into computer-ese using the programming language.

As an example, let's say you receive a request from the sales department for a program that will reverse all of the letters in any chunk of text provided to the program. "Our customers are clamoring for this; we need it by Tuesday," they say. Okay, so first you figure out the logic, and then you implement it in Visual Basic. Using **pseudo-code**, an artificial programming language that you make up yourself to help you write programs, you can sketch out the basics of this task (with leading line numbers).

```
01 Obtain the original text (or string) from the user.
02 If the user didn't supply any content, then quit now.
03 Prepare a destination for the reversed string, empty for now.
04 Repeat the following until the original string is empty:
05    Copy the last character from the remaining original string.
06    Put that character onto the end of the destination string.
07    Shorten the original string, dropping the last character.
08 [End of repeat section]
09 Show the user the destination string.
```

There are many ways that this logic could be written; this is just one example. This pseudo-code can now be converted into your language of choice; in this case, Visual Basic (don't worry about the syntax details for now).

```
01 originalText = InputBox("Enter text to reverse.")
02 If (Len(originalText) = 0) Then End
03 finalText = ""
04 Do While (originalText <> "")
05    oneCharacter = Right(originalText, 1)
06    finalText = finalText & oneCharacter
07    originalText = Left(originalText, _
         Len(originalText) - 1)
08 Loop
09 MsgBox("The reverse is: " & finalText)
```

This **source code** is now ready to be used in a Visual Basic program. And it also demonstrates several essential aspects of coding.

- The individual steps of the step-by-step instructions are called **statements**. In Visual Basic, each statement appears on a line by itself. Long statements can be broken into multiple lines by connecting the lines with a space-underscore pair, as shown in line 07 of the code. When a single statement is spread across multiple lines in this manner, the entire statement is sometimes called a **logical line**. Because a single logical line often includes only a single primary Visual Basic action (such as the *If* or *Do* actions, or the various assignment actions using the = sign), these actions are also referred to as statements.

- The statements of the code are processed one at a time, from top to bottom. However, certain statements alter the normal top-to-bottom flow of the program, as is done with the *Do While . . . Loop* block on lines 04 and 08 of the sample code. Such statements are called **flow control** statements, and include loops (repeating a block of code), conditions (optionally processing a block of code based on a comparison or calculated result), and jumps (moving immediately to some other section of the code).

- Data can be stored in **variables**, which are named containers for data values. The sample code block includes three variables: *originalText*, *oneCharacter*, and *finalText*, all of which store text (string) data. The .NET Common Type System allows you to create variables for four primary types of basic data values: text (both single characters and longer strings), numbers (both integer and decimal values), dates (and times), and Booleans (true or false values). You can also build more complex types of data by grouping the basic types.

- Data is stored in a variable through an **assignment**. Generally, this involves placing a variable name on the left side of an "=" assignment operator, and putting the data or calculation to store in that variable on the right side of that same equals sign. The statement *finalText* = "" on line 03 stores an empty string ("") in the variable *finalText*.

- Statements can include **function calls**, blocks of pre-written functionality, all squished down into a single name. Function calls do a bunch of work, and then **return** a final result, a data value. Function names are always followed by a set of parentheses, which may include zero or more **arguments**, additional data values supplied by the calling code that the function uses to generate its result.

    The sample code includes many examples of function calls, including the *Right* function on line 05. This function returns a copy of the right-most characters from another string. It accepts two parameters: the original string from which to extract the right-most characters, and an integer value indicating the number of characters to return. The code *Right(originalText, 1)* returns a copy of the right-most single (1) character from *originalText*.

When using a function in your source code, it acts a little like a variable; all the text of the function call, from the start of its name to the end of its closing parenthesis, could be replaced by a variable that contained the same resulting data. Function calls cannot appear on the left-hand side of an assignment statement, but they can appear almost anywhere else that a variable can appear. For example, the following two lines could be used to replace line 02 in the sample.

```
' Replacing --> If (Len(originalText) = 0) Then End
lengthOfText = Len(originalText)
If (lengthOfText = 0) Then End
```

■ In addition to functions, Visual Basic also includes **procedures**. Procedures bundle up pre-written code in a named package, just like functions, but they don't return a value. They must be used as stand-alone statements; you cannot use them where you would use a variable or a function call. The call to *MsgBox* on line 09 is a typical example of a procedure call in use.

This sample code listed previously could be made a little more efficient. In fact, it's entirely possible that Microsoft obtained an early draft of this book, because they included a string-reversal feature right in Visual Basic, and called it *StrReverse*.

```
originalText = InputBox("Enter text to reverse.")
If (Len(originalText) = 0) Then End
finalText = StrReverse(originalText)
MsgBox("The reverse is: " & finalText)
```

That's right, Visual Basic already includes a string reverse feature, some of that pre-written library code I keep taking about. Visual Basic includes many such **intrinsic functions** that are considered part of the language, and that bundle up useful pre-written functionality. Many of these functions appear in the *Microsoft.VisualBasic* namespace, which is automatically made available to your Visual Basic source code when you create a new VB project.

Data Types and Variables

Take my data . . . please! Ha, ha, that one always cracks me up. But it's actually what I ask my Visual Basic application to do: take data from some source (keyboard, hard disk, Internet, etc.) and present it in some useful way. All programs I write will actively manage at least some data in memory. Each data value is stored in a specific area of the computer's memory, as determined by the Common Language Runtime (CLR). The statements in Visual Basic exist primarily to manage and manipulate this data in useful and complex ways.

All data managed by the CLR is stored in the computer's memory, with each data value separated and protected from all others. It's as if each data value had its own individual teacup, as in Figure 2-1.

Figure 2-1 All types of teacups and data

All data values managed by the CLR have **content** and **type**. *Content* is the actual data: the text string "abc," the number 5, a sales invoice, orange pekoe. Whatever you put in the teacup, that's the content. In some cases, .NET allows you to store absolutely nothing in the teacup (only for "reference" types).

Type indicates the kind of content stored in the teacup. In Figure 2-1, this is shown by the shape of each teacup. Each teacup has limits on the type of data that can be poured into the teacup: a text string, an integer number, a customer invoice.

Literals

Some basic data values, such as numbers and text strings, can be entered into your source code and used just as they are. For instance, the *MsgBox* procedure displays a window with a supplied text message. The statement:

```
MsgBox("The answer is " & 42)
```

includes a **literal string**, *"The answer is,"* and a **literal integer** value, 42. (The "&" symbol is an operator that connects two values into a new string.) Literals are used once, and then they're gone. If I wanted to show the same "The answer is 42" message again, I would have to once again type the same literal values into a different part of the source code.

There are several types of basic literals supported by Visual Basic. **String literals** are always surrounded by quote marks. If you want to include a quote mark itself in the middle of a string, include two instead of one:

```
"This is ""literally"" an example."
```

String literals can be really, really long, up to about two billion characters in length; if you were to type just one character per second, it would take over 63 years to reach the maximum string length. Visual Basic also includes a **character literal** that is exactly one character in length; if you were to type just one character per second, well, never mind. These character literals are recognized by the "c" trailing after the string. The character literal "A" is entered as:

```
"A"c
```

Date and time literals are surrounded by number signs instead of quote marks. The date or time (or both) that you include can be in any format recognized by Microsoft Windows in your specific region. If you are using Visual Studio, it will reformat your date when you type in the literal.

```
#7/4/1776#
```

There are 11 different kinds of numeric data values—both integers and floating point values—that make up the "core" set of numeric teacups. And who needs more than 11? With these 11 teacups, you can manage numbers from zero all the way to 1×10^{300} and beyond. To use a numeric literal, type the number right in your code, like 27, or 3.1415926535. Visual Basic also lets you specify which of the 11 numeric teacups to use for a number, by appending a special character to the end of the number. Normally, 27 is an integer. To make it a currency-focused "decimal," append an @ sign:

```
27@
```

When I talk about data types in full detail in Chapter 6, "Data and Data Types," I will list the different special characters, like @, that set the data type for literal numbers.

The fourth and final type of Visual Basic literal is the Boolean literal. Boolean values represent the simplest type of computer data: the bit. Boolean values are either true or false, on or off, yes or no, delicious or disgusting, cats or dogs, zero or non-zero. Booleans always represent any two opposite values or states. George Boole invented *Boolean Algebra*, a language he used to represent logic statements as mathematical equations. It just so happens that computers *love* Boolean Algebra. All of the basic operations of a computer, such as addition, are implemented using Boolean functionality.

Visual Basic includes the Boolean literals **True** and **False**. No quotes. No number signs. Just the words True or False. Question: Is Tim Patrick telling the truth about this? Answer:

```
True
```

In certain cases, you can treat numbers as Boolean values. I'll talk about it more later, but for now just know that False equates to zero (0), and True equates to everything else (although generally, –1 is used for "everything else").

Variables

Literal data values are all well and good, but they are useful only once, and then they're gone. Each time you want to use a literal value, you must retype it. It's as if the data values are stored in disposable cups instead of fine china teacups. And besides, only programmers enter literal values, not users, so they are of limited use in managing user data.

Variables are not simply disposable cups; they are reusable. You can keep putting the same type of tea over and over into the teacup. A string variable teacup can hold a string for reuse over and over. For instance, in this block of code, *response* holds the various strings assigned to it.

```
01 response = "A"
02 MsgBox("Give me an 'A'!")
03 MsgBox(response)
04 MsgBox("Give me another 'A'!")
05 MsgBox(response)
```

```
06 MsgBox("What's that spell?")
07 response = StrDup(2, "A")
08 MsgBox(response)
```

The variable *response* is loaded twice with two different strings: an "A" and then "AA." It keeps whatever value was last assigned to it; both lines 03 and 05 display "A" in a message box window. And you don't just have to assign literal strings to it; anything that generates a string can assign its result to *response*. Line 07 uses a built-in Visual Basic function, *StrDup*, to return the two-character string "AA" and assign it to *response*.

Using variables is a two-step process. First you must **declare** the variable, and then you **assign** a value to it. The *Dim* statement takes care of the declaration part; it lets you indicate both the *name* and the *type* of a variable. Its basic syntax is pretty straightforward:

```
Dim response As String
```

where *response* is the name of the variable, and *String* is its type. Assignment occurs using the "=" assignment operator:

```
response = "The answer"
```

A single variable can have new values assigned to it over and over again. For those times when you want your variable to have some specific value immediately upon declaration, you can combine declaration and assignment into a single statement:

```
Dim response As String = "The answer"
```

Of course, you're not just limited to a single declaration; you can create as many variables as you need in your code. Each one normally uses its own *Dim* statement:

```
Dim question As String
Dim answer As String
```

These can also be combined into a single statement, although I think it's just plain ugly:

```
Dim question As String, answer As String
```

See, I told you it was ugly. This is just the start of what's possible with the *Dim* statement. I'll get into more details as the chapter progresses.

Value Types and Reference Types

I talked about **value types** and **reference types** in Chapter 1, "Introducing .NET." Value type variables store an actual value; the tea in a value type teacup is the content itself. All of the literal data values I mentioned previously, except for Strings, are value types.

Reference type variables store a "reference" to the actual data, data found somewhere else in memory. When you look into a reference type teacup, you have to read the tea leaves at the bottom to determine where the real data resides.

Reference types either have data or they don't. In the absence of data, a reference type has a value of *Nothing*, a Visual Basic keyword that indicates no data. Value types are never *Nothing*; they always contain some value, possibly the default value for that type (such as zero for numeric types).

Data Types

The *String* data type is useful, but it's only one of the teacup shapes at your disposal. The .NET Framework defines several core **data types**. Each data type is implemented as a specific class within the *System* namespace. The most basic data type, a large teacup that can hold any type of data, is called **Object**. More than just an object, this is object with a capital O. In the .NET Class Library namespace hierarchy, it's located at *System.Object*. It's the mother of all classes in .NET; all other classes, structures, enumerations, delegates, and other types, no matter where they reside in the namespace, whether they are written by Microsoft or by you, all derive from *System.Object*. There's no getting around it; you cannot create a class that ultimately derives from anything else.

So, back to these "core" data types I've been hinting at. They match the four types of literal data values I listed before: strings, dates, numbers, and Boolean values. Table 2-1 lists these core data types. Each of these types also has a Visual Basic-specific name that you can (and should) use instead.

Table 2-1 Core .NET and Visual Basic Data Types

VB Name	Data Type	Description
Boolean	Boolean	The Boolean data type supports only values of *True* and *False*. It's possible to convert numbers to Boolean values: 0 becomes *False*, and everything else becomes *True*. When you convert a Boolean back to a number, *False* becomes 0, and *True* becomes –1.[2]
Byte	Byte	A numeric data type, Byte stores single-byte (8-bit) unsigned integers, ranging from 0 to 255. The Byte data type is pretty useful for working with non-text data, such as graphic images.
Char	Char	The Char data type holds exactly one text character. Each Char data value represents 2 bytes (16 bits) of storage, so it can manage *Double Byte Character Sets*, providing support for languages such as Japanese that have a large number of characters. Although it is used to store single text characters, internally the Char data type maintains the characters as integer values, ranging from 0 to 65535.
Date	DateTime	This date and time data type handles all dates between Jan 1, 1 AD to Dec 31, 9999 AD, in the Gregorian calendar. The time can be included as well; if no time is specified, midnight is used. Internally, the Date data type stores the date and time as the number of "ticks" since midnight of January 1, 1 AD. Each tick is 100 nanoseconds.
Decimal	Decimal	The Decimal data type is designed with currency in mind. It is very accurate in mathematical calculations, and has a pretty good range, supporting numbers just beyond 79 octillion, positive or negative. (Did he say 79 octillion?) That's 29 digits long, and that's important to remember, because you only get 29 digits total on both sides of the decimal point. That 79-octillion number comes with the limitation of no digits to the right of the decimal point. If you want one decimal position, you have to give up one to the left (the mantissa) and only keep numbers up to 7.9 octillion. If you want 29 digits after the decimal, then you get a big fat zero for the mantissa. If you used to use Visual Basic 6.0, Decimal is similar to the Currency sub-data type.

(continues)

---

[2] This is only true in Visual Basic. In other .NET languages, such as C#, *False* becomes 0, but *True* becomes 1, not –1. If you keep a Boolean value as Boolean, it is normally not an issue. But if you first convert your Booleans to numbers, and then start passing them around willy-nilly between code from different .NET languages, you may get surprising results.

Table 2-1 Core .NET and Visual Basic Data Types *(continued)*

VB Name	Data Type	Description
Double	Double	The Double data type handles the largest possible numbers of all the core numeric data types. Its range is about 4.94×10^{-324} to $1.798 \times 10^{+308}$ for positive numbers, with a similar range for negative values. Although you may think you are in giganto-number heaven, it's not all harps and wings. The Decimal data type is notoriously inaccurate in complex calculations. Sometimes, a calculation that should result in zero will actually calculate as something like 0.00000000000005434, which is close. But comparisons of this number with zero will fail, because it is not zero.
Integer	Int32	The Integer data type is a 4-byte (32-bit) signed integer type. It handles numbers from –2,147,483,648 to 2,147,483,647. If you are a pre-.NET Visual Basic programmer, this new Integer data type is equivalent to the version 6.0 Long data type.
Long	Int64	The Long data type is even bigger than Integer; it's an 8-byte (64-bit) signed integer type. It handles numbers from –9,223,372,036,854,775,808 (wow!) to 9,223,372,036,854,775,807 (wow! wow!). It is not the same as the old Visual Basic 6.0 Long data type, as it has twice the storage capacity.
Object	Object	Object is the core type for all .NET types. It sits at the top of the class and type hierarchy; it is the ultimate base class for all other classes. It is a reference type, although value types eventually derive from it, too.
SByte	SByte	A numeric data type, SByte stores single-byte (8-bit) signed integers, ranging from –128 to 127. It is the signed version of the unsigned Byte data type.
Short	Int16	The Short data type is a 2-byte (16-bit) signed integer type. It stores numbers from –32,768 to 32,767. If you are a pre-.NET Visual Basic programmer, this new Short data type is equivalent to the version 6.0 Integer data type.

VB Name	Data Type	Description
Single	Single	The Single data type is pretty much like the Double data type, only smaller. Its range for positive numbers is about 1.4×10^{-45} to $3.4 \times 10^{+38}$, with a similar range for negative numbers. Like the Double data type, the single data type suffers from slight inaccuracies during calculations.
String	String	The String data type is a reference type that stores up to about two billion characters of text. It stores **Unicode** characters, which are 2-byte (16-bit) characters capable of storing characters from most languages in the world, including languages with large alphabets, such as Chinese.
UInteger	UInt32	UInteger stores 4-byte (32-bit) unsigned integers, ranging from 0 to 4,294,967,295. It is the unsigned version of the signed Integer data type.
ULong	UInt64	ULong stores 8-byte (64-bit) unsigned integers, ranging from 0 to 18,446,744,073,709,551,615. It is the unsigned version of the signed Long data type.
UShort	UInt16	UShort stores 2-byte (16-bit) unsigned integers, ranging from 0 to 65,535. It is the unsigned version of the signed Short data type.

The Microsoft developers in charge of Visual Basic data types lucked out on that job because all core Visual Basic data types are simply wrappers for specific data types implemented by .NET. The Visual Basic names given for each of these core data types are fully interchangeable with the .NET names. For example, *Integer* is fully equivalent to *System.Int32*. In fact, when writing Visual Basic code, it is better to use the Visual Basic synonyms, because most Visual Basic developers expect these data type names in the code they read and write.

Except for *Object* and *String*, all of these data types are value types. All value types are derived from *System.ValueType* (which in turn derives from *System.Object*).

The *SByte*, *UInteger*, *ULong*, and *UShort* data types were added to Visual Basic with its 2005 release, although their *System* namespace equivalents have been in .NET since its inception. Unlike the other core data types, these four types are not "CLS-compliant"; that is, they cannot be used to interact with .NET components and languages that limit themselves to just the very core required features of .NET. Generally this is not much of a limitation, but be on your guard when working with third-party components or languages.

Advanced Declaration

When I mentioned the need for *declaration* and *assignment* of variables, I was really focusing on value types. Reference types require one additional step: **instantiation**. Consider the following declaration statements:

```
Dim defaultValue As Integer
Dim nonDefaultValue As Integer = 5
Dim defaultReference As Object
```

These lines declare three separate variables: two value types (the Integers) and one reference type (the Object). Although only one variable has an explicit data assignment, all three have actually been assigned something, either explicitly or implicitly. Let's look at those statements again and see what is truly being assigned to each variable.

```
Dim defaultValue As Integer = 0
Dim nonDefaultValue As Integer = 5
Dim defaultReference As Object = Nothing
```

Both declaration and assignment already occurred for all of the variables, just by using the *Dim* statement. The *defaultValue* variable, with its default assignment of zero, can be used immediately in equations. However, the reference type variable *defaultReference* is just an empty teacup, with no default data to manipulate. There are features in Visual Basic that let you compare a reference type with *Nothing*, and you could do this immediately, but it's not really data. And remember, variables live to manage data.

Reference data values need instantiation, and instantiation needs the *New* keyword.

```
Dim defaultReference As Object = New Object
```

Now *defaultReference* points to a real object; now the *defaultReference* teacup has something consumable inside of it, but because it is just *System.Object*, it doesn't have much in the way of flavor. Strings are a little more interesting, and they also have more interesting *constructors*.

As you may recall from way back in Chapter 1, a constructor is a block of initialization code that runs when you create a new data value or object. Some objects allow you to supply extra information to a constructor, additional information that is used in the initialization process. A **default constructor** doesn't allow you to supply any extra information; it just works on its own, initializing data like it was nobody's business. There is no limit on the number of constructors in a class, but each one must vary in the type of extra information passed to it.

So back to Strings. You would expect the default String constructor to create a blank, zero-length string:

```
Dim worldsMostBoringString As String = New String
```

But the String class doesn't have a default constructor. Instead, you initialize the string with a literal:

```
Dim worldsMostBoringString As String = ""
```

That's because Strings are treated specially by Visual Basic. String literals are actually instantiations of *String* data values; it's as if you created a new *String* instance using the *System.String* class. But *String* also has more interesting constructors. (I'll delve into the details of constructors in Chapters 6 and 8, "Classes and Inheritance.") One of the constructors creates a new *String* instance initialized with a specific character repeated a number of times. For instance, to create a *String* instance with a 25-character string of the letter *M*, use the following syntax:

```
Dim mmGood As String = New String("M"c, 25)
```

If you're going to use the same data type just after the *As* keyword that you use right after the *New* keyword, you can use a collapsed syntax.

```
Dim mmGood As New String("M"c, 25)
```

As with value types, you can also break the statement into distinct declaration and assignment statements.

```
Dim mmGood As String
mmGood = New String("M"c, 25)
```

Constants

Literals don't change, but they can only be used once in your code. **Constants** are a cross between a literal and a variable; they have a single, never-changing value just like data literals, but they also have a name that can be reused over and over again, just like variables.

You declare constants using the *Const* keyword instead of the *Dim* keyword:

```
Const SpeedOfLight As Integer = 186000
```

Actual assignment of the value to the constant occurs in the statement itself, with the value following the = sign. Once your constant is declared and assigned, it's available for use in actual statements of your actual code:

```
MsgBox("Lightspeed in miles/second: " & SpeedOfLight)
```

Local Declaration and Fields

In the real world, there is some data that you need to keep private, for your use only. Your neighbors have other juicy bits of data and information that they share among themselves. And then there is public data that isn't hidden from anyone. But it's not just this way in the real world; the fake world of Visual Basic has different levels of access and privacy for your data.

A little later in the chapter, we'll see that your application's logic code will always appear in procedures, named blocks of source code. You declare **local variables** (and constants) in these same procedures when you need a short-lived and personal variable that is only for use within a single procedure. Other variables (and constants) can appear outside of procedures, but still within the context of a class or similar type. These **fields**, whether variable or constant, are immediately available to all of the different procedures that also call the current class home.

You define all local variables using the *Dim* keyword. The *Dim* statement works for field definitions, but it's more common to use special **access modifier** keywords instead. These modifiers determine what code can access the fields, from *Private* (only used by code inside of the class) to *Public* (also available outside of the class).

```
Private ForInClassUseOnly As Integer
```

There are five access modifiers in all. I'll talk more about them, and about fields in general, in Chapters 6 and 8.

Intermission

That was a lot to take in. Getting your mind around data and variables is probably the most complex part of programming in Visual Basic. Once you have the data in variables, it's pretty easy to manipulate.

Although the thought of a cup of tea may cause you to run out the room like a raving lunatic, you might want to take a few minutes, grab a cup, glass, saucer, or mug of your beverage of choice, and relax. I'll see you in about 20 or 30 minutes.

Comments

If you're an opera fan, you know how exciting a good opera can be, especially a classic work presented with the original foreign language *libretto*. If you're not an opera fan, you know how irritating it can be to listen to several hours of a foreign language *libretto*. With the advent of "supra titles" conveying the English-language interpretation of the content, those who until now have gotten little joy out of the opera experience will still find it repulsive, only this time in their native tongue. But at least now they will know why they don't enjoy the story.

That's really what comments do: tell you in your own language what is actually going on in a foreign language. In this book, the foreign language is Visual Basic, and English is the vernacular. You may find a particular block of Visual Basic code to be poorly written or even detestable, but if the accompanying comments are accurate, you can be disgusted in your own language, with a human language understanding of the process.

2. INTRODUCING VISUAL BASIC

Comments normally appear on lines by themselves, but you may also attach a comment to the end of an existing code line. If a logical line is broken into multiple physical lines using the "_" line continuation character, a trailing comment is only valid at the end of the final physical line.

```
' ----- This is a standalone comment, on a line by itself.
Dim counter As Integer    ' This is a trailing comment.
MsgBox("The counter starts at " & _   ' INVALID COMMENT HERE!
    counter)  ' But this one is valid.
```

Comments begin with the comment character, the standard single quote character (`'`). Any text following the comment character is a comment, and is ignored when your code is compiled into a usable application. Any single quote that appears within a literal string is not used as a comment marker.

```
MsgBox("No 'comments' in this text.")
```

Comments can also begin with the "REM" keyword (as in "REMark"), but most programmers use the single-quote variation instead.

Option Statements

A few code examples ago, you saw that Visual Basic would supply a default *assignment* to a variable—at least for value types—if you neglected to include one. In certain cases, Visual Basic will also supply the *declaration* if you leave it out. In the statement:

```
brandNewValue = 5
```

if there is no related *Dim* statement that defines *brandNewValue*, Visual Basic will declare the variable on your behalf, assigning it to the *Object* data type. *Don't let this happen to you!* You don't know what kind of trouble you will have if you allow such practices in your code. You will quickly find your code filled with mysterious logic bugs, esoteric data issues, recurrent head lice, and so on.

The problem is that Visual Basic will not complain if you mistype the name of your auto-declared variable. Left unchecked, this practice could lead to code like this:

```
brandNewValue = 5
MsgBox(brandNewVlaue)
```

My, my, my, look at that spelling mistake on the second line. What? Visual Basic compiled without any error? And now your message box displays nothing instead of 5? Such trauma could be avoided by judicious use of the **Option** statements included in the Visual Basic language. There are three such statements.

- **Option Explicit On.** This statement forces you to declare all variables using *Dim* (or a similar statement) before use. It's possible to replace "On" with "Off" in the statement, but don't do it.
- **Option Strict On.** Visual Basic will do some simple data conversions for you when needed. For instance, if you assign a 64-bit *Long* data value to a 32-bit *Integer* variable, Visual Basic will normally convert this data to the smaller size for you, complaining only if the data doesn't fit. This type of conversion—a **narrowing conversion**—is not always safe because the source data will sometimes fail to fit in the destination. (A **widening conversion**, as with storing *Integer* data in a *Long*, always works, because the destination can always hold the source value.) The *Option Strict On* statement turns off the automatic processing of narrowing conversions. You will be forced to use explicit conversion functions to perform narrowing conversions. This is good, because it forces you to think about the type of data your variables will hold. You can replace "On" with "Off" in this statement, but if I've warned you once, I've warned you twice: Don't even try it.
- **Option Compare Binary** and **Option Compare Text.** These two variations of the *Option Compare* statement instruct your code to use specific sorting rules for certain string comparison features. In general, "Binary" comparison is case-sensitive, while "Text" comparison is not. It's up to you which method you want to use; the default is "Binary."

These statements appear at the top of each source code file in your project, before any other code.

```
Option Explicit On
Option Strict On
```

Or, to save on precious disk space, set default values that apply to your entire project through the project's properties. In Visual Studio, select the **Project ➤ Properties** menu command. On the project's properties window that appears, select the **Compile** tab, and set your default choices for the **Option explicit**, **Option strict**, and **Option compare** fields (see Figure 2-2).

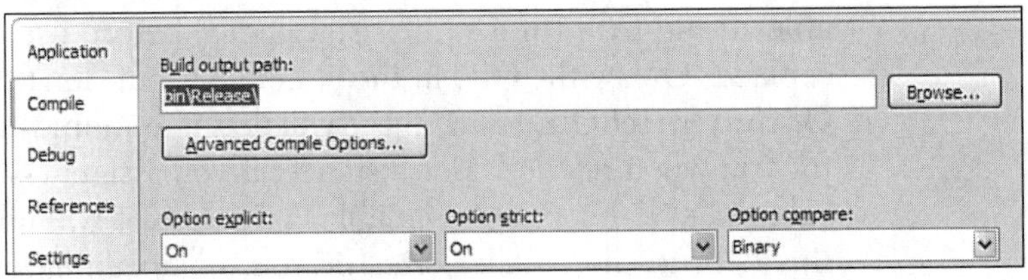

Figure 2-2 Options, options everywhere

Basic Operators

Visual Basic includes several basic operators that let you do what your code really wants to do: manipulate data. To use them, just dial zero from your phone. No, wait, those operators let you place operator-assisted calls for only $2.73 for the first minute. The Visual Basic operators let you perform mathematical, logical, bitwise, and string management functions, all at no additional cost.

The most basic operator is the assignment operator, represented by the equals sign (=). You've already seen this operator in use in this chapter. Use it to assign some value to a variable; whatever appears to the right of the operator gets assigned to the reference type or value type variable on the left. The statement:

```
fiveSquared = 25
```

assigns a value of 25 to the variable *fiveSquared*.

Most operators are **binary operators**—they operate on two distinct values, one to the operator's left and one to the right; the result is a single calculated value. It's as if the calculation is fully replaced by the calculated result. For instance, the addition operation:

```
seven = 3 + 4
```

becomes:

```
seven = 7
```

before the final application of the assignment (=) operator. A **unary operator** appears just to the left of its operand. For instance, the unary negation operator turns a positive number into a negative number.

```
negativeSeven = -7
```

I'll comment on each operator in detail in Chapter 6. But we'll need a quick summary for now so we can manipulate data before we get to that chapter. Table 2-2 lists the main Visual Basic operators and briefly describes the purpose of each one.

Table 2-2 Visual Basic Operators

Operator	Description
+	The addition operator adds two numbers together.
+	The unary plus operator retains the sign of a numeric value. It's not very useful until you get into operator overloading, something covered in Chapter 12, "Operator Overloading."
-	The subtraction operator subtracts the second operand from the first.
-	The unary negation operator reverses the sign of its associated numeric operand.
*	The multiplication operator multiplies two numeric values together.
/	The division operator divides the first numeric operand by the second, returning the quotient including any decimal remainder.
\	The integer division operator divides the first numeric operand by the second, returning the quotient, but with the decimal remainder truncated.

(continues)

2. INTRODUCING VISUAL BASIC

Table 2-2 Visual Basic Operators *(continued)*

Operator	Description
Mod	The modulo operator divides the first numeric operand by the second, and returns only the remainder as an integer value.
^	The exponentiation operator raises the first operand (the base) to the power of the second (the exponent).
&	The string concatenation operator joins two string operands together, and returns a new string with the combined results.
And	The conjunction operator returns *True* if both Boolean operands are also *True*.
AndAlso	This operator is just like the *And* operator, but it doesn't examine or process the second operand if the first one is *False*.
Or	The disjunction operator returns *True* if either of the operands is also *True*.
OrElse	This operator is just like the *Or* operator, but it doesn't examine or process the second operand if the first one is *True*.
Not	The negation operator returns the opposite of a Boolean operand.
Xor	The exclusive or operator returns *True* if exactly one of the operands is also *True*.
<<	The shift left operator shifts the individual bits in an integer operand to the left by the number of bit positions in the second operand.
>>	The shift right operator shifts the individual bits of an integer operand to the right by the number of bit positions in the second operand.
=	The equal-to comparison operator returns *True* if the operands are "equal" to each other.
<	The less-than comparison operator returns *True* if the first operand is "less than" the second.
<=	The less-than-or-equal comparison operator returns *True* if the first operand is "less than or equal to" the second.
>	The greater-than comparison operator returns *True* if the first operand is "greater than" the second.
>=	The greater-than-or-equal comparison operator returns *True* if the first operand is "greater than or equal to" the second.
<>	The not-equal-to comparison operator returns *True* if the first operand is "not equal to" the second.

Operator	Description
Like	The pattern comparison operator returns *True* if the first operand matches a string pattern specified by the second operand.
Is	The object equal-to comparison operator returns *True* if both operands truly represent the same instance of a data value in memory. Setting the second operand to *Nothing* lets you test a reference variable to see if it contains data or not.
IsNot	The object not-equal-to comparison operator is the opposite of the *Is* operator.

The *And*, *Or*, *Not*, and *Xor* operators also work as "bitwise" operators. I'll talk about that in the "Operators" section of Chapter 6.

As powerful as operators are, even more power comes when you combine them. This works because any of the operands can be a complex **expression** that includes its own operands. Parentheses grouped around clauses in operands ensure that values are processed in the order you expect.

```
circleArea = pi * (radius ^ 2)
```

In this statement, the second operand of the * multiplication operator is another expression, which includes its own operator.

Using Functions and Subroutines

Years ago I worked for a software company that sometimes published software developed outside of the organization, all for a non-Windows platform. While most of these programs were written in the C language, we also published software written in Pascal, assembly language, and good ol' BASIC. I inherited one such external application written entirely in BASIC, a program that assisted the user in 3-D modeling and graphic rendering. It was a complex program, containing about 30,000 lines of source code. The problem was that it was one large block of 30,000 source code lines. No comments, no variable names longer than a few characters, no extra-strength buffered aspirin product. Just thousands of lines of code with flow control statements jumping this way and that. And, of course, it had a bug.

2. INTRODUCING VISUAL BASIC

I was able to move past that event in my life without too much therapy, but at the time it was a shock to see code in that condition. And it was so unnecessary, because that flavor of BASIC was a **procedural language**, just like C and Pascal. Procedural languages allow you to break your code into named blocks of logic, called procedures. These procedures allow the programmer to take a "divide and conquer" approach to programming; you write procedures that accomplish a specific logical portion of the code within your entire application, and then access these procedures from other procedures.

Visual Basic includes three types of procedures.

- **Subroutines.** These procedures, also called "sub procedures," do a bunch of work and then return to the calling procedure. Data can be sent into the subroutine through its *argument list*, and some values may come back through that same list, but there is no official final result sent back from the procedure. A subroutine does its work, and once it is complete, the calling code continues on its merry way.
- **Functions.** Functions are just like subroutines, with one additional feature. You can return a single value or object instance from the function as its official result. Usually, the calling code takes this *return value* into consideration when it completes its own logic.
- **Properties.** When used, properties actually look like variables. You assign and retrieve values to and from properties just like you would for a variable. However, properties include hidden code, often used to validate the data being assigned to the property.

Subroutines, functions, and properties are the code members of each class or similar type. I'll delay discussion of properties until a little later in the chapter. For now, let's enjoy functions and subroutines, which together are also known as **methods**. Let's start with subroutines. To call a subroutine, type its name as a statement, followed by a set of parentheses. Any data you need to send to the subroutine goes in the parentheses. For instance, the following subroutine call does some work, passing the ID number of a customer and a starting date:

```
DoSomeWork(customerID, startDate)
```

Each subroutine defines the data type and order of the arguments you pass. This argument list may include one or more **optional arguments**, which are assigned default values if you don't include them. A subroutine might also be **overloaded**, defining different possible argument lists based on the number and data type of the arguments. We'll encounter a lot of these later.

Functions are a little more interesting because they return a usable value. Often, this value is assigned to a variable.

```
Dim balanceDue As Boolean
balanceDue = HasOutstandingBalance(customerID)
```

Then you can do something with this result. If you want, you can ignore the return value of a function, and we already have. The *MsgBox* function used earlier returns the identity of the on-screen button clicked by the user. If you only include an OK button (the default), you probably don't care which button the user presses.

```
MsgBox("Go ahead, click the OK button.")
```

But you can also capture the result of the button.

```
whichButton = MsgBox("Click Yes or No.", MsgBoxStyle.YesNo)
```

In this case, *whichButton* will either be *MsgBoxResult.Yes* or *MsgBoxResult.No*, two of the possible results defined by the *MsgBox* function.

Conditions

Sometimes, you just have to make some choices, and conditional expressions will help you do just that. Visual Basic includes support for **conditions**, which use data tests to determine which code should be processed next.

If Statements

The most common conditional statement is the *If* statement. It is equivalent to English questions in the form, "If such-and-such is true, then do so-and-so." For instance, it can handle, "If you have $20, then you can buy me dinner," but not, "If a train departs Chicago at 45 miles per hour, when will it run out of coal?"

If statements have a syntax that spans multiple source code lines.

```
01 If (hadAHammer = True) Then
02    DoHammer(inTheMorning, allOverThisLand)
03    DoHammer(inTheEvening, allOverThisLand)
04 ElseIf (hadAShovel = True) Then
05    DoShovel(inTheNoontime, allOverThisLand)
06 Else
07    TakeNap(allDayLong, onMySofa)
08 End If
```

The *If* statement lets you define **branches** in your code based on conditions. It is built from three main components.

1. **Conditions.** The expression found between the *If* (or *ElseIf*) keyword and the *Then* keyword is the condition. The sample includes two conditions, on lines 01 and 04. Conditions may be simple or complex, but they must already result in a Boolean *True* or *False* value. They can include calls to other functions and multiple logical and comparison operators.

   ```
   If ((PlayersOnTeam(homeTeam) >= 9) And _
         (PlayersOnTeam(visitingTeam) >= 9)) Or _
         (justPracticing = True) Then
       PlayBall()
   Else
       StadiumLights(turnOff)
   End If
   ```

   The original condition always follows the *If* keyword. If that conditions fails, you can specify additional conditions following an *ElseIf* keyword, as on line 04. You may include as many *ElseIf* clauses as you need.

2. **Branches.** Each condition's *Then* keyword is followed by one or more Visual Basic statements that are processed if the associated condition evaluates to *True*. All statements up to the next *ElseIf* or the final *End If* are included in that branch's statement block. You may include any number of statements in a branch block, including additional subordinate *If* statements. In the sample code, branch lines 02 and 03 are processed if the original "hadAHammer" condition is true. Line 05 is processed instead if the original condition fails, but the second "hadAShovel" condition passes. If none of the conditions are *True*, the *Else*'s branch, on line 07, executes.

3. **Statement keywords.** The *If* statement is one of several multi-line statements in Visual Basic, all of which end with the keyword *End* followed by the original statement keyword (*If* in this case). The *If* statement's keywords, which give the statement its structure, include *If*, *Then*, *ElseIf*, *Else*, and *End If*. All *ElseIf* and *Else* clauses and related branches are optional. The simplest *If* statement includes only an *If* branch.

```
If (phoneNumberLength = 10) Then
    DialNumber(phoneNumber)
End If
```

For conditions with simple single-statement branches and no *ElseIf* clauses, a single-line alternative can keep your code looking clean.

```
If (SaveData() = True) Then MsgBox("Data saved.")
If (TimeOfDay >= #13:00#) _
    Then currentStatus = WorkStatus.GoHome _
    Else currentStatus = WorkStatus.BusyWorking
```

If statements are cool because they make your code more than just a boring set of linear step-by-step instructions that never deviate for any reason. Software is written to support some real-world process, and real-world processes are seldom linear. The *If* statement makes it possible for your code to react to different data conditions, taking the appropriate branch when necessary.

Once the entire *If . . . End If* block completes, processing continues with the next statement that follows the *End If* statement.

Select Case Statements

Sometimes you might write an *If* statement that simply tests a variable against one possible value, then another, then another, then another, and so on.

```
If (billValue = 1) Then
   presidentName = "Washington"
ElseIf (billValue = 2) Then
   presidentName = "Jefferson"
ElseIf (billValue = 5) Then
   presidentName = "Lincoln"

   ...
```

2. INTRODUCING VISUAL BASIC

And on it goes, through many more *ElseIf* clauses. It's effective, but a little tedious, as your code must specifically test every case. The *Select Case* statement provides a cleaner alternative to simple value comparisons against a list.

```
01 Select Case billValue
02    Case 1
03       presidentName = "Washington"
04    Case 2
05       presidentName = "Jefferson"
06    Case 5
07       presidentName = "Lincoln"
08    Case 20
09       presidentName = "Jackson"
10    Case 50
11       presidentName = "Grant"
12    Case 10, 100
13       presidentName = "!! Non-president"
14    Case > 100
15       presidentName = "!! Value too large"
16    Case Else
17       presidentName = "!! Invalid value"
18 End Select
```

Unlike the *If* statement, which checks for a Boolean result, *Select Case* compares a single value against a set of test case values. In the example, the *billValue* variable is compared against the different values identified by each *Case* clause. All code that follows a *Case* clause (until the next *Case* clause) is the branch that is processed when a match is found. An optional *Case Else* condition (line 16) catches anything that is not matched by any other *Case*. Normally, *Case* clauses list single values for comparison. They can also include a list of comma-separated comparison values (line 12), or simple range comparison expressions (line 14).

IIf Function

Visual Basic includes a variation of the *If* statement for "in line" use. Consider the following statement.

```
If (gender = "F") Then fullGender = "Female" _
   Else fullGender = "Male"
```

Using the *IIf* function, this statement compresses into a single assignment statement with an embedded condition.

```
fullGender = IIf(gender = "F", "Female", "Male")
```

The *IIf* function has three comma-delimited arguments. The first is the condition, which must result in a Boolean *True* or *False* value. The second argument is returned by the function if the condition is *True*; a condition result of *False* returns the third argument. For simple conditions that are destined to return single values to a common variable, it's really a useful function. But with anything really useful, there are caveats. The caveat with *IIf* is that *anything appearing inside the IIf statement will be processed, even if it is not returned as a result.* Here's a dangerous example:

```
purgeResult = IIf(level = 1, PurgeSet1(), PurgeSet2())
```

The statement will correctly return the result of either *PurgeSet1()* or *PurgeSet2()* based on the value of *level*. The problem, or potential problem, is that both functions, *PurgeSet1()* and *PurgeSet2()*, will be called; if *level* is 1, both *PurgeSet1()* and *PurgeSet2()* will be called, even though only the function result from *PurgeSet1()* will be returned.

Loops

Visual Basic includes three major types of loops: *For . . . Next, For Each . . . Next*, and *Do . . . Loop*. Just as conditions allow you to break up the sequential monotony of your code through branches, loops add to the usefulness of your code by letting you repeat a specific block of logic a fixed or variable number of times.

For . . . Next Loops

The most common loop structure is the *For . . . Next* loop. This loop uses a numeric counter that increments from a starting value to an ending value, processing the code within the loop once for each incremented value.

```
Dim whichMonth As Integer
For whichMonth = 1 To 12
    ProcessMonthlyData(whichMonth)
Next counter
```

This sample loops 12 times (1 to 12), once for each month. You can specify any starting and ending values you wish; this range can also be specified using variables or functions that return numeric values. Once the starting and ending values are obtained, they are not recalculated each time through the loop, even if a function call is used to obtain one or both limits.

```
' ----- Month(Today) returns the numeric month
'       for the current date.
For whichMonth = 1 To Month(Today)
    ProcessMonthlyData(whichMonth)
Next counter
```

Normally, the loop increments by one (1) each time through. You can alter this default by attaching a *Step* clause to the end of the *For* statement line.

```
For countDown = 60 To 0 Step -1
    . . .
Next countDown
```

One additional syntax variation allows you to declare the loop counter variable within the statement itself. Such variables are available only within the loop, and cease to exist once the loop exits.

```
For whichMonth As Integer = 1 To 12
    ProcessMonthlyData(whichMonth)
Next whichMonth
```

For Each . . . Next Loops

A variation of the *For* loop, the *For Each . . . Next* loop, scans through a set of ordered and related items, from the first item until the last. Arrays and collection objects also work, as does any object that supports the *IEnumerable* interface (all these topics are covered in Chapter 6). The syntax is quite similar to the standard *For* statement.

```
For Each oneRecord In setOfRecords
    ProcessRecord(oneRecord)
Next oneRecord
```

Do . . . Loop Loops

Sometimes you want to repeat a block of code as long as a certain condition is true, or only until a condition is true. The *Do . . . Loop* structure performs both of these tasks. The statement includes a *While* or *Until* clause that specifies the conditions for continued loop processing. For instance, the following statement does some processing for a set of dates, from a starting date to an ending date.

```
Dim processDate As Date = #1/1/2000#
Do While (processDate < #2/1/2000#)
    ' ----- Perform processing for the current date.
    ProcessContent(processDate)

    ' ----- Move ahead to the next date.
    processDate.AddDays(1)
Loop
```

Processing in this sample will continue until the *processDate* variable exceeds 2/1/2000, which indicates the end of processing. The *Until* clause version is somewhat similar, although with a reversed condition result.

```
Do Until (processDate >= #2/1/2000#)
    . . .
Loop
```

Make the included condition as simple or as complex as you need. Putting the *Until* or *While* clause at the bottom of the loop guarantees that the statements inside of the loop will always be processed at least once.

```
Do
    . . .
Loop Until (processDate >= #2/1/2000#)
```

There is another loop that is similar to *Do . . . Loop* called the *While . . . End While* loop. However, it exists for backward compatibility only. Use the *Do . . . Loop* statement instead.

2. INTRODUCING VISUAL BASIC

Exit Statements

Normally, when you enter a loop, you have every intention of looping for the full number of times specified by the initial conditions of the loop. For *For* loops, you expect to continue through the entire numeric range or collection of elements. In *Do* loops, you plan to keep the loop going as long as the exiting condition has not yet been met. But there may be loops that you want to exit early. You accomplish this using an *Exit* statement.

There are two loop-specific exit statements.

- **Exit For.** Exits a *For . . . Next* or *For Each . . . Next* loop immediately.
- **Exit Do.** Exits a *Do . . . Loop* statement immediately.

Each *Exit* statement exits the loop that contains the statement; processing continues with the line immediately following the loop.

```
For whichMonth = 1 To 12
    If (ProcessMonthlyData(whichMonth) = False) Then Exit For
Next whichMonth
' ----- Code continues here no matter how the loop was exited.
```

The following sample is designed to loop through all 12 months. However, a processing failure for any of the 12 months will immediately exit the loop, abandoning all remaining month processing actions. The *Exit Do* statement similarly exits *Do . . . Loop* loops immediately.

When using an *Exit* loop statement within **nested loops** (where one loop appears within another), only the matching loop that immediately contains the statement is exited.

```
For whichMonth = 1 To 12
    For whichDay = 1 to DaysInMonth(whichMonth)
        If (ProcessDailyData(whichMonth, whichDay) = False) _
            Then Exit For
    Next whichDay
    ' ----- The Exit For statement jumps to this line.
    '       Processing continues with the next month.
Next whichMonth
```

Continue Statements

Because exiting a loop abandons all remaining passes through the loop, you may miss out on importing processing that would have happened in subsequent passes. Visual Basic includes a *Continue* statement that lets you abandon only the current pass through the loop.

There are different *Continue* statement variations for each of the loop types.

- **Continue For.** Immediately jumps to the end of the *For . . . Next* or *For Each . . . Next* loop and prepares for the next pass. The loop variable is incremented and compared with the range limits.
- **Continue Do.** Immediately jumps to the end of the *Do . . . Loop* statement and prepares for the next pass. The *Until* or *While* condition is reevaluated.

Because the loop conditions are reevaluated when using the *Continue* statements, there are times when *Continue* may cause the loop to exit, such as when it had been the final pass through the loop already.

In this example, the *Continue For* statement skips processing for months that have no data to process.

```
For whichMonth = 1 To 12
    If (DataAvailable(whichMonth) = False) The Continue For
    RetrieveData(whichMonth)
    ProcessData(whichMonth)
    SaveData(whichMonth)
Next whichMonth
```

Creating Your Own Procedures

All logic statements in your code must appear within a procedure, whether in a subroutine, a function, or a property. Although there are thousands of prewritten procedures for you to choose from in the Framework libraries, you can also add your own.

Subroutines

Subroutines begin with a *Sub* declaration statement and end with an *End Sub* statement. All of your subroutine's logic appears in between these two mighty jaws.

```
01 Sub ShowIngredients(ByVal gender As Char)
02    Dim theMessage As String = "Unknown."
03    If (gender = "M"c) Then
04       theMessage = "Snips and snails and puppy dog tails."
05    ElseIf (gender = "F"c) Then
06       theMessage = "Sugar and spice and everything nice."
07    End If
08    MsgBox(theMessage)
09 End Sub
```

Line 01 shows the subroutine's declaration line in its simplest form; throughout the book, you will find that there are additional keywords that decorate procedure declarations to change their behavior. The statement begins with the *Sub* keyword (for **sub**routine), followed by the name of the procedure, *ShowIngredients*.

The parentheses following this name contain the subroutine's **parameters**. Parameters allow another block of code that will use this procedure to pass data into the procedure, and optionally receive data back. You can include any number of parameters in the subroutine definition; simply separate them by commas. Each parameter specifies the name as it will be used in the procedure (*gender* in the sample) and its data type (*Char*). The arguments are treated as declared variables within the procedure, as is done with *gender* on lines 03 and 05.

The values supplied by the calling code are known as **arguments**. All arguments are passed **by value** or **by reference**. In the sample code, the argument passed into *gender* will be passed by value, as specified through the *ByVal* keyword. The related *ByRef* keyword indicates an argument to be passed by reference. If you don't include either keyword, *ByVal* is assumed. This passing method impacts whether changes made to the argument within the local procedure are propagated back to the calling code. However, the ability to update the original data is also influenced by whether the data is a *value type* or a *reference type*. Table 2-3 indicates the behavior for each combination of passing method and data type.

Table 2-3 Updating Data, the .NET Way

Passing Method	Data Type	Behavior
ByVal	Value Type	Changes made to the local version of the argument have no impact on the original version.
ByVal	Reference Type	Changes made to *members* of the data object immediately impact the original data object. However, the object itself cannot be changed or replaced with a completely new data object.
ByRef	Value Type	Changes made to the local version are returned to the calling procedure, and permanently impact the original data value.
ByRef	Reference Type	Changes made to either the data object or its members are also changed in the original. It is possible to fully replace the object sent in to the procedure.

In most cases, if you are interested in modifying the value of a parameter and having the changes return to the caller, use *ByRef*; otherwise, use *ByVal*.

Lines 02 through 08 in the sample code comprise the **body** of the procedure, where all of your logic appears. Any variables to be used solely in the routine are also defined here, as with the *theMessage* variable on line 02. The subroutine always concludes with an *End Sub* statement.

Functions

The syntax of a function differs only slightly from subroutines, to support a return value.

```
01 Function IsPrime(ByVal source As Long) As Boolean
02     ' ----- Determine if source is a prime number.
03     Dim testValue As Long
04     If (source < 2) Then
05         Return False
06     ElseIf (source > 2) Then
```

```
07        For testValue = 2 To source \ 2&
08            If ((source Mod testValue) = 0) Then
09                Return False
10            End If
11        Next testValue
12    End If
13    Return True
14 End Function
```

As with subroutines, the function's declaration line appears first (line 01), followed by the body (lines 02 through 13) and the closing *End Function* statement (line 14). The declaration line includes an extra data type definition after the parameter list. This is the data type of the final value to be returned to the calling code. Use this return value in the calling code just like any other value or variable. For example, the following line calls the *IsPrime* function and stores its Boolean result in a variable.

```
primeResult = IsPrime(23)
```

To indicate the value to return, use the *Return* statement (described later in the chapter). The sample code does this on lines 05, 09, and 13. (An older VB 6.0 syntax that lets you assign the return value to the name of the function still works.)

Properties

A little earlier I mentioned fields, variables or constants that appear within a class, but outside of any procedure definition.

```
01 Class PercentRange
02     Public Percent As Integer
03 End Class
```

Properties are similar to fields; they are used like class-level variables or constants. But they are programmed like functions, accepting parameters, having return values, and including as much logic as you require.

Properties are often used to protect private class data with logic that weeds out inappropriate values. The following class defines a single property that provides access to the hidden related field.

```
01 Class PercentRange
02    ' ----- Stores a percent from 0 to 100 only.
03    Private savedPercent As Integer
04    Public Property Percent() As Integer
05       Get
06          Return savedPercent
07       End Get
08       Set(ByVal value As Integer)
09          If (value < 0) Then
10             savedPercent = 0
11          ElseIf (value > 100) Then
12             savedPercent = 100
13          Else
14             savedPercent = value
15          End If
16       End Set
17    End Property
18 End Class
```

The *Percent* property (lines 04 to 17) protects access to the *savedPercent* field (line 03), correcting any caller-supplied values that exceed the 0 to 100 range. Properties include separate assignment and retrieval components, also called **accessors**. The *Get* accessor (lines 05 to 07) returns the property's monitored value to the caller. The *Set* accessor (lines 08 to 16) lets the caller modify the value of the property.

The property declaration statement (line 04) includes a data type that matches the data type passed into the *Set* accessor (line 08). This is the data type of the value set or retrieved by the caller. To use this sample *Percent* property, create an instance of the *PercentRange* class, and then use the property.

```
Dim activePercent As New PercentRange
activePercent.Percent = 107    ' An out-of-range Integer
MsgBox(activePercent.Percent)  ' Displays "100", not "107"
```

You can create read-only or write-only properties by including the *ReadOnly* or *WriteOnly* keyword just before the *Property* keyword in the declaration statement (line 04), and leaving out the unneeded accessor.

Properties do not need to be tied to fields. You can use properties to get and set any type of value, and store it or act upon it in any manner you wish.

Where to Put Your Procedures

Back in the good ol' days of Visual Basic 6.0, procedures could appear just about anywhere in your source code files. You would open a source file, type a function, and go; it was that easy. With the move to .NET, all Visual Basic procedures must now appear within a defined class (or a structure or module).

```
Class Employee
   Sub StartVacation()
      ...
   End Sub

   Function TotalVacationTaken() As Double
      ...
   End Function
End Class
```

When you create instances of your class later in code, the methods can be called directly through the object instance.

```
Dim executive As New Employee
...
executive.StartVacation()
```

Chapter 8 shows you how to use and build classes.

Other Flow Control Features

The loops and conditional statements available in Visual Basic let you reroute your code based on data. The language includes a few other statements that let you control the action in a more direct manner.

The GoTo Statement

The *GoTo* statement lets you jump immediately to some other location within the current procedure. The destination of a jump is always a **line label**, a named line position in the current procedure. All line labels appear at the start of a logical line, and end with a colon.

```
PromptUser:
   GetValuesFromUser(numerator, denominator)
   If (denominator = 0) Then GoTo PromptUser
   quotient = numerator / denominator
```

In this sample, the *GoTo* statement jumps back to the *PromptUser* label when the code detects invalid data. Processing continues with the line immediately following the *PromptUser* label. You can't use the same label name twice in the same procedure, although you can reuse label names in different procedures. If you want, include another logic statement on the same line as your label, right after the colon, although your code will be somewhat easier to read if you keep labels on their own lines.

```
LabelAlone:
   MsgBox("It's all alone.")
LabelAndCode: MsgBox("Together again.")
```

It's all right to include as many labels in your code as you need, but the *GoTo* statement is one of those elements of Visual Basic that is monitored closely by pesky international software agencies, such as the International Committee to Keep GoTo Always Gone (ICK-GAG). That group also scans computer books looking for derogatory references to their organization name; not that they would find anything like that in this book. But their core issue is that overuse of *GoTo* statements can lead to **spaghetti code**, such as the following.

```
Dim importantMessage As String = "Do"
GoTo Step2
Step6: importantMessage &= "AG!"
GoTo Step7
Step3: importantMessage &= "wit"
GoTo Step4
Step2: importantMessage &= "wn "
GoTo Step3
Step5: importantMessage &= "CK-G"
GoTo Step6
Step4: importantMessage &= "h I"
GoTo Step5
Step7: MsgBox(importantMessage)
```

Some people say that such code is hard to read. Others call it job security. No matter what you call it, it does make code very hard to maintain and review. You should probably keep an eye on your use of *GoTo* statements; if you don't, someone else might.

There are some limits placed on the use of *GoTo* by Visual Basic itself. You cannot jump into or out of certain multi-line statements that would result in improperly initialized code or data values. For instance, you cannot jump into the middle of a *For . . . Next* statement from outside of the statement, because the loop counter variable and the starting and ending ranges would not be properly initialized.

```
' ----- This GoTo statement will fail.
GoTo InsideTheLoop
For counter = 1 to 10
InsideTheLoop:
   MsgBox("Loop number: " & counter)
Next counter
```

However, once you are inside of the loop, you can jump to line labels that also appear in the loop, and it's acceptable to jump out of the loop using *GoTo*. Some other multi-line structures impose similar restrictions.

The Return Statement

Not only can you jump around within a procedure using *GoTo*, you can jump right out of a procedure anytime you want using the *Return* statement. Normally, a procedure exits when processing reaches the last line of code in the procedure; processing then continues with the code that called the procedure. The *Return* statement provides a way to exit the procedure before reaching the end.

In subroutines, the *Return* statement appears by itself as a standalone statement.

```
Return
```

In functions, the statement must include the value to be returned to the calling code: a variable, a literal, or an expression that must match the specified return value data type of the function.

```
Return 25
```

Pre-.NET releases of Visual Basic used an *Exit* statement to immediately leave a procedure. These are still supported in .NET. There are three variations.

- **Exit Sub.** Exits a subroutine.
- **Exit Function.** Exits a function.
- **Exit Property.** Exits a property.

When exiting from a function, the *Exit Function* statement does not include a way to specify a return value. You must set the return value separately by assigning the return value to the name of the function.

```
Function SafeDivide(ByVal numerator As Double, _
     ByVal denominator As Double) As Double
  ' ----- The "#" sign makes a number a Double.
  If (denominator = 0#) Then
     ' ----- Return 0 on invalid division.
     SafeDivide = 0#
     Exit Function
  End If
  Return numerator / denominator
End Function
```

The End and Stop Statements

The *End* and *Stop* bring an immediate halt to your Visual Basic application. The *End* statement exits your program immediately, aborting all further code and data processing (although certain acquired resources are cleaned up).

The *Stop* statement suspends processing only when you are running your application within a debugger, such as the Visual Studio development environment. *Stop* returns control to the environment, allowing the developer to examine and possibly alter data and code before continuing on with the program. If a *Stop* is encountered in a standalone application running outside of the debugger, it prompts the user to debug the application using any debugger installed on the workstation. Needless to say, the user will not be amused.

Events and Event Handlers

Visual Basic is an **event-driven language**. This is especially true of programs written to run on the Windows desktop. After some important initialization, the user is generally in control of all actions in the program. Who knows what the crazy user will do? He might click here. She might type there. It could be all mayhem and bedlam. But whatever the user does, your program will learn about it through **events**.

Since the first days of Windows, desktop programs have used a **message pump** to communicate user and system actions to your code. Mouse and keyboard input, system-generated actions, and other notifications from external sources flow into a program's common **message queue**. The message pump draws these messages out one by one, examines them, and feeds them to the appropriate areas of your code.

In traditional Windows programming, you craft the message pump yourself, including code that makes direct calls to event-handling procedures based on the message type. In a Visual Basic program (both in .NET and earlier), the language provides the message pump for you. It analyzes the messages as they are pumped out of the message queue, and directs them to the appropriate code. In .NET, this code appears within classes. Once a class has a chance to analyze the message, it can generate an event, which is ultimately processed by an **event handler**, a subroutine you write to respond to the action. This calling of the event handler is know as **firing an event**. So there are two parts of an event: (1) some code that decides to fire the event, and (2) an event handler that responds to the event.

Events are really just indirect calls to a procedure. Instead of having the main code call another subroutine directly, it asks .NET to call the other subroutine for it, passing specific arguments that the original code may wish to include. So why would I want to do this instead of just making the subroutine call directly? For one thing, this indirect method lets you add event handlers long after the initial event-firing code was written. This is good, because the event-firing code may be in a third-party assembly that was written years ago. A second benefit is that one event can target multiple event handlers. When the event fires, each of the event handlers will be called, and each can perform any custom logic found in the handler subroutine.

The code that fires the event passes event-specific data to the target event handler(s) through the handlers' parameter list. In order for the indirect subroutine call to work, the event handler needs to contain the correct number of arguments, in the right order, each of a specific and expected data type. The *Event* statement defines this contract between the event and the handler.

```
Public Event SalaryChanged(ByVal NewSalary As Decimal)
```

This *Event* statement defines an event named *SalaryChanged* with a single argument, a *Decimal* value. Any event handler wishing to monitor the event must match this argument signature.

```
Sub EmployeePayChanged(ByVal updatedSalary As Decimal) . . .
```

Events can occur for any reason you deem necessary; they need not be tied to user or system actions. In this sample class, an event fires each time a change is made to the employee's salary. The *RaiseEvent* statement performs the actual firing of the event, specifying the name of the event to fire, and a set of arguments in parentheses.

```
Public Class Employee
    Public Name As String
    Private currentSalary As Decimal

    Public Property Salary() As Decimal
      Get
         Return currentSalary
      End Get
      Set(ByVal value As Decimal)
         currentSalary = value
         RaiseEvent SalaryChanged(currentSalary)
      End Set
    End Property

    Public Event SalaryChanged(ByVal NewSalary As Decimal)
End Class
```

The event handlers are not added directly to the class. Instead, they are attached to an instance of the class. The instance, declared as a class field, must be defined using the special *WithEvents* keyword, which tells Visual Basic that this instance will process events.

```
Public WithEvents MonitoredEmployee As Employee
```

Event handlers are ordinary subroutines, but they include the *Handles* keyword to indicate which event is being handled.

```
Private Sub EmployeePayChanged( _
     ByVal updatedSalary As Decimal) _
     Handles MonitoredEmployee.SalaryChanged
   MsgBox("The new salary for " & _
     MonitoredEmployee.Name & " is " & updatedSalary)
End Sub
```

All that is needed is something to kick off the action.

```
Public Sub HireFred()
   monitoredEmployee = New Employee
   monitoredEmployee.Name = "Fred"
   monitoredEmployee.Salary = 50000    ' Triggers event
End Sub
```

When the salary is set, the *Employee* class' *Salary* property raises the *SalaryChanged* event using the Visual Basic *RaiseEvent* command. This fires the *EmployeePayChanged* event handler, which finally displays the message.

The events built into the Windows Forms classes in .NET work just like this, but instead of watching with me for a salary increase, they are watching for mouse clicks and keyboard clacks. All of these system events use a common argument signature.

```
Event EventName(ByVal sender As System.Object, _
     ByVal e As System.EventArgs)
```

The *sender* argument identifies the instance of the object that is firing the event, in case the caller needs to examine its members. The *e* argument is an object that lets the caller send event-specific data to the handler through a single class instance. The *System.EventArgs* class doesn't have much in the way of members, but many events use a substitute class that is derived from *System.EventArgs*.

As we pass through the chapters of this book, there will be no end to the number of event examples you will see and experience. I will save the more involved and interesting samples until then.

Namespaces

Classes, structures, modules, enumerations, interfaces, and delegates—the major .NET types—don't just float around in the code of your application. They must all be grouped and managed into **namespaces**. As described in Chapter 1, namespaces provide a hierarchy for your types, sort of a tree-shaped condominium where each type has a home. Some of those homes (or nodes), like *System*, get pretty crowded with all of those type families living there. Others, such as *System.Timers*, may have only a few types dwelling in its ample abode. But every type must live in the hierarchy; none of the types is adventurous enough to strike out on its own and build a ranch house.

At the very root of the hierarchy is *Global*, not a node itself, but a Visual Basic keyword that indicates the root of all roots. You can include *Global* when referencing your namespaces, but its use is only required when leaving it out would cause confusion between two namespace branches.

Directly under *Global* are the few top-level namespaces, including *System* and *Microsoft*. Each top-level namespace contains subordinate namespaces, and each of those can contain additional third-level namespaces, and so on. Namespaces nodes are referenced relative to each other using a "dot" notation.

```
System.Windows.Forms
```

This specifies the third-level *Forms* namespace. You could also have typed:

```
Global.System.Windows.Forms
```

which means the same thing. Relative namespaces are also supported.

```
Forms
```

However, to use relative namespaces, you must tell your Visual Basic code to expect them. There are so many namespaces out there, and there may be several *Forms* namespaces somewhere in the hierarchy.

Referencing Namespaces

Before namespaces can be used in your code, they must be **referenced** and optionally **imported**. Referencing a namespace identifies the DLL file that contains that namespace's types. Perform both of these actions through the *References* tab of each project's *Properties* form (see Figure 2-3).

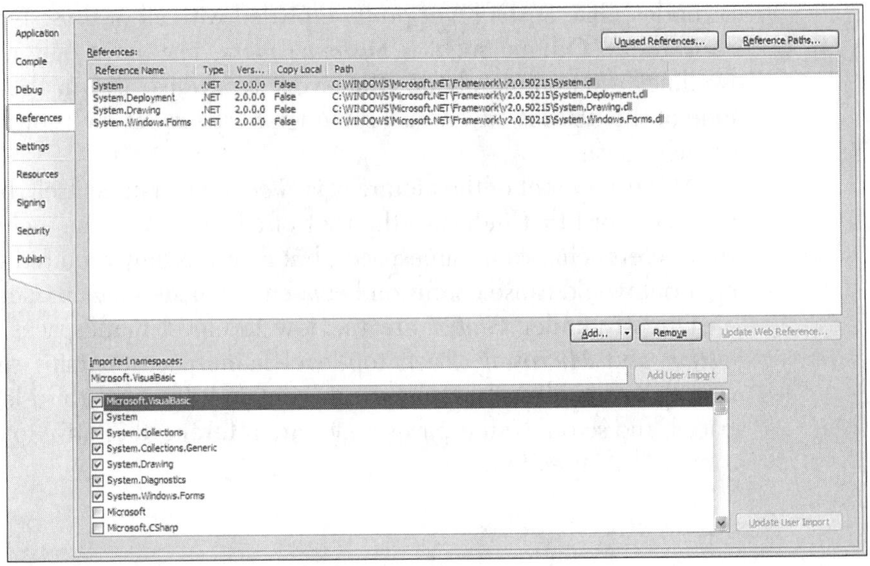

Figure 2-3 References and imports for a project

Actually, you are not referencing the namespaces in the DLL, but the types, all of which happen to live in specific namespaces. However, for the core type DLLs supplied with the .NET Framework, it feels like the same thing. In fact, Microsoft even named the DLLs to match the namespaces they contain. *System.dll* contains types within the *System* namespace. *System.Windows.Forms.dll* includes types specific to Windows Forms applications, and all of these types appear in the *System.Windows.Forms* namespace or one of its subordinates.

If you don't reference a DLL in your project, none of its types will be available to you in your code. Visual Studio loads several references into your project automatically based on the type of project you create.

Figure 2-3 shows the four default references included within a Windows Forms application: *System, System.Deployment, System.Drawing,* and *System.Windows.Forms.*

Once you have referenced a library of classes in your code, access any of its classes by specifying the full namespace to that class. For instance, the class for an on-screen form is referenced by *System.Windows.Forms. Form*. That's three levels down into the hierarchy, and some classes are even deeper. I hope that your health insurance plan covers carpel tunnel syndrome.

To avoiding typing all of those long namespaces over and over again, Visual Basic includes an *imports* feature. Imports are namespace-specific; once a namespace has been imported, you can access any of the types in that namespace without specifying the namespace name. If you import the *System.Windows.Forms* namespace, you only have to type "Form" to access the *Form* class. The bottom half of Figure 2-3 shows how to set these imports through the project's properties. The *Imported namespaces* list shows all available referenced namespaces. Simply check the ones you wish to import; *System.Windows.Forms* is already checked for you by default in Windows Forms applications.

You can also import a namespace directly in your source code. Use the *Imports* statement at the very start of a source code file.

```
Imports System.Windows.Forms
```

The *Imports* statement supports namespace abbreviations, short names that represent the full namespace in your code. Using the statement:

```
Imports Fred = System.Windows.Forms
```

lets you reference the *Form* class as "Fred.Form." Unlike the imports list in the project's properties, which impacts the entire project, the *Imports* statement affects only a single source code file.

Namespaces in Your Project

By default, all of the classes and types in your project appear in a top-level namespace that takes on the name of your project. For a Windows Forms application, this default namespace is called *WindowsApplication1*. To specify a different top-level namespace, modify it through the *Application* tab of the project's properties, in the **Root namespace** field. All of the types in your project appear in this namespace; if you specify an existing Microsoft-supplied namespace as your project's Root namespace, all of your types will appear in that specified namespace, mixed in with the pre-existing types. For standalone applications, this mixture will only be visible from your code.

From the root namespace, you can place types within subordinate namespaces by using the *Namespace* statement. *Namespace* is a block statement that ends with the *End Namespace* clause. Any types you create between the *Namespace* and *End Namespace* clauses will be contained in that subordinate namespace. For example, if your root namespace is *WindowsApplication1*, the following statements create a class whose full name is *WindowsApplication1.WorkArea.BasicStuff.BusyData*:

```
Namespace WorkArea.BasicStuff
    Class BusyData
    . . .
    End Class
End Namespace
```

You can include as many *Namespace* statements in your code as needed. Nesting of namespaces is also supported.

```
Namespace WorkArea.BasicStuff
    Namespace BasicStuff
        Class BusyData
        . . .
        End Class
    End Namespace
End Namespace
```

The My Namespace

Visual Basic 2005 includes a new "My" top-level namespace, which Microsoft is touting as one of the big new convenience features that will draw holdout Visual Basic 6.0 stalwarts into the .NET fold. But most of it is really not that dramatic. *My* collects commonly used features that are currently sprinkled around the FCL, and puts them in a mini-hierarchy for convenient access. It's really not much more complicated than that. The hierarchy is nicely organized, with sections for user, application, and computer-specific information. It's used just like any other part of the framework, although you cannot use the *Imports* keyword to access its components by a relative path.

Overall, *My* is very easy to use. To display the version number of your application, for instance, use the following statement.

```
MsgBox(My.Application.Info.Version.ToString)
```

Some areas of the *My* namespace are dynamic; classes are added or removed as you modify your source code. In Windows Forms applications, the *My.Forms* branch includes entries for each one of the project's forms. As you add new forms, new entries are added automatically. The *My.Forms* object then makes a reference to each form available for use in your code.

```
My.Forms.Form1.Text = "Welcome"
```

Summary

Sadly, this chapter has reached its conclusion. You may feel that it went by all so fast; you may feel that you didn't really learn how to write Visual Basic programs; you may feel that a mild sedative would be right just about now. But don't fret. This chapter served as an introduction to the syntax and major features of Visual Basic. Now begins the deeper training. As we start this book's main focus—the Library Project—you will encounter specific examples of all features covered only briefly in this chapter.

Project

In this chapter, we will use the Code Snippets feature of Visual Studio to insert source code into a basic sample code framework. Code snippets is a new Visual Studio feature that is basically a hierarchy of saved source code text. If you have installed the code for this book, you will find code snippets for most chapters included right in Visual Studio. In this chapter's project, I will show you how to use them to add chapter-specific code into your project.

Because we haven't officially started the Library Project, this chapter's project will simply extend the "Hello, World!" project we developed in Chapter 1, but with fun parts added. I will include some of the language features we discovered throughout this chapter.

Project Access Load the "Chapter 2 (Before) Code" project, either through the New Project templates, or by accessing the project directly from the installation directory. To see the code in its final form, load "Chapter 2 (After) Code" instead.

Each chapter's sample code includes a "Before" and "After" version. The "After" version represents the code as it will look when all the changes in that chapter's "Project" section have been applied. The before version doesn't have any of the chapter's project changes included, just placeholders where you will insert the code, one block at a time.

Like the project in Chapter 1, this chapter's project includes a basic Windows form with a single button on it. Clicking on the button displays the same "Hello, World!" message. However, this time, the message starts in an encoded form, and a separate class decodes the message and triggers an event that displays the form.

Once the project is open, view the source code attached to *Form1*. It should look somewhat like the following.

```
Public Class Form1
    ' *** Insert Code Snippet #2 here.

    Private Sub Button1_Click(ByVal sender As System.Object, _
        ByVal e As System.EventArgs) Handles Button1.Click
        ' *** Insert Code Snippet #3 here.
    End Sub

    ' *** Insert Code Snippet #4 here.
End Class

' *** Insert Code Snippet #1 here.
```

This sample uses a separate class to process the displayed message. The code for this class appears as snippet number 1. To insert the snippet, move the cursor *just after* the #1 snippet marker line, which reads:

```
' *** Insert Code Snippet #1 here.
```

To insert a snippet through the Visual Studio menus, select **Edit ➤ IntelliSense ➤ Insert Snippet**. The equivalent keyboard sequence is **Ctrl+K, Ctrl+X**. Or type a question mark (?) anywhere in the source code, followed by the **Tab** key. Any of these methods displays the first level of snippets (see Figure 2-4).

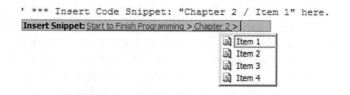

Figure 2-4 Snip, snip, snip

From the snippet list, select *Start-to-Finish Visual Basic 2005*, and then select *Chapter 2*. A list of the available snippet items for this chapter appears (see Figure 2-5).

Figure 2-5 Item, item, item

Finally, select *Item 1*. The content magically appears within the source code. All insertions of code snippets throughout this book occur exactly this way.

Snippet 1 inserts the *SayHello* class, part of the *HelloStuff* namespace, a portion of which appears here.

```
Namespace HelloStuff
    Friend Class SayHello
        Private secretMessage As String
        Private reverseFlag As Boolean
        Private decoded As Boolean

        Public Event MessageDecoded( _
            ByVal decodedMessage As String)

        Public Sub New(ByVal codedMessage As String, _
                ByVal reverseIt As Boolean)
            ...

        Public Sub DecodeMessage(ByVal rotationFactor As Integer)
            ...

        Public Sub ReportMessage()
            ...
    End Class
End Namespace
```

The *SayHello* class includes three private fields (*secretMessage*, *reverseFlag*, and *decoded*), which monitor the current status of the display message. A constructor (*New*) allows the user to create a new instance of *SayHello* with an initial message text, and a flag that indicates whether the text should be reversed before display. The *DecodeMessage* subroutine converts each letter of the encoded message to its final form by shifting each letter a *rotationFactor* number of places. If the letter "E" appears, and *rotationFactor* is 3, the letter E is shifted three spaces forward, to "H." A negative rotation factor shifts the letters lower in the alphabet. The alphabet wraps at the A-Z boundary. Only letters are rotated, and upper- and lowercase are handled independently.

The *ReportMessage* method fires the *MessageDecoded* event, sending the previously decoded message to the event as an argument. So where is this event handler? It's attached to an instance of *SayHello* that will be added to the *Form1* class.

Insert Snippet Insert Chapter 2, Snippet Item 2.

```
Private WithEvents HelloDecoder As HelloStuff.SayHello
```

The *HelloDecoder* class is an instance of the *HelloStuff.SayHello* class that we just wrote, and the snippet makes it a member of the *Form1* class. The *WithEvents* keyword says, "This instance will respond to events;" specifically, the *MessageDecoded* event from the *SayHello* class.

Let's add the code that triggers the message to display when the user clicks on the on-form button. This occurs in the button's click event.

Insert Snippet Insert Chapter 2, Snippet Item 3.

```
HelloDecoder = New HelloStuff.SayHello("!iqwtB ,tqqjM", True)
HelloDecoder.DecodeMessage(-5)
HelloDecoder.ReportMessage()
```

These three lines create an instance of the *SayHello* class, storing it in the *HelloDecoder* class field. Can't read the first argument in the constructor? It's encoded! It's a secret! And the *True* flag says that it's been reversed to make it an even bigger secret (you don't know what it is!). The *DecodeMessage* removes the secrets by shifting each letter as needed, although the reversal doesn't happen until the call to the *ReportMessage*.

The *ReportMessage* method doesn't actually display the message. Instead, it fires an event that makes the unscrambled message available to an event handler.

Insert Snippet Insert Chapter 2, Snippet Item 4.

```
Private Sub HelloDecoder_MessageDecoded( _
     ByVal decodedMessage As String) _
     Handles HelloDecoder.MessageDecoded
   ' ----- Show the decoded message.
   MsgBox(decodedMessage)
End Sub
```

The *Handles* keyword connects the subroutine with the fired event. The decoded message comes into the handler through the *decodedMessage* argument, and is splashed all over the screen with a simple yet powerful call to the *MsgBox* function.

That's it for the sample code. Now it's time to roll up your sleeves and embark on a full Visual Basic 2005 project.

CHAPTER 3

INTRODUCING THE PROJECT

You're sitting in your office, surfing the . . . I mean, reading up on the latest technology issues most pressing to software developers. You're minding your own business, when **boom**, someone walks up to your desk, and offers to pay you money to write them a program. It happens every day, all over corporate America; and sometimes it just makes me sick.

But enough about my health problems. This desk-hovering somebody informs you that you must develop a software application, possibly a database application with a user-friendly interface. Although the feature set will be specified by the primary users, you, as the lead (or only) programmer, will design, document, develop, and deliver discs dripping with distinguished, dazzling, and dynamic digital . . . um . . . software. (Darn.)

Well, that's what happened to me. A client of mine had a large collection of books that needed to be organized as a traditional library. Seeing that I was a reasonably codependent software architect, the client asked me to develop some software to manage the books and such. Out of this request came the *Library Project*.

As you read through this chapter, you will have to keep my day job in mind. I write custom Visual Basic applications for small- to medium-sized organizations. Most of the projects are sized so that I can complete them by myself, including all design and documentation requirements, in less than a year. All of my projects involve a "key user," one person—or sometimes a very small group—who speaks for the user community. These projects also involve someone who has "signature authority," a person authorized to pay for the project, or decide on its continued existence. This individual may be the same as the key user.

If you were developing, say, a replacement for Microsoft Word, you would likely lack a "key user." To obtain the specific requirements for the project, you may have to conduct general user interviews with dozens of user candidates. Or you might create a "virtual user," a fictional person who represents your intended target audience. Whichever method applies to you, the general discussion in this chapter should guide you to the happy conclusion: a design document that you will use to build the application.

The Library Project

My client needed a program that would manage a database of books and media items, and control how those items moved between bookshelves and patrons. The software needed to have both patron- and administrator-focused features. It would include various reports, including the printing of a receipt of checked-out items for the patron. And most of all, it needed to both print and read barcodes.

It sounds like a lot for one man to do, and it is a sizeable project. But I don't have to do it alone; you will help me. Together, through the pages of this book, you and I will design that program, and develop that code, and bring joy to the users, and collect that paycheck. Actually, I will collect the paycheck, although it wouldn't hurt to ask your boss to pay you to read this fine book.

The remainder of this section documents the key features of the Library management application.

Library Item Features

The Library system will manage an inventory of books and other media items, locate them, and manage the details and status of each copy of an item. To make this a reality, the Library program will:

- Allow patrons or administrators to search for items currently in inventory. The program allows searches based on several different properties of each item.
- Support multiple search methods, including by title, author name, subject or topic, a miscellaneous keyword, the name of the related publisher, the name of a series or group that contains the item, or a barcode number attached to the actual item.
- Limit search results by the location of the item, or by the type of media (book, CD, DVD, and so on).

- Support the definition and use of distinct physical locations. The client has books and media stored at three different sites within the building, including a storage closet for seldom-accessed items.
- Display the details of a retrieved item in a familiar browser-style interface. For instance, when looking up a book by title, the user clicks on the author's name to access all other items by that same author.
- Allow access to each library item through a barcode scan. As is common in most libraries today, the items in this library's collection each have a barcode affixed, which serves as a unique identifier for the individual item copy.

Patron Features

In addition to books and other items, the program manages a list of patrons, the "customers" of the library who are permitted to check out items. To support interaction with patrons, the application will include these patron-specific features:

- Items can be checked out to patrons, and checked back into the library inventory.
- All patrons are assigned a "PIN" that acts as their password.
- Patrons can check out items without librarian and administrator assistance. They can use a barcode scanner to scan a patron library card and library items.
- The "media type" of an item determines its checkout (and subsequently renewal) duration.
- Patrons can view their library record, including all books currently checked out, and a list of fines owed to the library.
- If permitted on a specific item, the patron can renew an item he or she has currently checked out.
- Patron-centric online help is available through the standard F1 key. This help file includes no information on administrative features, so as to reduce experimentation.
- Patrons can be divided into "patron groups" for the reporting and processing convenience of the administrative staff.

Administrative Features

Administrators include librarians, information technology staff, and others who need advanced access to application features. They are the primary users of the system, not the patrons. The application includes the following administrator-specific features:

- A login feature provides access to the administrative features of the application. Only authorized users can log in through an assigned password. The login feature is normally hidden from view from ordinary patrons.
- Administrators can view patron details just like patrons can, but they also have access to additional patron details. Specifically, administrators can add new patrons and manage their identity and demographic details. Administrators can also disable a patron record to prevent further item checkouts.
- Administrators collect and manage patron fines, including the ability to add non-standard fines, or dismiss unpaid fines.
- Administrators define the records for each item managed by the system's inventory database. This includes the basics of each item, such as title and authors. Each item includes one or more copies, which represent physical items that can be checked out. Barcodes are assigned to copies.
- Beyond the items and copies, administrators define all supporting values and lists, including author names and categories, the list of media types, publishers, book series names, status codes that identify the disposition of each item copy, and locations.
- Designated administrators can add, edit, and remove the accounts of other administrators. Each account includes feature-specific authorization settings (group rights).
- In addition to the scanning of barcodes, the program can assist administrators in the design and printing of both patron and item barcodes.
- A simple program-managed process allows the administrative staff to process overdue items and fines on a regular basis.
- The application allows holidays to be added and maintained. When a patron checks out a book, the program adjusts the due date of the item to avoid holidays.

- Administrator-centric online help provides assistance to the enhanced features of the application through the same F1 key available to patrons.
- The application includes some basic administrative reports, and the ability to "plug in" reports as needed in the future without the need to update the program itself.

The Application as a Whole

Beyond the basic features of the program as experienced by the patrons and administrators, there are a few other requirements.

- The program is "user friendly" and easy to navigate, especially for patrons, without much training or assistance.
- The application stores its data in a SQL Server database.
- Distribution of the application is done by administrative staff that has local administrative privileges, so a standard Windows installation package is sufficient.
- Configuration of the application uses standard XML methods.

Except for these general and feature-specific requirements, I was given design freedom. But where did the listed requirements come from? They came from the users, the masters of the application. It was their *needs*— the needs of my customers and theirs, who would be using the product day in and day out—that determined the list of requirements.

The Needs of the Users

Back in the old days of computers, there were no users. Who needed users? The only ones manly enough to approach the hallowed inner sanctum of the computing systems were the programmers. Only they touched the vacuum tubes, connected the cables, toggled the front panels, and fondled the punch cards that provided access to the heart of the machine. These programmers were tough, and their programs, tougher. "We don't need no stinking users" was their mantra.

Then came the '80s, with its *Greatest American Hero*-inspired attitude and its personal "personal" computers. Now there were users everywhere.

They were like the Blob, only with fewer computing skills. But they were the masters because most programs were written for them. Programmers rarely used the programs they wrote; they were simply the interface between the user and the heart of the computer. Programmers provided the element of *control* needed by both the computer and the users. In fact, that is a programmer's job: to provide highly controlled access to the computer and the data it contains.

Users have a lot of needs, most of which can't be met by a computer. But for those that can, the needs come in five parts: data and information, process, usability, commonality, and project-specific needs. The design process involves an examination of these needs and the subsequent massaging of those needs into a software product. By examining the current data and procedures, conducting user interviews, and performing other need-extraction methods, you gather the details you require to craft the right solution.

Data and Information

Your ability to provide convenient and specific access to the data and information required by the user is what makes you, the programmer, so loveable. Most users got along just fine before computers. They kept their information on 3-by-5 index cards, legal pads, scrolls of parchment, or in hermetically-sealed mayonnaise jars. But they had a reason to move to a computer-based storage medium: the convenience.

Data is the raw information stored by your program: names, numbers, images, or any other stand-alone values. **Information** is data in context: a customer record, an order, a slideshow. When you provide a quality program that moves data up to the level of information, you are providing the level of convenience the user needs to move from mayonnaise jars to silicon chips.

Process

When the user demands data back from the computer, you have three options.

1. Dump every single byte of data to the screen, printer, or disk, and let the user sort it out. Actually, this is the system that some users had before they started using a computer.
2. Protect the data from user access, insisting that the supplied password is invalid or expired, or that the data is unavailable. "Abort,

Retry, or Fail" anyone? Actually, this is the system that some other users had before they started using a computer.

3. Present the data as information, in a format that is both usable and accessible.

Although the first two choices are indeed tempting, the third option is the best. And given the amount of data that your application will likely manage, you will have to dole out the interaction with it a bit at a time, and in an appropriate sequence. This is *process*.

Through the implementation of a valid process, you not only control the user's data, but also you control the orderly interaction with that data. Most users need to supply or retrieve only a small portion of their data at a time. But when they do, it will usually be in the context of some process. For instance, in an order-taking situation, the user (1) enters or confirms the customer's contact information, (2) enters or updates the order details, and (3) prints or electronically communicates the order information so that it can be fulfilled. Your application (surprise!) manages this three-step process.

Usability

If your program presents data and information to the user, and in a specific arrangement or order, but is difficult to use, your users will hate you. They will loathe you. They will spread mean stories about you, true or not. And when they appear in groups, their vehemence can get downright ugly. I heard this story about an Excel user's group . . . but perhaps it was just a rumor.

As a programmer, it is your job to make the computer, and the software that runs on it, as usable as possible. And while you may not be able to control many of the basic system features, you are the king when it comes to your own software.

The more ease and usability you design into your programs, the happier your users will be. But I must warn you, ease-of-use for the user *always* means more work for the developer. *Always*. It's one of those unfair laws of the universe, and there is no way around it. But sometimes we try— to the user's peril.

Many, many years ago, I wrote some programs to demonstrate a hot new version of BASIC that ran on the Motorola 6809 processor. This release could handle programs that were twice the size of the previous version: a whopping 32Kb of source code. I was charged with testing the system, writing "big" programs that would show off the new functionality. I set to work in a fever of activity, but as my program approached about 27Kb, things started to happen, things that involved a shaking table and the smell of smoke. Seriously!

Since then, I have subconsciously feared the development of programs that I felt were too large for a particular system. So when I went to work on Visual Basic, I brought to my projects some of this apprehension. I tried to make my programs easy to use, but I also held back on the number of forms I would add to my projects. It wasn't an irrational fear; the original versions of Visual Basic did impose limits on code size, the number of unique variable names, and the maximum number of forms. I once hit the limit on the number of unique variable names, but I never came close on the number of forms. Still, I held back. I was sure that if I added too many forms, my users would require medical attention for smoke inhalation.

Unfortunately, my users were still suffering. I had put too much data on each form, to the point where it was no longer communicating information. My phone would ring constantly with the same user-sponsored question: "How do I use the fields on such-and-such a form?" Of course I always said, "Why don't you press the F1 key?" But it didn't make a bit of difference, because my online help pages were as long and complex as the forms they sought to simplify.

There did come a day when I escaped my phobia of form-laden applications. And on that day, I came up with the following rules for my own programs.

1. Don't put too much information on a single form. When in doubt, move some information to another form.
2. Only present the most necessary information and data to the user by default. Only show additional information if the user requests it.
3. Make it easy for the user to access the enhanced data, but allow the program to run properly without it.
4. Use text, graphics, and colors to the user's advantage.
5. Simplify the application so that user documentation becomes unnecessary.
6. Always provide user documentation. Make it simple enough so that calls to technical support become unnecessary.

These rules are generic enough to work with any type of application, and in-your-face enough to make them meaningful to us, the programmers, and to them, the users.

Commonality

Microsoft constantly touts *innovation*, and the ability to innovate has moved software products forward at a tremendous pace. But unfortunately, users can handle only so much innovation at a time. Consider the telephone. I inherited an old oak-boxed telephone from my grandparents (see Figure 3-1).

Figure 3-1 What a great phone!

It's a fun phone and so simple to use. When you want to make a call, you pick up the handset and crank the handle on the side of the unit for about three or four seconds. When the operator comes on the line, you tell her whom you wish to call. What could be simpler? What could be more user-friendly? What could be more expensive than an operator-assisted call? But it was simple, and everyone instinctively knew how to use it.

Today's phones use buttons instead of cranks. Most of the buttons are simple digits that let you directly dial a specific phone number. But there are other buttons as well: Mute, Redial, Pause, Flash, #, and *. I'm afraid to push the Flash button, and what's with the SND and CLR buttons on cell phones? The problem is not the buttons themselves, but that every phone has a different selection of buttons. They have lost the *commonality* that made crank phones easy to use. Sure they have many more features, but if the average person can't figure out how to use that functionality, what is the benefit?

Getting back to software: Even new and innovative programs must retain some commonality with the operating system, and with other installed programs. As you speak to users about their needs and think about the great advancements in software technology you will provide, don't forget about commonality. Don't forget about one of the user's core needs: the need to not be overwhelmed by new ways of doing tasks they thought they already could do. Users need consistency.

Project-Specific Needs

Beyond the general user needs required of every project, there are needs specific to each project. As an application designer or software architect, this is where you spend most of your time. If you have a lot of programming experience, you may be able to fulfill the other needs without ever meeting with a user. But the project-specific needs require an understanding of the tasks that the user needs to accomplish with the proposed application.

Once the users discover that you have a real interest in their needs, they may dump on you. They might start listing off a whole wish list of features, more features than they could ever use. That's okay. When they hear how much time it will take or how much it will cost to implement, they may back off of a few requests. The important thing is to *document everything*. Write down what the user asks for, combine it with a reasonable time schedule (always) and cost estimate (if required), and return it back to the key user for confirmation. If possible, have the user sign a document that says he agrees with the specific requirements listed in the document.

It is essential that there be *agreement* on the project design, at least for the initial phase or release. Because user's needs are so often a moving target, it is vital that an agreement on the project exist at some point in time. Later, after you have begun work on the project, the user will come to you, probably on a daily basis, and say, "Hey, that's not what I asked for." When that happens, point to the agreement and say, "Hey, yes it is." Changes will occur; I'll discuss how to handle those a little later in this chapter.

The Life of a Project

Projects have a lifetime all their own. Some are short-lived; I've written programs that were used for two weeks and then discarded when the business project was complete. Some programs go on forever, with continual improvements made over a series of version iterations. I'm typing into such a program right now.

As a developer, you should be aware of the lifetime of your project. Once you understand the lifetime, you can apply business processes to each major phase of the project's life. The skills needed to guide a project to its conclusion, or through each successive version of the project, are collectively called **project management**. Many organizations have dedicated project managers, especially for larger projects. For small projects, the programmer may have to carry the project management burden alone.

Fortunately, most project managers don't just make things up as they go (although I have met some who did). They work within a system, called a **project methodology framework**, which is a management system that keeps the project plan on track. I will hit the highlights of a typical framework in the remainder of this chapter. If you go back to the bookstore where you received a discount on this book, you will find a full shelf of project methodology framework resources. Microsoft even has its own recommended framework called the **Microsoft Solutions Framework (MSF)**. Because most of the projects Microsoft develops are renewed through successive versions, the MSF is *cyclical* or *iterative*. For applications that, at least for now, will have one major release only, a *linear* approach works well. (See Figure 3-2 for both approaches.)

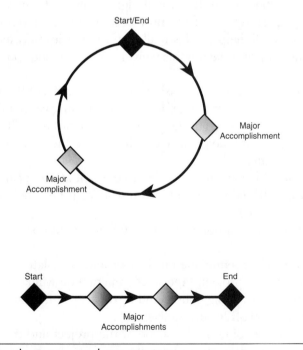

Figure 3-2 Two basic approaches to project management

Because this book will end with a completed project, and neither the next edition nor the movie rights have been arranged yet by my publisher, I will use the linear approach. Whichever approach you use, there are several major events that happen between the start and end of the line or iteration, beginning with the *project kickoff*.

Project Kickoff

Once everyone agrees that there should be a project, they all come to a big meeting to get things started. Everyone who is considered to be in charge of any part of the project is there: the technical lead (you), the key user, the project manager, and the person with signature authority. If you're writing a program for yourself, only you will be in the room, but you can still provide bagels. This event, the **project kickoff**, marks the official start of the project. This meeting of the minds usually determines the initial schedule for information and resource gathering.

Documentation

It's important to document everything as you go through the entire project, especially in the early design stages. Not only will this help you recall essential aspects of the project later during the development phase, but also it will help you keep all involved parties informed about the status of the project. Imagine this conversation with your boss:

Boss: Management is asking about the status of the Hazel project. Do you have anything up to date that I can give them?

You: Sure, I've got the project plan right here. I'll print you off a copy.

Boss: That'd be great. Hey, did you see the new car Bernie in accounting just got?

You: I know! How does an accountant afford a car like that?

Boss: Beats me. It makes you wonder if he's cooking the books or something.

You: Hey author, weren't we talking about documentation?

Oh yeah, documentation. Proper and complete documentation is important in any project. Precise documentation will keep Bernie from accounting out of the big house. And it will keep you in step with the project from initial kickoff to final delivery.

Depending on the scope of the project and the requirements of your organization, your project may need just some basic documentation, or it may need several three-inch binders filled with design documents that examine every nook and cranny of the system. Some project management documents require a signature before the project can continue. Others are informational only. As a programmer, the two most important documents are the main *project design* document (from which you will build the application) and the *schedule* (that lets you gauge progress during the project).

Project Goals

The first important item you will document is the set of **project goals**. If a project (or iteration) has a definite end, it should be possible to identify the major accomplishments needed for that ending event. These goals should be general, broad, and concerned with the final project **deliverables**. Deliverables are those items that are produced as a result of a project. They generally include software, user and technical documentation, installation media, and related materials. They can also include contractual and project management items, such as a proposed schedule for the next phase or iteration of the project.

The project's goals help determine its **scope**, the extent of the features and supporting materials that will be produced during the project's lifetime. Determining scope is important because it sets the constraints, the limits that will keep the project from going out of control. Although some aspects of the project may change throughout its lifetime, if you allow a project to continue without restraint, you will end up with something like Windows Vista: a useful product that was over a year late and had some features delayed until post-release.

Design and Planning

My mother recently gave me a rather old piece of paper with a drawing of a house floor plan. As I examined this paper in more detail, I found that the design matched the house in which I grew up, a house that is, alas, no longer part of the vast Patrick family real estate holdings. Yet it is still part of the vast Patrick family memory cells, and the home I remembered from my childhood was remarkably similar to the simple sketch. Some forgotten builder was able to take that sketch, add wood, windows and doors, red shag carpeting, and an avocado-green refrigerator, and turn it into a home.

Home builders don't work off of rough sketches. Between the sketch and the builder was an **architect**, a designer who set down on paper precise details about how to build the house. An architect provides a lot of detail, although not everything. The builder still has the choice of basic materials and construction methodology. But without the project plan—the blueprints—the builder would just be hammering boards together at random, and applying red shag carpet where it didn't belong.

During the design phase, you play the role of an architect, crafting the user's dreams and wishes into a design that can then be turned into a software creation. The level of detail required in these **specifications** will vary by project and organization. For the Library Project, the bullet items listed at the start of this chapter comprise the bulk of the design detail. (It parallels the level of detail my clients have agreed to in similar projects.) Other organizations require excruciating detail, demanding flowcharts, functional specifications and diagrams, and pseudo-code that is nearly as detailed as the final source code. For projects that include multiple programmers, you will likely have to specify the interfaces, the function or class member details that allow the code written by two different programmers to communicate accurately.

Whatever level of detail you include in your plan, you will also document certain key events that will happen throughout the entire project schedule. These **milestones** identify interim deliverables, results expected at specified moments throughout the timeline of the project. Comparing the milestone schedule against the actual results produced during development provides an overall view of how the project is progressing over time. Failing to meet several milestone deadlines may require an adjustment in the project schedule, cost, or scope.

Project Approval

A design document gives both the programmer and the user a point of agreement. Both sides can look at the design and say, "Yes, this is it; this is the plan." If the completed program is different from the proposed design, the user can say, "Hey, that wasn't what we agreed to." Sometimes the opposite happens; the programmer develops the application according to the plan, but the user claims that he requested something different. When this happens, the programmer can point to the design and say politely, "This is what we agreed to, and this is what was built."

To provide additional stability, the completed design usually includes a **project approval** document. This paper, signed by both the user representative and the development representative, says that (1) both sides have read the design document, (2) they agree with what it says, and (3) they commit to seeing the project through to completion as designed. As each representative **signs off** on the document, they pledge to give their support to the project.

The approval process also covers the **project cost** and **schedule**. A realistic estimate of the total time and costs needed to complete the project is as important as the project design itself. Any adjustments in the time and cost throughout the lifetime of the project can also provide valuable feedback on the progress being made.

Software and Other Development

Software development usually consumes most of a project's lifetime. Although the majority of work is done by the programmer or programming team, the user sometimes has a role in this step. By reviewing **prototypes** of specific portions of the application, and testing **beta versions** of the nearly completed product, the user remains an active participant in this long project phase.

Changes to the Project

In general, developers always complete projects on time, under budget, and with all features included, and the satisfied user joyfully installs the software, using it daily to meet demanding business challenges.

Ha ha. Now that you've had a good laugh, let's continue on with the chapter. Many projects do go well, and generally stick to the plan agreed to by the user and the developer. But other projects don't. Somewhere in the middle of the project's life, a change occurs. It may be due to difficulties in building the project, resulting in a **schedule change**. It may be due to new requirements in the user's needs (or desires), or in the related business process, resulting in a **scope change**.

Minor project changes may happen that neither the user nor the programmer is overly concerned about. But other changes can have a significant impact on cost or schedule, or both. Such changes can be documented and agreed to by both sides through a **scope change document**, sometimes called a "change order." If the development team must adjust the schedule, or reduce or change the included features of the application, communicating this to the user through a scope change document keeps the user from being surprised at the ever-advancing end of the project.

Using scope change documents, and requiring sign off from both sides, also helps prevent **scope creep**, the continual adjustment or expansion of software features included in the final product. As users see the progress you are making on the project, and what a great job you are doing, they may show their confidence in you by adding to the project, certain that you can complete the additional work well within the original timeline. Funneling all change requests through the scope change process provides a reality check to the user, giving him a sense of the effort (in terms of cost and schedule) required to develop software.

Acceptance Criteria Testing

There will come a day when you will say, "There, that's the last line of code I need to write for this project." Of course you will be wrong, but it will feel good to say it. The real last day of coding won't be for several more weeks, after all of the testing is done.

Unit testing concentrates on the individual components, even down to the class and method level. It ensures that each component or code block returns expected results when given specific input. Both good and bad inputs are sent into the components, and the results analyzed. Unit testing is actually the most cost effective form of testing, because it is not concerned with the complex interactions of the various components that make up the entire system.

Interface testing is concerned with these interactions. Components that interact with each other are tested as a group, to make sure that they work and play well together. Components that expose public interfaces are also tested for consistent results and secure access. **System testing** gives a chance for users to have at the product, doing all they can to certify that the entire application works in a real-life setting. **Beta testing** is part of the system testing process. System testing may also involve **stress testing**, where the system is tested in extreme computing conditions to see if it can support the load. Testing various installation scenarios ensures that the new software does not negatively impact other software or operating system components.

All of these testing phases are important, but there is one more type of testing that has a direct impact on the progression of the project: **acceptance criteria testing**. This involves a checklist of testable items that both the user and the programmer agree must pass successfully before the project is considered complete. This phase may cover items found in the other phases of testing, but it might also check for basic elements and features, such as the inclusion of quality documentation, or the delivery of the software on a certain medium, like a CD-ROM. Once acceptance criteria testing is complete, the user signs off on that phase, and the project moves to final acceptance.

Project Acceptance

You've worked long and hard. It's been difficult at times, and perhaps you weren't sure if you would ever finish. And I'm just talking about this chapter. Some projects take quite a while to complete, and by the end everyone should be ready to see the fruits of their labor. The final step in the agreement portion of the project is the **project acceptance document**. This paper, signed by the user, says that the project was completed as requested (or as modified through change orders). Once signed, the project is officially complete. The programmer is now handsomely paid, and takes a well deserved three days off.

Deployment and Distribution

The project is now ready for installation on each user's workstation. The method of distribution and delivery depends on the project and target audience. Whether it's an internal network distribution, CD distribution to a small number of locations, web-based distribution to the general public, or boxed media product for sale in retail stores, the programming team usually has limited interaction with the target workstations. Of course, that can change quickly once the technical support phone line is plugged in.

Ongoing Support

After the product has been in use by the user population for a while, reports of application errors or desired enhancements may trickle in to the development team. These can be collected for consideration in a future versioned release, or acted on immediately in "service release" updates of the product. As you may have multiple versions of the product in use within the user community, it is essential that you are able to identify and test against any particular release. **Source code control** systems (including *Microsoft Visual SourceSafe* that ships with some editions of Visual Studio) allow you to maintain version-specific images of the source code. You can also maintain an inventory of release executables and other files for later testing.

If your application was written for a single customer or organization, there may be a **warranty period** where some or all errors that are reported during the length of the warranty are fixed free of charge.

Summary

Projects are more than just source code. From design documents to project management tools to online help integration to web-based support functionality, a project encompasses resources that go way beyond the basic task of coding. If you are a lone developer, you will have to wear many hats to fully support the application. Those who are part of a larger product team don't have to worry about every possible component of the project, but they also lose out on some of the joy that comes with working on every aspect of a project.

Project

There are many tasks to complete before coding begins in a large project. The actual coding of the Library Project starts in Chapter 5, ".NET Assemblies." For this chapter, I will complete the project agreement document that describes the Library Project features.

This chapter does not include a Visual Studio project template that you can load and examine in Visual Studio. Instead, you must access the *Chapter 3* subdirectory from the book's installation directory. This subdirectory contains three files.

- **Project Agreement.doc.** This is the primary project document that identifies the features of the completed project. It is agreed upon by both the developer and user representatives. Deviation from this document only occurs through the "Change Order" process.
- **Change Order.doc.** This file is used to modify the original project through the "Change Order" process. When using this document, include a description of the change to be made to the project, and any schedule and cost impact.
- **Project Acceptance.doc.** This file is used when the project is complete, and the user is ready to accept the finished product. This document combines the "Acceptance Criteria Testing" and "Project Acceptance" elements described earlier in the chapter.

Please feel free to use these documents to support your own projects. However, the legal team at Addison-Wesley would like to remind you that if you choose to use these documents, you're on your own, bucko. These documents are meant as examples only. You should talk to a lawyer in your state if you wish to craft your own documents similar to these and have them be contractually binding.

The remainder of this section presents the "Project Agreement.doc" filled out with the details of the Library Project. Its primary content is a copy of the bullet items listed in the "The Library Project" section near the start of this chapter. It also documents some other project-specific requirements, and includes a typical estimate of project costs. For demonstration purposes, I have used an hourly rate of $25.00.

Project Agreement

Project Name: Library Project

User: The ACME Library

Date: November 7, 2005

This project agreement defines a project to be performed by the developer for the user. By signing this agreement, the user representative acknowledges that he or she has read the agreement, and accepts the terms of the agreement identified in this document. The terms of this agreement, or the services provided, may be modified at a later time through a Change Order document.

_____   _____

Authorized User Representative   Date

_____   _____

Authorized Developer Representative   Date

Project Objective

The ACME Company houses a small library for its employees, filled with business-specific documentation. The goal of this project is to develop a computer-based "library system" that tracks the inventory of books and other available library items. Patrons (employees) may check out items from the library. Librarians (administrators) have access to additional application features, including the ability to manage inventory and patron fines.

3. INTRODUCING THE PROJECT

Deliverables and Acceptance Criteria

Upon completion of the project tasks defined in this agreement, the developer will provide the following deliverables to the user. Also listed are any testable criteria that must be met for adequate project acceptance by the user:

- **The library application.** This Visual Basic 2005 application will be installed on each workstation within the library, and will include both patron and administrative features.
- **The library database.** This database, stored in SQL Server 2005, will manage all inventory, patron, and transaction data for the library.
- **Documentation.** The developer will supply both user documentation (online help, distinct for patrons and administrators) and technical documentation (especially concerning the database).
- **Installation image.** The developer will supply all scripts and supporting documentation needed for the installation of the database. For the client portion, the developer will supply a standard Windows install package to be run on each workstation. ACME's IT department will install this product from a shared network drive or CD.
- **User training.** The developer will provide up to five hours of administrator and librarian training.

Project Tasks

The developer will accomplish the following tasks for the user.

Library Item Features

- Allow patrons or administrators to search for items currently in inventory. The program allows searches based on several different properties of each item.
- Support multiple search methods, including by title, by author name, by subject or topic, by a miscellaneous keyword, by the name of the related publisher, by the name of a series or group that contains the item, or by a barcode number attached to the actual item.
- Limit search results by the location of the item, or by the type of media (book, CD, DVD, and so on).

- Support the definition and use of distinct physical locations. The client has books and media stored at three different sites within the building, including a storage closet for seldom-accessed items.
- Display the details of a retrieved item in a familiar browser-style interface. For instance, when looking up a book by title, the user clicks on the author's name to access all other items by that same author.
- Allow access to each library items through a barcode scan. As is common in most libraries today, the items in this library's collection each have a barcode affixed, which serves as a unique identifier for the individual item copy.

Patron Features

- Items can be checked out to patrons, and checked back into the library inventory.
- All patrons are assigned a "PIN" that acts as their password.
- Patrons can check out items without librarian and administrator assistance. They can use a barcode scanner to scan a patron library card and library items.
- The "media type" of an item determines its checkout (and subsequently renewal) duration.
- Patrons can view their library record, including all books currently checked out, and a list of fines owed to the library.
- If permitted on a specific item, the patron can renew an item he or she has currently checked out.
- Patron-centric online help is available through the standard F1 key. This help file includes no information on administrative features, so as to reduce experimentation.
- Patrons can be divided into "patron groups" for the reporting and processing convenience of the administrative staff.

Administrative Features

- A "login" feature provides access to the administrative features of the application. Only authorized users can log in through an assigned password. The login feature is normally hidden from view from ordinary patrons.
- Administrators can view patron details just like patrons can, but they also have access to additional patron details. Specifically, administrators can

add new patrons and manage their identity and demographic details. Administrators can also disable a patron record to prevent further item checkouts.

- Administrators collect and manage patron fines, including the ability to add non-standard fines, or dismiss unpaid fines.
- Administrators define the records for each item managed by the system's inventory database. This includes the basics of each item, such as title and authors. Each item includes one or more copies, which represent physical items that can be checked out. Barcodes are assigned to copies.
- Beyond the items and copies, administrators define all supporting values and lists, including author names and categories, the list of media types, publishers, book series names, status codes that identify the disposition of each item copy, and locations.
- Designated administrators can add, edit, and remove the accounts of other administrators. Each account includes feature-specific authorization settings (group rights).
- In addition to the scanning of barcodes, the program can assist administrators in the design and printing of both patron and item barcodes.
- A simple program-managed process allows the administrative staff to process overdue items and fines on a regular basis.
- The application allows holidays to be added and maintained. When a patron checks out a book, the program adjusts the due date of the item to avoid holidays.
- Administrator-centric online help provides assistance to the enhanced features of the application through the same F1 key available to patrons.
- The application includes some basic administrative reports, and the ability to "plug in" reports as needed in the future without the need to update the program itself.

The Application as a Whole

- The program is "user friendly" and easy to navigate, especially for patrons, without much training or assistance.
- The application stores its data in a SQL Server database.
- Distribution of the application is done by administrative staff that has local administrative privileges, so a standard Windows installation package is sufficient.
- Configuration of the application uses standard XML methods.

Page 4

Project Estimate and Timetable

The following table summarizes the estimated costs and time to complete the project.

Task	Description	Hourly Rate	Time Estimate	Price Estimate
1	Library Item Features	$25.00	30	$750.00
2	Patron Features	$25.00	35	$875.00
3	Administrative Features	$25.00	100	$2,500.00
4	Application as a Whole	$25.00	35	$875.00
	Task Subtotal		200	$5,000.00
5	SQL Server 2005 (estimate only)			$5,000.00
	Project Total			$10,000.00

Anticipated Project Start Date: November 15, 2005

Anticipated Project End Date: March 15, 2006

CHAPTER 4

DESIGNING THE DATABASE

Data. Databases. It just kind of makes sense. If you have data, you need to put it somewhere. And what better place to put it than in a "data" base?

Just to make sure I had all the "bases" covered, I did a quick search on the Internet for a useful definition. What a shock. According to virtually every web site I found, a database is "a collection of data organized for easy retrieval by a computer." With a definition like that, pretty much everything I put on my system is stored in a database. All of my disk files are organized for easy access. My saved emails can be sorted by subject or date received or sender, so they must be in a database, too. Even this document can be searched and sorted in any manner I wish. Is it a database?

Relational Databases

Perhaps that definition is too broad. These days, when we think of "database," it's generally a **relational database** system. Such databases are built on the "relational model" designed by Edgar Codd of IBM. In 1970, he issued "A Relational Model of Data for Large Shared Data Banks," the seminal paper on relational modeling, and later expanded on the basic concepts with C. J. Date, another "real programmer." Upon reading that 1970 paper—and if you have a free afternoon, you would really benefit from spending time with your family or friends rather than reading that paper—you will enter a world of n-tuples, domains, and expressible sets. Fortunately, you don't need to know anything about these terms to use relational database systems.

The relational databases that most programmers use collect data in **tables**, each of which stores of specific set of unordered **records**. For convenience, tables are presented as a grid of data values, with each **row** representing a single record, and each **column** representing a consistent **field** that appears in each record. Table 4-1 presents a table of orders, with a separate record for each line item of the order.

Table 4-1 Boy, a Lot of People Drink Coffee and Tea

Record ID	Order ID	Customer ID	Customer Name	Product ID	Product	Price	Quantity
92231	10001	AA1	Al Albertson	BEV01COF	Coffee	3.99	3
92232	10001	AA1	Al Albertson	BRD05RYE	Rye Bread	2.68	1
92233	10002	BW3	Bill Williams	BEV01COF	Coffee	3.99	1
92234	10003	BW3	Will Williams	BEV01COF	Tea	3.99	2
92235	10004	CC1	Chuck Charles	CHP34PTO	Potato Chips	0.99	7

Putting all of your information in a table is really convenient. The important data appears at a glance in a nice and orderly arrangement, and it's easy to sort the results based on a particular column. Unfortunately, this table of orders has a lot of repetition. Customer names and product names both repeat multiple times. Also, although the product ID "BEV01COF" indicates coffee, one of the lines lists it as "Tea." There are a few other problems inherent in data that's placed in a single **flat file** database table.

Mr. Codd, the brilliant computer scientist that he was, saw these problems, too. But instead of just sitting around and complaining about them like I do, he came up with a solution: **normalization**. By breaking the data into separate tables with data subsets, assigning a unique identifier to each record/row in every table (a **primary key**), and making a few other adjustments, the data could be "normalized" for both processing efficiency and data integrity. For the sample orders in Table 4-1, the data could be normalized into three separate tables: one for order line items, one for customers, and one for products (see Table 4-2, Table 4-3, and Table 4-4, respectively). In each table, I've put an asterisk next to the column title that acts as the primary key column.

Table 4-2 The Table of Customers

Customer ID *	Customer Name
AA1	Al Albertson
BW3	Bill Williams
CC1	Chuck Charles

Table 4-3 The Table of Products

Product ID *	Product Name	Unit Price
BEV01COF	Coffee	3.99
BRD05RYE	Rye Bread	2.68
BEV01COF	Coffee	3.99
CHP34PTO	Potato Chips	0.99

Table 4-4 The Table of Order Line Items

Record ID *	Order ID	Customer ID	Product ID	Quantity
92231	10001	AA1	BEV01COF	3
92232	10001	AA1	BRD05RYE	1
92233	10002	BW3	BEV01COF	1
92234	10003	BW3	BEV01COF	2
92235	10004	CC1	CHP34PTO	7

To get combined results from multiple tables at once, **join** (or link) their matching fields. For instance, you can link the *Customer ID* field in the table of line items with the matching *Customer ID* primary key field in the table of customers. Once joined, the details for a single combined line item record can be presented with the matching full customer name. It's the same for joins with any two tables that have linkable fields. Figure 4-1 shows the relationships between the customer, product, and order line tables.

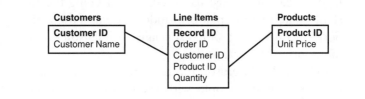

Figure 4-1 Three tables, and yet they work as one.

To join tables together, relational databases implement **query languages** that allow you to manipulate the data using **relational algebra** (from which the term "relational database" derives). The most popular of these languages, **SQL**, uses simple English-like sentences to join, order, summarize, and retrieve just the data values you need. The primary statement, **SELECT**, provides basic data selection and retrieval features. Three other common statements, **INSERT**, **UPDATE**, and **DELETE**, let you manipulate the records stored in each table. Together, these four statements make up the primary **data manipulation language (DML)** commands of SQL. SQL also includes **data definition language (DDL)** statements that let you design the tables used to hold the data, as well as other database features. I'll show examples of various SQL statements later in this chapter.

Vendor-specific systems, such as Microsoft's SQL Server, Oracle's "Oracle," Microsoft's Access, and IBM's DB2, extend these core DDL and DML features through additional data analysis and management tools. They also battle each other over important features such as data replication, crash-proof data integrity, the speed at which complex queries return the requested results, and who has the biggest private jet.

SQL Server 2005

Microsoft's primary business-level database tool is *SQL Server*. Although it began its life as a derivative of Sybase (another relational database), it has been given the Microsoft touch. Unlike Access (Microsoft's other relational database product), SQL Server includes advanced data management and analysis features, and a nifty price tag to go along with those features. Although Microsoft was somewhat late in joining the relational database game, it has done a pretty good job at playing catch-up. Oracle still gets high marks for at least its perception of being the most robust, the most stable, and the most platform-independent of the various players. But SQL Server scores big as well, especially with its somewhat lower costs, and its more intuitive visual tools.

Originally, Microsoft touted SQL Server as a business-minded tool for business-minded people with their business-minded agendas and their business-minded three-piece poly-knit double-breasted suits, and it is still viewed in this way. But Microsoft is increasingly identifying the database as a development tool, especially with the 2005 release. It was no coincidence that Microsoft chose to debut its newest version of SQL Server on

November 7, 2005, the same day as the release of Visual Studio 2005. All flavors of Visual Studio now include some version of SQL Server—even the low-end *Visual Studio 2005 Express Edition* products have access to a *SQL Server 2005 Express Edition* complement. (As of this writing, it was available at no cost from Microsoft's web site.) And it's a two-way relationship between the products: You could always use SQL Server data in your .NET applications, but SQL Server 2005 now allows you to craft embedded stored procedures using .NET code, along with the native and more traditional T-SQL scripting language.

SQL Server, as the name implies, is a "server" product. It runs in the background on a system and communicates with you, the user, by having you first establish a standard network connection with the server engine. This is true even if the SQL Server engine runs on your own workstation. Watching a server product is about as exciting as reading some of those other Visual Basic 2005 tutorial books that you wisely avoided, so Microsoft provides various client tools that let you manage databases, tables, and other relational database properties. *SQL Server Management Studio* is the standard enterprise-level client tool for managing SQL Server databases. For *SQL Server 2005 Express Edition*, Microsoft supplies a reduced yet friendlier tool, the *SQL Server Management Studio Express* (see Figure 4-2). This tool lets you manage databases and process DDL and DML statements. *Management Studio Express* is not included in *SQL Server 2005 Express Edition*; you must download or obtain it separately from Microsoft. As of this writing, it is available at no cost from Microsoft's web site.

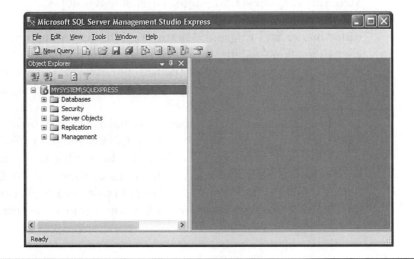

Figure 4-2 SQL Server Management Studio Express

SQL Server and This Book Because some readers of *Start-to-Finish Visual Basic 2005* may only have access to *SQL Server 2005 Express Edition* (and the related *SQL Server 2005 Management Studio Express* tool), all examples in this book are designed for use with that edition of the database engine. This only impacts the few times when I refer specifically to the client tools. All SQL statements (both DDL and DML) presented in this book and in the Library Project's source code will work with any edition of SQL Server 2005.

Although Microsoft continues to update and sell Microsoft Access, it is recommending more and more that professional developers use and distribute databases in SQL Server format. Microsoft will even permit you to redistribute *SQL Server 2005 Express Edition* with your application. To do this, you must first obtain a "SQL Server 2005 Express Edition redistribution license" from Microsoft. Fortunately, it's free and can be had for the asking from the *SQL Server 2005 Express Edition* web site, *http://www.microsoft.com/sql/express*.

SQL: Structured Query Language

Conducting business in Japan is pretty easy—once you know the language. The same is true of SQL Server: It's pretty easy to manipulate and access data, once you know the language. In this case, the language is SQL, or **Structured Query Language**. Originally developed by IBM, SQL has since become a standard across the database industry. Well, kind of. As with America and England, Microsoft's SQL Server and Oracle's "Oracle" are two relational databases divided by a common language. The core parts of the SQL language are pretty consistent between vendors, but each supplier adds a lot of extra features and syntax variations designed by Edgar Codd wannabes.

This section describes those DDL and DML statements that will be most useful in our development of the Library program. You'll be glad to know that SQL isn't too picky about the formatting of the various statements. Upper- and lowercase distinctions are ignored; *SELECT* is the same as *select* is the same as *SeLeCt*. (Traditional SQL code is mostly uppercase. I use uppercase for all keywords, and mixed case for tables, fields, and other custom items. Whatever you choose, consistency is important.) Also, employ whitespace as you see fit. You can put statements on one gigantic line, or put every word on a separate line. The only time whitespace and case matters is in the actual data text strings; whatever you type, that's how it stays.

SQL statements normally end with a semicolon, but some tools do not require you to include the semicolon, and other tools require that you exclude it. When using the SQL Server visual client tools (*Management Studio* and *Management Studio Express*), semicolons are optional, but it's a good idea to include them when you are using multiple statements together, one after another. SQL statements used in Visual Basic code never include semicolons.

Later, when you look at a SQL script I wrote, you will see the word "GO" from time to time. In SQL Server, this command says, "For all of the other statements that appeared so far, go ahead and process them now."

DDL Statements

This may come as a shock to you, but before you can store any data in a table, you have to create the table. SQL has just the tool to do this: the **CREATE TABLE** statement. It's one of the many DDL statements. The basic syntax is pretty straightforward.

```
CREATE TABLE tableName
(
    fieldName1    dataType    options,
    fieldName2    dataType    options,
    and so on...
)
```

Just fill in the parts, and you're ready to populate (data, that is). *Table and field names* are built from letters and digits; you can include spaces and some other special characters, but it makes for difficult coding later on. Each vendor has its own collection of *data types*; I'll stick with the SQL Server versions here. The *options* let you specify things such as whether the field requires data or not, whether it represents the table's primary key, and other similar **constraints**. Extensions to the syntax let you set up constraints that apply to the entire table, **indexes** (which let you sort or search a specific column more quickly), and data storage specifics.

Here's a sample CREATE TABLE statement that could be used for the table of order line items (refer to Table 4-4).

```
CREATE TABLE LineItems
(
    RecordID     bigint          IDENTITY PRIMARY KEY,
    OrderID      bigint          NOT NULL,
    CustomerID   varchar(20)     NOT NULL
        REFERENCES Customers (CustomerID),
    ProductID    varchar(20)     NOT NULL,
    Quantity     smallint        NOT NULL
)
```

The *IDENTITY* keyword lets SQL Server take charge of filling the *RecordID* field with data; it will use a sequential counter to supply a unique *RecordID* value with each new record. The *PRIMARY KEY* clause identifies the *RecordID* field as the unique identifying value for each record in the table. The *bigint* and *smallint* data types indicate appropriately sized integer fields, while the *varchar* type provides space for text, up to the maximum length specified in the parentheses (20 characters). The *REFERENCES* option clause identifies a relationship between this *LineItems* table and another table named *Customers*; values in the *LineItems.CustomerID* field match the key values from the *Customers.CustomerID* field. (Note the "dot" syntax to separate table and field names. It shows up everywhere in SQL.) References between tables are also known as **foreign references**.

If you need to make structure or option changes to a table or its fields after it is created, SQL includes an *ALTER TABLE* statement that can change almost everything in the table. Additionally, there is a related *DROP TABLE* statement used to get rid of a table and all of its data. You might want to avoid this statement on live production data as the users tend to get a bit irritable when their data suddenly disappears off the surface of the earth.

Table 4-5 summarizes the available data types used in SQL Server.

Table 4-5 SQL Server Data Types

Data Type	Description
bigint	An 8-byte (64-bit) integer field for values ranging from −9,223,372,036,854,775,808 to 9,223,372,036,854,775,807.
binary	Fixed-length binary data, up to 8,000 bytes in length. You specify the length through a parameter, as in "binary(100)."
bit	Supports three possible values: 1, 0, or NULL. Generally used for Boolean values. Internally, SQL Server stores multiple bit fields from a single record in a merged integer field.
char, nchar	Fixed-length standard (char) or Unicode (nchar) strings, up to 8,000 characters in length. You specify the length through a parameter, as in "char(100)."
cursor	This data type is used within stored procedures, and cannot be used to create a column.
datetime	A general date and time field for dates ranging from January 1, 1753 AD to December 31, 9999 AD. Time accuracy for any given value is within 3.33 milliseconds.
decimal, numeric	A fixed-precision and scale decimal field. You specify the maximum number of digits to appear on both sides of the decimal point (the precision) and the maximum number of those digits that can appear on the right side of the decimal point (the scale). For instance, a setting of "decimal(10,4)" creates a field with up to ten total digits, four of which may appear after the decimal point. The maximum precision value is 38. "numeric" is a synonym for "decimal," as is "dec."
float	A floating-point decimal field with variable storage. You can specify the number of bits used to store the value, up to 53. By default, all 53 bits are used, so a setting of "float" is equivalent to "float(53)." The pseudo-data type "real" is equivalent to "float(24)." The values stored are on the order of $\pm 1.0 \times 10^{\pm 38}$; the exact range and precision varies by the bits used for storage. This data type is susceptible to minor calculation errors.
image, text, ntext	Don't use these data types as they will eventually be removed from SQL Server.
int	A 4-byte (32-bit) integer field for values ranging from −2,147,483,648 to 2,147,483,647.

(continues)

Table 4-5 SQL Server Data Types *(continued)*

Data Type	Description
money	An 8-byte (64-bit) high-accuracy field for storing currency values, with up to four digits after the decimal point. Stored data values range from –922,337,203,685,477.5808 to 922,337,203,685,477.5807.
smalldatetime	A general date and time field for dates ranging from January 1, 1900 AD to June 6, 2079 AD. Time accuracy for any given value is within 1 minute.
smallint	A 2-byte (16-bit) integer field for values ranging from –32,768 to 32,767.
smallmoney	A 4-byte (32-bit) high-accuracy field for storing currency values, with up to four digits after the decimal point. Stored data values range from –214,748.3648 to 214,748.3647.
sql_variant	A generic type that stores values from many other type-specific fields.
table	A special field that temporarily stores the results of a query in a compacted table format. Defining a table field is somewhat complex, and its use naturally carries with it certain restrictions.
timestamp	This data type is used to record modification times on records. There are restrictions on its use, and it is not guaranteed to be unique within a table.
tinyint	A 1-byte (8-bit) unsigned integer field for values ranging from 0 to 255.
uniqueidentifier	A 16-byte globally unique identifier (GUID). The related NEWID function generates values for this field.
varbinary	Variable-length binary data, up to 8,000 bytes in length. You specify the length through a parameter, as in "varbinary(100)." The field consumes space only for the actual content currently stored in the field. A special setting of "varbinary(max)" allows entry of up to about two billion bytes.
varchar, nvarchar	Variable-length standard (varchar) or Unicode (nvarchar) strings, up to 8,000 characters in length. You specify the length through a parameter, as in "varchar(100)." The field consumes space only for the actual content currently stored in the field. A special setting of "varchar(max)" allows entry of up to about two billion characters.
xml	Provides storage for XML data.

DML Statements

Although DDL statements are powerful, they aren't used that much. Once you create your database objects, there's not much call for tinkering. The DML (Data Manipulation Language) statements are more useful for everyday data surfing.

The *INSERT* statement adds data records to a table. Data is added to a table one record at a time. (A variation of *INSERT* lets you insert multiple records, but those records must come from another existing table source.) To use the *INSERT* statement, specify the destination table and fields, and then the individual values to put into each field. One data value corresponds to each specified data column name.

```
INSERT INTO LineItems
   (OrderID, CustomerID, ProductID, Quantity)
   VALUES (10002, 'BW3', 'BEV01COF', 1)
```

Assuming this statement goes with the *CREATE TABLE* statement written earlier, this insert action will add a new record to the *LineItems* table with five new fields—four specified fields, plus the primary key automatically added to the *RecordID* field (because it was marked as *IDENTITY*). SQL Server also does a variety of data integrity checks on your behalf. Each data field you add must be of the right data type, but you already expected that. Because we designed the *CustomerID* field to be a reference to the *Customer* table, the insert will fail if customer 'BW3' does not already exist in the *Customer* table.

Numeric literals can be included in your SQL statements as needed without any additional qualification. String literals are always surrounded by single quotes, as is done for the customer and product IDs in this *INSERT* statement. If you need to include single quotes in the literal, enter them twice.

```
'John O''Sullivan'
```

Surround literal date and time values with single quotes.

```
'7-Nov-2005'
```

Such date and time values accept any recognized format, although you should use a format that is not easy for SQL Server to misinterpret.

Many field types support an "unassigned" value, a value that indicates that the field contains no data at all. Such a value is known as the "null" value, and is specified in SQL Server using the "NULL" keyword. You cannot assign *NULL* to primary key fields, or to any field marked with the "NOT NULL" option.

To remove a previously added record, use the *DELETE* statement.

```
DELETE FROM LineItems WHERE RecordID = 92231
```

The *DELETE* statement includes a "WHERE" clause (the "WHERE RecordID = 92231" part). *WHERE* clauses let you indicate one or more records in a table by making comparisons with data fields. Your *WHERE* clauses can include *AND* and *OR* keywords to join multiple conditions, and parentheses for grouping.

```
DELETE FROM LineItems WHERE OrderID = 10001
   AND ProductID = 'BRD05RYE'
```

Such a *DELETE* statement may delete zero, one, or 1,000 records, so precision in the WHERE clause is important. To delete all records in the table, exclude the *WHERE* clause altogether.

```
DELETE FROM LineItems
```

The *UPDATE* statement also uses a WHERE clause to modify values in existing table records.

```
UPDATE LineItems SET Quantity = 4
   WHERE RecordID = 92231
```

Assignments are made to fields with the *SET* clause; put the field name (*Quantity*) on the left side of the equals sign, and the new value on the right (*4*). To assign multiple values at once, separate each assignment with a comma. You can also include formulas and calculations.

```
UPDATE LineItems SET Quantity = Quantity + 1,
   ProductID = 'BEV02POP'
   WHERE RecordID = 92231
```

As with the *DELETE* statement, the *UPDATE* statement may update zero, one, or many records based on which records match the *WHERE* clause.

The final DML statement, and the one most often used, is *SELECT*.

```
SELECT ProductID, Quantity FROM LineItems
   WHERE RecordID = 92231
```

SELECT scans a table (*LineItems*), looking for all records matching a given criteria (*RecordID = 92231*), and returns a smaller table that contains just the indicated fields (*ProductID* and *Quantity*) for the matching records. The most basic query returns all rows and columns.

```
SELECT * FROM LineItems
```

This returns all records from the table in no particular order. The asterisk (*) means "include all fields."

The optional *ORDER BY* clause returns the results in a specific order.

```
SELECT * FROM LineItems
   WHERE Quantity > 5
   ORDER BY ProductID, Quantity DESC
```

This query returns all records that have a *Quantity* field value of more than five, and sorts the results first by the *ProductID* column (in ascending order), and then by the numeric quantity (in descending order, specified with *DESC*).

Aggregate functions and grouping features let you summarize results from the larger set of data. The following query documents the total ordered quantity for each product in the table.

```
SELECT ProductID, SUM(Quantity) FROM LineItems
   GROUP BY ProductID
```

You can use **joins** to link the data from two or more distinct tables. The following query joins the *LineItems* and *Customer* tables on their matching *CustomerID* columns. This *SELECT* statement also demonstrates the use of table abbreviations (the *LI* and *CU* prefixes) added through the *AS* clauses; they aren't usually necessary, but they can help make a complex query more readable.

```
SELECT LI.OrderID, CU.CustomerName, LI.ProductID
   FROM LineItems AS LI INNER JOIN Customer AS CU
   ON LI.CustomerID = CU.CustomerID
   ORDER BY LI.OrderID, CU.CustomerName
```

This table uses an "inner join," one of the five main types of joins, each of which returns different sets of records based on the relationship between the first (left) and second (right) table in the join.

- **Inner Join.** Returns only those records where there is a match in the linked fields. This type of join uses the "INNER JOIN" keywords.
- **Left Outer Join.** Returns every record from the left table, and only those records from the right table where there is a match in the linked fields. If a left table record doesn't have a match, it acts as if all the fields in the right table for that record contain NULL values. This type of join uses the "LEFT JOIN" keywords. One use might be to join the *Product* and *LineItems* tables. You could return a list of the full product name for all available products, plus the total quantity ordered for each one. By putting the *Product* table on the left of a left outer join, the query would return all product names, even if that product had never been ordered (and didn't appear in the *LineItems* table).
- **Right Outer Join.** This works just like a left outer join, but all records from the right table are returned, and just the left table records that have a match. This type of join uses the "RIGHT JOIN" keywords.
- **Full Outer Join.** Returns all records from the left and right tables, whether they have matches or not. When there is a match, it is reflected in the results. This type of join uses the "FULL JOIN" keywords.
- **Cross Join.** Also called a Cartesian Join. Returns every possible combination of left and right records. This type of join uses the "CROSS JOIN" keywords.

Joining focuses on the relationship that two tables have. (This use of "relationship," by the way, is not the basis for the term "relational database.") Some tables exist in a "parent-child" relationship; one "parent" record has one or more dependent "child" records in another table. This is often true of orders; a single "order header" has multiple "line items." This type of relationship is known as **one-to-many**, because one record is tied to many records in the other table. And the relationship is unidirectional; a given child record does not tie to multiple parent records.

A **one-to-one** relationship ties a single record in one table to a single record in another table. It's pretty straightforward, and is often used to enhance the values found in the original record through a supplementary record in a second table.

In a **many-to-many** relationship, a single record in one table is associated with multiple records in a second table, *and* a single record in that second table is also associated with multiple records in the first table. A real-world example would be the relationship between teachers and students in a college setting. One teacher has multiple students in the classroom, but each student also has multiple teachers each semester. Practical implementations of many-to-many relationships actually require three tables: the two related tables, and a "go between" table that links them together. I will show you a sample of such a table in the "Project" section of this chapter.

Beyond Basic SQL

The sample statements I listed here scratch only the surface of the data manipulation possibilities available through SQL. But by now you should have noticed that SQL is remarkably English-like in syntax, much more than even Visual Basic. In fact, the original name for the language— SEQUEL—was an acronym for "Structured *English* Query Language." As the SQL statements get more complex, they will look less and less like an eighth-grade essay, and more like random collections of English words.

The goal here is to introduce you to the basic structure of SQL statements. Most of the statements we will encounter in the Library Project will be no more complex than the samples included here. If you're hungry for more, the "Books Online" component installed with SQL Server (a separate download for the Express Edition) has some pretty good usage documentation. There are also several good books available on the ins and outs of SQL, including vendor-specific dialects.

Using Databases in Visual Basic

There are a few different ways that Visual Basic can interact with data stored in a database.

- Use ADO.NET, the primary data access technology included in the .NET Framework, to interact with database-stored content. This is the method used throughout the Library program to interact with its database. ADO.NET is discussed in Chapter 10, "ADO.NET," with examples of its use. I will also introduce ADO.NET-specific code into the Library Project in that chapter.

- Use the "data binding" features available in Visual Basic and Visual Studio. Binding establishes a connection between an on-screen data control or similar data-enabled object and content from a database. Code written for you by Microsoft takes care of all the communication work; you can even drag-and-drop these types of interactions. Although I will discuss data binding in Chapter 10 (because binding is based on ADO.NET), I tend to avoid it because it reduces the amount of control the programmer can exert on user data management. Data binding will not be used in the Library program.
- Extract the data from the database into a standard file, and use file manipulation features in Visual Basic to process the data. Hmm, that doesn't seem very useful, but I have actually had to do it, especially in the old days when some proprietary databases could not interact easily with Visual Basic code.
- Each time you need some of the data, tell the user that somehow the data has been lost, and that it must be reentered immediately. If you have ever been curious to know what the inside of an unemployment office looks like, this could be your chance.

If you are a former Visual Basic 6.0 (or earlier) programmer, you may think that your knowledge of ADO will translate directly into ADO.NET development. Ha! You couldn't be more wrong. Although the two data technologies share a partial name, the code written to use each method varies considerably. I will not discuss the older ADO technology at all in this book.

Documenting the Database

Technical content that describes the tables and fields in your application's database represents the most important piece of documentation generated during your application's lifetime. In fact, the need for good documentation is the basis for one of my core programming beliefs: Project documentation is as important, and sometimes more important, than source code.

You may think I'm joking about this. Although you will (hopefully) find a lot of humor in the pages of this book, this is something I don't joke about. If you are developing an application that centers on database-stored user content, complete and accurate documentation of every table and field used in the database is a must. Any lack in this area will—not might, not perhaps, but will—lead to data integrity issues and a longer-than-necessary development timeline. Figure 4-3 puts it another way.

This is your application

This is your application without database documentation

This is your application with database documentation

Figure 4-3 Any questions?

Why do I think that database documentation is even more important than user documentation or functional specifications? It's because of the impact the document will have on the user's data. If you have a documented database, you can make guesses about the functional specification, and probably come pretty close. If you lack user documentation, you can always write it when the program is done (as if there was any other way?). But if you lack database documentation, you are in for a world of hurt.

If you haven't worked on large database projects before, you might not believe me. But I have. I once inherited an existing enterprise-wide database system written in Visual Basic 3.0. The source code was bad enough, but the associated undocumented 100-table database was a mish-mash of inconsistently stored data values. The confusing stored procedure code wasn't much better. Because there wasn't a clear set of documentation on each field, the six programmers who originally developed the system had each made their own decisions about what range of data would be allowed in each field, or about which fields were required or not.

Tracing back through the uncommented 100,000 lines of source code to determine what every field did was not fun, and it took a few months to complete it with accuracy. Because the customer had paid for and expected a stable and coherent system, most of the extra cost involved in replacing the documentation that should have been there in the first place was borne by my development group. Don't let this happen to you!

Summary

Most Visual Basic applications target the business world, and are designed to interact with some sort of database. Understanding the database system used with your application is important; even more important is documenting the specific database features you incorporate into your application.

Because of the influence of relational databases and the SQL language on the database industry, it won't be hard to find a lot of resources to assist you in crafting SQL statements and complex data analysis queries. The Library Project in this book uses SQL Server 2005, but because of the generally consistent use of the core SQL language features, the application could just as easily have used Oracle, Access, or any of a number of other relational databases.

Project

To assist in my development of Visual Basic database projects, I always write a "Technical Resource Kit" document before I begin actual coding of the application. The bulk of this word-processing document consists of the table- and field-level documentation for the application's associated database. Also included are the formats for all configuration and custom data files, a map of the online help pages, and information about third-party products used in the application. Depending on the type of application, my expectations for the user, and the terms of any contract, I may supply none, some, or all of the Resource Kit's content to the user community.

Let's begin the Technical Resource Kit for the Library Project by designing and documenting the database tables to be used by the application. This Resource Kit appears in the book's installation directory, in the *Chapter 4* subdirectory, and contains the following three files.

- **ACME Library Resource Kit.doc.** A Microsoft Word version of the technical documentation for the project.
- **ACME Library Resource Kit.pdf.** A second copy of the Technical Resource Kit, this time in Adobe Acrobat (PDF) format.
- **Database Creation Script.sql.** A SQL Server database script used to build the actual tables and fields in the database.

4. DESIGNING THE DATABASE

Technical Resource Kit Content

This section includes a listing of the tables included in the Library database. Each table includes a general description to assist you in your understanding of the database structure. You will encounter all of these tables in successive chapters, along with associated source code, so don't freak out if some table or field seems unknowable right now.

Security-Related Tables

Although patrons do not need to log in to the application to look up items in the database, administrators must log in before they can access enhanced features of the program. The following four tables manage the security credentials of each administrator. The application uses SQL Server or Windows-based security credentials only to access the database initially, not to restrict features.

Activity

This table defines the features of the application that can be secured using group rights. These activities are linked with security groups (from the *GroupName* table) to establish the rights for a particular group.

Field	Type	Description
ID	bigint	Primary key. This key is not auto-generated; the value supplied matches internal values used within the Library application. Required.
FullName	varchar(50)	Descriptive name of this activity. Required.

The following activities are defined at this time.

- 1—Manage authors and names
- 2—Manage author and name types
- 3 —Manage copy status codes
- 4—Manage media types
- 5—Manage series

(continues)

- 6—Manage security groups
- 7—Manage library materials
- 8—Manage patrons
- 9—Manage publishers
- 10—Manage system values
- 11—Manage administrative users
- 12—Process and accept fees
- 13—Manage locations
- 14—Check out library items
- 15—Check in library items
- 16—Access administrative features
- 17—Perform daily processing
- 18—Run system reports
- 19—Access patrons without patron password
- 20—Manage barcodes
- 21—Manage holidays
- 22—Manage patron groups
- 23—View administrative patron messages

GroupName

Each record in this table defines a single security group. Librarians and other administrators each belong to a single security group.

Field	Type	Description
ID	bigint	Primary key; automatically assigned. Required.
FullName	varchar(50)	Name of this group. Required.

GroupActivity

This table connects records in the *Activity* table to records in the *GroupName* table (a many-to-many relationship) to establish the activities a security group can perform.

Field	Type	Description
GroupID	bigint	Primary key. The associated security group. Foreign reference to GroupName.ID. Required.
ActivityID	bigint	Primary key. The activity that members of the associated security group can perform. Foreign reference to Activity.ID. Required.

UserName

This table contains the actual records for each librarian or administrator. Each record includes the user's password and security group setting.

Field	Type	Description
ID	bigint	Primary key; automatically assigned. Required.
FullName	varchar(50)	Name of this user, administrator, or librarian. Required.
LoginID	varchar(20)	User ID that gives this user access to the system. It is entered into the Library program's "login" form, along with the password, to gain access to enhanced features. Required.
Password	varchar(20)	The password for this user, in an encrypted format. Optional.
Active	bit	Is this user allowed to access the system? 0 for False, 1 for True. Required.
GroupID	bigint	To which security group does this user belong? Foreign reference to GroupName.ID. Required.

Support Code Tables

Several tables exist simply to provide a list of values to other tables. In an application, these list tables often appear as the choices in a drop-down ("combo box") list control.

(continues)

CodeAuthorType

In the Library program, the word "author" is a generic term used for authors, illustrators, editors, and any other similar contributor to an item in the library's inventory. This table lets you define those roles.

Field	Type	Description
ID	bigint	Primary key; automatically assigned. Required.
FullName	varchar(50)	Name of this type of author or contributor. Required.

CodeCopyStatus

Copy status codes include things like "circulating," "being repaired," and any other primary status the library wishes to set. The checked-in or checked-out status is handled through other features, as is the flag that indicates whether an item is a reference item or not.

Field	Type	Description
ID	bigint	Primary key; automatically assigned. Required.
FullName	varchar(50)	Name of this status entry. Required.

CodeLocation

Physical locations where library items are stored. This could be separate sites, or rooms or areas within a common location.

Field	Type	Description
ID	bigint	Primary key; automatically assigned. Required.
FullName	varchar(50)	Name of this location. Required.
LastProcessing	datetime	The date when Daily Processing was last done for this location. If NULL, processing has not yet been done. Optional.

CodeMediaType
Types of media, such as book, magazine, video, CD, etc.

Field	Type	Description
ID	bigint	Primary key; automatically assigned. Required.
FullName	varchar(50)	Name of this media type. Required.
CheckoutDays	smallint	Number of days for which items in this type can be checked out, before renewal. Required.
RenewDays	smallint	Number of days to add to the original checkout period for a renewal of items within this type. Required.
RenewTimes	smallint	Maximum number of times the item can be renewed by a patron before it must be returned. Required.
DailyFine	money	Amount charged per day for an overdue item of this type. Required.

CodePatronGroup
Categories of groups into which patrons are placed. These are not security groups, but general groups for reporting purposes. This was added to support grouping of patrons by units within a company, or by class/grade within a school library setting.

Field	Type	Description
ID	bigint	Primary key; automatically assigned. Required.
FullName	varchar(50)	Name of this patron group. Required.

(continues)

CodeSeries

Some items appear as part of a larger series or collection. This table defines the collection and series names.

Field	Type	Description
ID	bigint	Primary key; automatically assigned. Required.
FullName	varchar(50)	Name of this series or collection. Required.

Library Items

The tables in this section manage the actual inventory of items. Because a library may own more than one copy of a single item, these tables manage the "named item" and its individual "copies" separately.

NamedItem

A library item, such as a book, CD, or magazine. This table represents a general item, and not the actual copy of the item.

Field	Type	Description
ID	bigint	Primary key; automatically assigned. Required.
Title	varchar(150)	Title of this item. Required.
Subtitle	varchar(150)	Subtitle of this item. Optional.
Description	varchar(max)	Full description of this item. Optional.
Edition	varchar(10)	Edition number for this item. Optional.
Publisher	bigint	This item's publisher. Foreign reference to Publisher.ID. Optional.
Dewey	varchar(20)	Dewey decimal number. Use "/" for line breaks. Optional.
LC	varchar(25)	Library of Congress number. Use "/" for line breaks. Optional.
ISxN	varchar(20)	ISBN, ISSN, or other standardized number of this item. Optional.
LCCN	varchar(12)	Library of Congress control number. Optional.

Field	Type	Description
Copyright	smallint	Year of original copyright, or of believed original copyright. Optional.
Series	bigint	The series or collection in which this item appears. Foreign reference to CodeSeries.ID. Optional.
MediaType	bigint	The media classification of this item. Foreign reference to CodeMediaType.ID. Required.
OutOfPrint	bit	Is this title out of print? 0 for False, 1 for True. Required.

ItemCopy

A single copy of a named item. Separate copies of the same item will appear as separate records in this table.

Field	Type	Description
ID	bigint	Primary key; automatically assigned. Required.
ItemID	bigint	The related named item record. Foreign reference to NamedItem.ID Required.
CopyNumber	smallint	Numbered position of this item within the set of copies for a named item. Required, and unique among items with the same ItemID field value.
Description	varchar(max)	Comments specific to this copy of the item. Optional.
Available	bit	Is this copy available for checkout or circulation? 0 for False, 1 for True. Required.
Missing	bit	Has this copy been reported missing? 0 for False, 1 for True. Required.
Reference	bit	Is this a reference copy? 0 for False, 1 for True. Required.
Condition	varchar(30)	Any comments relevant to the condition of this copy. Optional.

(continues)

Field	Type	Description
Acquired	datetime	Date this copy was acquired by the library. Optional.
Cost	money	Value of this item, either original or replacement value. Optional.
Status	bigint	The general status of this copy. Foreign reference to CodeCopyStatus.ID. Required.
Barcode	varchar(20)	Barcode found on the copy. At this time, only numeric barcodes are supported. Optional.
Location	bigint	The site or room location of this item. Foreign reference to CodeLocation.ID. Optional.

Publisher

An organization that publishes books or some other type of media.

Field	Type	Description
ID	bigint	Primary key; automatically assigned. Required.
FullName	varchar(100)	Name of the publisher. Required.
WebSite	varchar(255)	URL for this publisher's web site. Optional.

Author

Someone who writes, edits, illustrates, or in some other way contributes to a book or media item. In all cases, when the term "author" appears in this table, it refers to anyone who contributes to the item.

Field	Type	Description
ID	bigint	Primary key; automatically assigned. Required.
LastName	varchar(50)	Last name of this author. Required.
FirstName	varchar(30)	First name of this author. Optional.
MiddleName	varchar(30)	Middle name or initial of this author. Optional.
Suffix	varchar(10)	Name suffix, such as "Jr." Optional.
BirthYear	smallint	Year of birth. Use negative numbers for BC. Optional
DeathYear	smallint	Year of death. Use negative numbers for BC. Optional.
Comments	varchar(250)	Miscellaneous comments about this author. Optional.

ItemAuthor

An author, editor, and so on, for a specific named item. This table establishes a many-to-many relationship between the *NamedItem* and *Author* tables.

Field	Type	Description
ItemID	bigint	Primary key. The associated named item. Foreign reference to NamedItem.ID. Required.
AuthorID	bigint	Primary key. The author associated with the named item. Foreign reference to Author.ID. Required.
Sequence	smallint	Relative order of this author among the authors for this named item. Authors with smaller numbers appear first. Required.
AuthorType	bigint	The specific type of contribution given by this author for this named item. Foreign reference to CodeAuthorType.ID. Required.

(continues)

4. DESIGNING THE DATABASE

Keyword

Custom words that can be applied to named items to make searching easier.

Field	Type	Description
ID	bigint	Primary key; automatically assigned. Required.
FullName	varchar(50)	Name of this keyword. Required.

ItemKeyword

Connects a keyword with a named item through a many-to-many relationship between the *NamedItem* and *Keyword* tables.

Field	Type	Description
ItemID	bigint	Primary key. The associated named item. Foreign reference to NamedItem.ID. Required.
KeywordID	bigint	Primary key. The keyword to associate with the named item. Foreign reference to Keyword.ID. Required.

Subject

Subject headings used to classify named items.

Field	Type	Description
ID	bigint	Primary key; automatically assigned. Required.
FullName	varchar(150)	Name of this subject. Required.

ItemSubject

Connects a subject with a named item through a many-to-many relationship between the *NamedItem* and *Subject* tables.

Field	Type	Description
ItemID	bigint	Primary key. The associated named item. Foreign reference to NamedItem.ID. Required.
SubjectID	bigint	Primary key. The subject to associate with the named item. Foreign reference to Subject.ID. Required.

Patron-Related Tables

The tables in this section define the actual patron records, and their relationship to item copies (when such copies are checked out by the patron).

Patron

An identified library user. Patrons usually have check-out privileges.

Field	Type	Description
ID	bigint	Primary key; automatically assigned. Required.
LastName	varchar(30)	Last name of this patron. Required.
FirstName	varchar(30)	First name of this patron. Required.
LastActivity	datetime	Date of last checkout, renewal, or return. Optional.
Active	bit	Is this an active patron? 0 for False, 1 for True. Required.
Comments	varchar(max)	Any comments associated with this patron. Optional.
AdminMessage	varchar(500)	Comments that are displayed to administrative users when the patron's record is accessed. Optional.

(continues)

Field	Type	Description
Barcode	varchar(20)	Barcode found on this patron's library card. At this time, only numeric barcodes are supported. Optional.
Password	varchar(20)	Patron's password, in an encrypted format. Required.
Email	varchar(100)	Patron's email address. Optional.
Phone	varchar(20)	Patron's phone number. Optional.
Address	varchar(50)	Patron's street address. Optional.
City	varchar(20)	Patron's city. Optional.
State	varchar(2)	Patron's state abbreviation. Optional.
Postal	varchar(10)	Patron's postal code. Optional.
PatronGroup	bigint	The group in which this patron appears. Foreign reference to CodePatronGroup.ID. Optional.

PatronCopy

This table manages item copies currently checked out by a patron, or item copies that have been previously checked out and have since been returned.

Field	Type	Description
ID	bigint	Primary key; automatically assigned. Required.
Patron	bigint	The associated patron. Foreign reference to Patron.ID. Required.
ItemCopy	bigint	The item copy currently or previously checked out by the patron. Foreign reference to ItemCopy.ID. Required.
CheckOut	datetime	The date when this item copy was initially checked out. Required.
Renewal	smallint	The number of times this item copy has been renewed. Set to 0 when the item copy is first checked out. Required.
DueDate	datetime	Current due date for this item copy. Required.
CheckIn	datetime	The date when this item copy was returned. Optional.

Field	Type	Description
Returned	bit	Has the item copy been returned? 0 for False, 1 for True. Required.
Missing	bit	Is the item copy missing and considered lost? 0 for False, 1 for True. Required.
Fine	money	Total fine accumulated for this item copy. Defaults to 0.00. An administrator may reduce an accumulated fine. Required.
Paid	money	Total amount paid (in fees) for this item copy. Required.
ProcessDate	datetime	When an item copy is processed for overdue fines, this field contains the last date for which processing was done. Optional.

PatronPayment

Fines, payments, and dismissals on a patron copy record. Overdue fines are not recorded in this table, but administrator-initiated fines due to charges for missing items are recorded here.

Field	Type	Description
ID	bigint	Primary key; automatically assigned. Required.
PatronCopy	bigint	The associated patron. Foreign reference to PatronCopy.ID. Required.
EntryDate	datetime	Date and time when this entry was recorded. Required.
EntryType	varchar(1)	The type of payment entry. Required. The possible values are: ■ P = The patron made a payment. ■ F = A fine (other than a standard overdue fine) was imposed by an administrator. ■ D = A portion (or all) of the fine was dismissed. ■ R = A refund was given to the patron due to overpayment.

(continues)

Field	Type	Description
Amount	money	The amount associated with this entry. The value is always positive. Required.
Comment	varchar(50)	A short comment about this entry. Optional.
UserID	bigint	The user who added this payment event. Foreign reference to UserName.ID. Optional.

Barcode-Related Tables

There are three levels of definition to create a barcode: (1) the sheet on which a grid of labels prints, (2) a single label on the sheet, and (3) the individual items that appear on each label. The three tables in this section define those three levels.

BarcodeSheet

Describes the template for a single page of barcode labels.

Field	Type	Description
ID	bigint	Primary key; automatically assigned. Required.
FullName	varchar(50)	Name of this sheet template. Required.
UnitType	varchar(1)	Units used in the various measurements found in most fields in this record. Required. ■ I = Inches ■ C = Centimeters ■ P = Points ■ T = Twips
PageWidth	decimal(10,4)	Width of the entire page. Required.
PageHeight	decimal(10,4)	Height of the entire page. Required.
MarginLeft	decimal(10,4)	Left border, up to the edge of the printable label area. Required.
MarginRight	decimal(10,4)	Right border, up to the edge of the printable label area. Required.

Field	Type	Description
MarginTop	decimal(10,4)	Top border, up to the edge of the printable label area. Required.
MarginBottom	decimal(10,4)	Bottom border, up to the edge of the printable label area. Required.
IntraColumn	decimal(10,4)	The width of the blank area between label columns. Required.
IntraRow	decimal(10,4)	The height of the blank area between label rows. Required.
ColumnsCount	smallint	The number of label columns on this template. Required.
RowsCount	smallint	The number of label rows on this template. Required.

BarcodeLabel

Describes the template for a single label on a barcode sheet. There may be any number of labels on a single sheet, but they all have the same shape and format.

Field	Type	Description
ID	bigint	Primary key; automatically assigned. Required.
FullName	varchar(50)	Name of this label template. Required.
BarcodeSheet	bigint	The sheet template on which this label template appears. Foreign reference to BarcodeSheet.ID. Required.
UnitType	varchar(1)	Units used in the various measurements found in most fields in this record. Required. ■ I = Inches ■ C = Centimeters ■ P = Points ■ T = Twips

(continues)

BarcodeLabelItem

Describes a single item as found on a barcode label. Items include static and generated text, lines, rectangles, and generated barcodes.

Field	Type	Description
ID	bigint	Primary key; automatically assigned. Required.
Priority	smallint	Identifies the order in which items on the label are printed. Lower numbers are printed first. Required.
BarcodeLabel	bigint	The label template on which this item appears. Foreign reference to BarcodeLabel.ID. Required.
ItemType	varchar(1)	What type of item does this record represent? Required. ■ T = Static text ■ B = Barcode ■ N = Barcode number ■ L = Line ■ R = Rectangle
PosLeft	decimal(10,4)	Left edge of the item relative to the left edge of the label. Measured according to the related BarcodeLabel.UnitType field. Required.
PosTop	decimal(10,4)	Top edge of the item relative to the top edge of the label. Measured according to the related BarcodeLabel.UnitType field. Required.
PosWidth	decimal(10,4)	Width of the item, or of the box in which the item is drawn. For lines, this is the X-coordinate of the end point. Measured according to the related BarcodeLabel.UnitType field. Required.
PosHeight	decimal(10,4)	Height of the item, or of the box in which the item is drawn. For lines, this is the Y-coordinate of the end point. Measured according to the related BarcodeLabel.UnitType field. Required.

Field	Type	Description
Rotation	smallint	Rotation angle, in degrees, of the box in which the item is drawn. Zero (0) equals no angle, and increasing angles proceed clockwise. Ranges from 0 to 359. Only used when ItemType is T, B, N, or R. Optional.
FontName	varchar(50)	The name of the font used to write the text. Valid only when ItemType is T or N. Optional.
FontSize	decimal(10,4)	The size of the font used to write the text. Valid only when ItemType is T, B, or N. Optional.
StaticText	varchar(100)	The static text to display on the label. Valid only when ItemType is T. Optional.
FontStyle	varchar(4)	The style of the font text. May be any combination of the following four codes: ■ B = Bold ■ I = Italic ■ U = Underline ■ K = Strikeout Leave this field NULL to use the normal style. Valid only when ItemType is T or N. Optional.
Color1	bigint	The main color of the text, barcode, or line. When printing a rectangle, this is the border color. If NULL, black is used. A standard Windows 32-bit RGB color value. Optional.
Color2	bigint	The fill color when printing a rectangle. If NULL, white is used. A standard Windows 32-bit RGB color value. Optional.
Alignment	smallint	The alignment of the text within the bounding box. Valid only when ItemType is T, B, or N. ■ 1 = Align in top-left corner of box ■ 2 = Align in top-center area of box ■ 4 = Align in top-right corner of box

(continues)

Field	Type	Description
		■ 16 = Align in middle-left area of box ■ 32 = Align in middle-center area of box ■ 64 = Align in middle-right area of box ■ 256 = Align in bottom-left corner of box ■ 512 = Align in bottom-center area of box ■ 1024 = Align in bottom-right corner of box
PadDigits	smallint	The number of digits in which to pad the barcode number. Set to zero (0) to ignore padding. Ranges from 0 to 20. If the barcode length is less than the specified number of digits, it is padded on the left with zeros. Only applies to ItemTypes of B and N.

Other Miscellaneous Tables

Two additional tables provide support for features not handled through other tables.

Holiday

When checking out an item to a patron, the return date should not fall on a holiday (or any day that the library is closed) because the patron might not have a way to return the book on the day it's due. This table defines one-time and recurring holidays.

Field	Type	Description
ID	bigint	Primary key, automatically assigned. Required.
FullName	varchar(50)	Name of this holiday. Not necessarily unique. Required.

Field	Type	Description
EntryType	varchar(1)	The type of entry. Required. From the following list: ■ A = Annual (as in "every December 25") ■ E = Weekly (as in "every Sunday") ■ O = One-time (as in "2/16/2004 is President's Day")
EntryDetail	varchar(10)	Entry-type-specific detail. Required. Differs for each entry type.

Entry Type	Detail Value
A	Month and Day in "mm/dd" format.
E	Single digit: 1=Sunday through 7=Saturday.
O	Date in "yyyy/mm/dd" format.

SystemValue

This table stores miscellaneous enterprise-wide settings that apply to every workstation. Local workstation-specific settings are stored on each machine, not in the database.

Field	Type	Description
ID	bigint	Primary key; automatically assigned. Required.
ValueName	varchar(50)	Name of this value. Required.
ValueData	varchar(100)	Information associated with this entry. Optional.

(continues)

The following system values are defined at this time. The name of the code appears in the *ValueName* field. The corresponding value appears in the *ValueData* field.

- **BarcodeCode39.** Is the specified barcode in "code 39" or "code 3 of 9" format? If so, an asterisk will be placed before and after the barcode number before it is printed on a label. Use a value of 0 for False, or any non-zero value for True (−1 is preferred). If missing or NULL, False is assumed.
- **BarcodeFont.** The name of the font used to print barcodes. This font must be installed on any workstation that displays or prints barcodes. It is not needed to scan barcodes.
- **DatabaseVersion.** Which structural version of the database is currently in use? Right now, it is set to 1, and is reserved for future enhancement.
- **DefaultLocation.** CodeLocation.ID value for the location that is set as the default.
- **FineGrace.** Number of days that an item can be overdue without incurring a fine.
- **NextBarcodeItem.** The next starting value to use when printing item barcodes.
- **NextBarcodeMisc.** The next starting value to use when printing miscellaneous barcodes.
- **NextBarcodePatron.** The next starting value to use when printing patron barcodes.
- **PatronCheckOut.** Indicates whether patrons can check out items without being logged in as an administrative user. Use a value of 0 (zero) to indicate no check-out privileges, or any non-zero value to allow patron check out (−1 is preferred). If this value is missing or empty, patrons will not be allowed to check out items without administrator assistance.
- **SearchLimit.** Indicates the maximum number of results returned in any search or lookup. If this value is missing or invalid, a default of 250 is used. The allowed range is between 25 and 5,000, inclusive.
- **TicketHeading.** Display text to be printed at the top of check-out tickets. All lines are centered on the ticket. Include the vertical bar character ("|") to break the text into multiple lines.

- **TicketFooting.** Display text to be printed at the bottom of check-out tickets. All lines are centered on the ticket. Include the vertical bar character ("|") to break the text into multiple lines.
- **UseLC.** Indicates whether books are categorized by Dewey or by Library of Congress (LC) call numbers. Use a value of 0 (zero) to indicate Dewey, or any non-zero value for LC (–1 is preferred). If this value is missing or empty, Dewey is assumed.

Creating the Database

Adding the database to SQL Server is almost as easy as documenting it; in fact, it's less typing. The CREATE TABLE statements are straightforward, and they all pretty much look the same. I'm going to show only a few of them here. The *Database Creation Script.sql* file in this book's installation directory includes the full script content.

The instructions listed here are for *SQL Server 2005 Management Studio Express*. You can perform all of these tasks using *SQL Server 2005 Management Studio*, or even the command-line tools supplied with SQL Server, but the details of each step will vary. The same *CREATE TABLE* statements work with whichever tool you choose.

If you haven't done so already, install *SQL Server 2005 Express Edition* (or whichever version of the database you will be using). *SQL Server 2005 Management Studio Express* is a separate product from SQL Server itself, so you must install that as well.

Most of the tables in the library project are simple data tables with a single primary key. Their code is straightforward. The *Author* table is a good example.

```
CREATE TABLE Author
(
    ID          bigint          IDENTITY PRIMARY KEY,
    LastName    varchar(50)     NOT NULL,
    FirstName   varchar(30)     NULL,
    MiddleName  varchar(30)     NULL,
    Suffix      varchar(10)     NULL,
    BirthYear   smallint        NULL,
    DeathYear   smallint        NULL,
    Comments    varchar(250)    NULL
);
```

The fields included in each *CREATE TABLE* statement appear as a comma-delimited list, all enclosed in parentheses. Each field includes either a *NULL* or *NOT NULL* option that indicates whether *NULL* values may be used in that field or not. The *PRIMARY KEY* option automatically specifies *NOT NULL*.

Some fields create tables that link two other tables in a many-to-many relationship. One example is the *GroupActivity* table, which connects the *GroupName* table with the *Activity* table.

```
CREATE TABLE GroupActivity
(
    GroupID      bigint    NOT NULL,
    ActivityID   bigint    NOT NULL,
    PRIMARY KEY (GroupID, ActivityID)
);
```

The *Author* table had a single primary key, so the *PRIMARY KEY* option could be attached directly to its *ID* field. Because the *GroupActivity* table has a two-field primary key (which is common in relational databases), the *PRIMARY KEY* option is specified as an entry all its own, with the key fields specified as a parentheses-enclosed comma-delimited list.

Earlier in the chapter, I showed how you could establish a reference to a field in another table by using the *REFERENCES* constraint as part of the *CREATE TABLE* statement. You can also establish them after the tables are already in place, as I do in the script. Here is the statement that establishes the link between the *GroupActivity* and *GroupName* tables:

```
ALTER TABLE GroupActivity
    ADD FOREIGN KEY (GroupID)
    REFERENCES GroupName (ID);
```

Because I've already written the entire SQL script for you, I'll just have you process it directly using *Microsoft SQL Server 2005 Management Studio Express*. (If you will be using the full version of SQL Server or some other management tool, the provided script will still work, although the step-by-step instructions will differ.) Before adding the tables, we need to create a database specific to the Library project. Start up *Microsoft SQL Server 2005 Management Studio Express*.

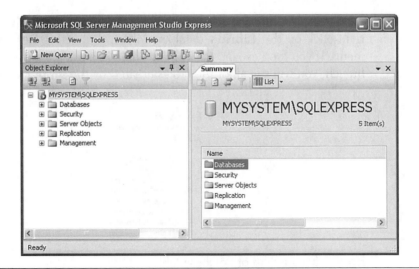

Figure 4-4 SQL Server 2005 Management Studio Express main form

To add a new database for the Library Project, right-click on the **Database** folder in the **Object Explorer**, and select **New Database** from the shortcut menu. On the **New Database** form that appears, enter "Library" in the **Database Name** field, and then click **OK**.

The Library database is a shell of a database; it doesn't contain any tables or data yet. Let's use the *Database Creation Script.sql* file from the book's installation directory to generate the tables and initial data. In *Management Studio Express*, select the **File ➤ Open ➤ File** menu command, and locate the *Database Creation Script.sql* file. (You may be prompted to log in to SQL Server again.) Opening this file places its content in a new panel within *Management Studio Express*.

All that's left to do is to process the script. In the toolbar area, make sure that "Library" is the selected database (see Figure 4-5). Then click the **Execute** toolbar button, or press the F5 key. It's a small script with not a lot going on (at least from SQL Server's point of view), so it should finish in just a few seconds.

Figure 4-5 If you don't select "Library," your tables will go somewhere else.

That's it! Close the script panel. Then, back in the **Object Explorer**, right-click on the **Library** database folder, and select **Refresh** from the menu. If you then expand the **Library** database branch and its **Tables** sub-branch, you will see all of the tables created by the script (see Figure 4-6).

Figure 4-6 Partial list of database tables

With the database done, it's time to start programming.

CHAPTER 5

.NET ASSEMBLIES

The mere mention of the word "assembly" takes me back to my days as a high school freshman. The assembly was actually held in the school gym, with 2000 screaming adolescents filling the bleachers around the basketball court. Because this was a school function, I naturally thought of an experience packed with fresh educational opportunities. School, education—the words just seem to go together. But then came the marching band, and the football players, and the cheerleaders, and the school mascot (a horse). For the next 30 minutes, the principal whipped the students into a controlled frenzy, attempting to prove the institution's place as the number-one school in the city. I still don't know what area we were supposed to be number one in, but it was all very exciting.

.NET assemblies are not that exciting. In fact, they're just files, EXE and DLL files, and without you to activate them, they just sit there taking up disk space. And as they are not doing anything else, let's take a moment to examine what they are and what they contain.

What Is an Assembly?

As I already mentioned in Chapter 1, "Introducing .NET," an assembly is a "unit of deployment," which in most cases is just a file. An assembly is a repository for compiled .NET application code; any code you write will eventually be stored in some EXE file (if it is an application) or DLL file (for code libraries or extensions to an application). Everything that .NET needs to know to load and run your application is stored in the assembly.

Assemblies are either private or public. **Private assemblies** are designed for use in a single application only. If there aren't any DLLs, then an EXE assembly *is* the application. Private assemblies appear in their own directory, the *installation directory* of the application or library. You can run two different private assemblies at the same time, and they won't bother each other. This is true even if each assembly uses the same combination of namespace and class names for its coded elements. If two application assemblies each implement a class named *WindowsApplication1.Class1*, they will not interfere with each other when running; they are private, and private means private.

Public assemblies are designed for shared use among multiple .NET applications. Public assemblies differ from private assemblies in two major ways.

1. Public assemblies have a **strong name**, an encrypted digital signature that is attached to an assembly to guarantee that it came from its named vendor or source. It's built from the assembly's name, version number, culture information, a "public key," and a digital signature generated from the assembly file that contains the manifest (described later). The .NET Framework includes a Strong Name generation tool (*sn.exe*) that assists in this process, and Visual Studio includes options that let you add a digital signature during the compilation process. (It's on the *Signing* tab of the project's properties.)

   The strong name of an assembly should be (and better be) unique; if two assemblies share a common strong name, they are copies of the same assembly. You can add a strong name to any assembly, even private assemblies.

2. Public assemblies are stored in the **global assembly cache (GAC)**. Although you can put a copy of your shared component in your application's install directory, it will only truly be shared once it reaches the GAC directory. The GAC lives in a directory named "assembly" within the computer's Windows directory. (On my system, it's in *c:\windows\assembly*.) Once a .NET assembly has a strong name applied, you can add it to the GAC by either dragging the file into the *assembly* directory, or by using the Global Assembly Cache Tool (*gacutil.exe*). Don't worry about your file being lonely if it's not communing with your other installed files. On my freshly installed copy of .NET, I found over 500 files already in the GAC directory, including all of the DLLs for the Framework Class Libraries.

.NET lets you install multiple versions of an assembly on a system and use them at the same time (a process called **versioning**). This applies both to applications (EXE) and libraries (DLL), and to private assemblies and shared assemblies in the GAC. Don't believe me? Open up the GAC's *assembly* folder, set the Explorer folder to a *Details* view, and then sort by *Assembly Name*. If you scroll down, you'll see the same file show up multiple times. Figure 5-1 shows a part of the cache. There are two copies of *System.Data* listed (from the *System.Data.dll* file), one for version 2.0 of the .NET Framework, and one for an older version. There are also several related *System.Data.resources* files, each one for a different language.

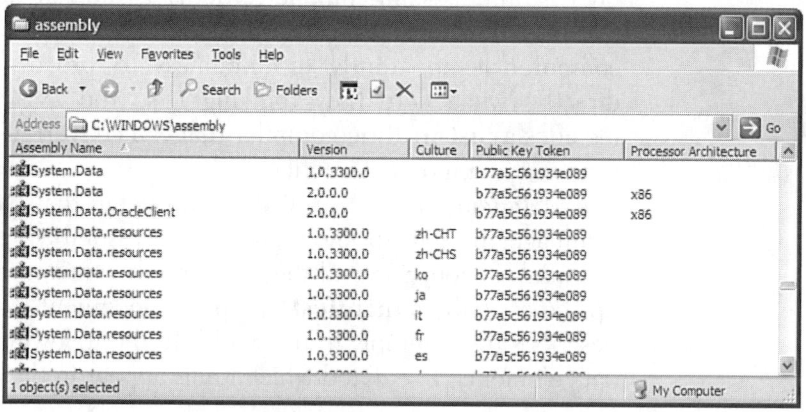

Figure 5-1 The GAC has this duplication under control.

Although there is usually a one-to-one relationship between files and assemblies, there may be cases when an assembly is made up of multiple files. For instance, an application might include an external graphics file in its assembly view. .NET keeps a close watch on these files. If any of the files are modified, deleted, or otherwise maimed, you will hear about it. For the purposes of discussion, the rest of this chapter only considers single-file assemblies.

What's Inside of an Assembly?

An assembly's EXE or DLL file is a standard "Portable Execution" (PE) file, the same file format used for non-.NET executables and code libraries (pretty much any Windows EXE or DLL file). What makes .NET PE files different is all the extra stuff found inside. As a general word, "assembly" indicates a gathering together of various parts into a single unit. In a .NET assembly, these "various parts" are specifically designed for use with .NET. A .NET PE file contains three main parts.

1. *A PE header.* Required of all PE files, this section identifies the locations of the other sections of the file.
2. *The MSIL code section.* The actual code associated with the assembly is stored as semi-compiled Microsoft Intermediate Language (MSIL or IL) code. Unfortunately, the Intel or AMD chip in your computer is apparently too brainless to process MSIL code directly (what were they thinking?), so the .NET Framework includes a **just-in-time** compiler that can convert MSIL to native x86 code at a moment's notice.
3. *The Metadata section.* All of the extra detail that .NET needs to rummage through to know about your assembly appears in this essential section. Some of these items, when taken together, make up the assembly's **manifest**, a type of document that completely describes the assembly to the world. In the following list of metadata elements, I've noted which items appear in the manifest.

   - *The name of the assembly.* (Part of the manifest.) This is defined on the *Application* tab of the project's properties.
   - *The version number of the assembly.* (Part of the manifest.) That's the four-part version number, as in 1.2.3.4. You've probably been wondering all day how you could set this number in your own projects. Your patience will be rewarded in this chapter's *Project* section, where I will demonstrate not just one, but two ways to set the assembly version number.
   - *Strong name content.* (Part of the manifest.) This includes the publisher's public key.
   - *Culture and language settings.* (Part of the manifest.) This is especially useful when you need to create language-specific resource files.
   - *Assembly file listing.* (Part of the manifest.) Single-file assemblies will show only the EXE or DLL file name, but some assemblies may include several files in this section. All files in an assembly must appear within the same directory, or in a directory subordinate to the assembly file that contains the manifest.

- *Exported type information.* (Part of the manifest.) Some assemblies "export" some of their types for use outside of the application. The details of those types appear here.
- *References.* (Part of the manifest, but in multi-file assemblies, each file will contain its own list of references.) The metadata includes a listing of all external assemblies referenced by your application, whether they are private or appear in the GAC. This list indicates which specific version, culture, and platform-target of the external assembly your assembly expects.
- *Internal type information.* (Not part of the manifest.) All types used in your assembly are fully described within the metadata. Also, any additional metadata you added to your types through Visual Basic's attribute feature appear here.

In multi-file assemblies, the manifest-specific elements only appear in the "main" file of the assembly.

The manifest is a subset of the metadata within your assembly. I hate to say that it's the most important part of the metadata—but it is. The manifest is the public expression of your assembly, and the only way that .NET knows whether it is legit. It's sort of like the "Nutrition Facts" label put on American food packaging (see Figure 5-2).

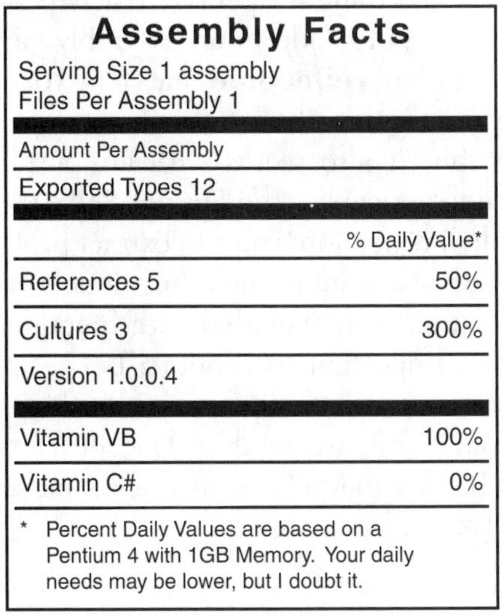

Assembly Facts

	% Daily Value*
Serving Size 1 assembly	
Files Per Assembly 1	
Amount Per Assembly	
Exported Types 12	
References 5	50%
Cultures 3	300%
Version 1.0.0.4	
Vitamin VB	100%
Vitamin C#	0%

* Percent Daily Values are based on a Pentium 4 with 1GB Memory. Your daily needs may be lower, but I doubt it.

Figure 5-2 Is that really good for me?

When you look at the food label, you know what the food package contains—although no one really knows what *riboflavin* is. When you look at the manifest for an assembly, you know at a glance what the assembly contains, and what requirements it has before it can be loaded and run.

Even before .NET burst onto the scene, executables and libraries already contained some "metadata," such as the version number of the file. But this data wasn't used to manage access between software components, nor was it organized in a generic and extensible way. The metadata in .NET embodies all of these attributes.

The presence of both the MSIL and metadata in each assembly make these files very readable and understandable. With the right tools, even I seem to understand them. And if I can, then anyone can, which leads to a big problem. Companies invest a lot of time and money in their software development efforts, and they don't want any rinky-dink two-bit startup reverse engineering their code and getting all of their algorithmic secrets. To prevent this casual reading of any .NET application, Microsoft and other third parties include **obfuscators**, software programs that scramble the contents of an assembly just enough so that it's hard for humans to understand, but not for the .NET Framework. I'll talk more about obfuscation in Chapter 21, "Licensing Your Application."

Reflection

It may be a bad thing for people to access the content of an assembly, but it's great when the code in an assembly can access itself. .NET includes a feature called **reflection** that lets you examine the contents of an assembly. You generally use this feature to access metadata in your own assembly, but it also works with any available assembly. All reflection-related code appears in the *System.Reflection* namespace.

Through reflection, you can extract pretty much anything stored in the metadata of an assembly, including details on all types, their members, and even the parameters included with function members. This is why obfuscation is so important to vendors; between the compiled MSIL and the metadata, you can virtually regenerate the entire source code for an application from just its executable. The source code would be in MSIL, but it wouldn't be that tough for someone to massage much of it back into Visual Basic or C#.

Assemblies and Applications

.NET applications (EXE files) are an instance of an assembly. But a single application can include multiple assemblies; in fact, it almost always does. I wrote a little program that uses reflection to list all assemblies actively being used by the program itself. When I ran the program against itself, it generated the following list.

```
mscorlib
Microsoft.VisualStudio.HostingProcess.Utilities
System.Windows.Forms
System
System.Drawing
Microsoft.VisualStudio.HostingProcess.Utilities.Sync
vshost
System.Deployment
Microsoft.VisualBasic
WindowsApplication1
System.Runtime.Remoting
```

Wow! Twelve assemblies, including *WindowsApplication1*, the main program. Most of the assemblies are Framework-supplied DLLs. For *Microsoft.Visual Basic*, it's the *Microsoft.VisualBasic.dll* assembly; for *System*, it's the *System.dll* assembly. All of the assemblies (except the main program assembly) are shared libraries from the GAC. The application can also support private assemblies loaded from local DLL files.

The .NET Framework automatically loaded these assemblies for me when *WindowsApplication1* started up; it figured out which ones needed to be loaded by looking in the manifest for *WindowsApplication1*. When the Framework loaded each assembly, it checked to see if those assemblies in turn needed additional assemblies loaded, and so on. Pretty soon, your once simple application becomes a dumping ground for assemblies all over the GAC. But that's OK, because the purpose of .NET is to manage it all.

5. .NET ASSEMBLIES

The 'My' Namespace and Assemblies

The .NET Framework, with its thousands of classes, contains a lot of packaged logic that I can use in my own programs. But I don't have all of the many assemblies and their classes memorized (yet), and it takes time to wander around the FCL documentation. With so many classes available, I sometimes shudder when I think of the effort it will take me to find just the right class or feature I need to accomplish some development task.

Fortunately, I'm not the only one who thinks this way; Microsoft agrees with me. Historically, Visual Basic programmers were sheltered from the complexities of Windows application development. Not that they needed to be; we all know that Visual Basic developers are generally a cut above the rest. But there was "the Visual Basic motto" to contend with: **Make Windows Development Fast and Easy**. And calling some esoteric method deep within the bowels of the *System* namespace just to get a minor piece of data is neither easy nor fast.

To bring back some semblance of the pleasant experience previously available in Visual Basic development, Microsoft introduced the *My* pretend namespace in its 2005 release of the language. The *My* pretend namespace collects a lot of useful features from all around the Framework Class Library, and organizes them in a much smaller hierarchy for simple and direct access. I briefly mentioned *My* in Chapter 1, but it's a good time to take a closer look at what it does.

The *My* pretend namespace looks a lot like other namespaces, such as *System*, *System.Reflection*, or *System.Windows.Forms*. But it's not really a namespace—it's pretend! For one thing, you can't use the *Imports* keyword to create a shortcut to branches within its hierarchy. Also, some sections of the hierarchy are dynamic; they change as your source code changes. Table 5-1 lists the major nodes of the hierarchy.

Table 5-1 Major Nodes in the My Namespace Hierarchy

Branch	Available Features
My.Application	Information about the current application, including culture settings and the deployment method.
My.Application.Info	Further details about the application and its assembly, including the name and version.

Branch	Available Features
My.Application.Log	Allows you to generate trace and logging output to registered logging destinations. Only used with client applications.
My.Computer	Provides access to general resources located on the local computer.
My.Computer.Audio	Plays named and system sounds through the computer's speakers.
My.Computer.Clipboard	Retrieves data from the system clipboard, and lets you add your own data to the clipboard in a variety of predefined and custom formats.
My.Computer.Clock	Gets the current system date and time dished up in a variety of ways.
My.Computer.FileSystem	Tools to examine and manipulate files and directories on local or networked file systems.
My.Computer.FileSystem. ➡ SpecialDirectories	References to special Windows folders such as "My Documents," "Desktop," and "Temp."
My.Computer.Info	Provides information about the installed operating system and other local system resources.
My.Computer.Keyboard	Exposes the current state of the keyboard and its keys.
My.Computer.Mouse	Makes available a few properties of the local computer's mouse.
My.Computer.Network	Reports on network availability, and provides features to interact with that network.
My.Computer.Ports	Lets you interact with the system's serial ports.
My.Computer.Registry	Reads and writes keys and values in the registry.
My.Forms	Presents a dynamic collection of all forms defined in the application. This node is only available in Windows Forms applications.

(continues)

Table 5-1 Major Nodes in the My Namespace Hierarchy *(continued)*

Branch	Available Features
My.Log	Allows you to generate trace and logging output to registered logging destinations. Only used with ASP.NET applications.
My.Request	This object is similar to the older Active Server Pages Request object. It is only available in ASP.NET applications.
My.Resources	Provides dynamic access to application-specific or locale-specific resources included with the application.
My.Response	This object is similar to the older Active Server Pages Response object. It is only available in ASP.NET applications.
My.Settings	Provides dynamic access to the new settings system included with Visual Basic 2005.
My.User	Identifies the current Windows user, including authentication information.
My.WebServices	Presents a collection of available Web Services for use in the application. This node is not available in ASP.NET applications.

The *My* namespace includes a lot of features you will use regularly, including access to the version number of the application. Instead of typing *System.Reflection.whatever* to get to the version number's "major" component, you can now just type:

```
My.Application.Info.Version.Major
```

Need a list of assemblies, but you're too lazy to type the word "Reflection?" Try:

```
My.Application.Info.LoadedAssemblies
```

Need to know the time right now in England?

```
My.Computer.Clock.GmtTime
```

Can you communicate over the local area network?

```
My.Computer.Network.IsAvailable
```

Who is running this computer anyway?

```
My.User.Name
```

There isn't much in the *My* namespace that you can't already do with standard FCL libraries. There are even a few parts of *My* that are repeats of features already included in the Visual Basic language, although with some enhancements. For instance, Visual Basic includes a *Kill* command that lets you delete files. The new *My.Computer.FileSystem.DeleteFile* method also removes files, but it includes new options, including one that lets you send the file to the Recycle Bin instead of just losing it forever.

Directives and Assemblies

Directives are Visual Basic statements—but then again, they're not. The two key directives—*#Const* and *#If*—provide instructions to the compiler on how to handle a block of Visual Basic source code. (There is a third directive, *#Region*, that helps to visually present source code within Visual Studio, but it has no impact on the compiler or the final compiled application.) By using directives, you can tell the compiler to include or exclude specific chunks of source code from the final project. So, they aren't really Visual Basic source code statements, but they are only available in Visual Basic.

Why would you want to include or exclude code in an application? Well, I can think of several good reasons, some of which involve the CIA and former Federal Reserve chairman Alan Greenspan. But the most common use is when you want to produce two different versions of your application, based on some condition. For example, you may sell an "express" version and a "professional" version of a product. Much of the code is identical for the two versions, but the professional version would include features not available in the express version. Also, the express version may include a simplified presentation for a feature that has a more complex usage in the professional edition.

Some software products fulfill this need by using standard Visual Basic conditions.

```
If (professionalVersion = True) Then
    ShowWhizBangFeatures()
Else
    ShowLaughableFeatures()
End If
```

This, of course, works just fine. But the express application still contains all of the enhanced features. But it can't access any of that code, so why even include it on the installation CD? If you use directives, you can mark down that problem as solved. Directives used conditional expressions, much like the *professionalVersion = True* condition in the previous block of code. But they are defined with the *#Const* statement, and are called **compiler constants**.

```
#Const fullVersion = True
```

This statement defines a Boolean compiler constant. It can only be used with directives; if you try to use *fullVersion* in a standard Visual Basic statement, the compiler will complain. But it will work just fine in the *#If* directive.

```
#If (fullVersion = True) Then
    ShowWhizBangFeatures()
#Else
    ShowLaughableFeatures()
#End If
```

This code looks a lot like the previous code block, but with the added "#" signs. It looks the same but it's not. With the plain *If* statement, the code that gets compiled into the final application is the following:

```
If (professionalVersion = True) Then
    ShowWhizBangFeatures()
Else
    ShowLaughableFeatures()
End If
```

Yeah, the whole block of code. But with the directives, what gets included in the compiled application depends on the value of *fullVersion*. If *fullVersion* is *True*, then this gets compiled into the compiled application:

```
ShowWhizBangFeatures()
```

The other four lines are gone; they've vanished . . . into thin air, as if they never existed. But in this case, it's a good thing. The goal was to have a version of the assembly completely devoid of the undesired code, and that's what happened.

To set the *fullVersion* compiler constant to generate the full version, you include this line at the top of each source code file that includes conditional *#If* code blocks:

```
#Const fullVersion = True
```

When you're ready to generate the "express" version, just change each of these lines to their *False* counterpart:

```
#Const fullVersion = False
```

Somehow, changing this line in every source code file that needs it seems like a lot of work, and it is. And what happens if I forget to set one of them to the right version? No good, I can tell you.

To keep Visual Basic developers from running down the halls screaming more than they normally would, Visual Studio provides a few different ways to set compiler constants once, and have them apply to every part of the application. The most common way to do this is through the project properties' *Compile* panel (see Figure 5-3). Click on the *Advanced Compile Options* button, and then add your global compiler constants to the *Custom constants* field.

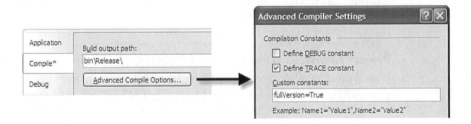

Figure 5-3 This is a whole lot easier than all that typing.

Now, by adding either *fullVersion=True* or *fullVersion=False* to this field, you can build different versions of the application. The Visual Basic compiler also provides features that let you set up different compile scripts for your project. I won't talk about it in this book, but you can read up on the MSBuild tool in the Visual Studio documentation if you need this level of control.

Besides Booleans, compiler constants can be numbers and strings. The Visual Studio environment also defines some compiler constants for you. The *DEBUG* and *TRACE* constants are *True* or *False* based on the *Define DEBUG constant* and *Define TRACE constant* checkboxes that appear in Figure 5-3. The *VBC_VER* constant identifies the version of the Visual Basic compiler being used; it is set to 8.0 in Visual Basic 2005.

Summary

Assemblies aren't just souped-up EXE or DLL files; they contain gobs of metadata, including the manifest, that make .NET applications **self-describing**. The compiler uses this information to correctly configure and process the managed MSIL code in each assembly. In later chapters, I'll show you how you can add your own content to the metadata area of the file assembly.

Although not actually parts of an assembly, this chapter also discussed the *My* namespace and directives, two Visual Basic features that impact what gets included in your assembly.

Project

This chapter's project officially kicks off the coding of the Library Project (muted applause). We'll start off with something simple: building the "About" form that provides basic information about the application, including its version number.

Project Access Load the "Chapter 5 (Before) Code" project, either through the New Project templates, or by accessing the project directly from the installation directory. To see the code in its final form, load "Chapter 5 (After) Code" instead.

Our goal is a pleasant form that conveys basic information about the program, a form that looks something like Figure 5-4.

About the Library Project

The Library Project
Version 1.0 Revision 0
Unlicensed

Developed by

Tim Patrick
Start-to-Finish Visual Basic 2005
In-book Project
http://www.timaki.com
tim@timaki.com

Copyright (c) 2006 by Tim Patrick

Close

Figure 5-4 Everything you wanted to know about the program

Like any Visual Basic application for Windows, the creation of this form involves two steps: (1) adding controls to the form; and (2) writing the related code.

Adding Controls

If there is one area where Visual Basic excels, it is form creation. Codeless programs can be created by the simple dragging and dropping of pre-built controls onto the surface of a pre-built form. It's all done from within the comfort and convenience of the Visual Studio Integrated Development Environment (IDE), as shown in Figure 5-5.

5. .NET ASSEMBLIES

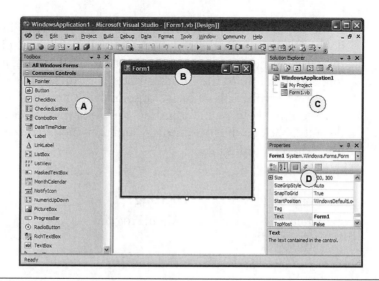

Figure 5-5 The Visual Studio environment

The displayed environment includes four key areas, which I've labeled with letters in Figure 5-5.

A. **The toolbox.** This listing of controls includes not only display controls, but controls that expose no specific user interface, such as the *Timer*. (If you don't see the toolbox, select the **View ➤ Toolbox** menu command.) To add a control to a form, double-click the control in the toolbox, drag it from the toolbox to the form, or draw the control on the form after first selecting it from the list.

B. **The form surface.** Place any control that exposes a user interface here. The form is WYSIWYG, so you can see the final result as you design the form.

C. **The Solution Explorer.** All files related to your project appear here. For the current project, you will only see the *My Project* entry and an entry for the form, *Form1.vb*. There are actually more files. If you click the second button from the left at the top of the Solution Explorer, it will show you additional files, most of which are managed by Visual Studio on your behalf.

D. **The Properties panel.** When you select a control on your form surface, or the form surface itself, or an item in the Solution Explorer, the properties of the selected item appear in this area. You can alter the settings of many properties by typing in the new setting. Some properties include special tools to assist you in setting the property value.

If you haven't done so already, open the form *Form1.vb* in design view by double-clicking it in the Solution Explorer. We'll add eight text labels, three shape and line elements, two web-style hyperlinks, a command button, and a picture to the form's surface. I've already added the picture to the form for you, with an image of some books, naming it *SideImage*.

Set up the form by adjusting the following properties from their defaults. Click on the form surface, and then modify these property values using the Properties panel.

Property	Setting
(Name)	AboutProgram
ControlBox	False
FormBorderStyle	FixedDialog

Property	Setting
Size	440, 311
StartPosition	CenterScreen
Text	About the Library Project

Next, add the eight basic text labels to the form's surface using the *Label* control. You'll find this control in the toolbox. As you add each *Label* control, use the following list of settings to set the properties for each label. The included text matches my situation, but feel free to modify the content as needed.

Label Name	Property Settings	
ProgramName	(Name):	ProgramName
	AutoSize:	True
	Font/Bold:	True
	Location:	136, 16
	Text:	The Library Project
ProgramVersion	(Name):	ProgramVersion
	AutoSize:	True
	Location:	136, 32
	Text:	Version X.Y Revision Z
LicenseInfo	(Name):	LicenseInfo
	AutoSize:	False
	Location:	136, 48
	Size:	280, 32
	Text:	Unlicensed
DevelopedBy	(Name):	DevelopedBy
	AutoSize:	True
	Location:	136, 88
	Text:	Developed By
DeveloperName	(Name):	DeveloperName
	AutoSize:	True
	Location:	160, 112
	Text:	Tim Patrick

Label Name	Property Settings	
DeveloperBook	(Name):	DeveloperBook
	AutoSize:	True
	Location:	160, 128
	Text:	Start-to-Finish Visual Basic 2005
DeveloperProject	(Name):	DeveloperProject
	AutoSize:	True
	Location:	160, 144
	Text:	In-book Project
CompanyCopyright	(Name):	CompanyCopyright
	AutoSize:	True
	Location:	136, 208
	Text:	Copyright (c) 2006 by Tim Patrick.

Let's add some lines and colored sections to the form. Visual Basic 6.0 included distinct shape controls for lines, rectangles, and ellipses that you could apply directly to the form surface. .NET no longer includes these items; you have to add them by hand using source code-specified drawing commands. But you can simulate lines and rectangles using the standard *Label* control, sans the text.

Label Name	Property Settings	
VersionDivider	(Name):	VersionDivider
	AutoSize:	False
	BackColor:	Black
	Location:	136, 80
	Size:	280,1
	Text:	*[Don't add any text]*

Label Name	Property Settings	
BackgroundSide	(Name):	BackgroundSide
	AutoSize:	False
	BackColor:	White
	Location:	0, 0
	Size:	120, 296
	Text:	*[Don't add any text]*
BackgroundDivider	(Name):	BackgroundDivider
	AutoSize:	False
	BackColor:	Black
	Location:	120, 0
	Size:	1, 296
	Text:	*[Don't add any text]*

If the *BackgroundSide* label obscures the graphic, right-click on the label, and select **Send To Back** from the shortcut menu that appears.

The *LinkLabel* control is similar to the more basic *Label* control, but you can include "links" in the text, clickable sections that are similar to the links on a web page. We'll use these to display the web site and email address. Add two *LinkLabel* controls to the form and use the following settings to configure each control's properties.

Label Name	Property Settings	
CompanyWeb	(Name):	CompanyWeb
	AutoSize:	True
	LinkBehavior:	HoverUnderline
	Location:	160, 160
	Text:	http://www.timaki.com
CompanyEmail	(Name):	CompanyEmail
	AutoSize:	True
	LinkBehavior:	HoverUnderline
	Location:	160, 176
	Text:	tim@timaki.com

The final control to add is a button that lets the user close the form. Add a *Button* control to the form with the following properties.

Label Name	Property Settings	
ActClose	(Name):	ActClose
	DialogResult:	Cancel
	Location:	344, 240
	Size:	80, 24
	Text:	Close

Forms can be configured so that a press of the Escape key triggers a *Button* control on the form. To do this, click on the form surface, and then set its *CancelButton* property to "ActClose." We had to delay this step until the button was actually added to the form; the *CancelButton* property would not have allowed a setting for a non-existent button.

Well, the form should look pretty good by now. The last thing I like to do is to set up the **tab order**, the order in which the user accesses each field on the form when pressing the Tab key on the keyboard. To edit the tab order, select the form surface, and then select the **View ➤ Tab Order** menu command. Each control on the form that can be given a tab order value will suddenly have a tab order number next to it. Click on each number or control in order until you get the arrangement you want. (See Figure 5-6 to view how I ordered the controls.) Finally, select the **View ➤ Tab Order** menu command again, or press the Escape key, to leave the tab ordering process.

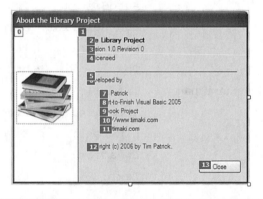

Figure 5-6 Nice and orderly

You can also set the tab order for each control by modifying its *TabIndex* property using a zero-based numbering system. However, it's usually faster to set these values by clicking on each control in order.

Adding the Code to the Form

Now it's time to add some real Visual Basic code. Not that we haven't added any until now. Everything we did on the form, although we didn't see it happen, was converted into Visual Basic source code. Let's take a quick look. In the *Solution Explorer*, click on the **Show All Files** button, the second button from the left. When all the files appear, click on the "plus sign" next to *Form1.vb*, and finally double-click on the *Form1.Designer.vb* file (see Figure 5-7).

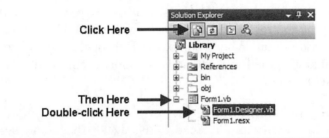

Figure 5-7 Accessing the hidden, secret, forbidden code. Yeah, it's out there.

Because it's over 200 lines of source code bliss, I won't be printing it here. But look it over; it's all pretty interesting. As you dragged-and-dropped controls on the form, and modified its properties, Visual Studio edited this file on your behalf. It's part of your form's class (all forms are classes that derive from *System.Windows.Forms.Form*). You can tell by the "Partial" keyword at the top.

```
Partial Public Class AboutProgram
    Inherits System.Windows.Forms.Form
```

Most of the action happens in the *InitializeComponent* procedure. When you are finished looking it all over, close up the designer code, and return to the form surface. To make our form a real and interesting form, we need it to do three things.

1. Show the actual version number of the application. This should be determined and displayed right when the form first appears.
2. Jump to the appropriate web site or email recipient when clicking on the link labels. This event gets processed in response to a user action.
3. Close the form when the user clicks the *Close* button. This is also a user-driven event.

Let's start with the easy one, closing the form. I'm sure you remember about **events** from Chapter 1. Events are blocks of code that are processed in response to something happening, most often a user action like a mouse click. All of the actions we want to perform on this form will be in response to a triggered event (lucky us). The easiest way to get to the "default" event for a control is to double-click the control. Try it now; double-click the *Close* button. When you do, the IDE opens the source code view associated with the form, and adds an empty event handler (the *ActClose_Click* subroutine).

```
Public Class AboutProgram
    Private Sub ActClose_Click(ByVal sender As System.Object, _
        ByVal e As System.EventArgs) Handles ActClose.Click


    End Sub
End Class
```

Every forms-based event (and in fact, most other types of events) in .NET have pretty much the same arguments: (1) a *sender* argument that indicates which object triggered this event; and (2) the *e* argument, which allows *sender* to supply any additional information that may be useful in the event. In this case, the *sender* argument will be a reference to the *ActClose* button, because that's the object that will generate the *Click* event. A button's *Click* event doesn't have any more useful information available, so *e* is the default object type, *System.EventArgs*, which is pretty much just a placeholder, and the object from which all of the more interesting *e* argument types derive.

The name of this event handler is *ActClose_Click*, but if you want to change it to *FredAndWilma*, that's fine; it won't mess up anything. But you must keep the *Handles ActClose.Click* clause intact. This is the part that links the event handler to the actual event.

The code to close the form is extremely simple. Enter it now, either by using the first code snippet for this chapter, or by typing it directly.

Insert Snippet Insert Chapter 5, Snippet Item 1.

```
' ----- Close the form.
Me.Close()
```

This statement says, "I'm the *AboutProgram* form/object, and I command myself to close." If you run the program right now (press the F5 key), you close the form by clicking on the *Close* button. Because the *AboutProgram* form was the only form in the application, closing it automatically ended the entire application, no questions asked.

Okay, back up to the second item, the web-style links. You could go back to the form surface and double-click on each link label to create an event handler for each label's default event (in this case, the *LinkClicked* event). But you can also add the event handler subroutines right in the editor, either by typing the code yourself (which is no fun), or by using the two drop-down lists just above the editor window (see Figure 5-8).

Figure 5-8 The Class Name and Method Name fields

The *Class Name* list appears on the left side. Selecting an entry from this list updates the right-hand list, the *Method Name* list. To add an event handler template for the *CompanyWeb's LinkClicked* event, first select "CompanyWeb" from the *Class Name* list, and then select "LinkClicked" from the *Method Name* list. The following code block appears in the code window.

```
Private Sub CompanyWeb_LinkClicked(ByVal sender As Object, _
      ByVal e As System.Windows.Forms. _
      LinkLabelLinkClickedEventArgs) _
      Handles CompanyWeb.LinkClicked

End Sub
```

This template's argument list is a little more interesting, because its *e* argument is an object of type *System.Windows.Forms.LinkLabelLinkClickedEventArgs*. The *LinkLabel* control allows you to have multiple web-style links in a single control, interspersed among regular text. The *e* argument has a *Link* property that tells you which of the links in the control was clicked by the user. Because our labels have only a single link, we won't bother to check it. We'll just show the web page immediately anytime the link is clicked.

Insert Snippet Insert Chapter 5, Snippet Item 2.

```
' ----- Show the company web page.
Process.Start("http://www.timaki.com")
```

The *Process* object is part of the *System.Diagnostics* namespace, and *Start* is one of its shared members that lets you start up external applications and resources. You pass it any valid URL, and it will run. Let's try it again with the *CompanyEmail's LinkClicked* event. Add in the template any way you choose, and then type or insert the code that starts a new message to an email address.

Insert Snippet Insert Chapter 5, Snippet Item 3.

```
' ----- Send email to the company.
Process.Start("mailto:tim@timaki.com")
```

The last event to design is one of the first events called in the lifetime of the form: the *Load* event. It's called just before the form appears on the screen. Double-clicking on the surface of the form creates an event handler template for the *Load* event. If you prefer to use the *Class Name* and

Method Name drop-down lists instead, select "(AboutProgram Events)" from the *Class Name* list before using the *Method Name* list.

```
Private Sub AboutProgram_Load(ByVal sender As Object, _
     ByVal e As System.EventArgs) Handles Me.Load

End Sub
```

Let's add code to this event handler that displays the correct version number, using the version information found in *My.Application.Info.Version*, an instance of the *System.Version* class.

Insert Snippet Insert Chapter 5, Snippet Item 4.

```
' ----- Update the version number.
With My.Application.Info.Version
    ProgramVersion.Text = "Version " & .Major & "." & _
        .Minor & " Revision " & .Revision
End With
```

This code uses a *With* statement to reduce the amount of typing needed in the main assignment statement. Inside of the *With . . . End With* statement, you aren't required to retype the object name that appears just after the *With* keyword—in this case, *My.Application.Info.Version.* You can just refer to that object's members by typing a dot (".") followed by the name of the member. You could forgo the *With* statement and type the full object name each time you wanted to use one of the version values, but this way keeps the code cleaner and less overwhelming.

Setting the Version Number

If you run the program, it will display the currently defined version number, "1.0 Revision 0," as shown in Figure 5-9.

Figure 5-9 The version number from the AboutProgram form

My question—and I hope I can answer it before the paragraph is finished—is, "Where is that version number defined, and how can it be changed?" It turns out that I do know the answer: The version values are stored as metadata within the assembly. Visual Studio includes a form that let's you modify the basic informational metadata stored in the assembly. To access the form, display the project's properties (double-click on "My Project" in the *Solution Explorer*), select the *Application* tab, and then click on the *Assembly Information* button (see Figure 5-10).

Figure 5-10 The Assembly Information form, filled out with some relevant values

Our *AboutProgram* form displays the assembly's version number, which is set using the four text fields next to the *Assembly Version* label. Those four fields represent the Major, Minor, Build, and Revision numbers of the assembly. Go ahead, set them to some other values, click *OK*, and run the program again.

Although this form is convenient, it's just another example of Visual Studio writing some of your project's code on your behalf. Every field on this form gets saved in a source code file included with your project. To view it, make sure you have the **Show All Files** button still selected in the *Solution Explorer*. Expand the *My Project* item using its "plus sign," and then double-click on the *AssemblyInfo.vb* item. This file defines several assembly-specific attributes (which we'll explore in Chapter 17, "GDI+"), including the following informational entries.

```
<Assembly: AssemblyTitle("The Library Project")>
<Assembly: AssemblyDescription( _
   "ACME Library Database System")>
<Assembly: AssemblyCompany("ACME")>
<Assembly: AssemblyProduct("Library")>
<Assembly: AssemblyCopyright( _
   "Copyright © 2006 by Tim Patrick")>
<Assembly: AssemblyTrademark("")>
<Assembly: AssemblyVersion("1.0.0.0")>
```

As you can see, this file has been updated with the values I typed into the *Assembly Information* form. Thank you, Visual Studio! You see the "AssemblyVersion" attribute defined here. If you modify these values, the changes will be reflected in the *Assembly Information* form, and also in your running application and final compiled assembly.

The last thing we will do for now to the *AboutProgram* form is to give it a meaningful file name. Currently, it is named "Form1.vb," but "AboutProgram.vb" would be much more descriptive. To change the name, select *Form1.vb* in the *Solution Explorer*, and modify the *File Name* property to "AboutProgram.vb" in the *Properties* panel. If you still have all the files showing, you will see Visual Studio also update the names of the file's two subordinate files, the designer file (*AboutProgram.Designer.vb*) and the resource file (*AboutProgram.resx*).

Now would be a great time to save your work (**File ➤ Save All**).

Adding the Main Form

As useful and full featured as the *AboutProgram* form is, such forms are seldom the core focus of an application. In the Library Project, this form will only be displayed when triggered from the "Main" form, so let's add a simple Main form now. In Visual Studio, select the **Project ➤ Add Windows Form** menu command. When the *Add New Item* form appears, select "Windows Form" from the list of available forms, and give it a name of "MainForm.vb" before clicking the **Add** button.

When the new form appears, adjust the following properties as indicated.

5. .NET ASSEMBLIES

Property	Setting
(Name)	MainForm
FormBorderStyle	FixedSingle
MaximizeBox	False
Size	576, 459
Text	The Library Project

From the toolbox, add a *Button* control to the form with the following properties.

Property	Setting
(Name)	ActHelpAbout
Size	80, 24
Text	&About . . .

If you're familiar with Visual Basic development from its pre-.NET days, you will recognize the "&" characters in the button's text. This special character sets the "shortcut" for the button. When you press the Alt key and the letter that follows "&" (in this case, "A"), the program acts as if you clicked on the button with the mouse.

Double-click on the button and add the following code to the click event procedure.

Insert Snippet Insert Chapter 5, Snippet Item 5.

```
' ----- Show the About form.
AboutProgram.ShowDialog()
```

Here we specify a direct reference to the *AboutProgram* form. Before the 2005 version of Visual Basic, showing a new form required that you create an instance of the form class before showing it.

```
(New AboutProgram).ShowDialog()
```

That syntax still works, and is the way to do if you need to display multiple copies of the same form on-screen at the same time. However the "AboutProgram.ShowDialog()" syntax is much cleaner for single-use forms, and more closely reflects how form presentation was done in Visual Basic since its initial release. Actually, this statement is using the *My* namespace. The full statement looks like this.

```
My.Forms.AboutProgram.ShowDialog()
```

The *My.Forms* collection allows you to reference any form within it without having to say "My.Forms" first. The members of the *My.Forms* collection represent **default instances** of each form in the project.

That's all the code we need for now, but if you run the program, it will still only show the *AboutProgram* form. That's because the *AboutProgram* form is set as the "startup" form. To alter this, open the project properties window, select the *Application* tab, and set the **Startup Form** field to "MainForm."

Because the *AboutProgram* form is now being shown as a "dialog" form (through the call to the *ShowDialog* method), its behavior is somewhat different. Each form includes a *DialogResult* property whose value is returned by the *ShowDialog* method when the form closes. Each button on your form can be configured to automatically set this property and close the form. The *Close* button on the *AboutProgram* form does just that; its own *DialogResult* property is set to *Cancel*, which is assigned to the form when the user clicks the *Close* button.

The upshot of that drawn-out paragraph is that you can now delete the event handler for the *Close* button's *Click* event, and the button will still close the form. Delete the *ActClose_Click* procedure from the *AboutProgram*'s source code, run the program, and see what happens. The *Close* button still closes the form, even without the event handler.

You could also have left the procedure there, cleared the *Close* button's *DialogResult*, and added the following statement to that button's event handler.

```
Me.DialogResult = Windows.Forms.DialogResult.Cancel
```

That brings to three the total different ways we can use to close the *AboutProgram* form. It's the flexibility of .NET at work; there are many different ways to accomplish the same task. So be creative!

5. .NET ASSEMBLIES

Extra Credit: Adding an Icon

If you've still got a little energy left, we can make one more change before this chapter runs out of paper: adding a custom icon to the main form. Just follow these step-by-step instructions:

1. Display the main form by double-clicking on the *MainForm.vb* item in the *Solution Explorer.*
2. Select the form's surface.
3. Select the form's *Icon* property in the Properties panel.
4. Click the "..." button in this property, and search for the *Book.ico* file in the "Chapter 5 Before" subdirectory of the book's installation directory. You can also use any other ".ico" file.

Save Your Work

Make sure you always save changes. By default, Visual Studio is configured to save your changes every time you run your program, but I like to save often just in case.

This chapter included a lot of manual instruction because there were just so many cool Visual Studio features to play with; I just couldn't help myself. We'll probably keep up this pace somewhat for a few chapters, but eventually there will be so much code that a lot of it will come from the code snippets.

CHAPTER 6

DATA AND DATA TYPES

Data is a funny word—although not as funny as datum. Our minds are filled with data: the useful and useless trivia that clogs thought; the millions of memories that keep superficial conversations going strong. But the word "data" rarely comes up in conversation. Unless you are a computer junkie, or you hang around the office all hours of the day or night waiting for reports of crunched numbers, you never have a need to use the term. I have never been asked to lend someone a cup of data. My friends never try to judge my health by asking, "How's your data going?" And you almost never hear it used as a character name in popular science fiction television shows.

Despite its lack of usage in everyday communication, data is extremely important. In the programming world, it is everything. In this chapter, we will discuss how Visual Basic uses and manipulates data within your applications, and how you can master the tools that make this manipulation possible.

The Nature of Computer Data

In Chapter 2, "Introducing Visual Basic," I mentioned how all data in a computer eventually breaks down to individual bits, electrical impulses that represent either one or zero, on or off, true or false. Because our decimal number system requires more than just those two values, computers work in the world of binary—a number system limited to only the numbers 0 and 1. Fortunately, it's pretty easy to represent basic decimal integer numbers using binary notation. You probably remember Mrs. Green back in second grade telling you about the different place values of multi-digit numbers, shown in Figure 6-1.

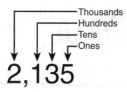

Figure 6-1 The fruits of Mrs. Green's labors

The same type of diagram can be used for binary numbers; only the position names and values are changed. For convenience, we call these positions by their decimal names, or use the related powers of two. All of this is shown in Figure 6-2.

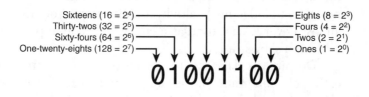

Figure 6-2 The positions of an 8-bit (8-digit) binary number

To figure out what this number is in decimal, just add up the columns. Let's see, there's one each of fours, eights, and sixty-fours, and none of the rest. 4+8+64, that's 76. Because any binary digit can never be more than 1, the counting is pretty simple. I showed an 8-bit (8-digit) binary example here—which can handle the numbers 0 through 255—but you can represent larger decimal numbers by adding more binary digits.

That's just fine for integer values, but how do you represent decimal and fractional numbers? What about negative numbers; where do they fit in this binary system? And it's not just numbers. My computer can process text data, arrays of numbers, graphic images, and customer records. How are those stored in binary form?

To handle the myriad data forms, every computer includes a small community of Lilliputians who are good at math, language, and art. No wait, I think that's from a story I'm reading my son at bedtime. Oh yes, now I remember. Computers implement **data types** to handle all the various forms of data to be managed. Each data type acts as an interpreter between a collection of bits and a piece of information that a computer user can better utilize and understand.

All data types ultimately store their content as individual bits of data, but they differ in how those bits get interpreted. Imagine a data type named *Vitamin* that indicated which vitamins were included in a food product. Figure 6-3 shows how the eight bits used earlier could be assigned and interpreted as vitamins.

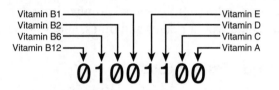

Figure 6-3 Loaded with vitamins B6, D, and E

With such a data type, you could assign vitamin values to food items tracked in your application. (This is just a sampling of vitamins; you would require more bits to handle all of the vitamins. This example should not be construed as an offer of medical services. Consult your doctor.)

For an example that is more in tune with Visual Basic, take that number 76 we were discussing earlier. It's easy enough to convert it to binary representation, 01001100. The .NET Framework includes a few data types that do this conversion automatically, varying only by the number of binary digits (bits) they can handle. In the computer world, 76 also represents a letter of the alphabet—the capital letter "L." That's because there's a data type that establishes a dictionary between binary values and alphabetic (and other) characters. Windows programs have long used **ASCII** (American Standard Code for Information Interchange) as its number-to-character dictionary. This eight-bit system documents how to convert the numbers 0 through 255 into all the various characters used in English, including punctuation and other miscellaneous characters. Another dictionary, **Unicode**, uses 16 bits of data to handle around 65,000 different characters. .NET uses Unicode for its character and "string" data types.

Another rule-bearing data type is Boolean, which uses a single bit to represent either True (a bit value of 1) or False (0). Negative integers, floating point and fixed point decimal values, and dates and times round out the kinds of basic data most often managed by computers and their applications. More complex **data structures** can be built up from these basic types.

Data in .NET

All data types in .NET are implemented as classes within the *System* name-space. One such data type is *System.Byte*, which implements an 8-bit integer value, just like we discussed earlier. It holds integer values from 0 to 255. These values are always stored using eight bits of binary data, but they magically appear in decimal form whenever you ask them to be presented.

The .NET Framework includes 15 core interpretive data types: eight for integers, three for decimal numbers, two for character data, one combined data type for dates and times, and a Boolean data type.

Integer Data Types

Based on the number of available data types (eight out of the 15 core types), you would think that most programmers worked with integers all day long—and you'd be right. Whether it's actual user data or loop counters or status codes or the storage method for enumerated data types, integers show up everywhere in .NET code.

The range of values for an integer data type depends directly on the number of binary digits managed by that data type; the more digits, the bigger the range. Also, half of the integer data types store both positive and negative values (called "signed" integers), while the other half supports only positive numbers ("unsigned"). Table 6-1 lists the eight integer data types included with .NET, and their associated ranges.

Table 6-1 Integer Data Types in .NET

.NET Data Type	Bits	Style	Range of Values
System.Byte	8	Unsigned	0 to 255
System.SByte	8	Signed	-128 to 127
System.Int16	16	Signed	-32,768 to 32,767
System.UInt16	16	Unsigned	0 to 65,535
System.Int32	32	Signed	-2,147,483,648 to 2,147,483,647
System.UInt32	32	Unsigned	0 to 4,294,967,295
System.Int64	64	Signed	-9,223,372,036,854,775,808 to 9,223,372,036,854,775,807
System.UInt64	64	Unsigned	0 to 18,446,744,073,709,551,615

Looking at these types another way, Table 6-2 shows the relationship between the types and their number of bits and range style.

Table 6-2 Bits and Signed Status for Integer .NET Data Types

	8 Bits	16 Bits	32 Bits	64 Bits
Signed	SByte	Int16	Int32	Int64
Unsigned	Byte	UInt16	UInt32	UInt64

Decimal Data Types

Once upon a time, life was happy. Strangers said "hello" when they met you on the street. Succulent fruit burst forth from trees. In short, God was in his heaven, and everything was right with the world—and then came fractions. At first, it didn't seem that bad, because so many fractions could be converted easily into a plain numeric form by inserting a "decimal point" in the number. $\frac{1}{2}$ became 0.5. $\frac{1}{4}$ became the longer yet smaller 0.25. $\frac{1}{3}$ became 0.3333 3333333333333333333333333333333333333333333333333333333333333333 3333333333333333333333333333333333333333333333333333333333333333… Hey, what's going on here? I can't write all of those 3s. The book would be 2,000 pages, or more. Eventually people discovered that in many cases, it just wasn't worth the bother of writing out all of the 3s, so they just stopped at some point, as in 0.33333333. It wasn't perfectly accurate, but it was good enough.

This is what life is like for computer-based decimal values. You can have perfect accuracy—up to a point. After that, you have to settle for good enough. The .NET Framework includes three decimal data types. Two of them accept limited accuracy in exchange for a large range of values. The third has perfect accuracy, but its range is more limited. Table 6-3 documents these three types.

Table 6-3 An Accurate List of the Inaccurate Decimal Data Types

.NET Data Type	Accuracy	Range	Description
System.Decimal	Perfect	Limited	The *Decimal* data type provides around 28 combined digits on both sides of the decimal point. And although it may truncate after the last available digit position, it is accurate within those digits. Because of this, it is perfect for working with money.
			The more digits you have on the left of the decimal, the fewer you have available for the right of the decimal, and vice-versa. For numbers with no decimal portion, the range is from −79,228,162,514,264,337,593,543,950,335 to 79,228,162,514,264,337,593,543,950,335. (That's 29 digits, but who's counting.) For numbers with only zero (0) to the left of the decimal, the range is −0.0000000000000000000000000001 to 0.0000000000000000000000000001.
System.Single	Imperfect	Big	The *Single* data type offers a much larger range than *Decimal* does, but it does have some accuracy problems. Sometimes, when you do a complex calculation that you know should result in zero, the actual calculated result might be 0.0000000000023. It's close to zero, but not exactly zero. But you can use very large or very small numbers. For negative values, the range is −3.402823E+38 to −1.401298E−45; for positive values, its range is 1.401298E−45 to 3.402823E+38.
System.Double	Imperfect	Huge	The *Double* data type is just like the *Single* data type, but with a bigger attitude—I mean a larger range. For negative values, the range is −1.79769313486231E+308 to −4.94065645841247E−324; for positive values, the range is 4.94065645841247E−324 to 1.79769313486232E+308.

Character Data Types

Hey, check this out. *ktuefghbiokh*. Pretty cool, eh? That's the power of a computer in action managing text data. So efficient; so graceful; so *lskjdfljsdfjl*. Although computers are really number machines, they handle text just as well. Of course, it's really just you doing all of the wordsmithing. In fact, the computer isn't even smart enough to tell the difference between numbers and letters; it's all bits to the CPU. Pretty mindless, if you ask me. I mean, what's the use of having all that computing power if you can't even think. Despite all of their speed and technology, computers are still just lumps of silicon wrapped up in a nice package. The computer I'm typing on doesn't even know that I'm insulting it; I can type these things on and on, and there's nutten that thiz komputre cann due about itt.

The Framework includes two text-related data types: *System.Char* and *System.String*. The *Char* data type holds a single character—no more, no less. At 16 bits, it holds any of the thousands of Unicode characters.

The *String* data type allows up to about two billion Unicode characters to be "strung" together into one long text block. Although *Char* and *String* are different data types, you can easily move data back and forth between them, because they are both based on basic 16-bit Unicode characters.

Date and Time Data Type

The *System.DateTime* data type lets you store either date or time values (or both) as data. Internally, *DateTime* is just a simple integer counter that displays a converted date or time format when needed. As a number, it counts the number of "ticks" since 12:00 a.m. on January 1, 1 AD. Each "tick" is exactly 100 nanoseconds, so it's pretty precise. The maximum allowed date is December 31, 9999 in the Gregorian calendar.

Boolean Data Type

The *System.Boolean* data type represents the true essence of computer data: the bit. It holds one of two possible values: *True* or *False*. Shockingly, the data type actually requires two bytes of data space to keep track of that single bit of data.

It turns out that Boolean values are very important in programs. As a developer, you are always testing to see if various conditions are met before you process a block of code. All of these conditions eventually boil down to Boolean values and operations. .NET even has ways to easily migrate data between integer values and the Boolean data type. In such conversions, zero becomes *False*, while the world of all other possible values becomes

True. When moving from Boolean to an integer equivalent, *False* becomes zero and *True* becomes –1. (If you ever use the C# language, you'll find that it converts *True* to 1, not –1. Internally in .NET, *True* does convert to 1, but for historical reasons, Visual Basic uses –1. This difference normally isn't a problem unless you store Boolean values as integers in a disk file and expect both Visual Basic and C# programs to interpret the data correctly.)

The System.Object Class

You already knew that .NET is an object-oriented development environment. What you probably didn't know is that some pranksters at Microsoft placed a bet to see if they could make the entire .NET system one big derived class. Well, the group that said it could be done won the bet. Everything in .NET—all code and all data—is derived from a single base class: *System.Object.* By itself, this class doesn't have too many features. It can tell you its name, its type, and whether two instances of an object are in fact one and the same object. Other than that, it isn't useful for much except to be used as a starting point for all other classes and types.

Because all classes in .NET—including all data types—derive from *System.Object,* you can treat an instance of any class (or data type) as *Object.* The data will remember what type it really is, so if you have a *System.Int32* posing as *System.Object,* you can change it back to *System.Int32* later.

Value Types and Reference Types

Back in Chapter 1, you read about the difference between **value types** and **reference types**: value types are buckets that contain actual data, while reference types contain instructions on where you can find the actual data. In general, value types contain simple and small data values, whereas reference types point to large and complex data blocks. This isn't always true, but for most data you work with, it will be true.

System.Object is a reference type from which all other types and classes derive. This includes all of the core data types, so you would think that they would be reference types as well. But there is another class stuck in between *System.Object* and most of the data types. This class, *System.ValueType,* implements the basic definition and usage of a value type. Table 6-4 lists some of the differences between value and reference types.

Table 6-4 Value Type and Reference Type Usage

Value Types	Reference Types
Ultimately derive from *System.ValueType*, which in turn derives from *System.Object*.	Ultimately derives from *System.Object*.
Derived core data types: *Boolean, Byte, Char, DateTime, Decimal, Double, Int16, Int32, Int64, SByte, Single, UInt16, UInt32, UInt64*	Derived core data types: *String*
Provides support for Visual Basic "structures."	Provides support for Visual Basic "classes."
Enumerations are derived as follows: *System.Object←System.ValueType←System.Enum*	Delegates, used as references to class methods, are derived as follows: *System.Object←System.Delegate*. One type of delegate, the "multicast delegate," is further derived through *System.MulticastDelegate*.
Value types cannot derive from other classes or structures, nor can further structures derive from them.	Reference types can be derived from other classes, and can be used as base classes.
Instances cannot be set to *Nothing*.	Instances can be set to *Nothing*.
Instances can contain data of the specified type only. For instance, *System.Int32* instances can contain 32-bit signed integer data only.	Instances usually refer to data of their defined type, but an instance can also point to a derived type. For instance, an instance of *System.String* could refer to any data that used *System.String* as a base class.
Cannot be used to implement Interfaces.	Can implement Interfaces.
Do not go through the full .NET garbage collection process.	Are destroyed through garbage collection.

(In addition to classes and structures, Visual Basic also defines "modules." The .NET documentation claims that modules are neither value types nor reference types.)

A value type can only contain data of its own type, but reference types can point to derived instances. This is important in .NET, because it was designed to allow a *System.Object* instance to refer to any data in an application. *System.Object* instances can refer to either value type or reference type data. For reference types, this is easy to understand because that instance will just point to some derived instance of itself. But if you assign a value type to a *System.Object* reference, .NET has to mark that instance in a special way to indicate that a reference type contains a value type. This process is called **boxing**, and the reverse process is called **unboxing**. You don't really need to know how it works, but if you ever appear on *Jeopardy* and select ".NET Data Types" for $500, you'll be able to give the right question.

Visual Basic Data Types

All of the data types implemented in the Visual Basic language are wrappers for the core .NET data types. Only some of the names have been changed to protect the innocent. Table 6-5 lists the Visual Basic data types and their .NET equivalents.

Table 6-5 Visual Basic Data Types and Related .NET Types

Visual Basic Type	.NET Type
Boolean	System.Boolean
Byte	System.Byte
Char	System.Char
Date	System.DateTime
Decimal	System.Decimal
Double	System.Double
Integer	System.Int32
Long	System.Int64
Object	System.Object
SByte	System.SByte
Short	System.Int16
Single	System.Single
String	System.String
UInteger	System.UInt32
ULong	System.UInt64
UShort	System.UInt16

All of the Visual Basic data types are fully interchangeable with their .NET equivalents. Any instance of *System.Int32* can be treated as if it were an instance of *Integer*, and vice-versa.

Literals

The quickest way to include values of a particular data type in your Visual Basic code is to use a **literal**. You've already seen literals in action in this book. Chapter 1 included a literal in its sample project.

```
MsgBox("Hello, World!")
```

This call to the *MsgBox* function includes a *String literal*. String literals always appear within a set of double quotes. Most numeric literals appear with a data-type-defining character on the end of the literal, but there are other variations. Table 6-6 lists the different literals values you can include in your code.

Table 6-6 Literals Supported by Visual Basic

Literal Type	Example	Description
Boolean	`True`	The *Boolean* data type supports two literal values: *True* and *False*.
Char	`"Q"c`	Single-character literals appear in double quotes with a trailing character *c*. A literal of type *Char* is not the same as a single-character literal of type *String*.
Date	`#11/7/2005#`	Date or time literals appear between a set of number signs. You can include dates, times, or a combination of both. The date or time values can be in any format recognized by Windows, although Visual Studio may reformat your date literal for conformity with its own standards.
Decimal	`123.45D` `123.45@`	Floating point values of type *Decimal* are followed by a capital *D*, or the character @.

(continues)

Table 6-6 Literals Supported by Visual Basic *(continued)*

Literal Type	Example	Description
Double	123.45R 123.45#	Floating point values of type *Double* are followed by a capital *R*, or the character #. Also, if you use a numeric literal with a decimal portion, but with no trailing data type character, that literal will be typed as a *Double*.
Hexadecimal	&HABCD	You can include hexadecimal literals in your code by starting the value with the "&H" character sequence, followed by the hex digits.
Integer	123.45I 123.45%	Integral values of type *Integer* are followed by a capital *I*, or the character %. Also, if you use a numeric literal that falls in the range of an *Integer*, but with no trailing data type character, that literal will be typed as an *Integer*.
Long	123.45L 123.45&	Integral values of type *Long* are followed by a capital *L*, or the character &. Also, if you use a numeric literal that falls in the range of a *Long* and outside the range of an *Integer*, but with no trailing data type character, that literal will be typed as a *Long*.
Octal	&O7654	You can include octal literals in your code by starting the value with the "&O" character sequence, followed by the octal digits.
Short	123.45S	Integral values of type *Short* are followed by a capital *S*.
Single	123.45F 123.45!	Floating point values of type *Single* are followed by a capital *F*, or the character *!*.
String	"Simple" "A ""B"" C"	String literals appear within a set of double quotes, with no special character following the closing quote. Use two quote characters within the string literal to embed a single quotation mark.

Constants

Literals are nice, but it isn't always clear what they mean. Encountering the number 12 in a formula, for instance, might cause the formula to generate correct results, but it would still be helpful to know what 12 means. Is it the number of months in a year, hours in a day, minimum number of teeth in a mouth to eat steak, or something even more sinister?

Constants provide a way to assign meaningful names to literal values. They are treated a lot like literal values, but once defined, they can be used over and over again in your code. Each use of a literal value, even if it has the same value, represents a distinct definition and instance of that value.

In Visual Basic, constants are defined using the *Const* keyword.

```
Const MonthsInYear As Short = 12
```

This constant definition has the following parts.

- **A name.** In this case, the name is *MonthsInYear*.
- **A data type.** This example defines a *Short* constant. The data type always follows the *As* keyword. If you leave out this *As* clause, the constant's data type will be whatever the assigned literal would have been on its own. Only the following data types can be used for constants: *Boolean, Byte, Char, Date, Decimal, Double, Integer, Long, Object, SByte, Short, Single, String, UInteger, ULong, UShort,* or the name of an enumeration (discussed in the next section).
- **An initializer.** The initializer assigned here is *12*. Once assigned, this value cannot be altered while your code is running. Constants are always value types, not reference types. Initializers are usually simple literals, but you can also include simple calculations.

```
Const Seven As Integer = 3 + 4
```

- **An access level.** The definition of *MonthsInYear* listed here represents the typical format of a constant definition included within a code procedure. You can also define constants outside of procedures, but still within a class or other type. When you do this, you generally add an *access modifier* keyword just before the *Const* keyword. This keyword indicates how much code will be able to use the constant. I'll describe access modifiers a little later in the section on variables. Constants defined within a procedure can only be used within that procedure.

Once you define a constant, you can use it anywhere you would use an equivalent literal.

```
Const GreatGreeting As String = "Hello, World!"
...Later...
MsgBox(GreatGreeting)
```

Enumerations

Enumerations, one of the core .NET types, allow you to group named, related integer values as a set. Once bound together, the enumeration can be used like any other data type; you can create variables that are specific instances of an enumeration.

Enumerations are a multi-line construct; the first line defines the name and underlying data type of the enumeration. Each enumeration member appears on a separate line, ending with a final closing *End Enum* line.

```
01 Enum CarType As Integer
02    Sedan = 1
03    StationWagon = 2
04    Truck = 3
05    SUV = 4
06    Other = 5
07 End Enum
```

The declaration line (line 01) includes the *Enum* keyword, the name of the enumeration (*CarType*) and the underlying data type (*Integer*). The *As* data type clause is optional; if you leave it off, the enumeration defaults to *Integer*. If you do supply a data type, it must be one of the following: *Byte*, *Integer*, *Long*, *SByte*, *Short*, *UInteger*, *ULong*, or *UShort*.

Each member of the enumeration (lines 02 to 06) must include at least a member name (such as *Sedan*). You can optionally assign a numeric value to some or all of the members, as I have done in the sample. If a member lacks an assignment, it is set to one more than the previous member. If none of the members have an assigned value, the first is assigned 0, the next to 1, and so on.

Once defined, enumeration members act a lot like integer constants; you can use them anywhere you would normally use a literal or constant.

When referencing the members of an enumeration in your code, include both the enumeration name and the member name.

```
CarType.Sedan
```

The *Enum* statement cannot be used within a method or procedure. Instead, you define an enumeration as a member of a type (class, structure, or module), or as its own stand-alone type, just like a class. The .NET Framework includes many useful predefined enumerations intended for use with Framework features. For instance, the *System.DayOfWeek* enumeration includes members for each day of the week.

Variables

Literals are nice, and constants and enumerations are nicer, but none of them can be altered once your program starts. This tends to make your application rigid and inflexible. If all of your customers are named "Fred," and they only place orders for $342.34, it probably won't be much of a limitation. But most users want more variety in their software. **Variables** are named containers for data, just like constants, but their contents can be modified throughout the run of an application. Also, they can contain both value types and reference types. Here's the basic syntax for defining a new variable.

```
Dim customerName As String
```

The *Dim* keyword—originally from the word "dimension"—defines a new variable; in this case, a variable named *customerName* with a data type of *String*. This named container is ready to hold any *String* value; assign to it string literals, other string variables, or the return value from functions that generate strings. Because it is a reference type, it can also be set to *Nothing*, a special Visual Basic value and keyword that means "this reference type has not yet been instantiated."

```
customerName = Nothing                        ' Nothing
customerName = "Fred"                          ' Literal
customerName = GetCustomerName(customerID)     ' Function result
```

All variables contain their default value until set to something else. For reference types, the default is *Nothing*; for numeric values, the default is zero. Booleans default to *False*. You can include an initial assignment as part of the *Dim* statement to override the default assignment.

```
Dim countdownSeconds As Short = 60
Dim processingDate As Date = Today
Dim customerName As String = GetCustomerName(customerID)
```

The last line in that code block shows a reference type—*String*—being assigned the *String* result of a function. You can also assign a brand-new instance of a reference instance to a reference type variable. And it's new. That is, it uses the special *New* keyword, which says, "I'm creating a new instance of the specific data type." There are a few different variations, but they all produce the same results.

```
' ----- One-line variation.
Dim someString As New String

' ----- Another one-line variation.
Dim someString As String = New String

' ----- Two-line variation.
Dim someString As String
someString = New String
```

Remember that reference types are buckets that contain directions for locating the actual data. When a reference data first springs into existence, it contains *Nothing*. That is, the bucket contains no instructions at all because there is no related data stored anywhere. When you assign a new instance to a reference type variable, that instance gets stored somewhere in memory, and instructions for locating that data are dumped into the bucket. In the previous code block, each use of the *New* keyword creates a new data instance somewhere in memory. This data's location is then assigned to the *someString* reference type variable.

Many classes include **constructors**, initialization routines that set up the initial values of the instance. You can call a constructor as part of the *New* clause. The *String* data type includes a constructor that lets you build an initial string. One of these special constructors lets you create a new string containing multiple copies of a specific character. The following statement assigns a string of 25 asterisks to the *lotsOfStars* variable.

```
Dim lotsOfStars As New String("*"c, 25)
```

Constructors are discussed in detail in Chapter 8, "Classes and Inheritance."

Dim statements can appear anywhere in a procedure, but by tradition they always appear right at the start of a procedure, before any other logic statements.

```
Sub MyProcedure()
    Dim myVariable As Integer
    ' ----- Additional code goes here...
End Sub
```

As with constants, variables can be defined either within a procedure, or outside of a procedure but within a type. (Variables and constants declared outside of procedures are known as **fields**. Variables and constants declared inside of a procedure are known as **local variables** and **local constants**, respectively.) The *Dim* keyword is always used with in-procedure variable declarations. At the type level, the *Dim* keyword is replaced by one of the following **access modifiers**.

- **Private.** *Private* variables can be used by any member or procedure within the type, but nowhere else. Each instance of a class or type contains its own version of the variable. If you derive a new class from a base class that includes a private type variable, the code in that derived class will have no access at all to that *Private* variable; it won't even know it exists.
- **Friend.** *Friend* variables are private to an assembly. They can be used by any code in their related type, but also by any code anywhere in the same assembly. Now that's friendly.
- **Public.** *Public* variables are available everywhere. It is possible to write an application or component that exposes its types to code beyond itself. Anything marked *Public* can be exposed in this way.
- **Protected.** *Protected* variables are like *Private* type variables, but code in derived classes can also access them. You can only use the *Protected* keyword in a class definition; it doesn't work in a structure or module.
- **Protected Friend.** *Protected Friend* variables combine all the features of *Friend* and *Protected*. They can only be used in classes.

A single class or type may contain both fields and local variables and constants.

```
Class MyClass
    ' ----- Here's a field.
    Private InternalUseOnly As Boolean

    Sub MyProcedure()
        ' ----- Here's a local variable.
        Dim myVariable As Integer

    End Sub
End Class
```

There are other syntax variations to the *Dim* statement, some of which I will discuss later in this chapter and in other chapters.

Scope and Lifetime

When you define a variable within a procedure, it has **procedure-level scope**. This means that you can use the variable anywhere within that procedure. Your procedure will likely have "block statements," those statements, such as *For...Next* and *If...Then*, that require more than one line of source code to complete. If you add a *Dim* statement between the starting and ending lines of one of these statements, that declared variable will have only **block-level scope**. It will be available only within that block of the procedure.

```
For counter = 1 To 10
    Dim processResult As Integer
    ' ----- More code here.
Next counter
MsgBox(processResult)  ' This line will fail
```

This code declares *processResult* within the *For...Next* block. So it's only available for use inside of that block; any attempted use outside of *processResult* outside of the *For* block generates an immediate error.

The **lifetime** of a procedure-level variable begins when the code first enters that procedure, and ends when the code exits the procedure. This is true for both procedure-level and block-level variables. This means that if you assign a block-level variable some value before exiting the block, it will still have that value if you reenter that block during the same procedure call.

For fields (class-level variables), the scope depends on the access level used when declaring the variable. The lifetime of a field begins when the class instance is created in code, and ends when the instance is destroyed or goes completely out of use.

Variable and Constant Naming Conventions

The names that you give to your variables will not have that much impact on how your application runs on the user's workstation, but it can affect the clarity of the source code. In the days before .NET, many Windows programming languages used a system called *Hungarian Notation* to craft variable names. Such names helped to communicate information about the data type and usage of a variable to anyone reading the source code. Unfortunately, the rules used to define Hungarian variable names were somewhat complex, and varied not only between programming languages, but between programmers using the same language.

When Microsoft released .NET back in 2002, its documentation included various programming recommendations. One of those recommendations was, "Stop using the Java programming language." Another recommendation encouraged programmers to cease from using Hungarian Notation, and instead embrace a new system that used casing rules to differentiate variables. The rules state that all variable names should employ mixed-case names (where each logical word in the variable name starts with a capital letter and continues with lowercase letters). The only differentiation comes in the capitalization of the initial letter.

- Set the first letter of all local variables and all method parameters to lowercase. This is known as *Camel Casing*.
- Set the first letter of all fields, methods, type members (including controls), and types to uppercase. This is known as *Pascal Casing*.

In the interest of full disclosure, I must tell you that I modified the original recommendations slightly from the documentation supplied with Visual Studio. The original rules were a little more complex when it came to field and method parameter names. Personally, I find the two rules listed here to be adequate for my needs.

You might give a local variable a name like *lookInThisVariable*, which capitalizes the first letter of each word, but not the initial letter. If you defined this variable as a field instead, you would change its name to *LookInThisVariable*, capitalizing the first letter.

Operators

Visual Basic includes a variety of **operators** that let you manipulate the values of your variables. You've already seen the *assignment operator* (=), which lets you assign a value directly to a variable. Most of the other operators let you build up **expressions** that combine multiple original values in formulaic ways for eventual assignment to a variable. Consider the following statement:

```
squareArea = length * width
```

This statement includes two operators: assignment and multiplication. The multiplication operator combines two values (*length* and *width*) using multiplication, and stores the product in the *squareArea* variable. Without operators, you would be hard pressed to calculate an area or any complex formula.

There are two types of non-assignment operators: **unary** and **binary**. Unary operators work with only a single value, or **operand**. Binary operators require two operands, but result in a single processed value. Operands include literals, constants, variables, and function return values. Table 6-7 lists the different operators with usage details.

Table 6-7 Visual Basic Non-Assignment Operators

Operator	Description
+	Addition. Adds two operands together, producing a sum. Some programmers also use this operator to perform string concatenation, but it's better to join strings using another operator (&) specifically designed for that purpose. Syntax: *operand1* + *operand2* Example: 2 + 3

Operator	Description
+	Unary plus. Ensures that an operand retains its current sign, either positive or negative. Because all operands automatically retain their sign, this operator is redundant, and removed from code automatically by Visual Studio. Normally this operator is meaningless in your code, but it may come in handy when we discuss "operator overloading" in Chapter 12, "Operating Overloading." Syntax: +*operand* Example: `+5`
-	Subtraction. Subtracts one operand (the second) from another (the first), and returns the difference. Syntax: *operand1* – *operand2* Example: `10 – 4`
-	Unary negation. Reverses the sign of its operand. When used with a literal number, it results in a negative value. When used with a variable that contains a negative value, it produces a positive result. Syntax: –*operand2* Example: `–34`
*	Multiplication. Multiplies two operands together, and returns the product. Syntax: *operand1* * *operand2* Example: `8 * 3`
/	Division. Divides one operand (the first) by another (the second), and returns the quotient. If the second operand contains zero, a divide-by-zero error occurs. Syntax: *operand1* / *operand2* Example: `9 / 3`

(continues)

6. DATA AND DATA TYPES

Table 6-7 Visual Basic Non-Assignment Operators *(continued)*

Operator	Description
\	Integer division. Divides one operand (the first) by another (the second), and returns the quotient, first truncating any decimal portion from that result. If the second operand contains zero, a divide-by-zero error occurs. Syntax: *operand1* \ *operand2* Example: 9 \ 4
Mod	Modulo. Divides one operand (the first) by another (the second), and returns the remainder as an integer value. If the second operand contains zero, a divide-by-zero error occurs. Syntax: *operand1* Mod *operand2* Example: 10 Mod 3
^	Exponentiation. Raises one operand (the first) to the power of another (the second). Syntax: *operand1* ^ *operand2* Example: 2 ^ 8
&	String concatenation. Joins two operands together, and returns a combined string result. Both operands are converted to their *String* equivalent before being joined together. Syntax: *operand1* & *operand2* Example: "O" & "K"
And	Conjunction. Performs a logical or bitwise conjunction on two operands, and returns the result. For logical (Boolean) operations, the result will be *True* only if both operands evaluate to *True*. For bitwise (integer) operations, each specific bit in the result will be set to 1 only if the corresponding bits in both operands are 1. Syntax: *operand1* And *operand2* Example: this And that

Operator	Description
Or	Disjunction. Performs a logical or bitwise disjunction on two operands, and returns the result. For logical (Boolean) operations, the result will be *True* if either operand evaluates to *True*. For bitwise (integer) operations, each specific bit in the result will be set to 1 if the corresponding bit in either operand is 1. Syntax: *operand1* `Or` *operand2* Example: `this Or that`
AndAlso	Short-circuited conjunction. This operator is equivalent to the logical version of the *And* operator, but if the first operand evaluates to *False*, the second operand will not be evaluated at all. This operator does not support bitwise operations. Syntax: *operand1* `AndAlso` *operand2* Example: `this AndAlso that`
OrElse	Short-circuited disjunction. This operator is equivalent to the logical version of the *Or* operator, but if the first operand evaluates to *True*, the second operand will not be evaluated at all. This operator does not support bitwise operations. Syntax: *operand1* `OrElse` *operand2* Example: `this OrElse that`
Not	Negation. Performs a logical or bitwise negation on a single operand. For logical (Boolean) operations, the result will be *True* if the operand evaluates to *False*, and *False* if the operand evaluates to *True*. For bitwise (integer) operations, each specific bit in the result will be set to 1 if the corresponding operand bit is 0, and set to 0 if the operand bit is 1. Syntax: `Not` *operand1* Example: `Not this`

(continues)

Table 6-7 Visual Basic Non-Assignment Operators *(continued)*

Operator	Description
Xor	Exclusion. Performs a logical or bitwise "exclusive or" on two operands, and returns the result. For logical (Boolean) operations, the result will be *True* only if the operands have different logical values (*True* or *False*). For bitwise (integer) operations, each specific bit in the result will be set to 1 only if the corresponding bits in the operands are different. Syntax: *operand1* Xor *operand2* Example: this Xor that
<<	Shift left. The *Shift Left* operator shifts the bits of the first operand to the left by the number of positions specified in the second operand, and returns the result. Bits pushed off the left end of the result are lost; bits added to the right end are always 0. This operator works best if the first operand is an unsigned integer value. Syntax: *operand1* << *operand2* Example: &H25 << 3
>>	Shift right. The *Shift Right* operator shifts the bits of the first operand to the right by the number of positions specified in the second operand, and returns the result. Bits pushed off the right end of the result are lost; bits added to the right end are always the same as the bit originally in the left-most position. This operator works best if the first operand is an unsigned integer value. Syntax: *operand1* >> *operand2* Example: &H25 >> 2
=	Equals (comparison). Compares two operands and returns *True* if they are equal in value. Syntax: *operand1* = *operand2* Example: one = two
<>	Not equals. Compares two operands and returns *True* if they are not equal in value. Syntax: *operand1* <> *operand2* Example: one <> two

Operator	Description
<	Less than. Compares two operands and returns *True* if the first is less in value than the second. When comparing string values, the return is *True* if the first operand appears first when sorting the two strings. Syntax: *operand1* < *operand2* Example: one < two
>	Greater than. Compares two operands and returns *True* if the first is greater in value than the second. When comparing string values, the return is *True* if the first operand appears last when sorting the two strings. Syntax: *operand1* > *operand2* Example: one > two
<=	Less than or equal to. Compares two operands and returns *True* if the first is less than or equal to the value of the second. Syntax: *operand1* <= *operand2* Example: one <= two
>=	Greater than or equal to. Compares two operands and returns *True* if the first is greater than or equal to the value of the second. Syntax: *operand1* >= *operand2* Example: one >= two
Like	Pattern comparison. Compares the first operand to the pattern specified in the second operand, and returns *True* if there is a match. The pattern operand supports some basic wildcard and selection options, and is fully described in the documentation supplied with Visual Studio. .NET also includes a feature called *Regular Expressions* that provides a much more comprehensive pattern matching solution. Syntax: *operand1* Like *operand2* Example: one Like pattern

(continues)

6. DATA AND DATA TYPES

Table 6-7 Visual Basic Non-Assignment Operators *(continued)*

Operator	Description
Is	Type comparison. Compares the first operand to another object, a data type, or *Nothing*, and returns *True* if there is a match. I will document this operator in more detail later in the text, and in Chapter 8. Syntax: *operand1* `Is` *operand2* Example: `one Is two`

IsNot	Negated type comparison. This operator is a shortcut for using the *Is* and *Not* operators together. The following two expressions are equivalent:
	
	`this IsNot that`
	
	`Not (this Is that)`
	
	Syntax: *operand1* `IsNot` *operand2*
	
	Example: `one IsNot two`

TypeOf	Instance comparison. Returns the data type of a value or variable. The type of every class or data type in .NET is implemented as an object, based on *System.Type*. The *TypeOf* operator can be used only with the *Is* operator: Syntax: `TypeOf` *operand1* `Is` *typeOperand* Example: `TypeOf one Is Integer`
AddressOf	Delegate retrieval. Returns a delegate (described in Chapter 8) that represents a specific instance of a procedure or method. Syntax: `AddressOf` *method1* Example: `AddressOf one.SomeMethod`
GetType	Type retrieval. Returns the data type of a value or variable, just like the *TypeOf* operator. However, *GetType* works like a function, and does not need to be used with the *Is* operator. Syntax: `GetType (`*operand1*`)` Example: `GetType(one)`

Non-assignment operators use their operands to produce a result, but they do not cause the operands themselves to be altered in any way. The assignment operator does update the operand that appears on its left side. In addition to the standard assignment operator, Visual Basic includes several operators that combine the assignment operator with some of the binary operators. Table 6-8 lists these assignment operators.

Table 6-8 Visual Basic Assignment Operators

Operator	Based On
=	Standard assignment operator
+=	+ (Addition)
-=	- (Subtraction)
*=	* (Multiplication)
/=	/ (Division)
\=	\ (Integer Division)
^=	^ (Exponentiation)
&=	& (Concatenation)
<<=	<< (Shift Left)
>>=	>> (Shift Right)

These assignment operators are just shortcuts for the full-bodied operators. For instance, to add one to a numeric variable, you can use either of these two statements.

```
' ----- Increment totalSoFar by 1.
totalSoFar = totalSoFar + 1


' ----- Another way to increment totalSoFar by 1.
totalSoFar += 1
```

Static Variables

Normally, the lifetime of a local procedure-level variable ends when the procedure ends. But sometimes you might want a variable to retain its value between each call into the procedure. Sometimes you might also want a million dollars, but you can't always have it. But you can have variables that keep their values if you want. They're called **static variables**. To declare a static variable, use the *Static* keyword in place of the *Dim* keyword.

```
Static keepingTrack As Integer = 0
```

The assignment of zero to *keepingTrack* is done only once, when creating the instance of the type that contains this statement. Thereafter, it keeps whatever value is assigned to it until the instance is destroyed. Static variables can be created only within procedures.

Arrays

Software applications often work with sets of related data, not just isolated data values. Visual Basic includes two primary ways of working with such sets of data: collections (discussed in Chapter 16, "Generics") and arrays. An **array** assigns a numeric position to each item included in the set, starting with zero and ending with one less than the number of items included. An array of five items has elements numbering from 0 to 4.

As an example, imagine that you were developing a zoo simulation application. You might include an array named *animals* that includes each animal name in your zoo:

- Animal #0: Aardvark
- Animal #1: Baboon
- Animal #2: Chimpanzee
- Animal #3: Donkey
- ...and so on...

Visual Basic identifies array elements by a parenthesized number after the array name. For our animals, a simple assignment puts the *String* name of each animal in an array element.

```
animal(0) = "Aardvark"
animal(1) = "Baboon"
animal(2) = "Chimpanzee"
animal(3) = "Donkey"
```

Using each array element is just as easy.

```
MsgBox("The first animal is: " & animal(0))
```

Each element of an array is not so different from a standalone variable. In fact, you could just consider the set of animals in the example code to be distinct variables: a variable named *animal(0)*, another variable named *animal(1)*, and so on. But they are better than ordinary variables because you can process them as a set. For instance, you can scan through each element using a *For...Next* loop. Consider an *Integer* array named *eachItem* with elements numbered from 0 to 2. The following code block adds the individual items of the array as if they were distinct variables.

```
Dim totalAmount As Integer
totalAmount = eachItem(0) + eachItem(1) + eachItem(2)
```

But because the items are in a numbered array, you can use a *For...Next* loop to scan through each element, one at a time.

```
Dim totalAmount As Integer = 0
For counter As Integer = 0 to 2
   ' ----- Keep a running total of the items.
   totalAmount += eachItem(counter)
Next counter
```

Before you assign values to array elements, or retrieve those elements, you must declare and size the array for your needs. The *Dim* statement creates an array just as it does ordinary variables; the *ReDim* statement resizes an array after it already exists.

```
Dim animal(0 To 25) As String   ' 26-element array
Dim moreAnimals() As String      ' An undefined String array
ReDim moreAnimals(0 To 25)       ' Now it has elements
```

Normally, the *ReDim* statement would wipe out any existing data stored in each array element. Adding the *Preserve* keyword retains all existing data.

```
ReDim Preserve moreAnimals(0 to 30)   ' Keeps elements 0 to 25
```

Each element of the array is an independent object that can be assigned data as needed. In this example, each element is a *String*, but you can use any value type or reference type you wish in the array declaration. If you create an array of *Object* elements, you can mix and match the data in the array; element 0 need not contain the same type of data as element 1.

The array itself is also an independent object—a class instance that manages its set of contained elements. If you need to specify the entire array, and not just one of its elements (and there are times when you need to do this), use its name without any parentheses or positional values.

Multidimensional Arrays

Visual Basic arrays support more than one **dimension** (or "rank"). The dimensions indicate the number of independent ranges supported by the array. A one-dimensional array, like the *animal* array earlier, includes a single range. A two-dimensional array includes two comma-delimited ranges, forming a grid arrangement of elements, with separate ranges for rows and columns.

```
Dim ticTacToeBoard(0 To 2, 0 To 2) As Char   ' 3 x 3 board
```

An array can have up to 60 different dimensions, although there are usually better ways to organize data than breaking it out into that many dimensions.

Array Boundaries

The **lower bound** of any array dimension is always zero, as indicated by the "0 To *x*" clause when defining or redimensioning the array. You can actually leave the "0 To" part out of the statement, and just include the upper bound.

```
' ----- These two lines are equivalent.
Dim animal(0 To 25) As String
Dim animal(25) As String
```

These two statements both create an array with 26 elements, numbered 0 through 25.

To determine the current lower or upper bound of an array dimension, use the *LBound* and *UBound* functions:

```
MsgBox("The board is " & (UBound(ticTacToeBoard, 1) + 1) & _
    " by " & (UBound(ticTacToeBoard, 2) + 1))
```

If your array only includes a single dimension, you don't have to tell *LBound* or *UBound* which dimension you want to check.

```
MsgBox("The upper element is numbered " & UBound(animal))
```

Each array also includes *GetLowerBound* and *GetUpperBound* methods that return the same results as *LBound* and *UBound*. However, the dimension number you pass to the *GetLowerBound* and *GetUpperBound* methods starts from zero, while *LBound* and *UBound* dimension values start the counting at 1.

```
MsgBox("The board is " & _
    (ticTacToeBoard.GetUpperBound(0) + 1) & _
    " by " & (ticTacToeBoard.GetUpperBound(1) + 1))
```

Common Visual Basic Functions

This final section includes a brief listing of the functions built-in to the Visual Basic language, many of which you will use regularly in your applications. Also listed here are some members of the FCL that replicate features that were part of the Visual Basic language before .NET, but were moved into the Framework for more general access. For the exact syntax required to use these functions, access the Visual Studio online help.

Conversion Functions

The conversion functions allow you to convert data of one Visual Basic data type to another. It's not a free-for-all, so don't go converting the string "hello" to an integer and expect it to work. But converting numbers from one numeric type to another, or converting values between string and numeric types, generally work just fine.

All of these statements (except *CType*) have the same basic syntax:

```
dest = CXxxx(source)
```

where *source* is the value to be converted by *CXxxx*. You don't have to assign the result to a variable; you can use the result anywhere you would use a similar literal or variable value. Table 6-9 lists the built-in conversion functions.

Table 6-9 Visual Basic Conversion Functions

Function	Description
CBool	Converts a value to a *Boolean*.
CByte	Converts a value to a *Byte*.
CChar	Converts a value to a *Char*. If the source value is a string, only the first character is converted.
CDate	Converts a value to a *Date*. If the source value is a string, it must be in a valid date or time format.
CDbl	Converts a value to a *Double*.
CDec	Converts a value to a *Decimal*.
CInt	Converts a value to an *Integer*.
CLng	Converts a value to a *Long*.
CObj	Converts a value to an *Object*. This is useful when you want to store a value type as an *Object* instance.
CSByte	Converts a value to an *SByte*.
CShort	Converts a value to a *Short*.
CSng	Converts a value to a *Single*.
CType	Converts a value to any defined type, class, or interface, either in your application or in the FCL. The syntax is: `CType(source, newType)` where *newType* is a data type. For instance: `CType(5, String)` converts the *Integer* 5 to a *String*. As with other conversion functions, you can't convert data from one type to another if the types are incompatible, or if there is no conversion available that knows how to generate the target type from the source type. Operator overloading, discussed in Chapter 12, provides a way to let the *CType* function convert between types that would otherwise be incompatible.
CUInt	Converts a value to a *UInteger*.
CULng	Converts a value to a *ULong*.
CUShort	Converts a value to a *UShort*.

Date-Related Functions

Visual Basic includes several functions designed to manage date and time values. Table 6-10 lists these functions. Most of these functions accept one or more source arguments, and return either *Date*, *String*, or numeric result.

Table 6-10 Visual Basic Date-Related Functions and Properties

Function	Description
DateAdd	Adds or subtracts time or date value to a starting date. For instance, you can add 12 minutes, or subtract three years, from a given date.
DateDiff	Returns the difference between two date or time values. You can specify the interval, such as months or seconds.
DatePart	Returns one component of a date or time, such as the hour or the year.
DateSerial	Returns a *Date* built from specific month, day, and year values.
DateString	Returns the current date as a string. You can also set the date on the local computer using this keyword.
DateValue	Returns the date portion of a combined date and time value; the time portion is discarded.
Day	Returns the day from a given date value.
FormatDateTime	Formats a given date or time as a string, using a small set of predefined formats. This function is included for backward compatibility with older VBScript code.
Hour	Returns the hour from a given time value.
IsDate	Indicates whether the data supplied to this function is a valid date or not.
Minute	Returns the minute from a given time value.
Month	Returns the month from a given date value.
MonthName	Returns the name of a month for a numeric month value.
Now	Returns the current date and time. Equivalent to *TimeOfDay*.
Second	Returns the seconds from a given time value.
TimeOfDay	Returns the current date and time. Equivalent to *Now*.

(continues)

6. DATA AND DATA TYPES

Table 6-10 Visual Basic Date-Related Functions and Properties *(continued)*

Function	Description
Timer	Returns the number of seconds that have elapsed since midnight of the current day. This function is reset to zero each midnight.
TimeSerial	Returns a *Date* built from specific hour, minute, and second values.
TimeString	Returns the current time as a string. You can also set the time on the local computer using this keyword.
TimeValue	Returns the time portion of a combined date and time value; the date portion is discarded.
Today	Returns the current date.
Weekday	Returns an integer that indicates the day of the week.
WeekdayName	Returns the name of a weekday for an integer day of the week.
Year	Returns the year from a given date value.

Variables created as *System.DateTime* (or Visual Basic *Date*) each include several properties and methods that provide features similar to the functions listed in Table 6-10. For instance, the *Second* property returns the number of seconds.

```
Dim meetingTime As Date
meetingTime = #11/7/2005 8:00:03am#
MsgBox(meetingTime.Second)    ' Displays '3'
MsgBox(Second(meetingTime))   ' Also displays '3'
```

You can use either the intrinsic Visual Basic functions or the equivalent *System.DateTime* methods and properties in your code. Each technique provides the same result.

Numeric Functions

Visual Basic programmers just love working with numbers; it's in their blood. Fortunately, Visual Basic includes lots of features for working wonders with numbers. In addition to the standard data manipulation operators, Table 6-11 lists several number-related functions.

Table 6-11 Visual Basic Number-Related Functions

Function	Description
Fix	Truncates the decimal portion of a number, returning only the whole portion. Similar to the *Int* function.
FormatCurrency	Formats a given number as a currency value, using a small set of predefined formats. This function is included for backward compatibility with older VBScript code.
FormatNumber	Formats a given number as a general number, using a small set of predefined formats. This function is included for backward compatibility with older VBScript code.
FormatPercent	Formats a given number as a percentage, using a small set of predefined formats. This function is included for backward compatibility with older VBScript code.
Hex	Formats a number as hexadecimal, and returns its string representation.
Int	Returns the whole number that is less than or equal to the supplied value. Similar to the *Fix* function.
IsNumeric	Indicates whether the data supplied to this function is a valid number or not.
Oct	Formats a number as octal, and returns its string representation.
Val	Extracts the first valid number from a string and returns it.

The .NET Framework includes the *System.Math* class, which contains several math-related function members. Some of these, such as *Round*, *Sin*, and *Log*, were implemented as intrinsic functions in Visual Basic 6.0, but have been moved from the language to the *Math* class in .NET.

Visual Basic also includes several functions used for financial and accounting calculations. These functions were also included in Visual Basic 6.0. As they are not relevant to the project discussed in this book, I will only list their names here: *DDB*, *FV*, *IPmt*, *IRR*, *MIRR*, *NPer*, *NPV*, *Pmt*, *PPmt*, *PV*, *Rate*, *SLN*, and *SYD*.

String Functions

String manipulation is a core part of Windows programming. The new XML features included with .NET are really just fancy string-manipulation routines, although with the complexities hidden from view. Visual Basic includes many functions designed to manipulate strings and characters. They are listed in Table 6-12.

As with most functions, these functions return a new string or value, leaving the original string or source values intact. The lone exception is the *Mid Statement*, which modifies the source string.

Table 6-12 Visual Basic String-Related Functions

Function	Description
Asc, AscW	Returns the numeric ASCII or Unicode value for a character.
Chr, ChrW	Given a number, these functions return the matching ASCII or Unicode character.
Filter	Returns an array that is a subset of a source array, but including only those elements that matched a pattern.
Format	Formats number, date, and time values using predefined or custom formatting codes.
GetChar	Extracts a single character from a larger string.
InStr	Returns the position of a substring within a larger string.
InStrRev	Returns the position of a substring within a larger string, searching from the end of the string until the beginning.
Join	Returns a string built from a concatenation of an array of strings.
LCase	Converts a string to its lowercase equivalent.
Left	Returns the left-most portion of a string.
Len	Returns the length of a string.
LSet	Left-aligns a string within a larger string of spaces.
LTrim	Removes spaces from the start of a string.
Mid	Extracts a substring from the middle of a larger string.
Mid Statement	Modifies a range of characters in an existing string with new content. This is not a function, but a special Visual Basic statement. Its syntax varies considerably from that of most other Visual Basic features.
Replace	Replaces occurrences of a substring with another substring, all within a larger string.
Right	Returns the right-most portion of a string.
RSet	Right-aligns a string within a larger string of spaces.

Function	Description
RTrim	Removes spaces from the end of a string.
Space	Generates a string containing a specified number of space characters. Similar to the *StrDup* function.
Split	Splits a string into an array of substrings based on a delimiter.
Str	Converts a number to its string representation.
StrComp	Compares two strings, and returns an integer indicating their sort order.
StrConv	Converts a string to a new format based on a conversion code. Some of the conversions involve changing the case of the content.
StrDup	Generates a string containing a specified number of a given character. Similar to the *Space* function, but works with any character.
StrReverse	Reverses the characters in a string.
Trim	Removes spaces from the start and end of a string.
UCase	Converts a string to its uppercase equivalent.

Variables created as *System.String* (or Visual Basic *String*) each include several properties and methods that provide features similar to the functions listed in Table 6-12. For instance, the *Length* property returns the number of characters in the string.

```
Dim simpleString As String = "abc"
MsgBox(simpleString.Length)   ' Displays '3'
MsgBox(Len(simpleString))     ' Also displays '3'
```

You can use either the intrinsic Visual Basic functions or the equivalent *System.String* methods and properties in your code. Each technique provides the same result, although the syntax details and options may vary.

Other Functions

Visual Basic includes several functions that refuse to be squeezed into any of the other categories. Table 6-13 documents these functions.

Table 6-13 Visual Basic Miscellaneous Functions

Function	Description
DirectCast	Converts a value from one data type to another. Similar to the *TryCast* and *CType* functions.
ErrorToString	Returns the string representation of an error code. This only works with the system error codes previously available in Visual Basic 6.0, although these codes are still available in .NET.
IsArray	Indicates whether the data supplied to this function is a valid array or not.
IsDBNull	Indicates whether the data supplied to this function is a valid NULL database value or not.
IsError	Indicates whether the data supplied to this function is a valid error condition or not.
IsNothing	Indicates whether the data supplied to this function is undefined, or set to *Nothing*.
IsReference	Indicates whether the data supplied to this function is a reference type or a value type.
QBColor	Returns a color code from a small set of predefined colors.
RGB	Returns a color code built from the individual red, green, and blue components.
SystemTypeName	Given a Visual Basic data type name, this function returns the equivalent .NET data type name.
TryCast	Converts a value from one data type to another. Similar to the *DirectCast* and *CType* functions.
TypeName	Returns a data type name that summarizes the data type of the supplied content. The returned string is not necessarily the name of the value's actual data type.
VarType	Returns a code indicating the general data type of the supplied content.

Summary

When you're working with Visual Basic, you're working with data. The data types included with Visual Basic are simply wrappers for the core data types in .NET, but Visual Basic also adds many functions and features that enhance your ability to manage and organize data.

Project

You look tired. Why don't you take a five-minute break, and then we'll dive into the project code.

Welcome back! In this chapter, we'll use the data type and function features we read about to design some general support routines that will be used throughout the program. All of this code will appear in a Visual Basic module named *General*, all stored in a project file named *General.vb*.

Project Access Load the "Chapter 6 (Before) Code" project, either through the New Project templates, or by accessing the project directly from the installation directory. To see the code in its final form, load "Chapter 6 (After) Code" instead.

I've already added the *General.vb* file with its module starting and ending blocks.

```
Friend Module General

End Module
```

All of the code we add in this chapter will appear between these two lines. Remember, modules are a lot like classes and structures, but you can't create instances of them; all of their members are shared with all parts of your source code. This allows them to be used anywhere in the application. We don't need to do anything special to make them available to the entire program, other than to set the access level of each member as needed.

First, we'll add some general constants used throughout the program. Back in Visual Basic 6.0, I would have called these "global constants." But now they are simply shared members of the *General* module. Add the following code just below the "Module General" statement.

Insert Snippet Insert Chapter 6, Snippet Item 1.

```
' ----- Public constants.
Public Const ProgramTitle As String = "The Library Project"
Public Const NotAuthorizedMessage As String = _
   "You are not authorized to perform this task."
Public Const UseDBVersion As Integer = 1


' ----- Constants for the MatchingImages image list.
Public Const MatchPresent As Integer = 0
Public Const MatchNone As Integer = 1

Public Enum LookupMethods As Integer
   ByTitle = 1
   ByAuthor = 2
   ...remaining items excluded for brevity...
End Enum

Public Enum LibrarySecurity As Integer
   ManageAuthors = 1
   ...remaining items excluded for brevity...
   ViewAdminPatronMessages = 23
End Enum
Public Const MaxLibrarySecurity As LibrarySecurity = _
   LibrarySecurity.ViewAdminPatronMessages
```

These constants and enumerations are pretty self-explanatory based on their Pascal-cased names. *UseDBVersion* will be used to ensure that the application matches the database being used when multiple versions of each are available. The *MatchPresent* and *MatchNone* constants will be used for library item lookups.

The two enumerations define codes that specify the type of library item lookup to perform (*LookupMethods*), and the security codes used to limit the features that a specific administrator will be able to perform in the application (*LibrarySecurity*).

It's time to add some methods. The first method, *CenterText*, centers a line of text within a specific width. For instance, if you had the string "Hello, World" (12 characters in length) and you wanted to center it on a line that could be up to 40 characters long, you would need to add

14 spaces to the start of the line (determined by subtracting 12 from 40, and then dividing the result by 2). The routine uses a couple of the string-specific Visual Basic functions (like *Trim*, *Left*, and *Len*) to manipulate and test the data, and the Integer Division "\" operator to help calculate the number of spaces to insert.

Insert Snippet Insert Chapter 6, Snippet Item 2.

```
Public Function CenterText(ByVal origText As String, _
     ByVal textWidth As Integer) As String
  ' ----- Center a piece of text in a field width. If the
  '       text is too wide, truncate it.
  Dim resultText As String

  resultText = Trim(origText)
  If (Len(resultText) >= textWidth) Then
     ' ----- Truncate as needed.
     Return Trim(Left(origText, textWidth))
  Else
     ' ----- Start with extra spaces.
     Return Space((textWidth - Len(origText)) \ 2) & _
        resultText
  End If
End Function
```

The function starts by making a copy of the original string (*origText*), removing any extra spaces with the *Trim* function. It then tests that result to see if it will even fit on the line. If not, it chops off the trailing characters that won't fit, and returns that result. For strings that do fit on a line *textWidth* characters wide, the function adds the appropriate number of spaces to the start of the string, and returns the result.

Code snippet #2 also added a function named *LeftAndRightText*. It works just like *CenterText*, but it puts two distinct text strings at the extreme left and right ends of a text line. Any questions? Great. Let's move on.

Code snippet #3 adds a routine named *DigitsOnly*. It builds a new string made of just the digits found in a source string, *origText*. It does this by calling the *IsNumeric* function for each character in *origText*, one at a time. Each found digit is then concatenated to the end of *destText*.

Insert Snippet Insert Chapter 6, Snippet Item 3.

```
Public Function DigitsOnly(ByVal origText As String) As String
    ' ----- Return only the digits found in a string.
    Dim destText As String
    Dim counter As Integer

    ' ----- Examine each character.
    destText = ""
    For counter = 1 To Len(origText)
        If (IsNumeric(Mid(origText, counter, 1))) Then _
            destText &= Mid(origText, counter, 1)
    Next counter
    Return destText
End Function
```

The last two functions, *CountSubStr* and *GetSubStr*, count and extract substrings from larger strings, based on a delimiter. Visual Basic includes two functions, *Mid* and *GetChar*, that also extract substrings from larger strings, but these are based on the position of the substring. The *CountSubStr* and *GetSubStr* examine substrings by first using a delimiter to break the larger string into pieces.

Insert Snippet Insert Chapter 6, Snippet Item 4.

The *CountSubStr* function counts how many times a given substring appears in a larger string. It uses Visual Basic's *InStr* function to find the location of a substring (*subText*) in a larger string (*mainText*). It keeps doing this until it reaches the end of *mainText*, maintaining a running count (*totalTimes*) of the number of matches.

```
Public Function CountSubStr(ByVal mainText As String, _
        ByVal subText As String) As Integer
    ' ----- Return a count of the number of times that
    '       a subText occurs in a string (mainText).
    Dim totalTimes As Integer
    Dim startPos As Integer
    Dim foundPos As Integer
```

```
      totalTimes = 0
      startPos = 1

      ' ----- Keep searching until we don't find it no more!
      Do
         ' ----- Search for the subText.
         foundPos = InStr(startPos, mainText, subText)
         If (foundPos = 0) Then Exit Do
         totalTimes = totalTimes + 1

         ' ----- Move to just after the occurrence.
         startPos = foundPos + Len(subText)
      Loop

      ' ----- Return the count.
      Return totalTimes
End Function
```

Just to be more interesting than I already am, I used a different approach to implement the *GetSubStr* function. This function returns a delimited section of a string. For instance, the following statement gets the third comma-delimited portion of *bigString*.

```
bigString = "abc,def,ghi,jkl,mno"
MsgBox(GetSubStr(bigString, ",", 3))  ' Displays: ghi
```

I used Visual Basic's *Split* function to break the original string (*origString*) into an array of smaller strings (*stringParts*), using *delim* as the breaking point. Then I return element number *whichField* from the result. Because *whichField* starts with 1 and the array starts at 0, I must adjust the position to return the correct element.

```
Public Function GetSubStr(ByVal origString As String, _
     ByVal delim As String, ByVal whichField As Integer) _
     As String
   ' ----- Extracts a delimited string from another
   '       larger string.
   Dim stringParts() As String

   ' ----- Handle some errors.
   If (whichField < 0) Then Return ""
   If (Len(origString) < 1) Then Return ""
   If (Len(delim) = 0) Then Return ""
```

```
' ----- Break the string up into delimited parts.
stringParts = Split(origString, delim)

' ----- See if the part we want exists and return it.
If (whichField > UBound(stringParts) + 1) Then Return "" _
    Else Return stringParts(whichField - 1)
End Function
```

If these functions seem simple to you, then great! Most Visual Basic code is no more difficult than these examples. Sure, you might use some unfamiliar parts of the Framework Class Library, or interact with things more complicated than strings and numbers. But the overall structure will be similar. Most source code is made up of assignment statements, tests using the *If* statement, loops through data using a *For...Next* or similar statement, and function calls. And that's just what we did in these short methods.

CHAPTER 7

WINDOWS FORMS

William Shakespeare wrote, "All the world's a form, and all the controls and labels merely players: They have their exit events and their entrance events; and one control in its time exposes many properties" (from "As You Code It," Act 2.7.0). Although .NET was still in beta when he penned these words, they apply perfectly to any Windows Forms application you write even today.

The .NET technology known as **Windows Forms** includes all of the classes and features needed to develop standard "desktop" applications for Microsoft Windows. In the early days of Windows, this was pretty much the only type of program you could write for the platform. But now it is just one of many application types, along with console applications, Web ("Web Forms") applications, and services.

Inside a Windows Application

If you're new to development on the Windows system, writing applications in the .NET Framework may keep you from a full appreciation of what really happens inside a Windows application, and from being involuntarily committed to an asylum. That's because the internals of Windows application are no fun.

Windows was originally developed as an application running within MS-DOS, and this had a major impact on the design of Windows and of any applications running within its pseudo-operation-system environment. The latest releases of Windows are true operating systems, no longer dependent on MS-DOS. But the programming methodology was left unchanged for backward compatibility. Applications written in Visual Basic for .NET still use this Windows 1.0 technology internally, but it is mostly hidden by the many well-designed classes of the Windows Forms package.

Everything Is a Window

Rumors abound about why Microsoft attached the name "Windows" to its flagship product. Some say it represented the "Windows of Usability and Opportunity" that users would gain by using the enhanced Graphical User Interface. Some believe it represents the building cavity through which Microsoft executives promised to toss several key developers and managers if the product bombed. But the name actually refers to the different elements that appear on-screen when using Windows and its included applications. In short, everything you see on the screen is either a window, or appears within a window: all form, all controls, all scroll bars, and all display elements. Figure 7-1 points out some of the windows within a typical Microsoft Windows 2.0 display.

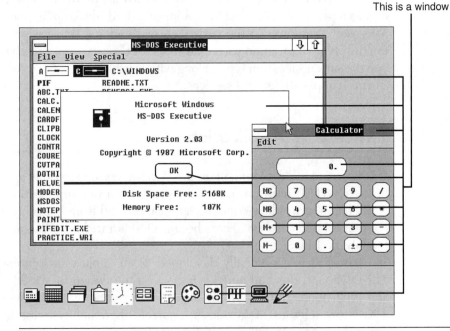

Figure 7-1 Some of the many windows of Windows 2.0

Every main application window was clearly a "window," as were all push buttons, text entry fields, checkbox and radio selection buttons, list boxes, and "combo" boxes (with a separate window for the "drop-down" portion). Static text and graphic images were drawn on a window's surface, and did not embody windows by themselves. But certainly there could be hundreds of windows on display at any one time.

Although the original developers on the Windows project team suffered from a deplorable lack of originality in the area of feature naming, Microsoft compensated for this somewhat with its release of Visual Basic. While everything was still a window internally, Microsoft divided the public world of windows into two hemispheres: **forms** and **controls**. There were always some internal differences between these two types of windows, and the new names did a lot to bring normalcy to the Windows application development situation. Microsoft elected to keep these useful monikers when it implemented the Windows Forms package.

Messages and the Message Pump

When you interact with Windows, it's pretty easy for you (as a human) to detect the different forms and controls on the screen. The image of Windows 2.0 I showed you in Figure 7-1 looks like a typical Windows screen, with its ability to interact with the keyboard and mouse, but it isn't. Go ahead; try to tap Figure 7-1 with your finger. You can tap all day long, but except for putting a hole in the page and not being able to get your money back on the book, nothing else will happen. But while you're tapping, you could shout out, "I just tapped on the 'OK' button," or "I just tapped on the '4' button of the 'Calculator' window."

This is what Microsoft Windows does for you. Windows keeps a list of all windows displayed on the screen, how they overlap and obscure each other, and which application each window belongs to. (Some applications are broken into multiple "threads" that all run at the same time. In such programs, Windows keeps track of all windows on a per-thread basis, not just on a per-application basis.) Each user input action (like mouse clicks and key presses) gets placed in the **system message queue** by the related device driver. As you click on the screen with your mouse, Windows extracts the system message from this queue, determines where you clicked, tries to figure out which window the mouse-click occurred on, and then informs that window's application about the mouse click by adding a **message** to the application's **message queue**. It does the same thing for keyboard input and other actions that a window might need to know about.

To function within the Windows environment, your application (or a specific thread within your application) includes a **message pump**, a block of code that monitors the message queue. Each incoming message includes the ID number of the intended window. The code extracts the message from the queue, and routes it to the **window procedure** (also called a **WndProc**) of the appropriate window for final processing. In the C language, this message pump looks somewhat like this.

```
while (!done)
{
    /* ----- Extract and examine the next message. */
    MSG msg;
    if (GetMessage(&msg, NULL, 0, 0))
    {
        /* ----- WM_QUIT means it's time to exit the program. */
        if (msg.message == WM_QUIT)
            done = true;

        /* ----- Send the message to the right window. */
        TranslateMessage(&msg);
        DispatchMessage(&msg);
    }
}
```

I know, I know. It makes you glad that you write in Visual Basic.

So, each application (actually, each thread within an application) has one message pump, but multiple window procedures. The message pump exists to route incoming messages to the correct window procedure.

Window Procedures

Just as the message pump dispatches messages to distinct window procedures, the WndProc routine directs processing to individual code blocks or procedures based on the type of incoming message. Here's a general logic outline (pseudocode) that shows the structure of a typical window procedure:

```
If (message type is a mouse click)
    Do mouse-click related code
Else If (message type is a key press)
    Do key-press related code
Else If (message type is a window resize)
   Do window-resizing-related code
Else...
```

(The pseudocode uses successive *If* statements, but an actual window procedure would more commonly use a *Select Case* type of statement to process the incoming message.) So the window procedure is like a vending machine. If the customer pushes the cola button, do the processing that returns a can of cola. If the customer presses the chewing gum button, do the processing that returns chewing gum. If the customer presses the coin return button, keep the money.

So, for each type of message (at least those that the program wants to handle), there is some related code that gets processed when a message arrives. Boy, that really sounds familiar, but I just can't seem to recall what . . . **events**! This sounds just like events in Visual Basic. And so it does. Even way back in Visual Basic 1.0, all generated applications included a message pump and WndProc procedures for each window. The primary task of these WndProc procedures was to call the code in your Visual Basic event handlers.

Windows in .NET

Take it from someone who used to write Windows applications in the 'C' language: Writing message pumps and window procedures isn't a lot of fun. Microsoft did try to mask some of the tedium with a variety of technologies, including "Message Crackers" and "MFC." It was Visual Basic that finally succeeded in burying the complexity under a programmer-friendly logical system.

The .NET Framework uses a system that is quite similar to that of older Visual Basic implementations, having the WndProc call custom event handlers written by you. It bundles up all this power and simplicity in a technology called Windows Forms. All of its classes appear in the *System.Windows.Forms* namespace. Many of these classes implement specific types of windows, such as ordinary main windows, buttons, text boxes, drop-down combo box lists, and so on.

If you really want to, you can still access the message pump and the various WndProc routines. Each window-specific class includes a *WndProc* method that you can override and craft yourself. The message pump is found in the *System.Windows.Forms.Application.Run* method. You could commandeer any of these components and control the whole ball of wax yourself, but you'll soon find out that the Windows Forms development process is so pleasant, you will work hard to forget what "message pump" even means.

Forms and Controls

In .NET, as in older versions of Visual Basic, windows are grouped into "Forms" and "Controls." But they are still all windows, built from the same core components. If you don't believe me, check out the classes for the various forms and controls in .NET. Both forms and controls derive from the common *System.Windows.Forms.Control* class, which abstracts the core Windows "window" functionality.

Some of the controls supplied with .NET (and also with the older Visual Basic) don't actually implement on-screen window elements. These controls—such as the "Timer" control—include no user interface experience, but do provide a programming experience that is similar to that of the visible controls. I'll list the specific controls a little later in this chapter, and indicate which ones are not user interface controls.

Designing Windows Forms Applications

Creating a Windows Forms application in Visual Basic is easy. Let's try it. Start Visual Studio and select **New Project . . .** from the **File** menu. The *New Project* form appears, as shown in Figure 7-2.

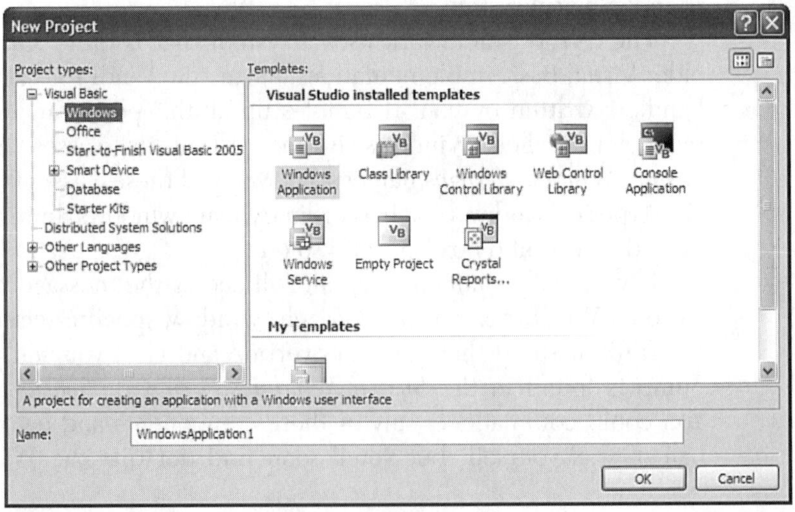

Figure 7-2 Visual Studio's New Project form

Give the project any name you want in the **Name** field, and then click **OK**. The new project has a single form ("Form1") all ready for you to use. At this point, Visual Studio has already added about 250 lines of source code to your application. If you click on the "Show All Files" button in the *Solution Explorer* panel (described way back in Chapter 1, Figure 1-13) and open the various files in the project, you can see the code for yourself. Some of the most interesting code is in the "Form1.Designer.vb" file, slightly edited here.

```
Partial Public Class Form1
    Inherits System.Windows.Forms.Form

    'Required by the Windows Form Designer
    Private components As System.ComponentModel.IContainer

    'NOTE: The following procedure is required by
    'the Windows Form Designer
    'It can be modified using the Windows Form Designer.
    'Do not modify it using the code editor.
    <System.Diagnostics.DebuggerStepThrough()> _
    Private Sub InitializeComponent()
        components = New System.ComponentModel.Container()
        Me.AutoScaleMode = _
            System.Windows.Forms.AutoScaleMode.Font
        Me.Text = "Form1"
    End Sub
End Class
```

All of the code that implements a form's behavior appears in the *Form* class in the *System.Windows.Forms* namespace. This project's initial form, *Form1*, inherits from that base form, receiving all of *Form*'s functionality and default settings. Any custom design-time changes made to *Form1*'s user interface, such as adding child controls, are added to the *InitializeComponent* procedure automatically as you use Visual Studio. Check out the routine periodically to see how it changes.

Most programs will have multiple forms. How does .NET know which of your forms should appear first when your program first runs? You indicate the starting location through the project's properties, via the **Startup Form** field on the *Application* tab (see Figure 7-3). (The project properties window appears when you select the **Project ▶ Properties** menu command in Visual Studio, or when you double-click on the "My Project" item in the *Solution Explorer*.)

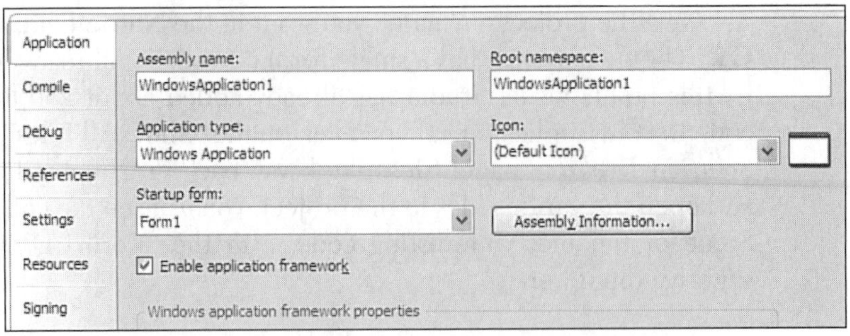

Figure 7-3 The startup options for a Windows Forms application

When a .NET application begins, the Framework calls a method named *Main* somewhere in your code. You indicate which form's *Main* routine is used through the **Startup Form** field. It includes a list of all forms; just choose the one you want. But wait, you haven't added a *Main* method to any of your forms? No problem. Visual Basic will write a simple *Main* routine on your behalf that will display the indicated form.

If you want to add a custom *Main* routine to your form, or to some other non-Form class in your application, that's no problem. If you uncheck the **Enable application framework** field on that same properties form, the **Startup Form** list changes to include any class in your application with a compatible *Main* routine. But the application framework, new with Visual Studio 2005, enables a lot of cool functionality, and all without any work on your part, so disable it only when you need precise control over the application's early lifetime.

If you do decide to write your own *Main* routine in a non-Form class, you'll eventually want to display your application's main form. Back in Visual Basic 6.0, whenever you wanted to display a form, you called its *Show* method:

```
Form1.Show
```

This simple syntax disappeared when the first .NET version of Visual Basic appeared in 2002, but it's returned with the 2005 release. Let's say that you wanted to start your application from a *Sub Main* procedure in a module separate from your main form. First, you need to add a new module to the project. Select the **Project ➤ Add Module** menu command. Modify the new *Module1* code module so that it looks like the following block of code.

```
Module Module1
   Public Sub Main()
      Form1.Show()
   End Sub
End Module
```

In the project's properties, uncheck the **Enable application framework** field, and select either "Module1" or "Sub Main" from the **Startup Form** list. That's pretty simple: Call *Module1*'s *Main* method, show the *Form1* form, and you're done. And in truth, if you run this program, you will be done pretty quickly. In fact, *Form1* will only appear for the briefest moment before exiting the program. Why didn't *Form1* stick around?

The program exited immediately because of that bothersome message pump, or more correctly, the lack of a message pump. Each window (or form or control) has a distinct *WndProc* procedure, but there is only one message pump for each application or thread. In this simple program, *Form1* has its own *WndProc* procedure, but it doesn't control the message pump by itself. You have to specifically tell the program to start running the message pump. Because the standard message pump for Windows Forms applications appears in the *System.Windows.Forms.Application.Run* method, altering the *Sub Main* code to include it will enable the pump and keep *Form1* displayed until the user closes the form or accidentally kicks the power cord out of the outlet.

```
Module Module1
   Public Sub Main()
      System.Windows.Forms.Application.Run(Form1)
   End Sub
End Module
```

You can add all sorts of initialization code to your *Sub Main* procedure, and show the main form only when your code is ready to interact with the user.

If you need to add a new form to your application, use the **Project ➤ Add Windows Form** menu command.

Working with Forms

In .NET, all forms are simply classes, variations of the *System.Windows. Forms.Form* class. Each time you create a new form, you are creating a derived class based on that common *Form* class. And your new class is loaded with functionality; it includes all of the fields, methods, bugs, properties, and events that make up the *Form* class. Visual Studio takes these elements and presents them in a way that makes it easy to program a form, both through source code and through the drag-and-drop interface of the Visual Studio Forms Designer.

When you first add a form to your application, it's kind of plain and boring. Use the Properties panel (see Figure 7-4) to adjust the form to your liking. This panel shows the principal properties for the currently selected item within the Visual Studio environment. It includes a separate entry for each property setting, most of which can be updated through simple text entry. For instance, you can alter the caption displayed at the top of the form by changing the content of the *Text* property from "Form1" to "Cool Form."

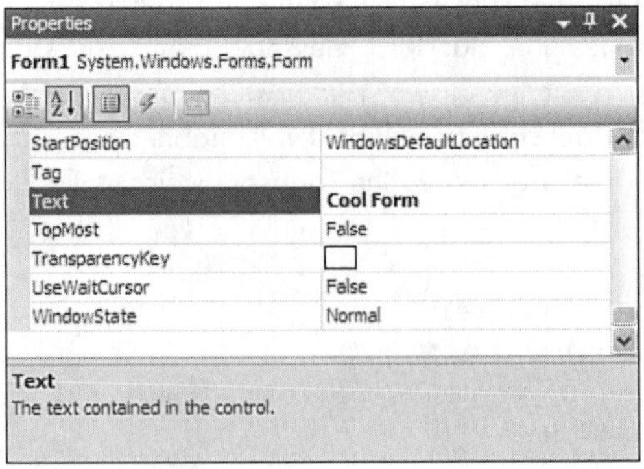

Figure 7-4 The properties of your form

Table 7-1 lists some of the more interesting form properties and their uses.

Table 7-1 Form Properties

Property	Description
(Name)	This is the name of the form, or more correctly, of the class that is the form. By default, it is named "Form*x*" where *x* is some number. It needs to be changed to something informative.
AcceptButton	Indicates which *Button* control already placed on the form should be triggered when the user presses the Enter key.
AutoScroll	If you set this field to True, the form automatically adds scroll bars that move around the contents of the form if the form is sized too small to show everything.
BackColor	The background color. Uses a specific or general system color.
BackgroundImage	Use this property, along with the *BackgroundImageLayout* property, to place a graphic on the background of the form.
CancelButton	This is just like the *AcceptButton* property, but the assigned button is triggered by the Escape key, not the Enter key.
ContextMenuStrip	This property lets you create a custom shortcut menu that appears when the user right-clicks on the background of the form. *ContextMenuStrip* refers to a separate control that you add to the form.
ControlBox	You hide or show the control box in the upper-left corner of the form through this property setting.
Cursor	Indicates the style of mouse cursor that appears when the mouse is over the form. This property demonstrates one of the many editors that appear within the properties window. If you click the "down arrow" at the right of the property setting, it displays a graphic list of all included mouse cursors. Click an image to get the one you want. (Other properties include custom editors designed for their type of content.) This list only includes the built-in cursors. You can also modify this property in the form's source code if you need to set the cursor to a custom graphic.
FormBorderStyle	This property indicates the type of form to display. The default is *Sizable*, which lets the user resize the form by dragging the bottom-right corner. If you set this property to *None*, the form's title bar and borders disappear. You would use this setting for an application's "Splash" welcome form, which normally has no form border.

(continues)

Table 7-1 Form Properties *(continued)*

Property	Description
Icon	Sets the graphic displayed in the upper-left corner of the form's border.
IsMdiContainer	Enables "multiple document interface" support on this form. This allows a master form to "contain" multiple child document forms. Visual Studio itself can display forms and source code windows in the MDI style.
KeyPreview	If you set this property to *True*, the form's *KeyDown* and *KeyPress* events will get to process any keys entered by the user, even if those keys were destined for a control contained on the form. This is useful when you need to capture keys that apply to the entire form, such as using the F1 key used to trigger online help.
Location	Sets the top and left position of the form on the screen. The *StartPosition* property also impacts the location of the form.
MainMenuStrip	Identifies the *MenuStrip* control to use for the form's main menu. The referenced *MenuStrip* control is added separately to the form.
MaximizeBox	Indicates whether the "maximum box" appears in the upper-right corner of the form. This button lets the user show a form in "full screen" mode.
MinimizeBox	Indicates whether the "minimize box" appears in the upper-right corner of the form. This button lets the user send the form to the system task bar.
MinimumSize	On forms that can be resized, this property indicates the minimum allowed size of the form. The user will not be able to size the form any smaller than this. This property, like some of the others, is a *composite property*, built by merging two or more other properties. In this case, it is built from distinct *Width* and *Height* sub-properties.
Opacity	Allows you to specify the level of transparency for a distinct color that appears on the form (set via the *TransparencyKey* field). Setting this field to 100% means that that color is fully displayed with no transparency; setting it to 0% makes that color fully transparent. You can set this property anywhere from 0% to 100%. Anything that appears behind the form will be partially or completely visible through the transparent portions of this form.

Property	Description
ShowInTaskbar	Specifies whether this form should appear as an item in the system task bar.
Size	Indicates the current size of the form through distinct *Width* and *Height* sub-properties.
StartPosition	Specifies how the form should be placed on the screen when it first appears. It is set through a list of predefined values, which actually link to an enumeration.
Tag	You can put any type of data you want in this property; it's there for your use.
Text	The form's display caption is set through this field.
TopMost	If set to *True*, this form will appear on top of all others, even when it is not the active form.
TransparencyKey	Indicates the color to use for transparency when the *Opacity* field is other than 100%.
Visible	Indicates whether the form is currently visible or not.
WindowState	Identifies the current state of the window: normal, maximized, or minimized.

I only listed about half of the available properties; clearly you have a lot of control over the form and how it is presented to the user. What's really interesting is that many of these properties are not limited to just forms. Some of these properties come from the shared *System.Windows.Forms.Control* class, and also appear in all other controls. This includes properties like *Visible*, *Location*, *BackColor*, and *Text*. Although the text displayed in a form's caption and the text displayed on a command button differ significantly in their presentation, the usage through code is identical.

```
Form1.Text = "This is a form caption."
Button1.Text = "This is a button caption."
```

Although you can set all of the properties in Table 7-1 through the Properties panel, you can also update and view them through code. In fact, if you've modified any of the properties through the Properties panel, then you've already updated them through source code, because Visual Studio is just updating your code for you. Try it out! Set the form's *TopMost* property to *True*, and then view the *InitializeComponent* routine in the *Form1.Designer.vb* file. You'll find the following new statement near the bottom of the method.

```
Me.TopMost = True
```

I know what you're thinking: "I'm a programmer, but my text editor is having all of the programming fun. When do I get a chance to modify properties through code?" That's a fair question. Properties are pretty easy to modify. You just name the object to be modified along with the property name and its new value, as Visual Studio did with the *TopMost* property.

```
Me.Text = "The Library Project"
```

You can also retrieve the property values by naming them.

```
MsgBox("The form's caption is: " & Me.Text)
```

You access the form's various methods in much the same way. For instance, the *Close* method closes the form.

```
Me.Close()
```

Of course, these statements need to appear within some valid procedure, such as an event handler. Let's add some code to the form's *Click* event so that when the user clicks on the form, the new code will alter the form's caption, remind us what that caption is, and close the form, causing the program to exit. What a great program! Access the form's source code by selecting *Form1.vb* in the *Solution Explorer*, and then clicking on the View Code button at the top of the *Solution Explorer*. The form's default code block appears.

```
Public Class Form1

End Class
```

As you remember from earlier in the chapter, this is the tourist portion of the *Form1* class, the part that Visual Studio shows to the public (you), and not the more interesting hidden parts (the part in *Form1.Designer.vb*). But we'll be able to make this section interesting in no time. Add a *Click* event to the form's surface by selecting "(Form1 Events)" from the **Class**

Name list (above and to the left of the code text editor), and then selecting "Click" from the **Method Name** drop-down list to its right, as shown in Figure 7-5.

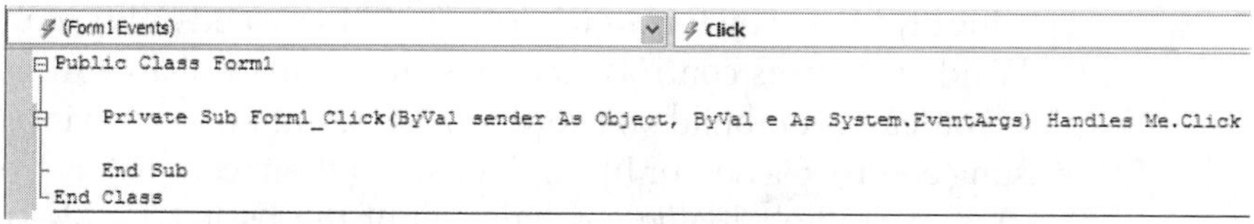

```
(Form1 Events)                                               Click
Public Class Form1

    Private Sub Form1_Click(ByVal sender As Object, ByVal e As System.EventArgs) Handles Me.Click

    End Sub
End Class
```

Figure 7-5 Adding a Click event to the form

Modify the event handler so that it displays the code listed here.

```
Private Sub Form1_Click(ByVal sender As Object, _
     ByVal e As System.EventArgs) Handles Me.Click
  Me.Text = "The Library Project"
  MsgBox("The form's caption is: " & Me.Text)
  Me.Close()
End Sub
```

If you run this code and click on the form's surface, a message box appears with the form's caption just before the application exits (see Figure 7-6).

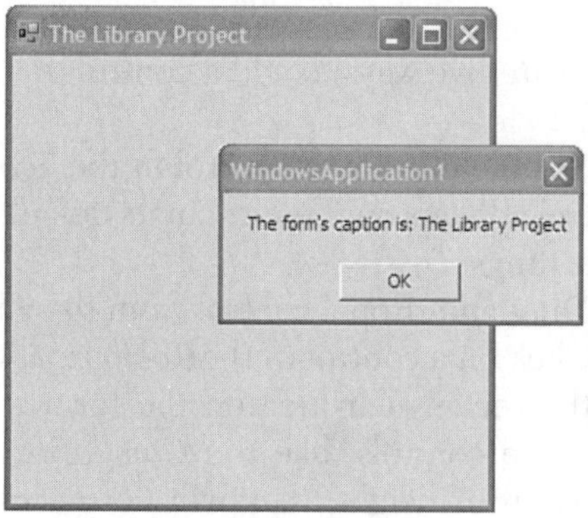

Figure 7-6 A program that communicates when clicked

Adding Controls

New forms are like blank canvases, and like the great painters before us, we have available a large palate of colorful tools at our disposal. In Visual Studio, these tools are in the form of **controls**, .NET classes designed specifically for use on form surfaces. Visual Basic and .NET include dozens of Windows Forms controls, and even more are available from third parties. You can even build your own controls, either by deriving them from existing control classes, or by implementing them completely from scratch.

Visual Studio's *Toolbox* includes all of the basic controls you need to build high-quality, or even pathetic low-quality, software applications. Access the *Toolbox*, part of which appears in Figure 7-7, through the **View** ➤ **Toolbox** menu command.

Figure 7-7 Visual Studio's Toolbox with Windows Forms controls

There are five ways to add a control to a form.

1. Double-click on a control in the *Toolbox*. An instance of the control appears on the form in its default location with all of its default settings.
2. Drag-and-drop a control from the *Toolbox* to the form.
3. Click on a control in the *Toolbox*, and then use the mouse to draw the rectangular area on the form where the control will appear. Some controls, like the *ComboBox* control, have limits on their width or height; they will not necessarily size themselves as you intend.
4. Ask someone else to add the control to the form. This option is for the faint of heart. If you are reading this book, this option is not for you.

5. Add the control to the form using Visual Basic source code. As you add controls to the form in Visual Studio, it is writing source code for you on your behalf. There is no reason why you can't add such code yourself. Although there are warnings in the *Form1.Designer.vb* file telling you not to edit the file, you can hand-modify the *InitializeComponents* routine if you properly conform to the code style generated by Visual Studio. You can also add controls in other areas of your code, such as in the form's *Load* event. Adding controls dynamically is beyond the scope of this book, but go ahead, experiment.

Some controls have no true user-interface presence in a running application. These controls, when added to your form, appear in a panel just below the form's surface. You can still interact with them just like form-based controls.

Once a control appears on the form, use the mouse to move the control, or resize it using the resizing anchors that appear when the control is selected. Some forms also include a small arrow-button, often near the upper-right corner of the control. These are **Smart Tags**, similar to the Smart Tags feature included in Microsoft Office. Clicking the Smart Tag provides access to useful features associated with the control, as shown in Figure 7-8.

Figure 7-8 The Smart Tag for a ComboBox control

Table 7-2 lists some of the more commonly used controls, all included by default with a new Windows Forms application. If you create a "Web Forms" application in Visual Studio—used to design web-based applications with ASP.NET—the available controls will differ from this list. See Chapter 22, "Web Development," for a discussion of ASP.NET applications.

Table 7-2 Windows Forms Controls Available in Visual Studio

Icon	Control	Description
	BackgroundWorker	.NET includes support for multi-threaded applications. The *BackgroundWorker* control lets you initiate a background task right from the comfort of your own form. It's especially useful when you wish to update form-based display elements interactively with the another "worker" thread. You kick off the new work task through this control's *RunWorkerAsync* method, and perform the actual work in its *DoWork* event.
	Button	A standard push button. A button's *Click* event is its most common programmatic feature, although you can also use its *DialogResult* property to trigger a dialog-specific action.
	CheckBox	This control implements a two-way (on, off) or three-way (on, off, other) "checked" selection field. The *ThreeState* property indicates the total number of choices. Use the *Checked* Boolean property for two-way checkboxes, or the *CheckState* property for three-way checkboxes.
	CheckedListBox	The *CheckedListBox* control combines the best of the *ListBox* and *CheckBox* worlds, giving you a list where each item can be checked in a two-way or three-way manner. The *GetItemChecked* and *GetItemCheckState* methods (and their "Set" counterparts) provide one of the many ways to examine the status of items in the list. Be aware of a similar control named *CheckBoxList*; it is for use in ASP.NET applications only.

Icon	Control	Description
	ColorDialog	Displays the standard Windows form used for color selection by the user. Display the color dialog using this control's *ShowDialog* method, getting the result via the *Color* property.
	ComboBox	This control implements the standard Windows drop-down *ComboBox* control, in all its various styles. The list of items can include any objects you wish; it is not just limited to strings. You can also provide custom "ownerdraw" code that lets you draw each list item yourself.
	ContextMenuStrip	This control lets you design a shortcut or "context" menu, to be displayed when the user right-clicks on the form or the control of your choice. It is designed and used in much the same way as the standard *MenuStrip* control.
	DataGridView	The *DataGridView* control implements a standard table-like grid used to display or edit data in individual cells. It is loaded with more display options than you can shake a stick at. The displayed data can be bound to some external data source, or you can make it up on the fly. A "virtual data" mode also lets you load data only as needed.
	DateTimePicker	The *DateTimePicker* control lets the user enter a date, a time, or both, either through basic text entry or mouse-based controls. Although not as free-form as a simple text field, it does enforce the selection of a date or time. You can set minimum and maximum boundaries on the user's selection. The *MonthCalendar* control provides an alternative interface for date-specific selection.

(continues)

Table 7-2 Windows Forms Controls Available in Visual Studio *(continued)*

Icon	Control	Description
	DomainUpDown	Through this control, the user selects one from among a list of choices that you define, choices that have a specific inherent order. Use this control as an alternative to a *ComboBox* or *TrackBar* control when warranted.
	FolderBrowserDialog	Displays the standard Windows form used for directory or folder selection by the user. Display the selection dialog using this control's *ShowDialog* method, getting the result via the *SelectedPath* property.
	FontDialog	Displays the standard Windows form used for font selection by the user. Displays the selection dialog using this control's *ShowDialog* method, getting the result via the *Font* property. Other properties provide access to components of the selected font.
	GroupBox	The *GroupBox* control provides a simple way to visibly group controls on a form. Subordinate controls are drawn or pasted directly onto the *GroupBox* control. To access similar functionality without the visible border or caption, use the *Panel* control.
	HelpProvider	The *HelpProvider* control lets you indicate online help details for other controls on the form. When used, it adds several extra "Help" pseudo-properties to each of the other form controls through which you can supply the help context details. When implemented properly, the indicated online help content will display when the user presses the F1 key in the context of the active control.

Icon	Control	Description
	HScrollBar	This control implements a horizontal scroll bar, allowing the user to scroll among a display region or list of choices. For a vertical implementation of this control, use the *VScrollBar* control. Several other controls include their own copy of these scroll bars.
	ImageList	The *ImageList* control encapsulates a set of small graphics or icons for use by other controls that support image lists. Image lists are commonly used by *ListView*, *Toolbar*, and *TreeView* controls.
A	Label	This control displays static text on a form. By using the various border and background properties, you can display simple lines and rectangles on a form. Visual Basic 6.0 included specific line and rectangle drawing controls, but they are not available in .NET. You must either simulate them using a *Label* control, or draw them yourself using the GDI+ drawing commands (which isn't that difficult—see Chapter 17, "GDI+").
A	LinkLabel	The *LinkLabel* control implements a static label that includes one or more "links" within the text content. These links are similar to the standard text links that appear in web browser content. The control calls its *LinkClicked* event handler when the user clicks on any of the embedded links.
	ListBox	This control implements the standard Windows list box control, displaying a list of items from which the user can select zero or more. The items can include any objects you wish; it is not just limited to strings. You can also provide custom "ownerdraw" code that lets you draw each list item yourself.

(continues)

Table 7-2 Windows Forms Controls Available in Visual Studio *(continued)*

Icon	Control	Description
	ListView	The *ListView* control presents a set of items with optional display properties. It is quite similar to the (pre-Vista) Windows File Explorer with all of its various display modes. You can add column-specific data for the "details" view. The items in the control appear as a set of *ListViewItem* class objects.
	MaskedTextBox	This variation of the standard text field helps the user enter formatted numeric or text data by displaying an entry template or mask. For instance, you can force the user to enter a telephone number in "xxx-xxx-xxxx" format by using a numeric mask with embedded hyphen characters.
	MenuStrip	This control lets you design standard form menus, which are displayed along the top of the user area of the form. Menus within the menu strip are implemented through *ToolStripMenuItem* class instances. The menu strip is a toolbar-like implementation of a standard Windows menu. (The older *MainMenu* control is still available if you need it.) You can add other types of controls to the menu, including toolbar-specific ComboBox controls. Context-sensitive menus, displayed when the user right-clicks on the form or a control, are implemented through the *ContextMenuStrip* control.
	MonthCalendar	The *MonthCalendar* control displays a subset of a calendar, focusing on a month-specific view. More than one month can be displayed at a time, in vertical, horizontal, or grid configurations. The *DateTimePicker* control provides an alternative interface for date-specific selection.

Icon	Control	Description
	NotifyIcon	The *NotifyIcon* control lets you place an icon in the "system tray" area of the Windows task bar, and communicate important messages to the user through this interface. Because this control has no form-specific user interface, it is possible to use it without having a standard form displayed.
	NumericUpDown	Allows the user to select a numeric value using a scrollable up/down section method. Use this control as an alternative to *HScrollBar*, *TextBox*, *TrackBar*, or *VScrollBar* controls when warranted.
	OpenFileDialog	Displays the standard Windows form used for "open" file selection by the user. The user can select one or more existing files from local or remote file systems. Display the selection dialog using this control's *ShowDialog* method, getting the result via the *FileName* or *FileNames* property. The *OpenFile* method provides a quick way to open the selected file.
	PageSetupDialog	Displays the standard Windows form used for page setup configuration by the user. Display the selection dialog using this control's *ShowDialog* method, getting the result via the *PageSettings* and *PrinterSettings* property.
	Panel	The *Panel* control logically groups controls on a form. Subordinate controls are drawn or pasted directly onto the *Panel* control. To access similar functionality with a visible border and user-displayed caption, use the *GroupBox* control.

(continues)

7. WINDOWS FORMS

Table 7-2 Windows Forms Controls Available in Visual Studio *(continued)*

Icon	Control	Description
	PictureBox	This control displays an image in a variety of formats. It should not be confused with the Visual Basic 6.0 *PictureBox* control, which is more closely related to the Windows Forms *Panel* control.
	PrintDialog	Displays the standard Windows form used for document printing and print properties selection by the user. Display the selection dialog using this control's *ShowDialog* method. This control is used in conjunction with an instance of the *System.Drawing.Printing.PrintDocument* class, which is created through code or via the *PrintDocument* control.
	PrintDocument	This control is used as part of the print and print preview process. It adds a wrapper around your custom print implementation, providing a consistent method of selecting and printing document pages.
	PrintPreviewDialog	This control provides a standardized interface for print preview, implementing all elements of the entire print preview dialog. When used with a *PrintDocument* class or control, it displays on-screen precisely what will appear on the final printed page. In fact, your printing code doesn't necessarily know if it is printing to the printer or the print preview display.
	ProgressBar	The *ProgressBar* provides graphical feedback to the user for a task completion range. Normally, the range goes from 0% to 100%, but you can supply a custom range. The *Value* property indicates the current setting between the *Minimum* and *Maximum* range limits.

Icon	Control	Description
	PropertyGrid	The *PropertyGrid* control allows the user to graphically edit specific members of an attached class instance. The Properties panel within the Visual Studio environment is an instance of this control. This control makes heavy use of class-based attributes to control the display and edit features of properties. Chapter 17 uses this control to support bar code label management in the Library Project.
	RadioButton	This control implements the standard Windows radio selection button. Although the circular "point" display is most common, the control can also appear as a toggle button by setting the *Appearance* property appropriately. The *Checked* property indicates the current value of a control. All *RadioButton* controls that appear within the same "group context" act in a mutually exclusive manner. Use the *Panel* and *GroupBox* controls to create specific group contexts.
	ReportViewer	The *ReportViewer* control allows you to design and display custom banded reports tied to collection or ADO.NET data sources. Using this control to design a report will add an ".rdlc" file to your project that contains the actual report design.
	SaveFileDialog	Displays the standard Windows form used for "save" file selection by the user. The user can select a new or existing file from local or remote file systems. The control optionally prompts the user to overwrite existing files. Display the selection dialog using this control's *ShowDialog* method, getting the result via the *FileName* property. The *OpenFile* method provides a quick way to open the selected file.

(continues)

Table 7-2 Windows Forms Controls Available in Visual Studio *(continued)*

Icon	Control	Description
	SplitContainer	This control adds a "split bar" by which you can divide your form into multiple sizeable regions, each of which contains a *Panel* control. Use the *Orientation* property to alter the direction of the split. The order in which you add *SplitContainer* controls to a form will impact the usability of the splits; experimentation is recommended.
	StatusStrip	This control displays a "status bar," usually along the bottom edge of a form, through which you can display status and other context-sensitive information to the user. The strip can contain multiple *ProgressBar*, *StatusStripPanel*, and *ToolStripLabel* controls. The older *StatusBar* control is still available if you need it.
	TabControl	The *TabControl* control lets you divide the controls of your form into multiple "tabbed" regions. Each named tab has an associated *TabPage* control, which works a lot like the *Panel* control. Add or paste subordinate controls directly to each *TabPage* control.
abl	TextBox	This control implements the standard Windows text box, both in its single-line and multi-line styles. The main body content is set through the *Text* property. The *PasswordChar* and *UseSystemPasswordChar* properties allow you to mask the input when accepting a user-supplied password.

7. WINDOWS FORMS

Icon	Control	Description
	Timer	This control triggers a timed event at an interval you specify. The size of the interval, in milliseconds, is set through the *Interval* property. If the *Enabled* property is set to *True*, the *Tick* event handler will be called at each met interval. Although you can set the interval as small as one millisecond, it is unlikely that you will achieve this frequency with today's hardware.
	ToolStrip	The *ToolStrip* control implements a toolbar on which other controls appear. It comes with a set of associated controls and classes that provide advanced rendering and user interaction features.
	ToolStripContainer	The *ToolStripContainer* control provides a convenient way to add *MenuStrip*, *StatusStrip*, and *ToolStrip* controls to the edges of a form.
	ToolTip	The *ToolTip* control lets you indicate a "tool tip" for other controls on the form. When used, it adds a "ToolTip" pseudo-property to each of the other form controls, through which you can supply the associated tool tip text. When the mouse hovers over a control with an assigned tool tip text, a small text window appears temporarily over the control to provide useful information to the user.
	TrackBar	The *TrackBar* control allows the user to make a selection among a small number of related and ordered values. Its real-world counterpart is the volume control on a radio. Use this control as an alternative to an *HScrollBar*, *NumericUpDown*, or *VScrollBar* control when warranted.

(continues)

Table 7-2 Windows Forms Controls Available in Visual Studio *(continued)*

Icon	Control	Description
	TreeView	The *TreeView* control presents a set of items in a hierarchical arrangement. It is quite similar to the "directory tree" portion of the (pre-Vista) Windows File Explorer. Each item in the tree is a "node" that can have zero or more child nodes.
	VScrollBar	This control implements a vertical scroll bar, allowing the user to scroll among a display region or list of choices. For a horizontal implementation of this control, use the *HScrollBar* control. Several other controls include their own copy of these scroll bars.
	WebBrowser	Implements a web browser within your application. You can use the standard web-based navigation features available within *Internet Explorer* for URL-based access, or provide your own custom HTML content through the *DocumentText* property or related properties.

Although there is no reasonable limit on the number of controls you can add to a form, there is a limit on how much information the user can experience on a single form without a direct wired connection to the brain. Don't go too wild.

Events and Delegates

Each form and control in a .NET application contains its own WndProc window procedure, and as it processes each incoming message from the message pump, it translates those messages into events. **Events** are the standard .NET technique that controls—and all other classes—use to say, "Hey, something is happening, and you might want to do something about it." When you include a form or control in your application, you can monitor one, some, or all of these events, and write custom code that responds appropriately. All of the custom code you write for each event appears in an **event handler**. But what actually happens between the finger of the user on the mouse and the logic in your custom event handler? Figure 7-9 shows you graphically what actually happens between action and custom logic.

1. The user clicks on a button.

Button1

2. Magic happens.

3. The event handler runs.

Private Sub Button1_Click(_
      ByVal sender As System. (
      ByVal e As System. Event/
      Handles Button1.Click
'–––––– Code here.
End Sub

Figure 7-9 What really happens when the user clicks a button

Clearly, there is still some mystery surrounding event processing.

Controls—and all classes—determine which events they will make available. For controls, many of the events parallel user-initiated actions: *Click*, *MouseDown*, *KeyPress*, *SizeChanged*. But there also many events that could only be triggered by modifications to the control through your source code: *TabIndexChanged* (when the tab-key order of the controls changes), *BackgroundImageChanged*, and *CursorChanged* are just three of the many events that the user cannot affect directly. A few final events tie to system-level changes, such as the *SystemColorsChanged* event, which fires when the user modifies the system-wide color scheme through the control panel.

Each event has not only a name (such as *Click*), but a set of parameters that the event handler will receive when called. Here's a typical event handler for a *Button* control.

```
Private Sub Button1_Click(ByVal sender As System.Object, _
   ByVal e As System.EventArgs) Handles Button1.Click

End Sub
```

This event handler receives two arguments from the triggering event: a *System.Object* instance (*sender*) and a *System.EventArgs* instance (*e*).

Other event handlers may use a slightly different set of arguments, so how do you know what to use? Any events defined within a control class must also indicate the number and type of arguments it will send to the event handler. Visual Basic includes an *Event* statement that defines events. Although the *Button* control was likely written in C#, here is a possible look at what the event definition for the *Button's Click* event might look like in Visual Basic.

```
Public Event Click(ByVal sender As System.Object, _
   ByVal e As System.EventArgs)
```

This definition sure looks a lot like the event handler, and it should. The *Event* statement establishes a parameter-passing contract between the control and any code that wants to receive event notifications. In this case, the *Click* event promises to send two arguments to the event handler. The first, *sender*, is a reference to the object that the event refers to. For *Button* controls, this parameter receives a reference to the *Button* instance itself. The second argument, *e*, provides a method for passing an entire object of additional information. The *System.EventArgs* class doesn't have much information, but some events use a variation of the second argument that uses *System.EventArgs* as its base class.

It turns out that the arguments used for the *Click* event are pretty common among the different controls and events. Instead of retyping the argument list in each *Event* statement, the designer of a control can define a **delegate**, a .NET type that defines an argument list and, for functions, a return value.

```
Public Delegate Sub StandardEventDelegate( _
   ByVal sender As System.Object, _
   ByVal e As System.EventArgs)
```

Event statements can then use the defined delegate as a shortcut for typing out the entire parameter list.

```
Public Event Click As StandardEventDelegate
```

Whether the *Event* statement uses a delegate or a full argument list, it has a firm grasp on what data it needs to send to any listening event handlers. And it sends those arguments using the Visual Basic *RaiseEvent* statement. Let's trace this process down for the *Button* control. When the user clicks on the button, the message pump finds a way to get a message to the WndProc procedure for the *Button* control. That control examines the message, sees it is a mouse click, and decides to tell event handlers about it. Then, from within the WndProc code, it raises the event.

```
RaiseEvent Click(Me, New System.EventArgs)
```

The Visual Basic *Me* keyword refers to the *Button* control instance itself. The *e* argument for a *Button* control contains no information beyond the default fields included in a *System.EventArgs* instance, so WndProc just sends a new empty instance. Controls with other event arguments would have created an instance first, filled it in with the relevant data, and passed that instance to the event handler.

If an event fires in an application, and there is no event handler to hear it, does it make a sound? Perhaps not. There is no requirement that an event have any active handlers listening. But when we do want to listen for an event, how do we do it? The standard way to do this in a Windows Forms application is a two-step process. First, the user of the control (your form class) needs to announce to the control, "I want to monitor your events." Then it attaches event handlers to specific events.

Earlier in the chapter, we saw that adding a control to the *Form1*'s user interface actually triggers Visual Studio to write source code in the *Form1.designer.vb* file. Here's the code added for a *Button* control named *Button1* (with line numbers).

```
01 Partial Class Form1
02    Inherits System.Windows.Forms.Form
03
04    Friend WithEvents Button1 As System.Windows.Forms.Button
05
06    Private Sub InitializeComponent()
07       Me.Button1 = New System.Windows.Forms.Button
08
09       Me.Button1.Location = New System.Drawing.Point(48, 16)
10       Me.Button1.Name = "Button1"
11       Me.Button1.Size = New System.Drawing.Size(75, 23)
12       Me.Button1.TabIndex = 0
13       Me.Button1.Text = "Button1"
14       Me.Button1.UseVisualStyleBackColor = True
15
16       Me.Controls.Add(Me.Button1)
17    End Sub
18 End Class
```

The code in the *InitializeComponent* method creates the *Button* control instance (line 07), modifies its properties to get just the look we want (lines 09 to 14), and attaches it to the form (line 16). But there is one additional line that defines the actual *Button1* reference type variable (line 04):

```
Friend WithEvents Button1 As System.Windows.Forms.Button
```

I talked about class-level fields in Chapter 6, "Data and Data Types," and *Button1* is just a typical class-level field. But it's the *WithEvents* keyword included in the statement that lets the control know that someone wants to monitor event notifications. Now, whenever a *Button1* event fires, it knows that *Form1* may contain event handlers that are watching and listening.

The second of our two-step event-to-handler connection process involves the actual connection of the handler. Let's look at the event handler definition again for the *Button1* instance.

```
Private Sub Button1_Click(ByVal sender As System.Object, _
    ByVal e As System.EventArgs) Handles Button1.Click


End Sub
```

It's just an ordinary class method, but with a *Handles* clause hanging off the end of the definition. This clause is what links the event with the *Button1.Click* event itself. You can follow the *Handles* keyword with multiple event names.

```
Private Sub ManyButtons_Click(ByVal sender As System.Object, _
    ByVal e As System.EventArgs) Handles Button1.Click, _
    Button2.Click, Button3.Click


End Sub
```

Now the single *ManyButtons_Click* event handler will listen for *Click* events from three different controls. You can even mix up the monitored events; one event handler can listen for different named events.

```
Private Sub ManyEvents(ByVal sender As System.Object, _
    ByVal e As System.EventArgs) Handles Button1.MouseDown, _
    Button2.MouseUp


End Sub
```

Another variation is to have multiple event handlers monitor a single event.

```
Private Sub FirstHandler(ByVal sender As System.Object, _
    ByVal e As System.EventArgs) Handles Button1.Click

End Sub

Private Sub SecondHandler(ByVal sender As System.Object, _
    ByVal e As System.EventArgs) Handles Button1.Click

End Sub
```

There is another way to connect events to event handlers that does not involve either the *WithEvents* keyword or the *Handles* keyword. Once you have an instance of an event-exposing class, you attach a handler to one of its events using the *AddHandler* statement. The following statement links *Button1's Click* event to an event handler named *MyHandler*. *MyHandler* must have the correct argument list for the defined event.

```
AddHandler Button1.Click, AddressOf MyHandler
```

A related *RemoveHandler* statement detaches a handler from an event.

There are a lot of complicated steps that take you from an initial user or system action to the code in an event handler. I've spent a lot of chapter space discussing exactly how events work, but with good reason. Events and event processing are core features of .NET application development. Eventually, you will spend so much time writing event handlers that it will all become second nature to you. But I also went into all of this detail so that you could take full advantage of this technology. Visual Basic not only lets you monitor controls for events, it lets you design new events into your own classes. You can use the *Delegate, Event, RaiseEvent, WithEvents, Handles, AddHandler,* and *RemoveHandler* keywords for your own custom events, triggered by whatever conditions you choose. If you have a class that represents an employee, you can have it trigger a *Fired* event whenever the employee loses his or her job. By adding custom events, you make it possible for custom code to be attached to your class logic, even if a programmer doesn't have access to your class' source code.

Making Forms Useful

Any form identified as your project's startup object appears automatically when the program begins. All other forms need to be displayed manually, using either the *Show* or *ShowDialog* methods of that form. For instance, if you have a form called *Form2*, you can display it using its *Show* method:

```
Form2.Show()
```

The *Show* method displays a **modeless form**. Modeless forms can be accessed independently from all other forms in the running application. All modeless forms can be activated at any time just by clicking on them; the form you click on will come to the front of the others and receive the input focus. A program might have one, two, or dozens of modeless forms open at once, and the user can move between them freely.

Modal forms take control of all input in the application for as long as they appear on-screen. Modal forms are commonly called "dialogs"; the user must complete a modal form and close it before any other open forms in the application can be accessed. The message box window that appears when you use the *MsgBox* function is a common modal dialog window. The *ShowDialog* method displays forms modally, and lets you return a value from that form. The values returned are the members of the *System.Windows.Forms.DialogResult* enumeration.

If you think of forms as works of literature by Alexandre Dumas, then modeless forms would be a lot like *The Three Musketeers*: All for one and one for all. They work with each other in support of the entire application. Modal forms are akin to *The Count of Monte Cristo*. Yes, there are other forms/characters in the application/story, but they are nothing when the Count is in view.

To display the Count—that is, a modal form—use the form's *ShowDialog* method, and optionally capture its return value.

```
Dim theResult As DialogResult
theResult = Form2.ShowDialog()
```

Modal dialogs are useful for editing some record that requires a click on the **OK** button when changes are complete. Let's say you were writing an application that displayed a list of books by Alexandre Dumas. It might include two forms: (1) a "parent" form that displays the list of books; and

(2) a "child" form that lets you type the name of a single book. Wouldn't it be great if you could return the name of the book (or, perhaps, an ID number of a record for the book as stored in a database) instead of a *DialogResult* value?

If the *ShowDialog* method, a public method of the underlying *Form* class, can return a result code, perhaps we can add another public method to a form that will return a result code that has actual meaning? Indeed we can. Consider the child form (named *BookEntry*) with a data entry field (*BookTitle*), and OK (*ActOK*) and Cancel (*ActCancel*) buttons, as shown in Figure 7-10.

Figure 7-10 Book title entry form

This simple form just returns whatever is typed in the field when the user clicks OK (first rejecting blank values), or returns a blank string on Cancel.

```
Public Class BookEntry
   Public Function EditTitle() As String
      ' ----- Show the form, and return what the user enters.
      If (Me.ShowDialog() = DialogResult.OK) Then
         Return BookTitle.Text.Trim
      Else
         Return ""
      End If
   End Function

   Private Sub ActCancel_Click(ByVal sender As System.Object, _
         ByVal e As System.EventArgs) Handles ActCancel.Click
      ' ----- Return a blank title for "Cancel."
      Me.DialogResult = DialogResult.Cancel
      ' ----- Continue with EditTitle()
   End Sub
```

```
Private Sub ActOK_Click(ByVal sender As System.Object, _
    ByVal e As System.EventArgs) Handles ActOK.Click
  ' ----- Only accept valid titles.
  If (Len(BookTitle.Text.Trim) = 0) Then
    MsgBox("Please supply a valid title.")
  Else
    Me.DialogResult = DialogResult.OK
    ' ----- Continue with EditTitle()
  End If
End Sub
End Class
```

To use this form, the parent calls the *EditTitle* method, which returns the book title entered by the user.

```
Dim newTitle As String = BookEntry.EditTitle()
```

The *EditTitle* routine shows the form modally with the *ShowDialog* method, and just sits there until the user closes the form. Closing the form is done through the OK or Cancel button events; setting the form's *DialogResult* property has the side effect of closing the form. Great!

Once the form closes, execution returns to *EditTitle*, which does a quick status check before returning the final value. And there we have it: a new public interface for a form's most important return value. We'll use this method a lot in the Library Project application.

Summary

Windows programming really hasn't changed much since Windows 1.0. It still does everything through messages, message queues, and window procedures. What has changed is the way that the code is abstracted for the benefit of the programmer. The .NET Framework's package for Windows development, Windows Forms, makes Windows desktop development easy and—dare I say it—fun!

Project

This chapter's project code implements the Library Project's basic "Main" form, as well as the "Splash" form that appears when the project first starts. Microsoft, knowing that this was a common need, included support for both main and splash forms in its new Application Framework system. By default, this system is enabled through the project properties' *Application* panel (see Figure 7-11).

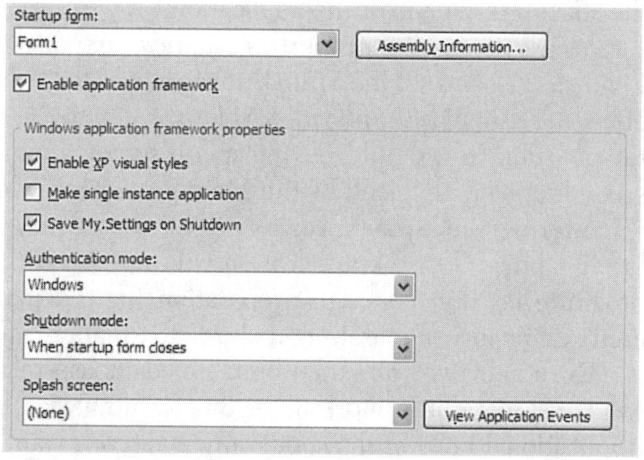

Figure 7-11 Main and splash fields identified through the project properties

The **Startup form** and **Splash screen** fields indicate the main and splash forms, respectively. It's quick, it's easy, and it's just the thing for us. So let's get to work. Now would be a great time to load the starter project for Chapter 7.

Project Access Load the "Chapter 7 (Before) Code" project, either through the New Project templates, or by accessing the project directly from the installation directory. To see the code in its final form, load "Chapter 7 (After) Code" instead.

Configuring the Splash Screen

I've already added a new form file to the project named *Splash.vb* (the form itself is named *Splash*), including some simple display elements to gussy it up somewhat. Check out the graphic on the form. It's presented through a *PictureBox* control, but it's stored in the application as a **resource**, a collection of strings and images attached to your source code. The *Resources* folder in the *Solution Explorer* includes this graphic file. It's linked into the picture box through that control's *Image* property. And it sure makes the form look pretty. Your job will be to attach this form into the startup sequence of the application.

Access the project properties' *Application* panel (which you just saw in Figure 7-11), and set the **Splash screen** field to "Splash." This has the side effect of setting *My.Application.SplashScreen* to the *Splash* form. Now run the program. You should see the splash screen appear for about 1/100 of a second, quickly replaced by the Main form. Hey, what was that?

Altering the **Splash screen** field does cause the splash screen to briefly appear, but the application will only keep it up until it thinks the program has done enough preparation for the main form. Because we aren't doing any preparation, it shows the main form right away.

Eventually we will add a bunch of database-related startup code that will consume a little more time. But for now we'll have to fake it. In the Application Framework model, any code you want to process when the program first begins appears in the application's *Startup* event. This event, new with Visual Basic 2005, is one of a small collection of events included with the *My* hierarchy. The source code for these events appears in the *ApplicationEvents.vb* file, a file that Visual Studio automatically adds to your project when needed. Use the **View Application Events** button on the project properties' *Application* panel to open that file's source code.

```
Namespace My
    Class MyApplication

    End Class
End Namespace
```

Let's pretend that the initialization required for the Library Project takes about three seconds. .NET includes a *Sleep* method that delays the code for a specific number of milliseconds. Code snippet 1 adds the *Startup* event handler for the application. Add it between *MyApplication's Class* and *End Class* keywords.

Insert Snippet Insert Chapter 7, Snippet Item 1.

```
Private Sub MyApplication_Startup(ByVal sender As Object, _
    ByVal e As Microsoft.VisualBasic.ApplicationServices. _
    StartupEventArgs) Handles Me.Startup
  ' ----- Take a three-second nap.
  System.Threading.Thread.Sleep(3000)
End Sub
```

Now run the program, and you will see the splash screen stick around for about three seconds (3,000 milliseconds). Eventually, we'll replace the *Sleep* statement with the actual database and application initialization code, but there's a good chance that it will take much less than three seconds. I mean, we're talking about SQL Server here. It's supposed to be blazing fast.

So it's clear that we still need to delay the removal of the splash screen. The *My.Application* object just happens to include the very property we need to enforce a delay. The *MinimumSplashScreenDisplayTime* property indicates the minimum number of milliseconds that the splash screen must be displayed. Setting this property in the *Startup* event is sufficient to postpone the delay of the main form for as long as we wish.

Delete the line containing the *Sleep* function call in the *Startup* event handler, and replace it with the following statement.

Insert Snippet Insert Chapter 7, Snippet Item 2.

```
' ----- Display the splash form for at least 3 seconds.
My.Application.MinimumSplashScreenDisplayTime = 3000
```

The last thing to do for the splash screen is to include some code that displays the version number. We already did this for the *About* form back in Chapter 5, ".NET Assemblies," so we'll just add similar code to the *Splash* form's *Load* event. We'll update the copyright message, too. Open the source code for the *Splash* form and add the following code.

Insert Snippet Insert Chapter 7, Snippet Item 3.

```
Private Sub Splash_Load(ByVal sender As Object, _
    ByVal e As System.EventArgs) Handles Me.Load
  ' ----- Update the version number.
  With My.Application.Info.Version
    ProgramVersion.Text = "Version " & .Major & "." & _
      .Minor & " Revision " & .Revision
  End With
  ProgramCopyright.Text = My.Application.Info.Copyright
End Sub
```

Run the program again and sit in awe as you witness a fully functional splash screen.

Configuring the Main Form

Although we designed a main form in an earlier chapter, it was pretty sparse, including only an About button. This chapter's project adds all of the user interface elements to the form. In fact, I've already added that form's controls to its surface for you (see Figure 7-12). But you can add some of the event handlers that will give some of its display pizzazz.

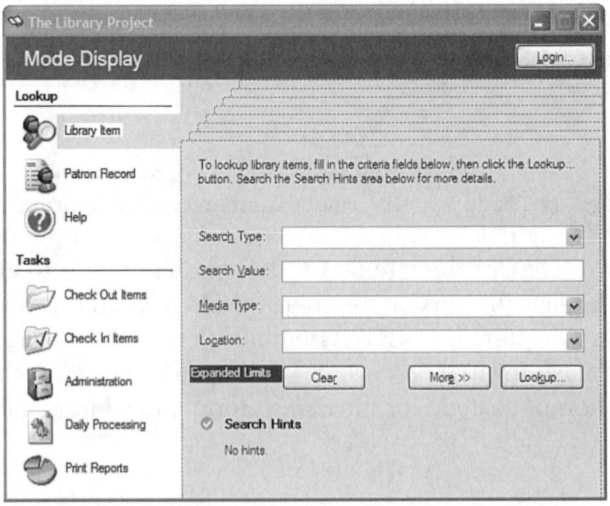

Figure 7-12 The basic look of the main form

All of the general event code for the form appears as code snippet number 4.

Insert Snippet Insert Chapter 7, Snippet Item 4.

Most of this code exists to move things around on the display. For example, different features of the form can be accessed by the user by clicking on the icons or related text labels along the left side of the form. Each of these icons and labels triggers one of seven common routines that exist to rearrange the furniture. The upper-left icon, *PicLibraryItem*, calls the common *TaskLibraryItem* routine when clicked.

```
Private Sub PicLibraryItem_Click( _
     ByVal sender As System.Object, _
     ByVal e As System.EventArgs) _
     Handles PicLibraryItem.Click
   ' ----- Library Item mode.
   TaskLibraryItem()
End Sub
```

The *TaskLibraryItem* procedure adjusts the various panels and fields on the display so that the user sees those fields needed to look up library items.

```
Private Sub TaskLibraryItem()
   ' ----- Update the display.
   AllPanelsInvisible()
   PanelLibraryItem.Visible = True
   ActLibraryItem.BackColor = SystemColors.Control
   LabelSelected.Location = New System.Drawing.Point( _
      LabelSelected.Left, PicLibraryItem.Top)
   Me.AcceptButton = ActSearch
End Sub
```

The *AllPanelsInvisible* routine also does some on-screen adjustment.

I like to have the existing text in a *TextBox* field selected when it becomes the active control. Each text control includes a *SelectAll* method that accomplishes this feat. We'll call that method during each *TextBox* control's *Enter* event, an event that occurs when a control receives the keyboard input focus.

```
Private Sub SearchText_Enter(ByVal sender As Object, _
     ByVal e As System.EventArgs) Handles SearchText.Enter
   ' ----- Highlight the entire text.
   SearchText.SelectAll()
End Sub
```

Using the mouse to access the different features of the form is good, but I'm a keyboard person. To support keyboard users like me, the code adds support for feature access using the F2 through F9 keys.

```
Private Sub MainForm_KeyDown(ByVal sender As Object, _
     ByVal e As System.Windows.Forms.KeyEventArgs) _
     Handles MyBase.KeyDown
   ' ----- The keys F2 through F9 access the different
   '       sections of the form.
   Select Case (e.KeyCode)
      Case Keys.F2
         TaskLibraryItem()
         e.Handled = True
      Case Keys.F3
         TaskPatronRecord()
         e.Handled = True
      Case Keys.F4
         ' ----- Allow form to handle Alt+F4.
         If (e.Alt = True) Then
            Me.Close()
         Else
            TaskHelp()
         End If
         e.Handled = True
      Case Keys.F5
         TaskCheckOut()
         e.Handled = True
      Case Keys.F6
         TaskCheckIn()
         e.Handled = True
      Case Keys.F7
         TaskAdmin()
         e.Handled = True
```

```
      Case Keys.F8
         TaskProcess()
         e.Handled = True
      Case Keys.F9
         TaskReports()
         e.Handled = True
   End Select
End Sub
```

As each keystroke comes into the *KeyDown* event handler, the *Select Case* statement examines it. When a matching *Case* entry is found, the code within the *Case* block executes. Pressing the F2 key triggers the code in the *Case Keys.F2* block. *Keys* is one of the many built-in enumerations that you can use in your .NET applications. Notice the special code for the F4 key. It allows the Alt+F4 key combination to exit the application, which is common among Windows programs.

Normally, all keystrokes go to the active control, not the form. To enable the *MainForm.KeyDown* event handler, the form's *KeyPreview* property must be set to *True*. Set this property back in the form designer.

Making the Program Single-Instance

The Library Project is designed for use only within a small library; it will run on only a few workstations at a time, perhaps up to ten at the most. And there's no need to run more than one copy on a single workstation, because each copy includes all of the available application features. One of the cool features included with Visual Basic 2005 is the ability to create a "single-instance application," one that enforces the one-at-a-time run policy on each workstation. Although you could create such applications before, it is now enabled with a single mouse click.

To make the Library Project a single-instance application, display the project properties' *Application* panel, and then select the **Make single-instance application** field. When the user tries to start up a second instance, .NET will refuse to carry out the request. Instead, it will trigger the application's *StartupNextInstance* event. Any special handling you wish to perform on a second instance startup will be done in this handler. Like the *Startup* event handler, the *StartupNextInstance* handler appears in the *ApplicationEvents.vb* file.

For the Library Project, the only thing we really need to do when the user tries to start a second instance is to make sure the application is displayed front and center, where the user can readily view it. Open the *ApplicationEvents.vb* file, and add the *StartupNextInstance* event handler.

Insert Snippet Insert Chapter 7, Snippet Item 5.

```
Private Sub MyApplication_StartupNextInstance( _
     ByVal sender As Object, _
     ByVal e As Microsoft.VisualBasic.ApplicationServices. _
     StartupNextInstanceEventArgs) _
     Handles Me.StartupNextInstance
   ' ----- Force the main form to the front.
   My.Application.MainForm.Activate()
End Sub
```

That's all the changes for this chapter. See you on the next page.

CHAPTER 8

CLASSES AND INHERITANCE

How many .NET programmers does it take to change a light bulb? None—they call a method on the light bulb object, and it changes itself. Ha, ha, ha! That's funny, but only if you understand the **object-oriented programming** (OOP) concepts that are the basic foundation of the .NET system. (Actually, it's not even that funny if you do understand OOP.) Without OOP, it would be difficult to support core features of .NET, such as the central *System.Object* object, which is the basic foundation of the .NET system. Also, productivity would go way down among Windows developers, who are the basic foundation of the .NET system.

Although I briefly mentioned OOP development concepts in both Chapters 1, "Introducing .NET," and 2, "Introducing Visual Basic," it was only to provide some context for other topics of discussion. But in this chapter, I hold back no longer. After a vigorous discussion of general OOP concepts, I'll discuss how you can use these concepts in your .NET code.

Object-Oriented Programming Concepts

If you've read this far into the book, it's probably okay to let you in on the secret of object-oriented computing. The secret is: It's all a sham, a hoax, a cover-up. That's right, your computer does not really perform any processing with objects, no matter what their orientation. The CPU in your computer processes data and logic statements the old-fashioned way: one step at a time, moving through specific areas in memory as directed by the logic, manipulating individual values and bits according to those same logic statements. It doesn't see data as collective objects; it sees only bits and bytes.

One moment, I've just been handed this important news bulletin. It reads, "Don't be such a geek, Tim. It's not the computer doing the object-oriented stuff, it's the programmer." Oh, sorry about that. But what I said before still stands: The final code as executed by your CPU isn't any more object-oriented than old MS-DOS code. But **object-oriented language compilers** provide the illusion that OOP is built into the computer. You design your code and data in the form of objects, and the compiler takes it from there. It reorganizes your code and data, adds some extra code to do the simulated-OOP magic, and bundles it all up in an EXE file. You could write any OOP program using ordinary procedural languages, or even assembly language. But applications that focus on data can often be written much more efficiently using OOP development practices.

The Object

The core of object-oriented programming is, of course, the **object**. An object is a person, place, or thing. Wait a minute, that's a noun. An object is *like* a noun. Objects are computer data-and-logic constructs that symbolize real-world entities, such as people, places, or things. You can have objects that represent people, employees, dogs, sea otters, houses, file cabinets, computers, strands of DNA, galaxies, pictures, word-processing documents, calculators, office supplies, books, soap opera characters, space invaders, pizza slices, majestic self-amortizing canals, plantations of ripening tea, a few of my favorite things, and sand.

Objects provide a convenient software means to describe and manage the data associated with one of these real-world objects. For instance, if you had a set of objects representing DVDs in your home video collection, the object could manage features of the DVD, such as its title, the actors performing in the content, the length of the video in minutes, whether the DVD was damaged or scratched, its cost, and so on. If you connected your application to the DVD-ROM player in your system, your object could even include a "play" feature that (assuming the DVD was in the drive) would begin to play the movie, possibly from a timed starting position or DVD "chapter."

Objects work well because of their ability to simulate the features of real-world objects through software development means. They do this through the four key attributes of objects: **abstraction**, **encapsulation**, **inheritance**, and **polymorphism**.

Throughout this chapter, the term "object" usually refers to an **instance** of something, a specific in-memory use of the defined element—an instance with its own set of data, not just its definition or design. **Class** refers to the design and source code of the object, comprising the **implementation**.

Abstraction

An abstraction indicates an object's limited view of a real-world object. Like an abstract painting, an abstracted object shows just the basic essentials of the real-world equivalent (see Figure 8-1).

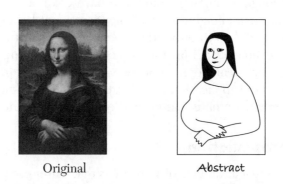

Original   Abstract

Figure 8-1 Actually, the one on the left is kind of abstract, too.

Objects can't perfectly represent real-world counterparts. Instead, they implement data storage and processes on just those elements of the real-world counterpart that are important for the application. Software isn't the only thing that requires abstraction. Your medical chart at your doctor's office is an abstraction of your total physical health. When you buy a new house, the house inspector's report is an abstraction of the actual condition of the building. Even the thermometer in your back yard is an abstraction; it cannot accurately communicate all of the minor temperature variations that exist just around the flask of mercury. Instead, it gathers the information it can, and communicates a single numeric result.

All of these abstract tools record, act on, or communicate just the essential information they were designed to manage. A software object, in a similar way, only stores, acts on, or communicates essential information about its real-world counterpart. For instance, if you were designing an object that monitored the condition of a building, you might record the following:

- Building location and address
- Primary construction material (wood, concrete, steel-beam, etc.)
- Age (in years)
- General condition (from a list of choices)
- Inspector notes

Although a building would also have color, a number of doors and windows, and a height, these elements may not be important for the application, and therefore would not be part of the abstraction. Those values that are contained within the object are called **properties**. Any processing rules or calculations contained within the object that act on the properties (or other supplied internal or external data) are known as **methods**. Taken together, methods and properties make up the **members** of the object.

Encapsulation

The great advantage of software is that a user can perform a lot of complex and time-consuming work quickly and easily. Actually, the software takes care of the speed and the complexity on behalf of the user, and in many cases, the user doesn't even care how the work is being done. "Those computers are just so baffling; I don't know and I don't care how they work as long as they give me the results I need" is a common statement heard in management meetings. And it's a realistic statement too, because the computer has **encapsulated** the necessary data and processing logic to accomplish the desired tasks.

Encapsulation carries with it the idea of **interfaces**. Although a computer may contain a lot of useful logic and data, if there was no way to interact with that logic or data, the computer would basically be a useless lump of plastic and silicon. Interfaces provide the means to interact with the internals of an object. An interface provides highly controlled entries and exits into the data and processing routines contained within the object. As a consumer of the object, it's really irrelevant how the object does its work internally, as long as it produces the results you expect through its publicly exposed interfaces.

Using the computer as an example, the various interfaces include (among other things) the keyboard, display, mouse, power connector, USB and 1394 ports, speakers, microphone jack, and the power button. Often, the things I connect to these interfaces are also **black boxes**, encapsulations with well-defined public interfaces. A printer is a mystery to me. How the printer driver can send commands down the USB cable, and eventually squirt ink onto 24-pound paper is just inexplicable; but I don't know and I don't care how it really works, as long as it does work.

Inheritance

Inheritance in .NET isn't like inheritance in real life; no one has to die before it works. But as in real life, **inheritance** defines a relationship between two different objects. Specifically, it defines how one object is descended from another.

The original class in the object relationship is called the **base class**. It includes various and sundry interface members, as well as internal implementation details. A **derived class** is defined using the base class as the starting point. Derived classes **inherit** the features of the base class. By default, any publicly exposed members of the base class automatically become publicly exposed members of the derived class, including the implementation. A derived class may choose to **override** one, some, or all of these members, providing its own distinct or supplementary implementation details.

Derived classes often provide additional details specific to a subset of the base class. For instance, a base class that defines *animals* would include interfaces for the common name, Latin species name, number of legs, and other common properties belonging to all animals. Derived classes would then enhance the features of the base class, but only for a subset of animals. A *mammal* class might define gestation time for birthing young, whereas a parallel *avian*-derived class could define the diameter of an egg. Both *mammal* and *avian* would still retain the name, species name, and leg count properties from the base *animal* class. An instance of *avian* would be an *animal*; an instance of *mammal* would be an *animal*. However, an instance of *avian* would not be a *mammal*. Also, a generic instance of *animal* could be considered as an *avian* only if it was originally defined as an *avian*.

Even though a base and derived class have a relationship, implementation details that are **private** to the base class are not made available to the derived class. The derived class doesn't even know that those private members exist. A base class may include **protected** members that, although hidden from users of the class, are visible to the derived class. Any member defined as **public** in the base class is available to the derived class, and also to all users of the base class. (Visual Basic defines another level named "**friend**." Members marked as friend are available to all code in the same assembly, but not to code outside of the assembly. Public members can be used by code outside of the defining assembly.)

Examples of inheritance do exist in the real world. A clock is a base object from which an alarm clock derives. The alarm clock exposes the public interfaces of a clock, and adds its own implementation-specific properties and methods. Other examples include a knife and its derived Swiss-army knife, a chair and its derived recliner, a table and its derived Periodic Table of the Elements.

Polymorphism

The concepts introduced so far could be implemented using standard procedural programming languages. Although you can't do true inheritance in a non-OOP language like C, you can simulate it using flag fields. If a flag field named "type" in a non-OOP class-like structure was set to "mammal," you could enable use of certain mammal-specific fields. There are other ways to simulate these features, and it wouldn't be too difficult.

Polymorphism is a different avian altogether. "Polymorphism" means "many forms." Because a derived class can have its own (overridden) version of a base class's member, if you treat a *mammal* object like a generic *animal*, there could be some confusion as to which version of the members should be used, the *animal* version or the *mammal* version. Polymorphism takes care of figuring all of this out, on an ad hoc basis, while your program is running. Polymorphism makes it possible for any code in your program to treat a derived instance as if it were its base instance. This makes for great coding. If you have a routine that deals with *animal* objects, you can pass it objects of type *animal*, *mammal*, or *avian*, and it will still work. This type of polymorphism is known as **subtyping polymorphism**, but who cares what its name is.

Another variation of polymorphism is **overloading**. Overloading allows a single class method (forget about derived classes for now) to have multiple forms, but still be considered as a single method. For instance, if you had a *house* object with a *paint* method (that would change the color of the house), you could have one *paint* method that accepted a single color (paint the house all one color) and another *paint* method that accepted two colors (main color plus a trim color). When these methods are overloaded in a single class, the compiler determines which version to call based on the data you include in the call to the method.

Interfaces and Implementation

OOP development differentiates between the public definition of a class, the code written to implement that class, and the resulting in-memory use of that class as an object. It's similar to how, at a restaurant, you differentiate between a menu, the cooking of your selection, and the actual food that appears at your table.

- The description of an item on the menu is (to some extent) its *interface*; it describes what the real object will expose publicly in terms of taste, smell, etc.
- The method used by the kitchen staff to prepare the food is the *implementation*; it's how the meal is prepared. There may be different implementations by different restaurants for the same menu item. In objects, the implementation is hidden from public view; in a restaurant, food preparation is thankfully hidden from view or no one would ever eat there.
- The food you receive from the kitchen is—ta da!—the object, the actual *instance* of what the menu described. Many hungry customers may each order the same menu item, and each would receive a distinct instance of the food.

OOP in Visual Basic and .NET

Conceptually, OOP really isn't that complex. Because both humans and programmers interact with real-world objects and instances every day, it's pretty easy to wrap their minds around the idea of programming with objects. But how easy is it to communicate these object concepts to the computer through the Visual Basic compiler and the .NET Framework? Can it be done without weekly sessions on a shrink's comfy sofa? Duh! It's Visual Basic; of course it's easy.

One reason objects are so easy in .NET is that they have to be. Everything in your .NET program is part of an object, and if everything about .NET was hard, you'd be reading a book on Macintosh development right about now. But it's not too hard because the Visual Basic implementation of objects parallels the conceptual ideas of objects.

Classes

Visual Basic uses **classes** to define objects. The *Class* keyword starts the definition.

```
Class Superhero
    ' ----- Class-related code goes here.
End Class
```

That's most of it: the *Class* keyword, and a name for the class ("Superhero" in this case). All classes reside in a namespace (discussed way back in Chapter 1). By default, your classes appear in a namespace that is named after your project. You can alter this in the project properties (to set the top-level namespace for your assembly) and with the *Namespace* statement (to indicate relative namespaces from your assembly's top-level namespace).

```
Namespace GoodGuys
    Class Superhero
    End Class
End Namespace
```

You can add any number of classes to a namespace. Classes that use the same name, but that appear in different namespaces, are unrelated.

The members of a class appear between the *Class* and *End Class* clauses. You can also split a class's definition into multiple source code files.

If you do split up a class like this, at least one of the parts must include the keyword *Partial* in the definition.

```
Partial Class Superhero
```

As with variable definitions, classes are defined using one of the access modifier keywords: *Public, Private, Protected, Friend,* or *Protected Friend.* Flip back to Chapter 6, "Data and Data Types," in the "Variables" section, if you need a refresher course.

The .NET Framework Class Libraries are simply loaded with classes and objects, and they are all pretty much defined with this simple keyword: *Class.*

Class Members

Calling your class *Superhero* won't endow it with any special powers if you don't add any **members** to the class. All class members must appear between the *Class* and *End Class* boundaries, although if you use the *Partial* feature to break up your class, you can sprinkle the members among the different class parts in any way you wish.

There are 11 different kinds of members you can include in your Visual Basic classes. Other books or documents may give you a different number, but they're wrong, at least if they organize things the way I do here.

- **Variable fields.** Value type and reference type variables can be added directly to your class as top-level members. As full class members, they are accessible by any code defined in the same class, and possibly by code that uses your class. Variables are defined using one of the access modifiers.

  ```
  Class Superhero
     Public Name As String
     Protected TrueIdentity As String
  End Class
  ```

- **Constant fields.** You define constants just like variable fields, but include the *Const* keyword. As with local procedure-level constants, you must assign a value to the constant immediately in source code, using literals or simple non-variable calculations.

```
Public Const BaseStrengthFactor As Integer = 1
```

- **Enumerations.** Enumerations define related integral values. Once defined, you can use them in your code just like other integer values.

```
Public Enum GeneralSuperPower
    Flight
    Strength
    Speed
    VisionRelated
    HearingRelated
    WaterRelated
    TemperatureRelated
    ToolsAndGadgets
    GreatCostume
End Enum
```

Enumerations can also be defined at the namespace level, outside of any specific class.

- **Sub methods.** Classes include two types of methods, *Subs* and *Functions*. All logic code in your application appears in one of these method types, so don't bother looking for such code in an enumeration. Sub methods perform some defined logic, optionally working on data passed in as **arguments**.

```
Public Sub DemonstrateMainPower( _
        ByVal strengthFactor As Integer)
    ' ----- Logic code appears here.
End Sub
```

The *DemonstrateMainPower* method, as a public member of your class, can be called either by code within the class, or by any code referencing an instance of your class. This method includes a single parameter, *strengthFactor*, through which calls to the method send in data arguments.

You can jump out of a sub method at any time by using the *Return* statement, or the older pre-.NET *Exit Sub* statement.

- **Function methods.** Function methods are just like sub methods, but they support a return value. You define the data type of the return value with an *As* clause at the end of the function definition. Assignment of the return value can be done using the *Return* statement, or by assigning the function name directly within the code.

```
Public Function GetSecretIdentity( _
      ByVal secretPassword As String) As String
   If (secretPassword = "Krypton") Then
      ' ----- I created a class field named
      '        TrueIdentity earlier.
      Return TrueIdentity
   Else
      GetSecretIdentity = "FORGET IT BAD GUY"
   End If
End Function
```

If you use the assignment-to-function-name style of return value assignment, use the *Exit Function* statement to return to the calling code at any time.

■ **Properties.** Properties combine the ideas of fields and methods. You can create read-write, read-only, or write-only properties through the *Get* and *Set* accessors. The following code defines a write-only property:

```
Public WriteOnly Property SecretIdentity() As String
   Set(ByVal value As String)
      TrueIdentity = value
   End Set
End Property
```

■ **Delegates.** Delegates define arguments and return values for a method, and encase them in a single object all their own. They are generally used to support the event process, callback procedures, and indirect calls to class methods.

```
Public Delegate Sub GenericPowerCall( _
   ByVal strengthFactor As Integer)
```

Because delegates are pretty generic, they can also be defined at the namespace level, outside of any class definition.

■ **Events.** Adding events to your class allows consumers of your class to react to changes and actions occurring within a class instance. The syntax used to define events looks a lot like a method definition, but an alternative syntax uses previously defined delegates to indicate the signature of the event.

```
' ----- Non-delegate definition.
Public Event PerformPower( _
    ByVal strengthFactor) As Integer


' ----- Delegate definition.
Public Event PerformPower As GenericPowerCall
```

- **Declares.** The *Declare* statement lets you call code defined in external DLL files, although it works only with pre-.NET DLL calls. The syntax for declares closely resembles the syntax used to define methods.

```
Public Declare Function TalkToBadGuy _
    Lib "evil.dll" (ByVal message _
    As String) As String
```

Once defined, an externally declared sub or function can be used in your code as if it were a built-in .NET sub or function definition. The .NET Framework does a lot of work behind the scenes to shuttle data between your program and the DLL. Still, care must be taken when interacting with such external "unmanaged" code, especially if the DLL is named "evil.dll."

- **Interfaces.** Interfaces allow you to define abstract classes and, in a way, class templates. A section near the end of this chapter discusses interfaces. Interfaces can also be defined at the namespace level, and usually are.

- **Nested types.** Classes can include other subordinate classes for their own internal or public use. If you make such a "child" class public, you can return instances of these classes to code that uses the larger "parent" class. (You can also return private class instances, but the caller wouldn't be able to do much with them.)

```
Class Superhero
    Class Superpower
    End Class
End Class
```

You can nest classes to any depth, but don't go overboard. Creating multiple classes within the same namespace will likely meet your needs without making the code overly complex. But that's just my idea; do what you want. It's your code after all. If you want to throw away your life on a career in the movies, that's fine with me.

Adding a nice variety of members to a class is a lot of fun. You can add class members in any variety, in any order, and in any quantity. If you add a lot of members, you might even get a quantity discount on Visual Studio from Microsoft, but I wouldn't hold your breath.

Shared Class Members

Normally, objects (class instances) are greedy and selfish; they want to keep everything to themselves and not share with others. That's why each instance of a class you create has its own version of the data elements defined as class members. Even class methods and properties give the appearance of being distinct for each class instance. It's as if each object was saying, "I've got mine; get your own." It's this attitude that has led to what is now commonly called "class warfare."

In an attempt to promote affability among software components and push for "kindlier and gentler" classes, Microsoft included the *Shared* keyword in its class design. The *Shared* keyword can be applied to Variable field, Sub method, Function method, and property members of your class. When defined, a **shared member** can be used *without the need to create an instance of that class*. You reference these shared members using just the class name and the member name.

```
Class ClassWithSharedValue
    Public Shared TheSharedValue As Integer
End Class
...later, in some other code...
ClassWithSharedValue.TheSharedValue = 10
```

Shared members are literally "shared" by all instances of your class, and if public, by code outside of the class as well. Because they don't require an object instance, they are also limited to just those resources that don't require an object instance. This means that a shared method cannot access a non-shared variable field of the same class. Any class members that are not marked *Shared* are known as **instance members**.

Overloaded Members and Optional Arguments

Overloading of a method occurs by attaching the *Overloads* keyword to each of the overloaded members.

```
Class House
    Public Overloads Sub PaintHouse()
        ' ----- Use the same color(s) as before.
    End Sub

    Public Overloads Sub PaintHouse(ByVal baseColor As Color)
        ' ----- Paint the house a solid color.
    End Sub

    Public Overloads Sub PaintHouse(ByVal baseColor As Color, _
            ByVal trimColor As Color)
        ' ----- Paint using a main and a trim color.
    End Sub

    Public Overloads Sub PaintHouse(ByVal baseColor As Color, _
            ByVal coats As Integer)
        ' ----- Possibly paint with many coats, of paint
        '         that is, not of fabric.
    End Sub
End Class
```

When you call the *PaintHouse* method, you must pass arguments that match one of the overloaded versions. Visual Basic determines which version to use based on the argument signature. If you pass the wrong type or number of arguments, the program will refuse to compile.

Two of the overloaded members in this class look alike, except for the second *coats* argument.

```
Public Overloads Sub PaintHouse(ByVal whichColor As Color)

Public Overloads Sub PaintHouse(ByVal baseColor As Color, _
    ByVal coats As Integer)
```

Instead of defining two distinct methods, I could have combined them into a single method, and defined an **optional argument** for the *coats* parameter.

```
Public Overloads Sub PaintHouse(ByVal baseColor As Color, _
    Optional ByVal coats As Integer = 1)
```

The *Optional* keyword can be used on any number of parameters, but no non-optional parameters can appear after them; the optional arguments must always be last in the list. Although the calling code might not pass a value for *coats*, .NET still requires that every parameter receive an argument. Therefore, each optional argument includes a **default value** using a simple assignment within the parameter definition. The optional argument *coats* uses a default value of 1 through the "= 1" clause.

Inheritance

Visual Basic supports inheritance, the joining of two classes in an ancestor-descendant relationship. To implement inheritance, define the base class, and then add the derived class using the keyword *Inherits*. What a surprise!

```
Class Animal
    ' ----- Animal class members go here.
End Class

Class Mammal
    Inherits Animal

    ' ----- All members of Animal are automatically
    '       part of Mammal. Add additional Mammal
    '       features here.
End Class
```

The *Inherits* statement must appear at the start of the class definition, before the definition for any class members. It must include the name of exactly one other class, the base class. If you split up your derived class using the *Partial* keyword, you only need to use the *Inherits* statement in one of the parts. And because a derived class can only use a single base class, you're pretty much limited to using the *Inherits* statement only once per class. (The base class can be used in several different derived classes, and the derived class can further be used as a base class for other derived classes.)

Derived classes automatically receive all defined members of the base class. If a derived class needs to provide special functionality for a member defined in the base class, it overrides the member in the base class. This is a two-step process: (1) the base class must allow its member to be overridden with the *Overridable* keyword; and (2) the base class must supply the overriding code using the *Overrides* keyword.

```
Class Animal
    Public Overridable Sub Speak()
       MsgBox("Grrrr.")
    End Sub
End Class

Class Canine
    Inherits Animal
    Public Overrides Sub Speak()
       MsgBox("Bark.")
    End Sub
End Class
```

Any class that derives from *Animal* can now supply its own custom code for the *Speak* method. But the same is true for classes derived from *Canine*; the *Overridable* keyword is passed down to each generation. If you need to stop this attribute at a specific generation, use the *NotOverridable* keyword. This keyword is valid only when used in a derived class, because base class members are non-overridable by default.

```
Class Canine
    Inherits Animal
    Public NotOverridable Overrides Sub Speak()
       MsgBox("Bark.")
    End Sub
End Class
```

There are times when it is not possible to write a truly generic method in the base class, and you want to require that every derived class define its own version of the method. Using the *MustOverride* keyword in the member definition enables this requirement.

```
Class Animal
    Public MustOverride Sub DefenseTactic()
End Class
```

Members marked as *MustOverride* include no implementation code of their own because it would go unused. (Also notice that *DefenseTactic* has no closing "End Sub" statement.) Because there is no code associated with this member, the entire *Animal* class has a deficiency. If you created an instance of *Animal* and called its *DefenseTactic* method, panic would ensue within the application. Therefore, it is not possible to create instances of classes that contain *MustOverride* members. To note this limitation, the class is also decorated with the *MustInherit* keyword.

```
MustInherit Class Animal
    Public MustOverride Sub DefenseTactic()
End Class
```

It won't be possible to create an instance of *Animal* directly, although you can derive classes from it, and create instances of those classes. Also, you can create an *Animal* variable (a reference type) and assign an instance of an *Animal*-derived class to it.

```
Dim zooMember As Animal
Dim monkey As New Simian   ' Simian is derived from Animal
zooMember = monkey
```

Such code doesn't really seem fair to the base class. I mean, it defined all the core requirements for derived classes, but it doesn't get any of the credit because it can't be directly instantiated. But there is a way for a base class to control its own destiny, to take all of the glory for itself. It does this with the *NotInheritable* keyword.

```
NotInheritable Class Animal
End Class
```

The only way to use a *NotInheritable* class is to create an instance of it; you cannot use it as the base class of another derived class.

Inherits, MustInherit, NotInheritable, Overrides, Overridable, NotOverridable—this certainly isn't your grandmother's Visual Basic anymore. And there's still one more of these inimitable keywords: *Shadows.* When you override a base class member, the new code must use a definition that is identical to the one provided in the base class. That is, if you override a function method with two *String* arguments and an *Integer* return code, the overriding code must use that same signature. Shadowed members have no such requirements. A shadowed member matches an item in the base class "in name only;" everything else is up for grabs. You can even change the member type. If you have a Sub method named *PeanutButter* in a base class, you can shadow it in the derived class with a variable field (or constant, or enumeration, or nested class) also named *PeanutButter*.

```
Class Food
    Public Sub PeanutButter()
    End Sub
End Class
Class Snack
    Inherits Food
    Public Shadows PeanutButter As String
        ' Hey, it's not even a "Sub"
End Class
```

Without the *Shadows* keyword in the *Snack* class, a compile-time error would occur.

Creating Instances of Classes

Step one: designing classes. Step two: deriving classes. Step three: creating class instances. Step four: cha-cha-cha. Visual Basic uses the *New* keyword to create instances of your custom classes.

```
Dim myPet As Animal = New Animal
' ----- Or...
Dim myPet As New Animal
' ----- Or...
Dim myPet As Animal
myPet = New Animal
```

The instance can then be used like any other .NET instance variable. Member access occurs using "dot" notation.

```
myPet.Name = "Fido"
```

You can also (within reason) pass instance variables between their base and derived variations.

```
Dim myPet As Animal
Dim myDog As Canine
myDog = New Canine
myDog.Name = "Fido"
myPet = myDog        ' Since Canine derives from Animal
MsgBox(myPet.Name)   ' Displays "Fido"
```

If you have *Option Strict* set to *On*, there will be limits on your ability to convert between types, especially narrowing conversions (where the source data type will not always "fit" in the target variable). In such cases, you must use the *CType* function (or one of a few similar .NET and Visual Basic supplied functions) to enable the conversion.

```
myDog = CType(myPet, Canine)
```

Referring to class instances is simply a matter of referring to the variable or object that contains the instance. That is true for code that uses an instance from outside of the class itself. For the code within your class (such as in one of its methods), you refer to members of your class as if they were local variables (with no qualification), or use the special *Me* keyword.

```
Class Animal
    Public Name As String
    Public Sub DisplayName()
        ' ----- Either of these lines will work.
        MsgBox(Name)
        MsgBox(Me.Name)
    End Sub
End Class
```

A similar keyword, *MyClass*, usually acts like the *Me* keyword, but it has some different functionality when a class instance is stored in a variable from a different (base or derived) class type. For instance, if you create an instance of *Canine*, but store it in an *Animal* variable, references using *Me* will focus on the *Canine* code, whereas references to *MyClass* will focus on the *Animal* code. I won't be using *MyClass* in the Library Project, and for most simple uses of class instances, you will never use it either. But there are times when it is important to differentiate between base and derived code, and this is the way to do it.

The *MyBase* keyword references elements of the base class from which the current class derives. It references only the closest base class; if you have a class named *Class5* that derives from *Class4*, which in turn derives from *Class3*, which derives from *Class2*, which derives from *Class1*, which eventually derives from *System.Object*, references to *MyBase* in the code of *Class5* refer to *Class4*. Well, that's almost true. If you try to use *MyBase.MemberName* and *MemberName* doesn't exist in *Class4*, *MyBase* will search back through the stack of classes until it finds the first definition of *MemberName*.

```
Class Animal
    Public Overridable Sub ObtainLicense()
        ' ----- Perform Animal-specific licensing code.
    End Sub
End Class

Class Canine
    Inherits Animal
    Public Overrides Sub ObtainLicense()
        ' ----- Perform Canine-specific licensing code, then...
        MyBase.ObtainLicense()  ' Calls code from Animal class
    End Sub
End Class
```

Constructors and Destructors

Class instances have a lifetime: a beginning, a time of activity, and finally, thankfully, an end. The beginning of an object's lifetime occurs through a **constructor**; its final moments are dictated by a **destructor** before passing into the infinity of the .NET garbage collection process.

Each class includes at least one constructor, whether explicit or implicit. If you don't supply one, .NET will at least perform minimal constructor-level activities, such as reserving memory space for each of the instance variable fields of your class. If you want a class to have any other startup-time logic, you must supply it through an explicit constructor.

Constructors in Visual Basic are Sub methods with the name *New*. A *New* constructor with no arguments acts as the **default constructor**, called by default whenever a new instance of a class is needed.

```
Class Animal
    Public Name As String
    Public Sub New()
        ' ----- Every animal must have some name.
        Name = "John Doe of the Jungle"
    End Sub
End Class
```

Without this constructor, new instances of *Animal* wouldn't have any name assigned to the *Name* field. And because *String* variables are reference types, *Name* would have an initial value of *Nothing*. Not very user friendly. A default constructor gives you a chance to provide at least the minimum needed data and logic for a new instance.

You can provide additional custom constructors by adding more *New* methods, each with a different argument signature.

```
Class Animal
    Public Name As String
    Public Sub New()
        ' ----- Every animal must have some name.
        Name = "John Doe of the Jungle"
    End Sub
    Public Sub New(ByVal startingName As String)
        ' ----- Use the caller-supplied name.
        Name = startingName
    End Sub
    Public Sub New(ByVal startingCode As Integer)
        ' ----- Build a name from a numeric code.
        Name = "Animal Number " & CStr(startingCode)
    End Sub
End Class
```

The following code demonstrates each constructor.

```
MsgBox((New Animal).Name)
    ' Displays "John Doe of the Jungle"

MsgBox((New Animal("Fido")).Name)
    ' Displays "Fido"

MsgBox((New Animal(5)).Name)
    ' Displays "Animal Number 5"
```

You can force the consumer of your class to use a custom constructor by excluding a default constructor from the class definition. Also, if you're deriving your class from anything other than *System.Object*, it's usually a good idea to call the base class's constructor as the first line of your derived constructor, although the default constructor in the base class will be called by default.

```
Class Canine
   Inherits Animal
   Public Sub New()
      MyBase.New()   ' Calls Animal.New()
      ' ----- Now add other code.
   End Sub
End Class
```

Killing a class instance is not as easy as it might seem. When you create local class instances in your methods, they are automatically **destroyed** when that method exits *if you haven't assigned the instance to a variable outside of the method*. If you create an instance in a method, and assign it to a class member, it will live on in the class member for the lifetime of the class, even though the method that created it has exited.

But let's think only about local instances for now. An instance is destroyed when the routine exits. You can also destroy an instance immediately by setting its variable to *Nothing*.

```
myDog = Nothing
```

Setting the variable to a new instance will destroy any previous instance stored in that variable.

```
myDog = New Canine
myDog.Name = "Fido"
myDog = New Canine   ' Sorry Fido, you're gone
```

When an object is destroyed, .NET calls a special method named *Finalize*, if present, to perform any final cleanup before removing the instance from memory. *Finalize* is implemented as a Protected method of the base *System.Object* class; you must override this method in your class to use it.

```
Class Animal
    Protected Overrides Sub Finalize()
        ' ----- Cleanup code goes here. Be sure to call the
        '       base class's Finalize method.
        MyBase.Finalize()
    End Sub
End Class
```

So what's with that crack about killing instances being so hard? The problem is that .NET controls the calling of the *Finalize* method; it's part of the garbage collection process. The Framework doesn't continually clean up its garbage. It's like the service at your house; it gets picked up by the garbage truck once in a while. Until then, it just sits there, rotting, decaying, decomposing, and not having its *Finalize* method called. For most objects, this isn't much of a problem; who cares if the memory for a string gets released now or 30 seconds from now? But there are times when it is important to release acquired resources as quickly as possible. For instance, if you acquire a lock on an external hardware resource and only release it in the destructor, you could be holding that lock long after the application has exited. Talk about a slow death.

There are two ways around this problem. One way is to add a separate cleanup method to your class that you expect any code using your class to call. This will work—until some code forgets to call the method. (You should therefore also call this routine from the destructor.) The second method is similar, but it uses a Framework-supplied interface called *IDisposable*. (I'll talk about interfaces in a minute, so don't get too worried about all the code shown here.)

```
Class Animal
    Implements IDisposable

    Protected Overrides Sub Finalize()
        ' ----- Cleanup code goes here. Be sure to call the
        '       base class's Finalize method.
        MyBase.Finalize()
    End Sub

    Public Overloads Sub Dispose() _
            Implements IDisposable.Dispose
```

```
' ----- Put cleanup code here. Also make these calls.
    MyBase.Dispose()    ' Only if base class is disposable.
    System.GC.SuppressFinalize(Me)
  End Sub
End Class
```

The *SuppressFinalize* method tells the garbage collector, "Don't call *Finalize*; I've already cleaned up everything." Any code that uses your class will need to call its *Dispose* method to perform the immediate cleanup of resources. So it's not too different from the first method, but it does standardize things a bit. Also, it enables the use of the Visual Basic *Using* statement. This block statement provides a structured method of cleaning up resources.

```
Using myPet As New Animal
    ' ----- Code here uses the myPet.
End Using
' ----- At this point, myPet is destroyed, and Dispose is
'       called automatically by the End Using statement.
```

Interfaces

The *MustOverride* and *MustInherit* keywords force derived classes to implement specific members of the base class. But what if you want the derived class to implement *all* members of the base class? You could use *MustOverride* next to each method and property, but a better way is to use an **interface**. Interfaces define **abstract classes**, classes consisting only of definitions, no implementation. (OOP purists will point out that a class with even just one *MustOverride* flag is also an abstract class. Fine.) The *Interface* statement begins the interface definition process. By convention, all interface names begin with the capital letter *I*.

```
Interface IBuilding
    Function FloorArea() As Double
    Sub AlterExterior()
End Interface
```

As you see here, the syntax is a somewhat simplified version of the class definition syntax. All interface members are automatically public, so access modifiers aren't included. Only the definition line of each member is needed because there is no implementation. In addition to function and sub methods, interface members also include properties, events, other interfaces, classes, and structures. Interfaces can also derive from other interfaces (using the *Inherits* keyword), and automatically include all of the members of the base interface.

Classes make use of interfaces as they wish. It's not like inheritance, where all base members become part of the derived class. A class can pick and choose which interface members to **implement**. Often you'll implement all interface members, but as a class designer, you have the power. You attach interfaces to your class using the *Implements* keyword. This same keyword is used later to indicate which class member defines which interface member.

```
Class House
    Implements IBuilding

    Public Function FloorArea() As Double _
            Implements IBuilding.FloorArea
        ' ----- Add implementation here.
    End Function

    Public Sub PaintHouse() Implements IBuilding.AlterExterior
        ' ----- Add implementation here.
    End Sub
End Class
```

Class implementations of interface members are not required to maintain the original interface member name (although the argument signature must match the one in the interface). In the sample code, the *FloorArea* kept the name of the equivalent interface member, but the *AlterExterior* member was implemented using the *PaintHouse* method. This makes possible some interesting code.

```
Dim someHouse As New House
Dim someBuilding As IBuilding
someBuilding = someHouse
someBuilding.AlterExterior()   ' Calls someHouse.PaintHouse()
```

Classes can only inherit from a single base class, but there is no limit on the number of interfaces that a class can implement.

```
Class House
    Implements IBuilding, IDisposable
```

Also, a single class member can implement multiple interface members.

```
Public Sub PaintHouse() Implements _
    IBuilding.AlterExterior, IContractor.DoWork
```

So, why use interfaces? Interfaces provide a generic way to access common functionality, even among objects that have nothing in common. Classes named *Animal*, *House*, and *Superhero* probably have nothing in common in terms of logic, but they may all need a consistent way to clean up their resources. If they each implement the *IDisposable* interface, they gain that ability without the need to derive from some common base class.

Modules and Structures

In addition to classes, Visual Basic provides two related object definition features: structures and modules. Although they have different names than "class," they still act a lot like classes, but with different features enabled or disabled.

Modules provide a place to include general global code and data values in your application or assembly. All members of a module are *Shared*. In fact, a module acts just like a class with the *Shared* keyword added to each member, yet with one major difference: There is no inheritance relationship allowed with modules. You cannot create a derived module from a base class or module, nor can you use a module as a base for any other type. Modules are a carryover from pre-.NET versions of Visual Basic, which included "Modules" for all non-Form code.

```
Friend Module GenericDataAndCode
    ' ----- Application-global constant.
    Public Const AllDigits As String = "0123456789"
```

```
' ----- Application-global function.
Public Function GetEmbeddedDigits( _
      ByVal sourceString As String) As String
   End Sub
End Module
```

You cannot create an instance of a module. As with classes, modules appear in the context of a namespace. Unlike a class with shared members, you do not need to specify the module name to use the module member. All module members act as global variables and methods, and can be used immediately in any other code in your application without further qualification.

Structures are much more like classes than are modules. Classes implement reference types, but structures implement value types. All structures derive from *System.ValueType* (which in turn derives from *System.Object*). As such, they act like the core Visual Basic data types, such as *Integer*. You can create instances of a structure using the same syntax used to create class instances. However, you cannot use a structure as the base for another derived structure. And while you can include a constructor in your structure, destructors are not supported.

Because of the way that structures are stored and used in a .NET application, they are well suited to simple data types. You can include any number of members in your structure, but it is best to keep things simple.

Related Issues

Let me take a few moments here before getting into the project code to discuss some issues that don't really fit into any particular chapter discussion, but that you might end up using a lot in your own applications.

The MsgBox Method

Although I've used it on practically every page of this book so far, I have never formally introduced you to the *MsgBox* method. Part of the *Microsoft.VisualBasic* namespace, *MsgBox* is a carryover from the *MsgBox* function in the original release of Visual Basic. It displays a simple message window, including a selection of response buttons and an optional icon. As a function, it returns a code indicating which button the user clicked to close the form, one of the *MsgBoxResult* enumeration values. The syntax is:

```
Public Function MsgBox(ByVal Prompt As Object, _
    Optional ByVal Buttons As _
    MsgBoxStyle = MsgBoxStyle.OKOnly, _
    Optional ByVal Title As Object = Nothing) _
    As MsgBoxResult
```

The *Prompt* parameter accepts a string for display in the main body of the dialog; *Buttons* indicates which buttons, icons, and other settings to use when displaying the dialog; and *Title* accepts a custom window title if you want something other than the application title to appear. The following statement displays the window in Figure 8-2.

```
Dim result As MsgBoxResult = MsgBox( _
    "It's safe to click; the computer won't explode.", _
    MsgBoxStyle.YesNoCancel Or MsgBoxStyle.Question, _
    "Click Something")
```

Figure 8-2 Communicating an important message

The *MsgBox* function is considered to be an intrinsic part of the language. But as a member of the *Microsoft.VisualBasic* namespace, it's valid within the Visual Basic language only. If you were to do some .NET coding in C#, you would need to find another way to display a message box. That way is through the *MessageBox.Show* method. It works pretty much like the *MsgBox* function, but its second and third arguments are reversed. Some .NET conformists insist that *MsgBox*—and anything that appears in the *Microsoft.VisualBasic* namespace—must be spurned in favor of class library alternatives. Personally, I find it to be a preference choice, but you may encounter just such a person insisting that your code is substandard.

You can read my views about such tactics in Chapter 25, "Project Complete."

Using DoEvents

Programs are designed to do a lot of thinking, and sometimes they think so much, they pretty much lock up the computer. This is especially true of Visual Basic methods that perform a lot of database-heavy transactions, one right after another. The system defers less-important screen updates so that more important data processing code can occur first. That's great, but sometimes the user thinks, "This stupid computer's dead again," and pulls the plug. If the screen would simply provide better updates, the user might be more patient.

Each control on your form (and the form itself) includes a *Refresh* method, but it can be a bother to constantly refresh everything. And refreshing the display wouldn't do much to enable the "Cancel" button that you want your user to click to abort all that lovely data processing. To make life easier, Visual Basic includes a *DoEvents* method. When called, the current method's code pauses temporarily, and messages in the thread's incoming message queue are processed, including "paint" (screen update) messages. *DoEvents* is part of the *My* namespace, and is used as a stand-alone statement.

```
My.Application.DoEvents()
```

Be warned that overuse of *DoEvents* can slow down your application, and can lead to problems related to an event being called too many times. In general, it should be used only in a processing-intensive block of code, and then it should be spread out so that it is called only a few times per second at the most.

ParamArray Arguments

Any method can enable optional arguments, and the calling code can choose to include or exclude those arguments. But what if you wanted to add an unlimited number of optional arguments to a method? How could you write, for instance, a function that would return the average of all supplied arguments, with no limits on the number of arguments? Although you could accept an array variable with the source data values, you could also use a **parameter array argument**, also called a "ParamArray" argument.

As with optional arguments, ParamArray arguments must appear at the end of a method's argument list, and there can be only one, because one is more than enough for any method. Parameter array arguments use the *ParamArray* keyword just before the argument name.

```
Public Function CalculateAverage( _
      ParamArray sourceData() As Decimal) As Decimal
   ' ----- Calculate the average for a set of numbers.
   Dim singleValue As Decimal
   Dim runningTotal As Decimal = 0@

   If (sourceData.GetLength(0) = 0) Then
      Return 0@
   Else
      For Each singleValue In sourceData
         runningTotal += singleValue
      Next singleValue
      Return runningTotal / sourceData.GetLength(0)
   End If
End Function
```

Calls to the *CalculateAverage* function now accept any number of decimal values.

```
MsgBox(CalculateAverage(1, 2, 3, 4, 5))   ' Displays: 3
```

Summary

The ability to extend classes through inheritance is truly the foundation on which complex yet manageable programs are built in .NET. And they are not overly complex either. Classes are simple containers for their members, and the variety and complexity of the available members is not that great. So it's really amazing that you can write almost any type of program, and implement any number of features, using these simple foundational tools. Oh yeah, the Visual Basic language helps, too.

As we add code to the Library Project throughout this book, you will become more and more familiar with classes, structures, modules, and their members. And while you'll never remember whether *ByRef* or *ByVal* is the default parameter-passing mechanism for methods, you will add properties, methods, events, fields, and other types to classes like you were born with the ability.

Project

This chapter's code implements two features of the Library Project: (1) a simple helper class used with *ListBox* and *ComboBox* controls to manage text and data; and (2) a set of generic forms used to edit lookup tables in the Library, such as tables of status codes.

Supporting List and Combo Boxes

In Visual Basic 6.0 and earlier, *ListBox* and *ComboBox* controls included two primary array-like collections: *List* (used to store the display text for each item) and *ItemData* (used to store a 32-bit numeric value for each item). The *List* array was important to the user because it presented the text for each item. But many programmers depended more on the *ItemData* array, which allowed a unique identifier to be attached to each list item.

```
cboMonth.AddItem "January"
cboMonth.ItemData(cboMonth.NewIndex) = 1
cboMonth.AddItem "February"
cboMonth.ItemData(cboMonth.NewIndex) = 2
...
cboMonth.AddItem "December"
cboMonth.ItemData(cboMonth.NewIndex) = 12
```

Later, after the user selected a value from the list, the numeric ID could be used for database lookup or any other designed purpose.

```
nMonth = cboMonth.ItemData(cboMonth.ListIndex)
```

The bad news is that neither *List* nor *ItemData* exists in the .NET variation of *ListBox* or *ComboBox* controls. The good news is that both are replaced with a much more flexible collection: *Items*. The *Items* collection stores any type of object you want—instances of *Integer*, *String*, *Date*,

Animal, Superhero, and you can mix them within a single *ListBox.* Because *Items* is just a collection of *System.Object* instances, you can put any type of object you wish in the collection. The *ListBox* (or *ComboBox*) uses this collection to display items in the list.

So, how does a *ListBox* control know how to display text for any mixture of objects? By default, the control calls the *ToString* method of the object. *ToString* is defined in *System.Object,* and you can override it in your own class. The ListBox control also includes a *DisplayMember* property that you can set to the field or property of your class that generates the proper text.

Let's see a *ListBox* in action. Add a new *ListBox* to a form, and then add the following code to the Form's *Load* event handler.

```
Public Class Form1
    Private Sub Form1_Load(ByVal sender As System.Object, _
        ByVal e As System.EventArgs) Handles MyBase.Load
        ListBox1.Items.Add(1)
        ListBox1.Items.Add("Easy")
        ListBox1.Items.Add(#5/3/2006#)
    End Sub
End Class
```

Running this code displays the form in Figure 8-3.

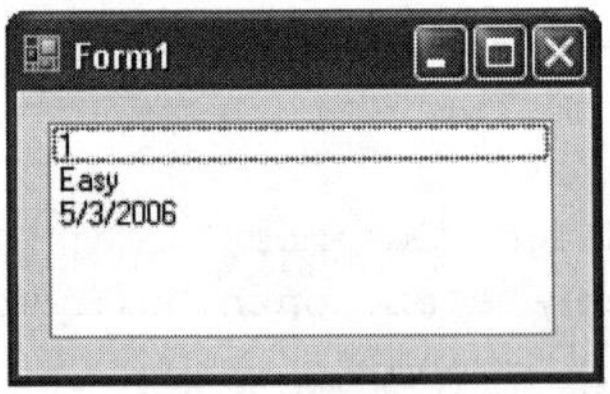

Figure 8-3 A simple ListBox with three different items

For the old *ItemData* value, the *ListBox* control includes a *ValueMember* property that identifies the identifier field or property for the objects in the *Items* collection. But you don't have to use *ValueMember.* Instead, you can simply extract the object in question from the *Items* collection, and examine its members with your own custom code to determine its identity. In reality, it's a little more work than the old

Visual Basic 6.0 method. But then again, because you can store objects of any size in the *Items* collection, you could opt to store entire database records, something you could never do before .NET.

Still, storing entire records in a *ListBox* or *ComboBox* control is pretty wasteful. It's usually much better to store just an ID number, and use it as a lookup into a database. That's what we'll do in the Library Project. To support this, we'll need to create a simple class that will expose a text and data value. First, let's go back into the Library code.

Project Access Load the "Chapter 8 (Before) Code" project, either through the New Project templates, or by accessing the project directly from the installation directory. To see the code in its final form, load "Chapter 8 (After) Code" instead.

Let's put the class in a source code file all its own. Add a new class file through the **Project ➤ Add Class** menu command. Name the class *ListItemData.vb* and click the **Add** button. The following code appears automatically.

```
Public Class ListItemData

End Class
```

This class will be pretty simple. It will include only members for text and item display. In case we forget to connect the text field to the *ListBox* or *ComboBox*'s *DisplayMember* property, we'll also include an override to the *ToString* function, plus a custom constructor that makes initialization of the members easier. Add the following code to the body of the class.

Insert Snippet Insert Chapter 8, Snippet Item 1.

```
Public ItemText As String
Public ItemData As Integer

Public Sub New(ByVal displayText As String, _
      itemID As Integer)
   ' ----- Initialize the record.
   ItemText = displayText
```

```
    ItemData = itemID
End Sub

Public Overrides Function ToString() As String
    ' ----- Display the basic item text.
    Return ItemText
End Function

Public Overrides Function Equals(ByVal obj As Object) _
        As Boolean
    ' ----- Allow IndexOf() and Contains() searches by ItemData.
    If (TypeOf obj Is Integer) Then
        Return CBool(CInt(obj) = ItemData)
    Else
        Return MyBase.Equals(obj)
    End If
End Function
```

Later, when it's time to populate a *ListBox*, we can use this object to add the display and identification values.

```
ListBox1.Items.Add(New ListItemData("Item Text", 25))
```

The override of the *Equals* method allows us to quickly look up items already added to a *ListBox* (or similar) control using features already included in the control. The *ListBox* control's *Items* collection includes an *IndexOf* method that returns the position of a matching item. Normally, this method will only match the object itself; if you pass it a *ListItemData* instance, it will report whether that item is already in the *ListBox*. The updated *Equals* code will also return *True* if we pass an *Integer* value that matches a *ListItemData.ItemData* member for an item already in the list.

```
Dim itemPosition As Integer = SomeListBox.Items.IndexOf(5)
```

Editing Code Tables

Back in Chapter 4, "Designing the Database," when we designed the database for the Library Project, several of the tables were designed to fill simple *ComboBox* lists in the application. All of these tables begin with the prefix "Code," and contain records that rarely, if ever, change in the lifetime of the application. One such table is *CodeCopyStatus*, which identifies the current general condition of an item in the library's collections (see Table 8-1).

Table 8-1 The CodeCopyStatus Table, Reprise

Field	Type	Description
ID	Long - Auto	Primary key; automatically assigned. Required.
FullName	Text(50)	Name of this status entry. Required.

Because all of these tables have basically the same format—an ID field and one or more content fields—it should be possible to design a generic template to use for editing these tables. A base (class) form would provide the basic editing features, to be developed in full through derived versions of the base form.

For the project, we will add two forms: a "summary" form (that displays a list of all currently defined codes) and a "detail" form (that allows editing of a single new or existing code). To make things even simpler, we will only include the most basic record-management functionality in the summary form. Most of the code needed to edit, display, and remove codes will appear in the detail forms.

The Generic Detail Form

Add a new form to the project (**Project ➤ New Windows Form**), naming it *BaseCodeForm.vb*. Alter the following properties as indicated.

Property	Setting
(Name)	BaseCodeForm
ControlBox	False
FormBorderStyle	FixedDialog
ShowInTaskbar	False
Size	406, 173
StartPosition	CenterScreen
Text	Code Form

Now access the source code for this class (**View ➤ Code**). The code will never create instances of this generic form directly, so let's disallow all direct instantiation by including the *MustInherit* keyword.

```
Public MustInherit Class BaseCodeForm

End Class
```

The main features of the form will be the adding of new code records, the editing of existing code records, and the removal of existing records. Add three function skeletons that support these features. We could have made them *MustOverride*, but as you'll see later, we will want the option to keep the default functionality from the base generic form.

Insert Snippet Insert Chapter 8, Snippet Item 2.

```
Public Overridable Function AddRecord() As Integer
    ' ----- Prompt to add a new record. Return the ID
    '        when added, or -1 if cancelled.
    Return -1
End Function

Public Overridable Function DeleteRecord( _
        ByVal recordID As Integer) As Boolean
    ' ----- Prompt the user to delete a record.
    '        Return True on delete.
    Return False
End Function

Public Overridable Function EditRecord( _
        ByVal recordID As Integer) As Integer
    ' ----- Prompt the user to edit the record. Return the
    '        record's ID if saved, or -1 on cancel.
    Return -1
End Function
```

The detail form will take responsibility for filling the *ListBox* control on the summary form with its items. Two methods will handle this: one that adds all items, and one that updates a single item. The derived class will be required to supply these features.

Insert Snippet Insert Chapter 8, Snippet Item 3.

```
' ----- Fill a ListBox control with existing records.
Public MustOverride Sub FillListWithRecords( _
    ByRef destList As ListBox, ByRef exceededMatches As Boolean)

' ----- Return the formatted name of a single record.
Public MustOverride Function FormatRecordName( _
    ByVal recordID As Integer) As String
```

The detail form must also display the proper titles and usage information on the summary form.

Insert Snippet Insert Chapter 8, Snippet Item 4.

```
' ----- Return a description of this editor.
Public MustOverride Function GetEditDescription() As String

' ----- Return the title-bar text for this editor.
Public MustOverride Function GetEditTitle() As String
```

While most of the tables will supply a short list of alphabetized codes, some tables will include a large number (possibly thousands) of codes. The summary form will support a search method, to locate an existing code quickly. Because only certain derived forms will use this feature, we won't include *MustOverride*.

Insert Snippet Insert Chapter 8, Snippet Item 5.

```
Public Overridable Sub SearchForRecord( _
        ByRef destList As ListBox, _
        ByRef exceededMatches As Boolean)
    ' ----- Prompt the user to search for a record.
    Return
End Sub
```

Finally, the detail form will indicate which of the available features can be used from the summary form. The summary form will call each of the following functions, and then enable or disable features as requested.

Insert Snippet Insert Chapter 8, Snippet Item 6.

```
Public Overridable Function CanUserAdd() As Boolean
    ' ----- Check the security of current user to see
    '          if adding is allowed.
    Return False
End Function

Public Overridable Function CanUserEdit() As Boolean
    ' ----- Check the security of this current to see
    '          if editing is allowed.
    Return False
End Function

Public Overridable Function CanUserDelete() As Boolean
    ' ----- Check the security of this current to see
    '          if deleting is allowed.
    Return False
End Function

Public Overridable Function UsesSearch() As Boolean
    ' ----- Does this editor support searching?
    Return False
End Function
```

That's it for the generic detail form. Later on in the book, we'll create derived versions for each of the code tables.

Generic Summary Form

The summary form is a little more straightforward, because it is just a plain form. When it starts up, it uses an instance of one of the derived detail forms to control the experience presented to the user. I've already added the form to the project; it's called *ListEditRecords.vb*, and looks like Figure 8-4.

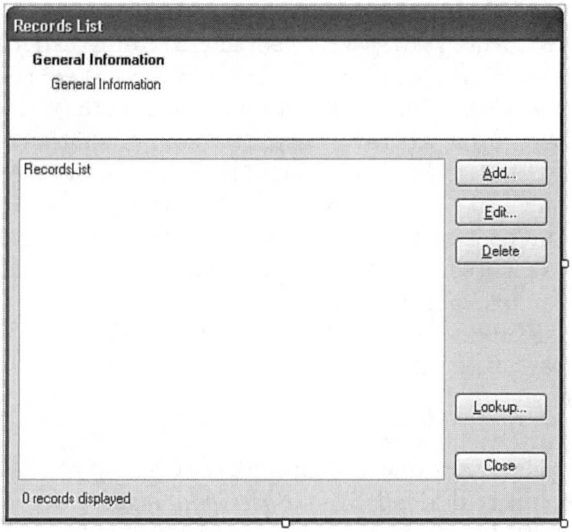

Figure 8-4 The Generic Summary form

A large *ListBox* control fills most of the form, a control that will hold all existing items. There are also buttons to add, edit, delete, and search for items in the list. There's a lot of code to manage these items; I've already written it in a code snippet. Switch to the form's source code view, and add the source code just after the "Public Class ListEditRecords" line.

Insert Snippet Insert Chapter 8, Snippet Item 7.

The first line of the added code defines a private instance of the generic detail form we just designed.

```
Private DetailEditor As Library.BaseCodeForm
```

This field holds an instance of a class derived from *BaseCodeForm*. That assignment appears in the public method *ManageRecords*.

```
Public Sub ManageRecords(ByRef UseDetail _
    As Library.BaseCodeForm)
    ' ----- Set up the form for use with this code set.
    Dim exceededMatches As Boolean
```

```
DetailEditor = UseDetail
RecordsTitle.Text = DetailEditor.GetEditTitle()
RecordsInfo.Text = DetailEditor.GetEditDescription()
Me.Text = DetailEditor.GetEditTitle()
ActAdd.Visible = DetailEditor.CanUserAdd()
ActEdit.Visible = DetailEditor.CanUserEdit()
ActDelete.Visible = DetailEditor.CanUserDelete()
ActLookup.Visible = DetailEditor.UsesSearch()
DetailEditor.FillListWithRecords(RecordsList, _
    exceededMatches)
RefreshItemCount(exceededMatches)
Me.ShowDialog()
End Sub
```

The code that calls *ManageRecords* passes in form instance, one of the forms derived from *BaseCodeForm*. Once assigned to the internal *DetailEditor* field, the code uses the public features of that instance to configure the display elements on the summary form. For instance, the detail form's *CanUserAdd* function, a *Boolean* value, sets the *Visible* property of the *ActAdd* button. The *FillListWithRecords* method call populates the summary *ListBox* control with any existing code values. After some more display adjustments, the *Me.ShowDialog* method displays the summary form to the user.

Although the user will interact with the controls on the summary form, most of these controls defer their processing to the detail form, *DetailEditor*. For example, a click on the "Add" button defers most of the logic to the detail form's *AddRecord* method. The code in the summary form doesn't do much more than update its own display fields.

```
Private Sub ActAdd_Click(ByVal sender As System.Object, _
    ByVal e As System.EventArgs) Handles ActAdd.Click
  ' ----- Let the user add a record.
  Dim newID As Integer
  Dim newPosition As Integer

  ' ----- Prompt the user.
  newID = DetailEditor.AddRecord()
  If (newID = -1) Then Return

  ' ----- Add this record to the list.
  newPosition = RecordsList.Items.Add( _
```

```
        (New Library.ListItemData( _
        DetailEditor.FormatRecordName(newID), newID)))
    RecordsList.SelectedIndex = newPosition
    RefreshButtons()
    RefreshItemCount(False)
End Sub
```

Most of the remaining code in the summary form is either just like this (for edit, delete, and search features), or is used to refresh the display based on user interaction with the form. Be sure to examine the code to get a good understanding of how the code works. In later chapters, when adding actual detail forms, you'll see this code in action.

CHAPTER 9

ERROR PROCESSING

Debugging and error processing are two of the most essential programming activities you will ever perform. There are three absolutes in life: death, taxes, and software bugs. Even in a relatively bug-free application, there is every reason to believe that a user will just mess things up royally. As a programmer, your job is to be the guardian of the user's data as managed by the application, and to keep it safe, even from the user's own negligence (or malfeasance) and also from your own source code.

I recently spoke with a developer from a large software company headquartered in Redmond, Washington; you might know the company. This developer told me that in any given application developed by this company, more than 50 percent of the code is dedicated to dealing with errors, bad data, system exceptions, and failures. Certainly, all this additional code slows down each application and adds a lot of overhead to what is already called "bloatware." But in an age of hackers and data entry mistakes, such error management is an absolute must.

Testing—although not a topic covered in this book—goes hand-in-hand with error management. Often, the report of an error will lead to a bout of testing, but it should really be the other way around: Testing should lead to the discovery of errors. When I first started work on this chapter, the daily news was reporting that NASA's *Mars Global Surveyor*, in orbit around the red planet, had captured images of the *Beagle 2*, a land-based research craft that crashed into the Martian surface in 2003. An assessment of the *Beagle 2*'s failure pinpointed many areas of concern, with a major issue being inadequate testing:

> This led to an attenuated testing programme to meet the cost and schedule constraints, thus inevitably increasing technical risk. (From Beagle 2 ESA/UK Commission of Inquiry Report, April 5, 2004, Page 4)

Look at all those big words. Boy, the Europeans sure have a way with language. Perhaps a direct word-for-word translation into American English will make it clear what the commission was trying to convey:

They didn't test it enough, and probably goofed it all up.

The Nature of Errors in Visual Basic

There are three major categories of errors that you will deal with in your Visual Basic applications.

1. **Compile-Time Errors.** Some errors are so blatant that Visual Basic will refuse to compile your application. Generally, such errors are due to simple syntax issues that can be corrected with a few keystrokes. But you can also enable features in your program that will increase the number of errors recognized by the compiler. For instance, if you set *Option Strict* to *On* in your application or source code files, implicit narrowing conversions will generate compile-time errors.

```
' ----- Assume: Option Strict On
Dim bigData As Long = 5&
Dim smallData As Integer
' ----- The next line will not compile.
smallData = bigData
```

Visual Studio 2005 includes new features that help you locate and resolve compile-time errors. Such errors are marked with a "blue squiggle" below the offending syntax. Some errors also prompt Visual Studio to display corrective options through a pop-up window, as shown in Figure 9-1.

```
Option Strict On

Public Class Form1
    Private Sub Form1_Click(ByVal sender As Object, _
            ByVal e As System.EventArgs) Handles Me.Click
        Dim bigData As Long = 5&
        Dim smallData As Integer
        ' ----- The next line will not compile.
        smallData = bigData
```

```
Option Strict On disallows implicit conversions from
'Long' to 'Integer'.
  ☆ |  Replace 'bigData' with 'CInt(bigData)'.
      Dim smallData As Integer
      ' ----- The next line will not compile
      smallData = CInt(bigData)bigData
☑ Expand All Previews
```

Figure 9-1 Error correction options for a narrowing conversion

2. **Run-Time Errors.** Run-time errors occur when a combination of data and code causes an invalid condition in what otherwise appears to be valid code. Such errors frequently occur when a user enters incorrect data into the application, but your own code can also generate run-time errors. Adequate checking of all incoming data will greatly reduce this class of errors. Consider the following block of code:

```
Public Function GetNumber() As Integer
    ' ----- Prompt the user for a number.
    '       Return zero if the user clicks Cancel.
    Dim useAmount As String

    ' ----- InputBox returns a string with whatever
    '       the user types in.
    useAmount = InputBox("Enter number.")
    If (IsNumeric(useAmount) = True) Then
        ' ----- Convert to an integer and return it.
        Return CInt(useAmount)
    Else
        ' ----- Invalid data. Return zero.
        Return 0
    End If
End Function
```

This code looks pretty reasonable, and in most cases, it is. It prompts the user for a number, converts valid numbers to integer format, and returns the result. The *IsNumeric* function will weed out any invalid non-numeric entries. Calling this function will, in fact, return valid integers for entered numeric values, and zero for invalid entries.

But what happens when a fascist dictator tries to use this code? As history has shown, a fascist dictator will enter a value such as "342304923940234." Because it's a valid number, it will pass the *IsNumeric* test with flying colors, but since it exceeds the size of the *Integer* data type, it will generate the dreaded run-time error shown in Figure 9-2.

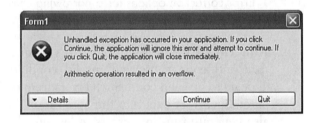

Figure 9-2 An error message only a fascist dictator could love

Without additional error-handling code or checks for valid data limits, the *GetNumber* routine generates this run-time error, and then causes the entire program to abort. Between committing war crimes and entering invalid numeric values, there seems to be no end to the evil that fascist dictators will do.

3. **Logic Errors.** Logic errors are the third, and the most insidious, type of error. They are caused by you, the programmer; you can't blame the user on this one. From process-flow issues to incorrect calculations, logic errors are the bane of software development, and result in more required debugging time than the other two types of errors combined.

Logic errors are too personal and too varied to directly address in this book. Many logic errors can be forced out of your code by adding sufficient checks for invalid data, and by adequately testing your application under a variety of conditions and circumstances.

You won't have that much difficulty dealing with compile-time errors. A general understanding of Visual Basic and .NET programming concepts, and a regular use of the tools included with Visual Studio 2005, will help you quickly locate and eliminate them.

The bigger issue is: What do you do with run-time errors? Even if you check all possible data and external resource conditions, it's impossible to prevent all run-time errors. You never know when a network connection will suddenly go down, or the user will trip over the printer cable, or a scratch on a DVD will generate data corruption. Any time you deal with resources that exist outside of your source code, you are taking a chance that run-time errors will occur.

Figure 9-2 showed you what Visual Basic does when it encounters a run-time error: It displays to the user a generic error dialog, and offers a chance to ignore the error (possible corruption of any unsaved data) or exit the program immediately (complete loss of any unsaved data).

Although both of these user actions leave much to the imagination, they don't instill consumer confidence in your coding skills. Trust me on this: The user will blame you for any errors generated by your application, even if the true problem was far removed from your code.

Fortunately, Visual Basic includes three tools to help you deal completely with run-time errors, if and when they occur. These three Visual Basic features—unstructured error handling, structured error handling, and unhandled error handling—can all be used in any Visual Basic application to protect the user's data—and the user—from unwanted errors.

Unstructured Error Handling

Unstructured error handling has been a part of Visual Basic since it first debuted in the early 1990s. It's simple to use, catches all possible errors in a block of code, and can be enabled or disabled as needed. By default, methods and property procedures include no error handling at all, so you must add error-handling code—unstructured or structured—to every routine where you feel it is needed.

The idea behind unstructured error handling is pretty basic. You simply add a line in your code that says, "If any errors occur at all, temporarily jump down to this other section of my procedure where I have special code to deal with it." This "other section" is called the **error handler**.

```
Public Sub ErrorProneRoutine()
    ' ----- Any code you put here, before enabling the
    '       error handler, should be pretty resistent to
    '       run-time errors.

    ' ----- Turn on the error handler.
    On Error GoTo ErrorHandler

    ' ----- More code here with the risk of run-time errors.
    '       When all logic is complete, exit the routine.
    Return

ErrorHandler:
    ' ----- When an error occurs, the code temporarily jumps
    '       down here, where you can deal with it. When you're
    '       finished, call this statement:
    Resume
    ' ----- which will jump back to the code that caused
    '       the error. The "Resume" statement has a few
    '       variations available. If you don't want to go
    '       back to main code, but just want to get out of
    '       this routine as quickly as possible, call:
    Return
End Sub
```

The *On Error* statement enables or disables error handling in the routine. When an error occurs, Visual Basic places the details of that error in a global *Err* object. This object stores the numeric error code, a text description of the error, related online help details, and other error-specific values. I'll list the details a little later.

You can include as many *On Error* statements in your code as you want, and each one could direct errant code to a different label. You could have one error handler for network errors, one for file errors, one for calculation errors, and so on. Or, you could have one big error handler that uses *If...Then...Else* statements to examine the error condition stored in the global *Err* object.

```
ErrorHandler:
    If (Err.Number = 5) Then
        ' ----- Handle error-code-5 issues here.
```

The Try Clause

Try statements are designed to monitor smaller chunks of code. Although you could put all the source code for your procedure within the *Try* block, it's more common to put only the statements that are likely to generate errors within that section.

```
Try
   My.Computer.FileSystem.RenameFile(existingFile, newName)
Catch...
```

"Safe" statements can remain outside of the *Try* portion of the *Try...End Try* statement. Exactly what constitutes a "safe" programming statement is topic of much debate, but there are two types of statements that are generally unsafe: (1) those statements that interact with external systems, such as disk files, network or hardware resources, or even large blocks of memory; and (2) those statements that could cause a variable or expression to exceed the designed limits of the data type for that variable or expression.

The Catch Clause

The *Catch* clause defines an error handler. As with unstructured error handling, you can include one global error handler in a *Try* statement, or you can include multiple handlers for different types of errors. Each handler includes its own *Catch* keyword.

```
Catch ex As ErrorClass
```

The *ex* identifier provides a variable name for the active error object that you can use within the *Catch* section. You can give it any name you wish; it can vary from *Catch* clause to *Catch* clause, but it doesn't have to.

ErrorClass identifies an exception class, a special class specifically designed to convey error information. The most generic exception class is *System.Exception*; other more specific exception classes derive from *System.Exception*. Because *Try...End Try* implements "object-oriented error processing," all the errors must be stored as objects. The .NET Framework includes many pre-defined exception classes already derived from *System.Exception* that you can use in your application. For instance,

System.DivideByZeroException catches any errors that (obviously) stem from dividing a number by zero.

```
Try
    result = firstNumber / secondNumber
Catch ex As System.DivideByZeroException
    MsgBox("Divide by zero error.")
Catch ex As System.OverflowException
    MsgBox("Divide resulting in an overflow.")
Catch ex As System.Exception
    MsgBox("Some other error occurred.")
End Try
```

When an error occurs, your code tests the exception against each *Catch* clause until it finds a matching class. The *Catch* clauses are examined in order from top to bottom, so make sure you put the most general one last; if you put *System.Exception* first, no other *Catch* clauses in that *Try* block will ever trigger because every exception matches *System.Exception*. How many *Catch* clauses you include, or which exceptions they monitor, is up to you. If you leave out all *Catch* clauses completely, it will act somewhat like an *On Error Resume Next* statement, although if an error does occur, all remaining statements in the *Try* block will be skipped. Execution continues with the *Finally* block, and then with the code following the entire *Try* statement.

The Finally Clause

The *Finally* clause represents the "do this or die" part of your *Try* block. If an error occurs in your *Try* statement, the code in the *Finally* section will always be processed after the relevant *Catch* clause is complete. If no error occurs, the *Finally* block will still be processed before leaving the *Try* statement. If you issue a *Return* statement somewhere in your *Try* statement, the *Finally* block will still be processed before leaving the routine. (This is getting monotonous.) If you use the *Exit Try* statement to exit the *Try* block early, the *Finally* block is still executed. If, while your *Try* block is being processed, your boss announces that a free catered lunch is starting immediately in the big meeting room and everyone is welcome, the *Finally* code will also be processed, but you might not be there to see it.

Finally clauses are generally optional, so you need to include it only when you need it. The only time that *Finally* clauses are required is when you omit all *Catch* clauses in a *Try* statement.

Unhandled Errors

I showed you earlier in the chapter how unhandled errors can lead to data corruption, crashed applications, and spiraling out-of-control congressional spending. All good programmers understand how important error-handling code is, and make the extra effort of including either structured or unstructured error-handling code. Yet there are times when I, even I, as a programmer, think, "Oh, this procedure isn't doing anything that could generate errors. I'll just leave out the error-handling code and save some typing time." And then it strikes, seemingly without warning: an unhandled error. Crash! Burn! Another chunk of user data confined to the bit bucket of life.

Normally, all unhandled errors "bubble up" the call stack, looking for a procedure that includes error-handling code. For instance, consider this code.

```
Private Sub Level1()
    On Error GoTo ErrorHandler
    Level2()
    Return

ErrorHandler:
    MsgBox("Error Handled.")
    Resume Next
End Sub

Private Sub Level2()
    Level3()
End Sub

Private Sub Level3()
    ' ----- The Err.Raise method forces an
    '       unstructured-style error.
    Err.Raise(1)
End Sub
```

When the error occurs in *Level3*, the application looks for an active error handler in that procedure, but finds nothing. So it immediately exits *Level3* and returns to *Level2*, where it looks again for an active error handler. Such a search will, sadly, be fruitless. Heartbroken, the code leaves *Level2* and moves back to *Level1*, continuing its search for a reasonable error handler. This time it finds one. Processing immediately jumps down to the *ErrorHandler* block and executes the code in that section.

If *Level1* didn't have an error handler, and no code farther up the stack included an error handler, the user would see the Error Message Window of Misery (refer to Figure 9-2), followed by the Dead Program of Disappointment.

Fortunately, Visual Basic does support a "catch all" error handler that traps such unmanaged exceptions and lets you do something about them. This feature works only if you have the **Enable application framework** field selected on the *Application* tab of the project properties. To access the code template for the global error handler, click the **View Application Events** button on that same project properties tab. Select "(MyApplication Events)" from the **Class Name** drop-down list above the source code window, and then select "UnhandledException" from the **Method Name** list. The following procedure appears in the code window.

```
Private Sub MyApplication_UnhandledException( _
    ByVal sender As Object, _
    ByVal e As Microsoft.VisualBasic. _
    ApplicationServices.UnhandledExceptionEventArgs) _
    Handles Me.UnhandledException


End Sub
```

Add your special global error-handling code to this routine. The *e* event argument includes an *Exception* member that provides access to the details of the error via a *System.Exception* object. The *e.ExitApplication* member is a *Boolean* property that you can modify either to continue or to exit the application. By default, it's set to *True*, so modify it if you want to keep the program running.

Even when the program does stay running, you will lose the active event path that triggered the error. If the error stemmed from a click on some button by the user, that entire *Click* event, and all of its called methods, will be abandoned immediately, and the program will wait for new input from the user.

Managing Errors

In addition to simply watching for them and screaming "Error!" there are a few other things you should know about error management in Visual Basic programs.

Generating Errors

Believe it or not, there are times when you might want to generate run-time errors in your code. In fact, many of the run-time errors you encounter in your code occur because Microsoft wrote code in the Framework Class Libraries that specifically generates errors. This is by design.

Let's say that you had a class property that was to only accept percentage values from 0 to 100, but as an *Integer* data type.

```
Private StoredPercent As Integer
Public Property InEffectPercent() As Integer
   Get
      Return StoredPercent
   End Get
   Set(ByVal value As Integer)
      StoredPercent = value
   End Set
End Property
```

There's nothing grammatically wrong with this code, but it will not stop anyone from setting the stored percent value to either 847 or –847, both outside the desired range. You can add an *If* statement to the *Set* accessor to reject invalid data, but properties don't provide a way to return a failed status code. The only way to inform the calling code of a problem is to generate an exception.

```
Set(ByVal value As Integer)
   If (value < 0) Or (value > 100) Then
      Throw New ArgumentOutOfRangeException("value", _
         value, "The allowed range is from 0 to 100.")
   Else
      StoredPercent = value
   End If
End Set
```

9. ERROR PROCESSING

Now, attempts to set the *InEffectPercent* property to a value outside the 0-to-100 range will generate an error, an error that can be caught by *On Error* or *Try...Catch* error handlers. The *Throw* statement accepts a *System.Exception* (or derived) object as its argument, and sends that exception object up the call stack on a quest for an error handler.

Similar to the *Throw* statement is the *Err.Raise* method. It lets you generate errors using a number-based error system more familiar to Visual Basic 6.0 and earlier environments. Personally, I recommend that you use the *Throw* statement, even if you employ unstructured error handling elsewhere in your code.

Mixing Error-Handling Methods

You are free to mix both unstructured and structured error-handling methods broadly in your application, but a single procedure or method may only use one of these methods. That is, you may not use both *On Error* and *Try...Catch...Finally* in the same routine. A routine that uses *On Error* may call another routine that uses *Try...Catch...Finally* with no problems.

Now you may be thinking to yourself, "Self, I can easily see times when I would want to use unstructured error handling, and other times when I would opt for the more structured approach." It all sounds very reasonable, but let me warn you in advance that there are error-handling zealots out there who will ridicule you for decades if you ever use an *On Error* statement in your code. For these programmers, "object-oriented purity" is essential, and any code that uses non-object methods to achieve what could be done through an OOP approach must be destroyed.

Warning I'm about to use a word that I forbid my nine-year-old son from using. If you have tender ears, cover them now, though it won't protect you from seeing the word on the printed page.

Rejecting the *On Error* statement like this is just plain **stupid**. As you may remember from earlier chapters, everything in your .NET application is object-oriented, because all the code appears in the context of an object. If you are using unstructured error handling, you can still get to the relevant exception object through the *Err.GetException()* method, so it's not really an issue of objects. Determining when to use structured or unstructured error handling is no different from deciding to use C# or Visual Basic to write your applications. For most applications, the choice is irrelevant. There may be some esoteric features that one language has that may steer you in that direction (such as optional method arguments in Visual Basic), but the other 99.9% of the features are pretty much identical.

The same is true of error-handling methods. There may be times when one is just plain better than the other. For instance, consider the following code that calls three methods, none of which include their own error handler.

```
On Error Resume Next
RefreshPart1()
RefreshPart2()
RefreshPart3()
```

Clearly I don't care if an error occurs in one of the routines or not. If an error causes an early exit from *RefreshPart1*, the next routine, *RefreshPart2*, will still be called, and so on. I often need more diligent error-checking code than this, but in low-impact code, this is sufficient. To accomplish this same thing using structured error handling would be a little more involved.

```
Try
    RefreshPart1()
Catch
End Try
Try
    RefreshPart2()
Catch
End Try
Try
    RefreshPart3()
Catch
End Try
```

That's a lot of extra code for the same functionality. If you're an *On Error* statement hater, then by all means, use the second block of code. But if you are a more reasonable programmer, the type of programmer who would read a book like this, then use each method as it fits into your coding design.

The System.Exception Class

The *System.Exception* class is the base class for all structured exceptions. When an error occurs, you can examine its members to determine the exact nature of the error. You also use this class (or one of its derived classes) to build your own custom exception in anticipation of using the *Throw* statement. Table 9-1 lists the members of this object.

Table 9-1 Members of the System.Exception Class

Object Member	Description
Data Property	Provides access to a collection of key-value pairs, each providing additional exception-specific information.
HelpLink Property	Identifies online help location information relevant to this exception.
InnerException Property	If an exception is a side effect of another error, the original error appears here.
Message Property	A textual description of the error.
Source Property	Identifies the name of the application or object that caused the error.
StackTrace Property	Returns a string that fully documents the current stack trace, the list of all active procedure calls that led to the statement causing the error.
TargetSite Property	Identifies the name of the method that triggered the error.

Classes derived from *System.Exception* may include additional properties that provide additional detail for a specific error type.

The Err Object

The *Err* object provides access to the most recent error through its various members. Anytime an error occurs, Visual Basic documents the details of the error in this object's members. It's often accessed within an unstructured error handler to reference or display the details of the error. Table 9-2 lists the members of this object.

Table 9-2 Members of the Err Object

Object Member	Description
Clear Method	Clear all of the properties in the *Err* object, setting them to their default values. Normally, you use the *Err* object only to determine the details of a triggered error. But you can also use it to initiate an error with your own error details. See the description of the *Raise* method later in the table.
Description Property	A textual description of the error.
Erl Property	The line number label nearest to where the error occurred. In modern Visual Basic applications, numeric line labels are almost never used, so this field is generally zero.
HelpContext Property	The location within an online help file relevant to the error. If this property and the *HelpFile* property are set, you or the user can access relevant online help information.
HelpFile Property	The online help file related to the active error.
LastDLLError Property	The numeric return value from the most recent call to a pre-.NET DLL, whether it is an error or not.
Number Property	The numeric code for the active error.
Raise Method	Use this method to generate a run-time error. Although this method does include some arguments for setting other properties in the *Err* object, you can also set the properties yourself before calling the *Raise* method. Any properties you set will be retained in the object for examination by the error-handler code that receives the error.
Source Property	The name of the application, class, or object that generated the active error.

The Debug Object

Visual Basic 6.0 (and earlier) included a handy tool that would quickly output debug information from your program, displaying such output in the "Immediate Window" of the Visual Basic development environment.

```
Debug.Print "Reached point G in code"
```

The .NET version of Visual Basic enhances the *Debug* object with more features, and a slight change in syntax. The *Print* method is replaced with *WriteLine*; a separate *Write* method outputs text without a final carriage return.

```
Debug.WriteLine("Reached point G in code")
```

Everything you output using the *WriteLine* (or similar) method goes to a series of "listeners" attached to the *Debug* object. You can add your own listeners, including output to a work file. But the *Debug* object is really only used when debugging your program. Once you compile a final release, none of the *Debug*-related features work anymore, by design.

If you wish to log status data from a released application, consider using the *My.Application.Log* object instead (or *My.Log* in ASP.NET programs). Similar to the *Debug* object, the *Log* object sends its output to any number of registered listeners. By default, all output goes to the standard debug output (just like the *Debug* object) and to a log file created specifically for your application's assembly. See the online help for the *My.Application.Log Object* for information on configuring this object to meet your needs.

Other Visual Basic Error Features

The Visual Basic language includes a few other error-specific statements and features that you may find useful:

- *ErrorToString Function.* This method returns the error message associated with a numeric system error code. For instance, *ErrorToString(10)* returns "This array is fixed or temporarily locked." It is useful only with older unstructured error codes.
- *IsError Function.* When you supply an object argument to this function, it returns *True* if the object is a *System.Exception* (or derived) object.

Summary

The best program in the world would never generate errors, I guess. But come on, it's not reality. If a multi-million dollar Mars probe is going to crash on a planet millions of miles away even after years of advanced engineering, then my customer-tracking application for a local video rental shop is certainly going to have a bug or two. But you can mitigate the impact of these bugs using the error-management features included with Visual Basic.

Project

This chapter's project code will be somewhat brief. Error-handling code will appear throughout the entire application, but we'll add it in little by little as we craft the project. For now, let's just focus on the central error-handling routines that will take some basic action when an error occurs anywhere in the program.

General Error Handler

As important and precise as error handling needs to be, the typical business application will not encounter a large variety of error types. Applications like the Library Project are mainly vulnerable to three types of errors: (1) data entry errors; (2) errors that occur when reading data from, or writing data to, a database table; and (3) errors related to printing. Sure, there may be numeric overflow errors or other errors related to in-use data, but it's mostly interactions with external resources, such as the database, that concern us.

Because of the limited types of errors occurring in the application, it's possible to write a generic routine that informs the user of the error in a consistent manner. Each time a run-time error occurs, we will call this central routine, just to let the user know what's going on. The code block where the error occurred can then decide whether to take any special compensating action, or continue on as if no error occurred.

Project Access Load the "Chapter 9 (Before) Code" project, either through the New Project templates, or by accessing the project directly from the installation directory. To see the code in its final form, load "Chapter 9 (After) Code" instead.

In the project, open the *General.vb* class file, and add the following code as a new method to *Module General*.

Insert Snippet Insert Chapter 9, Snippet Item 1.

```
Public Sub GeneralError(ByVal routineName As String, _
    ByVal theError As System.Exception)
  ' ----- Report an error to the user.
  MsgBox("The following error occurred at location '" & _
    routineName & "':" & vbCrLf & vbCrLf & _
    theError.Message, _
    MsgBoxStyle.OKOnly Or MsgBoxStyle.Exclamation, _
    ProgramTitle)
End Sub
```

Not much to that code, is there? So, here's how it works. When you encounter an error in some routine, the in-effect error handler calls the central *GeneralError* method.

```
Public Sub SomeRoutine()
    On Error GoTo ErrorHandler

    ' ----- Lots of code here.
    Return

ErrorHandler:
    GeneralError("SomeRoutine", Err.GetException())
    Resume Next
End Sub
```

You can use it with structured errors as well.

```
Try
    ' ----- Troubling code here.
Catch ex As System.Exception
    GeneralError("SomeRoutine", ex)
End Try
```

The purpose of the *GeneralError* global method is simple: Communicate to the user that an error occurred, and then move on. It's meant to be simple, and it is simple. You could enhance the routine with some additional features. Logging of the error out to a file (or any other active log listener) might assist you later if you needed to examine application-generated errors. Add the following code to the routine, just after the *MsgBox* command, to record the exception.

Insert Snippet Insert Chapter 9, Snippet Item 2.

```
My.Application.Log.WriteException(theError)
```

Of course, if an error occurs while writing to the log, that would be a big problem, so add one more line to the start of the *GeneralError* routine.

Insert Snippet Insert Chapter 9, Snippet Item 3.

On Error Resume Next
Unhandled Error Capture

As I mentioned earlier, it's a good idea to include a global error handler in your code, in case some error gets past your defenses. To include this code, display all files in the *Solution Explorer* using the "Show All Files" button, open the *ApplicationEvents.vb* file, and add the following code to the *MyApplication* class.

Insert Snippet Insert Chapter 9, Snippet Item 4.

```
Private Sub MyApplication_UnhandledException( _
     ByVal sender As Object, ByVal e As Microsoft. _
     VisualBasic.ApplicationServices. _
     UnhandledExceptionEventArgs) Handles _
     Me.UnhandledException
   ' ----- Record the error, and keep running.
   e.ExitApplication = False
   GeneralError("Unhandled Exception", e.Exception)
End Sub
```

Because we already have the global *GeneralError* routine to log our errors, we might as well take advantage of it here.

That's it for errors. In the next chapter, which covers database interactions, we'll make frequent use of this error-handling code.

ADO.NET

If you have ever read any programming books related to Microsoft development technologies, then you have already read a chapter just like this one. It seems that every Windows programming book has an obligatory chapter on database interaction. The reason for this widespread coverage comes as no surprise: Microsoft comes out with a new database technology every two years or so.

If you are new to Windows development, then you haven't yet been briefed on the following sometimes conflicting, sometimes complementary database interaction tools:

- ODBC—Open DataBase Connectivity
- ISAM—Indexed Sequential Access Method
- DAO—Data Access Objects
- RDO—Remote Data Objects
- OLE DB—Object Linking and Embedding for Databases
- ADO—ActiveX Data Objects

When you look at this list, you might think, "Wow, that's great. There are so many options to choose from." You would be foolish to think this. This list isn't great; it's terrible. Imagine, just for a moment, that we weren't talking about database interfaces, but about other, more practical issues. What if you had to replace the engine in your car every two years? What if the steering column had to be replaced annually? What if you had to replace the oil every 3,500 miles or three months, whichever came first? Could you imagine life in such a world?

Whenever Microsoft introduced a new database object technology into the mix, it was quickly followed by a flurry of reprogramming to bring older "legacy" Visual Basic (and other) applications up to the latest database technology. This wasn't always possible, as time and budget constraints kept organizations on older platforms. I still maintain a quarter-million-line application that uses DAO, a somewhat older technology. Although it will be converted to .NET someday, the cost to move it from DAO to the more flexible ADO platform was prohibitive.

So far, it seems that **ADO.NET** (ActiveX Data Objects for .NET) is different. It's been out for about six years (as of this writing), and Microsoft hasn't yet teased programmers with a replacement. ADO.NET is quite flexible, and that flexibility will hopefully allow it to stretch itself over new advances in technology for the foreseeable future.

If you are familiar with the ADO technology, then prepare to forget it. ADO.NET is not the natural successor to ADO. It's a completely new technology that is unrelated to ADO, and although it shares some terminology with ADO and other older tools, ADO.NET only does this to play with your mind.

What Is ADO.NET?

ADO.NET is a set of classes, included with the .NET Framework, that represents the primary method by which .NET applications interact with relational databases and other open and proprietary data management systems. But it's not just for interaction; ADO.NET is, in reality, a partial in-memory relational database all by itself. You can create tables and relationships (joins) with ADO.NET objects, add and remove records, query tables based on selection criteria, and do other simple tasks that are typical of stand-alone relational database systems.

All classes included with ADO.NET appear in the *System.Data* namespace; other subordinate namespaces provide derived classes geared toward specific database platforms. For instance, the *System.Data.SqlClient* namespace targets SQL Server databases, while *System.Data.OracleClient* focuses on Oracle RDBMS systems. Other database providers can develop streamlined implementations of the various ADO.NET classes for use with their own systems, and supply them as a separate namespace.

ADO.NET implements a **disconnected** data experience. In traditional database programming, especially in desktop applications, the connection between an application and its database was fixed and long-term. When the program started up, the connection started up. When the program exited many hours later, the connection finally ended. But in a world of massively scalable web sites, keeping a database connected for hours on end is wasteful and often impossible.

ADO.NET encourages you to open data connections just long enough to get the data that fulfills your immediate needs. Once you have the data, you drop the connection until the next time you need to retrieve, insert, or update database content. If you issue the following SQL statement:

```
SELECT * FROM Customer WHERE BalanceDue > 0
```

you have a choice of (1) scanning through all the records once in a quick and simple manner; and (2) loading the data into an in-memory table-like object, closing the connection, and working with the loaded records as if they were the original. If you use the first method, you can take your sweet time waltzing through the records, taking many minutes to process each one. But this type of selfish behavior is frowned upon by ADO.NET. The goal is to get in and get out as quickly as you can.

Because of the disconnected nature of ADO.NET, some techniques common in database applications need to change. For instance, the long-term locking of database records during a user modification ("pessimistic concurrency") is difficult to accomplish in ADO.NET's disconnected environment. You will have to use other methods, such as transactions or atomic stored procedure features, to accomplish the same goals.

Overview of ADO.NET

ADO.NET divides its world into two hemispheres: *providers* and the *DataSet*. Imagine your kitchen as the world of ADO.NET, with your refrigerator representing the provider, and the oven/stove as the *DataSet*. The provider "provides" access to some content, such as food, or an Oracle database (which normally appears in the meat-and-cheese drawer). It's a long-term storage facility, and content that goes in there usually stays in there for quite a while. If something is removed, it's because it is no longer valid, or has become corrupted.

To use your oven, you select content from the long-term storage of the refrigerator, update it by mixing, heating, and rearranging the content, and eventually return it to the refrigerator where it will again sit in storage. This analogy isn't perfect; in fact, something just doesn't smell right about it. But it conveys the basic idea: Providers give you access to stored data, some of which can be moved into and processed through an application and its *DataSet* on a short-term basis.

Providers

Large database systems, such as SQL Server and Oracle, are stand-alone "servers" (hence the "SQL *Server*" name) that interact with client tools and applications only indirectly. These systems generally accept network connections from clients through a TCP/IP port or similar connection. Once authenticated, the client makes all of its requests through this connection before disconnecting from the system.

Back in the early 1990s, Microsoft implemented **ODBC** (based on other existing standards) as a common system through which clients would connect to database servers, as well as other simpler data sources. Clients no longer had to worry about all of the networking protocols needed to talk with a database; all of that code was included in the ODBC driver.

Microsoft later released a similar data connection system called **OLE DB**, based on ActiveX technology. OLE DB drivers for common systems soon appeared, although you could still get to ODBC resources through a generic ODBC driver built in OLE DB.

In .NET, both ODBC and OLE DB are replaced by **providers**, libraries of code that provide all of the communication between the database and your application. Providers are an integral part of ADO.NET, and you will have to use them to get to your databases. Fortunately, providers exist for the main database systems, and an "OleDb provider" exists for systems without their own providers.

Four primary objects make up the programmer's view of the provider.

- **The Connection object.** This object directs communication between your program and the data source. It includes properties and methods that let you indicate the location or connection parameters for the data source. Multi-command transactions are managed at this object level.
- **The Command object.** This object takes the SQL statement you provide, and prepares it for transport through the *Connection* object. You can include parameters in your command for stored procedure and complex statement support.
- **The DataReader object.** The *DataReader* provides a simple and efficient way to retrieve results from a data query. It is used by other objects in ADO.NET to receive and redirect data for use within your program, but your code can use it directly to process the results of a SELECT statement or other data retrieval action.

- **The DataAdapter object.** This object is what makes communication between a *DataSet* and the rest of a provider possible. One of its primary jobs is to modify data manipulation statements (the SELECT, INSERT, UPDATE, and DELETE statements) generated by a *DataSet* into a format that can be used by the related data source.

Using these objects is a little involved, but not hard to understand. To connect to a typical relational database, such as SQL Server, and process data, follow these steps:

1. Establish a connection to your data source using a *Connection* object.
2. Wrap a SQL statement in a *Command* object.
3. Execute that *Command* object in the context of the established *Connection*.
4. If any results are to be returned, use either a *DataReader* to scan through the records, or use a combination of a *DataAdaptor* and *DataSet* (or *DataTable*) to retrieve or store the results.
5. Close all objects that you opened to process the data.

Although the .NET Framework includes data providers for a few different data systems, the remainder of this chapter's discussion focuses only on the SQL Server provider, exposed through the *System.Data.SqlClient* namespace.

Note SQL Server 2005 includes support for a new feature called "User Instances," for use with SQL Server 2005 Express Edition databases. This feature allows a low-privilege user to access a specific SQL Server Express database file without the need for an administrator to establish SQL Server security settings for that user. This feature is useful in environments where the related software was installed through the new *ClickOnce* deployment method (discussed in Chapter 24, "Deployment,") without administrator involvement. It also requires specific reconfiguration of the SQL Server Express installation before use. For more information on this feature, reference the "Working with User Instances" article in the ADO.NET portion of the MSDN documentation supplied with your Visual Studio installation.

DataSets

If you are going to do more than just quickly scan the data that comes back from a *DataReader* query, you will probably use a *DataSet* to store, manage, and optionally update your data. Each *DataSet* provides a generic disconnected view of data, whether it is data from a provider, or data that you build through code. While each provider is tied to a specific database platform (such as Oracle) or communication standard (such as OLE DB), the objects in the *DataSet* realm are generic, and can interact with any of the platform-specific providers.

Three main objects make up the world of *DataSets*.

- **The DataSet object.** Each *DataSet* object acts like a mini-database. You can add as many tables to a *DataSet* as you like, and establish foreign-key relationships between the fields of these tables. The internals of each *DataSet* are an unfathomable mystery, but you can export an entire *DataSet* to XML, and load it back in again later if you must.
- **The DataTable object.** Each table in your *DataSet* uses a separate *DataTable* object, accessible through the *DataSet's Tables* collection. *DataTables* are also useful as stand-alone objects. If you plan on only adding a single table to your *DataSet*, you might opt to just use a *DataTable* object alone without a *DataSet*. Within each *DataTable* object, separate *DataColumn* and *DataRow* objects establish the field definitions and the actual data values respectively.
- **The DataRelation object.** Use the *DataRelation* objects, stored within a *DataSet's Relations* collection, to establish field-level relationships and constraints between columns in your *DataTable* objects.

Although data sets are most often used with providers, you can use them independently to build your own in-memory collection of tables and relationships. This is similar to the "client-side record sets" that you could build with pre-.NET ADO objects, although the features included with ADO.NET make the *DataSet* much more powerful than the older *Recordset*.

Note Visual Basic 2005 includes "Typed DataSets," a feature used to integrate a *DataSet* with a specific data or record format. You may find them useful in your applications, but I won't be discussing them in this book.

DataSets Versus No DataSets

When used together, providers and *DataSets* give an end-to-end interface to individual data values, from the fields in your database tables, to the in-memory items of a *DataRow* record. Figure 10-1 shows this object interaction.

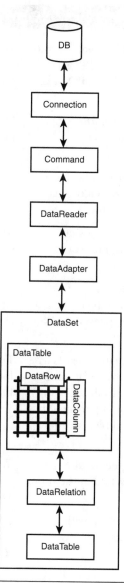

Figure 10-1 Providers and DataSets in action

When you interact with data from an external database, you always use the provider classes, but it's up to you whether you want to also use *DataSets*. There are pros and cons in both methods, some of which appear in Table 10-1.

Table 10-1 The Pros and Cons of Using DataSets

Without DataSet	With DataSet
You must supply all SQL statements, in the format expected by the provider. This is true for all SELECT, INSERT, UPDATE, and DELETE requests.	The *DataSet* and *DataAdapter* work together to craft many of the SQL statements on your behalf.
Data retrieved through the *DataReader* is read-only. You must issue separate commands to update data.	Data read from the database can be modified in-memory, and updated as a batch with a single method call.
Data transfers are very efficient, because there is no overhead needed to move data into a complex *DataSet* structure.	There may be a performance hit as the *DataSet* builds the necessary objects required for each transferred record.
Memory allocation is limited to a single record's worth of data fields, plus some minimal overhead.	Memory allocation is required for the entire result set, plus overhead for every table, field, column, and row in the result set.
Only a single *DataReader* can be open at a time (unless the provider supports MARS, which I'll discuss in just a bit).	Any number of *DataSets* can be in use at once.
A live connection to the database exists as long as a *DataReader* is in use. If it takes you five minutes to scan a result set because you are doing a lot of per-record analysis, the connection will be active for the full five minutes.	Data connections are maintained only long enough to transfer data from or to the database.
DataReaders present one record at a time. The records must be processed in the order they arrive.	You can jump around the records in a *DataSet*, and reorganize them to meet your needs.
You spend a lot of time working with Strings (for SQL statements) and raw data fields.	All data fields are organized logically, just like they are in the actual database. You can interact with them directly.

Without DataSet	With DataSet
Each *Command* and *Connection* works with a single provider-supported data source.	Different *DataTables* within your *DataSet* can connect to distinct data sources. Also, you can hand-craft data so that each *DataRow* contains data from different sources.
Because you manage all SQL statements, you have a (relatively) high level of control over the entire data interaction process.	Because the view of the data is abstracted, you have a (relatively) limited level of control over the entire data interaction process (although advanced use of *DataSets* does give you some additional control).

For me, the last entry in Table 10-1 is the clincher. The job of a programmer is to control the software experience of the user, and the more control, the better. That's why I generally hate "wizards" and "code generators" that take control away from me, the developer. There are limits to my paranoia, though; I put up with the basic template code supplied by Visual Studio when creating new projects. Still, you'll see my code-controlling personality in the Library Project, with my heavy dependence on *DataReaders* over *DataSets*. When I do store data long-term, I usually just stick the data in a *DataTable* without a containing *DataSet*.

MARS Support

I mentioned something called MARS in Table 10-1. MARS stands for Multiple Active Result Sets. Normally, a single *Connection* object only allows a single *DataReader* to be in use at any given moment. This limitation is bi-directional. If you are scanning a *DataReader* via a SELECT statement, you cannot issue INSERT, UPDATE, or DELETE statements on that same connection until you close the *DataReader*.

With the introduction of MARS, a single connection can now handle multiple data transmission activities in either direction. SQL Server adds MARS support with its 2005 release; Oracle has supported MARS-like features since the initial .NET release.

MARS connections seem like a feature you would always want to enable. But they do add additional overhead to your application that can slow it down. Also, MARS does not always mix well with multi-threaded applications.

Connecting to SQL Server with Visual Studio

Visual Studio has many built-in tools that make working with data as simple as drag-and-drop. Well, it's not really that quick. But by answering a few questions and dragging-and-dropping one item, you can build an entire application that lets you edit data in your database. Let's try it together.

Creating a Data Source

Start up a new Windows Forms project in Visual Studio—just a plain Windows Forms project, not one of the Library-specific projects. Selecting the **Data** ➤ **Show Data Sources** menu command brings up the *Data Sources* panel, as shown in Figure 10-2.

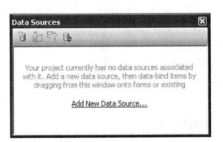

Figure 10-2 Where are the data sources?

New projects don't include any data sources by default, so we need to add one. Click on the **Add New Data Source** link in the *Data Sources* panel. The *Data Source Configuration Wizard* guides you through the data source creation process.

1. The first step asks, "Where will the application get data from?" Select "Database" and click the **Next** button.
2. The second step asks, "Which data connection should your application use to connect to the database?" We'll have to create a

new connection for the Library database we designed way back in Chapter 4, "Designing the Database." Click the **New Connection** button.

3. The *Add Connection* dialog appears to collect the details of the new connection. In the **Data source** field, click the **Change** button to choose the type of connection. Select "Microsoft SQL Server" from the list that appears. (It's possible that this *Change Data Source* sub-dialog popped up automatically on your system.)

4. Back on the *Add Connection* form, fill in the **Server name** field with the name of your SQL Server instance. Hopefully, this drop-down list already has the instances listed, but if not, you'll have to enter it yourself. The default for SQL Server Express is the name of your system with "\SQLEXPRESS" attached. If your system name is "MYSYSTEM," the instance name would be "MYSYSTEM\ SQLEXPRESS."

5. Configure your authentication settings in the **Log on to the server** section. I used standard Windows Authentication, but it depends on how you set up the database in Chapter 4.

6. In the **Connect to a database** section, either select or type in "Library" for the database name.

7. Click the **Test Connection** button to make sure it all works. When you're finished, click the **OK** button to create the new connection.

8. OK, we're back on the *Data Source Connection Wizard* form. The connection we just created should now appear in the list, as shown in Figure 10-3. Click **Next**.

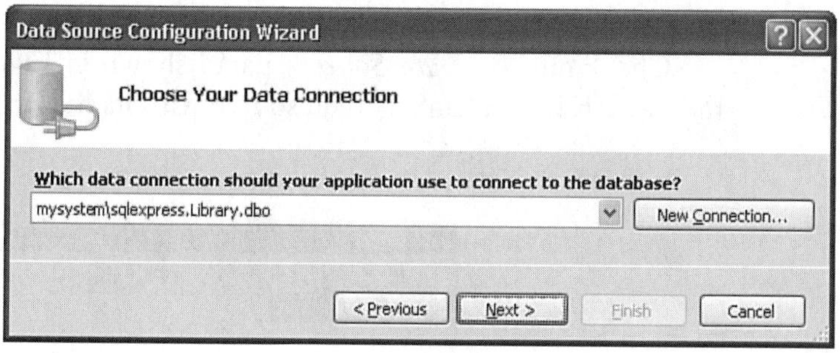

Figure 10-3 The new database connection, ready to use

9. The next panel asks whether this data source should become part of the configurable settings for this project. We'll get into the settings features of Visual Basic in Chapter 14, "Application Settings." For now, just accept the default and click **OK**.

10. We're almost there. Only 27 more steps to go! Just kidding. This is the last step in creating the data source. The final panel shows a list of the data-generating features in the Library database. Open the **Tables** branch, and select **Activity**, as shown in Figure 10-4. Then click **Finish**.

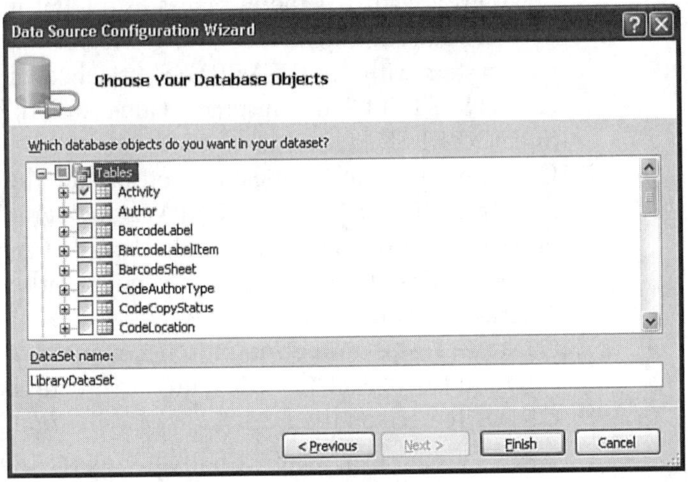

Figure 10-4 The final activity is selecting the Activity table.

Check out the *Data Sources* panel shown in Figure 10-5. It includes the new "LibraryDataSet" data source with its link to the *Activity* table.

Figure 10-5 Finally, a real data source

Using a Data Source

So, what is this data source anyway? It is simply a link to some portion of your database, wrapped up in a typical .NET object. Now that it's part of your project, you can use it to access the data in the *Activity* table through your project's code, or by drag-and-drop. In the *Data Sources* panel, you will find that the Activity entry is actually a drop-down list. Select "Details" from the list, as shown in Figure 10-6.

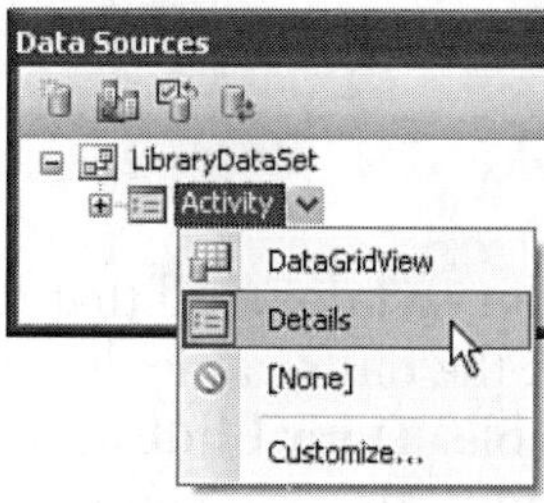

Figure 10-6 Select the Details view instead of DataGrid

Finally, drag-and-drop the Activity entry onto the surface of *Form1*. When you let go, Visual Studio will add a set of controls to the form, plus a few more non-user-interface controls just below the form (see Figure 10-7).

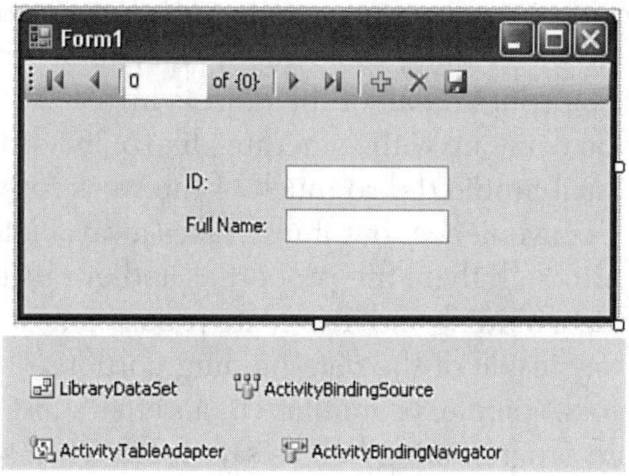

Figure 10-7 A complete program without writing a single line of code

By just dragging-and-dropping, Visual Studio added all of the necessary controls and links to turn your form into a turbo-charged *Activity* table editor. Try it now by pressing the F5 key. In the running program, you can use the Microsoft Access-style record access "VCR" control to move between the records in the *Activity* table. You can also modify the values of each record, add new records, or delete existing records (but please restore things back to their original state when you are done; we'll need all of the original records later). Talk about power! Talk about simplicity! Talk about unemployment lines! Who needs highly-paid programmers like us when Visual Studio can do this for you?

Data Binding

In reality, Visual Studio isn't doing all that much. It's using a feature called "data binding" to link the on-form fields with the data source, the Library database's *Activity* table. **Data binding** is a feature built into Windows Forms controls that allow them to automatically display and edit values in an associated data source, such as a database. It's all sorted out through the properties of the control.

Select the *FullNameTextBox* control added to this project's form, and then examine its properties. Right at the top is a property section named "(DataBindings)." Its *Text* sub-property contains "ActivityBindingSource - FullName," a reference to the *ActivityBindingSource* non-user-interface control also added by Visual Studio. *ActivityBindingSource*, in turn, contains a reference to the *LibraryDataSet* object, the data source we created earlier. That data source links to SQL Server, to the Library database, and finally to the *Activity* table and its *FullName* field. Piece of cake!

If you count up all of the objects involved in this data-binding relationship, you come up with something like 5,283 distinct objects. It's no wonder that Visual Studio did so much of the work for you. Data binding provides a lot of convenience, but it also takes away a lot of your *control* as a developer. Although there are properties and events that let you manage aspects of the data binding and its update process, most of the essential code is hidden away inside of the data binding portions of .NET. You may not touch, taste, fold, spindle, or mutilate it, and that's just bad. A quick look at one of my core programming beliefs says it all: *Good software includes maximum control for the developer, and minimum control for the user.*

Part of your job as a developer is to provide a highly scripted environment for the user to access important data. This requires that you have control over the user's experience through your source code. Certainly you will defer much of that control to others when you use any Microsoft or tools supplied by third-parties. As long as those tools allow you to control the user experience to your level of satisfaction, that's great. But I've always been disappointed with data binding, except for the read-only display of data from the database. Similar features were in Visual Basic long before .NET arrived, and they have always made it difficult for the developer to control the various data interactions on the form.

Fortunately, if you eschew the data-binding features, Visual Basic will pass to you the responsibility of managing all interactions between the database and the user.

Interacting with SQL Server in Code

Communicating with a database yourself is definitely more work than dragging-and-dropping data sources, but whoever said programming was a cake walk?

Building the Connection String

The first step on the road to the data-controlling lifestyle is to connect to the database using a **connection string**. If you have used ADO, then you are already familiar with the connection strings used in ADO.NET, for they are generally the same. You probably also know that it is through connection strings that Microsoft keeps a tight rein on Windows developers. It's not that they are complex; they are nothing more than strings of semicolon-separated parameters. But the parameters to include, and their exact format, are the stuff of legend. The MSDN documentation included with Visual Studio does provide some examples of connection strings, but not much detail. A third-party resource, http://www.connectionstrings.com, also provides numerous examples of valid connection string formats.

The connection string we will use to connect to the Library database, fortunately, isn't overly complex. If you use your Microsoft Windows login to connect to the database, the following string will meet your needs (as one unbroken line):

```
Data Source=instance_name;Initial Catalog=Library;
➥ Integrated Security=true
```

where *instance_name* is replaced by the name of your SQL Server instance or data source. The connection string we built visually earlier used "MYSYSTEM\SQLEXPRESS" for its data source name.

To use SQL Server user IDs and passwords, try this format.

```
Data Source=instance_name;Initial Catalog=Library;
➥ User ID=sa;Password=xyz
```

Of course, replace the user ID (*sa*) and password (*xyz*) with your own settings. If you want to include MARS support in your connection, add another semicolon-delimited component:

```
MultipleActiveResultSets=true
```

Note There are other connection string options that let you connect to a SQL Server Express (SSE) database file directly, alter the "user instancing" method (often used with *ClickOnce*-deployed databases), and make other adjustments. Although it is somewhat scattered about, you can find these options documented in the MSDN documentation that comes with Visual Studio.

Establishing the Connection

Use the connection string to create a *SqlConnection* object, and then open the connection.

```
' ----- Assumes:
'          Imports System.Data
Dim libraryDB As New SqlClient.SqlConnection( _
    "Data Source=MYSYSTEM\SQLEXPRESS;" & _
    "Initial Catalog=Library;Integrated Security=true")
libraryDB.Open()
```

Make sure you replace "MYSYSTEM" with your own system's name. This entire block of code sure seems a lot easier to me than those 10 or 15 steps you had to follow earlier when setting up the connection through Visual Studio.

Using SQL Statements

Once the connection is open, you can issue SELECT, INSERT, UPDATE, DELETE, or any other DML or DDL statement accepted by the database. A *SqlCommand* object prepares your SQL statement for use by the open connection. Here's a statement that returns the description for entry number 1 in the *Activity* table.

```
SELECT FullName FROM Activity WHERE ID = 1
```

Creating a *SqlCommand* object that wraps around this statement is easy. The constructor for the *SqlCommand* object takes a SQL statement, plus a *SqlConnection* object.

```
Dim sqlStatement As New SqlClient.SqlCommand( _
    "SELECT FullName FROM Activity WHERE ID = 1", libraryDB)
```

Processing the Results

The only thing left to do is to pass the SQL statement to the database, via the connection, and retrieve the results as a *SqlDataReader* object. Once we get the data, process each record using that object's *Read* method. You access individual fields by name through the default *Item* collection.

```
Dim sqlResults As SqlClient.SqlDataReader = _
    sqlStatement.ExecuteReader()
sqlResults.Read()
MsgBox(CStr(sqlResults.Item("FullName")))

' ----- Since Item is the default property, this works too...
MsgBox(CStr(sqlResults("FullName")))

' ----- This shortened syntax also works...
MsgBox(CStr(sqlResults!FullName))
```

Taking all these blocks of code together displays the message shown in Figure 10-8.

Figure 10-8 Basic data retrieved from a database

When you're finished, make sure that you close all of the connections you opened.

```
sqlResults.Close()
libraryDB.Close()
```

Modifying Data

Making changes to database tables is coded just like data retrieval, but no *SqlDataReader* is needed. Instead of using the *ExecuteReader* method, use the *ExecuteNonQuery* method, which returns no results.

```
Dim sqlStatement As New SqlClient.SqlCommand( _
    "UPDATE Activity SET FullName = 'Sleeps all day'" & _
    " WHERE ID = 1", libraryDB)
sqlStatement.ExecuteNonQuery()
```

SQL Server 2005 has a convenient new feature that will return a single field from a new record created via an INSERT statement. If you look back at the Library Project's database design, you will see that the ID fields in many of the tables are generated automatically. Traditionally, if you wanted to immediately retrieve the ID field for a new record, you first had to INSERT the record, and then perform a separate SELECT statement, returning the new record's ID field.

```
INSERT INTO CodeSeries (FullName)
    VALUES ('Children''s Books')

SELECT ID FROM CodeSeries
    WHERE FullName = 'Children''s Books'
```

A new *OUTPUT INSERTED* clause in SQL Server 2005 combines both of these statements into a single action.

```
INSERT INTO CodeSeries (FullName)
    OUTPUT INSERTED.ID
    VALUES ('Children''s Books')
```

When the INSERT is complete, SQL Server returns the ID field as a result set, just as if you had issued a separate SELECT statement. The *SqlCommand's ExecuteScalar* method is a simple way to retrieve a single value from a SQL statement.

```
sqlStatement = New SqlClient.SqlCommand( _
    "INSERT INTO CodeSeries (FullName) " & _
    "OUTPUT INSERTED.ID VALUES ('Children''s Books')", _
    libraryDB)
Dim newID As Integer = CInt(sqlStatement.ExecuteScalar())
```

Database Transactions

Transactions enable "all or nothing" actions across multiple SQL statements. Once started, SQL statements issued within the context of the transaction either all complete, or none of them complete. If you have ten data updates to perform, but the database fails after only five of them, you can **roll back** the transaction. The database reverses the earlier statements, restoring the data to what it was before the transaction began. (Updates from other users are not affected by the rollback.) If all statements succeed, you can **commit** the entire transaction, making all of its changes permanent.

For SQL Server databases, transactions are managed through the provider's *SqlTransaction* object. Like the other ADO.NET statements, it's easy to use. A transaction begins with a *BeginTransaction* method call on the connection.

```
Public atomicSet As SqlClient.SqlTransaction = _
    libraryDB.BeginTransaction()
```

To include a SQL statement in a transaction, assign the *SqlTransaction* object to the *SqlCommand* object's *Transaction* property.

```
sqlStatement.Transaction = atomicSet
```

Then call the appropriate *Execute* method on the command. When all commands complete, use the transaction's *Commit* method to make the changes permanent.

```
atomicSet.Commit()
```

If, instead, you need to abort the transaction, use the *Rollback* method.

```
atomicSet.Rollback()
```

Summary

There are programmers in this world who never have to access a database, who never worry about connections or transactions or record locking or INSERT statements or referential integrity. Yes, there are such programmers in the world—five, maybe six at last count. All other programmers must include code that manages external data of some sort, whether in a relational database, or an XML file, or a configuration file. ADO.NET is one of the .NET tools that make such data management easy. It's a lot different from the old ADO system, and I am still not convinced that having disconnected data 100 percent of the time is the way to go. But when I consider the power and flexibility of ADO.NET, I can't help feeling sorry for those six programmers who never use databases.

Project

It's likely that more than 50 percent of the code in the Library Project will directly involve database access, or manipulation of the data retrieved through ADO.NET. Constantly creating new *Command* and *DataReader* objects, while simple, is pretty hard on the fingers. Because so much of the code is repetitive, the code in this chapter's project will try to centralize some of that basic, boilerplate code.

Project Access Load the "Chapter 10 (Before) Code" project, either through the New Project templates, or by accessing the project directly from the installation directory. To see the code in its final form, load "Chapter 10 (After) Code" instead.

Reference the Data Namespaces

The Library Project code has references to several of the important .NET namespaces, such as *System*, *System.Windows.Forms*, and *Microsoft.VisualBasic*. However, it doesn't yet reference any of the ADO.NET namespaces. (Recall that "referencing" means accessing a .NET DLL in a project and using its types in your code.) Before using them in code, we need to create references to them. This is done through the project properties window, on the *References* tab. You'll see a list of those assemblies already referenced by the application (see Figure 10-9).

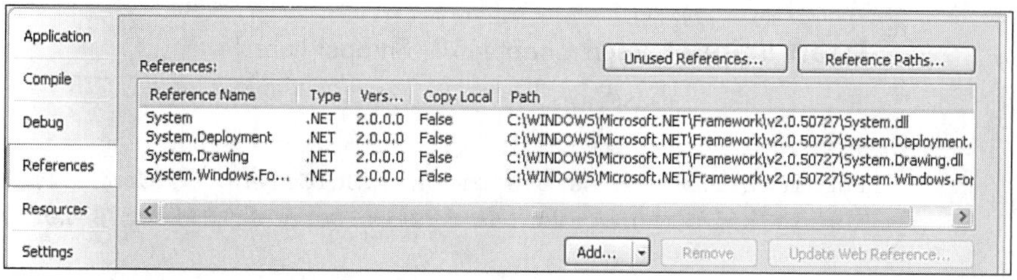

Figure 10-9 References included in the Library Project

To add new references, click the **Add** button just below the list, and select **Reference** if prompted for the type of reference to add. On the *Add Reference* form, the **.NET** tab should already be active. It's pretty amazing to see just how many .NET assemblies are installed on your system already. But don't just sit there gawking: Select both *System.Data* and *System.Xml* from the component list, and then click the **OK** button. The list of references in the project properties should now include both of the selected namespace libraries.

We can now refer to classes in the *System.Data* namespace directly. But typing "System.Data" before each use of a data-related class will get tedious. We could sprinkle "Imports System.Data" statements throughout the files in the project, but Visual Studio provides a more centralized solution. Since you still have the *References* tab open, look down to the **Imported namespaces** section. The large checklist indicates which namespaces should be automatically imported throughout your application. These namespaces don't require separate *Imports* statements in your code, but your source code acts as if you had added them anyway. Go ahead and select the checkbox next to the "System.Data" entry in this list. Then close the project properties window.

Most of the new code for this chapter appears in the *General.vb* file, so open it now. We will use two project-level (global) variables to manage the primary database connection to the Library database. The first variable, *LibraryDB*, is a *SqlConnection* object that uses our connection string for the Library database. A related object, *HoldTransaction*, will hold a *SqlTransaction* object when a transaction is in effect. Add these two lines to the *General* module. I put them just before the existing *CenterText* method.

Insert Snippet Insert Chapter 10, Snippet Item 1.

```
Public LibraryDB As System.Data.SqlClient.SqlConnection
Public HoldTransaction As System.Data.SqlClient.SqlTransaction
```

Connecting to the Database

Because the Library Project will depend so much on the database, we will build the *SqlConnection* object when first starting up the application.

Not-Really-Best Practices Warning Maintaining the connection throughout the application goes against the advice I provided earlier that database connections should be short-lived. However, to keep the code as simple as possible for purposes of tutorial demonstration, I have chosen this approach. Also, because the Library Project is designed for a small installation base, it does not have the requirement of being highly scalable.

---

10. ADO.NET

The *ConnectDatabase* procedure contains all the code needed to create this object. For now, I've just hard-coded the connection string into the routine. In a later chapter, we'll include that connection information as part of a configuration system. Add the following routine to your *General* module. Make sure you change the reference to "MYSYSTEM" to whatever is needed on your own system.

Insert Snippet Insert Chapter 10, Snippet Item 2.

```
Public Function ConnectDatabase() As Boolean
    ' ----- Connect to the database. Return True on success.
    Dim connectionString As String

    ' ----- Initialize.
    HoldTransaction = Nothing

    ' ----- Build the connection string.
    ' !!! WARNING: Hardcoded for now.
    connectionString = "Data Source=MYSYSTEM\SQLEXPRESS;" & _
        "Initial Catalog=Library;Integrated Security=true"

    ' ----- Attempt to open the database.
    Try
        LibraryDB = New SqlClient.SqlConnection(connectionString)
        LibraryDB.Open()
    Catch ex As Exception
        GeneralError("ConnectDatabase", ex)
        Return False
    End Try

    ' ----- Success.
    Return True
End Function
```

This project's "main" routine is actually the *MyApplication_Startup* application event, from the *ApplicationEvents.vb* source code file. (That's one that you will have to use the "Show All Files" button to see.) To build the connection object at startup, add the following code to the end of that event handler.

Insert Snippet Insert Chapter 10, Snippet Item 3.

```
' ----- Connect to the database.
If (ConnectDatabase() = False) Then
    Me.HideSplashScreen()
    e.Cancel = True
    Return
End If
```

When the user exits the Library application, the code will call the *CleanUpProgram* method to properly dispose of the connection object. Return to the *General.vb* module, and add the following method.

Insert Snippet Insert Chapter 10, Snippet Item 4.

```
Public Sub CleanUpProgram()
    ' ----- Prepare to exit the program.
    On Error Resume Next
    LibraryDB.Close()
End Sub
```

To simplify things, we'll call this routine from the application's *MyApplication_Shutdown* event handler, back in the *ApplicationEvents.vb* file.

Insert Snippet Insert Chapter 10, Snippet Item 5.

```
CleanUpProgram()
```

Interacting with the Database

Now that the database connection is established, it's time to do something with it. The first four centralized routines implement much of the code we discussed earlier: the creation of data readers and tables, and the processing of general SQL code. Add them to the *General* module.

Insert Snippet Insert Chapter 10, Snippet Item 6.

This snippet adds the following seven routines.

- **Function CreateDataTable.** Given a SQL statement, retrieve its results from the database, and put it all in a *DataTable* object. A *SqlDataAdapter* connects the *SqlDataReader* with the *DataTable*.
- **Function CreateReader.** Given a SQL statement, retrieve its results from the database, returning the associated *SqlDataReader* object.
- **Sub ExecuteSQL.** Sends a SQL statement to the database for processing.
- **Function ExecuteSQLReturn.** Sends a SQL statement to the database for processing, returning a single result value.
- **Sub TransactionBegin.** Begins a new transaction.
- **Sub TransactionCommit.** Commits the transaction, making all changes permanent.
- **Sub TransactionRollback.** Rolls back the transaction, undoing any changes that were part of the transaction.

None of these routines include their own error-processing code; they either suppress errors with an "On Error Resume Next" statement, or rely on the calling routine to trap errors. This lets the calling routine take specific action based on the type of error generated. All of these routines are pretty similar to each other. Here is the code for *CreateReader*; one interesting part is the use of the *HoldTransaction* object when a transaction is in effect.

```
Public Function CreateReader(ByVal sqlText As String) _
     As SqlClient.SqlDataReader
   ' ----- Given a SQL statement, return a data reader.
   Dim dbCommand As SqlClient.SqlCommand
   Dim dbScan As SqlClient.SqlDataReader

   ' ----- Try to run the statement. Note that no error
   '       trapping is done here. It is up to the calling
   '       routine to set up error checking.
   dbCommand = New SqlClient.SqlCommand(sqlText, LibraryDB)
   If Not (HoldTransaction Is Nothing) Then _
      dbCommand.Transaction = HoldTransaction
   dbScan = dbCommand.ExecuteReader()
   dbCommand = Nothing
   Return dbScan
End Function
```

10. ADO.NET

Processing Data Values

Building SQL statements by hand involves a lot of string manipulation, plus conditional processing for those times when data may be missing. For instance, if you want to store a text value in the database, you have to prepare it for use by a SQL statement (special processing for single quote marks), but if the text value is zero-length, you pass the word "NULL" in the statement instead. All of this data preparation can clog up your code, so why not centralize it? The eight routines in this section either prepare data for use in SQL statements, or adjust retrieved data for use in the application.

Insert Snippet Insert Chapter 10, Snippet Item 7.

- **DBCombo.** Takes the numeric code associated with a selected item in a *ComboBox* control and returns it as a string. If no item is selected, or if the value is –1, the routine returns "NULL."
- **DBDate(String).** Given a string containing a formatted date, returns a date ready for use in a SQL statement.
- **DBDate(Date).** Given a true date value, returns a string date ready for use in a SQL statement.
- **DBGetDecimal.** Returns a decimal number from a result set, even if the field contains a NULL value.
- **DBGetInteger.** Returns an integer number from a result set, even if the field contains a NULL value.
- **DBGetText.** Returns a string from a result set, even if the field contains a NULL value.
- **DBNum.** Prepares a number for use in a SQL statement.
- **DBText.** Prepares a string for use in a SQL statement.

Here is the code for the *DBText* routine. Strings in SQL statements must be surrounded by single quotes, and any embedded single quotes must be doubled.

```
Public Function DBText(ByVal origText As String) As String
    ' ----- Prepare a string for insertion in a SQL statement.
    If (Trim(origText) = "") Then
        Return "NULL"
```

```
   Else
      Return "'" & Replace(origText, "'", "''") & "'"
   End If
End Function
```

System-Level Configuration

The last blocks of code support the quick update and retrieval of system-wide configuration values stored in the *SystemValue* table of the Library database. The *GetSystemValue* routine returns the current setting of a configuration value when supplied with the value name. *SetSystemValue* updates (or adds, if needed) a named configuration value. Both of these routines appear in the *General* module.

Insert Snippet Insert Chapter 10, Snippet Item 8.

```
Public Function GetSystemValue( _
      ByVal valueName As String) As String
   ' ----- Return the data portion of a system value
   '        name-data pair.
   Dim sqlText As String
   Dim returnValue As String

   ' ----- Retrieve the value.
   returnValue = ""
   sqlText = "SELECT ValueData FROM SystemValue WHERE " & _
      "UPPER(ValueName) = " & DBText(UCase(valueName))
   Try
      returnValue = DBGetText(ExecuteSQLReturn(sqlText))
   Catch ex As Exception
      GeneralError("GetSystemValue", ex)
   End Try
   Return returnValue
End Function

Public Sub SetSystemValue(ByVal valueName As String, _
      ByVal valueData As String)
   ' ----- Update a record in the SystemValue table.
   Dim sqlText As String
```

```
      Try
         ' ----- See if the entry already exists.
         sqlText = "SELECT COUNT(*) FROM SystemValue WHERE " & _
            "UPPER(ValueName) = " & DBText(UCase(valueName))
         If (CInt(ExecuteSQLReturn(sqlText)) > 0) Then
            ' ----- Value already exists.
            sqlText = "UPDATE SystemValue " & _
               "SET ValueData = " & DBText(valueData) & _
               " WHERE UPPER(ValueName) = " & _
               DBText(UCase(valueName))
         Else
            ' ----- Need to create value.
            sqlText = "INSERT INTO SystemValue " & _
               (ValueName, ValueData) VALUES (" & _
               DBText(valueName) & ", " & _
               DBText(valueData) & ")"
         End If

         ' ----- Update the value.
         ExecuteSQL(sqlText)
      Catch ex As System.Exception
         GeneralError("SetSystemValue", ex)
      End Try
   End Sub
```

The *GetSystemValue* routine is clear. It simply retrieves a single value from the database. The *SetSystemValue* has to first check whether the configuration value to update already exists in the database. If it does, it modifies the records. Otherwise, it adds a full new record. To determine whether the record exists, it requests a count of records matching the system value name. It queries the database through our new *ExecuteSqlReturn* method, which returns a single value from a query. In this case, the value is the count of the matching records.

```
         sqlText = "SELECT COUNT(*) FROM SystemValue WHERE " & _
            "UPPER(ValueName) = " & DBText(UCase(valueName))
         If (CInt(ExecuteSQLReturn(sqlText)) > 0) Then
```

Using the *GetSystemValue* routine is easy, so let's use it right now. Go back to the *MyApplication_Startup* event handler in *ApplicationEvents.vb*, and add the following code to the end of the routine.

Insert Snippet Insert Chapter 10, Snippet Item 9.

```
' ----- Check the database version.
Dim productionDBVersion As String
productionDBVersion = Trim(GetSystemValue("DatabaseVersion"))
If (CInt(Val(productionDBVersion)) <> UseDBVersion) Then
    MsgBox("The program cannot continue due to an " & _
        "incompatible database. The current database " & _
        "version is '" & productionDBVersion & _
        "'. The application version is '" & _
        UseDBVersion & "'.", _
        MsgBoxStyle.OkOnly Or MsgBoxStyle.Critical, ProgramTitle)
    CleanUpProgram()
    Me.HideSplashScreen()
    e.Cancel = True
    Return
End If
```

Once in a while, I found it necessary to modify the structure of a database to such an extent that older versions of an application either crashed, or would cause major data headaches. To prevent this, I added a database version setting, "DatabaseVersion," and use this code block to test against it. If the program doesn't match the expected database version, it will refuse to run.

Now that we have some basic database access tools, we're ready to start adding some real data interaction code to the Library application.

10. ADO.NET

CHAPTER 11

SECURITY

Secrets are funny things. With billions of people on the planet, there is no shortage of really interesting events and stories, but none of them will hold our interest if there is a secret to be discovered somewhere else. For instance, former Associate Director of the FBI, W. Mark Felt, revealed himself to be the famous *Deep Throat* of Watergate fame, but not before 30 years of speculation and whispering about this secret identity had passed by. Other secrets are just as intriguing, even if we are in on the secret. Superman is fascinating in part due to his secret alter ego, Clark Kent. Many books include the word "Secret" in their titles to make them and their topics more interesting, titles such as *Japanese Cooking Secrets*.

In this era of information overload and increasingly permissive moral standards on television, secrets seem to be scarce. But everyone has important information that they need to keep protected from others, and that includes the users of your programs. Fortunately, .NET programs and related data can be as secure as you need, if you use the security features available to you in the .NET Framework.

Here's a secret that I'll expose right now: I really don't know that much about computer security issues. Back in the early '80s, I worked for a computer vendor that was coming out with its own UNIX System V implementation. They needed to confirm that it would be sufficiently secure for governmental sales, and I was tasked with building a bibliography of computer security resources, including the famous "Orange Book," a government security standards document whose title has no rhyme.

Although I don't recall many of the security details, I do remember that it would take several city garbage trucks to haul away all of the available materials on computer security. The bibliography I developed was over 40 pages long! And that was just the table of contents. One article that I do recall was quite interesting. It discussed how passwords are generated in UNIX systems, at least back when AT&T was in charge. The interesting part was that the entire algorithm was printed in a publicly available book.

Anyone could examine the book and see how the passwords were generated. And if you were familiar with UNIX, you knew that each user's encrypted password was stored in plaintext in the file */etc/passwd*. But it wasn't a big deal. Although the method for deriving the password was public knowledge, and although you could see everyone's encrypted password, UNIX was still considered secure enough for use even in the military.

Security Features in .NET

Security in .NET involves many features, but they fall generally into three major areas.

1. **Internal Security.** Classes and class members in .NET can be protected via user-based or role-based security. This *Code Access Security* (CAS) exists to keep unauthorized users from accessing powerful libraries of .NET features. Only those users meeting a minimum or specific set of rights can use those protected features.

2. **External Security.** Because anyone can develop and distribute a .NET application, it's important to protect system resources from malicious code. This is a big issue, especially with the ongoing reports of hackers taking advantage of "buffer overrun" problems in released software from Microsoft and other vendors. Just as CAS keeps code from accessing certain features of a class, it interacts with the operating system to keep rogue code from accessing some or all files and directories, registry entries, network resources, hardware peripherals, or other .NET assemblies based on in-effect security policies.

3. **Data Security.** Programs and computer resources aren't the only things that need to be protected. Some highfalutin users think that their precious data is so important, that it deserves to be protected through "special" software means. Encryption, digital signatures, and other cryptographic features provide the "special" support needed for such data.

Because the Library Project interacts with a major external resource—a SQL Server database—it does deal with External Security issues, although indirectly through ADO.NET and system security policies. Still, because of this book's focus on typical business application development, this chapter will not discuss either internal security or external security issues. Instead, it will focus on data security topics, especially the encryption of data.

Cryptography and Encryption

Knowing a secret is one thing. Keeping it safe and protected from others is another. Making sure an enemy doesn't alter it while we're blabbing—I mean, confiding—it to someone else is still another issue. Confirming that a secret coming from someone else is reliable is yet another issue. Making sure that I get the best deal on car insurance is again another issue entirely.

Clearly, data security is about more than just keeping a piece of data protected from prying eyes. And it's not only prying eyes that concern us. Just yesterday I experienced the Windows "blue screen of death" when I tried to synchronize the data on my desktop system with my electronic handheld scheduler. The potential for data corruption through the normal everyday use of technology is vast. Fortunately, the word processor I am using to type this chapter is free frôm su©h ¢or®uptioñ¡

Keeping Secrets

When people think about encryption and data security, they generally focus on the "keeping secrets" aspect. The ability to cryptographically encode content, keep it from an adversary, and still have it decoded by you or an associate at some later time is important. Encryption techniques range from simple language aberrations (such as Pig Latin) and replacement ciphers (letter substitutions, used in cryptogram puzzles) to complex enigma-machine-quality encoding systems.

Software-enabled encryption is now a part of our everyday experience. When you make credit card purchases from web sites, the chance is pretty good that your credit card information is encrypted and transferred in 128-bit secret fidelity.

Typical encryption methods make use of one or more **keys**, plus a combination of **hashing functions** and **encryption algorithms**, to convert sensitive content into a form that is not easily accessible without the original or related key. **Symmetric cryptography** is the name used for encryption methods using a single secret key.

Public-key encryption—also know as asymmetric cryptography—uses a pair of keys to encrypt and decrypt data. One of the keys, a **public key**, can be given to anyone who cares about communicating with you securely. You can even give it to your enemies; it's public. The related **private key** is kept safe for your use; you never show it to anyone, not even your mother. Content encrypted using one of the keys (and an encryption algorithm) can only be decrypted later using the other key. If your friend encrypts some information using the public key, nobody except you will be able to decrypt it, and it will require your private key. You can also encrypt data with your private key, but anyone would be able to decrypt it with the public key. We'll see uses for this seemingly insecure action a little bit later.

Data Stability

Data encryption helps ensure the integrity of a block of data, even if that data is not encrypted. If you send someone an email during a lightning storm, there is certainly the chance that some or all of the email content could be electronically altered before it reaches the recipient. Let's say that some static in the transmission line just happens to cause one sentence of the content to be duplicated. Let's say that some static in the transmission line just happens to cause one sentence of the content to be duplicated. How would you know whether it was the author trying to make some clever point, or simply a computer glitch?

Including a **checksum** with the content can help identify data problems during transmission. A checksum—sometimes called a **hash value**—takes the original content and passes it through a function that generates a short value that "represents" the original data. Checksum functions (or **hashing algorithms**) are very sensitive to even single-byte changes on the content, whether that single byte was altered, repositioned, added, or removed from the original data. By generating a checksum both before and after data transmission, you can confirm whether the content changed at all during the transfer.

Checksums represent a **unidirectional encryption** of the original data. It is impossible to use the checksum to obtain the original data content. That's all right, though, because the purpose of a checksum is not to deliver content secretly, but to deliver it unchanged. **Bidirectional encryption** is what I talked about in the "Keeping Secrets" section. If you have the right key and the right algorithm, bidirectional encryption restores original content from encrypted content.

Identity Verification

Let's say that you receive an email from your boss that says, "Order 50 copies of Tim Patrick's newest book, and hurry." How do you know this message is reliable, or really from your boss? In this case, the content alone should prove that it is trustworthy. But if you really wanted to verify the source, and your boss was unavailable, you could employ **digital signatures** to confirm the identity of the sender.

One method of using digital signatures employs public-key encryption to transmit an agreed-upon password or message, and passes that encrypted content along with the larger email. For instance, your boss could encrypt the text "I'm the boss" using his private key. When you receive the email, you could decrypt the digital signature using your boss's public key. If the decryption resulted in the "I'm the boss" message, you would know that the message did, in fact, come from your boss.

Encryption in .NET

The data encryption and security features included with .NET appear in the *System.Security.Cryptography* namespace. Most of the classes in this namespace implement various well-known encryption algorithms that have been accepted by organizations and governments as dependable encryption standards. For instance, the *DESCryptoServiceProvider* class provides features based on the Data Encryption Standard (DES) algorithm, an algorithm originally developed by IBM in the mid-1970s.

Symmetric Cryptography

Symmetric cryptography uses a single secret key to both encrypt and decrypt a block of data. Although these algorithms are often quite fast (when compared to asymmetric cryptography), the need to share the full secret key with others in order to share data may make them inherently less secure. Still, for many applications, "secret key encryption" is sufficient.

The .NET Framework includes support for four symmetric encryption algorithms.

- Data Encryption Standard (DES), a 56-bit block cipher with primary support through the *DESCryptoServiceProvider* class. This algorithm is generally secure, but due to its small key size (smaller keys are more easily compromised), it is inappropriate for highly sensitive data.
- RC2 (Rivest Cipher number 2), a 56-bit block cipher with primary support through the *RC2CryptoServiceProvider* class. The cipher was originally developed by Lotus for use in its Lotus Notes product. It is not excitingly secure, but for this reason, it was given more favorable export freedoms by the United States government.

- Rijndael (derived from the names of its two designers, Daemen and Rijmen), a variable bit (between 128 to 256 bits) block cipher with primary support through the *RijndaelManaged* class. It is related to a similar algorithm named Advanced Encryption Standard (AES), and is the most secure of the secret key algorithms provided with .NET.
- Triple DES, a block cipher that uses the underlying DES algorithm three times to generate a more secure result, with primary support through the *TripleDESCryptoServiceProvider* class. Although more secure than plain DES, it is still much more vulnerable than the Rijndael or AES standard.

The various "provider" classes are tools that must be used together with other cryptography classes to work properly. For instance, this sample code (based on code found in the MSDN documentation) uses the *DESCryptoServiceProvider* and *CryptoStream* classes, both members of *System.Security.Cryptography*, to jointly encrypt and decrypt a block of text.

```
Imports System
Imports System.IO
Imports System.Text
Imports System.Security.Cryptography

Class CryptoMemoryStream
    Public Shared Sub Main()
        ' ----- Encrypt then decrypt some text.
        Dim key As New DESCryptoServiceProvider
        Dim encryptedVersion() As Byte
        Dim decryptedVersion As String

        ' ----- First, encrypt some text.
        encryptedVersion = Encrypt("This is a secret.", key)

        ' ----- Then, decrypt it to get the original.
        decryptedVersion = Decrypt(encryptedVersion, key)
    End Sub

    Public Shared Function Encrypt(origText As String, _
            key As SymmetricAlgorithm) As Byte()
        ' ----- Uses a crytographic memory stream and a
        '          secret key provider (DES in this case)
        '          to encrypt some text.
```

```
Dim baseStream As New MemoryStream
Dim secretStream As CryptoStream
Dim streamOut As StreamWriter
Dim encryptedText() As Byte

' ----- A memory stream just shuffles data from
'         end to end. Adding a CryptoStream to it
'         will encrypt the data as it moves through
'         the stream.
secretStream = New CryptoStream(baseStream, _
    key.CreateEncryptor(), CryptoStreamMode.Write)
streamOut = New StreamWriter(secretStream)
streamOut.WriteLine(origText)
streamOut.Close()
secretStream.Close()

' ----- Move the encrypted content into a useful
'         byte array.
encryptedText = baseStream.ToArray()
baseStream.Close()
Return encryptedText
End Function


Public Shared Function Decrypt(encryptedText() As Byte, _
    key As SymmetricAlgorithm) As String
    ' ----- Clearly, this is the opposite of the
    '         Encrypt() function, using a stream reader
    '         instead of a writer, and the key's
    '         "decryptor" instead of its "encryptor."
Dim baseStream As MemoryStream
Dim secretStream As CryptoStream
Dim streamIn As StreamReader
Dim origText As String

' ----- Build a stream that automatically decrypts
'         as data is passed through it.
baseStream = New MemoryStream(encryptedText)
secretStream = New CryptoStream(baseStream, _
    key.CreateDecryptor(), CryptoStreamMode.Read)
streamIn = New StreamReader(secretStream)
```

```
'  ----- Move the decrypted content back to a string.
      origText = streamIn.ReadLine()
      streamIn.Close()
      secretStream.Close()
      baseStream.Close()
      Return origText
   End Function
End Class
```

This code combines a DES encryption class with a *Stream*, a common tool in .NET applications for transferring data from one state or location to another. (Streams are a primary method used to read and write files.) Streams are not too hard to use, but the code still seems a little convoluted. Why doesn't the *DESCryptoServiceProvider* class simply include *Encrypt* and *Decrypt* methods? That's my question, at least. I'm sure it has something to do with keeping the class generic for use in many data environments. Still, as chunky as this code is, it's sure a lot easier than writing the encryption code myself. And it's general enough that I could swap in one of the other secret key algorithms without very much change in the code.

Asymmetric Cryptography

In secret key cryptography, you can use any old key you wish to support the encryption and decryption process. As long as you keep it a secret, the content of the key itself isn't really too important. The same cannot be said, though, of asymmetric (public key) cryptography. Because separate keys are used to encrypt and decrypt the data, specific private and public keys must be crafted specifically as a pair. You can't just select random public and private keys and hope that they work together.

The components used to support asymmetric cryptography include "generators" that emit public and private key pairs. Once generated, these keys can be used in your code to mask sensitive data. And due to the large key size, it's very difficult for anyone to hack into your encrypted data.

Public key encryption is notoriously slow; it takes forever and a day to encode large amounts of data using the source key. This is one of the reasons that the Founding Fathers didn't use public key encryption on the *Declaration of Independence*. Because of the sluggish performance of asymmetric encryption, many secure data systems use a combination of public-key and secret-key encryption to protect data. The initial authorization occurs with public-key processes, but once the secure channel opens, the data passed between the systems gets encrypted using faster secret-key methods.

.NET includes two public key cryptography classes for your encrypting and decrypting pleasure.

- Digital Signature Algorithm (DSA), an algorithm designed by the United States government for use in digital signatures, with primary support through the *DSACryptoServiceProvider* class.
- The RSA algorithm (named after its founders: Ron Rivest, Adi Shamir, and Len Adleman), an older though generally secure asymmetric algorithm, with primary support through the *RSACryptoServiceProvider* class.

I won't be using asymmetric encryption in the Library Project. While the code needed to use these providers is interesting, and while the background information on prime number generation and large number factorization is fascinating, such discussions are beyond the scope of this book.

Hashing

Although hashing algorithms do not give you the ability to encrypt and decrypt data at will, they are useful in supporting systems that secure and verify data content. In fact, hashing is the one cryptography component that we will directly code in the Library Project, so stay alert.

Coming up with a hashing algorithm is easy. It took the best minds of the National Security Agency and the Massachusetts Institute of Technology to come up with reliable secret-key and public-key encryption systems, but you can develop a hashing algorithm in just a few minutes. A few years ago, I wrote my own hashing algorithm that I used for years in business applications. That fact alone should prove how simple and basic they can be. Here's a hashing algorithm I just made up while I was sitting here.

```
Public Function HashSomeText(ByVal origText As String) As Long
    ' ----- Create a hash value from some data.
    Dim hashValue As Long = 0&
    Dim counter As Long

    For counter = 1 To Len(origText)
        hashValue += Asc(Mid(origText, counter, 1))
        If (hashValue > (Long.MaxValue * 0.9)) Then _
            hashValue /= 2
    Next counter
    Return hashValue
End Function
```

In the code, I just add up the ASCII values of each character in the text string, and return the result. I do a check in the loop to make sure I don't exceed 90% of the maximum *Long* value; I don't want to overflow the *hashValue* variable and generate an error. Although *HashSomeText* does generate a hashed representation of the input data, it also has some deficiencies.

- It's pretty easy to guess from the hash value whether the incoming content was short or long. Shorter content will usually generate small numbers, and larger output values tend to indicate longer input content.
- It's not very sensitive to some types of content changes. For instance, if you rearrange several characters in the content, it probably won't impact the hash value. Changing a character will impact the value, but if you change one character from "A" to "B" and another nearby letter from "T" to "S," the hash value will remain unchanged.
- The shorter the content, the greater the chance that two inputs will generate the same hash value.

Perhaps you want something a little more robust. If so, .NET includes several hashing tools.

- Hash-based Message Authentication Code (HMAC) calculated using the Secure Hash Algorithm number 1 (SHA-1) hash function, made available through the *HMACSHA1* class. It uses a 160-bit hash code. There are no specific restrictions on the length of the secret key used in the calculation. While suitable for low-risk situations, the SHA-1 algorithm is susceptible to attack.
- Message Authentication Code (MAC) calculated using the Triple-DES secret key algorithms (described earlier), made available through the *MACTripleDES* class. The secret key used in the calculation is either 16 or 24 bytes long, and the generated value is 8 bytes in length.
- Message-Digest algorithm number 5 (MD5) hash calculation, made available through the *MD5CryptoServiceProvider* class. MD5 is yet another super-secret algorithm designed by Ron Rivest (that guy is amazing), but it has been shown to contain some flaws that could

make it an encoding security risk. The resulting hash value is 128 bits long.

- Like the *HMACSHA1* class, the *SHA1Managed* class computes a hash value using the SHA-1 hash function. However, it is written using .NET managed code only. *HMACSHA1* and some of the other cryptographic features in .NET are simply wrappers around the older Cryptography API (CAPI), a pre-.NET DLL library. *SHA1Managed* uses a 160-bit hash code.
- Three other classes—*SHA256Managed*, *SHA384Managed*, and *SHA512Managed*—are similar to the *SHA1Managed* class, but use 256-bit, 384-bit, and 512-bit hash codes, respectively.

Each of these algorithms uses a secret key that must be included each time the hash is generated against the same set of input data. As long as the input data is unchanged, and the secret key is the same, the resulting hash value will also remain unchanged. By design, even the smallest change in the input data generates major changes in the output hash value.

Other Security Features

That about sums up the major security features in .NET. There are a few other interesting security-related features that I won't discuss in detail, but they deserve at least a passing mention.

User Authentication and My.User

The Visual Basic *My.User* object includes several authentication features that can help you design security-enabled code. One useful member is the *Name* property, which supplies the name of the current authenticated user. The *IsInRole* method tells you whether or not the active user is included in, say, the *Administrators* security group.

For Windows Forms applications, the members of *My.User* will typically refer to the logged-in Windows user. However, you can use other authentication systems that meet your special development needs. Options include using the Internet-based Microsoft Passport system, other third-party authentication systems, or your own custom-designed user management system.

The SecureString Class

It's amazing that with all of these advanced tools, programmers still spend much of their time building and parsing string data. Fortunately, .NET includes a plethora of useful string manipulation tools. Unfortunately, they aren't very secure. You may recall that .NET strings are immutable; once created, they are never changed. Eventually, they will be destroyed by the garbage collection process. But until then, they sit around in memory, just waiting for some hacker-designed code to peruse. Internally, string data is stored as plain text, so if someone can get to the memory, they can copy the content for nefarious purposes.

SecureString to the rescue! The *System.Security.SecureString* class lets you store strings and get them back, but internally, the content of the string is encrypted. If anyone obtained the internal content of the class, it would look like gibberish.

Summary

When you write a business application for some other organization or department, you might not care all that much about the security and integrity of the data managed by the software tool. As long as the data gets from the user's fingertips to the database and back, it's all hunky-dory.

Although such views may work for many applications, there are systems and users that expect much more in the way of security. Sometimes, you need to ensure the security and integrity of the data managed by the application, especially if it will leave the confines of your software or associated database. The security features found in the *System.Security.Cryptography* namespace provide a fun variety of data hiding and restoration options.

Project

This chapter will see the following security-focused features added to the Library Project.

- The "login" form, which authenticates librarian and other administrative users.
- Security group and user management forms.
- A function that encrypts a user-supplied password.
- Activation of some application features that depend on user authentication.

Project Access Load the "Chapter 11 (Before) Code" project, either through the New Project templates, or by accessing the project directly from the installation directory. To see the code in its final form, load "Chapter 11 (After) Code" instead.

Authentication Support

Because all of the library's data is stored in a SQL Server database, we already use either Windows or SQL Server security to restrict access to the data itself. But once we connect to the database, we will use a custom authentication system to enable and disable features in the application. It's there that we'll put some of the .NET cryptography features into use.

Before adding the interesting code, we need to add some global variables that support security throughout the application. All of the global elements appear in the *General.vb* file, within the *GeneralCode* module.

Insert Snippet Insert Chapter 11, Snippet Item 1.

```
Public LoggedInUserID As Integer
Public LoggedInUserName As String
Public LoggedInGroupID As Integer
Public SecurityProfile(MaxLibrarySecurity) As Boolean
```

Although we added it in a previous step, the *LibrarySecurity* enumeration is an important part of the security system. Its elements match those found in the *Activity* table in the Library database. Each enumeration value matches one element in the *SecurityProfile* array that we just added to the code.

```
Public Enum LibrarySecurity As Integer
    ManageAuthors = 1
    ManageAuthorTypes = 2
    ...more here...
    ManagePatronGroups = 22
    ViewAdminPatronMessages = 23
End Enum
Public Const MaxLibrarySecurity As LibrarySecurity = _
    LibrarySecurity.ViewAdminPatronMessages
```

All of the newly added global variables store identity information for the active administrator. When a patron is the active user, the program sets all of these values to their default states. Because this should be done when the program first begins, we'll add an *InitializeSystem* routine that is called on startup. It also appears in the *General* module.

Insert Snippet Insert Chapter 11, Snippet Item 2.

```
Public Sub InitializeSystem()
    ' ----- Initialize global variables here.
    Dim counter As Integer

    ' ----- Clear security-related values.
    LoggedInUserID = -1
    LoggedInUserName = ""
    LoggedInGroupID = -1
    For counter = 1 To MaxLibrarySecurity
        SecurityProfile(counter) = False
    Next counter
End Sub
```

(The *SecurityProfile* array has items that range from 0 to *MaxLibrarySecurity*, but the loop at the end of this code starts from element 1. Because the *Activity* table starts its counting at 1, I decided to just skip element 0.) The *InitializeSystem* method is called from the *MyApplication_Startup* event in the *ApplicationEvents.vb* file, just before establishing a connection to the database. Let's add that code now.

Insert Snippet Insert Chapter 11, Snippet Item 3.

```
' ----- Perform general initialization.
InitializeSystem()
```

Each time that an administrator tries to use the system, and each time that the administrator logs off and returns the program to patron mode, all of the security-related global variables must be reset. This is done in the *ReprocessSecuritySet* method, added to the *General* module.

Insert Snippet Insert Chapter 11, Snippet Item 4.

```
Public Sub ReprocessSecuritySet()
    ' ----- Reload in the security set for the current
    '       user. If no user is logged in, clear all settings.
    Dim counter As Integer
    Dim sqlText As String
    Dim dbInfo As SqlClient.SqlDataReader = Nothing

    ' ----- Clear out the existing items.
    For counter = 1 To MaxLibrarySecurity
        SecurityProfile(counter) = False
    Next counter

    ' ----- Exit if there is no user logged in.
    If (LoggedInUserID = -1) Or _
        (LoggedInGroupID = -1) Then Return

    Try
        ' ----- Load in the security elements for this user.
        sqlText = "SELECT ActivityID FROM GroupActivity " & _
            "WHERE GroupID = " & LoggedInGroupID
        dbInfo = CreateReader(sqlText)
        Do While (dbInfo.Read)
            SecurityProfile(CInt(dbInfo!ActivityID)) = True
        Loop
        dbInfo.Close()
    Catch ex As Exception
        ' ----- Some database-related error.
        GeneralError("ReprocessSecuritySet", ex)
        If (dbInfo IsNot Nothing) Then dbInfo.Close()

        ' ----- Un-login the administrator through recursion.
        LoggedInUserID = -1
        LoggedInGroupID = -1
        ReprocessSecuritySet()
    Finally
        dbInfo = Nothing
    End Try
End Sub
```

11. SECURITY

This routine uses code built in Chapter 10, "ADO.NET," and other earlier chapters. When it detects an authorized user (the *LoggedInUserID* variable), it creates a *SqlDataReader* object with that user's allowed security features, and stores those settings in the *SecurityProfile* array. Once loaded, any array element that is *True* represents an application feature that the administrator is authorized to use. I'll discuss the *GroupActivity* table a little later in this project section.

If a database error occurs during processing, the code resets everything to patron mode, making a **recursive** call to *ReprocessSecuritySet* to clear the *SecurityProfile* array. (*Recursion* occurs when a routine directly or indirectly calls itself.)

Encrypting Passwords

The entire content of this chapter has been building to this very moment, the section where I reveal the winner of the next presidential election. Wait! Even better than that, I will use one of the .NET hashing methods to encrypt an administrator-supplied password before storing it in the database. One of the tables in the Library database, the *UserName* table, stores the basic security profile for each librarian or other administrative user, including a password. Because anyone who can get into the database will be able to see the passwords stored in this table, we will encrypt them to make them a little less tempting. (For patrons simply using the program, there shouldn't be any direct access to the database apart from the application, but you never know about those frisky patrons.)

To keep things secure, we'll scramble the user-entered password, using it to generate a hash value, and store the hash value in the database's password field for the user. Later, when an administrative user wants to gain access to enhanced features, the program will again convert the entered password into a hash value, and compare that value to the on-record hashed password.

Each .NET hashing function depends on a secret code. Because the Library Project will only perform a unidirectional encryption, and it will never ask any other program to re-encrypt the password, we'll just use the user's login name as the "secret" key. I decided to use the *HMACSHA1* hashing class, mostly for its ability to accept a variable-size key. Although it is reported to have security issues, that shouldn't be a problem for the way that we're using it. I mean, if someone actually got into the database trying to decrypt the passwords stored in the *UserName* table, they would already have full access to everything in the Library system.

Of course, the encryption code requires references to the *System.Security.Cryptography* namespace. We'll also need a reference to *System.Text* for some of the support code. Add the relevant *Import* statements to the top of the *General.vb* code file.

Insert Snippet Insert Chapter 11, Snippet Item 5.

```
Imports System.Text
Imports System.Security.Cryptography
```

The actual jumbling of the password occurs in the *EncryptPassword* routine, making its entrance in the *General* module.

Insert Snippet Insert Chapter 11, Snippet Item 6.

```
Public Function EncryptPassword(ByVal loginID As String, _
    ByVal passwordText As String) As String
  ' ----- Given a user name and a password, encrypt the
  '       password so that it is not easy to decrypt. There
  '       is no limit on password length since it is going
  '       to be hashed anyway.
  Dim hashingFunction As HMACSHA1
  Dim secretKey() As Byte
  Dim hashValue() As Byte
  Dim counter As Integer
  Dim result As String = ""

  ' ----- Prepare the secret key. Force it to uppercase for
  '       consistency, and then stuff it in a byte array.
  secretKey = (New UnicodeEncoding).GetBytes(UCase(loginID))

  ' ----- Create the hashing component using Managed SHA-1.
  hashingFunction = New HMACSHA1(secretKey, True)

  ' ----- Calculate the hash value. One simple line of code.
  hashValue = hashingFunction.ComputeHash( _
    (New UnicodeEncoding).GetBytes(passwordText))
```

```
' ----- The hash value is ready, but I like things in
'        plaintext when possible. Let's convert it to a
'        long hex string.
For counter = 0 To hashValue.Length - 1
    result &= Hex(hashValue(counter))
Next counter

' ----- Stored passwords are limited to 20 characters.
Return Left(result, 20)
End Function
```

The primary methods of interacting with the security providers in .NET are via a byte array or a stream. I opted to use the byte array method, converting the incoming string values through the *UnicodeEncoding* object's *GetBytes* method. Once stored as a byte array, I pass the login ID and password as arguments to the *HMACSHA1* class' features.

Although I could store the output of the *ComputeHash* method directly in a database field, I decided to convert the result into readable ASCII characters so that things wouldn't look all weird when I issued SQL statements against the *UserName* table. My conversion is basic: Convert each byte into its printable hexadecimal equivalent using Visual Basic's *Hex* function. Then just string the results together. The *UserName.Password* field only holds 20 characters, so I chop off anything longer.

Just to make sure that this algorithm generates reasonable output, I called *EncryptPassword* with a few different inputs.

```
MsgBox("Alice/none:      " & _
    EncryptPassword("Alice", "") & vbCrLf & _
    "Alice/password: " & _
    EncryptPassword("Alice", "password") & vbCrLf & _
    "Bob/none:        " & _
    EncryptPassword("Bob", "") & vbCrLf & _
    "Bob/password:   " & _
    EncryptPassword("Bob", "password"))
```

This code generated the following message.

```
Alice/none:     6570FC214A797C023F40
Alice/password: 4AEC6C914C65D88BD082
Bob/none:       7F544120E3AB9FB48C32
Bob/password:   274A56F047293EA0B97E
```

Undoing Some Previous Changes

The *UserName*, *GroupName*, and *GroupActivity* tables in the database define the security profiles for each administrative user. Every user (a record in *UserName*) is part of one security group (a *GroupName* record). Each group includes access to zero or more enhanced application features; the *GroupActivity* table identifies which features match up to each security group record.

To manage these tables, we need to add property forms that edit the fields of a single database record. We already wrote some of the code awhile back. Chapter 8, "Classes and Inheritance," defined the *BaseCodeForm.vb* file, a template for forms that edit single database records. That same chapter introduced the *ListEditRecords.vb* file, the "parent" form that displays a listing of already-defined database records. Our record editor for both users and security groups will use the features in these two existing forms.

Rant Alert Your friendly author, Tim Patrick, is about to rant on and on about something that really bugs him. Why not join him in this rant?

When we designed the code for *BaseCodeForm.vb* in Chapter 8, my goal was to show you the *MustInherit* and *MustOverride* class features included with Visual Basic. They are pretty useful features. Unfortunately, they just don't mix well with user interface elements, and here's why: Visual Studio actually creates instances of your forms at design time so that you can interact with them inside the editor. If you were to delve into the source code for, say, a *TextBox* control, you would find special code that deals with design-time presentation of the control. Interesting? Yes. Flexible? Yes. Perfect in all cases? No.

The problem—and *problem* is putting it mildly—is that Visual Studio won't (actually, can't) create an instance of a class defined as *MustInherit*. That's because you *must inherit it through another class first before you create instances*. What does this mean to you? It means that if you try to design a form that inherits from a *MustInherit* form template, Visual Studio will not present the user interface portion of the form for your editing enjoyment. You can still access the source code of the form, and if this is how you want to design the inherited form, that's fine. But you and I are looking for simplicity in programming, and we plunked down good money for Visual Studio, so we're certainly going to use its visual tools to edit our visual forms.

The upshot of all this ranting—and I'm almost at the end of my rant, but you can keep going on if you want—is that we must change the *BaseCodeForm.vb* file, removing the *MustInherit* and *MustOverride* keywords, and making other appropriate adjustments. I've already made the changes to both the before and after templates of the Chapter 11, "Security," code.

This is part of the reality of programming in a complex system like Visual Studio. Sometimes, even after you have done all of your research and carefully mapped out the application features and structure, you run in to some designer- or compiler-specific behavior that forces you to make some change. Once you learn to avoid the major issues, you find that it doesn't happen too often. But when it does occur, it can be a great time to rant.

Managing Security Groups

So, back to our *GroupName* record editor. I haven't added it to the project yet, so let's add it now. Because it will inherit from another form in the project, we have to allow Visual Studio to instantiate the base form by first compiling the application. This is easily done through the **Build ➤ Build Library** menu command.

To create the new form, select the **Project ➤ Add Windows Form** menu command. When the *Add New Item* window appears, select "Inherited Form" from the **Templates** list. Enter "GroupName.vb" in the **Name** field, and then click the **Add** button. When the *Inheritance Picker* form appears (see Figure 11-1), select "BaseCodeForm" from the list, and click **OK**. The new *GroupName* form appears, but it looks remarkably like the *BaseCodeForm* form.

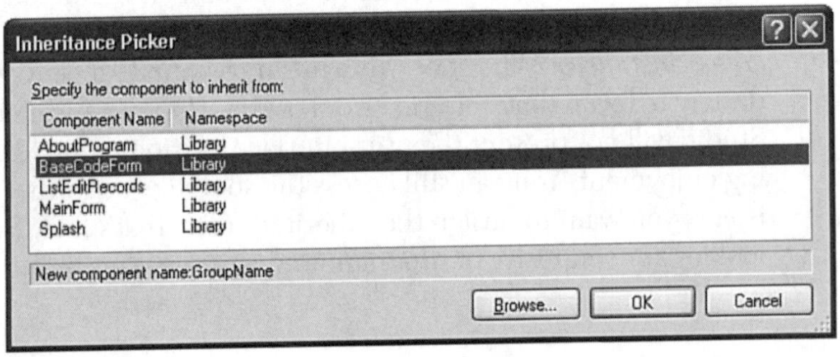

Figure 11-1 Who says you can't pick your own relatives?

Add two *Label* controls, two *TextBox* controls, two *Button* controls, and a *CheckedListBox* control from the Toolbox, and set their properties using the following settings.

Control Type	Property Settings	
Label	(Name):	LabelFullName
	AutoSize:	True
	Location:	8, 10
	Text:	&Security Group Name:
TextBox	(Name):	RecordFullName
	Location:	128, 8
	MaxLength:	50
	Size:	248, 20
Label	(Name):	LabelActivity
	AutoSize:	True
	Location:	8, 34
	Text:	&Allowed Activities:
CheckedListBox	(Name):	ActivityList
	Location:	128, 32
	Size:	248, 244
Button	(Name):	ActOK
	Location:	208, 288
	Size:	80, 24
	Text:	OK
Button	(Name):	ActCancel
	DialogResult:	Cancel
	Location:	296, 288
	Size:	80, 24
	Text:	Cancel
Form (GroupName)	(Name):	GroupName
	AcceptButton:	ActOK
	CancelButton:	ActCancel
	Size:	392, 351
	Text:	Edit Security Group

Don't forget to adjust the tab order of the controls on the form.

Let's add the code all at once. Add the next code snippet to the class source code body.

Insert Snippet Insert Chapter 11, Snippet Item 7.

Hey, that's nearly 300 lines of source code. Good typing. The class includes two private members. *ActiveID* holds the ID number of the currently displayed *GroupName* database record, or –1 when editing new records. The *StartingOver* flag is a little more interesting. Remember that we are using a shared summary form to display all of the already-entered *GroupName* records. To allow this generic form, *ListEditRecords.vb*, to work with the different record editors, we pass an instance of the detail form (*GroupName.vb* in this case) to the summary form.

```
ListEditRecords.ManageRecords(New Library.GroupName)
```

Within the *ListEditRecords* form's code, the instance of *GroupName* is used over and over, each time the user wants to add or edit a *GroupName* database record. If the user edits one record, and then tries to edit another, the leftovers from the first record will still be in the detail form's fields. Therefore, we will have to clear them each time we add or edit a different record. The *StartingOver* flag helps with that process by resetting the focus to the first detail form field in the form's *Activated* event.

```
Private Sub GroupName_Activated(ByVal sender As Object, _
      ByVal e As System.EventArgs) Handles Me.Activated
   ' ----- Return the focus to the main field.
   If (StartingOver) Then RecordFullName.Focus()
   StartingOver = False
End Sub
```

The related *PrepareFormFields* private method does the actual clearing and storing of data with each new Add or Edit call. For new records, it simply clears all entered data on the form. When editing an existing record, it retrieves the relevant data from the database, and stores saved values in the various on-form fields. The following statements display the stored group name in the *RecordFullName* field, a *TextBox* control.

```
' ----- Load in the values stored in the database.
sqlText = "SELECT FullName FROM GroupName WHERE ID = " & _
  .ActiveID
RecordFullName.Text = CStr(ExecuteSQLReturn(sqlText))
```

Most of the routines in the *GroupName* form provide simple overrides for base members of the *BaseCodeForm* class. The *CanUserAdd* method, which simply returns *False* in the base class, includes actual logic in the inherited class. It uses the *SecurityProfile* array we added earlier to determine if the current user is allowed to add group records.

```
Public Overrides Function CanUserAdd() As Boolean
   ' ----- Check the user for security access: add.
   Return SecurityProfile(LibrarySecurity.ManageGroups)
End Function
```

If you look through the added code, you'll find overrides for all of the *BaseCodeForm* members except for the *UsesSearch* and *SearchForRecord* methods. The derived class accepts the default action for these two members.

The user adds, edits, and deletes group name records through the *AddRecord*, *EditRecord*, and *DeleteRecord* overrides, respectively, each called by code in the *ListEditRecords* form. Here's the code for *EditRecord*.

```
Public Overrides Function EditRecord( _
     ByVal recordID As Integer) As Integer
   ' ----- Edit an existing record.
   ActiveID = recordID
   PrepareFormFields()
   Me.ShowDialog()
   If (Me.DialogResult = Windows.Forms.DialogResult.OK) Then _
     Return ActiveID Else Return -1
End Function
```

After storing the ID of the record to edit in the *ActiveID* private field, the code loads the data through the *PrepareFormFields* method, and prompts the user to edit the record with the *Me.ShowDialog* call. The form sticks around until some code or control sets the form's *DialogResult* property. This is done in the *ActOK_Click* event, and also through the

ActCancel button's *DialogResult* property, which Visual Basic will assign to the form automatically when the user clicks the *ActCancel* button.

The *AddRecord* routine is just like *EditRecord*, but it assigns −1 to the *ActiveID* member to flag a new record. The *DeleteRecord* routine is more involved, and uses some of the database code we wrote in the last chapter.

```
Public Overrides Function DeleteRecord( _
     ByVal recordID As Integer) As Boolean
  ' ----- The user wants to delete the record.
  Dim sqlText As String

  On Error GoTo ErrorHandler

  ' ----- Confirm with the user.
  If (MsgBox("Do you really wish to delete the " & _
     "security group?", MsgBoxStyle.YesNo Or _
     MsgBoxStyle.Question, ProgramTitle) <> _
     MsgBoxResult.Yes) Then Return False

  ' ----- Make sure this record is not in use.
  sqlText = "SELECT COUNT(*) FROM UserName " & _
     "WHERE GroupID = " & recordID
  If (CInt(ExecuteSQLReturn(sqlText)) > 0) Then
     MsgBox("You cannot delete this record because " & _
        "it is in use.", MsgBoxStyle.OkOnly Or _
        MsgBoxStyle.Exclamation, ProgramTitle)
     Return False
  End If

  ' ----- Delete the record.
  TransactionBegin()
  sqlText = "DELETE FROM GroupActivity " & _
     "WHERE GroupID = " & recordID
  ExecuteSQL(sqlText)
  sqlText = "DELETE FROM GroupName WHERE ID = " & recordID
  ExecuteSQL(sqlText)
  TransactionCommit()
  Return True

ErrorHandler:
  GeneralError("GroupName.DeleteRecord", Err.GetException())
  TransactionRollback()
  Return False
End Function
```

After confirming the delete with the user, a quick check is done to see if the group is still being used somewhere in the *UserName* table. If everything checks out fine, the record is deleted using a SQL *DELETE* statement. Because we need to delete data in two tables, I wrapped it all up in a transaction. If an error does occur, the error handler at the end of the routine will roll back the transaction through *TransactionRollback*.

Database Integrity Warning If you have a background in database development, you have already seen the flaw in the delete code. Although I take the time to verify that the record is not in use before deleting it, it's possible that some other user will use it between the time I check the record's use and the time when I actually delete it. Based on the code and database configuration I've presented so far, it would indeed be an issue. When I designed this system, I expected that a single librarian would manage administrative tasks such as this, so I didn't worry about such conflicts and "race conditions."

If you are concerned about the potential for deleting in-use records through code like this, you can enable **referential integrity** on the relationships in the database. I established a relationship between the *GroupName.ID* and *UserName.GroupID* fields, but it's for informational purposes only. You can reconfigure this relationship to have SQL Server enforce the relationship between the tables. If you do this, then it will not be possible to delete an in-use record; an error will occur in the program when you attempt it. That sounds good, and it is, but an overuse of referential integrity can slow down your data access. I will leave this configuration choice up to you.

When the user is done making changes to the record, a click on the **OK** button pushes the data back out to the database. The *ActOK_Click* event handler verifies the data, and then saves it.

```
If (ValidateFormData() = False) Then Return
If (SaveFormData() = False) Then Return
Me.DialogResult = Windows.Forms.DialogResult.OK
```

The *ValidateFormData* method does some simple checks for valid data, such as requiring that the user enter the security group name, and that it is unique. If everything looks good, the *SaveFormData* routine builds SQL statements that save the data.

11. SECURITY

```
Private Function SaveFormData() As Boolean
    ' ----- The user wants to save changes.
    '        Return True on success.
    Dim sqlText As String
    Dim newID As Integer = -1

    On Error GoTo ErrorHandler

    ' ----- Prepare to save the data.
    Me.Cursor = Windows.Forms.Cursors.WaitCursor
    TransactionBegin()

    ' ----- Save the data.
    If (ActiveID = -1) Then
        ' ----- Create a new entry.
        sqlText = "INSERT INTO GroupName (FullName) " & _
            "OUTPUT INSERTED.ID VALUES (" & _
            DBText(Trim(RecordFullName.Text)) & ")"
        newID = CInt(ExecuteSQLReturn(sqlText))
    Else
        ' ----- Update the existing entry.
        newID = ActiveID
        sqlText = "UPDATE GroupName SET FullName = " & _
            DBText(Trim(RecordFullName.Text)) & _
            " WHERE ID = " & ActiveID
        ExecuteSQL(sqlText)
    End If

    ' ----- Clear any existing security settings.
    sqlText = "DELETE FROM GroupActivity " & _
        "WHERE GroupID = " & newID
    ExecuteSQL(sqlText)

    ' ----- Save the selected security settings.
    For Each itemChecked As ListItemData In _
            ActivityList.CheckedItems
        sqlText = "INSERT INTO GroupActivity (GroupID, " & _
            "ActivityID) VALUES (" & newID & ", " & _
            itemChecked.ItemData & ")"
        ExecuteSQL(sqlText)
    Next itemChecked
```

```
' ----- Complete all changes.
TransactionCommit()
ActiveID = newID

' ----- This change may affect this user.
If (LoggedInGroupID = ActiveID) Then _
   ReprocessSecuritySet()

' ----- Success.
ActiveID = newID
Me.Cursor = Windows.Forms.Cursors.Default
Return True

ErrorHandler:
  Me.Cursor = Windows.Forms.Cursors.Default
  GeneralError("GroupName.SaveFormData", Err.GetException())
  TransactionRollback()
  Return False
End Function
```

Be sure to check out the other routines in the *GroupName* form; they exist to support and enhance the user experience.

Managing Users

We also need a form to manage records in the *UserName* table. Because the code for that form generally follows what we've already seen in the *GroupName* form, I won't bore you with the details. I've already added *UserName.vb* to your project, but to prevent bugs in your code while you were in the middle of development, I disabled it (at least in the "Before" version of the code). To enable it, select the file in the *Solution Explorer* window. Then in the *Properties* panel, change the *Build Action* property from "None" to "Compile."

The only interesting code in this form that is somewhat different from the *GroupName* form is the handling of the password. To keep things as secure as possible, I don't actually load the saved password into the on-form **Password** field. It wouldn't do any good anyway because I've stored the encrypted version.

Because I use the user's Login ID as the secret key when encrypting the password, I must regenerate the password if the user ever changes the

Login ID. The private *OrigLoginID* field keeps a copy of the Login ID when the form first opens, and checks for any changes when resaving the record. If changes occur, it regenerates the password.

```
passwordResult = EncryptPassword(Trim(RecordLoginID.Text), _
    Trim(RecordPassword.Text))
```

Using the *UserName* and *GroupName* editing forms requires some additional code in the main form. Add it to the body of the *General* module.

Insert Snippet Insert Chapter 11, Snippet Item 8.

The *AdminLinkGroups* and *AdminLinkUsers* controls are web-style link labels that we added to the program a few chapters back. The *LinkClicked* event—not the *Clicked* event—triggers the display of the code editor. Here's the code to edit the *GroupName* table.

```
Private Sub AdminLinkGroups_LinkClicked( _
        ByVal sender As Object, ByVal e As System.Windows. _
        Forms.LinkLabelLinkClickedEventArgs) _
        Handles AdminLinkGroups.LinkClicked
    ' ----- Let the user edit the list of security groups.
    If (SecurityProfile(LibrarySecurity.ManageGroups) _
            = False) Then
        MsgBox(NotAuthorizedMessage, MsgBoxStyle.OkOnly Or _
            MsgBoxStyle.Exclamation, ProgramTitle)
        Return
    End If

    ' ----- Edit the records.
    ListEditRecords.ManageRecords(New Library.GroupName)
    ListEditRecords = Nothing
End Sub
```

Per-User Experience

Now that we have all of the security support code added to the project, we can start using those features to change the application experience for patrons and administrators. It's not polite to tempt people with immense power, so it's best to hide those features that are not accessible to the lowly and inherently less powerful patron users.

First, let's provide the power of differentiation by adding the administrative login form, shown in Figure 11-2.

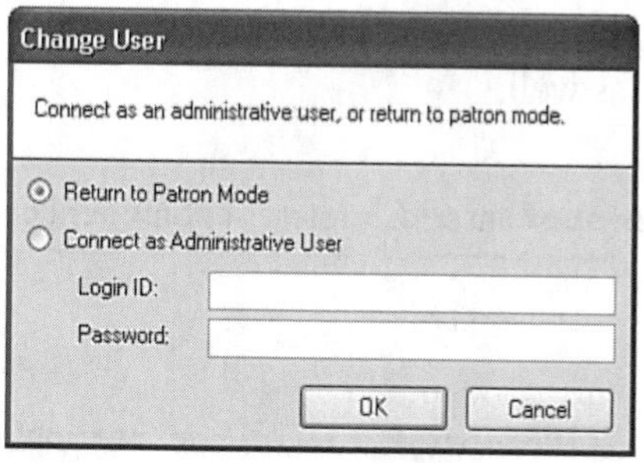

Figure 11-2 The official Library Project administrative login form

I've already added the *ChangeUser.vb* form to the project. If you're using the "Before" version of this chapter's code, select *ChangeUser.vb* in the *Solution Explorer*. Then change its *Build Action* property (in the *Properties* panel) from "None" to "Compile," just as you did with the *UserName.vb* form.

All of the hard work occurs in the form's *ActOK_Click* event. If the user selects the **Return to Patron Mode** option, all security values are cleared, and the Main form hides most features (through code added later).

```
LoggedInUserID = -1
LoggedInUserName = ""
LoggedInGroupID = -1
ReprocessSecuritySet()
```

This form gets connected into the application through the Main form's *ActLogin_Click* event. Open the *MainForm.vb* file, double-click on the **Login** button in the upper-right corner, and add the following code to the *Click* event template that appears.

Insert Snippet Insert Chapter 11, Snippet Item 9.

```
' ----- Prompt the user for patron or administrative mode.
ShowLoginForm()
```

That wasn't much code. Add the *ShowLoginForm* method's code to the form as well.

Insert Snippet Insert Chapter 11, Snippet Item 10.

```
Private Sub ShowLoginForm()
    ' ----- Prompt the user for patron or administrative mode.
    Dim userChoice As Windows.Forms.DialogResult
    userChoice = ChangeUser.ShowDialog()
    ChangeUser = Nothing
    If (userChoice = Windows.Forms.DialogResult.OK) Then _
        UpdateDisplayForUser()
End Sub
```

Let's also enable the F12 key to act as a login trigger. Add the following code to the *Select Case* statement in the *MainForm_KeyDown* event handler.

Insert Snippet Insert Chapter 11, Snippet Item 11.

```
Case Keys.F12
    ' ----- Prompt the user for patron or administrative mode.
    ShowLoginForm()
    e.Handled = True
```

The *ShowLoginForm* routine calls another method, *UpdateDisplayForUser*, that hides and shows various display elements on the main form based on the security profile of the current user. Add it to the *MainForm* class code. I won't show the code here, but basically it looks at the *LoggedInUserID* variable, and if it is set to –1, it hides all of the controls for advanced features.

Insert Snippet Insert Chapter 11, Snippet Item 12.

Currently, when you run the application, all of the advanced features appear, even though no administrator has supplied an ID or password. Calling *UpdateDisplayForUser* when the Main form first appears solves that problem. Add the following code to the end of the *MainForm_Load* method.

Insert Snippet Insert Chapter 11, Snippet Item 13.

```
' ----- Prepare for a patron user.
UpdateDisplayForUser()
```

The last update (five updates, actually) involves limiting the major sections of the form to just authorized administrators. For instance, only administrators who are authorized to run reports should be able to access the reporting panel on the main form. Locate the *TaskReports* method in the Main form, and find the line that displays the panel.

```
PanelReports.Visible = True
```

Replace this line with the following code.

Insert Snippet Insert Chapter 11, Snippet Item 14.

```
If (SecurityProfile(LibrarySecurity.RunReports)) Then _
    PanelReports.Visible = True
```

We need to do the same thing in the *TaskCheckOut*, *TaskCheckIn*, *TaskAdmin*, and *TaskProcess* methods. In each case, replace the line that reads:

```
Panel???.Visible = True
```

with code that checks the security settings before showing the panel.

Insert Snippet Insert Chapter 11, Snippet Items 15 through 18.

- Use Snippet 15 for *TaskCheckOut*.
- Use Snippet 16 for *TaskCheckIn*.
- Use Snippet 17 for *TaskAdmin*.
- Use Snippet 18 for *TaskProcess*.

Run the program, and you'll see that it's starting to look like a real application. If you want access to the enhanced features, try a Login ID of "admin" with no password. You can change that through the *UserName* form if you want!

Because we have a way to secure access to the data and features of the Library Project, let's move to the next chapter and start focusing on the data, the focal point of any business application.

CHAPTER 12

OPERATOR OVERLOADING

Do you ever wish you could do things beyond what people were designed to do? Like flying. We all dream about it, but we can't do it without several hundred pounds of jet fuel. Or what about bending steel with our bare hands? Does that sound like anyone you know? Then there's breathing underwater, doing long division in your head, speaking a foreign language fluently without much study, and having a successful career as an author of popular computer books. Ah, one can dream.

It's not that we want to do all of these things, but once in a while it would be nice to be *slightly enhanced* with the ability to do one or two of the things that are beyond our natural abilities. Unfortunately, it doesn't work for humans very often, but could it work for .NET operators?

You probably didn't even know that the humble Visual Basic addition operator (+) had dreams of flying, or of speaking Hungarian, or of bending steel. Well, operators are people, too. And now their dreams can be fulfilled because Visual Basic 2005 supports operator overloading.

What Is Operator Overloading?

Operator overloading allows your code to enhance the basic Visual Basic operators, and endow them with abilities not previously granted to them by the compiler. Overloading doesn't change the syntax used when employing operators, but it does change the types of objects that each operator can manage. For instance, the multiplication operator (*) normally only interacts with numbers, but you can augment it to work with your own custom *Bumblebee* class.

```
Dim swarm As Bumblebee
Dim oneBumblebee As New Bumblebee
Dim twoBumblebee As New Bumblebee
swarm = oneBumblebee * twoBumblebee
```

The meaning you apply to the overloaded operator is up to you. Although you would normally want to retain the additive nature of the addition operator when overloading it, you don't have to. In fact, you could overload the addition operator so that it subtracts one value from another. But I'd fire you if you did that working for me. Just so you know.

All operator overloading features tie directly to one or more of your classes. Overloaded features look curiously like standard function members, and appear as members of your classes.

Visual Basic includes two types of operators: **unary** and **binary**, defined based on the number of operands recognized by the operator. Unary operators accept a single operand, which always appears to the right of the operator name or symbol. The logical Not operator is a unary operator.

```
oppositeValue = Not originalValue
```

Binary operators accept two operands, one on each side of the operator. The multiplication operator is a binary operator.

```
ten = two * five
```

The nature of an operator is that once it has done its work, the operator and its input operand(s) are, in effect, fully replaced by the calculated result. The expression "10 / 5" is replaced by the calculated "2" result, and this result is used to complete whatever statement or expression the original operation appeared in. It works just like functions.

```
' ----- These two lines (probably) place the same
'       calculated result in theAnswer.
theAnswer = 2 * 5
theAnswer = DoubleIt(5)
```

To get ready for operator overloading, begin to alter your mind to see operators as functions. Look past the confines of your operator universe, and open your thoughts to the truth that the operators and the functions are one. If you've ever programmed in LISP, then I truly feel sorry for you. But you also already understand operators as functions. In LISP, everything is a function. To multiply two numbers together in LISP, you use "prefix" syntax, where the operator name comes first. The expression "seven times three" uses this syntax.

```
(* 7 3)
```

Once complete, the entire parenthesized expression is replaced, function-like, by its answer. The LISP expression:

```
(+ 2 (* 7 3))
```

becomes:

```
(+ 2 21)
```

becomes:

```
23
```

Defining overloaded operators in Visual Basic 2005 is somewhat similar. If you were to translate the definition of multiplication into Visual Basic function-ese, it might look like this:

```
Public Shared Function *( _
    ByVal firstOperand As Integer, _
    ByVal secondOperand As Integer) _
    As Integer
```

The operator (*) becomes a function name, with operands playing the role of function arguments, ultimately generating a value exposed through the function's return value. Although operators aren't defined as functions in this way in Visual Basic, overloads of those operators are.

To overload the multiplication operator in our imaginary *Bumblebee* class, we use the new *Operator* keyword to define a "multiplication function" for operands of the *Bumblebee* class.

```
Partial Class Bumblebee
    Public Shared Operator *(ByVal operand1 As Bumblebee, _
        ByVal operand2 As Bumblebee) As Bumblebee
        ' ----- Multiply two bumblebees together.
        Dim finalResult As New Bumblebee

        ' ----- Add special "multiplication" code here, then...
        Return finalResult
    End Operator
End Class
```

Now, when you multiply two *Bumblebee* instances together with the multiplication operator, Visual Basic recognizes the "operand1 * operand2" pattern as matching a multiplication operator overload with two *Bumblebee* arguments, and calls this class-based *Operator* function to get the result.

All *Operator* declarations must include the *Public* and *Shared* keywords. If they weren't shared, Visual Basic would be required to create an extra instance of the class just to access the operator overload code, and that wouldn't be very efficient.

What Can You Overload?

You can overload pretty much any of Visual Basic's standard operators (except for Is and IsNot), plus a few other features. This section describes each overloadable operator, grouped by general type. Each section includes a table of operators. To overload an operator in a class, use the name in the **Operator** column as the function name. If there were an operator named XX, the matching *Operator* statement would be as follows.

```
Public Shared Operator XX(...)
```

Mathematical Operators

Visual Basic defines ten mathematical or pseudo-mathematical operators. All but one of these exists to manipulate numbers. The leftover operator is the string concatenation operator (&), which works with strings, but kind of looks like the other mathematical operators in its syntax and use.

Two of the operators, plus (+) and minus (−), are both unary and binary operators. The minus sign (−) works as a unary "negation" operator (as in "−5"), and also as a binary "subtraction" operator (the common "5 − 2" syntax). When overloading these operators, the difference lies in the number of arguments included in the argument signature.

```
Public Shared Operator -(ByVal operand1 As SomeClass, _
      ByVal operand2 As SomeClass) As SomeClass
   ' ----- This is the binary "subtraction" version.
End Operator
```

```
Public Shared Operator -(ByVal operand1 As SomeClass) _
    As SomeClass
  ' ----- This is the unary "negation" version.
End Operator
```

Table 12-1 lists the mathematical operators that support overloading.

Table 12-1 The Overloadable Mathematical Operators

Operator	Type	Comments

+	Unary	The unary "plus" operator. You can already use this operator with numbers, as in "+5." But if you enter this value in Visual Studio, the plus operator gets stripped out because it is considered redundant. However, if you overload this operator on a class of your own, Visual Studio will retain the unary form of this operator when used in code.
		
		`' ----- Assuming the unary + operator`
		`'        is overloaded...`
		`Dim oneBuzz As New Bumblebee`
		`Dim moreBuzz As Bumblebee = +oneBuzz`
		
		Because this is a unary operator, only include a single argument when defining the *Operator* method.

+	Binary	The standard addition operator. Remember, just because the operator is called the "addition" operator doesn't mean that you have to retain that connotation. However, you should attempt to overload the operators as close to their original meaning as possible. Visual Basic itself overloads this operator to let it act a little like the string concatenation operator.
–	Unary	This is the unary "negation" operator that comes just before a value or expression.
–	Binary	The subtraction operator, although if you can figure out how to subtract one bumblebee from another, then you're a better programmer than I am.
*	Binary	The multiplication operator.
/	Binary	The standard division operator.

(continues)

Table 12-1 The Overloadable Mathematical Operators *(continued)*

Operator	Type	Comments
\	Binary	The integer division operator. Remember, you are not required to retain any sense of "integer" in this operator if it doesn't meet your class's needs.
^	Binary	The exponentiation ("to the power of") operator.
Mod	Binary	The modulo operator, sometimes called the remainder operator because it returns the remainder of a division action.
&	Binary	The string concatenation operator.

Comparison Operators

Visual Basic includes seven basic comparison operators, most often used in *If* statements and similar expressions that require a *Boolean* conditional calculation. The *Operator* methods for these comparison operators have the same syntax as is used for mathematical operators, but most of them must be implemented in pairs. For example, if you overload the Less Than (<) operator, Visual Basic requires you to overload the Greater Than (>) operator within the same class, and for the same argument signature.

All comparison operators are *Boolean* operators. Although you can alter the data types of the arguments passed to the operator, they must all return a *Boolean* value.

```
Public Shared Operator <=(ByVal operand1 As SomeClass, _
    ByVal operand2 As SomeClass) As Boolean
    ' ----- The <= operator returns a Boolean result.
End Operator
```

Table 12-2 lists six of the seven basic comparison operators that you can overload. Each entry includes a "buddy" value that identifies the matching operator that must also be overloaded.

Table 12-2 The Overloadable Comparison Operators

Operator	Buddy	Comments
=	<>	The Equal To operator compares two operands for equivalence, returning *True* if they are equal.
<>	=	The Not Equal To operator compares two operands for non-equivalence, and returns *True* if they do not match.
<	>	The Less Than operator returns *True* if the first operand is "less than" the second.
>	<	The Greater Than operator returns *True* if the first operand is "greater than" the second.
<=	>=	The Less Than Or Equal To operator returns *True* if the first operand is "less than or equal to" the second. Aren't you getting tired of reading basically the same sentence over and over again?
>=	<=	The Greater Than Or Equal To operator returns *True* if the first operand is "greater than or equal to" the second.

The seventh comparison operator is `Like`. In standard Visual Basic, it compares the first operand to a string "pattern," which is generally a set of matching characters and wildcards.

```
If (someValue Like somePattern) Then
```

You don't have to use the same pattern rules when overloading the `Like` operator, and you can accept any data type for the pattern operand, but you must still return a *Boolean* result.

```
Public Shared Operator Like(ByVal operand1 As Bumblebee, _
     ByVal operand2 As Integer) As Boolean
   ' ----- See if Bumblebee matches an Integer pattern.
End Operator
```

There is no "buddy" operator that you must implement when overloading the `Like` operator.

Bitwise and Logical Operators

Among the logical and bitwise operators included in Visual Basic, four already perform double duty as overloaded operators. The bitwise And, Or, Xor, and Not accept integer operands, generating a numeric result with values transformed at the individual bit level. They also work as logical operators, accepting and returning *Boolean* values, most often in conditional statements. But they can handle the stress of being overridden a little more.

When you do override these four operators, you are overriding the bitwise versions, not the logical versions. Basically, this means that you have control over the return value, and aren't required to make it *Boolean*.

Table 12-3 lists the eight overloadable bitwise and logical operators.

Table 12-3 The Overloadable Bitwise and Logical Operators

Operator	Comments

<<	The Shift Left operator performs bit-shifting on a source integer value, moving the bits to the left by a specified number of positions. Although you do not have to use this operator to perform true bit shifting, you must accept a shift amount (an *Integer*) as the second operand.
	
	`Public Shared Operator <<(ByVal operand1 As Bumblebee, _`
	`    ByVal operand2 As Integer) As Bumblebee`
	`    ' ----- Add shifting code here.`
	`End Operator`

>>	The Shift Right operator performs bit-shifting just like the Shift Left operator, but it moves the bits in the "right" direction. I guess that would make those bits more conservative. Your code can make the return value more liberal if you want, but as with the Shift Left operator, you must accept an *Integer* as the second operand.
Not	The bitwise negation operator. This operator is unary, and accepts only a single operand argument.
And	The bitwise conjunction operator. The original operator sets a bit in the return value if both equally-positioned bits in the source operands are also set.
Or	The bitwise disjunction operator. The original operator sets a bit in the return value if either of the equally positioned bits in the source operands is set.

Operator	Comments
Xor	The bitwise exclusion operator. The original operator sets a bit in the return value if only one of the equally-positioned bits in the source operands is set.
IsTrue	Overloading the Or operator does not automatically overload the related OrElse operator. To use OrElse, you must also overload the special IsTrue operator. It's not a real Visual Basic operator, and you can't call it directly even when overloaded. But when you use the OrElse operator in place of an overloaded Or operator, Visual Basic calls the IsTrue operator when needed. There are a few rules you must follow to use the IsTrue overload.

- The overloaded Or operator must return the class type of the class in which it is defined. If you want to use OrElse on the *Bumblebee* class, the overload of the Or operator in that class must return a value of type *Bumblebee*.

- The overloaded IsTrue operator must accept a single operand of the containing class's type (*Bumblebee*), and return a *Boolean*.

- You must also overload the IsFalse operator.

How you determine the truth or falsity of a *Bumblebee* is up to you.

Operator	Comments
IsFalse	The IsFalse overload works just like IsTrue, and has similar rules, but it applies to the And and AndAlso operators.

The CType Operator

The Visual Basic CType feature looks more like a function than an operator:

```
result = CType(source, type)
```

But looks are deceiving. It is not a true function, and as with the other conversion functions (like *CInt*), it is actually processed at compile time, long before the program even runs. By allowing you to overload it as an operator, Visual Basic enables you to create custom and special conversions between data types that don't seem compatible. The following method template converts a value of type *Bumblebee* to an *Integer*.

```
Public Shared Operator CType(ByVal operand1 As Bumblebee) _
    As Integer
    ' ----- Perform conversion here, returning an Integer.
End Operator
```

If you try to type that last block of code into Visual Basic, it will complain that you are missing either the "Widening" or "Narrowing" keyword (see Figure 12-1).

```
Class Bumblebee
```
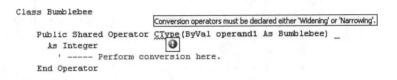
```
    Public Shared Operator CType(ByVal operand1 As Bumblebee) _
        As Integer
        ' ----- Perform conversion here.
    End Operator
```

Figure 12-1 Visual Basic complains about all things wide and narrow.

I mentioned widening and narrowing conversions in passing in Chapter 2, "Introducing Visual Basic," but let's examine them in more depth. When you convert between some core data types in Visual Basic, there is a chance that it will sometimes fail because the source value cannot fit into the destination value. This is true when converting a *Short* value to a *Byte*.

```
Dim quiteBig As Short = 5000
Dim quiteSmall As Byte
' ----- These next two lines will fail.
quiteSmall = quiteBig
quiteSmall = CByte(quiteBig)
```

And it's obvious why it fails: A *Byte* variable cannot hold the value 5000. But what about this code?

```
Dim quiteBig As Short = 5
Dim quiteSmall As Byte
' ----- These next two lines will succeed.
quiteSmall = quiteBig
quiteSmall = CByte(quiteBig)
```

It will run just fine, because 5 fits into a *Byte* variable with room to spare. (If *Option Strict* is set to *On*, the first assignment will still fail to compile.) Still, there is nothing to stop me from reassigning a value of 5000 to quiteBig and trying the assignment again. It's this *potential* for failure during conversion that is the issue.

When a conversion has the potential to fail due to the source data not being able to fully fit in the target variable, it's called a **narrowing**

conversion. Narrowing conversions are a reality, and as long as you have checked the data before the conversion, there shouldn't be any reason to permanently restrict such conversions.

Widening conversions go in the opposite direction. They occur when any source value in the original data type will always fit easily in the target type. A widening conversion will always succeed as long as the source data is valid.

Visual Basic allows widening conversions to occur automatically, implicitly. You don't have to explicitly use *CType* to force the conversion. If you had a widening conversion from *Bumblebee* to *Integer*, and you had set *Option Strict* to *On*, the following code would work just fine.

```
Dim sourceValue As New Bumblebee
Dim destValue As Integer = sourceValue
```

If the conversion from *Bumblebee* to *Integer* was narrowing, you would have to force the conversion using *CType* just so Visual Basic was sure you really wanted to do this.

```
Dim sourceValue As New Bumblebee
Dim destValue As Integer = CType(sourceValue, Integer)
```

When you create custom conversions with the overloaded *CType* operator, you must inform Visual Basic whether the conversion is widening or narrowing by inserting either the *Widening* or *Narrowing* keyword between the *Shared* and *Operator* keywords.

```
Public Shared Narrowing Operator CType( _
      ByVal operand1 As Bumblebee) As Integer
   ' ----- Perform narrowing conversion here.
End Operator
```

Other Operator Overloading Issues

There are a few other rules you must follow when overloading operators, but first let's look at a semi-useful *Bumblebee* class.

```
Class Bumblebee
   Public Bees As Integer
```

```
Public Sub New()
   ' ----- Default constructor.
   Bees = 0
End Sub

Public Sub New(ByVal startingBees As Integer)
   ' ----- Assign an initial number of bees.
   Bees = startingBees
End Sub

Public Shared Operator +(ByVal operand1 As Bumblebee, _
      ByVal operand2 As Bumblebee) As Bumblebee
   ' ----- Join bumblebee groups.
   Dim newGroup As New Bumblebee
   newGroup.Bees = operand1.Bees + operand2.Bees
   Return newGroup
End Operator

Public Shared Operator -(ByVal operand1 As Bumblebee, _
      ByVal operand2 As Bumblebee) As Bumblebee
   ' ----- Separate bumblebee groups.
   Dim newGroup As New Bumblebee
   newGroup.Bees = operand1.Bees - operand2.Bees
   If (newGroup.Bees < 0) Then newGroup.Bees = 0
   Return newGroup
End Operator

Public Shared Operator *(ByVal operand1 As Bumblebee, _
      ByVal operand2 As Bumblebee) As Bumblebee
   ' ----- Create a swarm.
   Dim newGroup As New Bumblebee
   newGroup.Bees = operand1.Bees * operand2.Bees
   Return newGroup
End Operator

Public Shared Widening Operator CType( _
      ByVal operand1 As Bumblebee) As Integer
   ' ----- Perform conversion here.
   Return operand1.Bees
   End Operator
End Class
```

The class is pretty simple; it exists to maintain a simple count of bees. But by overloading the addition, subtraction, multiplication, and *CType* operators, we can use instances of bees with a more natural syntax.

```
Dim studyGroup1 As New Bumblebee(20)
Dim studyGroup2 As New Bumblebee(15)
Dim swarmGroup As Bumblebee = studyGroup1 * studyGroup2
MsgBox("The swarm contains " & CInt(swarmGroup) & " bees.")
```

Running this code correctly generates a 300-bee swarm and the message in Figure 12-2.

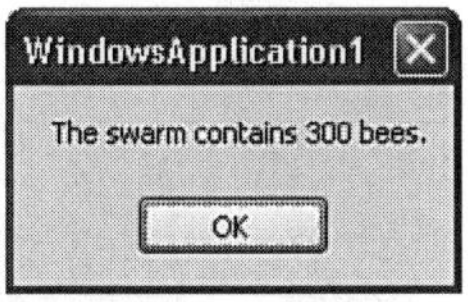

Figure 12-2 Bees sure know how to multiply.

Including a *CType* overload that generated an *Integer* allowed me to convert a *Bumblebee* using the *CInt* operator. I could also have changed the last line to use the true *CType* operator.

```
MsgBox("The swarm contains " & CType(swarmGroup, _
    Integer) & " bees.")
```

Declaration Requirements

As mentioned earlier, you must always make *Operator* methods *Public Shared*. And because the overloaded operators need some sort of intimate connection to their containing class, at least one of the operands or the return value must match the type of the containing class. (In some overloads, Visual Basic requires that it be one of the operands that match.)

Either of the two following overloads will work just fine, because *Bumblebee* is used for one of the operands.

```
Public Shared Operator <=(ByVal operand1 As Bumblebee, _
     ByVal operand2 As Integer) As Boolean
   ' ----- Compare a bumblebee to a value.
End Operator

Public Shared Operator <=(ByVal operand1 As Date, _
     ByVal operand2 As Bumblebee) As Boolean
   ' ----- Compare a date to a bumblebee.
End Operator
```

However, you cannot set both operands to a non-*Bumblebee* type at the same time and still keep the overload in the *Bumblebee* class.

```
Class Bumblebee
   Public Shared Operator <=(ByVal operand1 As Date, _
        ByVal operand2 As Integer) As Boolean
      ' ----- This will not compile.
   End Operator
End Class
```

Overloading Overloads

You can overload overloaded operators. No, dear editor, I didn't type the same word twice by mistake. You can add multiple argument-and-return-value signature variations of an overloaded operator to a single class.

```
Public Shared Widening Operator CType( _
     ByVal operand1 As Bumblebee) As Integer
   ' ----- Perform conversion to Integer here.
End Operator

Public Shared Widening Operator CType( _
     ByVal operand1 As Bumblebee) As Date
   ' ----- Perform conversion to Date here, somehow.
End Operator
```

As long as the argument signatures or return values differ, you can add as many overloads of an operator as you want. You don't need to use the *Overloads* keyword either.

Be Nice

That's right. Be nice. Just because you have the power to redefine addition to be division, you don't have to be so shocking. Don't make the maintenance programmers who have to modify your code later work harder because of your mischievous operator overloads. And I and my fellow maintenance programmers will thank you.

Summary

Operator overloading is a pretty neat feature, but you don't really need it. Anything you can do by overloading the addition operator, you can also do by adding an *Append* method to a class. But operator overloading does allow you to bring your classes more into the mainstream of Visual Basic syntax usage.

When you do overload your operators, make sure you include sufficient documentation or comments to make it clear what it means to left-shift a customer, or multiply a bank account. Hey, I'd like to know about that last one.

Project

This chapter's project will add a lot of code to the Library Program, as much as 25 percent of the full code base. Most of it is identical to code we added in earlier chapters, so I won't print it all here. There's a lot to read here, too, so I won't overload you with pasting code snippets right and left. But as you add each new form to the project, be sure to look over its code to become familiar with its inner workings.

Project Access Load the "Chapter 12 (Before) Code" project, either through the New Project templates, or by accessing the project directly from the installation directory. To see the code in its final form, load "Chapter 12 (After) Code" instead.

Overloading a Conversion

Operator overloading is new with Visual Basic's 2005 release. When I originally designed the Library Project using Visual Basic 2003, operator overloading was unknown in the language, and I had to make due with the features I had available. Looking back, it's not easy to say, "This section of code would work 100 times better through operator overloading." There just isn't much code like that in a typical business application that shuttles around SQL statements and related data.

But enough of my whining. Operator overloading is a useful tool, and I have grown especially fond of the *CType* overload. Let's add a *CType* overload to a class we first designed back in Chapter 8, "Classes and Inheritance": *ListItemData*. This class exposes both *ItemText* and *ItemData* properties, providing access to the textual and numeric aspects of the class content. Its primary purpose is to support the tracking of ID numbers in *ListBox* and *ComboBox* controls. If we need to know the ID number of a selected item in a *ListBox* control (let's name it *SomeList*), we use code similar to the following.

```
Dim recordID As Integer = _
    CType(SomeList.SelectedItem, ListItemData).ItemData
```

There's nothing wrong with that code. But I thought, "Wouldn't it be nice to convert the *ListItemData* instance to an *Integer* using the *CInt* function, and not have to mess with member variables like *ItemData*?"

```
Dim recordID As Integer = _
    CInt(CType(SomeList.SelectedItem, ListItemData))
```

Hmm. The code's not that different. But, hey, why not? Let's do it. To support this conversion, we need to add a *CType* overload to the *ListItemData* class. Open that class's file, and add the following code as a member of the class.

Insert Snippet Insert Chapter 12, Snippet Item 1.

```
Public Shared Widening Operator CType( _
      ByVal sourceItem As ListItemData) As Integer
   ' ----- To convert to integer, simply extract the
```

```
'        integer element.
   Return sourceItem.ItemData
End Operator
```

That's pretty simple. This widening conversion from *ListItemData* to *Integer* just returns the *Integer* portion of the instance. There are only about four or five places in the current Library Project that directly access the *ItemData* member, and it's not that important to go back and change them. But we'll use this conversion overload frequently in the new code added in this chapter.

Global Support Features

We need to add a few more global variables and common global routines to support various features used through the application. Two new global variables will track settings stored in the database's *SystemValue* table. Add them as members to the *General* module (in *General.vb*).

Insert Snippet Insert Chapter 12, Snippet Item 2.

```
Public DefaultItemLocation As Integer
Public SearchMatchLimit As Integer
```

The Library program identifies books and other items as stored in multiple locations, such as multiple branches or storage rooms. *DefaultItemLocation* indicates which one of these locations, from the *CodeLocation* table, is the default. The "DefaultLocation" entry of the *SystemValue* database table stores this value permanently.

When searching for books, authors, or other things that could result in thousands of matches, the *SearchMatchLimit* indicates the maximum number of matches returned by such searches. It's stored as the "SearchLimit" system value.

Because we're already in the *General* module, add three more helper functions.

Insert Snippet Insert Chapter 12, Snippet Item 3.

- **ConfirmDefaultLocation.** This routine verifies that a valid "DefaultLocation" entry exists in the *SystemValue* table. It returns *True* on success.
- **FormatAuthorName.** Given a *SqlDataReader* built from records in the *Author* table, this function formats and returns a friendly author name in the format "Public, John Q, Jr. (1900–1999)." Here's the main formatting code for just the name part, which does a lot of checking for empty (Null) fields:

```
authorName = CStr(dbInfo!LastName)
If (IsDBNull(dbInfo!FirstName) = False) Then
    authorName &= ", " & CStr(dbInfo!FirstName)
    If (IsDBNull(dbInfo!MiddleName) = False) Then _
        authorName &= " " & CStr(dbInfo!MiddleName)
End If
If (IsDBNull(dbInfo!Suffix) = False) Then _
    authorName &= ", " & CStr(dbInfo!Suffix)
```

Similar code for the birth and death years appears right after this code block.

- **GetCopyDisposition**. This routine provides a short description for the current status of a specific library item copy. It analyzes the item's and patron's records, and returns one of the following status code strings: New Item Copy, Checked In, Checked Out, Overdue, Missing, or Reference.

Record Editors and Supporting Forms

Now things really start to hop. We'll add 23 new forms to the application in this chapter. Most of them implement basic code editors, similar to the *UserName.vb* and *GroupName.vb* files we built in Chapter 11, "Security." Other forms exist to provide additional support for these record editors. I won't reprint anything I've gone over before, but I'll point out some interesting new code on our way through each of these 23 forms.

If you're following along in the "Before" version of this chapter's project, you will need to enable each form as you encounter it. To do this, select the file in the *Solution Explorer* window, and change the file's *Build Action* property (in the *Properties* panel) from "None" to "Compile."

Search-Limiting Forms

The first four forms allow the librarian to limit the information overload that comes through using a database with thousands of books, publishers, and authors. You probably remember that the generic *ListEditRecords* form displays all existing records from a table of records by default. This works fine for the security groups stored in the *GroupName* table since you probably won't have even a dozen of those. But listing all books in even a small library can generate quite an imposing list. And depending on the speed of your workstation, it can take a while to load all book titles into the list.

The four "search-limiting" forms help reduce the number of records appearing in the list at once. When the librarian accesses the list of books and other library items, the *ItemLimit* form (see Figure 12-3) provides a quick search prompt that reduces the listed results.

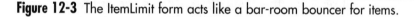

Figure 12-3 The ItemLimit form acts like a bar-room bouncer for items.

The form lets the user retrieve all records, or specific items based on item name (with wildcard support). Once the matches are loaded, the user can access this form again by clicking on the **Lookup** button on the *ListEditRecords* form for those types of code editors that support lookups (authors, items, patrons, and publishers).

We are ready to include these four search-limiting forms in the project.

- **AuthorLimit.vb.** This form limits author records as loaded from the *Author* table.
- **ItemLimit.vb.** This is the form we just talked about. It limits the display of library items from the *NamedItem* table.

12. Operator Overloading

- **PatronLimit.vb.** Just in case patrons are flocking to your library, this form lets you limit the records loaded from the *Patron* table.
- **PublisherLimit.vb.** This form limits records from the *Publisher* table.

Keyword and Subject Editors

While most record editors provide a full editing experience through the *ListEditRecords* form, some are subordinate to other editor forms. Keywords and subjects are a good example. Although they each have their own independent tables (*Keyword* and *Subject*), I chose to allow editing of them through the form that edits individual library items, the *NamedItem* form (added later). That form manages all interactions between the *Keyword* and *Subject* records and the *NamedItem* table, all through the intermediate many-to-many tables *ItemKeyword* and *ItemSubject*.

The *KeywordAdd* and *SubjectAdd* forms provide a simple text entry form for a single keyword or subject. Include each of these forms now into the project.

- *KeywordAdd.vb*
- *SubjectAdd.vb*

More Named Item Support Forms

As we'll see later, the *NamedItem* form is one of the most complex forms added to the Library Project so far. It manages everything about a generalized library item (like a book). Each item can have multiple copies, authors, keywords, subjects, and so on. It's simply too much editing power to include on a single form. We already added two of the subordinate forms: *KeywordAdd* and *SubjectAdd*. Let's add five additional support forms.

- **AuthorAddLocate.vb.** This form presents a wizard-like interface that lets the user add a new or existing author record to an item. "Authors" in the Library program is a generic term that refers to authors, editors, illustrators, performers, etc. This form's three wizard steps (1) let the user indicate the type of author via the *CodeAuthorType* table; (2) perform a search for an existing author by name; and (3) select from a list of matching author names. If the desired author isn't yet in the database, the last step allows a new author to be added. Figure 12-4 shows the first two of these steps.

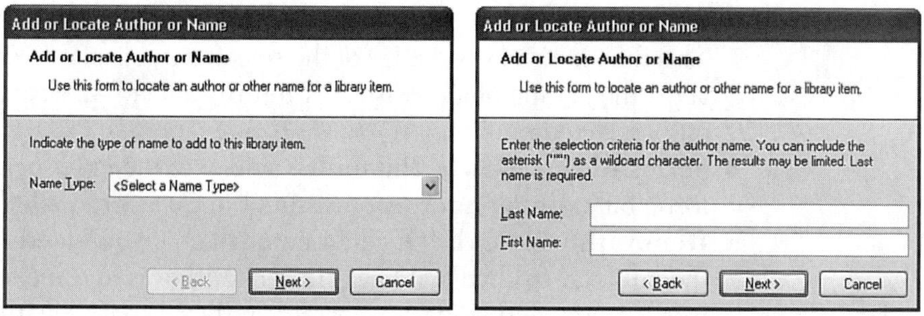

Figure 12-4 The first two of three author wizard steps

Most of the logic is controlled through the **Next** button's event handler. The code in this routine varies based on the current wizard panel in view (as indicated by the *ActivePanel* class-level variable). Here's the code that runs when the user clicks **Next** after selecting the author type.

```
' ----- Make sure a name type is selected.
If (CInt(CType(NameType.SelectedItem, _
      ListItemData)) = -1) Then
   MsgBox("Please select a name type from the list.", _
      MsgBoxStyle.OkOnly Or MsgBoxStyle.Exclamation, _
      ProgramTitle)
   NameType.Focus()
   Return
End If


' ----- Move to the search panel.
ActivePanel = PanelCriteria
SecondPanel.Visible = True
FirstPanel.Visible = False
ActBack.Enabled = True
LastName.Focus()
```

Did you see the first logic line in that code? We used the *CInt* conversion function to get an *ItemData* value from a list item. This calls our overloaded CType operator in the *ListItemData* class.

- **PublisherAddLocate.vb.** This form is just like the *AuthorAddLocate* form, but focuses on publishers. Its wizard only has two steps because publishers are not grouped by type. It locates or adds records in the *Publisher* table. When it's time to add a publisher to an item, the item editor form calls the public *PublisherAddLocate.PromptUser* function. This function returns the ID of the selected publisher record, or –1 to abort the adding of a publisher. A return value of –2 clears any previously selected publisher ID.

- **SeriesAddLocate.vb.** This form is similar to the *PublisherAddLocate* form, but it prompts for records from the *CodeSeries* table.

- **ItemAuthorEdit.vb.** Once an author has been added to an item, the only way to change it to a different author is to remove the incorrect author, and add the correct author separately through the *AuthorAddLocate* form. But if the user simply selected the wrong author type (like "Author" instead of "Illustrator"), it's kind of a burden to search for the author name again just to change the type. The *ItemAuthorEdit* form lets the user modify the type for an author already added to an item. It modifies the *ItemAuthor.AuthorType* database field.

- **ItemCopy.vb.** A library will likely have multiple copies of a particular book, CD, or other item. In the Library program, this means that each *NamedItem* record can have more than one *ItemCopy* record attached to it. Each copy is edited through the *ItemCopy* form (see Figure 12-5).

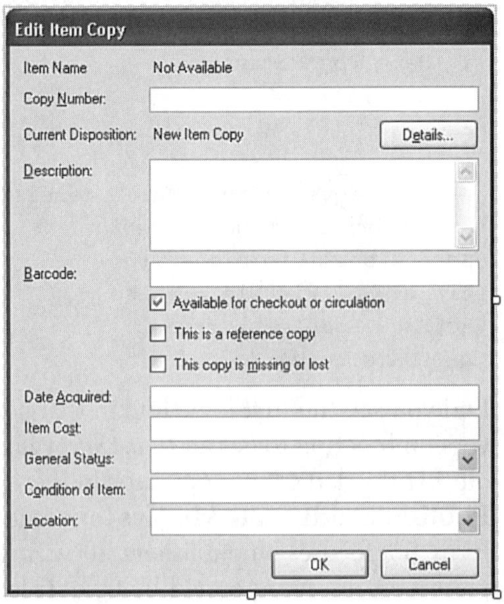

Figure 12-5 Details only a librarian could love

Although this code does not inherit from *BaseCodeForm* as other record editors do, it still has many of the features of those forms, including a *SaveFormData* routine that writes records to the database.

One interesting thing that this form does have is support for reading barcodes. Many barcode readers act as a "wedge," inserting the text of a scanned barcode into the keyboard input stream of the computer. Any program monitoring for barcodes simply has to monitor normal text input.

Barcode wedge scanners append a carriage return (the *Enter* key) to the end of the transmitted barcode. This lets a program detect the end of the barcode number. But in most of the Library program's forms, the *Enter* key triggers the **OK** button and closes the form. We don't want that to happen here. To prevent this, we'll add some code to this form that disables the auto-click on the **OK** button whenever the insertion point is in the **Barcode** text entry field.

Insert Snippet Insert Chapter 12, Snippet Item 4.

```
Private Sub RecordBarcode_Enter( _
      ByVal sender As Object, ByVal e As System.EventArgs) _
      Handles RecordBarcode.Enter
   ' ----- Highlight the entire text.
   RecordBarcode.SelectAll()

   ' ----- Don't allow Enter to close the form.
   Me.AcceptButton = Nothing
End Sub

Private Sub RecordBarcode_Leave( _
      ByVal sender As Object, ByVal e As System.EventArgs) _
      Handles RecordBarcode.Leave
   ' ----- Allow Enter to close the form again.
   Me.AcceptButton = ActOK
End Sub

Private Sub RecordBarcode_KeyPress(ByVal sender As Object, _
      ByVal e As System.Windows.Forms.KeyPressEventArgs) _
      Handles RecordBarcode.KeyPress
   ' ----- Ignore the enter key.
   If (e.KeyChar = ChrW(Keys.Return)) Then e.Handled = True
End Sub
```

With this code, when the user presses the *Enter* key in the **Barcode** field manually, the form will not close. But it's a small price to pay for barcode support.

Inherited Code Editors

Twelve of the forms added in this chapter inherit directly from the *BaseCodeForm* class. Add them to the project as I review each one.

- **Author.vb.** The *Author* form edits records in the *Author* database table. As a typical derived class of *BaseCodeForm*, it overrides many of the public elements of its base class. Two overrides that we haven't yet used in earlier chapters are the *UsesSearch* and *SearchForRecord* methods. These allow the user of the *ListEditRecords* form to limit the displayed authors through the prompting of the *AuthorLimit* form described earlier in this chapter. (The *FillListWithRecords* override also calls *SearchForRecord* to prompt the user for the initial list of authors to display.)

  In *SearchForLimit*, the call to *AuthorLimit.PromptUser* returns a comma-separated string in "Last, First" format.

  ```
  ' ----- Prompt the user for the limited author name.
  exceededMatches = False
  userLimit = (New AuthorLimit).PromptUser()
  If (userLimit = "") Then Return
  ```

  The user can include the "*" character as a wildcard in the first or last name parts. The asterisk has become a common character to use in all types of wildcard searches. Unfortunately, it is not supported in SQL Server SELECT statements. SQL Server uses the "%" character for a wildcard instead (as do many other SQL-compliant database platforms). As *SearchForLimit* extracts the first and last names, it ensures that the right wildcard character is used.

  ```
  ' ----- Use the limits to help prepare
  '       the search text.
  limitLast = Trim(GetSubStr(userLimit, ",", 1))
  limitFirst = Trim(GetSubStr(userLimit, ",", 2))
  If ((limitLast & limitFirst) = "") Then Return
  If (InStr(limitLast, "*") = 0) Then limitLast &= "*"
  If (InStr(limitFirst, "*") = 0) Then limitFirst &= "*"
  limitLast = Replace(limitLast, "*", "%")
  limitFirst = Replace(limitFirst, "*", "%")
  ```

This code uses our custom *GetSubStr* routine already added to the *General* module. Once the name parts are extracted, the Visual Basic *Replace* function replaces all instances of "*" with "%." You'll find similar code in the other record editors that allow limits on the list of records, such as the *Publisher* form added later.

While you have the source code open for this form, zoom up to the top. There, you'll find an interesting *Imports* statement.

```
Imports MVB = Microsoft.VisualBasic
```

Normally, *Imports* is followed immediately by a namespace. This variation includes the "MVB =" prefix, which defines a shortcut for the *Microsoft.VisualBasic* namespace for code in this file. With Visual Basic importing so many namespaces into an existing class that also defines a lot of public members, there are bound to be member name conflicts. In this case, the conflict is the *Left* form member. Because this source code for the *Author* form sees everything through the prism of that form, when you include the keyword *Left* in your logic, the code naturally assumes you mean the form's *Left* property, which sets the left position of the form. The problem is that *Left* is also a common string manipulation function that extracts the left-most characters from a larger string.

```
smallerString = Left(largerString, 5)
```

In a form, this code generates an error because it thinks *Left* means *Me.Left*. To use the string version of *Left*, you have to prefix it with its namespace.

```
smallerString = Microsoft.VisualBasic.Left( _
    largerString, 5)
```

The special *Imports* statement lets us substitute a shorter name for the rather long "Microsoft.VisualBasic" namespace.

```
smallerString = MVB.Left(largerString, 5)
```

You will find a few instances of such code in this and other forms that include the MVB prefix.

The *Author* form has one more notable element. A **Name Matches** label appears near the bottom of the form, as shown in Figure 12-6.

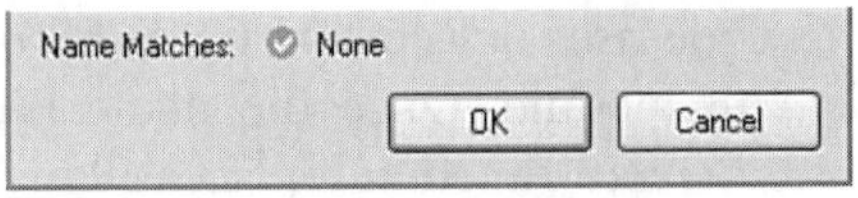

Figure 12-6 The bottom of the Author form showing "Name Matches"

This field helps the user avoid adding the same author to the database twice. As changes are made to the **Last Name** and **First Name** fields, the **Name Matches** field gets refreshed with matching author names found in the *Author* table. The *RefreshMatchingAuthors* routine counts the number of matching authors through the following code:

```
sqlText = "SELECT COUNT(*) AS TheCount " & _
    "FROM Author WHERE LastName LIKE " & _
    DBText(Trim(RecordLastName.Text))
If (Trim(RecordFirstName.Text) <> "") Then
    sqlText &= " AND FirstName LIKE " & _
        DBText(MVB.Left(Trim( _
        RecordFirstName.Text), 1) & "%")
End If
matchCount = CInt(ExecuteSQLReturn(sqlText))
```

This is similar to the lookup code in the *SearchForLimit* routine, but it only adds a wildcard to the first name before doing the search.

- **CodeAuthorType.vb.** The *CodeAuthorType* form edits records in the related *CodeAuthorType* table. Who knew?
- **CodeCopyStatus.vb.** This form edits records in the *CodeCopyStatus* database table.
- **CodeLocation.vb.** As expected, this form edits records in the *CodeLocation* table. Once you've added at least one record to that table, you'll be able to set the default location for the database. I'll discuss this again a little later in this chapter.
- **CodeMediaType.vb.** The *CodeMediaType* form, which edits records in the *CodeMediaType* table, includes a few more fields than the other "Code" table editors. Most of the fields accept numeric input. Although I do a final check for valid numeric data just before writing the record to the database, I try to prevent any non-numeric data from showing up in the first place by restricting

the acceptable keystrokes. For instance, the *RecordCheckoutDays* text field's *KeyPress* event includes this code:

```
' ----- Only allow digits and backspaces.
If (e.KeyChar = vbBack) Or _
   (IsNumeric(e.KeyChar)) Then Return
e.Handled = True
```

Setting the `e.Handled` property to *True* stops Visual Basic from doing anything else (pretty much) with the entered key. It's a quick and easy way to dispose of a user-entered keystroke.

- **CodePatronGroup.vb.** This form edits records in the *CodePatronGroup* table.
- **CodeSeries.vb.** This editor manages records in the *CodeSeries* table. Earlier I mentioned how series names and keywords are subordinate to named items. But it made sense to me to also provide direct management for series names, in case you wanted to build up a common list before adding individual library items. So this form performs double-duty: You can access it as a standard record editor through the *ListEditRecords* form, and it's also used for a specific named item through the not-yet-added *NamedItem* form.

When editing item-specific series names, the user first gets to search for a series name by typing it. Because I don't want them to have to retype the series name again in this editor form, I wanted to pass the typed series name into the *CodeSeries* form, but none of the overridden public methods supported this. So we'll need to add a new method that will accept the typed name. The *AddRecord* member already overrides the base function of the same name.

```
Public Overrides Function AddRecord() As Integer
    ' ----- Add a new record.
    ActiveID = -1
    PrepareFormFields()
    Me.ShowDialog()
    If (Me.DialogResult = Windows.Forms. _
       DialogResult.OK) Then _
       Return ActiveID Else Return -1
End Function
```

Let's add an overload to this function that includes a string argument. The caller will pass the originally typed text to this argument. We'll assign it to the *RecordFullName* control's *Text* property so that it shows up automatically when the form opens.

Insert Snippet Insert Chapter 12, Snippet Item 5.

```
Public Overloads Function AddRecord( _
      ByVal seriesText As String) As Integer
   ' ----- Add a new record, but use a starting value
   '       previously entered by the user.
   ActiveID = -1
   PrepareFormFields()
   RecordFullName.Text = seriesText
   Me.ShowDialog()
   If (Me.DialogResult = Windows.Forms.DialogResult.OK) _
   Then Return ActiveID Else Return -1
End Function
```

Yes, we could have used some name other than *AddRecord* for this function and avoided adding an overload. But it's nice to keep things consistent.

- **Holiday.vb.** This form manages the records in the *Holiday* table. In a later chapter, we'll add a cache of holidays within the program for quick access.
- **Patron.vb.** The *Patron* form provides editing services for records in the *Patron* table, and appears in Figure 12-7.

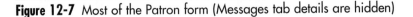

Figure 12-7 Most of the Patron form (Messages tab details are hidden)

This form includes a *TabControl* to help break up the amount of fields the user has to experience at once. If you have ever used the tab control included with Visual Basic 6.0, you'll quickly appreciate the .NET replacement. It manages all of the panel-switching logic automatically when the user selects a different tab. And each panel is a separate *TabPage* class instance. In your code, forcing the tab control to display a different tab is as easy as assigning the appropriate *TabPage* instance to the *TabControl* object's *SelectedTab* property, as with this code line from the *ValidateFormData* function.

```
TabPatron.SelectedTab = TabGeneral
```

Although this form looks quite complex, it's almost entirely made up of code we've seen in other forms. Beyond the standard overrides of *BaseCodeForm* members, this form includes barcode scanning support borrowed from the *ItemCopy* form, password logic stolen from the *UserName* form, and name-matching code similar to that used in the *Author* form.

I included a **Manage Patron's Items** button on the form, but its logic won't be added until a later chapter. An extra public function, *EditRecordLimited*, becomes important at that time.

■ **Publisher.vb.** The *Publisher* form lets the user edit the records in the *Publisher* table. It's a pretty simple form with only two data entry fields. A **Status** field indicates how many *NamedItem* records link to this publisher. A small button appears to the right of the text entry field for the publisher's web site. This is the "show me the web site" button, and when clicked, brings up the supplied web page in the user's default browser. To enable this button, add the following code to the *ShowWeb* button's *Click* event handler.

Insert Snippet Insert Chapter 12, Snippet Item 6.

```
' ----- Show the web site displayed in the field.
Dim newProcess As ProcessStartInfo

On Error Resume Next
If (Trim(RecordWeb.Text) = "") Then Return
newProcess = New ProcessStartInfo(Trim(RecordWeb.Text))
Process.Start(newProcess)
```

- **SystemValue.vb.** This code editor handles items in the *SystemValue* table. While we will connect it to a link on the main Library form in this chapter, we will change this access method in a future chapter.

Well, that's 11 of the 12 derived forms. The last one is the *NamedItem* form, shown here in Figure 12-8.

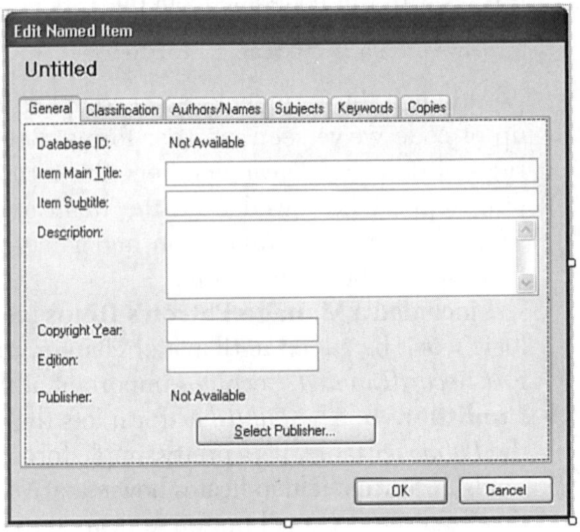

Figure 12-8 The NamedItem form with the General tab active

The *NamedItem* form is the largest and most complex of the forms that derive from *BaseCodeForm*. It edits primary library items recorded in the *NamedItem* database table. It's complex because it also directly or indirectly manages records in other subordinate tables: *ItemAuthor*, *ItemCopy*, *ItemKeyword*, *ItemSubject*, and indirectly *Author*, *Keyword*, *Publisher*, and *Subject*.

All of the fields on the *General* and *Classification* tabs are basic data entry fields that flow directly into the *NamedItem* table, just as is done with the other record-editing forms. The **Publisher** and **Series** fields use separate selection forms (*PublisherAddLocate* and *SeriesAddLocate*) to obtain the ID values stored in *NamedItem*. Here's the code that looks up the publisher.

```
' ----- Prompt the user.
newPublisher = (New PublisherAddLocate).PromptUser()
If (newPublisher = -1) Then Return

' ----- Check to clear the publisher.
If (newPublisher = -2) Then
    RecordPublisher.Text = "Not Available"
    PublisherID = -1
    Return
End If
```

The other four tabs—*Authors/Names*, *Subjects*, *Keywords*, and *Copies*—manage subordinate records. The code is pretty consistent between the four different tabs, so I'll limit my comments to the *Authors/Names* tab (see Figure 12-9).

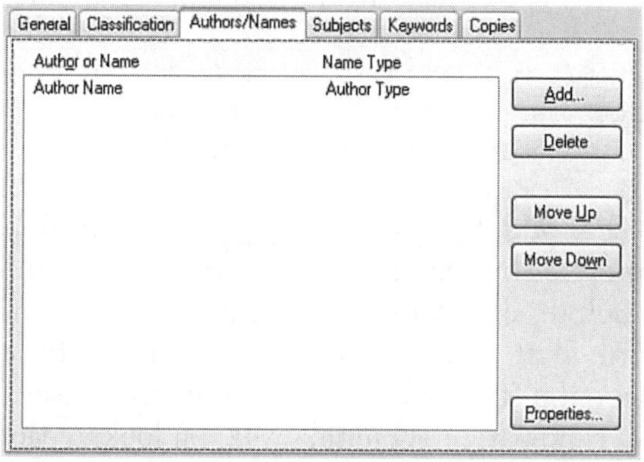

Figure 12-9 The NamedItem form with the Authors/Names tab active

The controls on this tab are quite similar to those on the *ListEditRecords* form; they exist to manage a set of records in a table. In this case, it's the *ItemAuthor* table. For the presentation list, I chose to use a *ListView* control instead of a standard *ListBox* control. By setting a *ListView* controls's *View* property to "Details," setting its *FullRowSelect* field to *True*, and modifying its *Columns* collection (see Figure 12-10), you can quickly turn it into a multi-column list box.

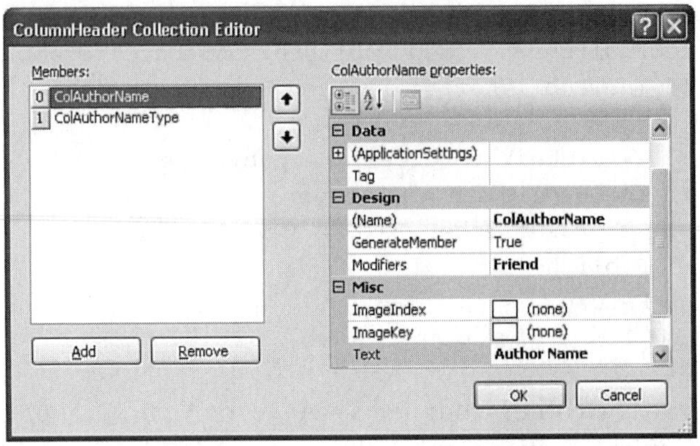

Figure 12-10 The ColumnHeader editor for a ListView control

When you add an item to this list, you also have to add "sub-items" to have anything appear in all but the first column.

```
Dim newItem As Windows.Forms.ListViewItem = _
    AuthorsList.Items.Add("John Smith")
newItem.SubItems.Add("Illustrator")
```

The **Add** button brings up the *AuthorAddLocate* form, while the **Properties** button displays the *ItemAuthorEdit* form instead.

Before any of the subordinate records can be added, the "parent" record must exist in the database. That's because the "child" records include the ID number of the parent record, and without a parent record, there is no parent ID number. If you look in each of the **Add** button routines on this form, you will find code like this.

```
' ----- The record must be saved first.
If (ActiveID = -1) Then
    ' ----- Confirm with the user.
    If (MsgBox("The item must be saved to the database " & _
        "before authors or names can be added. Would you " & _
        "like to save the record now?", _
        MsgBoxStyle.YesNo Or MsgBoxStyle.Question, _
        ProgramTitle) <> MsgBoxResult.Yes) Then Return

    ' ----- Verify and save the data.
    If (ValidateFormData() = False) Then Return
    If (SaveFormData() = False) Then Return
End If
```

If this is a brand-new *NamedItem* record (`ActiveID = -1`), this code will save it before allowing the user to add the subordinate record. Any invalid data that prevents the record from being saved will be caught in the call to *ValidateFormData*.

Actually, the calls to both *ValidateFormData* and *SaveFormData* are the same ones that occur when the user clicks on the **OK** button. Normally, that triggers a return of the new record's ID number to the calling form. But what if *SaveFormData* gets called by adding an author, but then the user clicks the **Cancel** button (which normally returns a –1 value to indicate "no record added")? To avoid that, the *SaveFormData* function sets a class-level variable named *SessionSaved*.

```
SessionSaved = True
```

This flag is cleared when the form first opens, but is set to *True* pretty much any time a subordinate record changes. The *NamedItem* form's overridden *AddRecord* and *EditRecord* functions check for this flag before returning to the calling form.

```
If (Me.DialogResult = Windows.Forms.DialogResult.OK) Or _
    (SessionSaved = True) Then Return ActiveID Else Return -1
```

There's lots of other interesting code in the *NamedItem* form. But at nearly 1,400 lines (not counting the related designer code), I'll have to let you investigate it on your own.

Connecting the Editors to the Main Form

OK, take a breath. That was a lot of code to go through. But if you run the program now, you won't see any difference at all. We still need to connect all of the record editors to the main form. They all connect through the *LinkLabel* controls on the main form's *Administration* panel (*PanelAdmin*). We need to add 12 *LinkClicked* event handlers to access all of the new and various forms. Go ahead and add them now to the *MainForm* class.

Insert Snippet Insert Chapter 12, Snippet Item 7.

Each of the *LinkClicked* event handlers is almost a mirror image of the other, except for a few object instance names here and there. Here's the code that handles a click on the *Publisher* link label.

```
Private Sub AdminLinkPublishers_LinkClicked( _
        ByVal sender As System.Object, ByVal e As _
        System.Windows.Forms.LinkLabelLinkClickedEventArgs) _
        Handles AdminLinkPublishers.LinkClicked
    ' ----- Make sure the user is allowed to do this.
    If (SecurityProfile(LibrarySecurity.ManagePublishers) = _
          False) Then
        MsgBox(NotAuthorizedMessage, MsgBoxStyle.OkOnly Or _
          MsgBoxStyle.Exclamation, ProgramTitle)
        Return
    End If

    ' ----- Let the user edit the list of publishers.
    ListEditRecords.ManageRecords(New Library.Publisher)
    ListEditRecords = Nothing
End Sub
```

After doing a quick security check, the code calls up the standard *ListEditRecords* form, passing it an instance of the record editor it is to use.

There are still a few inactive links on the *Administration* panel that we'll enable in later chapters.

Settings the Default Location

The program is now ready to run with all of its new features in place. Because we added only administrative features, you must click the **Login** button in the upper-right corner of the main form before gaining access to the *Administration* panel and its features. Unless you changed it, your login user name is "admin" with no password.

Although you can now run the program and access all of the record editors, you won't be able to add new item copies until you set a default location. To set the location:

1. Add at least one location through the **Locations** link on the *Administration* panel.

2. Obtain the ID number of the *CodeLocation* record you want to be the default. You can use *SQL Server Management Studio Express*'s query features to access the records in this table. If this is the first

time you've added records to the *CodeLocation* table, the first item
you add will have an ID value of 1.

3. Back in the Library program, edit the *SystemValue* table through
the **System Values** link on the *Administration* panel.

4. Add or modify the "DefaultLocation" system value, setting its
value to the ID number of the default location record.

Alternatively, you can update the "DefaultLocation" record in the
SystemValue table directly using *SQL Server Management Studio Express*.
If the ID of the location to use is 1, use this SQL statement to make the
change.

```
UPDATE SystemValue
   SET ValueData = '1'
   WHERE ValueName = 'DefaultLocation'
```

In a future chapter, we'll add a more user-friendly method to update
this default location.

Speaking of user friendly, we're about to enter the not-user-friendly
but logic-friendly world of text structured data: XML.

CHAPTER 13

XML

Because computers are computers and people are people, they generally have different requirements when it comes to getting their data into a usable format. XML is an attempt to arrange data in a structure that is usable for both people and software.

XML has really come into vogue in recent years, but its roots are quite old. It's derived from SGML (Standard Generalized Markup Language), as is HTML (cousins!). SGML in turn came from GML (Generalized Markup Language), a "metalanguage" (a language that describes another language) designed by IBM back in the 1960s. So, blame IBM if you want to, but either way, you will come in regular contact with XML as you develop .NET applications.

I might as well tell you right from the start: either you will love XML, or you will hate it, but probably both. It's a strange beast, this XML is, as you would expect from any acronym that takes letters from the middle of the words it represents (eXtensible Markup Language). XML represents an alphabet of data manipulation technologies, an alphabet that strangely has seven Xs. But enough of the teasing; let's *extend* our understanding of this basic .NET technology.

What Is XML?

XML is nothing more than a data format that is both human readable and machine readable. Have you ever tried to open a Microsoft Word document with Notepad? Good luck (see Figure 13-1). Although you can usually sift out the main text of the document, most of what you see is gobbledygook. That's because it is in a *proprietary binary* format. It's proprietary because, frankly, you shouldn't be poking your fingers in there. That's what Microsoft Word is for. And it's *binary* because you can store a lot of information conveniently in a little bit of disk space. With such a file, I can store my data anyway I choose. In fact, I can write my data out willy-nilly, and not have to get permission from anyone, because it's mine, mine, all mine.

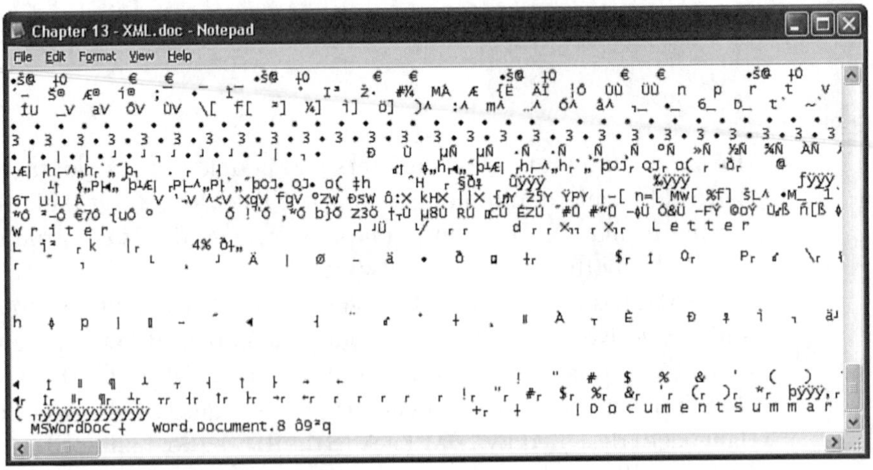

Figure 13-1 This chapter in Notepad

Binary files are great for storing any kind of data: numbers, strings, base-64 encrypted images, streams of networking data chatter, anything. The problem is that unless you know the exact structure that you used to write it out, there is little chance of ever getting the data back. This is good if your goal is secrecy, but if you ever need to share that data with another person or program, or worse yet, debug the output from your errant program, you're in for a tough time. If one little byte gets messed up, the whole file might be useless.

There are, of course, other ways to store your data. For files that store records of data, tab-delimited and CSV (comma-separated values) files provide a convenient transfer medium, in a more human-friendly format. For instance, consider this data from Microsoft's sample "Northwind Traders" database, stored as comma-separated values.

```
ProductID,ProductName,SupplierID,Category,UnitPrice,Available
"1","Chai","652","Beverages","$18.00","Yes"
"2","Chang","9874","Beverages","$19.00","No"
"3","Aniseed Syrup","9874","Condiments","On Sale","Yes"
```

Now that's better. This data is pretty easy to understand. Each piece of data is grouped by commas, and the first row indicates what each column contains. And the best part is, many programs already know how to read files in this format. If you save this data in a text file with a ".csv" extension, and open it in Microsoft Excel, the data automatically appears in columns as expected.

But it could be better. For instance, what do those "652" and "9874" values refer to anyway? And is it correct that the unit price of Aniseed Syrup is "On Sale?" Sure, I can load this data into my program, but can I do anything with it? At least it's an easy read for both people and computer programs, and isn't that what I said XML was all about?

Well, yes. Although XML includes rules and features that make it more flexible than your average text data file, it's not that different. For all the hype, XML is just a way of storing data. Any of the fancy-schmancy XML traits discussed in this chapter could be performed easily with data stored in more simple text or binary proprietary formats. In fact, it is often quicker and more convenient to develop using a proprietary format, because your data will contain exactly and only what you need, without any fluff.

That being said, XML does include many aspects that make it a strong contender when considering a data format.

- **It's straightforward to read.** Each data element includes a type of title. Good titles make for good reading.
- **It's easy to process.** All data includes starting and ending tags, so a program can process the data without much effort. And one bad element won't necessarily ruin the whole file.
- **It's flexible.** You can store any type of data in XML. It is just a text file, after all. If you have a certain XML file format used in version 1 of your program, and you add features to it in version 2, you can do it in a way that still allows version 1 programs to use version 2 files without breaking.
- **It's self-describing.** XML includes several methods that let you describe the content of a given XML file. Two of the most popular are: DTD (Document Type Definition) and XSD (XML Schema Definition). You use these tools to indicate exactly what you expect your data file to contain. Additionally, XML allows you to embed comments in the content without impacting the actual data.
- **It's self-verifying.** There are tools available, including tools in .NET, which can confirm the integrity and format of an XML file by comparing the content to the associated DTD or XSD. This lets you verify a file before you even process it.
- **It's an open standard.** XML has gained widespread acceptance, even across divergent computer platforms.

- **It's built into .NET.** This is going to be the biggest reason for using it. In fact, you won't be able to get away from XML in .NET, even if you try. It's everywhere.

But there's bad news, too.

- **It's bulky.** XML content contains a lot of repetitive structural information, and generally lots of whitespace. You could abbreviate many of the structure elements, and remove all the whitespace (XML doesn't require it), but that would remove the human-readable aspects of the data. Some platforms, such as cell phone browsers, like to keep data small. XML is anything but small.
- **It's text.** Wait a minute, this is a good thing—most of the time. Sometimes you just need to store binary data, like pictures. You can't really store true binary data in an XML file without breaking one of the basic rules about XML: text only! Often, binary data is encoded in a text-like format, such as base-64 (which uses readable characters to store binary data).
- **It's inefficient.** This comes from having data in a verbose semi-human-readable format, rather than in terse, compact binary form. It simply takes longer for a computer to scan text looking for matching angle brackets than it does to move a few bytes directly from a lump of binary data into a location in memory.
- **It's human readable.** There are not many secrets in an XML file. And while you could encrypt the data elements in the file, or the entire file for that matter, that would kind of defeat the purpose of using XML.
- **It's machine readable.** If you are expecting the average Joe to pick up an XML printout and read it in his easy chair, think again. XML is not appropriate for every type of data file.
- **It's not immune to errors.** As I keep repeating, XML is just a text file. If you open it in Notepad and let your five-year-old pound on the keyboard, the content will have problems. XML is not a panacea; it's just a useful file format.

The XML Rule

Before we look at some actual XML, you need to know **The Rule**. You must obey **The Rule** with every piece of XML text you write.

The Rule If you open it, close it.

That's it. Don't forget it. Obey it. Live it. I'll explain what it means later.

XML Content

There's no better way to learn about XML then to start looking at it. If you've never used XML, but you've written some HTML, then this should look somewhat familiar.

Some Basic XML

Here's a simple chunk of XML for you to enjoy.

```
<?xml version="1.0"?>
<hello>
   <there>
      <!-- Finally, real data here. -->
      <world target="everyone">think XML</world>
      <totalCount>694.34</totalCount>
      <goodbye />
   </there>
</hello>
```

Hey, I didn't say it was going to be interesting. As I mentioned before, it's just data, but it is useful data, and here's why.

- **It's obviously XML.** This is clear from the first line, which always starts with "`<?xml....`" This line also indicates the XML version number, which tells XML processing routines (parsers) to adjust behavior if needed. That's foresight.
- **It's structured.** XML is a hierarchical data structure. That is, you can have data **elements** embedded inside of other data elements to any depth you want. Every element is bounded by a set of **tags**. In this sample, the tags are *hello, there, world, totalCount,* and *goodbye.* Tags always appear inside of <angle brackets>, and always appear in pairs, as in <hello>...</hello>. (This is where **The Rule**, "If you open it, close it," comes in.) Don't forget the "/" just before the tag name in the closing bracket. This syntax lets you

organize your data into specifically arranged named units. For tag pairs that have nothing in between them, you can use the shortened syntax "`<tagname />`," as I did with the *goodbye* tag. By the way, XML tags are case sensitive, so type carefully.

- **It's readable.** It's human readable, thanks to all the whitespace, although you could remove it all and still have XML. It's also computer readable because of the consistent use of tags.
- **It's a single unit of data.** All XML files have a single *root element* in which all other elements must appear. In the sample, `<hello>` is the root element. Once that element is closed (through its ending tag), you can't add any additional elements. Nope. Nada.
- **It's got comments.** See that "`<!--...-->`" line? That's a comment. You can stick comments here and there just like they were free-floating tags.
- **It's got attributes.** XML supports two varieties of data: real data and attributes. Real data values come between the in-most tag pairs, as with `think XML` and `694.34` in the sample. Attributes provide extended information about the tags themselves. I included an attribute named *target* in the *world* element. The content of all attributes must be in quotes. I could have made this attribute a sub-element instead, and a lot of people do. There is disagreement among programmers as to when data should be an element or an attribute. Let your conscience be your guide.

So there you have it—some clean, clear XML data.

Some Basic—and Meaningful—XML

Let's see what that comma-delimited data from Northwind Traders I listed previously could look like in XML.

```
<?xml version="1.0"?>
<productList>
   <supplier ID="652" fullName="Beverages R Us">
      <product ID="1" available="Yes">
         <productName>Chai</productName>
         <category>Beverages</category>
         <unitPrice>18.00</unitPrice>
      </product>
   </supplier>
```

```
<supplier ID="9874" fullName="We Sell Food">
   <product ID="2" available="No">
      <productName>Chang</productName>
      <category>Beverages</category>
      <unitPrice>19.00</unitPrice>
   </product>
   <product ID="3" available="Yes" onSale="true">
      <productName>Aniseed Syrup</productName>
      <category>Condiments</category>
      <unitPrice>12.00</unitPrice>
   </product>
</supplier>
</productList>
```

Moving the data to XML has greatly increased the size of the content. But with an increase in size comes an increase in processing value. I was immediately able to get some benefit from the hierarchical structure of XML. In the original data, supplier was just another column. But in the XML version, all the data is now grouped into supplier sections, which makes sense (at least, if that is how I was planning to use the data).

You can also see that I followed **The Rule**. Every opening tag has a matching closing tag. Whatever you do, don't forget **The Rule**.

Now, you're saying to yourself, "Tim, I could have grouped the data by supplier once I loaded the comma-delimited data into my program." And to that I say, "You're right." I told you that XML was just another data format. By itself, the XML content is not all that sexy. It's really the tools that you use with your XML data that make it zoom. Because XML uses a consistent yet generic structure to manage data, it was a snap to develop tools that could process consistent yet generic data in ways that look interesting and specific.

What About the Human-Readable Part?

One of the tools used with XML is the double acronym **XSLT**, which stands for XSL Transformations (XSL stands for eXtensible Stylesheet Language). XSLT is a hard-to-use scripting language that lets you transform some XML data into whatever other data or output format you want. It's just one of a handful of XSL-related languages created to manipulate XML data in complex ways. Ready for some hands-on XSL fun? Take the useful chunk of XML listed previously (the <productList> sample), and replace the first "?xml" line with the following two lines:

```
<?xml version="1.0"?>
<?xml-stylesheet type="text/xsl" href="hello.xsl"?>
```

Save all of that beautiful XML text to a file on your desktop as *hello.xml*. Next, put the following XSLT script into another file on your desktop named *hello.xsl*. (Notice that I break one line with the ➥ marker so that the content could fit in this book. Please don't really break the comma-separated list on that line in the file.)

```
<?xml version="1.0"?>
<xsl:stylesheet
      xmlns:xsl="http://www.w3.org/1999/XSL/Transform"
      version="1.0">
  <xsl:template match="/">
    <xsl:text>
    ProductID,ProductName,SupplierID,Category,
    ➥ UnitPrice,Available
    </xsl:text>
    <BR/>
    <xsl:apply-templates/>
  </xsl:template>
  <xsl:template match="supplier">
    <xsl:variable name="supID" select="@ID"/>
    <xsl:for-each select="product">
      "<xsl:value-of select="@ID"/>",
      "<xsl:value-of select="productName"/>",
      "<xsl:value-of select="$supID"/>",
      "<xsl:value-of select="category"/>",
      "<xsl:choose>
        <xsl:when test="@onSale='true'">On Sale</xsl:when>
        <xsl:otherwise>
          $<xsl:value-of select="unitPrice"/>
        </xsl:otherwise>
      </xsl:choose>",
      "<xsl:value-of select="@available"/>"
      <BR/>
    </xsl:for-each>
  </xsl:template>
</xsl:stylesheet>
```

I told you it was hard to use, and even harder to look at. OK, now for the show. I have Internet Explorer 6 installed on my system, but this should work with most current browsers. Open the *hello.xml* file in your browser, and *voilà*, the following beautifully formatted text should appear.

```
ProductID,ProductName,SupplierID,Category,UnitPrice,Available
"1","Chai","652","Beverages","$18.00","Yes"
"2","Chang","9874","Beverages","$19.00","No"
"3","Aniseed Syrup","9874","Condiments","On Sale","Yes"
```

Now that's more like it. XML and XSLT together have made this advance in data technology possible. (I did cheat a little in this example. You will notice the `<BR/>` entries in the XSLT script that don't appear in the final output. I added these just to make it look right in your browser.) But seriously, while I was able to generate a comma-separated data set with XSLT, more common tasks for XSLT include generating nicely-formatted HTML based on XML data, or generating a new XML document with a specific alternative view of the original data. How does it work? Basically, the `<xsl:template>` elements tell the parser to look for tags in the XML document that match some pattern (like "supplier"). When it finds a match, it applies everything inside the `<xsl:template>` tags to that matching XML tag and its contents. The pattern specified in the "match" attributes uses an XML technology called *XPath*, a system to generically search for matching tags within your XML document.

Sounds confusing? Well, it is, and don't get me started on how long it took to write that short little XSLT script. XSLT scripting is, blissfully, beyond the scope of this book. Of course, there are tools available to make the job easier. But XSLT is useful only if the XML data it manipulates is correct. You could write an XSL Transformation to report on data inconsistencies found in an XML document, but it won't work if some of the tags in your document are misspelled or arranged in an inconsistent manner. For that, you need another advancement in XML technology: XSD.

XML Schemas

XSD (XML Structure Definitions) lets you define the **schema**—the "language" or "vocabulary"—of your particular XML document. Remember, XML is a wide-open generic standard; you can define the tags any way you want and nobody will care, at least until you have to process the tags with your software. If they aren't correct, then your processing will likely fail. XSD lets you define the rules that your XML document **must** follow if it is to be considered a valid document for your purposes. (DTD, or Document Type Definition, is a similar, though older, technology. It's widely support by XML tools, but it is not as flexible as XSD. There are also other schema definition languages similar to XSD, but because XSD is built right in to .NET, we'll focus on that.)

XSD schemas are every bit as endearing as XSLT scripts. Let's create an XSD for our original sample `<productList>` XML listed previously. First, we need to change the top of the XML to let it know that an XSD schema file is available. Change this:

```
<?xml version="1.0"?>
<productList>
```

to this:

```
<?xml version="1.0"?>
<productList xmlns="SimpleProductList"
      xmlns:xsi="http://www.w3.org/2001/XMLSchema-instance"
      xsi:noNamespaceSchemaLocation="hello.xsd">
```

These directives tell the XML parser to look in *hello.xsd* for the schema. They also define a namespace; more on that later. The *hello.xsd* file contains the following schema.

```
<xs:schema xmlns:xs="http://www.w3.org/2001/XMLSchema"
    targetNamespace="SimpleProductList">
  <xs:element name="productList" type="ProductListType"/>

  <xs:complexType name="ProductListType">
    <xs:sequence>
      <xs:element name="supplier" type="SupplierType"
        maxOccurs="unbounded"/>
    </xs:sequence>
  </xs:complexType>

  <xs:complexType name="SupplierType">
    <xs:sequence>
      <xs:element name="product" type="ProductType"
        maxOccurs="unbounded"/>
```

13. XML

```
    </xs:sequence>
    <xs:attribute name="ID" type="xs:integer"/>
    <xs:attribute name="fullName" type="xs:string"/>
  </xs:complexType>

  <xs:complexType name="ProductType">
    <xs:sequence>
      <xs:element name="productName" type="xs:string"/>
      <xs:element name="category" type="xs:string"/>
      <xs:element name="unitPrice" type="xs:decimal"/>
    </xs:sequence>
    <xs:attribute name="ID" type="xs:integer"/>
    <xs:attribute name="available" type="YesOrNoType"/>
    <xs:attribute name="onSale" type="xs:boolean"/>
  </xs:complexType>

  <xs:simpleType name="YesOrNoType">
    <xs:restriction base="xs:string">
      <xs:enumeration value="Yes"/>
      <xs:enumeration value="No"/>
    </xs:restriction>
  </xs:simpleType>
</xs:schema>
```

It looks nasty, doesn't it? Actually, it's more straightforward than XSLT. Basically, the schema says that for each element (or "tag" or "node") in my XML document, here are the sub-elements and attributes they contain, and the data type of each of them. You can even create your own pseudo-data types (actually, limiting factors on existing data types), as I did with the "YesOrNoType" data type, which limits the related value to the strings "Yes" and "No."

You can look at the XML file with the attached XSD schema in your browser, but it wouldn't be all that interesting. It just shows you the XML. But schemas will be useful when you need to assess the quality of XML data coming into your software applications from external sources.

XML Namespaces

The product list in the XML shown earlier is nice, but someone else could come up with a product list document that is just as nice, but with different naming and formatting rules. For instance, they might create a document that looks like this:

```
<?xml version="1.0"?>
<allProducts>
    <vendor ID="652" vendorName="Beverages R Us">
        <item ID="1" available="Yes">
            <itemName>Chai</itemName>
            <group>Beverages</group>
            <priceEach>18.00</priceEach>
        </item>
    </vendor>
</allProducts>
```

The data is all the same, but the tags are different. Such a document would be incompatible with software written to work with our original document. Running the document through our XSD would quickly tell us that we have a bogus data set, but it would be nicer if something told us that from the start. Enter *namespaces*. Namespaces provide a convenient method to say, "This particular tag in the XML document uses this XSD-defined language." Notice the start of the XSD schema shown previously.

```
<xs:schema xmlns:xs="http://www.w3.org/2001/XMLSchema">
```

This line sets up a namespace named xs by using the xmlns attribute. (The ":xs" part tells XML what you want to call your namespace.) The value of the attribute is a URI (Uniform Resource Identifier), just a unique value that you are sure no one else is going to use. Typically, you use a web site address for your own company; the web site doesn't have to exist. You could even put your phone number there, just as long as it is unique.

The most common way to use a namespace is to prefix the relevant tags in your XML document with the new namespace name, as in xs:schema instead of just schema. This tells the parser, "If you are checking my syntax against an XSD schema, then use the one that I defined for the xs namespace." You can also use a "default" namespace for a given element and all its descendants by including the xmlns attribute in the outermost element. Then all elements within that outermost element will use the specified namespace. I used this method in one of the preceding examples.

```
<productList xmlns="SimpleProductList"...
```

For basic XML files that will be used only by your program, you may not need to bother with namespaces. They really come in handy when you are creating XML data that uses some publicly published standard. There are also instances where a single XML file might contain data related to two or more distinct uses of XML. In this case, different parts of your XML file could refer to different namespaces.

As with other parts of the XML world, XSD and namespaces are not all that easy to use, but they are flexible and powerful. As usual, there are tools, including tools in Visual Studio, which let you build all of this without having to think about the details.

As I keep saying, XML is just data, and if your program and data don't understand each other, you might as well go back to chisel and stone. XML and its related technologies provide a method to help ensure your data is ready to use in your application.

Using XML in .NET with System.Xml

XML is used internally in the .NET Framework to pass all types of data around. From ADO.NET to Web Services, XML is the data format of choice for shuffling information to and from Framework services. Fortunately, we aren't reprogramming the entire Framework, so most of that isn't really important to our understanding of .NET development. But some Framework classes expose XML services right out there for the programmer to use.

Because XML is no fun to manage as a big chunk of text, .NET includes several classes that manage XML data. All of these tools appear in the *System.Xml* namespace and its subordinate namespaces.

- **System.Xml.** The main collection of XML-related classes.
- **System.Xml.Schema.** Classes that create and use XSD schemas.
- **System.Xml.Serialization.** Classes that read and write XML documents via a standard .NET stream.
- **System.Xml.XPath.** Classes that implement the XPath technology used to search XML documents.
- **System.Xml.Xsl.** Classes that enable XSL Transformations.

The features included in each class tie pretty closely to the structure of the XML, XSD, and XSLT documents themselves. They include a whole lot of features that weren't covered previously, because there are gobs of ways to manipulate XML data.

The Basic XML Classes, Basically

The *System.Xml* namespace includes the most basic classes you will use to manage XML data. An *XmlDocument* object is the in-memory view of your actual XML document:

```
Dim myData As New System.Xml.XmlDocument
```

Your document is made up of declarations (that `<?xml...?>` thing at the top), data elements (all the specific tags in your document), attributes (inside of each starting element tag), and comments. These are represented by the *XmlDeclaration*, *XmlElement*, *XmlAttribute*, and *XmlComment* classes, respectively. Together, these four main units of your document are called *nodes*, represented generically by the *XmlNode* class. (The four specific classes all inherit from the more basic *XmlNode* class.) Usually, when you build an XML document by hand in memory, you use the individual classes like *XmlElement*. Later on, when you need to scan through an existing document, it is easier to use the generic *XmlNode* class.

Let's build a subset of our sample XML product data.

```
<?xml version="1.0"?>
<productList>
    <!-- We currently sell these items. -->
    <supplier ID="652" fullName="Beverages R Us">
        <product ID="1" available="Yes">
            <productName>Chai</productName>
            <category>Beverages</category>
            <unitPrice>18.00</unitPrice>
        </product>
    </supplier>
<productList>
```

Declare all the variables you will use, and then use them.

```
Dim products As XmlDocument
Dim prodDeclare As XmlDeclaration
Dim rootSet As XmlElement
Dim supplier As XmlElement
Dim product As XmlElement
Dim productValue As XmlElement
Dim comment As XmlComment
```

```
' ----- Create the document with a valid declaration.
products = New XmlDocument
prodDeclare = products.CreateXmlDeclaration("1.0", _
    Nothing, String.Empty)
products.InsertBefore(prodDeclare, products.DocumentElement)

' ----- Create the root element, <productList>.
rootSet = products.CreateElement("productList")
products.InsertAfter(rootSet, prodDeclare)

' ----- Add a nice comment.
comment = products.CreateComment( _
    " We currently sell these items. ")
rootSet.AppendChild(comment)

' ------ Create the supplier element, <supplier>.
'         Include the attributes.
supplier = products.CreateElement("supplier")
supplier.SetAttribute("ID", "652")
supplier.SetAttribute("fullName", "Beverages R Us")
rootSet.AppendChild(supplier)

' ----- Create the product element, <product>, with the
'         subordinate data values.
product = products.CreateElement("product")
product.SetAttribute("ID", "1")
product.SetAttribute("available", "yes")
supplier.AppendChild(product)

productValue = products.CreateElement("productName")
productValue.InnerText = "Chai"
product.AppendChild(productValue)

productValue = products.CreateElement("category")
productValue.InnerText = "Beverages"
product.AppendChild(productValue)

productValue = products.CreateElement("unitPrice")
productValue.InnerText = "18.00"
product.AppendChild(productValue)
```

It really works, too. To prove it, put this code in the click event of a button, and end it with the following line:

```
products.Save("c:\products.xml")
```

Run the program and view the *c:\products.xml* file to see the XML product data. There are many different ways to use the XML classes to create an XML document in memory. For instance, although I used the *SetAttribute* method to add attributes to the supplier and product nodes, I could have created separate attribute objects, and appended them on to these nodes, just like I did for the main elements.

```
Dim attrData As XmlAttribute
attrData = products.CreateAttribute("ID")
attrData.Value = "652"
supplier.SetAttributeNode(attrData)
```

So, this is nice and all, but what if you already have some XML in a file, and you just want to load it into an *XmlDocument* object? Simply use the *XmlDocument* object's *Load* method.

```
Dim products As XmlDocument
products = New XmlDocument
products.Load("c:\products.xml")
```

For those instances where you just want to read or write some XML from or to a file, and you don't care much about manipulating it in memory, the *XmlTextReader* and *XmlTextWriter* classes let you quickly read and write XML data via a text stream. But if you are going to do things with the XML data in your program, the *Load* and *Save* methods of the *XmlDocument* object are a better choice.

Finding Needles and Haystacks

In our sample data, all of the products appear in supplier groups. If we just wanted a list of products, regardless of supplier, we ask the *XmlDocument* to supply that data via an *XmlNodeList* object.

```
Dim justProducts As XmlNodeList
Dim oneProduct As XmlNode
```

```
' ----- First, get the list.
justProducts = products.GetElementsByTagName("product")

' ----- Then do something with them.
For Each oneProduct In justProducts
    ' ----- Put interesting code here.
Next oneProduct
MsgBox("Processed " & justProducts.Count.ToString() & _
    " product(s).")
```

For a more complex selection of nodes within the document, the *System.Xml.XPath* namespace implements the XPath searching language, which gives you increased flexibility in locating items. The Visual Studio documentation describes the methods and searching syntax used with these classes.

Schema Verification

An *XmlDocument* object can hold any type of random yet valid XML content, but you can also verify the document against an XSD schema. If your XML document refers to an XSD schema, includes a document type definition (DTD), or uses XDR (XML Data Reduced Schemas, similar to XSD), an *XmlReader*, when configured with the appropriate *XmlReaderSettings*, will properly compare your XML data against the defined rules, and throw an exception if there's a problem.

```
Dim products As New XmlDocument
Dim xmlRead As XmlTextReader
Dim withVerify As New XmlReaderSettings
Dim xmlReadGood As XmlReader

' ----- Open the XML file and process schemas
'       referenced within the content.
withVerify.ValidationType = ValidationType.Schema
xmlRead = New XmlTextReader("c:\temp\products.xml")
xmlReadGood = XmlReader.Create(xmlRead, withVerify)

' ----- Load content, or throw exception on
'       validation failure.
products.Load(xmlReadGood)

' ----- Clean up.
xmlReadGood.Close()
xmlRead.Close()
```

XML Transformations

Before we move on to the project code, let's look at XSL Transformations in the .NET classes. It's no more difficult than any of the other manipulations of XML. Just as there are many ways to get XML source data (from a file, building it by hand with *XmlDocument*, and so on), there are many ways to transform the data. If you just want to go from input file to output file, the following code provides a quick and efficient method. XSL Transformation is generally a performance-poor activity. But you can speed up performance by putting your source XML document into an *XPathDocument* object instead of a plain *XmlDocument* object.

```
' ----- Above: Imports System.IO
'              Imports System.Xml
'              Imports System.Xml.Xsl
'              Imports System.Xml.Xpath
Dim xslTrans As XslTransform
Dim inFile As XPathDocument
Dim outFile As StreamWriter
Dim outWriter As XmlTextWriter

' ----- Open the source file using XPath.
inFile = New XPathDocument("c:\input.xml")

' ----- Open the XSL file as a transformation.
xslTrans = New XslTransform()
xslTrans.Load("c:\convert.xsl")

' ----- Open the output file as a stream.
outFile = New System.IO.StreamWriter("c:\output.txt")
outWriter = New XmlTextWriter(outFile)

' ----- Convert and save the output.
outWriter.Formatting = Formatting.Indented
xslTrans.Transform(inFile, Nothing, outWriter, Nothing)
outFile.Close()
```

Summary

There are a lot of useful features in the various *System.Xml* namespaces, and you can manage complex data in very effective ways. It's not always the most efficient way to manage data, but if you have structured hierarchical data, it may be the most direct and clear method.

Although XML lurks everywhere in the .NET Framework, and in all applications written using .NET, you could actually write large and interesting applications without looking at a single line of XML content. Even if your application needs to interact with XML content, the classes in the *System.Xml* namespace effectively shield you from the text manipulation nightmare that is XML.

XML is a very useful and flexible data format that is here to stay. Although it will always lack the speed of more compact data standards, its benefits are numerous. There is a move to introduce a "binary XML" format as a standard. Currently it's meeting with much resistance from the standards and development communities. As a .NET programmer, you won't really have to worry about that. If binary XML does become a standard, you will likely continue to use the same classes and methods introduced in this chapter, with the possible addition of an *OutputFormat* ("Text" or "Binary") property.

Project

The administrator of the Library system will want to see statistics and information at a glance, or run various reports that provide meaningful summary or detail views of system data. As a programmer, I could try to add every conceivable type of report that the user may need, but I have learned from experience that this is not possible. Users always want the moon, usually in the form of some weird esoteric report that I know they will use once and never look at again (although they will call once a year asking for the same report to be written again). I don't like recompiling and re-releasing the entire application every time a user needs a new report. Instead, I keep the reports outside the application, stored as separate programs. Then, from one form in the main application, I make all of those external reports available in a nice convenient list.

To implement this generic feature, I use a report configuration file, a simple XML file that contains information on the available reports, and how to run them. I want my selection list to have indented items, so that I can visibly group reports for convenience. To do this, I will make my XML file into an unlimited depth hierarchy, with each level representing a further level of displayed indent. For instance, let's say I wanted the following outline of reports (with report group titles in bold).

Detail Reports
> Daily Report
> > **Monthly Reports**
> > > Monthly Value
> > > Monthly Inventory
> **Summary Reports**
> > Inventory Summary

The XML configuration would follow this structure.

```
<Group name="Detail Reports">
   <Item name="Daily Report"/>
   <Group name="Monthly Reports">
      <Item name="Monthly Value"/>
      <Item name="Monthly Inventory"/>
   </Group>
</Group>
<Group name="SummaryReports">
   <Item name="Inventory Summary"/>
</Group>
```

Of course, this is greatly simplified (not to mention non-compliant) XML. In addition to the hierarchy, I also want to include support for a variety of reporting methods. To keep things simple, the Library project will include three methods of initiating reports.

1. **Built-in Reports.** The application includes a limited number of reports that are permanently built in to the main application (assembly). The reports are numbered, starting from 1, and at this time I have five reports in mind. The designer of the XML configuration file can choose to include these in the display of reports or not by simply including or not including them in the file. In the absence of a configuration file, these reports will appear in the list by default. In addition to the report number (1 to 5), each entry has a display text and a long description.

2. **Application Reports.** These reports are separate and distinct EXE files, and are started via standard application initiation methods. Each entry includes a display text, the full path to the application, optional arguments, a flag to pass the identity of the user initiating the report, and a long description.

3. **URL Reports.** These reports are simply calls to web pages, or any other valid URL. For instance, you could include a report entry that does a "mailto:" to the local organization's help desk. Each entry includes the display text, the URL itself, and a long description.

The project activities in this chapter involve both coding and documentation of the new external resource (the XML file format).

Project Access Load the "Chapter 13 (Before) Code" project, either through the New Project templates, or by accessing the project directly from the installation directory. To see the code in its final form, load "Chapter 13 (After) Code" instead.

Update Technical Documentation

First, let's add clear documentation on the structure of the XML configuration file. There is no easy way to communicate the structure of an XML file to an ordinary user. Although such documentation is a requirement, hopefully the application will also include a tool to let an administrator build the configuration file. Such a program, sadly, is not included in this book's project. It is left as an exercise for the reader. (I always wanted to say that.)

Report Configuration File

The library application can be configured to run any number of reports through the Reports form. The list of available reports is managed through an XML report configuration file, a file containing "groups" and "items." All items are reports, and appear within a group. You can nest groups within groups to any depth, and the list of reports displayed in the Library program will indent each subordinate group to help the user see the organization of the reports. There is no limit to the nesting of groups.

The root element of the XML file must be named **<reportList>**, and it may contain any number of **<reportGroup>** and **<reportItem>** data elements.

- **<reportItem>**—Represents a single report entry. This entry has one required attribute, and up to five subordinate data elements depending on the setting of the attribute.
- **type** (attribute)—Set to one of the following values:
- **built-in**—Run one of the built-in programs. This type of report uses the **<displayText>**, **<reportPath>**, and **<description>** data elements.
- **program**—Runs a separate EXE program. This type of report uses the **<displayText>**, **<reportPath>**, **<reportArgs>**, **<reportFlags>**, and **<description>** data elements.
- **url**—Starts a URL, such as a web page or a "mailto" email to a recipient address. This type of report uses the **<displayText>**, **<reportPath>**, and **<description>** data elements.
- **<displayText>**—A short name or description for this report, as it will appear in the list of report choices. This element is required for all types of reports.
- **<reportPath>**—The full path, URL, or number of the report, depending on the type of report. For program (EXE) reports, this is the full UNC or driver letter-based path to the report, without additional arguments. For built-in reports, this is a report number, from 1 to 5 (values and their meanings are listed later in this section). For URL reports, this is the actual URL, as in "http://mysite.com/myreport.aspx" or "mailto:helpdesk@mysite.com." This element is required for all types of reports.
- **<reportArgs>**—For program (EXE) reports, this entry includes any command-line arguments to be included when running the program. This element is only valid for program (EXE) reports, and is always optional.
- **<reportFlags>**—For program (EXE) reports, this entry indicates the optional flags that should be appended to the application command as arguments. At this time, the only flag is the **U** flag. When this element is set to **U**, the argument "-u *userid*"

is appended to the command string (where *userid* is the user's login ID, from the database field UserName.LoginID). This element is only valid for program (EXE) reports, and is always optional.

- **<description>**—This is a longer, verbose description of the report, up to about 200 characters, which will appear on the Report form when the user selects the report from the list. This description should assist the user in selecting the right report. This element is valid for all types of reports, but is always optional.

- **<reportGroup>**—Represents a category group, used to visibly group and indent reports in the display list. This element must contain exactly one **<displayText>** element, but may contain any number of **<reportItem>** or **<reportGroup>** elements.

  - **<displayText>**—A short name or description for this group, as it will appear in the list of report choices. This element is required.

When using the "built-in" report type, the **<reportPath>** element is set to one of the following integer values.

- 1—Items Checked Out Report
- 2—Items Overdue Report
- 3—Items Missing Report
- 4—Fines Owed by Patrons Report
- 5—Library Database Statistics Report

This technical description appears in the Technical Resource Kit document, originally developed in Chapter 4, "Designing the Database."

Create Report Entry Class

With .NET's ability to store whole objects as *ListBox* items, we can create a custom class that contains all the information needed to select and run a report from the list of reports. This class is fairly simple, with nothing but basic public fields, plus an overridden *ToString* function, used by the *ListBox* control to properly display each list item.

13. XML

In the Library Project, add a new class file named *ReportItem.vb* through the **Project ➤ Add Class** menu command. Add the following enumeration to the file, but add it outside the *Class . . . End Class* boundaries. This enumeration indicates what type of entry each list item represents.

Insert Snippet Insert Chapter 13, Snippet Item 1.

```
Public Enum ReportItemEnum
    ' ----- The type of item in the report select list.
    GroupLabel = 0
    BuiltInCheckedOut = 1
    BuiltInOverdue = 2
    BuiltInMissing = 3
    BuiltInFinesOwed = 4
    BuiltInStatistics = 5
    ExeProgram = 6
    UrlProgram = 7
End Enum
```

To this same file, add the members of the *ReportItem* class. This class contains all the information we need to run reports loaded from the configuration file.

Insert Snippet Insert Chapter 13, Snippet Item 2.

```
' ----- Instance of report selection items used
'       in the ReportSelect form.
Public ItemType As ReportItemEnum
Public Indent As Integer      ' Indent level. Starts with 0.
Public DisplayText As String
Public ReportPath As String   ' ExeProgram / UrlProgram only
Public ReportArgs As String   ' ExeProgram only
Public Description As String

Public Overrides Function ToString() As String
    ' ----- Display an indented string. Prepend with spaces.
    Return StrDup(Indent * 5, " ") & DisplayText
End Function
```

Design the Report Form

Librarians and administrators use the *Select Report* form (see Figure 13-2) to view reports. The form includes a *ListBox* control that displays all reports and report groups, a **Run** button that starts a report, and a **Close** button that returns the user to the main form. A label displays the full description of a report, when available, just below the *ListBox*.

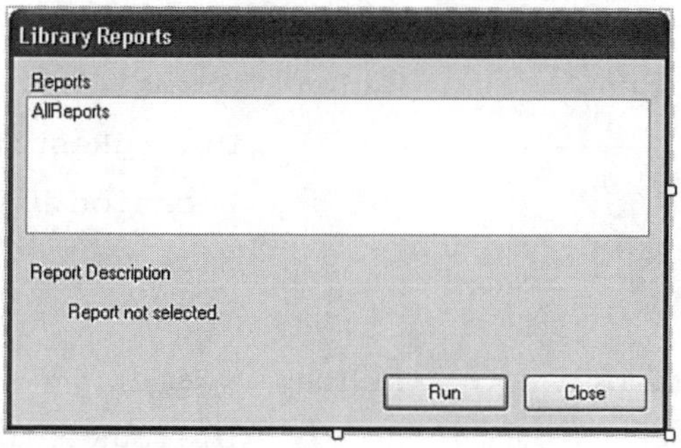

Figure 13-2 The Select Report form

Add a new form file named *ReportSelect.vb* through the **Project ➤ Add Windows Form** menu command. Add the controls and settings as listed here.

Control/Form	Type	Settings	
LabelReports	Label	(Name):	LabelReports
		Location:	8, 8
		Text:	&Reports
AllReports	ListBox	(Name):	AllReports
		Location:	8, 24
		Size:	392, 160
LabelDescription	Label	(Name):	LabelDescription
		Location:	8, 200
		Text:	Report Description

(continues)

13. XML

Control/Form	Type	Settings	
FullDescription	Label	(Name):	FullDescription
		AutoSize:	False
		Location:	32, 224
		Size:	368, 64
		Text:	Report not selected.
		UseMnemonic:	False
ActRun	Button	(Name):	ActRun
		DialogResult:	None
		Location:	232, 304
		Size:	80, 24
		Text:	Run
ActClose	Button	(Name):	ActClose
		DialogResult:	Cancel
		Location:	320, 304
		Size:	80, 24
		Text:	Close
ReportSelect	Form	(Name):	ReportSelect
		AcceptButton:	ActRun
		CancelButton:	ActClose
		ControlBox:	False
		FormBorderStyle:	FixedDialog
		StartPosition:	CenterScreen
		Text:	Library Reports

Adjust the tab order of the new controls by selecting the form, and then using the **View ➤ Tab Order** menu command.

Although the administrator has probably given useful names to each report, the terseness of each report name may still confuse the user. Each report includes an optional full description. As the user selects reports from the list, an event handler updates the *FullDescription* label just below the main list. Add this event handler member to the class.

Insert Snippet Insert Chapter 13, Snippet Item 3.

```
Private Sub AllReports_SelectedIndexChanged( _
     ByVal sender As Object, ByVal e As System.EventArgs) _
     Handles AllReports.SelectedIndexChanged
   ' ----- Display a description of the report, if available.
   Dim reportEntry As Library.ReportItem

   ' ----- Clear any previous description.
   FullDescription.Text = "No report selected."
   If (AllReports.SelectedIndex <> -1) Then
      ' ----- Locate the content and display it.
      reportEntry = CType(AllReports.SelectedItem, _
         Library.ReportItem)
      FullDescription.Text = reportEntry.Description
   End If
End Sub
```

Populate Reports from Configuration File

The *RefreshReportList* method loads the data from the report configuration file, and processes the results. Eventually, the location of this file will be recorded in the application's configuration file, but we won't be adding that until a later chapter. For now, let's put in a hard-coded test file location, and mark it for later update.

Insert Snippet Insert Chapter 13, Snippet Item 4.

```
Private Sub RefreshReportList()
   ' ----- Load in the list of available reports.
   Dim configFile As String
   Dim configData As Xml.XmlDocument
   Dim reportEntry As ReportItem
   Dim counter As Integer

   On Error GoTo ErrorHandler
```

```
' ----- Clear the existing list.
AllReports.Items.Clear()

' ----- Get the location of the configuration file.
' TODO: Load this from the application's configuration.
'       For now, just hard-code the value.
configFile = "c:\ReportConfig.txt"

' ----- Load the configuration file.
If (configFile <> "") Then
   If (System.IO.File.Exists(configFile)) Then
      ' ----- Load in the file.
      configData = New Xml.XmlDocument
      configData.Load(configFile)

      ' ----- Process the configuration file.
      LoadReportGroup(configData.DocumentElement, 0)
   End If
End If

' ----- If the configuration file resulted in no reports
'       appearing in the list, add the default reports.
If (AllReports.Items.Count = 0) Then
   For counter = 1 To _
         CInt(ReportItemEnum.BuiltInStatistics)
      ' ----- Build the report entry.
      reportEntry = New ReportItem
      reportEntry.Indent = 0
      reportEntry.ItemType = CType(counter, ReportItemEnum)
      Select Case reportEntry.ItemType
         Case ReportItemEnum.BuiltInCheckedOut
            reportEntry.DisplayText = "Items Checked Out"
         Case ReportItemEnum.BuiltInOverdue
            reportEntry.DisplayText = "Items Overdue"
         Case ReportItemEnum.BuiltInMissing
            reportEntry.DisplayText = "Items Missing"
         Case ReportItemEnum.BuiltInFinesOwed
            reportEntry.DisplayText = "Patron Fines Owed"
         Case ReportItemEnum.BuiltInStatistics
            reportEntry.DisplayText = "Database Statistics"
      End Select
```

```
      ' ----- Add the report entry to the list.
         AllReports.Items.Add(reportEntry)
      Next counter
   End If
   Return

ErrorHandler:
   GeneralError("ReportSelect.RefreshReportList", _
      Err.GetException())
   Resume Next
End Sub
```

Because the report configuration file allows nested report groups to any level, we need to use a recursive routine to repeatedly descend to each successive level. The *LoadReportGroup* routine, called by *RefreshReportList*, adds all report items and report groups within a starting report group. It's initially called from the reference point of the root <reportList> element. Each time that it finds a child <reportGroup> element, it calls itself again, but this time starting from the reference point of the child <reportGroup> element.

Insert Snippet Insert Chapter 13, Snippet Item 5.

```
Private Sub LoadReportGroup(ByVal groupNode As Xml.XmlNode, _
      ByVal indentLevel As Integer)
   ' ----- Add the groups and items at this level,
   '        and recurse as needed.
   Dim scanNode As Xml.XmlNode
   Dim detailNode As Xml.XmlNode
   Dim reportEntry As ReportItem

   ' ----- Process each item or group.
   For Each scanNode In groupNode.ChildNodes
      ' ----- Build a content item for the list.
      reportEntry = New ReportItem
      reportEntry.Indent = indentLevel

      ' ----- Get the display name.
      detailNode = scanNode.SelectSingleNode("displayText")
      If (detailNode Is Nothing) Then Continue For
      reportEntry.DisplayText = Trim(detailNode.InnerText)
```

```
If (scanNode.Name = "reportGroup") Then
   ' ----- Start a new display group.
   reportEntry.ItemType = ReportItemEnum.GroupLabel
   AllReports.Items.Add(reportEntry)

   ' ----- Recurse to child items.
   LoadReportGroup(scanNode, indentLevel + 1)
ElseIf (scanNode.Name = "reportItem") Then
   ' ----- This is an item. Record its location.
   detailNode = scanNode.SelectSingleNode("reportPath")
   If Not (detailNode Is Nothing) Then _
      reportEntry.ReportPath = _
      Trim(detailNode.InnerText)

   ' ----- Get any command-line arguments.
   detailNode = scanNode.SelectSingleNode("reportArgs")
   If Not (detailNode Is Nothing) Then _
      reportEntry.ReportArgs = _
      Trim(detailNode.InnerText)

   ' ----- Get any item-specific flags.
   detailNode = scanNode.SelectSingleNode("reportFlags")
   If Not (detailNode Is Nothing) Then
      ' ---- "U" adds "-u loginid" to the command.
      If (InStr(UCase(detailNode.InnerText), "U") > 0) _
         And (LoggedInUserName <> "") Then _
         reportEntry.ReportArgs = _
         Trim(reportEntry.ReportArgs & " -u " & _
         LoggedInUserName)
   End If

   ' ----- Store the full description.
   detailNode = scanNode.SelectSingleNode("description")
   If Not (detailNode Is Nothing) Then _
      reportEntry.Description = _
      Trim(detailNode.InnerText)

   ' ----- So, what type of entry is it?
   If (scanNode.Attributes("type").Value = _
         "built-in") Then
      ' ----- Built-in program. Check for valid ID.
      If (IsNumeric(reportEntry.ReportPath) = False) Or _
         (Val(reportEntry.ReportPath) < 1) Or _
```

```
                    (Val(reportEntry.ReportPath) > _
                    CInt(ReportItemEnum.BuiltInStatistics)) Then _
                    Continue For
                reportEntry.ItemType = CType(CInt( _
                    reportEntry.ReportPath), ReportItemEnum)
                AllReports.Items.Add(reportEntry)
            ElseIf (scanNode.Attributes("type").Value = _
                    "program") Then
                ' ----- EXE program-based report.
                If (reportEntry.ReportPath = "") Then Continue For
                reportEntry.ItemType = ReportItemEnum.ExeProgram
                AllReports.Items.Add(reportEntry)
            ElseIf (scanNode.Attributes("type").Value = _
                    "url") Then
                ' ----- URL-based report.
                If (reportEntry.ReportPath = "") Then Continue For
                reportEntry.ItemType = ReportItemEnum.UrlProgram
                AllReports.Items.Add(reportEntry)
            End If
        End If
    Next scanNode
    Return

ErrorHandler:
    GeneralError("ReportSelect.LoadReportGroup", _
        Err.GetException())
    Resume Next
End Sub
```

Add the form's *Load* event, which loads in the content from the configuration file.

Insert Snippet Insert Chapter 13, Snippet Item 6.

```
Private Sub ReportSelect_Load(ByVal sender As Object, _
        ByVal e As System.EventArgs) Handles MyBase.Load
    ' ----- Display the list of reports.
    RefreshReportList()
End Sub
```

Running the Reports

Now that all of the groups and items appear in the list, we have to run the actual reports. The *ActRun* button's *Click* event handles this duty. For now, we will just add the framework to support the calling of each report. The built-in reports will be added in Chapter 20, "Reporting."

Insert Snippet Insert Chapter 13, Snippet Item 7.

```
Private Sub ActRun_Click(ByVal sender As System.Object, _
     ByVal e As System.EventArgs) Handles ActRun.Click
  ' ----- Run the selected report.
  Dim reportEntry As Library.ReportItem

  On Error GoTo ErrorHandler

  ' ----- Make sure a report is selected.
  If (AllReports.SelectedIndex = -1) Then
     MsgBox("Please select a report from the list.", _
        MsgBoxStyle.OKOnly Or MsgBoxStyle.Exclamation, _
        ProgramTitle)
     Return
  End If

  ' ----- Different code for each type of entry.
  reportEntry = CType(AllReports.SelectedItem, _
     Library.ReportItem)
  Me.Cursor = Windows.Forms.Cursors.WaitCursor
  Select Case reportEntry.ItemType
     Case ReportItemEnum.GroupLabel
        ' ----- No report for group entries.
        MsgBox("Please select a report from the list.", _
           MsgBoxStyle.OKOnly Or MsgBoxStyle.Exclamation, _
           ProgramTitle)
     Case ReportItemEnum.BuiltInCheckedOut
        ' ----- Items Checked Out
        ' TODO: Write BasicReportCheckedOut()
     Case ReportItemEnum.BuiltInOverdue
```

```
                ' ----- Items Overdue
                ' TODO: Write BasicReportOverdue()
           Case ReportItemEnum.BuiltInMissing
                ' ----- Items Missing
                ' TODO: Write BasicReportMissing()
           Case ReportItemEnum.BuiltInFinesOwed
                ' ----- Fines Owed by Patrons
                ' TODO: Write BasicReportFines()
           Case ReportItemEnum.BuiltInStatistics
                ' ----- Library Database Statistics
                ' TODO: Write BasicReportStatistics()
           Case ReportItemEnum.ExeProgram
                ' ----- Start a program.
                Process.Start("""" & reportEntry.ReportPath & _
                    """ " & reportEntry.ReportArgs)
           Case ReportItemEnum.UrlProgram
                ' ----- Start a URL.
                Process.Start(reportEntry.ReportPath)
      End Select
      Me.Cursor = Windows.Forms.Cursors.Default
      Return

ErrorHandler:
      GeneralError("ReportSelect.ActRun_Click", _
         Err.GetException())
      Resume Next
End Sub
```

For external reports, the event handler calls the *Process.Start* method. This amazing method accepts either a standard command-line expression, or any valid URL or web page address.

Connecting the Select Report Form

To make the reports available to the user, we must enable a link to the report form from the main form. We included a distinct panel on that form just for printing reports. The *ActDoReports* button on that panel triggers a call to the new report selection form. Create a new event handler for the *ActDoReports* button and add the following code.

Insert Snippet Insert Chapter 13, Snippet Item 8.

```
' ----- Show the reports form.
ReportSelect.ShowDialog()
```

Now that we have a firm grasp on the world of XML, we'll let Visual Basic do all the hard work of manipulating it for application configuration purposes.

CHAPTER 14

APPLICATION SETTINGS

Over seven score years ago, President Abraham Lincoln began his famous Gettysburg Address with, "Four score and seven years ago...." Why this poetic reference to the founding of America 87 years earlier? He could have started the speech with, "Last week, I was talking with members of my cabinet," or even, "These three confederate soldiers walked into a bar...." But he stuck with the decades-old anecdote.

Lincoln understood that his listeners, as humans, had a tie with the past, a fondness for the familiar, a love of fast sports cars, and a desire to see the stability of a former era restored. This is how people are. They like peace, not war. They like the status quo, not change. They like dinner on the table when they return home from a hard day at the office. They like short lines at the amusement park. They like seeing their favorite football team win once again.

People like to know that things are configured in a way that makes sense to them, set up in a way that is familiar and known. They expect this in life, and they expect this in their software. That's why Visual Basic 2005 includes features that let you maintain user-specific and application-specific settings, to give the people what they want.

A Short History of Settings

Since that short yet dynamic speech by Lincoln, programmers have sought a convenient way to maintain configurable values in their applications. In the early days of MS-DOS development, it was a configuration free-for-all; each program provided its own settings system. Many applications needed no specialized configuration, but those that did often stored configuration settings together with the application's managed data, all in proprietary ".dat" files.

With the advent of mainstream Windows development, Microsoft introduced file-based settings management through its **application programming interface** (API). The "private profile" API calls (GetPrivateProfileInt, GetPrivateProfileString, SetPrivateProfileString, and a few others) supplied a standard way to store short configuration values in an open and easy-to-understand text file format. Microsoft used these "INI" files (named for their ".ini" file extension) for its own configuration. A few of these files still reside in your system's *Windows* folder. (Visual Studio 2005 even installs a couple of them for its purposes.) Here's the content I found in my system's *win.ini* file.

```
; for 16-bit app support
[fonts]
[extensions]
[mci extensions]
[files]
[Mail]
MAPI=1
[CDWINSETUP]
AUTOUNLOAD=No
[MSUCE]
Advanced=0
CodePage=Unicode
Font=Arial
```

The format of an INI file was simple to understand. Each file included named sections defined within square brackets, as in "[fonts]." Each section maintained a set of key-value pairs in the form "key=value." The format was simple enough that anyone could use Notepad to make changes. It wasn't even that hard for a program to write its own INI-file management routines, but having them included in the Windows API made them that much more attractive.

But then came the clutter. With so many programs opting to store their configuration files in a known central location, the *Windows* folder quickly became the file equivalent of Grand Central Station at 5:00 p.m. on a Friday. Speed was an issue too, because the constant parsing and rewriting of INI files consumed precious CPU resources.

Microsoft came up with a solution: the **registry**. This hierarchical database of key-value pairs cleaned up the file system and brought speed improvements to configuration management. It also added new administrator-defined security settings for access to the registry, and provided support for some limited strongly-typed data. But the new API features weren't the most intuitive (although Visual Basic did include simple commands, such as *GetSetting*, that provided limited access to registry keys and values).

The registry threw technology at the configuration values problem, but it wasn't a full triumph. With so many vendors stuffing gobs of data in the registry, bloat once again became an issue. And with the system managing all access to the registry, the larger the registry, the worse the performance.

.NET's initial release included application-specific configuration files, a sort-of return to those days of INI-file yesteryear. In some ways, "app.config" and "web.config" files were better than INI files because they contained structured XML content. But big whoop. INI files had structure, and you could update them in Notepad. .NET config files were notoriously difficult to update, either within a .NET application or externally in Notepad (due to some weird caching issues). Also, .config files had neither the security nor the strong data typing available in the registry.

Configuration settings have been giving programmers at least some level of angst since Windows first appeared. But Visual Basic 2005 seeks to change all that with a new and improved settings system.

Settings in Visual Basic 2005

The new settings system in Visual Basic 2005 is a multi-file, XML-based, strongly-typed, and easy-to-manage configuration approach. Its file-focused methodology includes these features and benefits.

- Data is stored in XML format for efficient processing by .NET libraries. Although it is not freeform text, XML is not overwhelmingly difficult when manual updates need to be made by mere mortals.
- The data stored in each settings-specific file is strongly typed, reducing errors from the processing of invalid data.
- Settings are managed on a per-application, per-user, and even per-assembly-version basis to promote security and reduce conflicts. You can also store multiple sets of settings per application as you require, such as one set of settings per document opened by your application. (I won't discuss it in this chapter, but you can search for "SettingsKey property" in the online help for additional information on this feature.)

- Visual Studio includes a user-friendly management tool used to configure settings within an application.
- Visual Basic has its own simple interface to make the use and update of settings at runtime easier.

But it's not all fun and games. As a developer, you have to do some of the heavy lifting, like coming up with meaningful names for each setting ("MainFormLocation," "DatabaseConnection," and so on), and altering the behavior of your program as needed based on the stored settings.

The actual settings appear in XML files scattered throughout the file system.

- At design time, all the settings you create get stored in a *Settings.settings* file, stored in the *My Project* subdirectory of your source code folder. Here's the *Settings.settings* file as it exists so far in the Library Project.

```
<?xml version='1.0' encoding='utf-8'?>
<SettingsFile xmlns="http://schemas.microsoft.com/
    ➥VisualStudio/2004/01/settings"
    CurrentProfile="(Default)">
  <Profiles>
    <Profile Name="(Default)" />
  </Profiles>
  <Settings />
</SettingsFile>
```

- At runtime, all user-specific settings appear in a *user.config* file, typically stored in *C:\Documents and Settings\<user>\Local Settings\Application Data\<company>\<appdata>\<version>*, where *<user>* is the Windows username, *<company>* is the company name recorded in the assembly, *<appdata>* is a combination of values that help differentiate the settings based on use, and *<version>* is the four-part version number of the assembly. It seems like a difficult place to store settings, but it keeps things nice and ordered. (The location of the *user.config* file is a little different if you deploy an application using *ClickOnce*, a method described in Chapter 24, "Deployment.")

  You're probably wondering if this contributes to disk bloat. Yes! Each time you bump up the version number of your application, .NET creates a new settings file to go with it. There's a way to mitigate this somewhat, but with 120GB hard drives, no one's really complaining about disk space usage anymore.

■ Some settings are application-focused, and apply to all users of the application on a particular workstation. These are stored in the *app.config* file that appears in the same folder as your assembly's executable. This file existed in .NET applications before the 2005 release. The new 2005-style settings appear in an XML branch named *<applicationSettings>* within this file. Application-focused settings cannot be modified by the application; you must manually update the *app.config* file to force a change.

The settings system is a great place to store **state**, things that you want the program to remember from the last time it was run, but that shouldn't be hard-coded into the source code.

Adding Settings to a Project

The *Project Properties* window within Visual Studio 2005 provides centralized control of the settings for an application. The *Settings* panel of this window, shown in Figure 14-1, provides access to the application's custom settings.

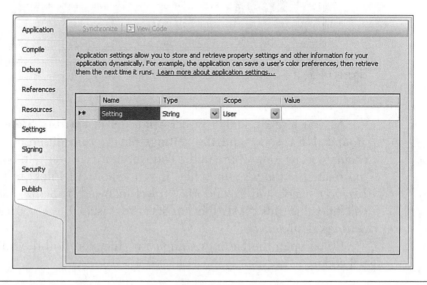

Figure 14-1 The Settings panel with no defined settings

To add a setting, type in its **Name**, select its data **Type** from the drop-down list, choose the **Scope** (*User* or *Application*), and enter its **Value** using whatever value editor is available for the selected type. The **Type** list includes many default selections, including the basic Visual Basic data types, fonts, colors, and drawing-related sizes. Also included is a "(Connection string)" type that, when selected, enables a **Connection Properties** string builder in the **Value** column.

It's important that you select the correct type for each stored setting; otherwise, your workstation will explode. Actually, I think they fixed that in a later beta. It's really because all settings are strongly typed. If you assign the type to *Integer*, you won't be able to stuff the word "None" in there as a special flag as you could have done with an INI file. You can choose any valid .NET type for the data type, although complex types without their own custom editors will require that you set their value through code.

What happens when you add a new setting to your Visual Basic project? Let's find out. I'll add two settings to a new Windows Forms project: an *Integer* named *WarningLimit*, and a *System.Drawing.Font* named *NoticeFont* (see Figure 14-2).

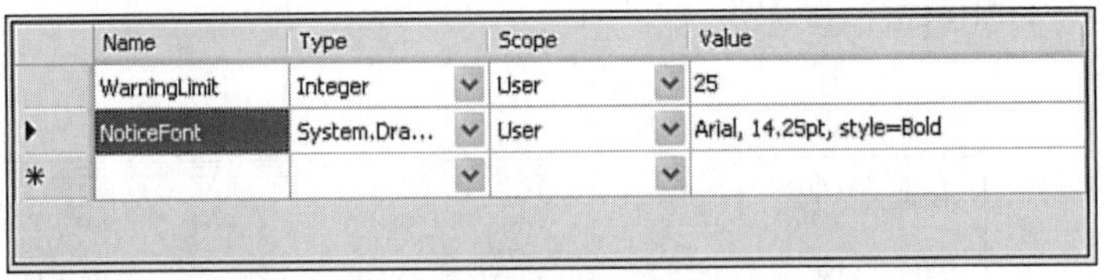

	Name	Type		Scope		Value
	WarningLimit	Integer	∨	User	∨	25
▸	NoticeFont	System.Dra...	∨	User	∨	Arial, 14.25pt, style=Bold
∗			∨		∨	

Figure 14-2 The Settings panel with two new settings

As you already know, Visual Studio is just a user-friendly wrapper around .NET code, and the settings panel is no different. So the real changes occur somewhere in the code, or more correctly, in both code and the related *Settings.settings* file. If you "Show All Files" in the *Solution Explorer* panel, and expand *My Project* followed by *Settings.settings*, you will find that this XML file has its own Visual Basic source code file, *Settings.Designer.vb*.

If you open the *Settings.Designer.vb* file, you find the following partial code.

```
Namespace My
    Partial Friend NotInheritable Class MySettings
        Inherits Global.System.Configuration. _
            ApplicationSettingsBase

        <Global.System.Configuration. _
            UserScopedSettingAttribute(),  _
            Global.System.Diagnostics. _
            DebuggerNonUserCodeAttribute(),  _
            Global.System.Configuration. _
            DefaultSettingValueAttribute("25")>  _
        Public Property WarningLimit() As Integer
            Get
                Return CType(Me("WarningLimit"),Integer)
            End Get
            Set
                Me("WarningLimit") = value
            End Set
        End Property

        <Global.System.Configuration. _
            UserScopedSettingAttribute(),  _
            Global.System.Diagnostics. _
            DebuggerNonUserCodeAttribute(),  _
            Global.System.Configuration. _
            DefaultSettingValueAttribute( _
            "Arial, 14.25pt, style=Bold")>  _
        Public Property NoticeFont() _
                As Global.System.Drawing.Font
            Get
                Return CType(Me("NoticeFont"), _
                    Global.System.Drawing.Font)
            End Get
            Set
                Me("NoticeFont") = value
            End Set
        End Property
    End Class
End Namespace
```

I excluded a lot of the extra code. It's amazing how much code Microsoft loads up in prewritten attributes, and it's not really possible to know what goes on inside. I can guess what the *DefaultSettingValueAttribute* attribute does for each setting (assigns the initial default value of the setting), but some of the others are mysteries. Oh well. Even the ancients didn't have answers for everything.

But the code that remains is quite clear. Visual Studio generates two properties within the *My.MySettings* class, properties named—amazingly enough—*WarningLimit* and *NoticeFont*. Here's the property entry for *NoticeFont*.

```
Public Property NoticeFont() As Global.System.Drawing.Font
   Get
      Return CType(Me("NoticeFont"), _
         Global.System.Drawing.Font)
   End Get
   Set
      Me("NoticeFont") = value
   End Set
End Property
```

You won't find any private class members that store the hidden *WarningLimit* and *NoticeFont* values. Instead, somewhere else in this partial class is a default property (named *Item*) that gets and sets each defined property value, accessed through `Me("something")`.

The settings available through this default property are loaded directly from the XML stored in the *Settings.settings* file. (This file is compiled into the application; you don't have to distribute *Settings.settings* with the application.) Here's the content from that file with our two new configuration values.

```
<?xml version='1.0' encoding='utf-8'?>
<SettingsFile xmlns="http://schemas.microsoft.com/
   ➥ VisualStudio/2004/01/settings"
   CurrentProfile="(Default)"
   GeneratedClassNamespace="My"
   GeneratedClassName="MySettings"
   UseMySettingsClassName="true">
   <Profiles />
   <Settings>
     <Setting Name="WarningLimit"
        Type="System.Int32" Scope="User">
       <Value Profile="(Default)">25</Value>
     </Setting>
     <Setting Name="NoticeFont"
```

```
      Type="System.Drawing.Font" Scope="User">
    <Value Profile="(Default)">
      Arial, 14.25pt, style=Bold</Value>
  </Setting>
 </Settings>
</SettingsFile>
```

Each setting contains distinct *Name*, *Type*, *Scope*, and *Value* attributes or entries, matching the four columns that appeared in the Visual Studio settings editor.

My.Settings

Visual Basic creates an instance of the *My.MySettings* class we just saw previously, and makes it available as *My.Settings*. As you add settings to your project, they become strongly-typed class members of *My.Settings*. To access one, simply reference it directly in your code.

```
MsgBox("The font for notices is: " & _
   My.Settings.NoticeFont.ToString())
```

(The output for this code appears in Figure 14-3.) The *My.Settings.NoticeFont* is an actual instance of a *System.Drawing.Font* that you can use like any other *Font* instance.

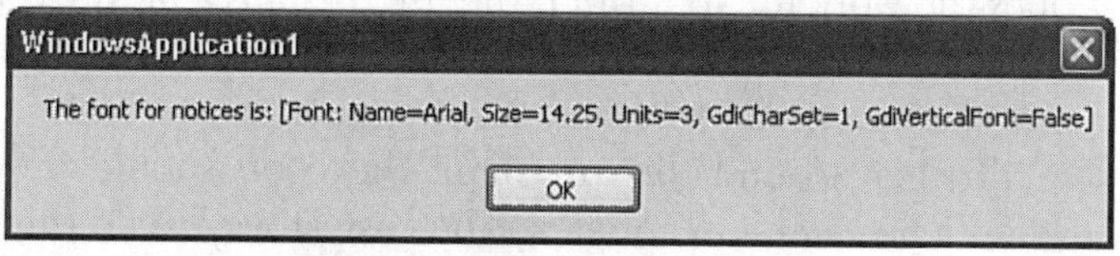

Figure 14-3 Be sure to take "notice" of this font

You can modify the value of any setting scoped as "User," and have the new value preserved for your next use of the application (that is, for the current user's next use of the application).

```
My.Settings.WarningLimit = 30
```

All changes made to these settings are saved automatically to the user-specific setting files by default. If you don't want the updates saved automatically, set the *My.Application.SaveMySettingsOnExit* flag to *False*.

Then, when you are ready to save the new settings, use the *My.Settings.Save* method.

Settings come in three delicious flavors: default, persisted, and current. *Default settings* are those values defined by the programmer through the Visual Studio settings editor. *Persisted settings* include the saved changes to specific settings, and the default settings for those that have never been altered by the user. *Current settings* include any changes made to the settings during the current session, but not yet saved. You can play with these states using members of the *My.Settings* object.

- The *Save* method, as mentioned previously, saves all current settings to a persisted state.
- The *Reload* method restores any current values with the persisted versions.
- The *Reset* method wipes out all current and persisted settings, and returns all configuration entries to their default values.

One of the strangest aspects of settings is that they are version-specific. If you release your application as version 1.0.0.0, and then later release version 1.1.0.0, each user will lose all of the previously persisted settings. Actually, they won't be lost, but they will be stuck in 1.0.0.0-land. If you always want to have the most up-to-date settings as modified by the user, you will have to make sure that older settings are "upgraded" when installing a new version. *My.Settings* includes an *Upgrade* method that does the work for you. But if the user installs a newer version and upgrades the settings, makes changes to those settings, and then calls *Upgrade* again, any changes made since the last upgrade will be lost.

To get around this problem, the code should only upgrade settings when a new version appears. The easiest way to do this is to include a setting called something like *SettingsUpgraded* and set it to *False*. Check this flag before calling *Upgrade*. If it is still *False*, then it is safe to call *Upgrade*. Once the code upgrades the settings, change *SettingsUpgraded* to *True*.

```
If (My.Settings.SettingsUpgraded = False) Then
   My.Settings.Upgrade()
   My.Setttings.SettingsUpgraded = True
End If
```

This need to upgrade settings whenever even minor version number changes are made to an assembly seems a bit over the top. But it's necessary to support .NET's goal of side-by-side installation. The user should be able to install two different versions of your application on the same workstation, and use each one without interference from the other. Storing version-specific settings helps achieve this goal.

Bound Settings

Although using and updating your own custom configuration values can be exciting, even more exciting is that the fields in your Windows Forms and related controls can interact with the persisted settings automatically. By **binding** form- and control-specific properties to the settings system, Visual Basic automatically saves and restores user-controlled preferences within the user interface.

A typical use for bound settings is to have the application remember where a particular form appeared on the screen when the program was last run. The form's *Location* property maintains its on-screen position. Recording this value to the settings requires two steps. First, create a setting of type *System.Drawing.Point* to hold the persisted location value. Second, indicate in the form's properties that its *Location* value should persist to the new settings entry.

Perform the first step by adding a new user-scoped *System.Drawing.Point* setting in the project properties' *Settings* panel. Let's name it "MainFormPosition," and leave the *Value* field blank for now.

Back in the form editor, select the form object itself, and then access the *Properties Windows.* Expand the *(ApplicationSettings)* property to locate the *(PropertyBinding)* sub-property. Clicking the "..." button for this entry displays the *Application Settings* dialog. This selection process appears in Figure 14-4.

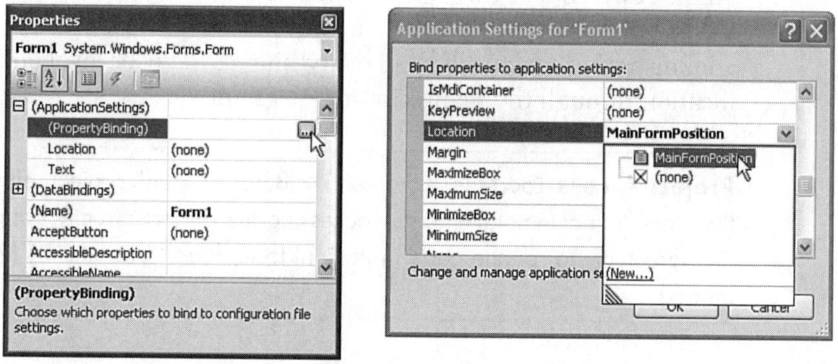

Figure 14-4 Bringing up the application settings dialog for a form

Find the *Location* entry in the list, and choose "MainFormPosition" for its value. Now, each time you run the application containing this bound setting, the modified form will "remember" its previous location.

Summary

As with XML, the .NET settings system is one of those internal, behind-the-scenes, don't-let-the-boss-know features that makes your program great to use, but without all of the whiz-bang showing-off stuff. Personally, I found it a little hard to part with my precious INI files and all of their simplicity. But the automation attached to the new settings system makes the migration painless.

Project

Of course we will add settings to the Library Project in this chapter, but we'll also go back and start using some of those settings in code that we previously entered as hard-coded values.

I really struggled over whether to use application-scoped or user-scoped configuration values for some of the rarely changing settings, such as the database connection string. I finally decided on the user area so that they could be modified through the features of the program. Application-scoped settings are read-only and can only be updated outside of the program, so that idea is out. The expectation with application-scoped settings is that the system administrator will manage them, either by using Notepad on the XML file, or through some custom administrative tool. Because we aren't going to take the time in this book's project to write a separate administration tool, we'll keep everything at the user level and allow modification through the main Library Program.

Project Access Load the "Chapter 14 (Before) Code" project, either through the New Project templates, or by accessing the project directly from the installation directory. To see the code in its final form, load "Chapter 14 (After) Code" instead.

Update Technical Documentation

Let's document the settings used by the application in the project's *Resource Kit*. Add the following content to the *Resource Kit* word processing file.

User Settings

The Library project uses Visual Basic's *settings* system to track user-specific state values maintained between uses of the application. All of these settings are stored in an XML file in the user's portion of the *C:\Documents and Settings* (or equivalent) directory in a format dictated by .NET. The following is a list of the settings recognized by the Library program.

- **DBConnection** (String)—A properly formatted connection string that identifies the SQL Server database used by the application. If missing, the application will prompt for the location of the database on startup.
- **HelpFile** (String)—Indicates the UNC or drive letter-based location of the basic application online help file, with a ".chm" extension.
- **HelpFileAdmin** (String)—Indicates the UNC or drive letter-based location of the administrative application online help file, with a ".chm" extension.
- **HideLogin** (Boolean)—Indicates whether the *Login* button in the upper-right corner of the main Library form should be hidden from view when in patron (non-administrative) mode. Use *True* to hide the button, or *False* to show the button. If this field is missing, *False* is assumed.
- **MainFormPosition** (System.Drawing.Point)—The position of the upper-left corner of the main Library form. This value is updated each time the application closes.
- **ReceiptPostlude** (String)—Any raw character data to send to the receipt printer at the end of each ticket. This text may include the following special characters.
  - \n—A newline character (ASCII 10).
  - \r—A carriage return character (ASCII 13).

- \e—An escape character (ASCII 27).
- \x??—Any ASCII value, where "??" is a two-character hexadecimal code.
- \\—The backslash character ("\").

- **ReceiptPrinter** (String)—The UNC pathname to the receipt printer used by this workstation to print out patron check-out receipts and payment receipts.
- **ReceiptWidth** (Integer)—The width, in characters, of each line on the receipt printer. If missing or empty, the program uses a default width of 40 characters.
- **ReportConfig** (String)—Indicates the UNC or drive letter-based location of the XML report configuration file. This file has the XML format described in the *Report Configuration File* section of this document. This file indicates the reports available in the application.
- **SettingsUpgraded** (Boolean)—When upgrading the application from an older release, this flag indicates whether the settings associated with that older release have already been upgraded into this new version. It defaults to *False* for all new releases.
- **UseReceipts** (Boolean)—Indicates whether printed receipts are to be used at this workstation. If this field is missing, *False* is assumed.

This technical description appears in the Technical Resource Kit document, originally developed in Chapter 4, "Designing the Database," and updated in subsequent chapters. Some of the content added here refers to features and technical content that won't be added until later chapters, so don't spend too much time thinking about features that you thought you already forgot.

Add the Settings

Because we know all of the settings we will add to the application, let's add them now. Open the project properties window and select the *Settings* tab. Add each setting to the application using Table 14-1 as a guide. If a setting in Table 14-1 has no listed value, leave the **Value** field blank in the settings editor as well.

Table 14-1 Default Settings for the Library Project

Name	Type	Scope	Value
DBConnection	*String*	User	
HelpFile	*String*	User	
HelpFileAdmin	*String*	User	
HideLogin	*Boolean*	User	False
MainFormPosition	*System.Drawing.Point*	User	
ReceiptPostlude	*String*	User	
ReceiptPrinter	*String*	User	
ReceiptWidth	*Integer*	User	40
ReportConfig	*String*	User	
SettingsUpgraded	*Boolean*	User	False
UseReceipts	*Boolean*	User	False

Make sure you type the settings names as listed. The application will not be able to match up incorrectly spelled names.

Positioning the Main Form

I showed you how to link a form's or control's property value to one of the settings earlier in this chapter, so let's do it for real in the project. We'll link the main form's *Location* property to the *MainFormPosition* setting. Just to refresh your memory, follow these steps to enable the link.

1. Open *MainForm.vb* in Design view.
2. Make sure the form itself is selected, not one of its subordinate controls.
3. In the *Properties* panel, expand the *(ApplicationSettings)* property.
4. Select the *(PropertyBinding)* sub-property, and click on the "..." button in its value area.
5. Locate the *Location* property in the binding list.
6. Select the *MainFormPosition* setting for the *Location* property's value. It should be the only setting available, because it is the only one we defined as type *System.Drawing.Point*.
7. Click the *OK* button to enable the link.

Caching and Using Settings

Although all the settings are as close as typing "My.Settings.*something*" in the code, some settings may initially be undefined, and using them could involve a lot of repetitive code that checks for valid settings. In order to reduce overall code and CPU cycles, we will cache some of the settings for easy use throughout the application.

Let's add three more global variables to cache some of the settings. Open the *General.vb* module, and add these three new class members.

Insert Snippet Insert Chapter 14, Snippet Item 1.

```
Public MainHelpFile As String
Public MainAdminHelpFile As String
Public FineGraceDays As Integer
```

Let's give these variables initial values in the *InitializeSystem* method, where the code already initializes some other values. Add the following statements to that routine in the *General* module.

Insert Snippet Insert Chapter 14, Snippet Item 2.

```
FineGraceDays = -1

' ----- Locate the online help files.
MainHelpFile = My.Settings.HelpFile & ""
MainAdminHelpFile = My.Settings.HelpFileAdmin & ""
```

In an earlier chapter, we stored some settings in the *SystemValue* table that apply to all workstations that connect to the database. Because we're caching settings anyway, we should add some code to cache these database-stored values so that we don't have to keep opening and closing the database. Add the *LoadDatabaseSettings* method to the *General* module.

Insert Snippet Insert Chapter 14, Snippet Item 3.

```
Public Sub LoadDatabaseSettings()
   ' ----- Get some system-level values from
   '        database storage.
   Dim holdText As String

   On Error Resume Next

   ' ----- Get the default location.
   holdText = GetSystemValue("DefaultLocation")
   If (holdText = "") Then holdText = "-1"
   DefaultItemLocation = CInt(holdText)

   ' ----- Get the maximum number of search maches.
   holdText = GetSystemValue("SearchLimit")
   If (holdText = "") Then holdText = "-1"
   SearchMatchLimit = CInt(holdText)

   ' ----- Get the number of days to wait before
   '        charging fines.
   holdText = GetSystemValue("FineGrace")
   If (holdText = "") Then holdText = "-1"
   FineGraceDays = CInt(holdText)
End Sub
```

We will call this routine during application startup, just after we open and confirm the database. Add the following code to the end of the *MyApplication_Startup* event handler. If it's been a while, remember that this handler is in the *ApplicationEvents.vb* file, one of the files normally hidden from view in the *Solution Explorer*.

Insert Snippet Insert Chapter 14, Snippet Item 4.

```
' ----- Load some settings that reside in the database.
LoadDatabaseSettings()
```

It's time to actually use a setting. The *My.Settings.HideLogin* setting indicates whether the "Login" button (*ActLogin*) on the main Library application form should appear when running in non-administrator (non-librarian) mode. The administrator can still bring up the login form through the F12 key, even if the button is hidden. In an environment where the patrons may be unknown, the system will be slightly more secure if the temptation of a "Login" button is removed.

The *UpdateDisplayForUser* routine in the *MainForm* class includes code for user mode (*LoggedInUserID = -1*) and administrator mode (*LoggedInUserID <> -1*). In the user mode block (the first block), replace this line:

```
ActLogin.Visible = True
```

with the following code.

Insert Snippet Insert Chapter 14, Snippet Item 5.

```
' ----- Show or hide the Login button per the settings.
ActLogin.Visible = Not My.Settings.HideLogin
```

Adding Configuration Forms

It's time to add the forms that will manage all of the various application settings, both those stored locally in the user-focused settings file, and the system-wide settings stored in the database. Most of the settings are pretty simple—just basic strings, numbers, and Boolean flags—so it shouldn't overwhelm the administrator to have them all appear on a single form. But before we get to that form, we'll add a form that lets us manage the database connection.

I thought about calling up the connection properties dialog that Visual Studio uses to establish connection strings. I'm sure it's possible, but it provides way more flexibility than we need in this project. For instance, it supports the configuration of non-SQL Server databases, which is of no interest to the Library Project. Instead, we'll design a simpler form that collects only those data values that we need to build the Library connection string. The *LocateDatabase* form appears in Figure 14-5.

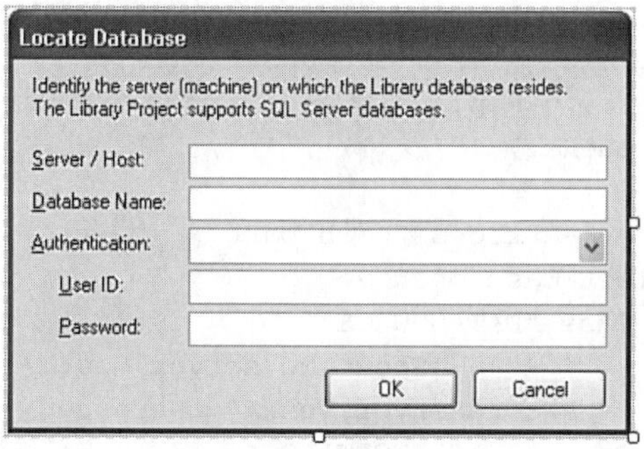

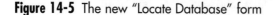

Figure 14-5 The new "Locate Database" form

I've already added the form and its controls to the project. Open the *LocateDatabase.vb* file to see the form. Four of the fields on this form are basic text entry fields (one with a password mask character). The third entry field, *Authentication*, lets the user select between Microsoft Windows authentication and SQL Server authentication.

Most of the form's code parallels what we've seen in many of the other forms already in the application. Go ahead and add in all of the form's code now.

Insert Snippet Insert Chapter 14, Snippet Item 6.

The significant work in this form occurs in the *Load* event when the existing connection string is parsed out into distinct data entry fields, and in the *PromptUser* routine where the parts are put back together.

There are many different ways you could chop up the connection string into its base parts. I took the basic divide-and-conquer approach, extracting out each semicolon- and equals-sign-separated component. Here's the main block of code from the *Load* event handler that does the chopping and extracting.

```
' ----- Load in the existing data.
connectionString = My.Settings.DBConnection & ""
For counter = 1 To CountSubStr(connectionString, ";") + 1
    ' ----- Each comma-delimited part has the format
    '         "key=value".
```

```
oneKey = GetSubStr(connectionString, ";", counter)
oneValue = Trim(GetSubStr(oneKey, "=", 2))
oneKey = Replace(UCase(Trim(GetSubStr( _
   oneKey, "=", 1))), " ", "")


' ----- Process each part.
Select Case oneKey
   Case "DATASOURCE"
      ' ----- Show the server host.
      RecordServer.Text = oneValue
   Case "INITIALCATALOG"
      ' ----- Show the default database name.
      RecordDatabase.Text = oneValue
   Case "INTEGRATEDSECURITY"
      ' ----- Only check for "true". False is assumed.
      If (UCase(oneValue) = "TRUE") Then _
         RecordAuthentication.SelectedIndex = _
         RecordAuthentication.Items.IndexOf( _
         AuthenticationTypeWindows)
   Case "USERID"
      ' ----- A user ID forces SQL authentication.
      RecordAuthentication.SelectedIndex = _
         RecordAuthentication.Items.IndexOf( _
         AuthenticationTypeSQL)
      RecordUser.Text = oneValue
   Case "PASSWORD"
      ' ----- A password forces SQL authentication.
      RecordAuthentication.SelectedIndex = _
         RecordAuthentication.Items.IndexOf( _
         AuthenticationTypeSQL)
      RecordPassword.Text = oneValue
   End Select
Next counter
```

Putting the parts together is less complicated. Here's the needed string concatenation code found in the *PromptUser* routine.

```
newConnection = "Data Source=" & Trim(RecordServer.Text) & _
   ";Initial Catalog=" & Trim(RecordDatabase.Text)
If (CInt(CType(RecordAuthentication.SelectedItem, _
   ListItemData)) = AuthenticationTypeWindows) Then
```

```
' ----- Use Windows security.
    newConnection &= ";Integrated Security=true"
Else
    ' ----- Use SQL Server security.
    newConnection &= ";User ID=" & Trim(RecordUser.Text) & _
        ";Password=" & Trim(RecordPassword.Text)
End If
```

Although the *LocateDatabase* form does the difficult work of parsing and building the connection string, it doesn't actually update the saved setting. Instead, it returns the newly built connection string, and depends on the calling code to save it.

Now, back to our single-form configuration editor, *Maintenance.vb*. This form does all of the direct modification of the values in both the database and the local *My.Settings* items. Figure 14-6 and Figure 14-7 show the two main panels of the *Maintenance* form. The centralized settings stored in the database are "system-wide," and the "workstation-specific" values are those accessed through *My.Settings*.

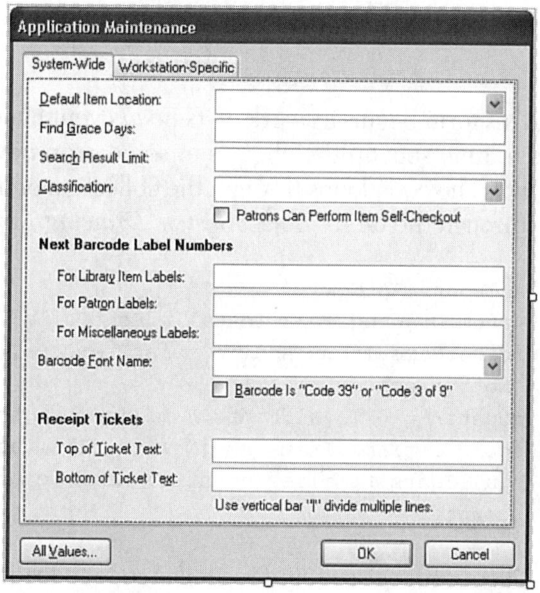

Figure 14-6 The new "Maintenance" form showing the "System-Wide" panel

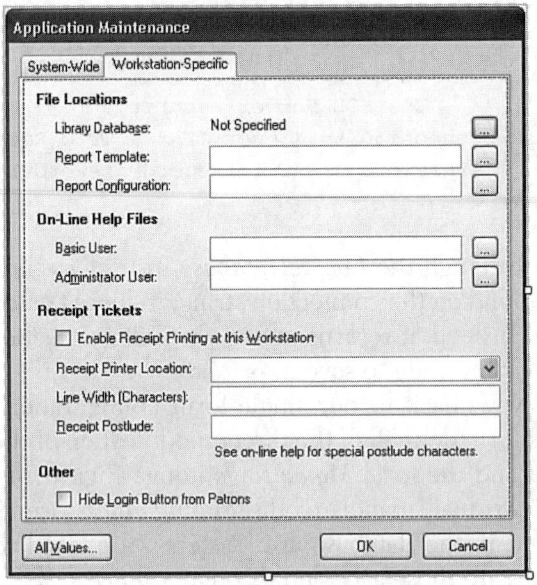

Figure 14-7 The new "Maintenance" form showing the "Workstation-Specific" panel

This form begins its work in its *Load* event handler, *Maintenance_Load*. This routine sets up the choices in some drop-down fields, including a list of fonts. The code loops through the collection of installed fonts made available through the GDI+ object *System.Drawing.Text.InstalledFontCollection*.

```
Dim allFonts As New _
   System.Drawing.Text.InstalledFontCollection
RecordFontName.Items.Add(New ListItemData( _
   "<Not Selected>", -1))
For counter = 0 To allFonts.Families.Length - 1
   RecordFontName.Items.Add(New ListItemData( _
      allFonts.Families(counter).Name, counter))
Next counter
```

The routine also includes similar code to load a list of installed printers.

```
For Each installedPrinter As String In _
     PrinterSettings.InstalledPrinters
   RecordPrinterLocation.Items.Add(installedPrinter)
Next installedPrinter
```

Once everything is set up, the *PopulateCurrentValues* procedure completes the initialization. Its code retrieves all the current values from both the database and the *My.Settings* object, and stores those values in the various on-screen data entry fields. I've already added the database-specific code. Go ahead and add in the settings-specific code.

Insert Snippet Insert Chapter 14, Snippet Item 7.

```
LibraryConnection = My.Settings.DBConnection & ""
RecordDBLocation.Text = GetDBDisplayText(LibraryConnection)
RecordConfigLocation.Text = My.Settings.ReportConfig & ""
RecordBasicHelp.Text = My.Settings.HelpFile & ""
RecordAdminHelp.Text = My.Settings.HelpFileAdmin & ""
EnableReceipts.Checked = My.Settings.UseReceipts
RecordPrinterLocation.Text = My.Settings.ReceiptPrinter & ""
RecordPrinterWidth.Text = CStr(My.Settings.ReceiptWidth)
RecordPostlude.Text = My.Settings.ReceiptPostlude & ""
HideLogin.Checked = My.Settings.HideLogin
```

Most of the code in this form deals with basic user interaction while the form is in use. For example, the *ActDBLocation_Click* event handler displays the *LocateDatabase* form we added earlier. Add the relevant source code to that event handler template.

Insert Snippet Insert Chapter 14, Snippet Item 8.

```
' ----- Prompt for the database connection details.
Dim newConnection As String

' ----- Prompt the user for the new setting.
newConnection = LocateDatabase.PromptUser()
If (newConnection = "") Then Return

' ----- Store the new value.
LibraryConnection = newConnection
RecordDBLocation.Text = GetDBDisplayText(LibraryConnection)
```

Several of the settings specify the locations of files used by the application, such as the online help files. The user can type in the path to the file directly, or use the Open File Dialog to locate the file visually. To display this dialog, I've added an *OpenFileDialog* control named *LocateFile*. Using it is a matter of setting the various file-specific properties and calling the *ShowDialog* method. Here's some of the code already included in the *ActBasicHelp_Click* event handler used to locate the non-administrative online help file.

```
' ----- Set up the file structure.
LocateFile.DefaultExt = "chm"
LocateFile.FileName = RecordBasicHelp.Text
LocateFile.Filter = "Help Files (*.chm)|*.chm|" & _
    "All Files (*.*)|*.*"
LocateFile.FilterIndex = 1
LocateFile.Title = "Locate Help"

' ----- Prompt the user.
If (LocateFile.ShowDialog() <> _
    Windows.Forms.DialogResult.OK) Then Return

' ----- Save the file path.
RecordBasicHelp.Text = LocateFile.FileName
```

Once the user has made the various setting changes, a click on the *OK* button saves each new setting to its storage area. I've included the database-focused saving code in the *SaveFormData* routine. I'll let you add the settings-focused code, near the end of that routine.

Insert Snippet Insert Chapter 14, Snippet Item 9.

```
My.Settings.DBConnection = LibraryConnection
My.Settings.ReportConfig = Trim(RecordConfigLocation.Text)
My.Settings.HelpFile = Trim(RecordBasicHelp.Text)
My.Settings.HelpFileAdmin = Trim(RecordAdminHelp.Text)
My.Settings.HideLogin = HideLogin.Checked
My.Settings.UseReceipts = EnableReceipts.Checked
My.Settings.ReceiptPrinter = Trim(RecordPrinterLocation.Text)
My.Settings.ReceiptPostlude = RecordPostlude.Text
```

```
' ----- Save the receipt printer width.
If (Trim(RecordPrinterWidth.Text) = "") Then
   My.Settings.ReceiptWidth = DefaultReceiptPrinterWidth
Else
   My.Settings.ReceiptWidth = CInt(RecordPrinterWidth.Text)
End If
```

Although the *Maintenance* form provides a user-friendly interface to the database-stored settings, you probably remember that we already wrote code to update *SystemValue* table records through the *SystemValue.vb* file. In Chapter 12, "Operator Overloading," we connected that form to the main form, but we're going to alter that logic. First, we'll add the call to the *SystemValue* form to the *Maintenance* form's *ActAllValues_Click* event handler.

Insert Snippet Insert Chapter 14, Snippet Item 10.

```
' ----- Let the user edit the list of system values.
Dim RecordsForm As Library.ListEditRecords

' ----- Edit the records.
RecordsForm = New Library.ListEditRecords
RecordsForm.ManageRecords(New Library.SystemValue)
RecordsForm = Nothing

' ----- Refresh the display elements.
PopulateCurrentValues()
```

Then we'll change the *AdminLinkValues_LinkClicked* event handler back in *MainForm.vb*. Currently, it calls the *SystemValue* editor directly. Replace that part of the *LinkClicked* handler's code with code that calls the *Maintenance* form instead.

Insert Snippet Insert Chapter 14, Snippet Item 11.

```
' ----- Access the maintenance portion of the program.
Maintenance.ShowDialog()
```

Connecting to the Configured Database

The last change in this chapter uses the configured connection string to establish the connection to the database. When we originally wrote the *ConnectDatabase* routine in the *General* module, we added a hard-coded connection string just to get the program working.

```
' ----- Build the connection string.
' !!! WARNING: Hardcoded for now.
connectionString = "Data Source=MYSYSTEM\SQLEXPRESS;" & _
    "Initial Catalog=Library;Integrated Security=true"
```

Now that we have a user-configured connection string available, we will use that instead. The changes we must make to this routine are somewhat extensive, so just replace the function's existing content with the updated code.

Insert Snippet Insert Chapter 14, Snippet Item 12.

```
' ----- Connect to the database. Return True on success.
Dim connectionString As String
Dim configChanged As Boolean

' ----- Initialize.
HoldTransaction = Nothing
configChanged = False

' ----- Obtain the connection string.
If (Trim(My.Settings.DBConnection & "") = "") Then
    ' ----- Inform the user about the need to configure
    '       the database.
    If (MsgBox("This copy of the application has not " & _
        "been configured to connect to the library " & _
        "database. If you know the database settings, " & _
        "you can configure it now. Would you like to " & _
        "proceed?", MsgBoxStyle.YesNo Or _
        MsgBoxStyle.Question, ProgramTitle) _
        <> MsgBoxResult.Yes) Then Return False
```

```
' ----- Prompt for the new connection details.
connectionString = LocateDatabase.PromptUser()
If (connectionString = "") Then Return False
configChanged = True
Else
connectionString = My.Settings.DBConnection
End If

TryConnectingAgain:

' ----- Attempt to open the database.
Try
    LibraryDB = New SqlClient.SqlConnection(connectionString)
    LibraryDB.Open()
Catch ex As Exception
    ' ----- Some database failure.
    GeneralError("ConnectDatabase", ex)

    ' ----- Perhaps it is just a configuration issue.
    If (MsgBox("The connection to the database may " & _
        "have failed due to invalid configuration " & _
        "settings. Would you like to change the " & _
        "database configuration at this time?", _
        MsgBoxStyle.YesNo Or MsgBoxStyle.Question, _
        ProgramTitle) <> MsgBoxResult.Yes) Then Return False

    ' ----- Prompt for new details.
    connectionString = LocateDatabase.PromptUser()
    If (connectionString = "") Then Return False
        configChanged = True
    GoTo TryConnectingAgain
End Try

' ----- Save the udpated configuration if needed.
If (configChanged = True) Then _
    My.Settings.DBConnection = connectionString

' ----- Success.
Return True
```

The basic gist of the code involves setting the *connectionString* variable to the persisted connection string, and using that to open the

LibraryDB object. The new code obtains the connection string from *My.Settings.DBConnection*. If for any reason the connection string is missing or fails to generate an open database connection, the user is prompted to supply or correct the connection string through our new *LocateDatabase* form.

The program is back to a condition where you can run it. The first time you run the program, it will prompt you to supply the database connection information. The values you supply will match the hard-coded version that used to be in the *ConnectDatabase* routine.

- Set *Server/Host* to "MYSERVER\SQLEXPRESS" or to the name of your actual SQL Server host.
- Set *Database Name* to "Library" or any other name you previously assigned to your library database.
- Set *Authentication* to "Microsoft Windows" if you use Windows integrated security. If you need to connect using SQL Server's security system, set this field to "SQL Server," and enter a valid *User ID* and *Password*.

In the next chapter, we'll focus on file manipulation techniques. Although we did update the settings file in this chapter, it was done indirectly through features provided by the Framework. Chapter 15, "Files and Directories," will discuss more direct approaches to file manipulation.

FILES AND DIRECTORIES

Software development in the 21st century has really turned programmers into a bunch of softies (no pun intended). In the old days of computers, developers had to solder programs into the computer by hand. Complex calculations could take days to set up, and one misplaced wire meant lead poisoning or worse. The suffering was real, and older issues of *Popular Electronics* are riddled with articles by former programmers who went crazy in their attempt to craft one more ballistics calculation algorithm.

Life improved tremendously for programmers when John von Neumann and others suggested that a computer could store internally the logic for an algorithm, and process it directly from memory instead of through hard-wired configurations. Engineers were soon putting their programs onto punch cards and paper tapes. The danger of lead poisoning was quickly replaced by the larger evil of paper cuts.

Punch cards were great—until you dropped your stack that took you hours or days to assemble. Some programmer somewhere dropped one too many card stacks and proclaimed, "That's it! I'm going to invent the hard disk and related technologies such as IDE and SCSI. Sure I'll become fabulously wealthy, but at least I won't have to deal with these stupid cards anymore."

And thus was born the file system, the structured storage of programs and information on a disk surface. File systems have been a part of Microsoft technologies since Bill Gates first wooed IBM. It's no coincidence that the "DOS" in "MS-DOS" stands for *Disk Operating System*. Bill knew how essential file systems were, and so do you.

In this chapter, we'll talk about interactions with files and directories, the main units of storage and organization in the Windows file system. We'll also see some of the technologies and features .NET provides to manipulate files and their content. Just make sure you turn the pages carefully; I wouldn't want you to get a paper cut.

Traditional Visual Basic File Management

Visual Basic has included significant file management features since its first release. In fact, there are more features in Visual Basic that deal with file and directory manipulation than with pretty much anything else.

Most of the functions that allow you to read and modify file content use a *file handle*, a numeric identifier that refers to a specific open file. This file handle is generated with the *FreeFile* function, and must be obtained before calling any of the traditional Visual Basic file features.

```
Dim fileID As Integer
fileID = FreeFile()
FileOpen(fileID, "C:\TestData.txt", OpenMode.Append)
PrintLine(fileID, "Important output to file.")
FileClose(fileID)
```

File handle-based file manipulation works just fine, but it is so early-'90s. It's not really a .NET technology, and is not object-based at all (unless you consider that an *Integer* is an object). Therefore, we won't be covering it in this book, or using it in the Library Project. Table 15-1 lists the major Visual Basic features that use file handles. If you need to know about the handle-based features in Visual Basic, or if your work involves migrating pre-.NET Visual Basic applications, use this table to help you locate full feature details in the technical documentation supplied with Visual Basic.

Table 15-1 Visual Basic Features That Use File Handles

Feature	Description
EOF	Returns a *Boolean* indicating whether the current position in the file is at or past the end of the file. Use this function to determine when to stop reading existing data from a file.
FileAttr	Indicates the file attributes currently set on an open file handle.
FileClose	Closes a specific file opened using a file handle.

Feature	Description
FileGet	Retrieves structured data from a file and stores it in a matching object.
FileGetObject	Same as `FileGet`, but with slightly different data typing support.
FileOpen	Opens a file for input or output.
FilePut	Writes an object to a file in a structured manner.
FilePutObject	Same as `FilePut`, but with slightly different data typing support.
FileWidth	Sets the default line width for formatted text output files.
FreeFile	Returns the next available file handle.
Input	Retrieves a value previously written to a file using `Write` or `WriteLine`.
InputString	Retrieves a specific number of characters from an input file.
LineInput	Returns a complete line of input from a file.
Loc	Returns the current byte or record location in the file.
Lock	Locks a file or specific records in a file so that others cannot make changes.
LOF	Returns the length of an open file, in bytes.
Print	Sends text output to a file.
PrintLine	Sends text output to a file, ending it with a line terminator.
Reset	Closes all files currently opened with file handles.
Seek	Gets or sets the current position in a file.
SPC	This function helps format text for output to columnar text files.
TAB	This function helps format text for output to columnar text files.
Unlock	Removes locks previously set with `Lock`.
Write	Writes data to a file using a consistent format that can be easily read later.
WriteLine	Same as `Write`, but ends the output with a line terminator.

Manipulating Files Through Streams

The .NET Framework includes a new object-oriented approach to reading and writing files: **streams**. The abstract *Stream* object, found at *System.IO.Stream*, defines a generic interface to a chunk of data. It doesn't matter where that data is: In a file, in a block of memory, in a *String* variable. If you have a block of data that can be read or written one byte at a time, you can design a derived stream class to interact with it.

Stream Features

The basic features of a *Stream* object include the *Read* and *Write* methods that let you read or write bytes. As data is read from or written to a stream, the *Stream* object maintains a "current position" within the stream that you can adjust using the *Seek* method, or examine using the *Position* property. The *Length* property indicates the size of the readable data. The class also exposes variations of these basic features to allow as much flexibility as possible.

Not every stream supports all features. Some streams are read-only, forward-only constructs that don't support writing or seeking. Other streams support all possible features. The features available to you depend on the type of stream you use. Because *Stream* itself is abstract, you must create an instance of one of its derived classes. .NET defines several useful streams ready for your use:

- **FileStream.** The *FileStream* object lets you access the content of a file using the basic methods of the generic *Stream* class. *FileStream* objects support reading, writing, and seeking, although if you open a read-only file, you won't be able to write to it.
- **MemoryStream.** A stream based on a block of raw memory. You can create a memory stream of any size, and use it to temporarily store and retrieve any data.
- **NetworkStream.** This class abstracts data coming over a network socket. Whereas most of the derived stream classes reside in *System.IO*, this class sits in *System.Net.Sockets*.
- **BufferedStream.** Adds buffering support to a stream to improve performance on streams with latency issues. You wrap a *BufferedStream* object around another stream to use it.
- **CryptoStream.** This stream allows you to attach a cryptographic service provider to it, resulting in encrypted output from plain input, or vice versa. Chapter 11, "Security," includes examples that use this type of stream.

- **DeflateStream** and **GZipStream.** Lets you use a stream to compress or decompress data as it is processed, all using standard compression algorithms.

Streams are useful on their own, but you can also combine streams so that an incoming network stream can be immediately encrypted, compressed, and stored in a block of stream memory.

Using a Stream

Using a stream is simple; first you create it, and then you start reading and writing bytes left and right. Here's some sample code I wrote that moves data into and out of a memory stream. It's loosely based on the code you'll find in the MSDN documentation for the *MemoryStream* class.

```
' ----- The Stream, or There and Back Again.
Dim position As Integer
Dim memStream As IO.MemoryStream
Dim sourceChars As Byte()
Dim destBytes As Byte()
Dim destChars As Char()
Dim asUnicode As New System.Text.UnicodeEncoding()

' ----- Create a memory stream with room for 100 bytes.
memStream = New IO.MemoryStream(100)

' ----- Convert the text data to a byte array.
sourceChars = asUnicode.GetBytes( _
   "This is a test of the emergency programming system.")

Try
   ' ----- Store the byte-converted data in the stream.
   memStream.Write(sourceChars, 0, sourceChars.Length)

   ' ----- The position is at the end of the written data.
   '       To read it back, we must move the pointer to
   '       the start again.
   memStream.Seek(0, IO.SeekOrigin.Begin)

   ' ----- Read a chunk of the text/bytes at once.
   destBytes = New Byte(CInt(memStream.Length)) {}
```

```
   position = memStream.Read(destBytes, 0, 25)

   ' ----- Get the remaining data one byte at a time,
   '        just for fun.
   While (position < memStream.Length)
      destBytes(position) = CByte(memStream.ReadByte())
      position += 1
   End While

   ' ----- Convert the byte array back to a set of characters.
   destChars = New Char(asUnicode.GetCharCount( _
      destBytes, 0, position)) {}
   asUnicode.GetDecoder().GetChars(destBytes, 0, _
      position, destChars, 0)

   ' ----- Prove that the text is back.
   MsgBox(destChars)
Finally
   memStream.Close()
End Try
```

The comments hopefully make the code clear. After creating a memory stream, I push a block of text into it, and then read it back out. (The text stays in the stream; reading it did not remove it.) Actually, the stream code is pretty simple. Most of the code deals with conversions between bytes and characters. If it looks overly involved, that's because it is.

Beyond Stream Bytes

For me, all that converting between bytes and characters is for the birds. When I write business applications, I typically deal in dates, numbers, and strings: customer names, order dates, payment amounts, and so on. I rarely have a need to work at the byte level. I sure wish there was a way to send this byte stuff down a programming stream of its own so I wouldn't have to see it anymore.

Lucky me! .NET makes some wishes come true. Although you can manipulate streams directly if you really want to or need to, the *System.IO* namespace also includes several classes that provide a more programmer-friendly buffer between you and the stream. These classes—implemented as distinct readers and writers of stream data—provide simplified methods of storing specific data types, and retrieving them back again.

The readers and writers are designed for single-direction start-to-finish processing of data. After creating or accessing a stream, you wrap that stream with either a reader or a writer, and begin traversing the extent of the stream from the beginning. You always have access to the underlying stream if you need more fine-tuned control at any point.

There are three main pairs of readers and writers:

- **BinaryReader** and **BinaryWriter.** These classes make it easy to write and later read the core Visual Basic data types to and from a (generally) non-text stream. The *BinaryWriter.Write* method includes overloads for writing *Bytes*, *Chars*, signed and unsigned integers of various sizes, *Booleans*, *Decimals* and *Doubles*, *Strings*, and arrays and blocks of *Bytes* and *Chars*. Curiously missing is an overload for *Date* values.

  The *BinaryReader* counterpart includes separate *Read* methods for each of the writable data types. The *ReadDouble* method returns a *Double* value from the stream, and there are similar methods for the other data types.

- **StreamReader** and **StreamWriter.** These classes are typically used to process line-based text files. The *StreamReader* class includes a *ReadLine* method that returns the next text line in the incoming stream as a standard *String*. The related *StreamWriter.Write* method includes all the overloads of *BinaryWriter.Write*, and also has a version that lets you format a string for output. The reader includes features that let you read data one character at a time, a block at a time, or an entire file at a time.

- **StringReader** and **StringWriter.** This pair of classes provides the same features as the *StreamReader* and *StreamWriter*, but uses a standard *String* instance for data storage instead of a true *Stream*.

There is one additional pair—*TextReader* and *TextWriter*—that provides the base class for the other non-binary readers and writers. You can't create instances of them directly, but they do let you treat the stream and string versions of the readers and writers generically.

15. FILES AND DIRECTORIES

With these new tools, it's easier to process non-*Byte* data through streams. Here's a rewrite of the simple memory stream code I wrote earlier, adjusted to use a *StreamReader* and *StreamWriter*.

```
' ----- The Stream, or There and Back Again.
Dim memStream As IO.MemoryStream
Dim forWriting As IO.StreamWriter
Dim forReading As IO.StreamReader
Dim finalMessage As String
Dim asUnicode As New System.Text.UnicodeEncoding()

' ----- Create a memory stream with room for 100 bytes.
memStream = New IO.MemoryStream(100)

Try
    ' ----- Wrap the stream with a writer.
    forWriting = New IO.StreamWriter(memStream, asUnicode)

    ' ----- Store the original data in the stream.
    forWriting.WriteLine( _
        "This is a test of the emergency programming system.")
    forWriting.Flush()

    ' ----- The position is at the end of the written data.
    '        To read it back, we must move the pointer to
    '        the start again.
    memStream.Seek(0, IO.SeekOrigin.Begin)

    ' ----- Create a reader to get the data back again.
    forReading = New IO.StreamReader(memStream, asUnicode)

    ' ----- Get the original string.
    finalMessage = forReading.ReadToEnd()

    ' ----- Prove that the text is back.
    MsgBox(finalMessage)
Finally
    memStream.Close()
End Try
```

That code sure is a lot nicer without all of that conversion code cluttering up the works. (It could be simplified even more by leaving out all of the optional Unicode encoding stuff.) Of course, everything is still being converted to bytes under the surface; the memory stream only knows about bytes. But *StreamWriter* and *StreamReader* take that burden away from us, performing all of the messy conversions on our behalf.

Reading a File via a Stream

Most *Stream* processing involves files, so let's use a *StreamReader* to process a text file. Although we already decided in Chapter 14, "Application Settings," that INI files are a thing of the past, it might be fun to write a routine that extracts a value from a legacy INI file. Consider a file containing this text.

```
[Section0]
Key1=abc
Key2=def

[Section1]
Key1=ghi
Key2=jkl

[Section2]
Key1=mno
Key2=pqr
```

Now there's something you don't see everyday, and with good reason! Still, if we wanted to get the value for *Key2* in section *Section1* (the "jkl" value), we would have to fall back on the *GetPrivateProfileString* API call from those bad old pre-.NET programming days. Or, we could implement a *StreamReader* in a custom function all our own.

```
Public Function GetINIValue(ByVal sectionName As String, _
    ByVal keyName As String, ByVal iniFile As String) _
    As String
' ----- Given a section and key name for an INI file,
'       return the matching value entry.
Dim readINI As IO.StreamReader
Dim oneLine As String
```

15. FILES AND DIRECTORIES

```
Dim compare As String
Dim found As Boolean

On Error GoTo ErrorHandler

' ----- Open the file.
If (My.Computer.FileSystem.FileExists(iniFile) = False) _
    Then Return ""
readINI = New IO.StreamReader(iniFile)

' ----- Look for the matching section.
found = False
compare = "[" & Trim(UCase(sectionName)) & "]"
Do While (readINI.EndOfStream = False)
    oneLine = readINI.ReadLine()
    If (Trim(UCase(oneLine)) = compare) Then
        ' ----- Found the matching section.
        found = True
        Exit Do
    End If
Loop

' ----- Exit early if the section name was not found.
If (found = False) Then
    readINI.Close()
    Return ""
End If

' ----- Look for the matching key.
compare = Trim(UCase(keyName))
Do While (readINI.EndOfStream = False)
    ' ----- If we reach another section, then the
    '       key wasn't there.
    oneLine = Trim(readINI.ReadLine())
    If (Len(oneLine) = 0) Then Continue Do
    If (oneLine.Substring(0, 1) = "[") Then Exit Do

    ' ----- Ignore lines without an "=" sign.
    If (InStr(oneLine, "=") = 0) Then Continue Do
```

```
' ----- See if we found the key. By the way, I'm
'         using Substring() instead of Left() so
'         I don't have to worry about conflicts with
'         Form.Left in case I drop this routine into
'         a Form class.
If (Trim(UCase(oneLine.Substring(0, _
        InStr(oneLine, "=") - 1))) = compare) Then
    ' ----- Found the matching key.
    readINI.Close()
    Return Trim(Mid(oneLine, InStr(oneLine, "=") + 1))
End If
Loop

' ----- If we got this far, then the key was missing.
readINI.Close()
Return ""

ErrorHandler:
    ' ----- Return an empty string on any error.
    On Error Resume Next
    If (readINI IsNot Nothing) Then readINI.Close()
    readINI = Nothing
    Return ""
End Function
```

This routine isn't an exact replacement for *GetPrivateProfileString*; it doesn't support a default return value, or perform file caching for speed. You could improve the routine with better error handling. But it does retrieve the value we seek, and it does it by reading the INI file one line at a time through a *StreamReader*.

```
MsgBox(GetINIValue("Section1", "Key2", iniFilePath))
    ' ----- Displays 'jkl'
```

File Management with the My Namespace

The *My* namespace includes several file management features in its *My.Computer.FileSystem* branch, including features that create streams for reading and writing.

My Namespace Versus Visual Basic Commands

Most of the *My.Computer.FileSystem* object's members exist to replace or supplement file management features already present in Visual Basic. Table 15-2 lists some of the long-standing file and directory interaction features in Visual Basic, and their equivalents in *My.Computer.FileSystem*.

Table 15-2 Two Ways of Doing the Same Thing

Visual Basic Feature	Purpose	My.Computer.FileSystem Equivalent
ChDir	Change the current "working" directory on a specified or default drive.	The *FileSystem.CurrentDirectory* property gets and sets the current "working" directory as understood by the application. You set the active directory through an absolute or relative path string.
ChDrive	Change the current "working" drive.	The *FileSystem.CurrentDirectory* property not only reports or changes the active directory; it also modifies the active drive.
CurDir	Identify the current "working" directory and drive as a full path string.	Once again, *FileSystem.CurrentDirectory* is the substitute for this Visual Basic directory feature. *CurDir* does have a little more flexibility; it allows you to determine the current directory on a drive other than the current drive. This can't be done with *FileSystem.CurrentDirectory*.
Dir	Retrieve files and directories in a parent directory that match a specific name pattern.	The *FileSystem.GetDirectories* and *FileSystem.GetFiles* methods both support wildcard patterns when retrieving matching directory and file names. *Dir* requires that you call it once for each entry to return, and it doesn't work well when processing nested directories. The *FileSystem* equivalents return collections of matching items, and can optionally descend the entire subdirectory tree of a base path.

Visual Basic Feature	Purpose	My.Computer.FileSystem Equivalent
FileCopy	Make a copy of a file.	The *FileSystem.CopyFile* provides a few additional user-friendly features beyond *FileCopy*. But what's the deal with the reversal of "File" and "Copy?"
FileDateTime	Retrieve the creation or modification date and time of a file.	Use the *FileSystem.GetFileInfo* method to retrieve a *FileInfo* object replete with details about a file. You'll probably focus on the *FileInfo.LastWriteTime* property, but you can also get the original creation time and the last access time, features not available through the lowly and now disgraced *FileDateTime* function.
FileLen	Retrieve the length, in bytes, of a file.	Obtain a *FileInfo* object through the *FileSystem.GetFileInfo* method, and access that object's *Length* property to get the file size in bytes.
GetAttr	Retrieve the attributes of a file as a bit field.	Get details on a file through the *FileSystem.GetFileInfo* method, and use the returned *FileInfo* object's *Attributes* property to examine your attribute of choice. This object also exposes an *IsReadOnly* Boolean value.
Kill	Delete a file or empty directory.	The *FileSystem.DeleteFile* and *FileSystem.DeleteDirectory* methods replace the *Kill* procedure, and provide additional options not available with *Kill*. Plus, you won't have the police knocking at your door asking why you constantly type *Kill, Kill, Kill*.
MkDir	Create a new directory.	The *FileSystem.CreateDirectory* method is a gentle replacement for *MkDir*. Anyway, "mkdir" is an old UNIX command, and you're not programming on UNIX, are you?

(continues)

Table 15-2 Two Ways of Doing the Same Thing *(continued)*

Visual Basic Feature	Purpose	My.Computer.FileSystem Equivalent
Rename	Change the name of a file or directory.	*Rename* is replaced by distinct *FileSystem.RenameFile* and *FileSystem.RenameDirectory* methods.
RmDir	Delete a directory, even if it contains files.	The *FileSystem.DeleteDirectory* deletes directories that still contain other files, an action that *RmDir* rejected. There's also an option to send the files to the Recycle Bin.
SetAttr	Modify the attributes of a file using a bit field.	Same process listed for *GetAttr* previously. The *FileInfo* object's *Attributes* and *IsReadOnly* properties are read/write values, assuming you have the necessary security rights to change attributes.

Why would Microsoft introduce so many new *My* features that duplicate existing Visual Basic features? Perhaps it's a way to bring consistency to file-based programming practices through a more object-oriented approach. Or maybe it's yet another move by Microsoft, the United States government, the Knights Templar, Burger King, and other groups set on world domination by controlling you, your family, and your community through the "hidden hand" of extra-long source code statements.

Reading and Writing Files Through My

The *My.Computer.FileSystem.OpenTextFileReader* and parallel *OpenTextFileWriter* methods provide shortcuts to the filename-based constructor for *StreamReader* and *StreamWriter* objects. This statement:

```
Dim inputStream As IO.StreamReader = _
   My.Computer.FileSystem.OpenTextFileReader( _
   fileNamePath)
```

is identical to:

```
Dim inputStream As New IO.StreamReader(fileNamePath)
```

For me, the second version is better due to its terse nature, but it's between you and your source code review team as to which one you will use.

If you want to load the entire contents of a file into either a *String* or a *Byte* array, there's no need to open a stream now that *My* includes the *My.Computer.FileSystem.ReadAllText* and related *ReadAllBytes* methods. This statement dumps the entire content of a file into a *String*.

```
Dim wholeFile As String = _
    My.Computer.FileSystem.ReadAllText( _
    fileNamePath)
```

The *My.Computer.FileSystem.WriteAllText* and *WriteAllBytes* methods do the same thing, but in the opposite direction. There's an *append* Boolean argument that lets you either append or replace the new content relative to any existing content in the file.

```
My.Computer.FileSystem.WriteAllText( _
    fileNamePath, dataToWrite, True)   ' True=append
```

One feature that has always been missing from Visual Basic is the ability to conveniently scan a delimited file (such as tab-delimited or comma-delimited) or a fixed-width-field file, and extract the fields on each line without a lot of extra parsing code. Visual Basic now includes the *Microsoft.VisualBasic.FileIO.TextFieldParser* object that simplifies this process. This object lets you indicate either a field delimiter (such as the tab character) or an array of column sizes. Once you associate it with a file path, it reads each data line, breaking up the distinct fields for you into a string array. The *My.Computer.FileSystem.OpenTextFieldParser* method opens the file and defines the parsing method in one fell swoop.

```
Dim dataFields() As String
Dim sourceFile As FileIO.TextFieldParser

' ----- Open the file with tab-delimited fields.
sourceFile = My.Computer.FileSystem.OpenTextFieldParser( _
    sourceFilePath, vbTab)
```

```
' ----- Process each line.
Do While Not sourceFile.EndOfData
   dataFields = sourceFile.ReadFields()
   ' ----- dataFields is a simple string array,
   '       so you can examine each field directly.
   If (dataFields(0) = "NEW") Then
   ' ----- and so on...
Loop
sourceFile.Close()
```

The *TextFieldParser* can also detect comment lines and ignore them silently. I am sure that it's using a *StreamReader* secretly hidden inside the object's black box. While the internals are hidden from view, the exposed features of this object make it a snap to process field-based text files.

Summary

Managing and manipulating files isn't brain surgery. But with the file system as a major focus of any operating system, tools and methods for reading and updating files just seem to multiply like rabbits. The .NET Framework uses the *Stream* as its primary file interaction method, so this should help make things simpler. Of course, it piles dozens of wrapper classes on top of the basic stream, but that's another issue.

As for the management of files and directories, .NET is going in the opposite direction, giving you more and more language and object features to perform the same basic tasks. Beyond the traditional Visual Basic and *My* namespace features introduced in this chapter, there are additional duplicate features in the .NET class libraries. Use the methods that meet your needs, and "file" the others away for future reference.

Project

I have some good news and some bad news. The bad news is that the Library Project does not make direct reads or writes of standard files, and has no need for file streams. That means we won't be adding any code to the project in this chapter at all. The good news is that we still have interesting things to talk about. Besides, I figured that since you had reached the half-way point of the book, you could use a break.

Project Access Chapter 15 does not include any project templates, so don't bother looking in Visual Studio for them.

Configuring Log Output

Whenever an error occurs in the Library application, the *GeneralError* routine first shows the error message to the user, and then logs it to any configured "log listeners."

```
Public Sub GeneralError(ByVal routineName As String, _
     ByVal theError As System.Exception)
  ' ----- Report an error to the user.
  On Error Resume Next

  MsgBox("The following error occurred at location '" & _
     routineName & "':" & vbCrLf & vbCrLf & _
     theError.Message, MsgBoxStyle.OkOnly Or _
     MsgBoxStyle.Exclamation, ProgramTitle)
  My.Application.Log.WriteException(theError)
End Sub
```

So, who's listening? If you are running the program within Visual Studio, Visual Basic always configures a log listener that displays the text in the *Immediate Window* panel. But that doesn't do much good in a compiled and deployed application.

You can design your own log listeners, but .NET also includes several predefined listeners, all of which can be enabled and configured through the application's *app.config* file. If you access the "After" version of the project in Chapter 14, you will find content in its *app.config* file that sets up one such listener. Here's a portion of that file, showing just the relevant sections.

```
<system.diagnostics>
  <sources>
    <!-- This section defines the logging configuration
        for My.Application.Log -->
    <source name="DefaultSource" switchName="DefaultSwitch">
      <listeners>
        <add name="FileLog"/>
      </listeners>
```

```
      </source>
   </sources>

   <switches>
     <add name="DefaultSwitch" value="Information" />
   </switches>

   <sharedListeners>
     <add name="FileLog" type=
➡        "Microsoft.VisualBasic.Logging.FileLogTraceListener,
➡        Microsoft.VisualBasic, Version=8.0.0.0, Culture=neutral,
➡        PublicKeyToken=b03f5f7f11d50a3a,
➡        processorArchitecture=MSIL"
➡        initializeData="FileLogWriter"/>
   </sharedListeners>
</system.diagnostics>
```

The <sharedListeners> section defines the details for a particular log listener. In this case, it's the *FileLogTraceListener* listener, a class in the *Microsoft.VisualBasic.Logging* namespace. It's enabled in the <source>/<listeners> section, where it's included through an <add> tag. There's a lot of stuff here that seems bizarre or extremely picky (such as the public key token). Fortunately, it's all documented in MSDN if you ever need the details.

The *FileLogTraceListener* listener sends relevant logging data to an application-specific log file. By default, the file resides in the following:

```
C:\Documents and Settings\username\Application Data\
➡  Company\Product\Version\AppName.log
```

The *username* part is replaced by the name of the current logged-in user. The *Company*, *Product*, and *Version* parts represent the company name, product name, and version number of your assembly as defined in its assembly attributes. *AppName* is the name of your application with the ".exe" extension stripped off. On my system, the log file for the Library Project appears here.

```
C:\Documents and Settings\username\Application Data\
➡  ACME\Library\1.0.0.0\Library.log
```

If you don't like that location, you can change the output to any location you choose. To do it, you'll need to alter the *<add>* tag in the *<sharedListeners>* section, adding two additional attributes to that tag.

```
<sharedListeners>
  <add name="FileLog" type=
➥    "Microsoft.VisualBasic.Logging.FileLogTraceListener,
➥    Microsoft.VisualBasic, Version=8.0.0.0, Culture=neutral,
➥    PublicKeyToken=b03f5f7f11d50a3a,
➥    processorArchitecture=MSIL"
➥    initializeData="FileLogWriter"
➥    location="Custom"
➥    customLocation="c:\temp\" />
</sharedListeners>
```

The new *location* and *customLocation* attributes do the trick. Set the *customLocation* attribute to the directory where the log file should go. These attributes link to properties of the same name in the *FileLogTraceListener* class. Visual Studio's documentation describes these properties and attributes, plus others that are available for you to configure through *app.config*.

This *app.config* change is based on an MSDN article named "How to: Write Event Information to a Text File" that you can search for in your online help. (Use the *Search* feature, not the *Index* feature.)

Other Log Output Options

Another MSDN article, "Walkthrough: Changing Where My.Application.Log Writes Information," describes how to send log output to more than just a simple text file. It discusses ways to log application information to the system Event Log, to a delimited file, to an XML-formatted file, and to the console display.

Some of the changes you need to make to the *app.config* file are, again, mysterious, so I'll just list them here for your examination. Add the following content to the *app.config* file to define the available listeners.

```
<add name="EventLog"
  type="System.Diagnostics.EventLogTraceListener,
➥    System, Version=2.0.0.0,
➥    Culture=neutral, PublicKeyToken=b77a5c561934e089"
```

```
➥     initializeData="sample application"/>

<add name="Delimited"
  type="System.Diagnostics.DelimitedListTraceListener,
➥     System, Version=2.0.0.0,
➥     Culture=neutral, PublicKeyToken=b77a5c561934e089"
➥     initializeData="c:\temp\SomeFile.txt"
➥     delimiter=";;;"
➥     traceOutputOptions="DateTime" />

<add name="XmlWriter"
  type="System.Diagnostics.XmlWriterTraceListener,
➥     System, Version=2.0.0.0,
➥     Culture=neutral, PublicKeyToken=b77a5c561934e089"
➥     initializeData="c:\temp\SomeFile.xml" />

<add name="Console"
  type="System.Diagnostics.ConsoleTraceListener,
➥     System, Version=2.0.0.0,
➥     Culture=neutral, PublicKeyToken=b77a5c561934e089"
➥     initializeData="true" />
```

The *initializeData* attribute in each entry contains the values sent to
the arguments of the relevant class constructor. Other attributes (except
for *type*) modify the properties of the same name in the class specified
through the *type* attribute. For all the options available to you for each listener, look up its class entry in the Visual Studio documentation.

To enable any of these listeners, use an *<add>* tag in the *<source>*/
<listeners> section. The following XML block enables all the listeners
defined in this chapter project.

```
<sources>
  <!-- This section defines the logging configuration
       for My.Application.Log -->
  <source name="DefaultSource" switchName="DefaultSwitch">
    <listeners>
      <add name="FileLog"/>
      <add name="EventLog" />
      <add name="Delimited" />
      <add name="XmlWriter" />
```

```
        <add name="Console" />
      </listeners>
    </source>
</sources>
```

Obtaining a Barcode Font

Because we have a little time left, let's talk about obtaining a barcode font. The Library Project will include barcode printing support, but only if you have a barcode font installed on your system. It's no emergency, but you should obtain one before you reach Chapter 17, "GDI+," where we develop the barcode configuration code.

When you downloaded the code for this book, it didn't include a barcode font. It's all due to licensing issues and the like, you understand. But barcode fonts are easy to get. You can purchase a professional barcode font if you want to, and if you plan on deploying this project into an actual library setting, you probably should. But if you're only reading this book for the great humor, you can download one of the many free barcode fonts available on the Internet. I've included some links to barcode font providers on the Web site where you obtained the source code for this book. Even if you don't plan on using the barcode printing features, I recommend that you download a free barcode font just so you can try out some of the Chapter 17 features.

Once you've installed the font, you will need to tell the Library program to use it. The settings form designed in the previous chapter included a selection field for this font. It's the **Barcode Font Name** field on the **System-Wide** tab of the *Maintenance* form. You can see it in the middle of Figure 14-6. I made it a system-wide setting because it seemed best to have all administrators in a single library using a common font.

If your font is a "Code 3 of 9" barcode font (also called "Code 39"), make sure you select the **Barcode is "Code 39" or "Code 3 of 9"** field on that same form. (The provider of the font will let you know if it is a Code 3 of 9 font or not.) These fonts require an asterisk before and after the barcode number. Selecting this field will cause the Library program to add the asterisk characters automatically.

Well, I'm getting tired of talking about files, be they fonts or config files. In the next chapter, we'll go back into the world of code and its fraternal twin, data.

CHAPTER 16

GENERICS

When I was in high school, my family sometimes shopped at a local grocery warehouse named *Fedmart*. Signs on the window clearly stated that there was "no connection between Fedmart and the Federal government," but people continued to shop there anyway. They had these small one-dollar frozen cheese pizzas that my mom would buy in bulk for me and my friends, teenage boys who didn't care much about what went down the esophagus.

Most of the store stocked the typical grocery products, but there was one aisle near the south border of the store that only sold "generic" products. Walking into this section was like walking into a black-and-white television; all of the product labels were plain clear or white, with simple black lettering. And they were cheap. They did the job, but just barely. You would never want to run out of name-brand ketchup in the middle of a celebratory barbeque with your friends, and offer up a bottle of generic ketchup as a replacement. Somehow I remember clearly reading the black lettering on the white label of that watery ketchup substitute, about how it met the requirements for federal ketchup standards. At that moment I had an epiphany, a sudden realization that would change the way I thought about life in these United States forever: The government has a federal ketchup standard!

Sadly, Fedmart closed down before I finished my senior year, leaving a vacuum in the generic ketchup and aluminum foil marketplace. But as a Visual Basic programmer, you can still gain access to generics, through .NET's generics technology. **Generics**—the ability to use placeholders for data types—is new in Visual Basic 2005 and the related .NET Framework 2.0. This chapter provides you with the "specifics" on generics.

What Are Generics?

In .NET, "generics" is a technology that lets you define data type place-holders within types or methods. Let's say you needed to define a class to track customer data, but you didn't want to enforce a specific format on the customer "ID" value. Part of your code needs to interact with customer objects using an *Integer* ID value, while another part of the code will use an alphanumeric key for the customer. You might ask, "Why don't you just include both types of identifiers as distinct fields in your customer record?" That wouldn't work because I am trying to come up with a reasonably simple example and answering that question would just distract me. So, here's the numeric version of the class.

```
Class CustomerWithNumberID
    Public ID As Integer
    Public FullName As String
End Class
```

Here's the variation that uses a string ID.

```
Class CustomerWithStringID
    Public ID As String
    Public FullName As String
End Class
```

Of course, you could define *ID* as *System.Object*, and stick anything you wanted in that field. But *System.Object* is considered "weakly typed," and there is nothing to stop you from mixing in *Integer* and *String* ID values for different instances in an array of customer objects.

What you want is a system that lets you define the class generically, and hold off on specifying the data type of *ID* until you actually create an instance of the class, or a complete collection of related class instances. With such a system, you could define a general-purpose version of the customer class.

```
Class CustomerWithSomeID
    Public ID As <DatatypePlaceholder>
    Public FullName As String
End Class
```

Later, when it was time to create an instance, you could tell the language which data type to use for the placeholder.

```
Dim oneCustomer As CustomerWithSomeID(replacing _
    <DatatypePlaceholder> with Integer)
```

This is what generics let you do. Here's the actual Visual Basic syntax that defines the non-specific customer class.

```
Class CustomerWithSomeID(Of T)
    Public ID As T
    Public FullName As String
End Class
```

The general placeholder, *T*, appears in a special *Of* clause, just after the class name. (You don't have to name the placeholder *T*, but it's become a tradition when presenting sample code using generics.) As a data type, *T* can be used anywhere within the class definition where you don't want to define the data type up front. The class, and its *ID* member, are now ready for instantiation with an actual replacement data type for *T*. To create a new instance, try this code:

```
Dim numberCustomer As CustomerWithSomeID(Of Integer)
```

By attaching "(Of Integer)" to the end of the class definition, Visual Basic acts as if you had actually declared a variable for a class that had an *Integer* member named *ID*. In fact, you did. When you create an instance of a generic class, the compiler defines a separate class that looks like a non-generic class with all of the placeholders replaced.

```
Dim customer1 As New CustomerWithSomeID(Of Integer)
Dim customer2 As New CustomerWithSomeID(Of Integer)
Dim customer3 As New CustomerWithSomeID(Of String)
```

These lines define two instances of *CustomerWithSomeID(Of Integer)*, and one instance of *CustomerWithSomeID(Of String)*. *customer1* and *customer2* are truly instances of the same data type, but *customer3* is an instance of a completely different data type. Assignments between *customer1* and *customer2* will work, but you can't mix either of them with *customer3* without performing an explicit conversion.

```
' ----- This works just fine.
customer1 = customer2

' ----- This will not compile.
customer3 = customer1
```

As true compile-time data types generated automatically by the compiler, they exhibit all of the personality of other non-generic classes. Even Visual Studio's *IntelliSense* properly detects the substituted data type. Figure 16-1 includes a tool tip, just to the right of the instance member selection list, which properly identifies the *customer1.ID* member as *Integer*.

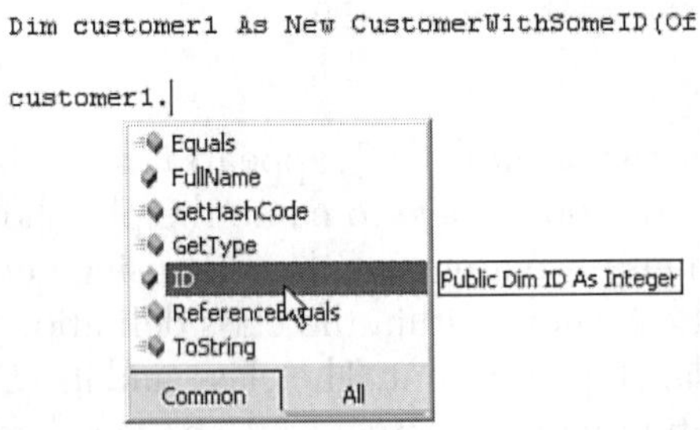

```
Dim customer1 As New CustomerWithSomeID(Of Integer)

customer1.|
```

Figure 16-1 Congratulations, Mr. and Mrs. Generic: It's an Integer.

Within the class definition, the *T* placeholder can appear anywhere, even within argument lists and local variable declarations.

```
Class SomeClass(Of T)
    Public Function TransformData(ByVal sourceData As T) As T
        ' ----- Add generic transformation code here.
        Dim workData As T
        ...
    End Function
End Class
```

Generics work with structures and interfaces as well.

```
Structure SomeStructure(Of T)
    Public GenericMember As T
End Structure

Interface ISomeInterface(Of T)
    Sub DoWorkWithData(ByVal theData As T)
End Interface
```

Variations of Generic Declaration

If there were a minimum federal government data type placeholder requirement, the implementation of generics just described would certainly meet it. It's kind of nice to postpone the definition of data types until the last minute. But .NET generics don't stop there.

Multiple Placeholders

Generic placeholders—also known as **type parameters**—are like those knives you buy on late-night TV. You don't get one; you get more! As many as you need, it turns out. Each generic class can include multiple placeholders by adding them to the initial *Of* clause.

```
Class MultiTypes(Of T1, T2)
    Public Member1 As T1
    Public Member2 As T2
End Class
```

As before, you aren't required to use the boring names *T1* and *T2*. Whatever names you choose, include them as a comma-separated list just after the *Of* keyword. When you're ready to create an instance, replicate the comma-delimited list in the same order, but using actual types. In this statement, *Integer* replaces *T1*, while *String* replaces *T2*.

```
Dim useInstance As MultiTypes(Of Integer, String)
```

Data Type and Interface Constraints

The type parameters you included in a generic, such as *T*, accept any valid data type, including *Integer, String, System.Windows.Forms.Form*, or your own custom types. That is, *T* can be replaced by anything that derives from *System.Object*, which is everything. You can even imagine the statement:

```
Class SomeClass(Of T)
```

being replaced by:

```
Class SomeClass(Of T As System.Object)
```

adding the *As* clause to make it look like other Visual Basic declarations. Well, you can stop imagining and start acting: Placeholders support the *As* clause. If you don't include an *As* clause, Visual Basic assumes you mean *As System.Object*, but you can follow *As* with any type you want.

```
Class FormOnlyClass(Of T As System.Windows.Forms.Form)
```

By adding a specific class with the *As* clause, you enforce a **constraint** on the generic type, a limitation that must be met to use the type. In this case, the constraint says, "You may supply any class value for *T* as long as **it is or it derives from** *System.Windows.Forms.Form*. This means you can create an instance of *FormOnlyClass* using one of your application's forms, but not using non-Form classes.

```
' ----- This works.
Dim usingForm As FormOnlyClass(Of Form1)
```

```
' ----- This doesn't work.
Dim usingForm As FormOnlyClass(Of Integer)
```

When you add a constraint to a type parameter, it impacts the features you can use with that type parameter. Consider this generic class destined to work with forms, but not declared that way.

```
Class WorkWithForms(Of T)
    Public Sub ChangeCaption(ByVal whichForm As T, _
        ByVal newCaption As String)
        ' ----- The following line will not compile.
        whichForm.Text = newCaption
    End Sub
End Class
```

In this class, the assignment to *whichForm.Text* will fail because the *WorkWithForms* class does not know that you plan to use it with forms. It only knows that you plan to use *T*, and *T* is, by default, of type *System.Object*. There's no *Text* property in the *System.Object* class; I checked.

If we change the definition of *WorkWithForms* to accept *Form* objects, the outlook for compiling this code changes dramatically.

```
Class WorkWithForms(Of T As Windows.Forms.Form)
    Public Sub ChangeCaption(ByVal whichForm As T, _
        ByVal newCaption As String)
```

```
      ' ----- Yes! It now compiles.
      whichForm.Text = newCaption
    End Sub
End Class
```

Becaue *T* has to be a *Form* type or something derived from *Form*, Visual Basic knows that all the members of the *Form* class, including *Text*, are available to all things *T*. Therefore, the assignment to *whichForm.Text* works.

In addition to classes, you can also use interfaces to constrain your generic types.

```
Class ThrowAwayClass(Of T As IDisposable)
```

Instances of *ThrowAwayClass* can be created as needed, but only if the type supplied with the declaration implements the *IDisposable* interface.

```
' ----- This works. Pens use IDisposable.
Dim disposablePen As ThrowAwayClass(Of System.Drawing.Pen)

' ----- This doesn't work, since the Integer data type
'       doesn't implement IDisposable.
Dim disposableNumber As ThrowAwayClass(Of Integer)
```

But wait, there's more! See, I told you it was like shopping for knives on TV. Besides your run-of-the-mill types and interfaces, you can also follow the *As* clause on the generic placeholder with the *New* keyword.

```
Class SomeClass(Of T As New)
```

The *As New* clause says to the generic type, "Accept any type for *T*, but only if that type includes a constructor that requires no arguments." That is, *T* must include a default constructor. Once defined, you'll be able to create new instances of *T*—whatever type it actually turns out to be—in your generic type.

```
Class SomeClass(Of T As New)
   Public Sub SomeSub()
      Dim someVariable As New T
   End Sub
End Class
```

If your generic class includes multiple type parameters, each parameter can include its own *As* class with a distinct type or interface constraint.

Simultaneous Constraints

It's nice that each of those knives you purchased can slice a watermelon, but what if you want to chop wood with that same knife, or use it to upgrade that electrical work you've been postponing? You're looking for a multi-functional tool, just like you find in each generic placeholder. If you need one placeholder to include a constraint for a specific class, an interface, and "New" all at once, you can do it. After the *As* keyword, include the multiple constraints in curly braces.

```
Class SomeClass(Of T As {Windows.Forms.Form, _
    IDisposable, New})
```

Now, any type you supply in the *Of* clause when creating an instance of this class **must meet all of the constraints**, not just one of them. And here's something new: You can include more than one interface constraint at a time.

```
Class SomeClass(Of T As {ISerializable, IDisposable})
```

And you can still include a class constraint and the *New* constraint, even with those multiple interfaces. (You can't include more than one class constraint for a single placeholder.) If your generic type includes multiple type parameters, each of them can have their own multiple constraints set.

Nesting Generic Types

Generic types can include their own nested types.

```
Class Level1(Of T1)
    Public Level1Member As T1
    Class Level2(Of T2)
        Public Level2Member1 As T1
        Public Level2Member2 As T2
    End Class
End Class
```

You can nest the generics as deeply as you need.

Non-Generic Types with Generic Members

If generic types seem a little scary or overwhelming, don't fret. You don't have to create a full generic type to use the new generic features. You can add generic support to just a single method within an otherwise normal class.

```
Class SomeClass
    ' ----- The class itself does not have the generic
    '       Of clause, so it's not generic. But...

    Public Shared Sub ReverseValues(Of T) _
          (ByRef first As T, ByRef second As T)
        ' ----- This method is generic with its own Of clause.

        ' ----- Reverse the contents of two variables.
        Dim holdFirst As T

        holdFirst = first
        first = second
        second = holdFirst
    End Sub
End Class
```

Generic methods are useful when you need to have a local variable of the placeholder's type within the method (as is done with *holdFirst* here), but you don't know the type in advance. Using this shared *ReverseValues* method works like any other method, with the extra *Of* clause stuck in.

```
Dim x As Integer = 5
Dim y As Integer = 10
SomeClass.ReverseValues(Of Integer)(x, y)
MsgBox(x)   ' Displays 10
```

If you will be using the placeholder for one or more of the method arguments, Visual Basic will infer the type based on the passed value. If Visual Basic is able to guess the type in this way, you don't even need the *Of* clause when calling the generic method.

```
SomeClass.ReverseValues(x, y)
```

As with generic types, generic methods allow you to add constraints to the placeholders.

Overloading Generic Types and Members

Earlier I mentioned how the compiler essentially creates separate classes for each instance variation of a generic class that you create. This means that these two instances actually use completely different and generally unrelated classes.

```
Dim numberVersion As SomeClass(Of Integer)
Dim textVersion As SomeClass(Of String)
```

So *SomeClass(Of Integer)* and *SomeClass(Of String)* are completely different classes, even though they have the same base name. In a way, Visual Basic is *overloading* the class name for you, letting you use it in two (or more) different ways.

Generics also let you get involved in the class-overloading game. Normally, you can only create a single class with a given name (inside of a particular namespace, that is). But with generics, you can reuse a class name, as long as the placeholders used among the classes are different enough, either in their number or in their applied constraints.

```
Class SomeClass(Of T1)
   ' ----- This is a generic class with one placeholder.
End Class

Class SomeClass(Of T1, T2)
   ' ----- This is a completely different generic
   '       class with two placeholders.
End Class
```

Visual Basic will figure out which version to use based on the *Of* clause you include with the instance declaration.

```
Dim simpleVersion As SomeClass(Integer)
Dim complexVersion As SomeClass(Integer, String)
```

Generics and Collections

Generics really shine in the area of collections. The initial release of .NET had, among the thousands of possibly useful classes, a set of "collection" classes, all in the *System.Collections* namespace. Each collection lets you stuff as many other object instances as you want inside of that collection, and retrieve them later. The collections differ in how you stuff and retrieve, but they all allow you to stick any type of object in the collection.

One of the collection classes is the *System.Collections.Stack* class. Stacks let you store objects like pancakes: the first object you add to the stack goes on the bottom, and each one you add goes on top of the previous object. When you're ready to eat a pancake—I mean, remove an item—it comes off the top. The *Push* and *Pop* methods manage the addition and removal of objects. (There is also a *Peek* method that looks at the top-most item, but doesn't remove it from the stack.)

```
Dim numberStack As New Collections.Stack
numberStack.Push(10)
numberStack.Push(20)
numberStack.Push(30)
MsgBox(numberStack.Pop())    ' Displays 30
MsgBox(numberStack.Pop())    ' Displays 20
MsgBox(numberStack.Pop())    ' Displays 10
```

The thing with stacks (and other similar collections) is that you don't have to put just one type of object into the stack. You can mix any ol' type of objects you want.

```
Dim numberStack As New Collections.Stack
numberStack.Push(10)                    ' Integer
numberStack.Push("I'm sneaking in.")    ' String
numberStack.Push(Me.Button1)            ' Control
```

The stack doesn't care, because it's just treating everything as *System.Object*. But what if you needed to ensure that **only integers** were put into the stack? What if you wanted to limit a stack to any specific data type, but didn't want to write separate stack classes for each possible type?

This sure sounds like a job for generics to me. It sounded that way to Microsoft, too. So they added a bunch of new generic collections to the Framework. They appear in the *System.Collections.Generic* namespace. There are a few different classes in this namespace, including classes for linked lists, queues, chocolate chip cookies, and dictionaries. And hey, there's a class called *Stack(Of T)*. That's just what we need.

```
Dim numberStack As New Collections.Generic.Stack(Of Integer)
numberStack.Push(10)
numberStack.Push(20)
numberStack.Push(30)
```

Now, if we try to add anything other than an *Integer* to *numberStack*, an error occurs.

```
' ----- This won't work.
numberStack.Push("I'll try again.")
```

Summary

Adding generics to .NET development is really the next logical step in providing a flexible and general use programming system. You always had the ability to use placeholders for data—they're called *variables*. Generics provide that same placeholder functionality, but with data types instead of just plain data.

When you control all development aspects of an application, you might think that generics aren't for you. After all, you're not going to let an *Integer* variable slip into a collection of dates. But they are quite handy for enforcing standards within your code, which is always good.

Project

This chapter's project code adds two major features to the application. The first task adds holidays to the system. When a patron checks out a book or other library item, the due date is automatically calculated based on a number of days stored in the *CodeMediaType.CheckoutDays* database field. But what happens if that calculated date is a holiday, and the library is closed? The patron might not be able to return the book until the next day, and would incur a fine. This fine, though small, could start a chain reaction in the patron's life that would lead to poverty, despair, and an addiction to soap operas. Fortunately, this can all be avoided by adding a list of holidays to the project. If an item's return date falls on a documented holiday, the program adjusts the date forward until it finds a non-holiday date.

In the second part of the project code, we finally add what many consider to be the heart of a library system: the lookup of books and other library items by patrons.

Project Access Load the "Chapter 16 (Before) Code" project, either through the New Project templates, or by accessing the project directly from the installation directory. To see the code in its final form, load "Chapter 16 (After) Code" instead.

Managing Holidays

As a small, stand-alone application that fully manages its own data, there isn't necessarily a pressing need for generics in the Library application. However, generics provide more advantages than just limiting the types of data stored in a class or collection. They also enhance data conversion and *IntelliSense* support, because Visual Basic can tell immediately, for instance, what type of data will appear in a collection.

We'll store all holidays managed by the Library Project in the *Holiday* database table. The contents of this table will seldom change, and will be frequently accessed during the checkout process. To speed things up, we'll cache the data inside of the application. And to simplify management of that cache, we'll store the holidays in a generic collection.

First, let's create the class that holds a single holiday entry. Add a new class to the project through the **Project ➤ Add Class** menu command, and give it the name *HolidaySet.vb*. The familiar structure of an empty class appears.

```
Public Class HolidaySet

End Class
```

The *Holiday* database table includes two main fields used in calculating holidays: *EntryType* and *EntryDetail*. Let's store these as members of the class, and add a flag that ensures the entry is valid.

Insert Snippet Insert Chapter 16, Snippet Item 1.

```
Private HolidayType As String
Private HolidayDetail As String
Private IsValid As Boolean
```

We'll populate these private members through the class constructor.

Insert Snippet Insert Chapter 16, Snippet Item 2.

```
Public Sub New(ByVal entryType As String, _
     ByVal entryDetail As String)
   ' ----- Create a new holiday entry instance.
   HolidayType = Left(Trim(UCase(entryType)), 1)
   HolidayDetail = entryDetail

   ' ----- See if the details are valid.
   IsValid = True
   Select Case HolidayType
      Case "A"
         ' ----- The detail should be in mm/dd format.
         IsValid = IsDate(entryDetail & "/2004")
      Case "E"
         ' ----- The detail is a number from 1 to 7.
         If (Val(entryDetail) < 1) Or _
            (Val(entryDetail) > 7) Then IsValid = False
      Case "O"
         ' ----- The detail should be a valid date.
         IsValid = IsDate(entryDetail)
      Case Else
         ' ---- Invalid. This should never happen.
         IsValid = False
   End Select
End Sub
```

Clearly, the holiday entries have a coding system all their own, and it wouldn't be fair to force code elsewhere in the application to deal with all of the complexities of holiday date comparisons. So let's add a public method to the class that indicates whether or not a given date matches the holiday stored in an instance.

Insert Snippet Insert Chapter 16, Snippet Item 3.

```
Public Function IsHoliday(ByVal whatDate As Date) As Boolean
   ' ----- Given a date, see if it matches the entry
   '       type in this instance.
   Dim buildDate As String

   ' ----- If this record is invalid, then it is never a
   '       holiday match.
   If (IsValid = False) Then Return False

   Select Case HolidayType
      Case "A"
         ' ----- Annual.
         buildDate = HolidayDetail & "/" & Year(whatDate)
         If (IsDate(buildDate)) Then
            Return CBool(CDate(buildDate) = whatDate)
         Else
            ' ----- Must be 2/29 on a non-leap-year.
            Return False
         End If
      Case "E"
         ' ----- Day of the week.
         Return CBool(Val(HolidayDetail) = _
            Weekday(whatDate, FirstDayOfWeek.Sunday))
      Case "O"
         ' ----- See if this is an exact one-time match.
         Return CBool(CDate(HolidayDetail) = whatDate)
   End Select
End Function
```

We're done with that class. Now we just need a place to keep our cached holiday records. The *System.Collections.Generic* namespace includes a few different collection classes that we could use. Because the only thing we really need to do with the holidays once they are in the collection is scan through them, looking for matches, the standard no-frills list seems best. Its class name is *List(Of T)*, and its primary feature, according to the .NET documentation, is that it lets you access members by index. That's fine.

Open up the *General.vb* file and find where the global variables appear, somewhere near the top. Then add a definition for the global collection that will store all of the holidays.

Insert Snippet Insert Chapter 16, Snippet Item 4.

```
Public AllHolidays As Collections.Generic.List( _
   Of Library.HolidaySet)
```

There it is! There it is! The *Of* clause. This is a generic collection. Yeah! Okay, party's over; let's move on.

Locate the *InitializeSystem* method, still in the *General.vb* file, and add the code that will initialize the global holiday cache.

Insert Snippet Insert Chapter 16, Snippet Item 5.

```
AllHolidays = New Collections.Generic.List(Of HolidaySet)
```

That's it for infrastructure. Let's add some routines that access this generic list. We need a routine that will tell us, *True* or *False*, whether a given date (the planned due date of a library item) matches any of the holidays or not. Add the function *IsHolidayDate* to *General.vb*.

Insert Snippet Insert Chapter 16, Snippet Item 6.

```
Public Function IsHolidayDate(ByVal whatDate As Date) _
     As Boolean
   ' ----- See if the given date is a holiday.
   Dim oneHoliday As Library.HolidaySet

   ' ----- Scan through the holidays, looking for a match.
   For Each oneHoliday In AllHolidays
      If (oneHoliday.IsHoliday(whatDate)) Then Return True
   Next oneHoliday

   ' ----- Not a holiday.
   Return False
End Function
```

This routine, *IsHolidayDate*, shows where generics really come in handy. It's all in the *For Each* statement that the magic occurs. In a normal collection, we wouldn't be sure what type of items were stored in the collection, be they *HolidaySet* or *String* or *Integer*. Well, *we* would know because *we* are the developer, but Visual Basic plays dumb in this area, and assumes you mixed up the data types in one collection.

But because we tied the *AllHolidays* collection to the *HolidaySet* class using the *Of HolidaySet* clause, Visual Basic now understands that we are only going to store items of *HolidaySet* in the *AllHolidays* collection. That means that we don't have to explicitly convert items retrieved from the collection to the *HolidaySet* data type. If we weren't using a generic class, the code would look something like this.

```
Dim scanHoliday As System.Object
Dim oneHoliday As Library.HolidaySet

For Each scanHoliday In AllHolidays
    oneHoliday = CType(scanHoliday, Library.HolidaySet)
    If (oneHoliday.IsHoliday(whatDate)) Then Return True
Loop
```

Because non-generic collections boil everything down to *System.Object*, we would have to explicitly convert each collection object to *HolidaySet* using *CType* or similar conversion function. But with a generic collection, Visual Basic takes care of it for us.

We still need to cache the holidays from the database, so add a *RefreshHolidays* method to *General.vb* that does this.

Insert Snippet Insert Chapter 16, Snippet Item 7.

```
Public Sub RefreshHolidays()
    ' ----- Load in the list of holidays.
    Dim sqlText As String
    Dim dbInfo As SqlClient.SqlDataReader
    Dim newHoliday As Library.HolidaySet

    On Error GoTo ErrorHandler
```

```
' ----- Clear the current list of holidays.
AllHolidays.Clear()

' ----- Get the holidays from the database.
sqlText = "SELECT * FROM Holiday"
dbInfo = CreateReader(sqlText)
Do While dbInfo.Read
   newHoliday = New Library.HolidaySet( _
      CStr(dbInfo!EntryType), CStr(dbInfo!EntryDetail))
   AllHolidays.Add(newHoliday)
Loop
dbInfo.Close()
Return

ErrorHandler:
   GeneralError("RefreshHolidays", Err.GetException())
   On Error Resume Next
   If Not (dbInfo Is Nothing) Then _
      dbInfo.Close() : dbInfo = Nothing
   Return
End Sub
```

You've seen a lot of code like this already, code that loads records from a database table into the program. I won't sport with your intelligence by explaining it to you line by line.

There are two places where we need to call *RefreshHolidays*: when the program first starts up, and later whenever changes are made to the list of holidays. We won't worry about other users changing the list; we'll just focus on when the local application updates the list. First, open the sometimes-hidden *ApplicationEvents.vb* file, and add this code to the *MyApplication_Startup* event handler, just after the existing call to *LoadDatabaseSettings()*.

Insert Snippet Insert Chapter 16, Snippet Item 8.

```
RefreshHolidays()
```

One down, and one to go. Open the *MainForm.vb* file, and locate the *AdminLinkHolidays_LinkClicked* event handler. This is the handler that lets the user edit the list of holidays. Add the same *RefreshHolidays()* line to the end of this routine.

Insert Snippet Insert Chapter 16, Snippet Item 9.

```
' ----- Reload the holidays if they changed.
RefreshHolidays()
```

As you can see right in this routine, we already added the editor to manage the list of holidays. The only thing left to do is to actually access the holiday list when checking out items. We'll do that in a future chapter.

Looking Up Library Items

When we built the main Library form back in Chapter 7, "Windows Forms," we included fields that allowed a patron to search for library items. But that's about all we did; we didn't enable the fields or make them usable. We also didn't include any place to display a list of matching items. Let's complete those components in this chapter. We'll start with the matching items list.

I've added a form to the project named *ItemLookup.vb* that displays the results of a search for library items. It includes a few buttons at the top of the form, and three main display panels.

1. **PanelMatches.** Contains a large list box that displays non-item matches. For instance, it displays a list of matching author or publisher names as searched for by the patron. When this panel appears, the patron selects a match from the *MatchingGeneral* list, and clicks the *Lookup* button to display items tied to that selected author, publisher, or other entry.
2. **PanelItems.** Contains a large list box that displays items from the *NamedItem* database table. That is, it displays a list of library items matching some criteria. Selecting an item from the *MatchingItems* list and clicking the *Lookup* button displays the details of that item.
3. **PanelOneItem.** Contains a *WebBrowser* control that displays details about a single library item. The detail content is built using standard HTML, and may contain links that return you to the *PanelItems* panel with a new set of matching items displayed. For instance, if you are viewing the details of an award-winning (one can hope) Visual Basic 2005 programming book and click on the publisher name for that item, the *PanelItems* panel appears, listing all items made by that publisher.

The form also includes a set of *Back* buttons (in the upper-left corner) that work like the Back button in your web browser, a *Close* button that returns to the main form, and a menu (*BackMenu*), used to support the *Back* button feature. Figure 16-2 shows the form with the *PanelItems* panel out in front, since it looks a little more interesting than the other two panels.

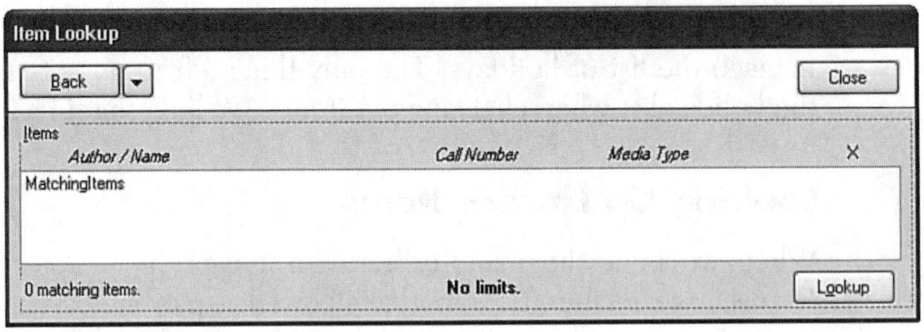

Figure 16-2 The panel of matching items, with column headings

The associated source code weighs in at around 1,000 lines, much of it focused on filling in the two list boxes and the HTML detail content. The search performed on the main form calls into this lookup form through the *InitiateSearch* method. The actual database search for matching items occurs in the *PerformLookup* method, which is called by *InitiateSearch*. *PerformLookup* includes distinct SQL queries for each type of search: title, author, subject, keyword, publisher, series, barcode, and some ID number searches, mostly for internal use. The type of search performed determines which of the three panels gets displayed (via the *resultType* variable). An author search displays *PanelMatches* with a list of matching author names; a title lookup displays matching items on the *PanelItems* panel. Here's the code that performs a lookup by publisher name based on a patron-supplied *searchText*.

```
sqlText = Trim(searchText)
If (InStr(sqlText, "*") = 0) Then sqlText &= "*"
sqlText = Replace(sqlText, "*", "%")
sqlText = "SELECT ID, FullName FROM Publisher " & _
    "WHERE FullName LIKE " & DBText(sqlText) & _
    " ORDER BY FullName"
resultType = "M"
```

This code ensures that a wildcard character appears somewhere within the search text; if the user doesn't supply it, the code appends one to the end of *searchText*. Recall that SQL Server uses the percent (%) character for its wildcard, although the program lets the user enter the more familiar asterisk (*) character.

After processing this query through a data reader, the *resultType* = *"M"* flag moves the code to fill in the *MatchingGeneral* list.

```
MatchingGeneral.Items.Clear()
Do While dbInfo.Read
    ' ----- General list item.
    MatchingGeneral.Items.Add(New ListItemData( _
        CStr(dbInfo!FullName), CInt(dbInfo!ID)))
Loop
```

This is just more of the same code you've seen in previous chapters. It loads the *ListBox* control with *ListItemData* objects, each containing a display name and an ID number from the database. That's fine for a list with simple display requirements. But if you look back to Figure 16-2, it's clear we want something a little more interesting for the list of matching items. We want columns, and columns require reasonable data for each column.

To store this data, we'll make up a new class, called *MatchingItemData*, which works just like *ListItemData*, but has more data fields.

```
Private Class MatchingItemData
    Public ItemID As Integer   ' NamedItem.ID
    Public Title As String
    Public Subtitle As String
    Public Author As String
    Public MediaType As String
    Public CallNumber As String

    Public Overrides Function ToString() As String
        ' ----- Build a simple display string.
        If (Subtitle = "") Then
            Return Title & ", by " & Author
        Else
            Return Title & ": " & Subtitle & ", by " & Author
        End If
    End Function
End Class
```

Because this class will be used only to display matching items on this form, I've made it a subordinate class within the larger *ItemLookup* form class. The *ToString* method outputs the text that appears in the list. We won't generate the actual columnar output until the next chapter. For now, we'll just display the title and author.

The *PanelMatches* and *PanelItems* panels each include a *Lookup* button that initiates a new call to *PerformLookup* based on the item selected in the list. The *Lookup* button on the *PanelItems* panel retrieves the selected *MatchingItemData* object from the list, and performs the new search.

```
Private Sub ActItemLookup_Click( _
    ByVal sender As System.Object, _
    ByVal e As System.EventArgs) _
    Handles ActItemLookup.Click
   ' ----- Look up the item with the selected ID.
   Dim itemID As Integer

   ' ----- Ignore if no match is selected.
   If (MatchingItems.SelectedIndex = -1) Then Return
   itemID = CType(MatchingItems.SelectedItem, _
      MatchingItemData).ItemID

   ' ----- Perform the lookup.
   If (PerformLookup(LookupMethods.ByDatabaseID, _
      CStr(itemID), False) = False) Then Return

   ' ----- Store the history.
   AddLookupHistory(LookupMethods.ByDatabaseID, CStr(itemID))
End Sub
```

The call to *PerformLookup* starts the process all over again.

Maintaining Search History

Let's say you have a patron with a lot of time on his hands, and he wants to look up the book *War and Peace*.

- Starting from *InitiateSearch* and moving on to the *PerformLookup* code, the initial title search ("War and Peace") displays a list of matching titles on the *PanelItems* panel.
- The patron locates the book in this list, and clicks the *Lookup* button, which calls the *ActItemLookup_Click* event handler.

- This event handler in turn calls *PerformLookup* again, this time doing a precise lookup based on a database ID within the *NamedItem* table.
- The detail of the item appears on the *PanelOneItem* panel. (I'll discuss how it's done later in this chapter.)
- The detail includes a link to "Tolstoy, Leo," the long-suffering author of the book. When the patron clicks on this link, it initiates another call to *PerformLookup*, this time by author ID.
- We're back to the *PanelItems* panel, viewing a list of books and other items by Tolstoy, assuming he had time to write anything else.

So the patron now has an experience with three search panels: (1) titles matching the name "War and Peace;" (2) the detail for the selected "War and Peace" item; and (3) items written by Leo Tolstoy. The history feature included in this form lets the patron return to any previous search page, just like the feature in your web browser.

It's possible that some of the searches performed could return hundreds of results. We don't want to store all of that content in memory, because it's possible the patron will never use the *Back* button. Instead, we will do just what your web browser does: store the minimum information needed to perform the query again. Your web browser maintains just the name and URL of visited paths in its "back" list. (File and image caching is not part of the history feature.) The *ItemLookup.vb* form needs to store only those values needed by *PerformLookup* to do the search again: the type of search, and the numeric or text criteria used in the search.

Patron history is accessed on a "last in, first out" basis. The most recent page viewed is the one the patron wants to see first when using the *Back* button. We discussed just such a last-in, first-out, or LIFO, structure earlier in this chapter: the stack. Each time the user views a panel, we'll make note of it, *pushing* just those values we will need later onto the stack. Later, when the user wants to view history, we will *pop* the most recent panel off the stack and update the display.

The *ItemLookupHistory* class, another subordinate class within the *ItemLookup* class, stores the values we need to manage history in the stack.

```
Private Class ItemLookupHistory
    Public HistoryDisplay As String
    Public LookupType As Library.LookupMethods
    Public LookupData As String
End Class
```

16. GENERICS

HistoryDisplay provides a short display name to help the user scan through history. *LookupType* and *LookupData* are the values that get passed to *PerformLookup*. It's all nice and neat. To make things even neater, we'll use a generic stack for actual storage. It's declared as a field of the *ItemLookup* class.

```
Private LookupHistorySet As _
    Collections.Generic.Stack(Of ItemLookupHistory)
```

As the patron visits each panel, calls to the *AddLookupHistory* method populate the stack with each new visited item.

```
Private Sub AddLookupHistory( _
    ByVal searchType As Library.LookupMethods, _
    ByVal searchText As String)
' ----- Add an item to the lookup history.
Dim newHistory As ItemLookupHistory
Dim displayText As String

' ----- Build the text for display in the new item.
displayText = BuildDisplayText(searchType, searchText)

' ----- Build the new history item.
newHistory = New ItemLookupHistory
newHistory.LookupType = searchType
newHistory.LookupData = searchText
newHistory.HistoryDisplay = displayText
LookupHistorySet.Push(newHistory)

' ----- Update the back button.
RefreshBackButtons()
End Sub
```

Later, when the patron clicks one of the *Back* buttons, the *BackMenuItems_Click* event handler examines the history stack, and calls *PerformLookup* as needed. And because we stored the *ItemLookupHistory* objects in a generic stack, we don't have to specifically convert them from *System.Object*; the program just knows what data type they are.

```
Private Sub BackMenuItems_Click( _
     ByVal sender As System.Object, _
     ByVal e As System.EventArgs) _
     Handles BackMenu1.Click, ..., BackMenu10.Click
   ' ----- One of the back menu items was clicked.
   Dim whichItem As Integer
   Dim counter As Integer
   Dim scanHistory As ItemLookupHistory

   ' ----- Determine the clicked item.
   whichItem = CInt(DigitsOnly(CType(sender, _
      System.Windows.Forms.ToolStripMenuItem).Name))
   If (whichItem >= LookupHistorySet.Count) Then Return

   ' ----- Get rid of the in-between items.
   For counter = 1 To whichItem
      LookupHistorySet.Pop()
   Next counter

   ' ----- Perform a lookup as requested.
   scanHistory = LookupHistorySet.Peek
   If (PerformLookup(scanHistory.LookupType, _
      scanHistory.LookupData, False) = False) Then Return
   RefreshBackButtons()
End Sub
```

Showing Item Detail

The *BuildHTMLAndLinks* function builds the HTML content that appears on the *PanelOneItem* panel. This panel includes *SingleItemDetail*, a *WebBrowser* control included with .NET. It's basically a version of Internet Explorer that you embed in your applications. Normally, you supply it with a URL to display, but you can also provide custom content through the control's *DocumentText* property. The *resultType* = "S" branch of the *PerformLookup* method assigns this property with content returned from *BuildHTMLAndLinks*.

```
SingleItemDetail.DocumentText = BuildHTMLAndLinks(itemID)
```

The content supplied by this routine is standard HTML, but with some specially crafted links that let the library program perform additional lookups based on the details of the displayed library item.

Most of the HTML is boilerplate, and it seems a shame to waste brain cells doing string concatenation just to include it. So instead, I stored much of the HTML as a text file resource through the *Resources* panel of the project properties. On that panel, I clicked the *Add Resource* button, selected *Add New Text File* (see Figure 16-3), and gave it the name *ItemLookupBody*.

Figure 16-3 Adding a new text file resource

In the text editor window that appeared, I added the following HTML content.

```
<html>
<head>
<style type="text/css">
body { font-family: "Arial"; }
h1 { font-family: "Arial"; margin-top: 0px;
    margin-bottom: 0px; font-size: 18pt; font-weight: bold; }
h2 { font-family: "Arial"; margin-top: 20px;
    margin-bottom: 0px; font-size: 15pt; font-weight: normal; }
h3 { font-family: "Arial"; margin-top: 0px;
    margin-bottom: 0px; font-size: 15pt; font-weight: normal;\
    font-style: italic;   }
p { margin-top: 2px; margin-bottom: 2px;
    margin-left: 15px; font-family: "Arial"; font-size: 12pt; }
table { border: solid black 1px; margin-left: 15px; }
th { border: solid black 1px; background-color: black;
    color: white; white-space: nowrap; text-align: left; }
```

```
td { border: solid black 1px; white-space: nowrap; }
a:visited { color: blue; }
</style>
</head>
<body>
```

If you're familiar with HTML, you recognize most of the content as an embedded Cascading Style Sheet. Its various formatting rules will bring a specific and consistent look and feel to the browser content that appears within the item lookup form. This is not a book on Cascading Style Sheets, but there are some good books at your local bookstore that can talk you through the rules and syntax if you're interested.

You can find the HTML content portion in the *Solution Explorer*, within the *Resources* branch. You've probably already noticed that the closing `</body>` and `</html>` tags aren't included. We'll attach those in the *BuildHTMLAndLinks* method. Because string concatenation is notoriously slow, I choose to use a *StringBuilder* class, a special string-like class that is custom designed for speed when repeatedly adding content to a base string. You attach content to the end of the *StringBuilder* using its *Append* and *AppendLine* methods, and retrieve the entire string through the standard *ToString* method.

We'll begin the content with the boilerplate HTML listed previously. Because we added it as a resource, it already appears in the *My.Resources* object under the name we gave it.

```
Dim detailBody As New System.Text.StringBuilder
detailBody.Append(My.Resources.ItemLookupBody)
```

Most of the code adds plain text to the *detailBody* string builder using its *AppendLine* method. Here's the code that adds the main book title.

```
sqlText = "SELECT Title, Subtitle FROM NamedItem " & _
   "WHERE ID = " & itemID
dbInfo = CreateReader(sqlText)
dbInfo.Read()
detailBody.AppendLine("<h1>" & _
   HTMLEncode(CStr(dbInfo!Title)) & "</h1>")
```

The *HTMLEncode* function, called in this block, is included in the *ItemLookup* class. It does some simple modification of special characters as required by HTML. It's called repeatedly throughout *BuildHTMLAndLinks*.

So that's the HTML, but what about the links? If I put a standard link to, say, *http://www.microsoft.com*, the embedded browser will jump to that page when the link is clicked. But that doesn't help me do database lookups. The *WebBrowser* control doesn't really expose a "link clicked" event, but it has a *Navigating* event that is close. This event fires whenever the browser is about to move to a new page. Fortunately, one of the data values passed to the event handler is the target URL. So all we have to do is build a link that contains the information we need to perform the database lookup.

I decided to store the relevant database lookup details as a collection (similar to the history stack), and create fake URL-like links that indicate which item in the collection to use. After a lot of thought and contemplation, I decided on the format of my fake URL links:

```
library://x
```

where *x* gets replaced by an index into the collection of links. It's simple, and it works. The collection of search details is a generic dictionary collection stored as a field within the form class.

```
Private Class SingleItemLink
    Public LinkType As Library.LookupMethods
    Public LinkID As Integer
End Class

Private ItemLinkSet As Collections.Generic.Dictionary( _
    Of Integer, SingleItemLink)
```

Then back in the HTML-building code, I add fake URLs and *SingleItemLink* objects in tandem. Here's some of the code used to add in author links, given a data reader with author name fields. (The *entryID* value supplies the *x* in library://x.)

```
Do While dbInfo.Read
    ' ----- Add in this one author name.
    holdText = FormatAuthorName(dbInfo)
    entryID += 1
    detailBody.AppendLine("<p><a href=""library://" & _
        entryID & """>" & HTMLEncode(holdText & " [" & _
        CStr(dbInfo!AuthorTypeName) & "]") & "</a></p>")

    ' ----- Add in an author link.
    newLink = New SingleItemLink
```

```
        newLink.LinkType = General.LookupMethods.ByAuthorID
        newLink.LinkID = CInt(dbInfo!ID)
        ItemLinkSet.Add(entryID, newLink)
    Loop
```

When the user clicks on a link in the embedded web browser, it triggers the *Navigating* event handler.

```
Private Sub SingleItemDetail_Navigating( _
        ByVal sender As Object, ByVal e As System.Windows. _
        Forms.WebBrowserNavigatingEventArgs) _
        Handles SingleItemDetail.Navigating
    ' ----- Follow the clicked link.
    If (e.Url.Scheme = "library") Then _
        FollowItemLink(CInt(e.Url.Host()))
End Sub
```

The *e.Url.Scheme* property returns the portion of the URL before the ":://" characters, while *e.Url.Host* returns the first slash-delimited component just after these characters. That's where we stored the index into the *ItemLinkSet* dictionary. The *FollowItemLink* method extracts the lookup details from *ItemLinkSet*, and calls our trusty *PerformLookup* method, resulting in a new search that gets stored in the search history. Once again, generics come to our aid, letting us assign *scanLink* in this code block without explicit data type conversion.

```
Private Sub FollowItemLink(ByVal entryID As Integer)
    ' ----- Given a character position in the single item
    '       text panel, follow the link indicated by that item.
    Dim scanLink As SingleItemLink

    ' ----- Access the link.
    scanLink = ItemLinkSet.Item(entryID)
    If (scanLink Is Nothing) Then Return

    ' ----- Perform a lookup as requested.
    If (PerformLookup(scanLink.LinkType, _
        CStr(scanLink.LinkID), False) = False) _
        Then Return

    ' ----- Store the history.
    AddLookupHistory(scanLink.LinkType, CStr(scanLink.LinkID))
End Sub
```

Enabling the Search Features

The *ItemLookup* form is ready to use. We just need to call it from the search fields on the main form. The *PanelLibraryItem* panel in *MainForm.vb* includes several *ComboBox* selection controls, but there is no code to fill them in. Let's add that code now. Access the source code for *MainForm.vb*, and locate the *MainForm_Load* event. There's already some code there that adjusts the form elements. Append the new list-filling code to the end of this routine.

Insert Snippet Insert Chapter 16, Snippet Item 10.

Here's the portion of that new code that fills in the list of search methods.

```
' ----- Load in the list of search types.
SearchType.Items.Add(New ListItemData( _
   "Lookup By Title", LookupMethods.ByTitle))
SearchType.SelectedIndex = 0
SearchType.Items.Add(New ListItemData( _
   "Lookup By Author", LookupMethods.ByAuthor))
SearchType.Items.Add(New ListItemData( _
   "Lookup By Subject", LookupMethods.BySubject))
SearchType.Items.Add(New ListItemData( _
   "Lookup By Keyword (Match Any)", _
   LookupMethods.ByKeywordAny))
SearchType.Items.Add(New ListItemData( _
   "Lookup By Keyword (Match All)", _
   LookupMethods.ByKeywordAll))
SearchType.Items.Add(New ListItemData( _
   "Lookup By Publisher", LookupMethods.ByPublisher))
SearchType.Items.Add(New ListItemData( _
   "Lookup By Series Name", LookupMethods.BySeries))
SearchType.Items.Add(New ListItemData( _
   "Lookup By Barcode", LookupMethods.ByBarcode))
```

The *Clear* button on the search panel resets all of the search fields and prepares them for a new search. Add a new *ActSearchClear_Click* event handler either by using the method selection fields just above the code editor window, or by double-clicking on the *Clear* button on the form itself. Then add the following code to the handler.

Insert Snippet Insert Chapter 16, Snippet Item 11.

```
' ----- Clear the current search criteria.
SearchType.SelectedIndex = SearchType.Items.IndexOf( _
   CInt(LookupMethods.ByTitle))
SearchText.Text = ""
SearchMediaType.SelectedIndex = _
   SearchMediaType.Items.IndexOf(-1)
SearchLocation.SelectedIndex = _
   SearchLocation.Items.IndexOf(-1)
```

Because the Library application will probably be used by many different patrons throughout the day, we should assume that a different person is using the program each time they return to the search panel. Let's simulate a click on the *Clear* button whenever the user returns to the search panel. Locate the existing *TaskLibraryItem* method, and add the following code to the end of the routine, just before the *SearchText.Focus()* statement.

Insert Snippet Insert Chapter 16, Snippet Item 12.

```
ActSearchClear.PerformClick()
If (ActSearchLimits.Top = LabelMoreLimitsTop.Top) Then _
   ActSearchLimits.PerformClick()
```

In the interest of being as user friendly as possible, let's add some "help text" to the search panel that varies based on the search type selected in the *Search Type* drop-down list. Add a new *SearchType_SelectedIndexChanged* event handler, and then add its code.

Insert Snippet Insert Chapter 16, Snippet Item 13.

I won't list it all here because it's rather repetitive. The code simply examines the current selection in the *SearchType* control, and sets the *LabelSearchHintsData* label to some helpful descriptive text.

16. GENERICS

We're getting close. The only thing left to do is to perform the search when the user clicks the *Lookup* button. Add an event handler for *ActSearch_Click*, and then add its code.

Insert Snippet   Insert Chapter 16, Snippet Item 14.

Most of this routine checks for valid input before calling the *ItemLookup* form through its *InitiateSearch* public method.

```
Call (New ItemLookup).InitiateSearch( _
   CType(searchMethod, Library.LookupMethods), _
   Trim(SearchText.Text), mediaLimit, locationLimit)
```

You've done it, doctor. You've added a heart to the patient. The program is ready to run and use for item lookups! If you've already added some named items, you can locate them using any of the relevant search methods. Try doing a title search, using just the "*" wildcard character for the search criteria.

Although the search feature works, you will find that some of the display elements on the *ItemLookup* form don't work perfectly. We never did get those columns working on the item results panel. Improvements are coming soon. With the next chapter's focus on GDI+, we'll soon be able to customize the display to our heart's content.

CHAPTER 17

GDI+

A picture is worth a thousand words—or several thousand lines of source code, if you're generating a bitmap image of it. Writing code to manipulate images of varying color depths, or to trace out multi-layer vector art, can be a nightmare of geometric contortions and linear algebra. It makes one yearn for those days of pre-screen computers. The first programming class I took used a *DECWriter*, a printer-based terminal that had no screen, and included the graphics capabilities of a jellyfish. It was perfect for me. I couldn't draw a straight line anyway, and I didn't need some fancy schmancy "video display terminal" reminding me of it.

The graphics included in early display systems weren't much better. "Dumb terminals," like the popular VT100, included some simple character graphics that displayed basic lines and blocks. Each graphic part was exactly one character in size, and any images you sought to display had to fit in a clunky 80 by 24 grid.

Fortunately for art aficionados everywhere, computers have come a long way in the graphics department. GDI+ includes complex drawing features that would make a *DECWriter* cry. Built upon the older Windows' Graphics Device Interface (GDI) technology, GDI+ includes commands for drawing lines, text, and images in the Picasso-enhanced world of 2D graphics.

Overview of GDI+

Before .NET, Windows programmers depended on the GDI system to draw pretty much anything on the screen, even if they didn't know that GDI existed. In addition to bitmap images, all controls, labels, window borders, and icons appeared on the screen thanks to GDI. It was a giant step forward from character graphics. GDI presented a basic set of drawing features from which you could potentially output any type of complex image. But it wasn't easy. The graphic primitives were—well—primitive, and you had to build up complex systems from the parts. Most programmers weren't into making things beautiful, so they tried to avoid the complexities of GDI. But sometimes you had to draw a line or a circle, and there was no way around it.

GDI+, new with .NET, builds on GDI, providing the basic primitives of GDI, but also supplying some more complex groupings of graphic features into easy-to-use functions. The simplicity has brought about a Renaissance of programmer-initiated graphic work. Take a look at Figure 17-1, which shows an image drawn using the older GDI, and that same image generated with just a few quick commands in GDI+.

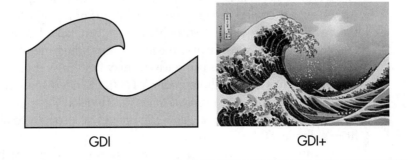

GDI   GDI+

Figure 17-1 The marvel that is GDI+

The GDI+ system makes its home in the *System.Drawing* namespace, and includes multitudes of classes that represent the drawing objects, surfaces, and embellishment features that enable display graphics. But it's not just about display. GDI+ generalizes bitmap and vector drawing on all available output surfaces: bitmaps or line drawings on the screen (including form and control surfaces), report output on a printer, graffiti on the back wall of your local supermarket, image content destined for a JPEG file—they are all the same to GDI+. All destinations use the same drawing methods and objects, making it easier for you to generalize your drawing code.

GDI+'s features include surfaces, drawing inks, drawing elements, and transformations.

- GDI+ generalizes drawing **surfaces** through the *System.Drawing.Graphics* class. This object represents a drawing canvas, with attributes for color depth and size (width and height). The canvas may link to a region of the workstation screen, an internal holding area for final output to the printer, or a general graphics canvas for manipulating content in-memory before outputting it to a display or a file. Another type of surface, the **path** (*System.Drawing.Drawing2D.GraphicsPath*), is like a macro recorder for vector (line) graphics. Drawing done within a path can be "replayed" back on a standard drawing surface, or used to supply boundaries for other drawing commands.
- Colors and inks appear in the form of **colors** (opaque or semi-transparent color values), **brushes** (bitmap-based pseudo-pens used for fills and tiling), and **pens** (colored line-drawing objects with a specific thickness).
- **Drawing elements** include rectangles, ellipses, lines, and other standard or custom-edge shapes. They also include fonts, both bitmapped and outline-based versions.
- **Transformations** let you resize, rotate, and skew drawings as you generate them. When a transformation is applied to a surface, you can draw objects as if there were no transformation applied, and the changes will happen in real time.

The Windows Forms controls that you use in desktop applications generally take care of their own display features. However, some controls let you take over some or all of the drawing responsibilities. For instance, the *ListBox* control displays simple single-color text for each list item. However, you can override the drawing of each list item, providing your own custom content, which may include multi-color text or graphics. This ability to supply some of the drawing code to a control is known as **owner draw**, and it works through the same generalized *Graphics* object used for other drawing. We'll include some owner draw code in the Library Project.

In the interest of full disclosure, you should know that this chapter will cover probably only one percent of the available GDI+ features, if even that. GDI+ is complex and vast, and you could spend three years delving into every little feature, just in time for the next major release of GDI+ (it will be called Windows Presentation Foundation and was formerly known as Avalon). I'll give you a brief overview of the system so you get a feel for some of the basics. If you need to manipulate images and text beyond what is listed here (and you probably will), try the MSDN documentation or another resource dedicated to deciphering GDI+.

Selecting a Canvas

Most drawing in .NET occurs in the context of a *Graphics* object. (For those familiar with pre-.NET development in Windows, this is similar to a *device context*.) *Graphics* objects provide a canvas on which you draw lines, shapes, bitmap images, and pre-recorded drawing macros. *Graphics* objects do not contain the graphics surface itself; they are simply generic conduits to the actual canvas. There is always some surface behind the *Graphics* object, whether it is a portion of the screen, a *Bitmap* object, or the simulated surface of a printed page. Any drawing that is done to the *Graphics* object immediately impacts the underlying surface.

The *Graphics* object includes dozens of methods that let you draw shapes and images on the graphics surface, and perform other magical 2-D activities. We'll cover many of them in this chapter.

Obtaining and Creating Graphics Objects

Getting a *Graphics* object for an on-screen form or control is as easy as calling the form or control's *CreateGraphics* method.

```
Dim wholeFormGraphics As Graphics = _
    Form1.CreateGraphics()
Dim buttonOnlyGraphics As Graphics = _
    Button1.CreateGraphics()
```

Some events, most notably the *Paint* event for forms and controls, provide access to a *Graphics* object through the event arguments.

```
Private Sub PictureBox1_Paint(ByVal sender As Object, _
        ByVal e As System.Windows.Forms.PaintEventArgs) _
        Handles PictureBox1.Paint
    Dim holdGraphics As Graphics = e.Graphics
End Sub
```

You can also create a *Graphics* object that is unrelated to any existing display area by associating it to a bitmap.

```
Dim workBitmap As New Bitmap(50, 50)
Dim workGraphics = Graphics.FromImage(workBitmap)
```

Remember, all changes made to the *workGraphics* instance will impact the *workBitmap* image.

Disposing of Graphics Objects Properly

When you are finished with a *Graphics* object **that you create**, you must dispose of it by calling its *Dispose* method. (This rule is true for many different GDI+ objects.) Don't keep it around for a rainy day because it won't be valid later. You must, must, must dispose of it when you are finished with it. If you don't, it could result in image corruption, memory usage issues, or worse yet, international armed conflict. So, please dispose of all *Graphics* objects properly.

```
workGraphics.Dispose()
```

If you create a *Graphics* object within an event, you really need to dispose of it before exiting that event handler. There is no guarantee that the *Graphics* object will still be valid in a later event. Besides, it's easy to re-create another *Graphics* object at any time.

If you use a *Graphics* object that is passed to you from another part of the program (like that *e.Graphics* reference in the preceding *Paint* event handler), you should not dispose of it. Each creator is responsible for disposing of its own objects.

Choosing Pens and Brushes

A lot of graphics work involves drawing primitives: using lines, ellipses, rectangles, and other regular and irregular shapes to build up a final display. As in real life, you draw these primitives using a *Pen* object. For those primitives that result in a fillable or semi-fillable shape, a *Brush* object specifies the color or pattern to use in that filled area. GDI+ includes many predefined pens and brushes, or you can create your own.

Pens

Pens are line-drawing tools used with the drawing commands of a *Graphics* object. A basic pen has a solid color and a thickness.

```
' ----- A red pen five units wide.
Dim redPen As New Pen(Color.Red, 5)
```

As with *Graphics* objects, any *Pen* you create using the *New* keyword **must be disposed of properly** when you are finished with it.

```
redPen.Dispose()
```

There are several predefined pens made available through the *System.Drawing.Pens* class, all named by their color, as in *Pens.Red*. If you use one of these pens, you don't have to dispose of it.

You can create a lot of interesting pens that vary by line style, end decoration, and color variations. The following code generates the image displayed in Figure 17-2.

```
Private Sub PictureBox1_Paint(ByVal sender As Object, _
    ByVal e As System.Windows.Forms.PaintEventArgs) _
    Handles PictureBox1.Paint
' ----- Draw some fancy lines.
Dim usePen As Pen

' ----- Blank out the background.
e.Graphics.Clear(Color.White)

' ----- Draw a basic 1-pixel line using the title
'         bar color.
usePen = New Pen(SystemColors.ActiveCaption, 1)
e.Graphics.DrawLine(usePen, 10, 10, 200, 10)
usePen.Dispose()

' ----- Draw a thicker dashed line with arrow and ball
'         end caps. Each dashed segment has a triangle end.
usePen = New Pen(Color.FromName("Red"), 5)
usePen.DashCap = Drawing2D.DashCap.Triangle
usePen.StartCap = Drawing2D.LineCap.ArrowAnchor
usePen.EndCap = Drawing2D.LineCap.RoundAnchor
usePen.DashStyle = Drawing2D.DashStyle.Dash
e.Graphics.DrawLine(usePen, 10, 30, 200, 30)
usePen.Dispose()
```

```
' ----- A semi-transparent black pen with three line
'        parts, two thin and one thick.
usePen = New Pen(Color.FromArgb(128, 0, 0, 0), 10)
usePen.CompoundArray = _
   New Single() {0.0, 0.1, 0.4, 0.5, 0.8, 1.0}
e.Graphics.DrawLine(usePen, 10, 55, 200, 55)
usePen.Dispose()
End Sub
```

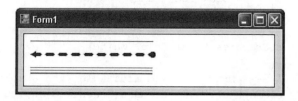

Figure 17-2 Yes sir, yes sir, three lines full

The code shows that there are a few different ways to specify a color, either by its predefined name (*Color.White* and *SystemColors.ActiveCaption*), a string name (using *Color.FromName*), or its Alpha-Red-Green-Blue value (*Color.FromArgb*). That last version lets you supply distinct values for the "alpha blend" (which sets the transparency level, from 0 for fully transparent, to 255 for fully opaque), red, green, and blue components of the full color.

Most of the pen-specific properties I demonstrated here are somewhat self-explanatory. As with most of GDI+, the mind-numbing amount of available features makes it impossible to completely document in a small chapter, let alone provide a good night's sleep for authors designing such chapters. I will simply refer you to the online documentation for the *Pen* class to get all of the luscious details.

Brushes

Brushes are used for filling in spaces between drawn lines, even if you make those lines fully invisible. GDI+ includes a variety of brush types, including *solid brushes* (your basic single-color brush), *hatch brushes* (pattern brushes that are pleasant but general), *texture brushes* (where a custom bitmap is used for the brush), and *gradient brushes* (which slowly fade from one color to another across the brush). The *System.Drawing.Brushes* class

17. GDI+

includes some predefined solid brushes based on color name. As with pens, you must dispose of brushes that you create, but not the solid system-defined brushes.

The following block of code draws some simple rectangles with a variety of brush styles. The results appear in Figure 17-3.

```
Private Sub PictureBox1_Paint(ByVal sender As Object, _
    ByVal e As System.Windows.Forms.PaintEventArgs) _
    Handles PictureBox1.Paint
' ----- Draw some fancy rectangles.
Dim useBrush As Brush

e.Graphics.Clear(Color.White)

' ---- Draw a filled rectangle with a solid color.
e.Graphics.FillRectangle(Brushes.Cyan, 10, 10, 150, 50)

' ----- Draw a hatched rectangle. Use black for the
'        background, and white for the pattern foreground.
useBrush = New Drawing2D.HatchBrush( _
    Drawing2D.HatchStyle.LargeConfetti, _
    Color.White, Color.Black)
e.Graphics.FillRectangle(useBrush, 10, 70, 150, 50)
useBrush.Dispose()

' ----- Draw a left-to-right linear gradient rectangle.
'        The gradient's own rectangle determines the
'        starting offset, based on the Graphics surface
'        origin.
useBrush = New Drawing2D.LinearGradientBrush( _
    New Rectangle(200, 10, 75, 25), Color.Blue, _
    Color.Yellow, Drawing2D.LinearGradientMode.Horizontal)
e.Graphics.FillRectangle(useBrush, 200, 10, 150, 50)
useBrush.Dispose()

' ----- Use an image for the brush. I'm using the
'        "LookupItem.bmp" graphic used in the Library
'        Project.
useBrush = New TextureBrush(Image.FromFile( _
    "LookupItem.bmp"))
e.Graphics.FillRectangle(useBrush, 200, 70, 150, 50)
useBrush.Dispose()
End Sub
```

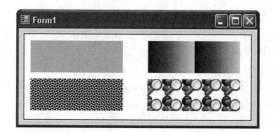

Figure 17-3 Kind of square if you ask me

Flowing Text from the Font

Circles and squares are okay, but they don't always communicate much, unless you are Joan Miró. Most of us depend on text to say what we mean. Fortunately, GDI+ has features galore that place text on your graphics surface.

Before graphical user interfaces were all the rage, text wasn't really an issue; you either used the characters built into the system, or nothing. On the screen, each letter of the alphabet was designed into the hardware of the computer or monitor, and any particular character could only appear within each square of the predefined 80×24 grid. Printers were a little better, becaue you could backspace and retype over previously typed positions to generate either bold or underscore text. Still, you were generally limited to one font, or just a small handful of basic fonts embedded in the printer's memory.

Such limitations are a thing of the past. All text in Microsoft Windows appears courtesy of *fonts*, descriptions of character shapes that can be resized or stretched or emphasized to meet any text need. And because the user can add fonts to the system at any time, and from any third-party source, the variety of these fonts is amazing. But you already know all this. Let's get on to the code.

To gain access to a font for use in your graphics, create an instance of the *System.Drawing.Font* class, passing it at least the font name and point size, and an optional style reference.

```
Dim basicFont As New Font("Arial", 14, FontStyle.Italic)
```

17. GDI+

Naturally, the list of available fonts varies by system; if you're going to go beyond the basic preinstalled fonts supplied with Windows, you should confirm that a named font is really available, and have a fallback option if it is not. You can get a list of all fonts by asking GDI+ nicely. All fonts appear in "families," where each named family may have bold, italic, and other variations installed as separate font files. The following code block adds a list of all installed font families to a *ListBox* control.

```
Dim allFonts As New Drawing.Text.InstalledFontCollection()
For Each oneFamily As Drawing.FontFamily In allFonts.Families
    ListBox1.Items.Add(oneFamily.Name)
Next oneFamily
```

If the font you need isn't available and you aren't sure what to use, let GDI+ choose for you. It includes a few generic fonts for emergency use.

```
Drawing.FontFamily.GenericMonospace
Drawing.FontFamily.GenericSansSerif
Drawing.FontFamily.GenericSerif
```

Getting back to using fonts in actual drawing: The *Graphics* object includes a *DrawString* method that blasts out some text to the canvas.

```
Private Sub PictureBox1_Paint(ByVal sender As Object, _
    ByVal e As System.Windows.Forms.PaintEventArgs) _
    Handles PictureBox1.Paint
  Dim basicFont As New Font("Arial", 14, FontStyle.Italic)
  e.Graphics.DrawString("This is a test", basicFont, _
    Brushes.Black, 0, 0)
  basicFont.Dispose()
End Sub
```

Figure 17-4 shows the output for this code block. In most of the sample code in this chapter, I'll be outputting content to a *PictureBox* control named *PictureBox1* that I've placed on the form of a new Windows Forms application. I've also set that control's *BorderStyle* property to *FixedSingle*, and its *BackColor* property to white, so that I can visualize the edges of the canvas. Drawing occurs in the *Paint* event handler, which gets called whenever the picture box needs to be refreshed, as when another window obscures it and then goes away. In the remaining code examples, I won't be including the "Sub PictureBox1_Paint" method definition, just the code that goes inside of it.

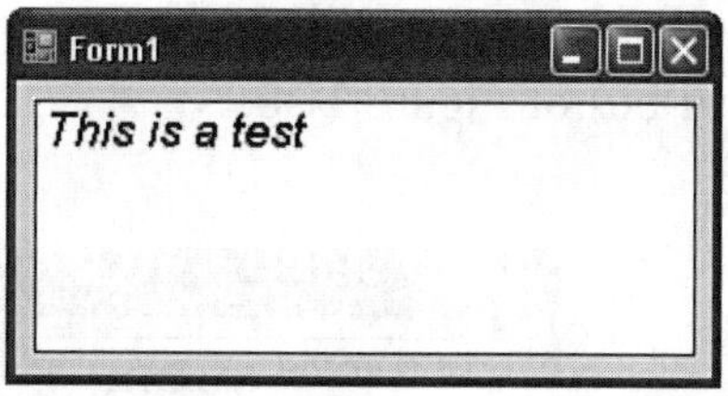

Figure 17-4 This is a test for sure.

Of course, you can mix and match fonts on a single output canvas. This code includes text using Arial 14 and Arial 18.

```
Dim basicFont As New Font("Arial", 14)
Dim strongFont As New Font("Arial", 18, FontStyle.Bold)
Dim offset As Single = 0.0
Dim showText As String
Dim textSize As Drawing.SizeF

showText = "This is some "
textSize = e.Graphics.MeasureString(showText, basicFont)
e.Graphics.DrawString(showText, basicFont, _
   Brushes.Black, offset, 0)
offset += textSize.Width

showText = "strong"
textSize = e.Graphics.MeasureString(showText, strongFont)
e.Graphics.DrawString(showText, strongFont, _
   Brushes.Black, offset, 0)
offset += textSize.Width

showText = "text."
textSize = e.Graphics.MeasureString(showText, basicFont)
e.Graphics.DrawString(showText, basicFont, _
   Brushes.Black, offset, 0)
offset += textSize.Width

strongFont.Dispose()
basicFont.Dispose()
```

The output of this code appears in the top box of Figure 17-5, and it's okay. But I want the bottom edges of the main body parts of each text block—that is, the *baselines* of each block—to line up properly, as shown in the lower box of Figure 17-5.

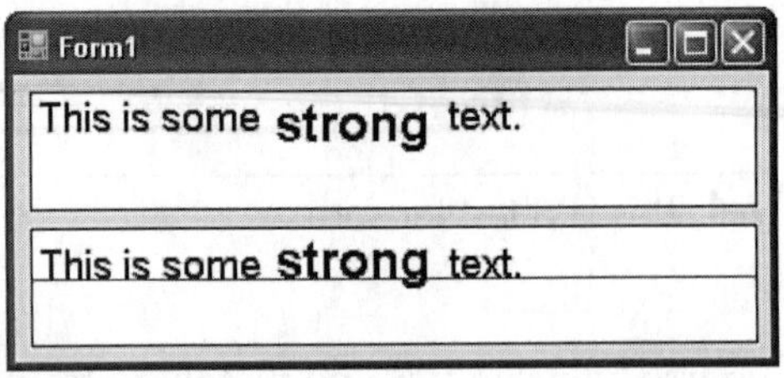

Figure 17-5 The good and the bad; both ugly

Doing all of the fancy font-lining-up stuff is kind of a pain in the neck. You have to do all sorts of measuring based on the original font design as extrapolated onto the pixel-based screen device. Then you connect the knee bone to the thigh bone, and so on. Here's the code I used to generate the second lined-up image.

```
Dim basicFont As New Font("Arial", 14)
Dim strongFont As New Font("Arial", 18, FontStyle.Bold)
Dim offset As Single = 0.0
Dim showText As String
Dim textSize As Drawing.SizeF
Dim basicTop As Single
Dim strongTop As Single
Dim strongFactor As Single
Dim basicFactor As Single

' ----- The Font Family uses design units, probably
'       specified by the original designer of the font.
'       Map these units to display units (points).
strongFactor = strongFont.FontFamily.GetLineSpacing( _
   FontStyle.Regular) / strongFont.Height
basicFactor = basicFont.FontFamily.GetLineSpacing( _
   FontStyle.Regular) / basicFont.Height

' ----- Determine the location of each font's baseline.
strongTop = (strongFont.FontFamily.GetLineSpacing( _
   FontStyle.Regular) - strongFont.FontFamily.GetCellDescent( _
   FontStyle.Regular)) / strongFactor
```

```
basicTop = (basicFont.FontFamily.GetLineSpacing( _
   FontStyle.Regular) - basicFont.FontFamily.GetCellDescent( _
   FontStyle.Regular)) / basicFactor

' ----- Draw a line that proves the text lines up.
e.Graphics.DrawLine(Pens.Red, 0, strongTop, _
   e.ClipRectangle.Width, strongTop)

' ----- Show each part of the text.
showText = "This is some "
textSize = e.Graphics.MeasureString(showText, basicFont)
e.Graphics.DrawString(showText, basicFont, _
   Brushes.Black, offset, strongTop - basicTop)
offset += textSize.Width

showText = "strong"
textSize = e.Graphics.MeasureString(showText, strongFont)
e.Graphics.DrawString(showText, strongFont, _
   Brushes.Black, offset, 0)
offset += textSize.Width

showText = "text."
textSize = e.Graphics.MeasureString(showText, basicFont)
e.Graphics.DrawString(showText, basicFont, _
   Brushes.Black, offset, strongTop - basicTop)
offset += textSize.Width

strongFont.Dispose()
basicFont.Dispose()
```

There's a lot more calculating going on in that code. And I didn't even try to tackle things like kerning, ligatures, or anything else having to do with typography. Anyway, if you need to perform complex font manipulation, GDI+ does expose all of the details so that you can do it properly. If you just want to output line after line of text using the same font, call the font's *GetHeight* method for each line displayed.

```
verticalOffset += useFont.GetHeight(e.Graphics)
```

Enough of that complex stuff. There are easy and cool things to do with text, too. Did you notice that text output uses brushes and not pens? This means that you can draw text using any brush you can create. This block of code uses the Library Project's "LookupItem" bitmap brush to display some bitmap-based text.

```
Dim useBrush As Brush = New TextureBrush( _
   Image.FromFile("LookupItem.bmp"))
Dim useFont As New Font("Arial", 60, FontStyle.Bold)
e.Graphics.DrawString("Wow!", useFont, useBrush, 0, 0)
useFont.Dispose()
useBrush.Dispose()
```

The output appears in Figure 17-6.

Figure 17-6 The merger of text and graphics

Imagining Images

Probably more than anything else, the Internet has fueled the average computer user's need for visual stimuli. Web sites are awash with GIF, JPG, TIFF, and a variety of other image formats. Even if you deal with non-web applications, it's likely that you, as a programmer, will come into more frequent contact with graphic images. Fortunately, GDI+ includes features that let you manage and manipulate these images with ease.

The "BMP" file format is the native bitmap format included in Microsoft Windows, but it's not all that common in the web world. But none of that matters to GDI+. It can load and manage files using the following graphics formats.

- Windows "BMP" bitmap files of any color depth and size.
- CompuServe Graphics Interchange Format (GIF) files, commonly used for non-photo images on the Internet.

- Joint Photographic Experts Group (JPEG) files, commonly used for photos and other images on the Internet. JPEG files are compressed internally to reduce file size, but with the possible loss of image quality.
- Exchangeable Image File (EXIF) files, a variation of JPEG that stores professional photographs.
- Portable Network Graphics (PNG) files, which are similar to GIF files, but with some enhanced features.
- Tag Image File Format (TIFF) files, which are kind of a combination of all other file formats. Some government organizations store scanned images using TIFF.
- Metafiles, which store vector line art instead of bitmap images.
- Icon (ICO) files, used for standard Microsoft Windows icons. You can load them as bitmaps, but there is also a distinct *Icon* class that lets you treat them in more icon-like ways.

There are three primary classes used for images: *Image* (an abstract base class for the other two classes), *Bitmap*, and *Metafile*. I'll discuss the *Metafile* class a little later.

Bitmaps represent an image as drawn on a grid of bits. When a bit in the grid is *on*, that grid cell is visible or filled. When the bit is *off*, the grid cell is invisible or empty. Figure 17-7 shows a simple image using such a bitmap grid.

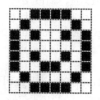

Figure 17-7 An 8x8 monochrome bitmap containing great art

Because a bit can support only two states, "1-bit bitmap files" are monochrome, displaying images using only black and white. To include more colors, bitmaps add additional "planes." The planes are stacked on each other, so that a cell in one plane matches up with that same position cell in all other planes. A set of eight planes results in an "8-bit bitmap

17. GDI+

image," and supports 256 colors per cell (because $2^{planes} = 2^8 = 256$). Some images include as many as 32 or even 64 bits (planes), although some of these bits may be reserved for "alpha blending," which makes perceived transparency possible.

Unless you are a hardcore graphics junkie, manipulating all of those bits is a chore. Fortunately, you don't have to worry about it, because it's all done for you by the *Bitmap* class. You just need to worry about loading and saving bitmaps (using simple *Bitmap* methods, of course), using a bitmap as a brush or drawing object (as we did in some sample code in this chapter already), or writing on the bitmap surface itself by attaching a *Graphics* object to it.

If you have a bitmap in a file, you can load it via the *Bitmap* class constructor.

```
Dim niceImage As New Bitmap("LookupItem.bmp")
```

To save a bitmap object to a file, use its *Save* method.

```
niceImage.Save("LookupItem.jpg")
```

Another constructor lets you create new bitmaps in a variety of formats.

```
' ---- Create a 50-50 pixel bitmap, using 32 bit-planes
'         (eight each for the amounts of red, green, and blue
'         in each pixel, and eight bits for the level of
'         transparency of each pixel, from 0 to 255).
Dim niceImage As New Bitmap(50, 50, _
    Drawing.Imaging.PixelFormat.Format32bppArgb)
```

To draw a bitmap on a graphics surface, use the *Graphics* object's *DrawImage* method.

```
e.Graphics.DrawImage(niceImage, leftOffset, topOffset)
```

That statement draws the image to the graphics surface as is, but that's kind of boring. You can stretch and crop the image as you draw it, or even generate a thumbnail. I'll try all these methods using the image from the Library Project's "splash" welcome form (*SplashImage.jpg*).

```
Dim splashImage As New Bitmap("SplashImage.jpg")

' ----- Draw it at half width and height.
e.Graphics.DrawImage(splashImage, New RectangleF(10, 50, _
    splashImage.Width / 2, splashImage.Height / 2))

' ----- Stretch it with fun!
e.Graphics.DrawImage(splashImage, New RectangleF(200, 10, _
    splashImage.Width * 1.25, splashImage.Height / 4))

' ----- Draw the middle portion.
e.Graphics.DrawImage(splashImage, 200, 100, New RectangleF( _
    0, splashImage.Height / 3, splashImage.Width, _
    splashImage.Height / 2), GraphicsUnit.Pixel)
```

Figure 17-8 shows the output for the previous block of code. But that's not all the drawing you can do. The *DrawImage* method includes 30 overloads. That would keep me busy for 37 minutes at least!

Figure 17-8 Three views of a reader: a masterpiece by the author

Exposing Your True Artist

Okay, we've covered most of the basic GDI+ features used to draw images. It's all now just a matter of issuing the drawing commands for shapes, images, and text on a graphics surface. Most of the time, you'll stick with the methods included on the *Graphics* object, all 12 bazillion of them. Perhaps I over-counted, but there are quite a few. Here's just a sampling.

- *Clear* method. Clear the background with a specific color.
- *CopyFromScreen* method. If the "Prnt Scrn" button on your keyboard falls off, this is the method for you.
- *DrawArc* method. Draw a portion of an arc along the edge of an ellipse. Zero degrees starts at three o'clock. Positive arc sweep values move in a clockwise direction; use negative sweep values to move counterclockwise.
- *DrawBezier* and *DrawBeziers* methods. Draw one Bezier spline, or a continuing curve made up of multiple connected splines.
- *DrawCurve*, *DrawClosedCurve*, and *FillClosedCurve* methods. Draw "cardinal" curves, with an optional brush fill.
- *DrawEllipse* and *FillEllipse* methods. Draw an ellipse or a circle (which is a variation of an ellipse).
- *DrawIcon*, *DrawIconUnstretched*, *DrawImage*, *DrawImageUnscaled*, and *DrawImageUnscaledAndClipped* methods. Different ways of drawing images and icons.
- *DrawLine* and *DrawLines* methods. Draw one or more lines with lots of options for making the lines snazzy.
- *DrawPath* and *FillPath* methods. I'll discuss "graphic paths" a little later.
- *DrawPie* and *FillPie* methods. Draw a pie-slice border along the edge of an ellipse.
- *DrawPolygon* and *FillPolygon* methods. Draw a regular or irregular geometric shape based on a set of points.
- *DrawRectangle*, *DrawRectangles*, *FillRectangle*, and *FillRectangles* methods. Draw squares and rectangles.
- *DrawString* method. We used this before to output text to the canvas.
- *FillRegion* method. I'll discuss regions later in the chapter.

Here's some sample drawing code.

```
' ----- Line from (10, 10) to (40, 40).
e.Graphics.DrawLine(Pens.Black, 10, 10, 40, 40)


' ----- 90degree clockwise arc for 40-pixel diameter circle.
e.Graphics.DrawArc(Pens.Black, 50, 10, 40, 40, 0, -90)
```

```
' ----- Filled 40x40 rectangle with a dashed line.
e.Graphics.FillRectangle(Brushes.Honeydew, 120, 10, 40, 40)
Dim dashedPen As New Pen(Color.Black, 2)
dashedPen.DashStyle = Drawing2D.DashStyle.Dash
e.Graphics.DrawRectangle(dashedPen, 120, 10, 40, 40)
dashedPen.Dispose()

' ----- A slice of elliptical pie.
e.Graphics.FillPie(Brushes.BurlyWood, 180, 10, 80, 40, _
    180, 120)
```

And so on. You get the idea. Figure 17-9 shows the output for this code.

Figure 17-9 Some simple drawings

Paths: Drawings on Macro-Vision

The *GraphicsPath* class lets you collect several of the more primitive drawing objects (like lines and arcs, and even rectangles) into a single grouped unit. This full path can then be replayed onto a graphics surface such as a macro.

```
Dim thePath As New Drawing2D.GraphicsPath

thePath.AddEllipse(0, 0, 50, 50)
thePath.AddArc(10, 30, 30, 10, 10, 160)
thePath.AddRectangle(New Rectangle(15, 15, 5, 5))
thePath.AddRectangle(New Rectangle(30, 15, 5, 5))

e.Graphics.DrawPath(Pens.Black, thePath)

thePath.Dispose()
```

17. GDI+

This code block draws a smiley face on the canvas (see Figure 17-10).

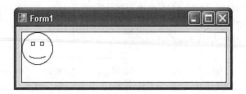

Figure 17-10 Drawing with a GraphicsPath object

That's cute. Fortunately, there are other uses for graphics paths, some of which I'll discuss in the following section.

Keeping It Regional

Usually, when you draw images, you have the entire visible canvas to work with. (You can draw images and shapes off the edge of the canvas if you want, but if a tree draws an image in the forest and no one is there to admire it, does it appear?) But there are times when you may want only a portion of what you draw to appear. Windows uses this method itself to save time. When you obscure a window with another one, and then expose the hidden window, the application has to redraw everything that appeared on the form or window. But if only a portion of that background window was hidden and then made visible again, why should the program go through the trouble of drawing everything again? It really only has to redraw the part that was hidden, the part that was in the hidden region.

A **region** specifies an area to be drawn on a surface. And regions aren't limited to boring rectangular shapes. You can design a region based on simple shapes, or you can combine existing regions into more complex regions. For instance, if you have two rectangular regions, you can overlap them and request a new combined region that contains (1) all of the original two regions; (2) the original regions but without the overlapped parts; or (3) just the overlapped parts. Figure 17-11 shows these combinations.

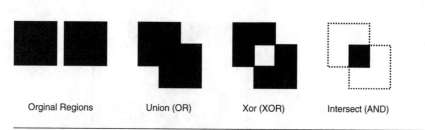

Figure 17-11 Different combinations of regions

During drawing operations, regions are sometimes referred to as "clipping regions" because any content drawn outside of the region is clipped off and thrown away. The following code draws an image, but masks out an ellipse in the middle by using (ta-da!) a graphics path to establish a custom clipping region.

```
' ----- Load the image. We'll show it smaller than normal.
Dim splashImage As New Bitmap("c:\temp\SplashImage.jpg")
Dim thePath As New Drawing2D.GraphicsPath()

' ----- Create an elliptical path that is the size of the
'       output image.
thePath.AddEllipse(20, 20, splashImage.Width \ 2, _
   splashImage.Height \ 2)

' ----- Replace the original clipping region that covers
'       the entire canvas with just the rectangular region.
e.Graphics.SetClip(thePath, Drawing2D.CombineMode.Replace)

' ----- Draw the image, which will be clipped.
e.Graphics.DrawImage(splashImage, 20, 20, _
   splashImage.Width \ 2, splashImage.Height \ 2)

' ----- Clean up.
thePath.Dispose()
```

The output for this code appears in Figure 17-12.

17. GDI+

Figure 17-12 Ready to hang in your portrait gallery

Regions are also useful for "hit testing." If you draw a non-rectangular image on a form, and you want to know when the user clicks on the image, but not on any pixel just off of the image, you can use a region that is the exact shape of the image to test for mouse clicks.

Twisting and Turning with Transformations

Normally, anything you draw on the graphics canvas is laid down directly on the bitmap surface. It's like a giant grid, and your drawing commands are basically dropping colored inks directly into each grid cell. The *Graphics* object also gives you the ability to pass your drawing commands through a geometric transformation before their output goes to the canvas surface. For instance, a rotation transformation would rotate your lines, shapes, and text by the amount you specify (in degrees), and then apply the result to the surface. Figure 17-13 displays the results of the following code, which applies two translations: (1) moving the (0, 0) origin right by 100 pixels, and down by 75 pixels; and (2) adding a clockwise rotation of 270 degrees.

```
e.Graphics.DrawString("Normal", _
    SystemFonts.DefaultFont, Brushes.Black, 10, 10)
e.Graphics.TranslateTransform(100, 75)
e.Graphics.RotateTransform(270)
e.Graphics.DrawString("Rotated", _
    SystemFonts.DefaultFont, Brushes.Black, 10, 10)
```

Figure 17-13 Normal and rotated text

Transformations are cumulative; if you apply multiple transformations to the canvas, any drawing commands will pass through all of the transformations before arriving at the canvas. The order in which transformations occur is important. If the code we just ran had reversed the *TranslateTransform* and *RotateTransform* statements, the rotation would have altered the x-y coordinates for the entire canvas world. The subsequent translation of (100, 75) would have moved up the origin 100 pixels, and then to the right 75 pixels.

The *Graphics* class includes these methods that let you apply transformations to the "world view" of the canvas during drawing.

- *RotateTransform*. Rotates the world view in clockwise degrees, from 0 to 359. The rotation can be positive or negative.
- *ScaleTransform*. Sets a scaling factor for all drawing. Basically, this increases or decreases the size of the canvas grid when drawing. Changing the scale impacts the width of pens. If you scale the world by a factor of two, not only do distances appear to be twice as far apart, but all pens draw twice as thick as when unscaled.
- *TranslateTransform*. Repositions the origin based on an *x* and *y* offset.
- *MultiplyTransform*. A sort of master transformation method that lets you apply transforms through a *Matrix* object. It has more options than just the standard transforms included in the *Graphics* object. For instance, you can apply a shearing transformation that skews all output in a rectangle-to-parallelogram type of change.
- *ResetTransform*. Removes all applied transformations from a canvas.
- *Save*. Saves the current state of the transformed (or untransformed) graphics surface to an object for later restoration. This allows you to apply some transformations, save them, apply some more, and then restore the saved set, wiping out any transformations applied since that set was saved.
- *Restore*. Restores a saved set of transformations.

17. GD+

Enhancing Controls Through Owner Draw

There are a lot more drawing features included in .NET, but what we've seen here should be enough to whet your appetite. You can do a lot of fancy drawing with GDI+, but let's face it: You and I are programmers, not artists. If we were artists, we'd be raking in six figures using a floor mop to draw traditional abstract cubist Italian landscapes with Bauhausian accents.

Fortunately, there are practical semi-artistic things you can do with GDI+. One important drawing feature is owner draw, a sharing of drawing responsibilities between a control and you, the programmer. (You are the "owner.") The *ComboBox* control supports owner drawing of the individual items in the drop-down portion of the list. Let's create a *ComboBox* control that displays color names, including a small sample of the color to the left of the name. Create a new Windows Forms application, and add a *ComboBox* control named *ComboBox1* to *Form1*. Make these changes to *ComboBox1*.

- Change its *DropDownStyle* property to *DropDownList*.
- Change its *DrawMode* property to *OwnerDrawFixed*.
- Alter its *Items* property, adding multiple color names as distinct text lines in the *String Collection Editor* window. I added Red, Green, and Blue.

Now, add the following code to the source code area of *Form1*'s class.

```
Private Sub ComboBox1_DrawItem(ByVal sender As Object, _
    ByVal e As System.Windows.Forms.DrawItemEventArgs) _
    Handles ComboBox1.DrawItem
' ----- Ignore the unselelected state.
If (e.Index = -1) Then Return

' ----- Create a brush for the display color, based on
'       the name of the item.
Dim colorBrush As New SolidBrush(Color.FromName( _
    CStr(ComboBox1.Items(e.Index))))

' ----- Create a text brush. The color varies based on
'       whether this item is selected or not.
```

```
Dim textBrush As Brush
If ((e.State And DrawItemState.Selected) = _
      DrawItemState.Selected) Or _
      ((e.State And DrawItemState.HotLight) = _
      DrawItemState.HotLight) Then
   textBrush = New SolidBrush(SystemColors.HighlightText)
Else
   textBrush = New SolidBrush(SystemColors.ControlText)
End If

' ----- Get the shape of the color display area.
Dim colorBox As New Rectangle(e.Bounds.Left + 4, _
   e.Bounds.Top + 2, (e.Bounds.Height - 4) * 2, _
   e.Bounds.Height - 4)

' ----- Draw the selected or unselected background.
e.DrawBackground()

' ----- Draw the custom color area.
e.Graphics.FillRectangle(colorBrush, colorBox)
e.Graphics.DrawRectangle(Pens.Black, colorBox)

' ----- Draw the name of the color to the right of
'        the color.
e.Graphics.DrawString(CStr(ComboBox1.Items(e.Index)), _
   ComboBox1.Font, textBrush, 8 + colorBox.Width, _
   e.Bounds.Top + ((e.Bounds.Height - _
   ComboBox1.Font.Height) / 2))

' ----- Draw a selected rectangle around the item,
'        if needed.
e.DrawFocusRectangle()

' ----- Clean up.
textBrush.Dispose()
colorBrush.Dispose()
End Sub
```

Run the code and play with the combo box, as shown in Figure 17-14.

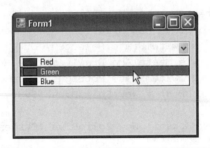

Figure 17-14 Our custom color combo box

Enhancing Classes with Attributes

Class-modifying attributes are something we discussed way back in Chapter 1, "Introducing .NET," and they have nothing to do with GDI+. I just wanted to refresh your memory, because they will be used in this chapter's project code.

Class- or member-modifying attributes appear just before the definition of the class or member, and within angle brackets. This code attaches the *ObsoleteAttribute* attribute to the *SomeOldClass* class.

```
<ObsoleteAttribute> _
Class SomeOldClass
    ...class details here...
End Class
```

(You can leave the "Attribute" part of an attribute's name off if the first part of the name doesn't conflict with any Visual Basic keyword.) Attributes appear as metadata in the final compiled assembly, and they are used by classes and applications that, by design, extract meaning from specific attributes. In this chapter's code, we'll make use of the *PropertyGrid* control, the control that implements the *Properties* panel within the Visual Studio development environment, and is often used to modify Form and Control properties. This control is available for your use in your own applications. To use it, assign a class instance to the control's *SelectedObject* property. Then, magically, all of the object's properties appear in the controls list of properties.

Nice as this is, it's not always desirable. Your object may have properties that should not be displayed. The *PropertyGrid* control is designed to be generic; it doesn't know about your object's needs, so it doesn't know which properties to exclude. That is, it doesn't know until you tell it through attributes. By adding specific attributes to your class's properties, you tell the *PropertyGrid* control how to treat members of your object. For instance, the *BrowsableAttribute* attribute tells the *PropertyGrid* to include (*True*) or exclude (*False*) the property.

```
<Browsable(False)> _
Public Property SecretProperty() As String...
```

I'll supply additional details about this when we use the *PropertyGrid* control later in this chapter.

Summary

While many parts of GDI+ are pretty much wrappers around the old GDI system, it still manages to provide power and simplicity that goes way beyond the original implementation. In business development, you won't always have a need to use the more interesting aspects of the *System.Drawing* namespace. But when you do, you'll encounter a simple and coherent system for displaying images, text, and custom vector elements on the screen or other output medium.

Project

The Library Project has used features of GDI+ since the moment the first form appeared in the newly created project, but it all came for free through code included in the Framework. Now it's time for you, the programmer, to add your own GDI+ contribution to the application. In this chapter's project code, we'll use GDI+ to enhance the normal display of a control through owner draw features. Plus, we'll finally begin to implement some of the barcode features I tempted you with in earlier chapters.

Project Access Load the "Chapter 17 (Before) Code" project, either through the New Project templates, or by accessing the project directly from the installation directory. To see the code in its final form, load "Chapter 17 (After) Code" instead.

17. GDI+

Install the Barcode Font

If you haven't yet obtained a barcode font, now is the time to do it. The features included in this chapter's project code will require you to use such a font. The publisher web site for this book (listed in Appendix A, "Installing the Software") includes suggested resources for obtaining a font at little or no cost for your personal use. You may also purchase a professional barcode font. Make sure the font you obtain is a TrueType font.

Using Owner Draw

In the previous chapter, we added the *ItemLookup.vb* form with its multiple views of library items. One of those views included the *MatchingItems* control, a multi-column list box displaying "Author/Name," "Call Number," and "Media Type" columns. Although we stored the column-specific data within each item already, we didn't actually display the individual columns to the user.

The thing about multi-column lists and other limited-space text displays is that some of the text is bound to overrun its "official" area if you let it. For instance, the text in one list column may overlap into another column of text. In such cases, it has become the tradition to chop off the extended content, and replace it with an ellipsis (" . . . "). So we'll need a routine that will determine if a string is too long for its display area, and perform the chopping and ellipsizing as needed. Add the *FitTextToWidth* method to the *General.vb* file's module code.

Insert Snippet Insert Chapter 17, Snippet Item 1.

```
Public Function FitTextToWidth(ByVal origText As String, _
     ByVal pixelWidth As Integer, _
     ByVal canvas As System.Drawing.Graphics, _
     ByVal useFont As System.Drawing.Font) As String
   ' ----- Given a text string, make sure it fits in the
   '        specified pixel width. Truncate and add an
   '        ellipsis if needed.
   Dim newText As String

   newText = origText
```

```
    If (canvas.MeasureString(newText, useFont).Width() > _
        pixelWidth) Then
      Do While (canvas.MeasureString(newText & "...", _
          useFont).Width() > pixelWidth)
        newText = Left(newText, newText.Length - 1)
        If (newText = "") Then Exit Do
      Loop
      If (newText <> "") Then newText &= "..."
    End If
    Return newText
End Function
```

The *ItemLookup.vb* form has a web-browser-like *Back* button with a drop-down list of recent entries. The items added to this list may include long book titles and author names. Let's use the new *FitTextToWidth* method to limit the size of text items in this list. Open the source code for the *ItemLookup* form and locate the *RefreshBackButtons* method. About halfway through this routine is this line of code:

```
whichMenu.Text = scanHistory.HistoryDisplay
```

Replace this line with the following lines instead.

Insert Snippet Insert Chapter 17, Snippet Item 2.

```
whichMenu.Text = FitTextToWidth(scanHistory.HistoryDisplay, _
    Me.Width \ 2, useCanvas, whichMenu.Font)
```

That will limit any menu item text to half the width of the form, which seems reasonable to me. That *useCanvas* variable is new, so add a declaration for it at the top of the *RefreshBackButtons* method.

Insert Snippet Insert Chapter 17, Snippet Item 3.

```
Dim useCanvas As Drawing.Graphics = Me.CreateGraphics()
```

Also, we need to properly dispose of that created graphics canvas at the very end of the method.

Insert Snippet Insert Chapter 17, Snippet Item 4.

```
useCanvas.Dispose()
```

Now let's tackle owner draw list items. *ListBox* controls allow you to use your own custom drawing code for each visible item in the list. You have two options when you are managing the item drawing by yourself: You can keep every item a consistent height, or you can make each list item a different height based on the content for that item. In the *MatchingItems* list box, we'll use the same height for every list item.

To enable owner draw mode, open the *ItemLookup* form design editor, select the *MatchingItems* list box on the form or through the *Properties* panel, and change its *DrawMode* property to *OwnerDrawFixed*.

Each matching list item will include two rows of data: (1) the title of the matching item, in bold; and (2) the three columns of author, call number, and media type data. Add the following code to the form's *Load* event handler that determines the entire height of each list item, and the position of the second line within each item.

Insert Snippet Insert Chapter 17, Snippet Item 5.

```
' ----- Prepare the form.
Dim formGraphics As System.Drawing.Graphics

' ----- Set the default height of items in the matching
'       items listbox.
formGraphics = Me.CreateGraphics()
MatchingItems.ItemHeight = CInt(formGraphics.MeasureString( _
   "A" & vbCrLf & "g", MatchingItems.Font).Height()) + 3
SecondItemRow = CInt(formGraphics.MeasureString("Ag", _
   MatchingItems.Font).Height()) + 1
formGraphics.Dispose()
```

I used the text "Ag" to make sure that the height included all of the font's ascenders and descenders (the parts that stick up and stick down from most letters). I think the calculation would include those values even if I used "mm" for the string, but better safe than sorry, I always say. Setting the *MatchingItems.ItemHeight* property here indicates the size of all items in the list. If we had decided to use variable-height items instead of fixed-height items, we would have handled the control's *MeasureItem* event. With fixed items, we can ignore that event, and move on to the event that does the actual drawing: *DrawItem*.

Here is what the code is going to do for each list item: (1) create the necessary brushes and font objects we will use in drawing; (2) draw the text strings on the list item canvas; and (3) clean up. Becasue list items can also be selected or unselected, we'll call some framework-supplied methods to draw the proper background and foreground elements that indicate item selections.

When we draw the multiple columns of text, it's possible that one column of text will be too long, and intrude into the next column area. This was why we wrote the *FitTextToWidth* function earlier. But it turns out that GDI+ already includes a feature that adds ellipses to text at just the right place when it doesn't fit. It's found in a class called *StringFormat*, in its *Trimming* property. Setting this property to *EllipsisCharacter* and using it when drawing the string will trim the string when appropriate. When we draw the string on the canvas, we will provide a rectangle that tells the string what its limits are. Here is the basic code used to draw one column of truncated text.

```
Dim ellipsesText As New StringFormat
ellipsesText.Trimming = StringTrimming.EllipsisCharacter
e.Graphics.DrawString("Some Long Text", e.Font, someBrush, _
    New Rectangle(left, top, width, height), ellipsesText)
```

The code we'll use to draw each list item in the *MatchingItems* list will use code just like this. Let's add that code now to the *MatchingItems.DrawItem* event handler.

17. GDI+

Insert Snippet Insert Chapter 17, Snippet Item 6.

```vbnet
' ----- Draw the matching items on two lines.
Dim itemToDraw As MatchingItemData
Dim useBrush As System.Drawing.Brush
Dim boldFont As System.Drawing.Font
Dim ellipsesText As StringFormat

' ----- Draw the background of the item.
If (CBool(CInt(e.State) And CInt(DrawItemState.Selected))) _
   Then useBrush = SystemBrushes.HighlightText _
   Else useBrush = SystemBrushes.WindowText
e.DrawBackground()

' ----- The title will use a bold version of the main font.
boldFont = New System.Drawing.Font(e.Font, FontStyle.Bold)

' ----- Obtain the item to draw.
itemToDraw = CType(MatchingItems.Items(e.Index), _
   MatchingItemData)
ellipsesText = New StringFormat
ellipsesText.Trimming = StringTrimming.EllipsisCharacter

' ----- Draw the text of the item.
e.Graphics.DrawString(itemToDraw.Title, boldFont, useBrush, _
   New Rectangle(0, e.Bounds.Top, _
   ItemColEnd.Left - MatchingItems.Left, _
   boldFont.Height), ellipsesText)
e.Graphics.DrawString(itemToDraw.Author, e.Font, useBrush, _
   New Rectangle(ItemColAuthor.Left, _
   e.Bounds.Top + SecondItemRow, _
   ItemColCall.Left - ItemColAuthor.Left - 8, _
   e.Font.Height), ellipsesText)
e.Graphics.DrawString(itemToDraw.CallNumber, e.Font, _
   useBrush, New Rectangle(ItemColCall.Left, _
   e.Bounds.Top + SecondItemRow, _
   ItemColEnd.Left - ItemColType.Left, _
   e.Font.Height), ellipsesText)
e.Graphics.DrawString(itemToDraw.MediaType, e.Font, _
   useBrush, New Rectangle(ItemColType.Left, _
```

```
        e.Bounds.Top + SecondItemRow, _
        ItemColType.Left - ItemColCall.Left - 8, _
        e.Font.Height), ellipsesText)

    ' ----- If the ListBox has focus, draw a focus rectangle.
    e.DrawFocusRectangle()
    boldFont.Dispose()
```

See, it's amazingly easy to draw anything you want in a list box item. In this code, the actual output to the canvas via GDI+ amounted to just the four *DrawString* statements. Although this library database doesn't support it, we could have included an image of each item in the database, and displayed it in this list box, just to the left of the title. Also, the calls to *e.DrawBackground* and *e.DrawFocusRectangle* let the control deal with properly highlighting the right item (although I did have to choose the proper text brush). Figure 17-15 shows the results of our hard labor.

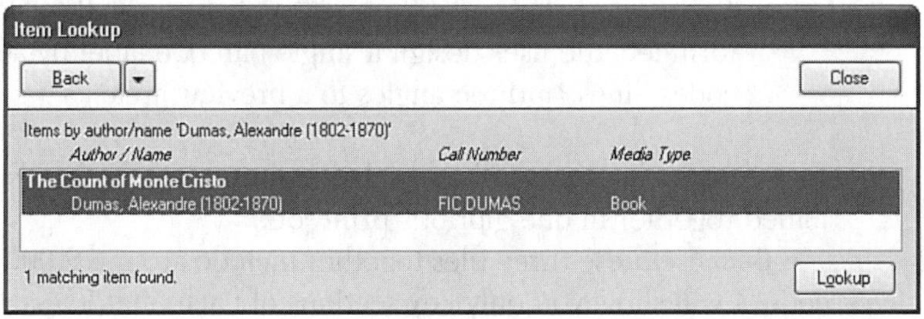

Figure 17-15 A sample book with two lines and three columns

Barcode Design

The Library Project includes generic support for barcode labels. I visited a few libraries in my area and compared the barcodes added to both their library items (like books) and their patron ID cards. What I found is that the variety was too great to shoehorn into a single predefined solution. Therefore, the Library application allows an administrator or librarian to design sheets of barcode labels to meet their specific needs. (There are businesses that sell preprinted barcode labels and cards to libraries that don't want to print their own. The application also supports this method, because barcode generation and barcode assignment to items are two distinct steps.)

To support generic barcode design, we will add a set of design classes and two forms to the application.

- *BarcodeItemClass.vb.* This class file contains six distinct classes, one of which is a base class for the other five derived classes. The derived classes design the static text elements, barcode images, barcode numbers, lines, and rectangles that the user will add to the surface of a single barcode label.
- *BarcodePage.vb.* An editor form derived from *BaseCodeForm*, the same base form used for the various code editors in the application. This form specifies the arrangement of labels sheets. Users will probably purchase label sheets from their local office supply store. By entering the number of label rows and columns, the size of each label, and any spacing between and around each label, the user can design on pretty much any regular sheet of labels.
- *BarcodeLabel.vb.* Another editor based on *BaseCodeForm*. This form lets the user design a single barcode label by adding text, barcodes, lines, and rectangles to a preview area.

In a future chapter, we'll add label printing, where labels and pages are joined together in one glorious print job.

Because these three files together include around 2,000 lines of source code, I will show you only key sections of each one. I've already added all three files to your project code, so let's start with *BarcodeItemClass.vb*. It defines each type of display item that the user will add to a label template in the *BarcodeLabel.vb* form. Here's the code for the abstract base class, *BarcodeItemGeneric*.

```
Imports System.ComponentModel
Public MustInherit Class BarcodeItemGeneric
   <Browsable(False)> Public MustOverride ReadOnly _
      Property ItemType() As String
   Public MustOverride Overrides _
      Function ToString() As String
End Class
```

Not much going on here. The class defines two required members: a read-only *String* property named *ItemType*, and a requirement that derived classes provide their own implementation for *ToString*. The other five derived classes in this file enhance the base class to support the distinct types of display elements included on a barcode label. Let's look briefly at one of the classes, *BarcodeItemRect*. It allows an optionally filled rectangle to appear on a barcode label, and includes private members that track the details of the rectangle.

```
Public Class BarcodeItemRect
    ' ----- Includes a basic rectangle element in a
    '        barcode label.
    Inherits BarcodeItemGeneric

    ' ----- Private store of attributes.
    Private StoredRectLeft As Single
    Private StoredRectTop As Single
    Private StoredRectWidth As Single
    Private StoredRectHeight As Single
    Private StoredRectColor As Drawing.Color
    Private StoredFillColor As Drawing.Color
    Private StoredRectAngle As Short
```

The rest of the class includes properties that provide the public interface to these private members. Here's the code for the public *FillColor* property.

```
<Browsable(True), DescriptionAttribute( _
"Sets the fill color of the rectangle.")> _
Public Property FillColor() As Drawing.Color
    ' ----- The fill color.
    Get
        Return StoredFillColor
    End Get
    Set(ByVal Value As Drawing.Color)
        StoredFillColor = Value
    End Set
End Property
```

Like most of the other properties, it just sets and retrieves the related private value. Its declaration includes two attributes that will be read by

17. GDI+

the *PropertyGrid* control later on. The *Browsable* property says, "Yes, include this property in the grid," while *DescriptionAttribute* sets the text that appears in the bottom help area of the *PropertyGrid* control.

When you've used the *Property* panel to edit your forms, you've been able to set colors for a color property using a special color selection tool built into the property. Just having a property defined using *System.Drawing.Color* is enough to enable this same functionality for your own class. How does it work? Just as the *FillColor* property has attributes recognized by the *PropertyGrid* control, the *System.Drawing.Color* class also has such properties, one of which defines a custom property editor class for colors. Its implementation is beyond the scope of this book, but it's cool anyway. If you're interested in doing this for your own classes, you can read an article I wrote about property grid editors a few years ago.[1]

Before we get to the editor forms, I need to let you know about four supporting functions I already added to the *General.vb* module file.

- *BuildFontStyle* function. Font styles (like bold and italic) are set in *Font* objects using members of the *System.Drawing.FontStyle* enumeration. But when storing font information in the database, I chose to store these style settings using letters (like "B" for bold). This function converts the letters back to a *FontStyle* value.
- *ConvertPageUnits* function. The label editors let you position items in a few different measurement systems, including inches or centimeters. This function converts measurements between the different systems.
- *DBFontStyle* function. This is the opposite of the *BuildFontStyle* function, preparing a *FontStyle* value for insertion into a database record.
- *GetBarcodeFont* function. Returns the name of the barcode font, if configured.

The *BarcodePage* form lets the user define a full sheet of labels—not the labels themselves, but the positions of multiple labels on the same printed page. Figure 17-16 shows the fields on the form with some sample data.

Collectively, the fields on the form describe the size of the page and the size of each label that appears on the page. As the user enters in the values, the *Page Preview* area instantly refreshes with a preview of what the page will look like.

---

1. You can find the article referenced on my web site, http://www.timaki.com, in the articles section.

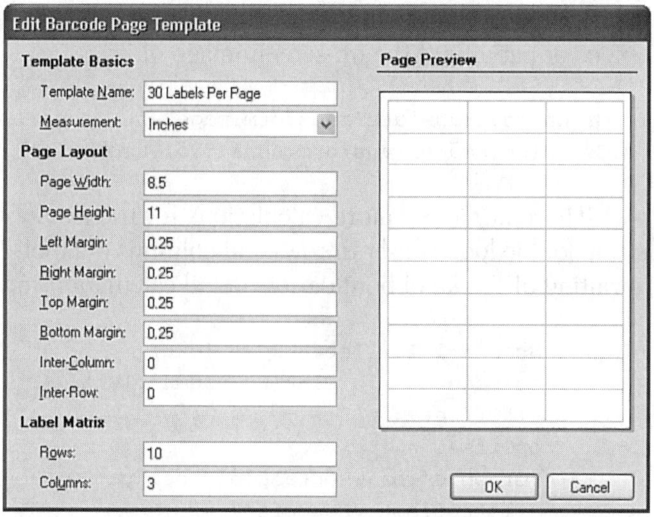

Figure 17-16 The BarcodePage form

As a code editor derived from *BaseCodeForm*, you're already familiar with some of the logic in the form; it manages the data found in a single record from the *BarcodeSheet* table. What's different is the GDI+ code found in the *PreviewArea.Paint* event handler. Its first main block of code tries to determine how you scale down an 8.5×11 piece of paper to make it appear in a small rectangle that is only 216×272 pixels in size. It's a lot of gory calculations that, when complete, determine the big-to-small-paper ratio, and lead to the drawing of the on-screen piece of paper with a border and a drop shadow.

```
e.Graphics.FillRectangle(SystemBrushes.ControlDark, _
    pageLeft + 1, pageTop + 1, pageWidth + 2, pageHeight + 2)
e.Graphics.FillRectangle(SystemBrushes.ControlDark, _
    pageLeft + 2, pageTop + 2, pageWidth + 2, pageHeight + 2)
e.Graphics.FillRectangle(Brushes.Black, pageLeft - 1, _
    pageTop - 1, pageWidth + 2, pageHeight + 2)
e.Graphics.FillRectangle(Brushes.White, pageLeft, _
    pageTop, pageWidth, pageHeight)
```

Then, before drawing the preview outlines of each rectangular label, it repositions the grid origin to the upper-left corner of the on-screen piece of paper, and transforms the world scale based on the ratio of a real-world piece of paper and the on-screen image of it.

```
e.Graphics.TranslateTransform(pageLeft, pageTop)
e.Graphics.ScaleTransform(useRatio, useRatio)
```

There are a few more calculations for the size of each label, followed by a double loop (for both rows and columns of labels) that does the actual printing of the label boundaries (detail calculations omitted for brevity).

```
For rowScan = 1 To CInt(BCRows.Text)
   For colScan = 1 To CInt(BCColumns.Text)
      leftOffset = ...
      topOffset = ...
      e.Graphics.DrawRectangle(Pens.Cyan, _
         leftOffset, topOffset, _
         oneWidthTwips, oneHeightTwips)
   Next colScan
Next rowScan
```

The *BarcodeLabel* form is clearly the more interesting and complex of the two barcode editing forms. While the *BarcodePage* form defines an entire sheet of labels with nothing inside of each label, *BarcodeLabel* defines what goes inside of each of those labels. Figure 17-17 shows this form with a sample label.

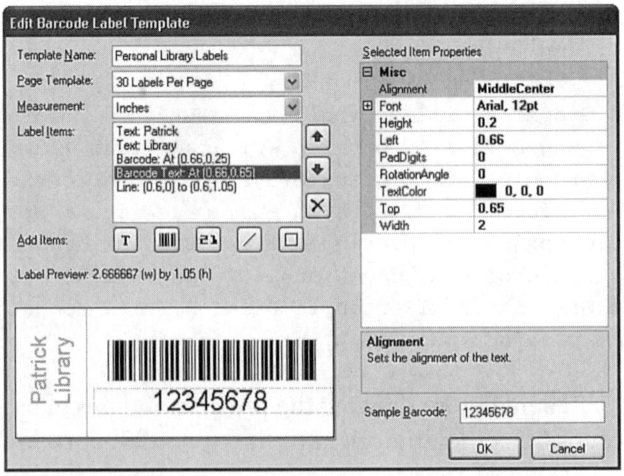

Figure 17-17 The BarcodeLabel form

The *BarcodeLabel* form does derive from *BaseCodeForm*, so much of its code deals with the loading and saving of records from the *BarcodeLabel* and *BarcodeLabelItem* database tables. Each barcode label is tied to a specific barcode page template (which we just defined through the *BarcodePage* form), and stores its primary record in the *BarcodeLabel* table. This table defines the basics of the label, such as its name and measurement system. The text and shape items placed on that label are stored as records in the related *BarcodeLabelItem* table.

The *PrepareFormFields* routine loads existing label records from the database, creating instances of classes from the new *BarcodeItemClass.vb* file, and adds them to the *DisplayItems ListBox* control. Here's the section of code that loads in a "barcode image" (the actual displayed barcode) from an entry in the *BarcodeLabelItems* table.

```
newBarcodeImage = New Library.BarcodeItemBarcodeImage
newBarcodeImage.Alignment = CType(CInt(dbInfo!Alignment), _
    System.Drawing.ContentAlignment)
newBarcodeImage.BarcodeColor = _
    System.Drawing.Color.FromArgb(CInt(dbInfo!Color1))
newBarcodeImage.BarcodeSize = CSng(dbInfo!FontSize)
newBarcodeImage.Left = CSng(dbInfo!PosLeft)
newBarcodeImage.Top = CSng(dbInfo!PosTop)
newBarcodeImage.Width = CSng(dbInfo!PosWidth)
newBarcodeImage.Height = CSng(dbInfo!PosHeight)
newBarcodeImage.RotationAngle = CShort(dbInfo!Rotation)
newBarcodeImage.PadDigits = _
    CByte(DBGetInteger(dbInfo!PadDigits))
DisplayItems.Items.Add(newBarcodeImage)
```

The user can add new shapes, text elements, and barcodes to the label by clicking on one of the five "Add Items" buttons that appear just below the *DisplayItems* control. Each button adds a default record to the label, which can then be modified by the user. As each label element is selected from the *DisplayItems*, its properties appear in the *ItemProperties* control, an instance of a *PropertyGrid* control. Modification of a label element is a matter of changing its properties. Figure 17-18 shows a color property being changed.

17. GDI+

Figure 17-18 Modifying a label element property

As with the *BarcodePage* form, the real fun in the *BarcodeLabel* form comes through the *Paint* event of the label preview control, *PreviewArea*. This 300+ line routine starts out drawing the blank surface of the label with a drop shadow. Then it processes each element in the *DisplayItems* list, one by one, transforming and drawing each element as its properties indicate. As it passes through the element list, the code applies transforms to the drawing area as needed. To keep things tidy for each element, the state of the surface is saved before changes are made, and restored once changes are complete.

```
For counter = 0 To DisplayItems.Items.Count - 1
   ' ----- Save the current state of the graphics area.
   holdState = e.Graphics.Save()

   ...main drawing code goes here, then...

   ' ----- Restore the original transformed state of
   '       the graphics surface.
   e.Graphics.Restore(holdState)
Next counter
```

Each element type's code performs the various size, position, and rotation transformations needed to properly display the element. Let's take a closer look at the code that displays static text elements (code that is also called to display barcode text). After scaling down the world view to the label surface preview area, any user-requested rotation is performed about the upper-left corner of the rectangle that holds the printed text.

```
e.Graphics.TranslateTransform(X1, Y1)
e.Graphics.RotateTransform(textAngle)
```

Next, a gray dashed line is drawn around the text object to show its selected state.

```
pixelPen = New System.Drawing.Pen(Color.LightGray, _
    1 / e.Graphics.DpiX)
pixelPen.DashStyle = Drawing2D.DashStyle.Dash
e.Graphics.DrawRectangle(pixelPen, X1, Y1, X2, Y2)
pixelPen.Dispose()
```

After setting some flags to properly align the text vertically and horizontally within its bounding box, the standard *DrawString* method thrusts the text onto the display.

```
e.Graphics.DrawString(textMessage, useFont, _
    New System.Drawing.SolidBrush(textColor), _
    New Drawing.RectangleF(X1, Y1, X2, Y2), textFormat)
```

We will somewhat duplicate the label drawing code included in the *BarcodeLabel* class when we print actual labels in a later chapter.

The only thing left to do is to link up these editors to the main form. Because I've had so much fun with these forms, I'll let you play for a while in the code. Open the code for *MainForm*, locate the event handler for the *AdminLinkBarcodeLabel.LinkClicked* event, and add the following code.

Insert Snippet Insert Chapter 17, Snippet Item 7.

```
' ----- Let the user edit the list of barcode labels.
If (SecurityProfile( _
     LibrarySecurity.ManageBarcodeTemplates) = False) Then
   MsgBox(NotAuthorizedMessage, MsgBoxStyle.OkOnly Or _
   MsgBoxStyle.Exclamation, ProgramTitle)
   Return
End If
```

```
' ----- Edit the records.
ListEditRecords.ManageRecords(New Library.BarcodeLabel)
ListEditRecords = Nothing
```

Do the same for the *AdminLinkBarcodePage.LinkClicked* event handler. Its code is almost identical except for the class instance passed to *ListEditRecords*.

Insert Snippet Insert Chapter 17, Snippet Item 8.

```
' ----- Let the user edit the list of barcode pages.
If (SecurityProfile( _
      LibrarySecurity.ManageBarcodeTemplates) = False) Then
   MsgBox(NotAuthorizedMessage, MsgBoxStyle.OkOnly Or _
   MsgBoxStyle.Exclamation, ProgramTitle)
   Return
End If

' ----- Edit the records.
ListEditRecords.ManageRecords(New Library.BarcodePage)
ListEditRecords = Nothing
```

Fun with Graphics

GDI+ isn't all about serious drawing stuff; you can also have some fun. Let's make a change to the *AboutProgram.vb* form so that it fades out when the user clicks its *Close* button. This involves altering the form's *Opacity* property to slowly increase the transparency of the form. From our code's point of view, there is no GDI+ involved. But it's still involved through the hidden code that responds to the *Opacity* property.

Open the source code for the *AboutProgram.vb* file, and add the following code to the end of the *AboutProgram.Load* event handler.

Insert Snippet Insert Chapter 17, Snippet Item 9.

```
' ----- Prepare the form for later fade-out.
Me.Opacity = 0.99
```

Although this statement isn't really necessary, I found that the form tended to blink a little on some systems when the opacity went from 100% (1.0) to anything else (99%, or 0.99, in this case). This blink was less noticeable when I made the transition during the load process.

In the event handler for the *ActClose.Click* event, include this code.

Insert Snippet Insert Chapter 17, Snippet Item 10.

```
' ----- Fade the form out.
Dim counter As Integer

For counter = 90 To 10 Step -20
   Me.Opacity = counter / 100
   Me.Refresh()
   Threading.Thread.Sleep(50)
Next counter
Me.DialogResult = Windows.Forms.DialogResult.Cancel
```

This code slowly fades out the form over the course of 250 milliseconds, in five distinct steps. So that the form doesn't close abruptly before the cool fade-out, open the form designer, select the *ActClose* button, and change its *DialogResult* property to *None*.

Another thing we never did was to set the primary icon for the application. Although this isn't strictly GDI+, it does involve graphic display, which impacts the user's perception of the program's quality. I've included an icon named *Book.ico* in the project's file set. Open the project properties, select the *Application* tab, and use the *Icon* field to browse for the *Book.ico* file.

While testing out the icon, I noticed that the splash window appeared (with the default Visual Studio icon) in the Windows task bar. In fact, each opened form appeared in the task bar, right alongside the main form's entry. This is non-standard, and it's all due to the *ShowInTaskbar* property setting included in each form. I've taken the liberty of going through all the forms (except for *MainForm*) and setting this property to *False*. Most of the forms were already set properly, so I altered the dozen or so that were set improperly.

The Library application is really starting to bulk up with features. In fact, by the next chapter, we will have added more than 95 percent of its total code. I can see the excitement on your face. Go ahead, turn the page, and add to your coding enjoyment.

17. GDI+

CHAPTER 18

LOCALIZATION AND GLOBALIZATION

Bienvenue à chapitre dix-huit! My apologies to those of you who don't speak French—and also to those who actually do. I took four full years of the language in high school, but for some reason, it didn't stick. I can still remember some of the important sentences, such as, «Je suis un garçon» and «Où est le crayon». We even read *Candide* and *Le Petite Prince* in class, but to no avail. I did take Japanese in college, and found it much easier to digest than French. So perhaps I should say instead 第十八章にようこそ.

In an attempt to expand this book beyond the shores of English-speaking nations, I localized that previous paragraph. In an attempt to expand the appeal of your own applications beyond the English-speaking world, .NET provides features that let you *localize* your project in another language, even after your software has been compiled and released.

Coverage of all localization features in .NET would include lunar- and emperor reign-based calendars, and right-to-left writing systems. This chapter only covers some of the more common user interface localization features. Hopefully, it will entice you to push the language limits of your own applications, reaching out to *les étoiles*.

Defining Globalization and Localization

Microsoft has hundreds of for-sale and freely available software applications, and the company makes a lot of money worldwide providing these software products to consumers. Most of their products are developed in the United States, written by programmers who speak mainly English, directed by technical leads and product managers who make decisions in English, marketed by a sales team that plans out campaigns in English, and dogged by competitors and detractors who blast the motives and business practices behind each product in English. So how is it possible that Microsoft can sell software to non-English speakers around the globe?

The key lies in the globalization and localization of their products. Sure, Microsoft or any other company could develop distinct yet identical products, each in a different language, and sell them in the appropriate markets. But that would be expensive and time consuming. Instead, they write a single program, and then enhance it with language- and culture-specific features.

Globalization is the process of preparing software so that it can be easily adjusted for each language and culture market. No foreign terms are added to software during the globalization process. Instead, the developers design the application so that all relevant English (in my case) terms and American cultural elements (such as currency displays in U.S. dollars) can be quickly and easily replaced by foreign substitutes, all without impacting the core software elements.

Windows applications have traditionally used **resources** to keep applications globally generic. Resources contain text strings, images, and other non-code elements that are replaced at runtime based on the active language and culture of the operating system. On a German-language system, the application loads its German-language resources (if available) and displays them instead of the default resources. The .NET Framework continues to use resources for this purpose, although it enhances resource development through XML-based resource files and tools.

Localization adds the actual non-native language and culture elements to an application. It is in this step that, say, English-language form labels get translated into Swahili, or some other target language. Visual Studio lets you localize an application within the development environment itself, or through external tools that translators who have no access to the application source code can use.

The good news for .NET developers is that Microsoft pretty much took care of the globalization part for you. You mainly need to focus on localizing your application. Your local community college offers foreign language instruction in a dozen or so languages, so I'll let you choose your first localization target.

Resource Files

Resource files are the key to language localization in .NET programs. Visual Studio will write the files for you, but it's good to know something about how they work, because you may want to craft your own resource files (if you have a lot of time on your hands). The life of a resource moves through three phases, as determined by the type of file in which it appears.

- **Source.** An application's resources start out their lives in a resource source file. Before .NET, resources appeared in "resource script" files, which merged all the best of C-language development and UPPER CASE SCRIPT COMMANDS, and used an ".rc" file extension. In Visual Basic 2005, you use XML-based ".resx" files. Every new Windows Forms application already includes a *Resources.resx* file just waiting to be joyfully filled with your application resources.

  Beyond the core resource source files, other file types can be included as resources, although they are still referenced through the *.resx* file content. Common external resource files include image files (such as .gif and .jpg files) and plain text files (.txt). The Library Project uses a file named *SplashImage.jpg* as a resource for the splash screen, and another file named *ItemLookupBody.txt* that contains HTML content used when displaying items through the *ItemLookup.vb* form.

- **Intermediate.** Once you have your resource sources ready, they are converted into an intermediate form, and stored with a ".resources" file extension, through a process called *resource generation*. Visual Studio normally does this step behind the scenes for you, but you can also use a tool supplied with the .NET SDK (called *resgen.exe*) to generate these files yourself. Intermediate resource files include binary content only, and are not designed for browsing in Notepad.

- **Compiled.** Intermediate resource files aren't much use to your deployed application. The term "intermediate" kind of gave this secret away, didn't it? Before employing the resources in your program, they need to be compiled into a DLL or EXE file. Perhaps you already knew that these files contained multiple sections, including distinct code and data sections. A compiled resource file contains only a data section with the resources; there is no code in a compiled resource file, although standard compiled code files may also include compiled resources.

  In .NET, compiled resource files are *satellite assemblies*. They support your primary application assembly, and are not generally useful apart from that master assembly.

18. LOCALIZATION AND GLOBALIZATION

Figure 18-1 shows the lifetime of a resource through these three stages.

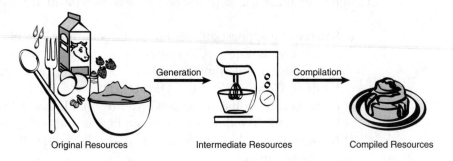

Generation   Compilation

Original Resources   Intermediate Resources   Compiled Resources

Figure 18-1 The edible life of a resource

There are some standard resource types stored in .NET resource (*.resx*) files.

- **Strings.** We'll focus primarily on string resources in this chapter. Each string resource includes a name and a string value.
- **Images.** Visual Basic applications can include JPEG, GIF, TIFF, PNG, and BMP image files. Each image, as with all resources, includes an associated name, which may differ from the original name of the graphic file.
- **Icons.** Program icons used with forms and the application itself appear as standard resources. Icons have an ".ico" file extension.
- **Audio.** Resources can include named audio files, based on WAV audio content.
- **Files.** If the file types listed so far don't meet your needs, you can include whole files of any type as a named resource.
- **Other.** Beyond files, you can store the content of any valid .NET data type as a resource. The resources in a *.resx* file are actually strongly typed to .NET types, so there's really no limit to the type of data you can place there. You can also modify the underlying *.resx* file to include "non-standard" resources. Non-standard resources are beyond the scope of this chapter.

The project properties window includes a manager for application-wide resources (see Figure 18-2). The IDE also includes special editors that let you edit standard and a few non-standard resources types.

Figure 18-2 The resource manager for the Library Project in Visual Studio

The My.Resources Object

We discussed this in earlier chapters, but as a reminder, you can access an application's resources through the *My.Resources* object. If you have a string resource named *MainFormCaption*, the following reference returns its value:

```
My.Resources.MainFormCaption
```

All resources are strongly typed. In this case, *MainFormCaption* is of type *System.String*. The *SplashImage* image resource included in the Library Project is declared as type *System.Drawing.Bitmap*. Because each resource is strongly typed, you can use the *My.Resources* reference in your code just like any data of the resource's type.

In new Windows Forms applications, all application-wide resources appear in the *Resources.resx* file, found in the *My Project* directory within the application's source code directory. You can view it in Notepad if you want. It's a pretty big XML file that doesn't immediately interest me, except that it works! Here's the portion of the Library Project's *Resources.resx* file that specifies our two existing resources. (I've wrapped some of the lines to make it fit on the page.) I've highlighted the name of each resource, and their strong data types.

```
<data name="ItemLookupBody"
  type="System.Resources.ResXFileRef, System.Windows.Forms">
  <value>..\Resources\ItemLookupBody.txt;System.String,
    mscorlib, Version=2.0.0.0, Culture=neutral,
    PublicKeyToken=b77a5c561934e089;Windows-1252</value>
</data>
```

18. LOCALIZATION AND GLOBALIZATION

```
<data name="SplashImage"
  type="System.Resources.ResXFileRef, System.Windows.Forms">
  <value>..\Resources\SplashImage.jpg;System.Drawing.Bitmap,
    System.Drawing, Version=2.0.0.0, Culture=neutral,
    PublicKeyToken=b03f5f7f11d50a3a</value>
</data>
```

Each form you add to your project also has its own private resource file. The one for *Form1* is called *Form1.resx*. These files end up being a big plus in the localization of Windows Forms applications.

Behind the scenes, your application is taking an object-oriented approach to resource management. It's using the *System.Resources.ResourceManager* class to locate and return instances of each resource when you need it. And this same class makes decisions about which language-specific or culture-specific resources, from the dozens I'm sure you'll have added to your application, will be made visible to the user.

Localizing Forms within Visual Studio

There's no sense postponing the introduction to the localization features of Visual Studio, because they are so easy to use. You already know about the application-wide project properties resource editor. Instead, let's look at the amazing part: localizing forms and controls right in the Visual Studio form editor. You might as well start up Visual Studio and try it out with me, because it's just so fun.

Here's a cute but relatively harmless Windows Forms application that writes your name upside down. I've added some *Label* controls, a *TextBox* control, and a *PictureBox* control to a form, as shown in Figure 18-3.

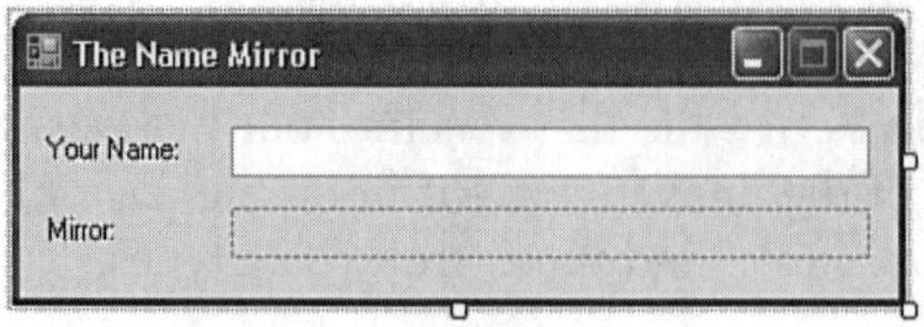

Figure 18-3 A typical Windows Forms application

Then I added the following source code to the form.

```
Private Sub TextBox1_TextChanged( _
     ByVal sender As System.Object, _
     ByVal e As System.EventArgs) _
     Handles TextBox1.TextChanged
   ' ----- Force a redraw.
   PictureBox1.Invalidate()
End Sub

Private Sub PictureBox1_Paint(ByVal sender As Object, _
     ByVal e As System.Windows.Forms.PaintEventArgs) _
     Handles PictureBox1.Paint
   ' ----- Draw the blank background.
   e.Graphics.Clear(SystemColors.Window)
   e.Graphics.DrawRectangle(SystemPens.InactiveCaption, _
     0, 0, PictureBox1.Width - 1, PictureBox1.Height - 1)

   ' ----- Change the orientation of the display.
   Dim saveState As Drawing2D.GraphicsState = _
     e.Graphics.Save()
   Dim mirrorMatrix As New Drawing2D.Matrix( _
     1, 0, 0, -1, 0, PictureBox1.Height)
   e.Graphics.Transform = mirrorMatrix

   ' ----- Draw the text.
   e.Graphics.DrawString(TextBox1.Text, TextBox1.Font, _
     SystemBrushes.WindowText, 1, 4)

   ' ----- Put everything back.
   e.Graphics.Restore(saveState)
End Sub
```

When you run the program, it creates a mirror image of whatever you type in the *TextBox* control. Figure 18-4 shows me playing with the program instead of meeting this chapter's submission deadline.

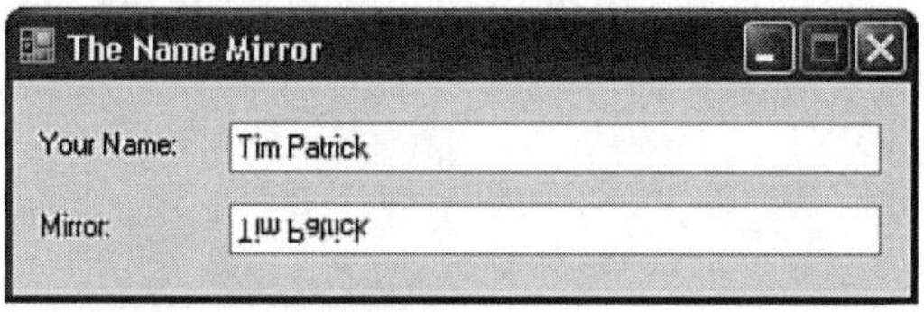

Figure 18-4 Look Ma, I'm upside down.

As interesting as this program may be, it is neither fully globalized nor localized. It's *almost* globalized. All we need to fully globalize it is to "throw the switch" on the form that enables later localization. This is done through the form's *Localizable* property. Change this property from *False* to *True*. Ta da! Your form is globalized!

Now for part 2: localization. Here are the steps to localize the form.

1. Determine which language or language-culture combination you want to localize.
2. Select that language or language-culture from the form's *Language* property. When you open this property list, it includes languages alone, such as "French," and languages combined with a culture or country, as with "French (Canada)." The language-alone entries are known as "neutral language" entries. You can use either type for localization. If you select, for instance, "French," users of your application in either France or French-speaking Canada will use the French resources. If you localize using "French (Canada)," French-Canadian users will access the localized resources, but not French-language users in France.
3. Modify any of the properties of the form or its controls.

That's it. Whenever the form's *Language* property is changed to something other than *(Default)*, Visual Studio starts recording all form and control changes into a separate form-specific *and* language- or language-culture-specific resource file.

You can localize the form with multiple languages. Each time you change the *Language* property to another language or language-culture selection, the changes to the form or controls apply only to that selection. Whatever you change gets saved in a separate resource file.

Let's try it with the sample mirror program. I'm going to choose Japanese for the localization language. First, I set the form's *Language* property to "Japanese." The form momentarily blinks, but there is no other noticeable change. It looks just as it did in Figure 18-3.

Next, I change the *Text* properties of the form and of each of the label controls to their Japanese language equivalents (see Figure 18-5).

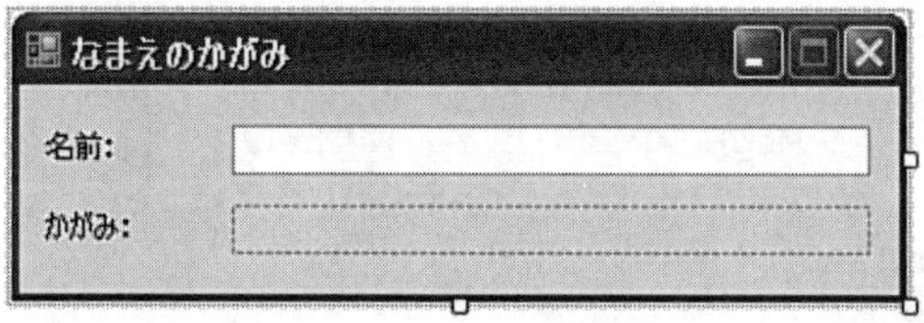

Figure 18-5 The name-mirror program in Japanese

Do you notice how the shorter Japanese language labels are farther away from the text and mirror display fields? Does it bother you as much as it bothers me? To get it out of my mind, I will resize the two fields a little larger by stretching them to the left, as I've done in Figure 18-6.

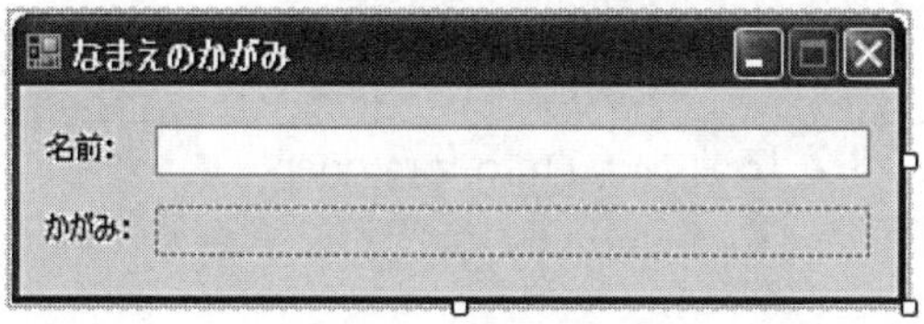

Figure 18-6 The Japanese version with adjusted fields

The amazing part is that if you set the form's *Language* property back to "(Default)," not only will the labels return to English, but the resized text and mirror fields will return to their "natural" sizes. Although I haven't checked out every property, the localization feature seems to impact all display elements of each control.

The program is now fully localized for English (the default language) and Japanese. Normally, the Japanese resource would be used only on a system running the Japanese version of Microsoft Windows. But we can force the program to use Japanese by changing its "user interface culture." In the application's startup code (the *MyApplication_Startup* routine in the *ApplicationEvents.vb* file), I add the following code.

```
Private Sub MyApplication_Startup(ByVal sender As Object, _
    ByVal e As Microsoft.VisualBasic.ApplicationServices. _
    StartupEventArgs) Handles Me.Startup
```

```
If (MsgBox("Switch from English to Japanese?", _
      MsgBoxStyle.Question Or MsgBoxStyle.YesNo) = _
      MsgBoxResult.Yes) Then
   My.Application.ChangeUICulture("ja-JP")
 End If
End Sub
```

And sure enough, running the program and saying "Yes" to the "Switch to Japanese" prompt presents a form in Japanese, as shown in Figure 18-7. (If you answer "No" to the question, the default language, English, appears.)

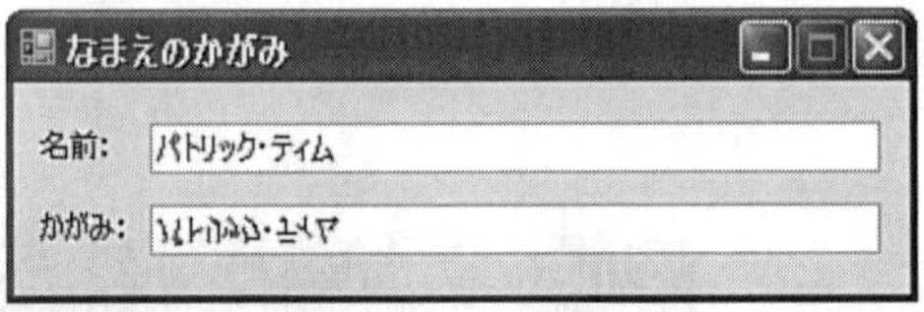

Figure 18-7 Look Ma, I'm a foreigner.

Let's look at the files created in this project. (Look in the installation directory of this book's code for the *Foreign Names* subdirectory. I've placed a copy of this mirror-text project there for you.) The source code directory includes a *Form1.resx* file, added by default to all new Windows Forms applications. But there is also a *Form1.ja.resx* file, the *Form1* resource file for the Japanese language. Visual Studio will compile this file into a language-specific resource when it builds the project. At that time, the code's *bin\Release* subdirectory will contain a further *ja* subdirectory with a file named *ForeignNames.resources.dll*. This is the satellite assembly that contains all of the Japanese language resources. If the application had included multiple forms, all of the Japanese resources for all forms would appear in that single DLL file.

Adding Resources Outside of Visual Studio

Visual Studio makes localization quite easy. But it's rare that the developer of a major application would also be fluent in multiple target languages. And you certainly don't want non-programmers gaining access to your forms and code in Visual Studio, where they can do who-knows-what to its logic.

To keep foreign-language eyes and fingers where they belong, Microsoft wrote the *Windows [Forms] Resource Localization Editor*, and included it with the .NET Framework SDK. (On my system, it's found at **Start ➤ [All] Programs ➤ Microsoft .NET Framework SDK v2.0 ➤ Tools ➤ Microsoft Resource Localization Editor**. Its command-line name is *winres.exe*.) When you are ready to have a translator convert a form to a specific language, you need only to provide them with this program, and the form's *.resx* file (such as *Form1.resx*). The program simulates the display of the form as it appears in Visual Studio, and lets the translator modify any relevant form or control properties for a specific language. Figure 18-8 shows *ForeignNames*'s *Form1* in the Localization Editor.

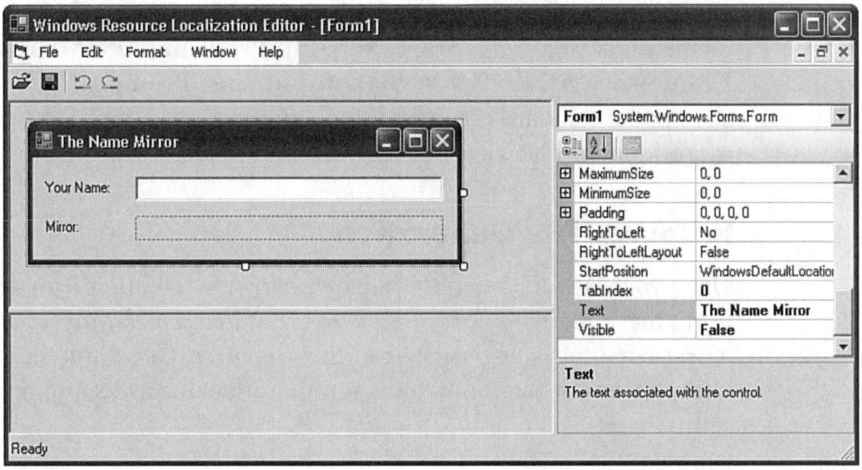

Figure 18-8 An amazing likeness of Form1, ready for translation

The program prompts for the target language or language-culture when you try to save changes. It outputs a language-specific *.resx* file (like *Form1.ja.resx* for Japanese) that can be used in your application. Once you get the foreign resource files back from the translators, store them (the files, not the translators) in the project's source directory, and rebuild the project to generate the correct satellite assemblies.

18. LOCALIZATION AND GLOBALIZATION

Manually Compiling Resources

It's possible to generate the satellite assemblies manually from the source *.resx* files without rebuilding the entire project in Visual Studio. You will have to use the Windows command line (*cmd.exe*), and you will need access to the main assembly's EXE or DLL file. It's not for the faint of heart; and a single mistyped character could cost the American taxpayers millions.

Figure 18-1 summarized the steps needed to move a *.resx* file into a satellite assembly. The "generate" and "compile" steps can be done using two command-line utilities: *resgen.exe* and *al.exe*. Doesn't that sound like great fun?

As with other .NET command-line tools, these tools need the command-line environment to be set up just so, or they will have a snit and refuse to run. To ensure you have the correct environment, you need to open the special .NET version of the command line. The .NET SDK was installed when you installed the Framework, so you should be able to find a Start-menu entry for it at **Start ➤ [All] Programs ➤ Microsoft .NET Framework SDK v2.0 ➤ SDK Command Prompt**. Alternatively, you can open a standard command line and run the *SDK\v2.0\bin\sdkvars.bat* script found in the Visual Studio installation directory.

Resource File Generation

Once you have a *.resx* file available, either by creating it manually or by using the *Windows [Forms] Resource Localization Editor*, you generate a *.resources* file using *resgen.exe*, the *Resource Generator* command-line utility. It accepts an input and an output filename as its arguments.

```
resgen.exe Form1.ja.resx Form1.ja.resources
```

If you omit the output filename, *resgen* will simply replace the *.resx* extension with *.resources*.

If you have multiple foreign-language assemblies (for multiple forms, for instance), generate resource files for all of them. Then you will be ready to compile the satellite assembly.

Compiling Satellite Assemblies

The *Assembly Linker* program *al.exe* is used by .NET to compile all of your .NET applications to their file assembly files. We'll use this same program to generate the satellite assemblies. Its command-line arguments were designed by a secret society, so getting them just right will take some work. Let's look at the command first, and then I'll explain it.

```
al.exe /target:lib
➡ /embed:Form1.ja.resources,ForeignNames.Form1.ja.resources
➡ /culture:ja
➡ /out:ForeignNames.resources.dll
➡ /template:bin\Release\ForeignNames.exe
```

These lines should be entered as one long line. I had to wrap them in the book because the publisher didn't want to do one of those fold-out pages that you see in some children's books. They also didn't like my interactive "pop-up" Visual Studio environment idea either. Something about keeping the book below $100 per copy.

The options provided to *al.exe* work all of the magic.

- **/target:lib.** The "lib" part says, "Output a DLL-style file."
- **/embed.** This option indicates which source files you want to include in the output assembly. The first comma-delimited part indicates source *filename*. The second part indicates the *name* by which this resource will be known in the application. The *name* must be in the format *"basename.cultureName.*resources," where *basename* is the application name (for application-wide resources) or the class name (qualified with its namespace) for a specific class, like *Form1*. Because my application and its default top-level namespace are both "ForeignNames," I've included that in the name component. You can add as many *embed* options as you have resource files to include.
- **/culture.** Although you will eventually put the satellite assembly in a folder named for the target culture, Visual Basic doesn't trust you. Instead, it wants a record of the culture embedded in the assembly itself. You do that through this command-line option.
- **/out.** This option specifies the output name of the satellite file. You really need to use the name *"application.*resources.dll" for the file, where *application* is the same as your application's name before the ".exe" part. If you don't do this, it won't work. Well, you could still get it to work by adjusting the application's *app.config* file, but that file is just plain scary, so you don't want to go there.
- **/template.** This is the option that says, "I'm making a satellite assembly, and the related primary assembly is *x*."

18. LOCALIZATION AND GLOBALIZATION

To use the satellite assembly, locate the directory that contains the main EXE assembly. Create a new subdirectory right there, giving it the name of the language or language-culture key used to create the assembly ("ja" in my case; "ja-JP" would have been an option if I created the assembly using "Japanese (Japan)"). Then put the new satellite assembly in that subdirectory.

Other Localization Features

Localization is more than just words on a screen. There are also issues of how you display times, dates, and monetary values to the user. The good news is that these features will work automatically if you *globalize* your program properly. Just as each .NET program maintains a "user interface culture" (which we played with in the sample program previously), it also has a "general culture" used for string manipulation of times, dates, financial values, and other similar culture-dependent things.

If you use core methods like *CDate* to extract date values, instead of scanning through a user-entered date string by hand, you get culture-specific date processing for free. Also for output, if you use the predefined formats for the *Format* method (and other similar string output methods), you get correct culture-specific formatting for no additional effort on your part. Let's try a quick sample that displays money using the local currency.

I'm creating a new Windows Forms application. I'll add the following code to the *ApplicationEvents.vb* file.

```
Private Sub MyApplication_Startup(ByVal sender As Object, _
    ByVal e As Microsoft.VisualBasic.ApplicationServices. _
    StartupEventArgs) Handles Me.Startup
  If (MsgBox("Switch from English to Japanese?", _
      MsgBoxStyle.Question Or MsgBoxStyle.YesNo) = _
      MsgBoxResult.Yes) Then
    My.Application.ChangeCulture("ja-JP")
  End If
End Sub
```

This code block is almost identical to the one we used in the previous sample, but I'm calling *My.Application.ChangeCulture* instead of *My.Application.ChangeUICulture* (the "UI" part is missing). This changes the string-manipulation culture instead of the user interface culture.

Now I'll add the following code to *Form1*'s class.

```
Private Sub Form1_Load(ByVal sender As System.Object, _
     ByVal e As System.EventArgs) Handles MyBase.Load
   MsgBox(Format("500", "Currency"))
End Sub
```

Figure 18-9 shows the results of this code when run in both English and Japanese modes.

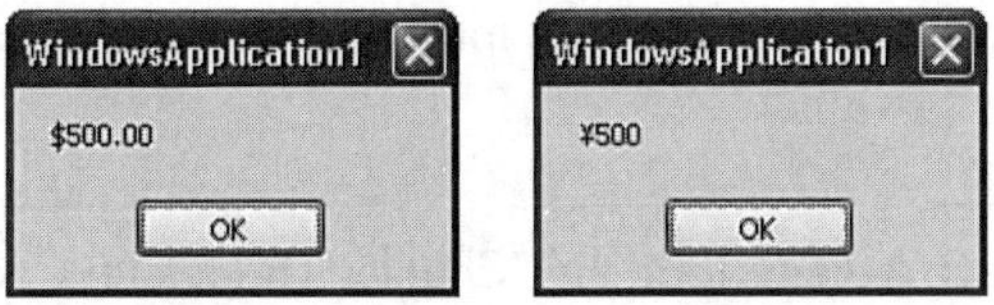

Figure 18-9 Spending money in two places at once

The Framework Class Libraries include even more culture management features in the *System.Globalization* namespace. The classes in this namespace let you manually adjust the output of culture-sensitive strings to meet your needs. Most of them are pretty esoteric and intended for specific culture groups, so I won't be discussing them here.

Summary

It's a small world, after all. And the culture-specific features in .NET have helped to make it that way, at least for your software. I'm still amazed that I'm able to use Japanese on my English version of Microsoft Windows. (I first had to enable support for East Asian languages in the Control Panel's *Regional and Language Options* applet.) And now it's not just Windows or Microsoft Office that can automatically shift with the current culture. Politicians can do it, too. Oops, I mean that your own applications can do it, too. By taking advantage of culture-specific resources and the automatic and manual formatting features included with .NET, you'll soon be selling your snazzy business application in six of the seven continents.

18. LOCALIZATION AND GLOBALIZATION

Project

I know you're expecting me to localize all of the forms in the Library Project into Greek, and it is a tempting idea. But in the interests of brevity (and my sanity), I'll leave that as an exercise for the reader. (Muffled laughter.)

What we will do in this chapter's project code is to enable the remaining patron-specific tracking and management features. Those features include the management of fines for naughty patrons who don't return their library books on time. We'll use the generic currency formatting features discussed in this chapter to make the application as globally accessible as possible.

Project Access Load the "Chapter 18 (Before) Code" project, either through the New Project templates, or by accessing the project directly from the installation directory. To see the code in its final form, load "Chapter 18 (After) Code" instead.

Tracking Patron Payments

Let's create a class that exposes the important features of each set of payments applied to a specific checked-in item. Of course, they'll all be stored in the Library database. But keeping a summary of payments temporarily cached in memory simplifies some processing.

Add a new class item to the Library Project, giving it the name *PaymentItem.vb*. Define it using the following code.

Insert Snippet Insert Chapter 18, Snippet Item 1.

```
Public Class PaymentItem
    ' ----- Used to track and print payment tickets.
    Public ItemTitle As String
    Public PatronCopyID As Integer
    Public FeesPaid As Decimal
    Public BalanceDue As Decimal
End Class
```

Each instance of this class identifies the collected fines and payments for a specific library item (*ItemTitle*) and for the patron who turned in the item late (*PatronCopyID*).

Calculating Patron Fines

We also need to know the total fines owed by a patron for all items, even when we're not showing the details. Add the *CalculatePatronFines* function to the *General.vb* module.

Insert Snippet Insert Chapter 18, Snippet Item 2.

```
Public Function CalculatePatronFines(_
     ByVal patronID As Integer) As Decimal
   ' ----- Given a patron ID, calculate the fines due.
   Dim sqlText As String

   On Error GoTo ErrorHandler

   ' ----- Retrieve the fine records for the patron.
   sqlText = "SELECT SUM(Fine - Paid) FROM PatronCopy " & _
      "WHERE Patron = " & patronID
   Return DBGetDecimal(ExecuteSQLReturn(sqlText))

ErrorHandler:
   GeneralError("CalculatePatronFines", Err.GetException())
   Return 0@
End Function
```

It's pretty basic code, actually, because the database does all of the work of adding up the values. I checked the database documentation and confirmed that *Fine* and *Paid* are required fields, and will never be NULL. This keeps the SQL code terse.

Patron Record Access

Before reviewing a patron's record, the user must identify the patron. This is done through a *Patron Record Access* form, sort of a login form for patrons. Each patron is assigned a password, which must be supplied before the patron can access his or her own record. Administrators can access a patron's record without providing the password.

I've already added the *PatronAccess.vb* form to your project; it appears in Figure 18-10.

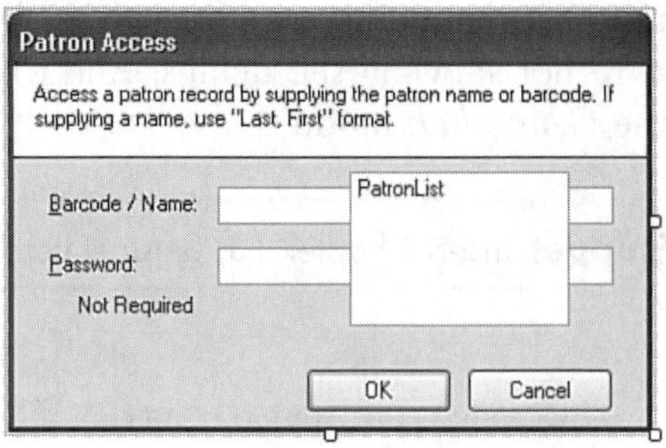

Figure 18-10 The Patron Access form, PatronAccess.vb

This form's code is a lot like that found in the *ChangeUser.vb* form, a form that provides administrative access to the program, and that we added back in Chapter 11, "Security." The Patron Access form behaves a little differently for administrators and regular patrons.

- Regular patrons must provide either their barcode, or supply their name (full last name, optional wildcards on the first name) **and** their password. If they use a partial name instead of a barcode, and a search of that name results in multiple matches, they will have to provide a more correct entry of their name. (If two patrons have the same name, they will have to depend on barcodes; but this program is for a *small* library, so name conflicts should be rare.)
- Administrators enter the patron's name or barcode, but no password is needed. If there are multiple name matches, the form presents all matching names in a list, and the administrator can select the correct entry from the list. This gives an administrator full access to all patron records. It's obviously important for an administrator to log out when finished using a workstation that is available to patrons.

The *PatronAccess* form's *SelectPatron* method provides the interface to the form for both administrators and ordinary patrons. The function returns the ID of the selected patron, or –1 if the user didn't successfully access a patron record.

Patron Password Modification

Although administrators can change the password of each patron through the *Patron.vb* form, we don't want to give ordinary patrons access to that form and all of its raw, unadulterated power. But we still want the patrons to be able to change their own passwords, because it's the nice and secure thing to do. I've added the *PatronPassword.vb* form to your project to fulfill this purpose (see Figure 18-11).

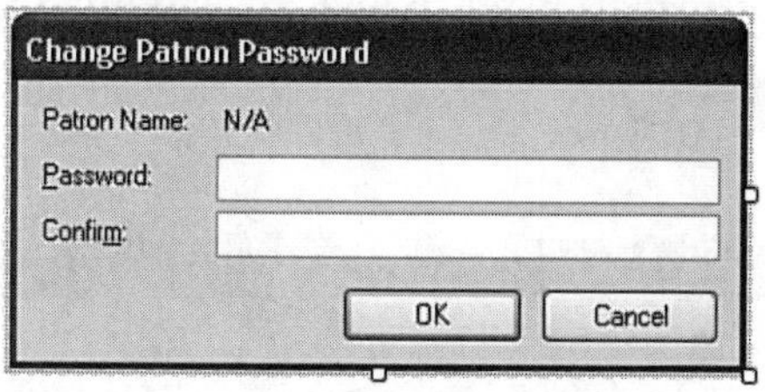

Figure 18-11 The Patron Password form, PatronPassword.vb

The form is basically a dramatically reduced subset of the full *Patron.vb* form. Because it needs to deal with active patrons only, it doesn't have a lot of the *Patron.vb* code that differentiates between new and existing patron records. The focus of the *Patron Password* form is the update statement that sets the patron's password, in the *SaveFormData* method.

```
sqlText = "UPDATE Patron SET [Password] = " & _
   DBText(EncryptPassword("patron", _
   Trim(RecordPassword.Text))) & _
   " WHERE ID = " & ActiveID
ExecuteSQL(sqlText)
```

The word "Password" is a reserved keyword in SQL Server, so we need to "escape" it with square brackets when referring to the field in SQL statements.

Collecting Patron Payments

In a perfect world, patrons would never let their books and other library items reach the overdue state. Of course, in a perfect world, libraries would let you keep books you like indefinitely. And give me a break with those incessant overdue notices. What's up with that?

But for those small libraries that insist on charging fines for overdue items, the Library Project includes features for assigning and tracking fines. In a later chapter, we'll add the code that automatically calculates the fines for overdue items. Right now, we'll implement the form that lets you document patron payments and other financial adjustments to items in the patron's record.

I've added the *PatronPayment.vb* form to the collection of project files, but it's not yet integrated into the project. Select the *PatronPayment.vb* file in the *Solution Explorer*, and then change its *Build Action* property (in the *Properties* panel) from "None" to "Compile." Figure 18-12 shows the controls on this form.

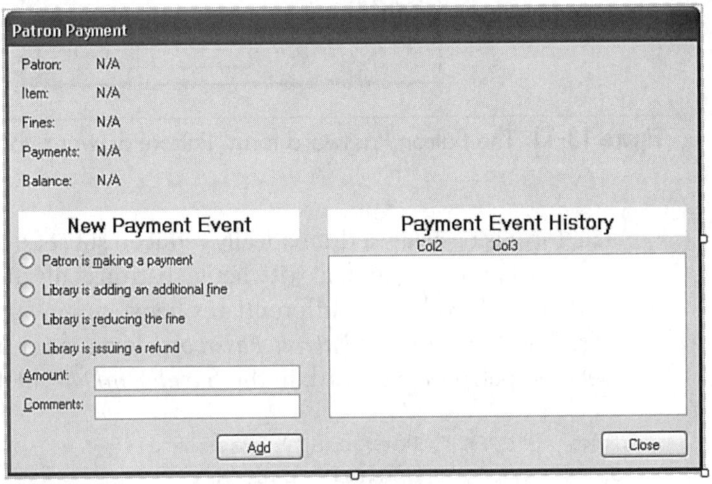

Figure 18-12 The Patron Payment form, PatronPayment.vb

Fines that are automatically added to an overdue item appear in the *PatronCopy.Fine* database field. While that value is displayed on the *Patron Payment* form, it's not the primary focus of that form. Instead, the form exists to allow a librarian to enter charges and payments for a previously checked-out item, storing these updates in the *PatronPayment* database table. This table tracks four types of financial events for each item checked out by a patron.

1. Additional fines imposed by a librarian or administrator. For example, a librarian may add the value of an item as a fine if it turns out that the patron has lost the item. Additional fine entries use the letter "F" in the *PatronPayment.EntryType* database field.
2. Payments made by the patron for an overdue item. "P" is the entry type.
3. A dismissal of some or all of the pending fines for an overdue item, indicated by a "D" entry type.
4. If entry type is "R," the record indicates a refund paid to the patron by the library.

Each *PatronPayment* table record includes a transaction date, the amount of the transaction, optional comments, and the identity of the administrative user recording the entry. To make the code a little clearer, the letter codes in the database table are converted into enumeration values from the *EventEntryType* enumeration.

```
Private Enum EventEntryType
    NotDefined
    PatronPayment
    FineAdded
    FineDismissal
    RefundToPatron
    OverdueFines
End Enum
```

The *OverdueFines* entry allows the *PatronCopy.Fines* value to be part of the displayed financial history on the form.

The librarian uses the fields in the "New Payment Event" section of the *PatronPayment* form to add charge and payment records. All previously added records appear in the *EventHistory* list, in the "Payment Event History" section of the form.

The calling form (added later in this chapter) needs to pass in the *PatronCopy.ID* value to identify the proper record. But the plan is to have payments added on this form flow back to the parent form. The two forms will share a set of *PaymentItem* objects, using the class we added a few sections earlier in this chapter. We'll store it in a local member variable as a generic set.

```
Private PaymentsOnly As Generic.List(Of PaymentItem)
```

The entry point into the form will be a public method named *ManagePayments*. Add that code now to the *PatronPayment* class.

Insert Snippet Insert Chapter 18, Snippet Item 3.

```
Public Sub ManagePayments(ByVal patronCopyID As Integer, _
    ByVal sessionPayments As Generic.List(Of PaymentItem))
  ' ----- Manage the payments for an item.
  ActivePatronCopyID = patronCopyID
  PaymentsOnly = sessionPayments
  Me.ShowDialog()
End Sub
```

This method records the patron-copy ID number and the collection of payments for that checked-out item. Processing then moves on to the form's *Load* event handler. It's in this routine that we will add our localized financial management code. In the *PatronPayment_Load* routine, scan down about one-third of the way through the method to the code that loads in the "summary details" from the database. Just after the line:

```
RecordItem.Text = CStr(dbInfo!Title)
```

add in the statements that will globally format currency values for the **Fines**, **Payments**, and **Balance** summary labels that appear near the top of the form.

Insert Snippet Insert Chapter 18, Snippet Item 4.

```
originalFine = CDec(dbInfo!Fine)
RecordFine.Text = Format(originalFine, "Currency")
RecordPayments.Text = Format(CDec(dbInfo!Paid), "Currency")
balanceDue = originalFine - CDec(dbInfo!Paid)
RecordBalance.Text = Format(balanceDue, "Currency")
```

The rest of the *Load* event handler's code loads existing records from the *PatronPayment* table, plus the original overdue fine, if any, from the *PatronCopy.Fine* database field.

Later, when the user clicks the **Add** button to add a new financial event to the patron-and-item-copy entry, the *SaveEventData* routine—equivalent to the *SaveFormData* method in most of the other forms we've developed so far—saves the updated information in the database. This routine needs to save the new charge or payment in the *PatronPayment* table, plus update the charge and payment summary in the *PatronCopy* record. Add the code that writes out these records, just after the calculations for the *fineAmount* and *paidAmount* variables in the *SaveEventData* method.

Insert Snippet Insert Chapter 18, Snippet Item 5.

```
' ----- Add the entry to the database.
TransactionBegin()
sqlText = "INSERT INTO PatronPayment (PatronCopy, " & _
    "EntryDate, EntryType, Amount, Comment, UserID) " & _
    "OUTPUT INSERTED.ID VALUES (" & ActivePatronCopyID & _
    ", GETDATE(), " & DBText(entryCode) & ", " & _
    RecordAmount.Text & ", " & _
    DBText(Trim(RecordComment.Text)) & _
    ", " & LoggedInUserID & ")"
newID = CInt(ExecuteSQLReturn(sqlText))

sqlText = "UPDATE PatronCopy SET Fine = " & fineAmount & _
    ", Paid = " & paidAmount & " WHERE ID = " & _
    ActivePatronCopyID
ExecuteSQL(sqlText)
TransactionCommit()
```

I've wrapped up both database statements in a transaction to help ensure the integrity of the data. Once the database is up to date, it's time to update the screen. The on-screen list of charges and payments needs this new record. That list uses the local *EventHistoryItem* class, a variation of the application-wide *ListItemData* class that we usually use in *ListBox* controls. *EventHistoryItem* has fields that are specific to displaying financial information in the *EventHistory* list box. Add the code that builds an *EventHistoryItem* record and add it to the *EventHistory* list, immediately after the database update code we just added.

Insert Snippet Insert Chapter 18, Snippet Item 6.

```
' ----- Add an item to the entry list.
historyItem = New EventHistoryItem
historyItem.PaymentID = newID
historyItem.EntryDate = Today
historyItem.PaymentAmount = CDec(RecordAmount.Text)
historyItem.Comments = Trim(RecordComment.Text)
historyItem.EntryType = entryType
EventHistory.Items.Add(historyItem)
```

This code block is followed by similar code that updates the *PaymentsOnly* list, the *Generic.List(Of PaymentItem)* that was passed in from the calling form. The code either updates the existing payment summary record, or adds a new record to the generic list.

```
' ----- Add a new payment.
scanPayment = New PaymentItem
scanPayment.PatronCopyID = ActivePatronCopyID
scanPayment.ItemTitle = RecordItem.Text
scanPayment.FeesPaid = paidAmount
scanPayment.BalanceDue = fineAmount - paidAmount
PaymentsOnly.Add(scanPayment)
```

Before leaving this function, we need to refresh the three financial summary values near the top of the form, the ones we set when the form first loaded. Add this code just after the update to the *PaymentOnly* list.

Insert Snippet Insert Chapter 18, Snippet Item 7.

```
' ----- Update the on-screen values.
RecordFine.Text = Format(fineAmount, "Currency")
RecordPayments.Text = Format(paidAmount, "Currency")
RecordBalance.Text = Format(fineAmount - paidAmount, _
   "Currency")
```

The *EventHistory* list is a variable-line-height owner draw control, similar to one we designed in Chapter 17, "GDI+." Its *MeasureItem* event handler sets the height of each list item (comments appear on a second line when available), while its *DrawItem* event handler does the actual drawing of each data column and the comments.

Managing All Fines and Payments

The *Patron Payment* form lets a librarian enter individual fines and payments, but the program still needs a form to manage all fines and payments for a single patron, a form that calls up the *Patron Payment* form when needed. The new *PatronRecord.vb* form fulfills this need. I've added this form to your project, although you need to enable it. Select it in the *Solution Explorer*, and change its *Build Action* property (in the *Properties* panel) from "None" to "Compile." Figure 18-13 shows the controls on this form.

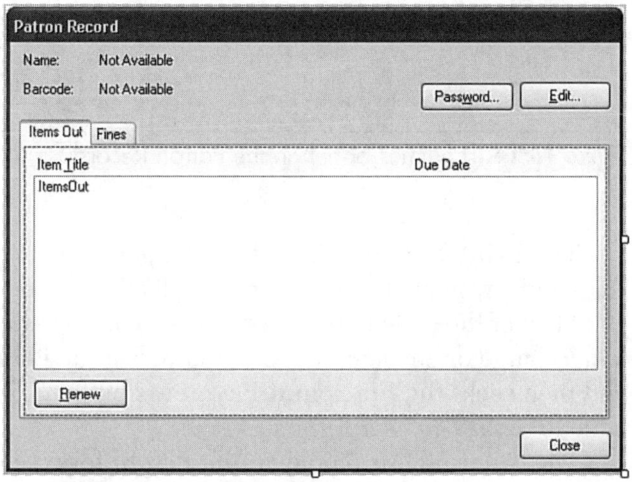

Figure 18-13 The Patron Record form, PatronRecord.vb

This form is available to both administrators and patrons, although some of the fields are hidden from patron view.

The **Password** button leads to the *Change Patron Password* form we added earlier in this chapter. The **Edit** button, only available to administrators, provides access to the full *Patron.vb* form. The main section of the *Patron Record* form displays a list of all items the patron currently has checked out. It includes a **Renew** button that lets a patron extend the due date for a checked-out item. We'll add the code for that feature in a later chapter.

The form also displays a summary of all pending fines and payments. Figure 18-14 shows the **Fines** tab and its fields.

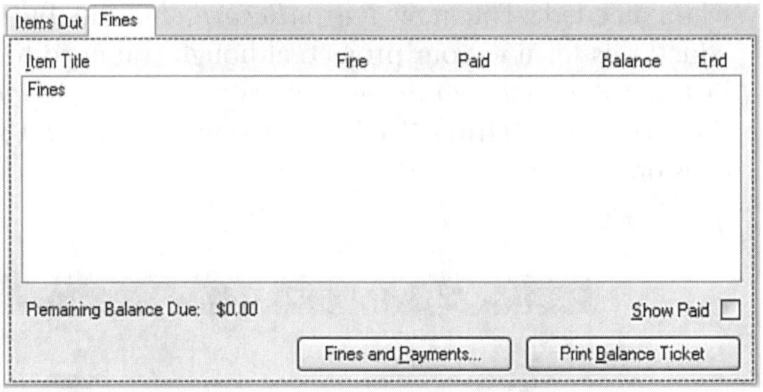

Figure 18-14 The Fines panel on the Patron Record form

The **Print Balance Ticket** button generates a printed receipt of all fines and payments for the patron. We'll add its code in a later chapter.

Most of the code in this form exists to manage fines and payments. To add a charge or payment, the librarian selects an item from the **Fines** list, and then clicks the **Fines and Payments** button. This brings up the just-added *Patron Payment* form.

The two main lists on the *Patron Record* form will each forgo the standard *ListItemData* class, and use a more property-rich class to support the display needs of each list. We'll add this *PatronDetailItem* as a separate public class because (as we'll see in a later chapter) it will be used elsewhere in the Library Project. Create a new class named *PatronDetailItem.vb*, and use the following code for its content.

Insert Snippet Insert Chapter 18, Snippet Item 8.

```
Private Class PatronDetailItem
    Public DetailID As Integer
    Public TitleText As String
    Public DueDate As Date
    Public FineAmount As Decimal
    Public PaidAmount As Decimal
    Public BalanceDue As Decimal
End Class
```

Now back to the *PatronRecord* form. As you can tell from looking at the form, the **Fines** list displays several columns of currency values. Let's add the code that correctly formats the currency according to the regional monetary settings. First, locate the *RefreshPaymentFines* method. This routine adds up all fines and payments, and displays the result through the *BalanceDue Label* control.

Near the top of this routine is a comment that states, "Clear the current list." Add the following code just after this comment.

Insert Snippet Insert Chapter 18, Snippet Item 9.

```
Fines.Items.Clear()
totalBalance = 0@
BalanceDue.Text = Format(0@, "Currency")
Me.Cursor = Windows.Forms.Cursors.WaitCursor
```

We could have just set the *BalanceDue* field to "$0.00," but this would not be properly globalized. Using the *Format* function with "Currency" as the formatting rule still results in "$0.00" when used in America, but properly adjusts for other cultures as well.

The *RefreshPaymentFines* method does a whole bunch of calculations, and ends up with the remaining patron balance in the *totalBalance* local variable. Locate the comment that reads, "Show the total balance," and add the following code just after it.

18. LOCALIZATION AND GLOBALIZATION

Insert Snippet Insert Chapter 18, Snippet Item 10.

```
BalanceDue.Text = Format(totalBalance, "Currency")
```

The **Fines** list, an owner draw *ListBox* implementation, also displays currency values. This is another list that forgoes the standard *ListItemData* class, using the local *PatronDetailItem* class instead for its item management. Locate the *Fines_DrawItem* event handler, and the "Extract the details from the list item" comment within that handler. Add the following code just after the comment.

Insert Snippet Insert Chapter 18, Snippet Item 11.

```
itemDetail = CType(Fines.Items(e.Index), PatronDetailItem)
titleText = itemDetail.TitleText
fineText = Format(itemDetail.FineAmount, "Currency")
paidText = Format(itemDetail.PaidAmount, "Currency")
balanceText = Format(itemDetail.BalanceDue, "Currency")
If (itemDetail.BalanceDue = 0@) Then useNotice = useBrush
```

This block properly formats the each currency value. By default, all due amounts appear in red in the list. The last line in this code block resets the color to the neutral list item color if no balance is due.

Connecting Patron Features to the Main Form

That does it for the new patron-specific forms. Let's enable access to them through the main Library form. Wow! It's been awhile since I really looked at this form. I've forgotten what it looks like. Ah, yes. One of the main icons provides access to a patron's record (see Figure 18-15).

Figure 18-15 Accessing patron records from the Main form

All we need to do is add an event handler for the **Patron** button. Locate the *ActAccessPatron_Click* event handler in the form's source code. Then add the following code to that handler.

Insert Snippet Insert Chapter 18, Snippet Item 12.

```
' ----- Look up the record of an active patron.
Dim patronID As Integer

' ----- Get the ID of the patron.
patronID = (New PatronAccess).SelectPatron()
If (patronID = -1) Then Return

' ----- Show the patron record.
Call (New PatronRecord).ViewPatronRecord(patronID, True)
```

This code makes direct calls to two of the forms we added in this chapter: *PatronAccess* and *PatronRecord*. It first prompts the user to select a patron record, and then displays its details through the *Patron Record* form.

Dueling Patron Management Forms

Let's make one more change regarding patron records. Way back in an earlier chapter, we included a **Manage Patron Items** button on the *Patron.vb* form. This button existed to provide access to the future *PatronRecord.vb* form, but it's pretty much been dead weight until now. But with the *PatronRecord.vb* form in place, we're ready to make patron management history.

Open the source code for the *Patron.vb* form, and locate the *ActItems_Click* event handler. Then add the following code to it.

Insert Snippet Insert Chapter 18, Snippet Item 13.

```
Call (New PatronRecord).ViewPatronRecord(ActiveID, False)
```

18. LOCALIZATION AND GLOBALIZATION

This is all well and good, but you are probably thinking to yourself, "The *Patron* form now lets you open the *Patron Record* form. And that form has an **Edit** button that lets you once again open the *Patron* form. If you get a rogue librarian, there may be millions of patron management forms on the screen at once." And that's all true. So we had to add some code to prevent that from happening. The second "False" argument to *PatronRecord.ViewPatronRecord* is a flag that says, "Don't show the **Edit** button on the *Patron Record* form." Similar code exists in the *Patron Record* form that stops the recursion.

```
Private Sub ActEditPatron_Click...
    If ((New Patron).EditRecordLimited( _
        ActivePatronID) <> -1) Then...
```

The *EditRecord**Limited*** method hides the **Manage Patron Items** button on the *Patron.vb* form. Whichever form you start with, you can access the other form, but you won't be able to generate a new copy of the initial form.

There was a lot of new code in this chapter, but it was all very pedestrian. We could have made even more culturally sensitive changes. For example, the **Due Date** column in the list of checked-out items on the *PatronRecord.vb* form uses a hard-coded date format for its display.

```
dueDate = Format(itemDetail.DueDate, "MMM d, yyyy")
```

This could be changed to "Short Date" or another culture-neutral setting. Whichever method you choose really depends on your target audience. If you do need to develop applications for global markets, you might want to consider reading another great Addison-Wesley book, *.NET Internationalization: The Developer's Guide to Building Global Windows and Web Applications*, by Guy Smith-Ferrier. But wait, let's finish this book first! Chapter 19, "Printing," is next.

PRINTING

When Microsoft released its original version of MS-DOS, it included printing features that supported the then-available printers: chisel and stone. Fortunately, printing has come a long way since then. These days, advanced color laser printers and even "paperless" printing systems (like Adobe Acrobat) provide printer support that rivals that of professional four-color offset printing facilities.

Although the .NET Framework does not replace the print spooler system built into each version of Windows, it makes it greatly accessible. As you'll read in this chapter, a printer is now treated like any other .NET drawing surface. The statements you use to draw on a form or control can be copied and pasted directly into your printing code.

This chapter provides a general discussion of .NET printing support. A discussion of report printing appears in the next chapter. If you are reading this chapter in its electronic format through the *Safari* publishing system, you can still rush right out and plunk down the funds for a hard-copy version of this book. Having that tactile response from the surface of the page should get you in the mood for this chapter's discussion of ink and paper.

Printing in Windows

Printers are a lot like people. Oh, I don't mean that they are cantankerous, or that they quickly run out of ink. Like the people of the world, printers speak many different languages. At the basic end of the language scale, many printers simply output the characters they receive. Others add "escape sequences," special combinations of characters that enable special features like font selection or double-wide text. At the complex end of the scale is PostScript, an English-like printer language with commands that are somewhat similar to those in GDI+.

It would be every programmer's worst nightmare to adjust application code so it targets all likely printers that a user may have. Each new printer language would mean another bout of development and testing. And printer makers are just giddy enough to come up with new language variations on a monthly basis.

Fortunately, Windows implements a system of printer-specific drivers that shield the developer from most printer variations. These drivers all speak a common language—let's call it "Printish"—which the driver translates into the printer's native tongue. As developers, we need only design software that speaks Printish.

The .NET Framework's printing system adds yet another level of language translation. .NET programs do not directly communicate with the printer drivers. Instead, they use GDI+ commands—the same commands used for screen updates—to output content to an in-memory printer canvas. The Framework then converts these commands to Printish and sends the output on to the appropriate printer driver, and finally to the printer. Figure 19-1 shows a summary of the steps involved in .NET printing.

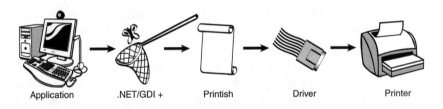

Application　　.NET/GDI +　　Printish　　Driver　　Printer

Figure 19-1 From programmer to canvas: printing with .NET

Printing in .NET

Having both screen and printer output generated through identical GDI+ commands means that I can make this a really short chapter, referring you back to Chapter 17, "GDI+, " for details. But it also means that there needs to be a canvas—a *System.Drawing.Graphics* object—where the printer-specific GDI+ commands target their output. The *System.Drawing.Printing.PrintDocument* class provides you with the output canvas you need for both ordinary printing and "print preview" output. There are three ways to use the *PrintDocument* class.

1. Add a *PrintDocument* control to a form from the Windows Forms toolbox. This control appears by default in the Toolbox's "Printing" section. Assign its properties and respond to its events as with any other control.
2. Create a class-level instance of the *PrintDocument* class. Include the *With Events* clause in the definition to get event management.
3. Create a local instance of *PrintDocument*, and connect any events using *AddHandler*.

These are standard methods in .NET, but having a control variation makes the class that much more convenient. We'll get into the actual printing code a little later.

There are four other printer-specific controls available for Windows Forms projects.

- **PageSetupDialog.** This control presents a standard Windows printer settings dialog that lets the user configure a specific print job, or all print jobs for the application. The control's *ShowDialog* method displays the form shown in Figure 19-2. The control also exposes properties related to the user's selection. Its *PageSettings* member exposes specific user preferences as defined on the form, while the *PrinterSettings* member identifies the selected printer and its properties. You can retain these members and later assign them to other printer-specific classes that include similar members.

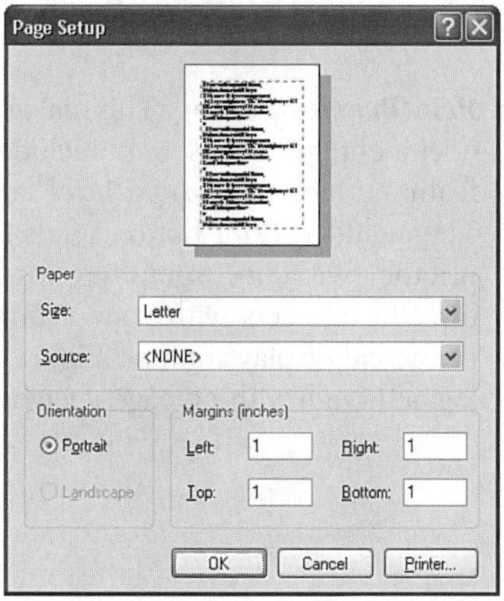

Figure 19-2 The Page Setup dialog

19. PRINTING

■ **PrintDialog.** Figure 19-3 shows this control's dialog, the standard dialog that appears in most programs when the user selects the **File ➤ Print** menu command. This control also exposes a *PrinterSettings* member used to assign or retrieve the selected printer and related options.

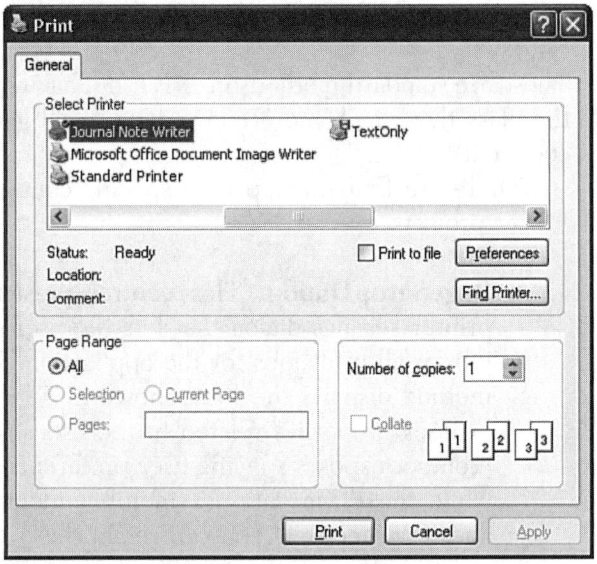

Figure 19-3 The Print dialog

■ **PrintPreviewDialog.** This dialog displays a preview of your printed document to the user. It includes standard preview presentation features, including zoom level and a pages-to-see-at-once control. The included *Print* button sends the preview content to the default printer (without prompting for printer selection). This control directly interacts with your *PrintDocument* instance, which drives the actual display content. Figure 19-4 shows the *Print Preview* dialog, although with no page-specific content.

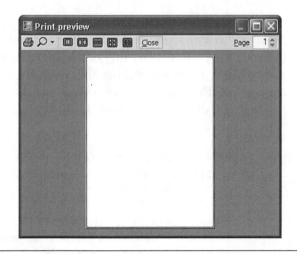

Figure 19-4 The Print Preview dialog

- **PrintPreviewControl.** The *PrintPreviewDialog* control includes basic preview management features (such as the zoom feature) that meet the needs of most applications. Unfortunately, that control is a sealed black box, and you cannot easily add your own custom features to it, or remove features that you don't want. The *PrintPreviewControl* control provides an alternative interface that lets you fully customize the print preview experience. Instead of a full dialog, it implements just the page-display portion of the form. You must implement all toolbars and other features, and link their functionality with the preview control. I won't be discussing this control in this chapter. If you're interested in using this advanced control, you can read an article I wrote about print preview a few years ago. (You can find the article referenced on my web site, http://www.timaki.com, in the articles section.)

Before you print, you need to know which printer your user wants to target for the output. You may also need to know about available features of the printer, such as whether it supports color or not. An early beta release of Visual Basic 2005 included a *My.Computer.Printers* collection. Unfortunately, that feature did not make it into the final product, so you will have to use more indirect means to access the printers.

The *System.Drawing.Printing.PrinterSettings* class includes a shared *InstalledPrinters* string collection that lists the path to each configured printer. You can assign any of these strings to the *PrinterSettings'* *PrinterName* member, making the specific printer available within the application. The following code chunk lets the user select from the list of printers, and displays some basic information about the selected printer.

```
Private Sub Form1_Load(ByVal sender As System.Object, _
    ByVal e As System.EventArgs) Handles MyBase.Load
  ' ----- Display the list of printers.
  Dim scanPrinter As String

  For Each scanPrinter In Drawing.Printing. _
      PrinterSettings.InstalledPrinters
    ListBox1.Items.Add(scanPrinter)
  Next scanPrinter
End Sub

Private Sub Button1_Click(ByVal sender As System.Object, _
    ByVal e As System.EventArgs) Handles Button1.Click
  ' ----- Display information about the selected printer.
  Dim selectedPrinter As Drawing.Printing.PrinterSettings

  If (ListBox1.SelectedIndex = -1) Then Return
  selectedPrinter = New Drawing.Printing.PrinterSettings()
  selectedPrinter.PrinterName = ListBox1.Text
  MsgBox(selectedPrinter.ToString)
End Sub
```

Printing a Document

Earlier we saw that many Windows components work together to generate your printed output. Within your .NET code, you will also use many components (classes) to drive the printing process. There are four main steps involved (at least directly) in printing a document from your code.

1. Create an instance of a *PrintDocument* class (or add it as a control to your form).
2. Set the *PrintDocument*'s various printer settings, either by using a *PrintDialog* (or related) class/control, or by using the default or manual settings.

3. Add an event handler for the *PrintDocument*'s *PrintPage* event. This event is called once for each page, and receives a *System.Drawing.Graphics* object for the printer canvas. Your event handler code prints a single page, and updates a flag telling the document whether there are more pages to come.
4. Call the *PrintDocument*'s *Print* method to start the ball rolling.

Let's try a little code to see how this printing beast eats. Or prints. Or whatever it does. How about a simple program that prints a five-page document on the user's selected printer? The output will be a large single-digit page number, perfect for the Sesame Street set. First, let's create a new Windows Forms application, and add a single button to *Form1* named *ActPrint*. We'll also add a *PrintDocument* control (named *CountingDoc*), and a *PrintDialog* control (named *UserPrinter*). Figure 19-5 shows the form and its supporting controls.

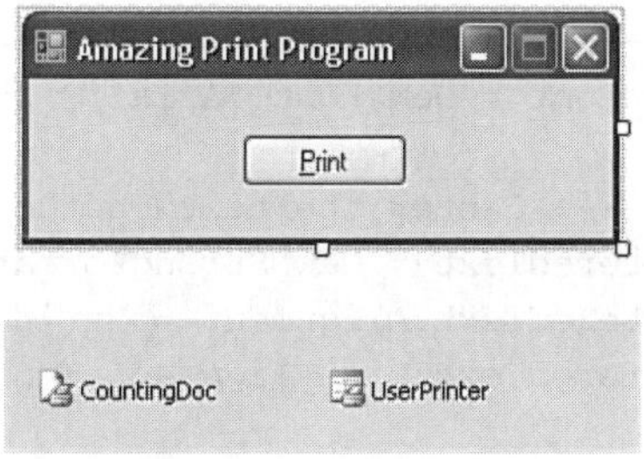

Figure 19-5 A program with only printing on its mind

These controls implement the first two of our four-step printing process. Next, we'll add the source code.

```
Public Class Form1
    Private WhichPage As Integer

    Private Sub ActPrint_Click(ByVal sender As System.Object, _
        ByVal e As System.EventArgs) Handles ActPrint.Click
        ' ----- Prompt the user for printer settings, and
        '       start printing.
        UserPrinter.Document = CountingDoc
```

```vb
      If (UserPrinter.ShowDialog() = _
         Windows.Forms.DialogResult.OK) Then _
         CountingDoc.Print()
   End Sub

   Private Sub CountingDoc_BeginPrint(ByVal sender As Object, _
         ByVal e As System.Drawing.Printing.PrintEventArgs) _
         Handles CountingDoc.BeginPrint
      ' ----- Start the counting over.
      WhichPage = 1
   End Sub

   Private Sub CountingDoc_PrintPage(ByVal sender As Object, _
         ByVal e As System.Drawing.Printing. _
         PrintPageEventArgs) Handles CountingDoc.PrintPage
      ' ----- Print a single page.
      Dim hugeFont As Font
      Dim centeredText As StringFormat

      ' ----- Let's go overboard on the font: 256 points!
      hugeFont = New Font("Arial", 256)

      ' ----- Center the text on the page.
      centeredText = New StringFormat()
      centeredText.Alignment = StringAlignment.Center
      centeredText.LineAlignment = StringAlignment.Center

      ' ----- Print the number.
      e.Graphics.DrawString(CStr(WhichPage), hugeFont, _
         Brushes.Black, e.MarginBounds, centeredText)

      ' ----- Draw the page margins to make it clear where
      '       they are.
      e.Graphics.DrawRectangle(Pens.Blue, e.MarginBounds)

      ' ----- Limit the output to five pages.
      WhichPage += 1
      If (WhichPage <= 5) Then e.HasMorePages = True _
         Else e.HasMorePages = False
   End Sub
End Class
```

This code implements steps three (*ActPrint_Click*) and four (*CountingDoc_PrintPage*). The *ActPrint* button's *Click* event handler links the document and the *Print Dialog* so that they both refer to the same settings. It then prompts the user to select a printer and various options through the *ShowDialog* call. If the user clicks the *OK* button on that dialog, it triggers a call to the document's *Print* method.

The action then moves to the events of the *PrintDocument* instance. I've implemented two of the events: a *BeginPrint* event handler that performs some initialization, and a *PrintPage* event handler that does the hard work. (Other events include *EndPrint*, used to clean up when printing is complete, and *QueryPageSettings*, where you change the orientation and settings of each page of the document.) Actually, it's not all that hard, especially since we saw similar code in the chapter on GDI+. The biggest difference is the amount of space available on a printed page, allowing us to play with fonts in the hundreds of point sizes.

Figure 19-6 shows page two of the output from this program. I printed to the pseudo-printer installed with Microsoft's *Windows Journal* application. You can see in the bottom-right corner that it did properly record five output pages.

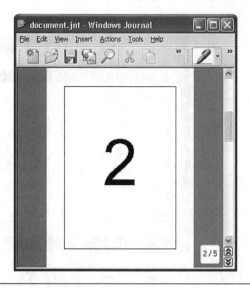

Figure 19-6 This page is brought to you by the number 2.

Print Preview

Adding a print preview interface is so easy, you should probably ask your boss for a really hard project to do first, and then come back when you're worn out. Let's build on our simple number-printing application, adding a new *Button* control named *ActPreview*. We will also add a *PrintPreviewDialog* control named *UserPreview*. Once these are in place, add the following preview button *Click* event handler.

```
Private Sub ActPreview_Click(ByVal sender As System.Object, _
     ByVal e As System.EventArgs) Handles ActPreview.Click
   ' ----- Display a preview of the document.
   UserPreview.Document = CountingDoc
   UserPreview.ShowDialog()
End Sub
```

Hey, that's even simpler than the code that initiates printing to a real printer, even though print preview technology seems to be more complex than plain printing. There almost ought to be a law against code that simple. Fortunately, there's not. Figure 19-7 shows the preview window, after using the two-pages-at-once toolbar button.

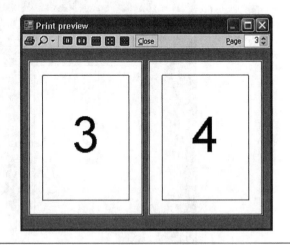

Figure 19-7 The preview displays multiple pages at once with no extra effort on our part.

Let's dwell just a little longer on how simple that code was. I can accept that the *PrintPreviewDialog* class includes a lot of amazing code for previewing printed output. But the remarkable part of the code is that we didn't have to rewrite the custom GDI+ drawing logic. The same set of GDI+ statements now drives the preview display and the actual output. All we had to do was assign the *PrintDocument* object to the correct dialog control.

Counting and Numbering Pages

During the printing (or preview) process, the *PrintDocument*'s *PrintPage* event handler gets called once for each output page. But here's the tricky thing: When the *PrintPage* handler was called the first time, it was not to print "page 1" of the document, but to print "the first page in need of printing," whatever its page number. Search all you want through the properties of the *PrintDocument* class, but you will never find a *PageNumber* property. The *PrintDocument* does not know about the page numbers in your document, and—despite all of the nice things it does for you—it does not care. All it knows is that you have a bunch of pages to print, and it will call your *PrintPage* event handler until you say "enough!"

If you turn back to Figure 19-3, you'll see that the *Print* dialog includes a "Page Range" section, although most of its controls are disabled by default. The *PrintDialog* control includes three Boolean properties that let you enable specific controls in that section: *AllowCurrentPage*, *AllowSomePages*, and *AllowSelection*. Setting any of these properties to *True* enables the matching option control. Later, after the user has made a choice, you can query the *PrintDocument* object's *PrinterSettings.PrintRange* property to determine which choice it is.

Let's add code that enables page range selection. We'll still limit the allowed pages to just those numbered one to five, but the user will be able to choose a sub-range within that set. Return to the *Click* event handler for the *ActPrint* button, and insert a few new lines of code (the ones in bold).

```
Private Sub ActPrint_Click(ByVal sender As System.Object, _
    ByVal e As System.EventArgs) Handles ActPrint.Click
    ' ----- Prompt the user for printer settings, and
    '       start printing.
    UserPrinter.Document = CountingDoc
```

```
UserPrinter.AllowSomePages = True
CountingDoc.PrinterSettings.MinimumPage = 1
CountingDoc.PrinterSettings.MaximumPage = 5
CountingDoc.PrinterSettings.FromPage = 1
CountingDoc.PrinterSettings.ToPage = 5

If (UserPrinter.ShowDialog() = _
    Windows.Forms.DialogResult.OK) Then _
    CountingDoc.Print()
End Sub
```

When the user clicks on the **Print** button this time, the "Print Range" section of the dialog has enabled the *Pages* field, and it's already filled in with the minimum and maximum pages in the range "1-5" (see Figure 19-8).

Figure 19-8 Support for page ranges

If the user adjusts this field to "1-6," an error occurs stating that the valid range is somewhere within "1-5" only. But whether the user selects "All Pages" or "1-5" or "1-4" or "2-3" or "Current Page" or "Selection," the *PrintPage* event handler will be called in exactly the same manner. In fact, the handler will be called dozens, even hundreds of times, until you tell it to stop. The user's selection impacts the *PrinterSettings.PrintRange* property and some other properties, but it does not directly impact the print process. It is up to you to alter the print behavior based on these settings.

Let's pretend that the user entered a print range of "2-3." We cannot let the *PrintDocument* fire the *PrintPage* event for all five pages because, even if we generated output for pages two and three only, we would still get three other blank pages out of the printer. What we want is to only have the event fire twice, once for page two and once for page three. We'll need to adjust the use of the *WhichPage* class-level tracking variable to compensate for the indicated range. First, let's change the *BeginPrint* handler to use the correct starting page number.

```
Private Sub CountingDoc_BeginPrint(ByVal sender As Object, _
    ByVal e As System.Drawing.Printing.PrintEventArgs) _
    Handles CountingDoc.BeginPrint
    ' ----- Start the counting over.
    WhichPage = CountingDoc.PrinterSettings.FromPage
End Sub
```

In the *PrintPage* event handler, we must modify the code that determines when to quit the print process.

```
WhichPage += 1
If (WhichPage <= CountingDoc.PrinterSettings.ToPage) _
    Then e.HasMorePages = True Else e.HasMorePages = False
```

Because the print preview code shares the same document settings, we need to adjust the preview code to force it to always print all pages.

```
Private Sub ActPreview_Click(ByVal sender As System.Object, _
    ByVal e As System.EventArgs) Handles ActPreview.Click
    ' ----- Display a preview of the document.
    UserPreview.Document = CountingDoc
    CountingDoc.PrinterSettings.PrintRange = _
        Printing.PrintRange.AllPages
    UserPreview.ShowDialog()
End Sub
```

If you run the program and adjust the print range, you should get just the pages you requested. I've placed a copy of this program in the book's installation directory. You'll find it in the *Print Preview Test* subdirectory.

Printing in "Raw" Mode

Using GDI+ to generate printed pages is pretty straightforward. For complex pages, you may have to do a lot of positioning and measuring of text strings and whatnot, but it all boils down to "draw this text or this shape at this position."

Sadly, not all printers support the application-to-printer-via-GDI-and-Printish way of doing things. This is especially true of printers used to print thermal credit card receipts at your favorite pizza place. Although some of these printers may have Windows drivers, they are really designed for direct communication with an application via their special "escape sequence" language. For such printers, you need to write directly to the printer in "raw" mode, where you control exactly which characters get sent to the printer. (Actually, you don't have to go directly to the printer. You can still write to the printer's queue, and let Windows manage the scheduling of the print job.)

It is with even more sadness that I must inform you of .NET's lack of raw printer support. Although there is a DLL included with Windows that enables this direct printing method, a managed .NET wrapper for it does not ship with the Framework. You, and other overburdened programmers everywhere, must take up the charge yourselves.

Well, it's not all that bad. Microsoft and other developers have published code that maps the unmanaged DLL calls to managed equivalents. We'll be using a variation of some of this code in the Library Project in this chapter to support the printing of check-out slips, paper receipts that let a patron know which items were just checked out and when they are all due back.

Summary

I recommend that you peruse the printer-specific classes and controls discussed in this chapter. They include many properties that let you fine-tune the output of your printed page based on the user's specified settings. For instance, I promised you earlier in the chapter that you could discover whether a printer supported color or not. The *PrinterSettings.SupportsColor* property gives you a straight-up yes or no answer to this feature question. If you know that a printer does not support color, you can adjust your *PrintPage* code to present the page content in a slightly different format.

Project

As advertised, this chapter's project focuses on the printing of check-out and fine-payment receipts. But we'll also add all of the code that lets patrons and librarians check in and check out books and other library items.

Project Access Load the "Chapter 19 (Before) Code" project, either through the New Project templates, or by accessing the project directly from the installation directory. To see the code in its final form, load "Chapter 19 (After) Code" instead.

Supporting Raw Printing

In the interest of frank and honest discussion, I must tell you that I didn't come up with the basic code for raw printing in this section. Oh, some of the code is mine, both stylistically and imaginatively. But I didn't figure out all of the links between the application and the *winspool.drv* file. That code originally came from Microsoft Knowledge Base article number 322090, which describes raw printing support from .NET applications. It uses a feature of .NET known as "interop" that allows .NET code to "interoperate" with older unmanaged COM-based components and applications.

Boy, am I glad that I got that off my chest. I mean, if anyone thought I was the one who came up with the code you are about to see, there would be angry mobs storming my house nightly, and general turmoil in the streets. The code, contained in the *RawPrinterHelper* class, is just plain ugly. Well, there's no sense postponing it any longer. Create a new class named *RawPrinterHelper.vb*, and use the following code for its definition.

Insert Snippet Insert Chapter 19, Snippet Item 1.

```vb
Imports System.Runtime.InteropServices

Public Class RawPrinterHelper
    ' ----- The code in this class is based on Microsoft
    '       knowledge base article number 322090.
    '       Web: http://support.microsoft.com/?id=322090

    ' ----- Structure and API declarations.
    <StructLayout(LayoutKind.Sequential, _
    CharSet:=CharSet.Unicode)> _
    Private Structure DOCINFOW
        <MarshalAs(UnmanagedType.LPWStr)> _
        Public pDocName As String
```

```vb
        <MarshalAs(UnmanagedType.LPWStr)> _
            Public pOutputFile As String
        <MarshalAs(UnmanagedType.LPWStr)> _
            Public pDataType As String
    End Structure


    <DllImport("winspool.Drv", EntryPoint:="OpenPrinterW", _
        SetLastError:=True, CharSet:=CharSet.Unicode, _
        ExactSpelling:=True, _
        CallingConvention:=CallingConvention.StdCall)> _
    Private Shared Function OpenPrinter(ByVal src As String, _
        ByRef hPrinter As IntPtr, ByVal pd As Long) As Boolean
    End Function


    <DllImport("winspool.Drv", EntryPoint:="ClosePrinter", _
        SetLastError:=True, CharSet:=CharSet.Unicode, _
        ExactSpelling:=True, _
        CallingConvention:=CallingConvention.StdCall)> _
    Private Shared Function ClosePrinter( _
        ByVal hPrinter As IntPtr) As Boolean
    End Function


    <DllImport("winspool.Drv", EntryPoint:="StartDocPrinterW", _
        SetLastError:=True, CharSet:=CharSet.Unicode, _
        ExactSpelling:=True, _
        CallingConvention:=CallingConvention.StdCall)> _
    Private Shared Function StartDocPrinter( _
        ByVal hPrinter As IntPtr, ByVal level As Int32, _
        ByRef pDI As DOCINFOW) As Boolean
    End Function


    <DllImport("winspool.Drv", EntryPoint:="EndDocPrinter", _
        SetLastError:=True, CharSet:=CharSet.Unicode, _
        ExactSpelling:=True, _
        CallingConvention:=CallingConvention.StdCall)> _
    Private Shared Function EndDocPrinter( _
        ByVal hPrinter As IntPtr) As Boolean
    End Function


    <DllImport("winspool.Drv", EntryPoint:="StartPagePrinter", _
        SetLastError:=True, CharSet:=CharSet.Unicode, _
        ExactSpelling:=True, _
        CallingConvention:=CallingConvention.StdCall)> _
```

```
Private Shared Function StartPagePrinter( _
   ByVal hPrinter As IntPtr) As Boolean
End Function

<DllImport("winspool.Drv", EntryPoint:="EndPagePrinter", _
   SetLastError:=True, CharSet:=CharSet.Unicode, _
   ExactSpelling:=True, _
   CallingConvention:=CallingConvention.StdCall)> _
Private Shared Function EndPagePrinter( _
   ByVal hPrinter As IntPtr) As Boolean
End Function

<DllImport("winspool.Drv", EntryPoint:="WritePrinter", _
   SetLastError:=True, CharSet:=CharSet.Unicode, _
   ExactSpelling:=True, _
   CallingConvention:=CallingConvention.StdCall)> _
Private Shared Function WritePrinter( _
   ByVal hPrinter As IntPtr, ByVal pBytes As IntPtr, _
   ByVal dwCount As Int32, ByRef dwWritten As Int32) _
   As Boolean
End Function

Public Shared Function SendStringToPrinter( _
     ByVal targetPrinter As String, _
     ByVal stringContent As String, _
     ByVal documentTitle As String) As Boolean
   ' ----- Send an array of bytes to a printer queue.
   '       Return True on success.
   Dim printerHandle As IntPtr
   Dim errorCode As Int32
   Dim docDetail As DOCINFOW = Nothing
   Dim bytesWritten As Int32
   Dim printSuccess As Boolean
   Dim contentBytes As IntPtr
   Dim contentSize As Int32

   On Error Resume Next

   ' ----- Set up the identity of this document.
   With docDetail
      .pDocName = documentTitle
      .pDataType = "RAW"
   End With
```

```
        ' ----- Convert the string to ANSI text.
        contentSize = stringContent.Length()
        contentBytes = Marshal.StringToCoTaskMemAnsi( _
            stringContent)

        ' ----- Open the printer and print the document.
        printSuccess = False
        If OpenPrinter(targetPrinter, printerHandle, 0) Then
            If StartDocPrinter(printerHandle, 1, docDetail) Then
                If StartPagePrinter(printerHandle) Then
                    ' ----- Send the content to the printer.
                    printSuccess = WritePrinter(printerHandle, _
                        contentBytes, contentSize, bytesWritten)
                    EndPagePrinter(printerHandle)
                End If
                EndDocPrinter(printerHandle)
            End If
            ClosePrinter(printerHandle)
        End If

        ' ----- GetLastError may provide information on the
        '          last error. For now, just ignore it.
        If (printSuccess = False) Then errorCode = _
            Marshal.GetLastWin32Error()

        ' ----- Free up unused memory.
        Marshal.FreeCoTaskMem(contentBytes)

        ' ----- Complete.
        Return printSuccess
    End Function
End Class
```

Although ugly, the code is relatively clear-cut. The *SendStringToPrinter* method prepares a string for printing by forcing it to a standard ANSI format. It then uses the functions in the *winspool.drv* library to open a new print job, and send the prepared content to it. There's a whole lot of "marshalling" going on in the code through members of the *Marshall* class. Because *winspool.drv* is an unmanaged library, all data calls must be shuttled indirectly between the managed Library application and the unmanaged *winspool.drv* library.

Printing Tickets

Now that we have a convenient class that will send any raw content to any specific printer, let's add some code to use it. First, we need to add a helper class for a portion of the ticket printing. Create a new class file named *CheckedOutItem.vb*, and replace its empty class template with the following code.

Insert Snippet Insert Chapter 19, Snippet Item 2.

```
Public Class CheckedOutItem
    ' ----- Used to store the details of each checked out
    '       on the main form, although it also supports
    '       receipt printing.
    Public ItemTitle As String
    Public CopyNumber As Integer
    Public Barcode As String
    Public DueDate As Date
End Class
```

We'll use this class to convey the details to be printed on the receipt when checking out items. Speaking of ticket printing, let's add the class that does the actual printing. Create a new module file (not a class) named *TicketPrinting.vb*. Replace its empty module definition with the snippet code.

Insert Snippet Insert Chapter 19, Snippet Item 3.

The code includes three methods that drive printing: *PrintCheckoutTicket*, *PrintBalanceTicket*, and *PrintPaymentTicket*. These methods are called from other parts of the application when it's time to present a printed ticket to the user. The *TicketPrinting* module also includes a few other methods that support these three primary methods. Because these three methods are somewhat similar in structure, let's just look at *PrintCheckoutTicket*.

```
Public Sub PrintCheckoutTicket(ByVal patronID As Integer, _
    ByVal checkedOutItems As ListBox)
```

```
' ----- Print out a ticket of what the patron checked
'       out. The supplied ListBox control contains
'       objects of type CheckedOutItem.
Dim ticketWidth As Integer
Dim ticketText As System.Text.StringBuilder
Dim counter As Integer
Dim patronFines As Decimal
Dim itemDetail As CheckedOutItem

On Error GoTo ErrorHandler

' ----- Ignore if there is nothing to print.
If (patronID = -1) Or (checkedOutItems.Items.Count = 0) _
   Then Return

' ----- Get the width of the ticket.
ticketWidth = My.Settings.ReceiptWidth
If (ticketWidth <= 0) Then ticketWidth = 40

' ----- Build the heading.
ticketText = GetTicketHeader(patronID, ticketWidth)
If (ticketText Is Nothing) Then Return

' ----- Process each checked-out item.
For counter = 0 To checkedOutItems.Items.Count - 1
   ' ----- Extract the detail from the list.
   itemDetail = CType(checkedOutItems.Items(counter), _
      CheckedOutItem)

   ' ----- Add the item name.
   ticketText.AppendLine(Left(itemDetail.ItemTitle, _
      ticketWidth))

   ' ----- Add the barcode number and due date.
   ticketText.AppendLine(LeftAndRightText( _
      itemDetail.Barcode, "Due: " & _
      Format(itemDetail.DueDate, "MMM d, yyyy"), _
      ticketWidth))
   ticketText.AppendLine()
Next counter
```

```
' ----- If there are fines due, print them here.
patronFines = CalculatePatronFines(patronID)
If (patronFines > 0@) Then
   ticketText.AppendLine("Fines Due: " & _
      Format(patronFines, "$#,##0.00"))
   ticketText.AppendLine()
End If


' ----- Add the bottom display text.
ticketText.Append(GetTicketFooter(ticketWidth))


' ----- Send the ticket to the printer.
RawPrinterHelper.SendStringToPrinter( _
   My.Settings.ReceiptPrinter, _
   ticketText.ToString(), "Checkout Receipt")
Return

ErrorHandler:
   GeneralError("TicketPrinting.PrintCheckoutTicket", _
      Err.GetException())
   Return
End Sub
```

The code builds a string (actually a *StringBuilder*) of display content, adding details about each checked-out item to a string buffer. Then it calls *SendStringToPrinter* to send the content to the configured receipt printer (*My.Settings.ReceiptPrinter*).

We'll add the code that calls *PrintCheckoutTicket* later. Right now, let's add code that calls the two other methods. When the *Payment Record* form closes, we want to automatically print a receipt of all payments made while the form was open. Add the following code to the *PatronRecord.ActClose_Click* event handler, just before the code already found in that handler.

Insert Snippet Insert Chapter 19, Snippet Item 4.

```
' ----- Print out a ticket if needed.
If (SessionPayments.Count > 0) Then _
   PrintPaymentTicket(ActivePatronID, SessionPayments)
SessionPayments.Clear()
SessionPayments = Nothing
```

Then, add some code to the *ActBalanceTicket_Click* event handler, also in the *PatronRecord* class, that prints a balance ticket when the user requests it.

Insert Snippet Insert Chapter 19, Snippet Item 5.

```
' ----- Print a ticket of all balances.
PrintBalanceTicket(ActivePatronID, Fines)
```

Printing Barcodes

The Library Project prints three types of barcodes: (1) item barcodes that you can stick on books, CDs, and anything else that can be checked-out or managed by the system; (2) patron barcodes that can be made into patron identification cards; and (3) miscellaneous barcodes that a library can use for any other purpose. All three barcode types are printed through the new *BarcodePrint* form. Figure 19-9 shows the controls included on this form.

Figure 19-9 One form, three barcode types, many happy labels

I've already added this form to the project, including its code. Here's the code for the *Preview* button, which should look familiar after I beat its concepts into you throughout this chapter.

```
Private Sub ActPreview_Click(ByVal sender As System.Object, _
     ByVal e As System.EventArgs) Handles ActPreview.Click
   ' ----- The user wants to preview the labels.
   On Error Resume Next

   ' ----- Make sure the user supplied valid data.
   If (VerifyFields() = False) Then Return

   ' ----- Load in all of the page-specific details to be
   '         used in printing.
   If (LoadPageDetails() = False) Then Return

   ' ----- Create the preview dialog.
   Me.Cursor = Windows.Forms.Cursors.WaitCursor
   PageSoFar = 0
   PreviewMode = True
   BarcodeDoc = New System.Drawing.Printing.PrintDocument

   ' ----- Display the preview.
   BarcodePreview.Document = BarcodeDoc
   BarcodePreview.ShowDialog()
   BarcodeDoc = Nothing
   Me.Cursor = Windows.Forms.Cursors.Default
End Sub
```

The **Print** button's code is almost exactly the same, but it uses a *PrintDialog* instance instead of *PrintPreviewDialog*. It also keeps track of the final printed barcode number so that it can help avoid overlaps the next time they are printed.

The *BarcodeDoc_PrintPage* event handler does the actual barcode printing. Its code combines the *BarcodeLabel.PreviewArea_Paint* and *BarcodePage.PreviewArea_Paint* event handlers into one glorious printing machine.

To enable use of the barcode printing form, add the following statements to the *ActReportsBarcode_Click* event handler in the *MainForm* class.

Insert Snippet Insert Chapter 19, Snippet Item 6.

```
' ----- Make sure the user is allowed to do this.
If (SecurityProfile(LibrarySecurity. _
        ManageBarcodeTemplates) = False) Then
    MsgBox(NotAuthorizedMessage, MsgBoxStyle.OkOnly Or _
        MsgBoxStyle.Exclamation, ProgramTitle)
    Return
End If


' ----- Show the barcode label printing form.
Call (New BarcodePrint).ShowDialog()
```

Renewal of Checked-Out Patron Items

For a library patron, the only thing more important than checking out
and in items is being able to read those items. The Library Project won't
help anyone with that, but it will do that check-in, check-out transaction
thing through the code we add in this chapter. Let's start by adding the
renewal code for currently checked-out items. The **Renew** button on
the *Patron Record* form initiates the process. Add the code to the
PatronRecord.ActRenewItemsOut_Click event handler that does the
renewal.

Insert Snippet Insert Chapter 19, Snippet Item 7.

The code does some calculations to determine the new due date
(avoiding holidays), and then updates the database in a transaction.

```
TransactionBegin()

' ----- Update the record.
sqlText = "UPDATE PatronCopy SET DueDate = " & _
    DBDate(dueDate) & ", Renewal = " & renewsSoFar & _
    " WHERE ID = " & itemDetail.DetailID
ExecuteSQL(sqlText)

' ----- Update the patron record.
sqlText = "UPDATE Patron SET LastActivity = Now " & _
    "WHERE ID = " & ActivePatronID
ExecuteSQL(sqlText)

TransactionCommit()
```

Support for Check-In and Check-Out

If a library adds barcode labels to all of its items, then check-in and check-out will be via a barcode reader. But a very small library using the program may not have the staff time available to barcode everything on the shelves. Therefore, the Library Project needs to support check-in and check-out by title. During check-out or check-in, the user enters either a barcode or a title (partial or complete). Non-numeric entries are assumed to be titles, and initiate a title search. The new *CheckLookup.vb* form, pictured in Figure 19-10, displays all matches for the entered title.

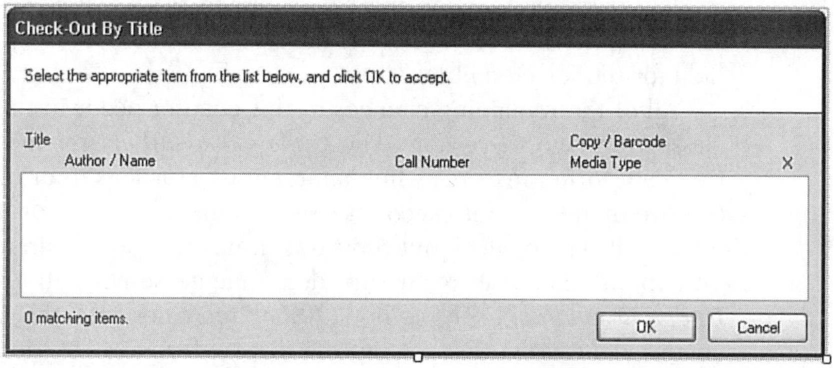

Figure 19-10 A title matching form for both check-in and check-out

Although the fields on the form initially indicate that they are for check-out only, the form does double duty, altering its visage for check-in purposes. Additionally, check-in listings are limited to only those items already checked out.

I've already added this form to the project, along with its source code. Most of the code queries the database for matching library items and displays the results using an owner draw list box. It is a subset of the code found in the *ItemLookup.vb* form. The only real difference between check-in and check-out occurs in the *PerformLookup* method. This code block starts to build the main item selection SQL command, and then ends it with these statements.

```
If (asCheckIn) Then sqlText &= " AND IC.ID IN" _
   Else sqlText &= " AND IC.ID NOT IN"
sqlText &= " (SELECT ItemCopy FROM PatronCopy " & _
   "WHERE Returned = 0)"
```

So the difference is "IN" versus "NOT IN."

The *CheckItemByTitle* function is the main interface to the form's logic.

```
Public Function CheckItemByTitle(ByVal CheckIn As Boolean, _
   ByVal searchText As String) As Integer
```

You pass this function the user-supplied title (*searchText*) and a flag indicating check-in or check-out, and it returns the *ItemCopy.ID* database field for the selected library item.

All of the remaining changes in this chapter occur in the *MainForm* class, so let's go there now. The *UpdateDisplayForUser* method adjusts the main form's features when an administrator logs in or out. One feature we didn't take into account before is the administrator-defined ability for patrons to check out their own items without librarian assistance. To support that feature, we need to change some of the code in the *UpdateDisplayForUser* method. About ten lines into the code, in the conditional section that sets up the display for patrons, you'll find these four lines.

```
LabelTasks.Visible = False
LineTasks.Visible = False
PicCheckOut.Visible = False
ActCheckOut.Visible = False
```

Replace these four lines with the following code.

Insert Snippet Insert Chapter 19, Snippet Item 8.

```
' ----- See if patrons can check out items by themselves.
Dim userCanCheckOut As Boolean = _
   CBool(Val(GetSystemValue("PatronCheckOut")))
```

```
LabelTasks.Visible = userCanCheckOut
LineTasks.Visible = userCanCheckOut
PicCheckOut.Visible = userCanCheckOut
ActCheckOut.Visible = userCanCheckOut
```

We also need to add similar security-related code to the *TaskCheckOut* method. Here are the first few lines of code from that method.

```
' ----- Update the display.
AllPanelsInvisible()
If (SecurityProfile(LibrarySecurity.CheckOutItems)) Then _
   PanelCheckOut.Visible = True
```

Replace these lines with the following code.

Insert Snippet Insert Chapter 19, Snippet Item 9.

```
' ----- Check Out mode.
Dim userCanCheckOut As Boolean

' ----- See if patrons can check out items by themselves.
userCanCheckOut = CBool(Val(GetSystemValue("PatronCheckOut")))

' ----- Update the display.
AllPanelsInvisible()
If (userCanCheckOut Or _
   SecurityProfile(LibrarySecurity.CheckOutItems)) Then _
   PanelCheckOut.Visible = True
```

The actual check-out of items occurs on the main form itself. First, a patron is identified, and then the items to check out get processed. Let's add a class-level variable to *MainForm* that keeps track of the patron. And as long as we're adding definitions, we'll also add two constants that refer to images stored in the *MainForm.StatusImages* control. These constants will be used in some check-in-related code added a little later. Add the following code to the start of the class definition.

Insert Snippet Insert Chapter 19, Snippet Item 10.

```
Private ActiveCheckOutPatron As Integer = -1

Private Const StatusImageBad As Integer = 0
Private Const StatusImageGood As Integer = 1
```

When the user identifies the patron to use for check-out, and then starts checking items out, the last step is a click of the **Finish** button, indicating the end of the check-out process for that patron. (Skip ahead to Figure 19-11 if you want to see the **Finish** button now.) However, there is nothing to stop the user from jumping to another part of the program, or from exiting the program completely, without first pushing the **Finish** button. We must anticipate this rude behavior so typical of software users. To ensure that check-out completes properly, we will add some code to three places in *MainForm* that should catch any such discourteous actions by the user. Add the following code to **the start** of these three methods: (1) the *MainForm_FormClosing* event handler; (2) the *ShowLoginForm* method; and (3) the *AllPanelsInvisible* method.

Insert Snippet Insert Chapter 19, Snippet Item 11 **three times**.

```
' ----- Finish the in-process check-out if needed.
If (ActiveCheckOutPatron <> -1) Then _
   ActFinishCheckOut.PerformClick()
```

Checking Out Items

All of the check-out code (except for the code in the *CheckLookup.vb* form) appears in the main form's class. Check-out is one of the eight main display panels accessed through this form (see Figure 19-11).

Here's the process for checking out items from the check-out panel.

1. The user clicks the **Patron** button and identifies the patron who will check out items.
2. The user enters the title or barcode for each item to check out, and clicks the **Check Out** button for each one.
3. The user clicks the **Finish** button when check-out is complete.

Let's add the code for each of these three buttons. First, add code to the *ActCheckOutPatron_Click* event handler.

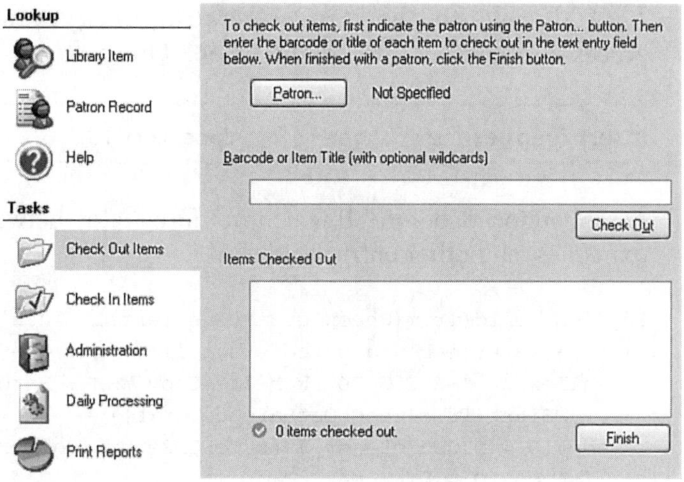

Figure 19-11 The check-out panel on the main form

Insert Snippet Insert Chapter 19, Snippet Item 12.

This code prompts the user for patron selection, and displays the remaining fields if successful. Here's the part of the code that does the prompting.

```
' ----- Get the ID of the patron.
patronID = (New PatronAccess).SelectPatron()
If (patronID = -1) Then Return

' ----- Get the patron name.
sqlText = "SELECT FirstName + ' ' + LastName FROM Patron " & _
   "WHERE ID = " & patronID
patronName = CStr(ExecuteSQLReturn(sqlText))

' ----- Is this patron active?
sqlText = "SELECT Active FROM Patron WHERE ID = " & patronID
If (CBool(ExecuteSQLReturn(sqlText)) = False) Then
   MsgBox("Patron '" & patronName & _
      "' is marked as inactive.", MsgBoxStyle.OkOnly Or _
      MsgBoxStyle.Exclamation, ProgramTitle)
   Return
End If
```

Add code to the *ActDoCheckOut_Click* event handler, which processes each item through the **Check Out** button.

Insert Snippet Insert Chapter 19, Snippet Item 13.

As I mentioned before, this code differentiates between numeric entry (barcodes) and other entries (titles).

```
If (IsNumeric(Trim(CheckOutBarcode.Text))) Then
   ' ----- Probably a barcode supplied. Get the related ID.
   sqlText = "SELECT ID FROM ItemCopy WHERE Barcode = " & _
      DBText(Trim(CheckOutBarcode.Text))
   copyID = DBGetInteger(ExecuteSQLReturn(sqlText))
   If (copyID = 0) Then
      ' ----- Invalid barcode.
      MsgBox("Barcode not found.", MsgBoxStyle.OkOnly Or _
         MsgBoxStyle.Exclamation, ProgramTitle)
      CheckOutBarcode.Focus()
      CheckOutBarcode.SelectAll()
      Return
   End If
Else
   ' ----- Look up by title.
   copyID = (New CheckLookup).CheckItemByTitle(False, _
      Trim(CheckOutBarcode.Text))
   If (copyID = -1) Then Return
End If
```

Eventually, after verifying that the item is available for patron use, the code checks out the item by updating the relevant records in the database.

```
TransactionBegin()

' ----- Update patron copy record.
sqlText = "INSERT INTO PatronCopy (Patron, ItemCopy, " & _
   "CheckOut, Renewal, DueDate, Returned, Missing, " & _
   "Fine, Paid) VALUES (" & ActiveCheckOutPatron & ", " & _
   copyID & ", " & DBDate(Today) & ", 0, " & _
   DBDate(untilDate) & ", 0, 0, 0, 0)"
ExecuteSQL(sqlText)
```

19. PRINTING

```
' ----- Update the patron record.
sqlText = "UPDATE Patron SET LastActivity = GETDATE() " & _
    "WHERE ID = " & ActiveCheckOutPatron
ExecuteSQL(sqlText)

TransactionCommit()
```

The last of the three buttons is the **Finish** button. Add code to the *ActFinishCheckOut_Click* event handler.

Insert Snippet Insert Chapter 19, Snippet Item 14.

This code simply resets the display fields in preparation for the next patron check-out.

The list box on the check-out panel needs to display two columns of data: (1) the due date; and (2) details of the item such as title and barcode. These values were added to the list using the *CheckedOutItem* class we added a little earlier in the chapter. Add code to the *CheckedOutItems_DrawItem* event handler.

Insert Snippet Insert Chapter 19, Snippet Item 15.

Checking In Items

Checking in items is much simpler, because we don't need to first identify the patron. The barcode or title of the check-in item is sufficient to complete all processing. Figure 19-12 shows the check-in panel.

This panel includes a date indicating when the item will be checked in. Normally, that's today, but if library items are turned in through a nighttime repository after business hours, the librarian might want to adjust the date to "Yesterday," just in case any of these items were turned in before midnight. Let's add some code so that the panel indicates "Today" or "Yesterday" or some other day when a date changes. Add the following code to the *CheckedInDate_ValueChanged* event handler.

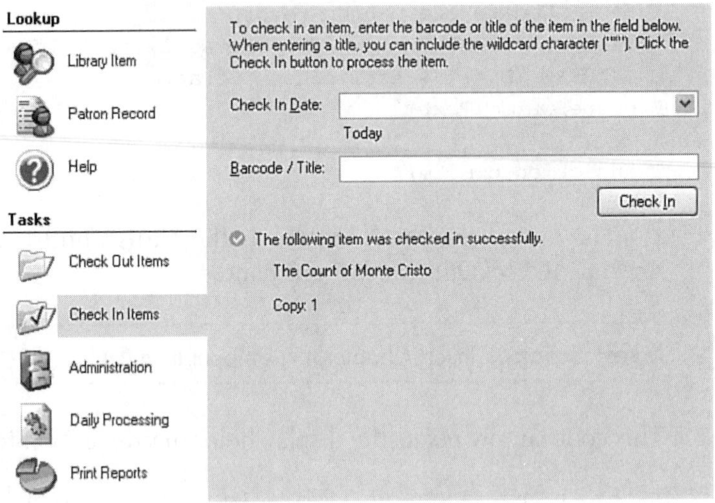

Figure 19-12 The check-in panel on the main form

Insert Snippet Insert Chapter 19, Snippet Item 16.

```
' ----- Adjust the day in the display.
Select Case DateDiff(DateInterval.Day, _
      CheckInDate.Value, Today)
   Case 0     ' ----- Today
      CheckInDay.Text = "Today"
      CheckInDay.BackColor = SystemColors.Control
      CheckInDay.ForeColor = SystemColors.ControlText
   Case 1     ' ----- Yesterday
      CheckInDay.Text = "Yesterday"
      CheckInDay.BackColor = Color.Red
      CheckInDay.ForeColor = Color.White
   Case Else  ' ----- X days ago
      CheckInDay.Text = DateDiff(DateInterval.Day, _
      CheckInDate.Value, Today) & " days ago"
      CheckInDay.BackColor = Color.Red
      CheckInDay.ForeColor = Color.White
End Select
```

The actual check-in occurs when the user enters a barcode or title in the text field, and clicks the **Check In** button. Add code to the *ActDoCheckIn_Click* event handler.

Insert Snippet Insert Chapter 19, Snippet Item 17.

After doing some lookups and confirmation checks, the code checks in the item through database updates.

```
' ----- Do the check-in in a transaction.
TransactionBegin()

' ----- Update patron copy record.
sqlText = "UPDATE PatronCopy SET CheckIn = " & _
    DBDate(CheckInDate.Value) & _
    ", Returned = 1 WHERE ID = " & patronCopyID
ExecuteSQL(sqlText)

' ----- Update the patron record.
sqlText = "UPDATE Patron SET LastActivity = " & _
    "GETDATE() WHERE ID = " & patronID
ExecuteSQL(sqlText)

TransactionCommit()
```

That's it for the check-in and check-out procedures, and all ticket printing. It's pretty good code, but not yet perfect. What we haven't yet added is code to properly process fines on items before they are checked in, or as they are adjusted in other ways. We will postpone this logic until Chapter 21, "Licensing Your Application." Until then, let's look at another application printing feature: reports.

CHAPTER 20

REPORTING

For the business application developer, reports are a fact of life. You may want to spend your time developing cool user interfaces or figuring out the core algorithms used in Generally Accepted Accounting Principles. But instead, you invest many boring hours each week turning out report after report. And these reports take a significant toll on the programming community. In America alone, the Centers for Disease Control and Prevention estimates nearly 850 report-related deaths each year—and that's doesn't even count those who read the reports. I once had a customer who printed off 20 copies of a 600-page report every month for his top-level managers. Clearly stupefied by the amount of tree pulp just to generate this report, the staff was unable to come up with a more interesting name than "the monthly report."

So if you are a business programmer, reports are in your future. But while your forebears had to deal with languages like RPG III, you get to use .NET. Hey, reports won't be so bad after all. And even without resorting to third-party reporting tools, Visual Studio and .NET include several report-focused features and tools you can use right out of the box.

This chapter discusses some of those reporting resources, and delves a little deeper into the reporting controls used in the Library Project.

Report Options in .NET

Reporting involves displaying and printing basic or summarized data to the user for specific business purposes. Visual Basic 2005 Professional Edition includes five primary methods of accomplishing this goal. Other editions add to or reduce this set of choices, and you can always enhance this list using third-party tools.

PrintDocument-Based Printing

As we learned in the previous chapter, the .NET Framework includes a full object-based printing system that uses GDI+ commands to draw text and graphics on each printed page. Because you can put anything you want on each page, you could develop your own custom reports using this method. The responsibility for positioning each label and calculated field on the page, and determining when to move to a new page, will rest entirely on your shoulders. Still, the GDI+ commands are straightforward, and developing some basic reports using this method would not be overwhelming.

If you want to take this route for your reports, I refer you back to Chapter 19, "Printing," and the basic printing concepts presented in that chapter.

HTML/Web Pages

Besides being a significant timewaster, the Internet (and its HTML-based page description language) is a great medium for data-report communication. The table-formatting tags in HTML (such as <td>) let you organize tabular output without much effort. Sure, it's a chore stringing all of those baby-sized text strings together to build the page, but there are ways around that, too.

Back in Chapter 13, "XML," I discussed XSLT (XSL Transformations), a way to take XML-based data, and reshape it into any form you want—including great works of art by Michelangelo, or nicely crafted HTML. However you obtain the HTML, you have a choice of display methods as well. The most direct method involves storing the generated HTML in a disk file, and starting the user's default browser to display it using a command such as:

```
Process.Start("c:\temp\MyReport.htm")
```

If you want the report to have a more "integrated" look in your application, you can display the HTML content in a web browser control. We did this in the project code for Chapter 16, "Generics," when we displayed the details of a library item as HTML.

Reporting Services and Controls

Visual Studio includes a set of classes in the *Microsoft.Reporting* namespace that are specifically designed to report data. The key class in this namespace is the *ReportViewer* control/class. Actually, it's two controls:

one for Windows Forms, and one for Web Forms. These controls are based, in part, on the technology found in *Microsoft SQL Server Reporting Services*, although you can use the controls without SQL Server.

The Library Project will use the *WinForms.ReportViewer* control for its built-in reports. We'll spend most of this chapter discussing the control and its use in Windows Forms applications. (I won't be discussing the Web Forms version of the control here, although its use closely parallels that of the Windows Forms version.)

Crystal Reports

If you have at least the Professional Edition of Visual Studio 2005, you received a complementary copy of Crystal Reports. The included version is a functional subset of Crystal Reports version XI, Developer Edition. If you are new to Visual Basic, then you have missed out on the previous versions of Crystal Reports that have been included with the language since its earliest releases. Because of this long-time relationship with Visual Basic, Crystal Reports has become one of the most widely used reporting packages on the market.

Crystal Reports is a third-party product, currently owned by a company called Business Objects. The product has changed ownership hands several times over the past 15 years, but Business Objects seems to be taking care of it for now. (I won't be discussing Crystal Reports in this book.)

Integration with Microsoft Office

Visual Basic has been the primary macro language of the Microsoft Office suite of applications since the untimely death of WordBasic. But I'm talking about pre-.NET Visual Basic; Microsoft Office does not yet include direct support for .NET integration. But that doesn't mean you can't interact with the Office products *indirectly*. How you interact with Office depends on whether the Office document or the Visual Basic application is the primary focus for the user.

If the goal is to have the user open an Office document (such as a Word or Excel file) and have that document interact with managed code, use the new *Visual Studio Tools for the Microsoft Office System* (abbreviated as VSTO, or "visto"). VSTO installs a small component that shuttles data and events between your Visual Basic code and the unmanaged COM world of Office. Visual Studio includes templates for building VSTO projects right in the development environment.

If the user will access Office features only indirectly through your Visual Basic application (for instance, if you want your program to initiate a Microsoft Word mail merge), use the Microsoft Office *Primary Interop Assemblies* (PIA) supplied by Microsoft. Like VSTO, these libraries marshal data between your managed code and the unmanaged Office COM libraries, but with the focus on your code instead of the Office document.

I won't be talking about Microsoft Office integration in this book. Use the Visual Studio MSDN documentation, and look in the index for "Visual Studio Tools for Office" if you need additional development information on these resources.

Using Reporting Controls in .NET

Let's spend the remainder of this chapter discussing the standard reporting tools provided in Visual Studio. As mentioned earlier, there are two *ReportViewer* classes included in Visual Studio: one for desktop development and one for web development. I'll only be talking about the desktop variation in this chapter. The designer used to develop these reports does not differentiate between the report target (desktop or browser). There are some differences in deployment, but I'll have to leave the web deployment to a future best-selling programming book, or to your own research.

The *ReportViewer* control integrates directly with *Microsoft SQL Server Reporting Services*, displaying whole pages generated by that server-based system. Because we're assuming that you are using SQL Server Express for your development (which does not include Reporting Services), I'll focus instead on the control's "local" mode presentation. This lets you display any data from any source you choose on each report display page, including SQL Server.

And Now, the Bad News The *ReportViewer* control is not the easiest control in the world to use, but it's even harder to use when it doesn't even come with your copy of Visual Studio. If you are using *Visual Basic 2005 Express Edition*, you will not find the *ReportViewer* in your toolbox. Microsoft does make it available as a separate download (look in the download area of http://msdn.microsoft.com, the MSDN web site, for "Microsoft Report Viewer Redistributable 2005"), but that will only get you halfway. I'll be discussing a visual reporting designer later that is also not in the *Express Edition*. Although you can still manually create the XML content that is normally generated by the visual designer, that's no fun at all.

If you are using the *Express Edition*, you can still use the project code in this book. You just won't be able to visually design new reports. But you can run the prewritten reports that I already included, because they are just XML content.

If, after all of that, you are still an *Express Edition* user, please download and install the *Microsoft Report Viewer Redistributable 2005* file from Microsoft's web site.

In the vein of "those who can, do; those who can't, teach," let me walk you through the steps needed to visually design a simple report using the *ReportViewer* class. We'll create a report that lists the records in the Library Project's *Activity* table, a table that will have data in it even if you haven't used the Library program yet. This works best if you follow along in front of your computer, because reading about report design is a lot like reading about brain surgery: It's more interesting if you actually do it. Start by creating a new Windows Forms application.

Add the Data Source

Add a data source to the project that refers to the *Activity* database table. We already did this back in Chapter 10, "ADO.NET," in the "Creating a Data Source" section. Select the **Data ➤ Add New Data Source** menu command, and use the *Data Source Configuration Wizard* to locate your Library database. When you reach the list of database objects, check the box next to the *Activity* table, and click the **Finish** button. You should now have a data source named *LibraryDataSet*. Figure 20-1 shows the elements added to the *Solution Explorer* and the *Data Sources* panel by this action.

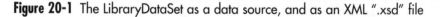

Figure 20-1 The LibraryDataSet as a data source, and as an XML ".xsd" file

Add a Report Design Surface

Use the **Project ➤ Add New Item** menu command to add a new Report item. Figure 20-2 shows the item report in the *Add New Item* dialog. Make sure that you choose "Report" and not "Crystal Report" from the list.

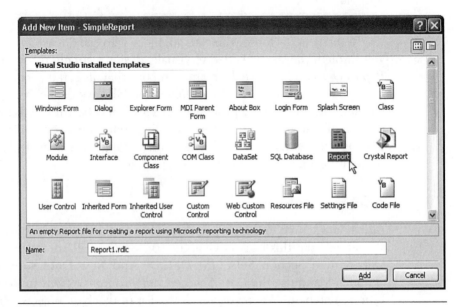

Figure 20-2 Adding a new report to the project

Click the *Add* button to insert the report into the project. A new *Report1.rdlc* file appears in your project, and its designer opens automatically. "RDLC" is short for "Report Definition Language - Client," and files of this type contain XML content that describes the layout of a locally designed report. Figure 20-3 shows the designer for the added *Report1.rdlc* file, plus the controls in the toolbar that you can add to the report surface. I will refer to reports created through this designer as "RDLC reports" throughout the rest of this chapter.

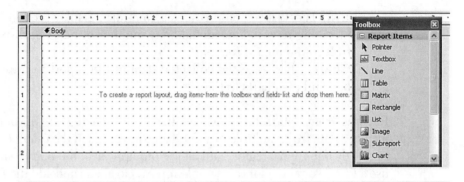

Figure 20-3 The report designer and related toolbar

Design the Report Surface

If you've written reports in Microsoft Access or in some other common reporting tool, then you are probably familiar with "banded" reports. These reports have separate "bands," or stripes, that represent a portion of the printed page. Bands include page headers and footers, report headers and footers, the record detail section, and group headers and footers used to visually and logically group the detail entries. As the report runs, an imaginary horizontal page-wide line runs from the top to the bottom of the page. As the line hits each band, the report processes the fields in that band until there are no more records to process.

RDLC reports are a little bit different from those banded reports. There are only three bands: page header, page footer, and everything else (a band called "Body"). Instead of adding bands for records and groups, you add fields to *data regions*. These special controls process the records linked to the report according to the shape of the data region. There are four data region controls in the toolbox.

- **Table.** This region presents an unlimited number of data rows, but with a predefined set of data columns. It's designed for tabular presentation of data records, with each column generally displaying a single source or calculated data field. Each row of the table represents a source data record.
- **Matrix.** This control is similar to the *Table* region, but it allows for a flexible number of data columns, not just rows.

20. REPORTING

- **List.** The List region provides a free-form display section for each incoming record. You can add any number of fields or display controls to the record section.
- **Chart.** Charts use the collected data of the report to present line, bar, and pie charts to the user.

Records from data sets are always tied to a data region. If your report includes data from multiple distinct data sources, each data source will link to exactly one report region, and all regions appear in the *Body* band. We'll use a *List* data region for this sample report. Go ahead and add the *List* control to the *Body* band on the report surface. You can now add other items to either the band surface itself, or to the *List* control surface. Items added to the *List* control are reprocessed for each record in the incoming data source. These items can be either controls from the Toolbox, or database fields displayed in the *Data Sources* panel. Using the *Activity* table in the *Data Sources* panel, drag the *FullName* field to the *List* control surface. Figure 20-4 shows the display just after performing this drag operation.

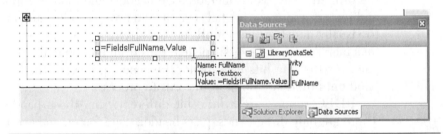

Figure 20-4 A List control with a field from the data set

When we dragged the field from the data source to the *List* control, Visual Studio established a link between them. The *list1* control's *DataSetName* field now refers to "LibraryDataSet_Activity," the name of the data source. It also added a *TextBox* control to the list's surface, and added an expression (=Fields!FullName.Value) that displays the contents of that field from the database for each processed record.

I'm going to resize the *List* control, the text box, and the *Body* band itself so that the *FullName* text box field is pretty much all there is in the report (see Figure 20-5).

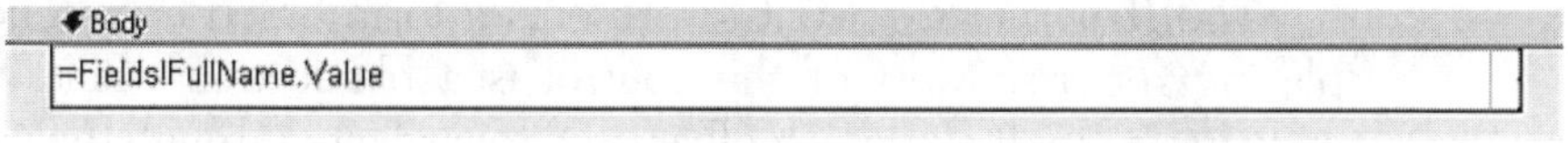

⬧ Body

=Fields!FullName.Value

Figure 20-5 A resized version of the report

The report is ready to use. As we designed the report surface, Visual Studio was busy generating XML and storing it in the *Report1.rdlc* file.

Using a Report Control

The RDLC file is only an XML definition of a report; it doesn't have any ability to display itself. To view the report, we must add a report control to a form or web page that knows how to properly merge the XML design content with the data from the specified data source. Return to *Form1*, and add a *ReportViewer* control to its surface from the Toolbox (it's in the *Data* section of the Toolbox on my system).

The added control includes a small "smart tags" button in its upper-right corner. Clicking this button displays the ReportViewer Tasks fly-out window, which appears in Figure 20-6.

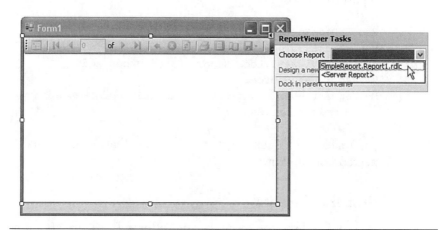

Figure 20-6 The ReportViewer control on the form surface

The *ReportViewer* control presents a form-based experience for displaying reports. Most of the control is a blank area where the report appears. It also includes a toolbar used to navigate through the pages of the report. The user can also initiate an export or a print-out of the report through these controls. If you don't need the toolbar or one of its controls, use the various *Show...* properties of the *ReportViewer* control to hide the unneeded elements.

The report viewer is generic and report-independent. If you have several RDLC files in your project, you can display any of them (one at a time) through the same report viewer. We have only one report in our project, so let's connect it (*SimpleReport.Report1.rdlc*) to the viewer by using the *Choose Report* task from the report viewer's smart tag button. Also, click on the *Dock in parent container* task in the fly-out window to expand the report to the form's size.

The RDLC report, the data from the data source, and the *ReportViewer* control are all joined in one glorious report display by the magic of data binding. When you linked the report to the viewer control, three more controls appeared on the form: *LibraryDataSet*, *ActivityBindingSource*, and *ActivityTableAdapter*. *LibraryDataSet* is a reference to the actual data source we added earlier. The other two controls wrap up that data in a form that can be bound to the report viewer. Although you can't see it in the designer, the hidden form code connects these controls and the XML report to the viewer.

```
ReportDataSource1.Name = "LibraryDataSet_Activity"
ReportDataSource1.Value = Me.ActivityBindingSource
Me.ReportViewer1.LocalReport.DataSources.Add( _
    ReportDataSource1)
Me.ReportViewer1.LocalReport.ReportEmbeddedResource = _
    "SimpleReport.Report1.rdlc"
```

Yeah, I don't really get it either. But that's okay. Visual Studio connected it all up for us.

Run the Report

Press F5 and see the results of your efforts. In Figure 20-7, I adjusted the view by clicking on the Page Layout button, and setting the size to 100%.

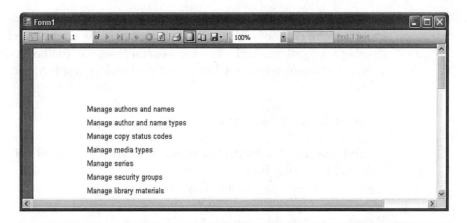

Figure 20-7 Reporting the essential contents of the *Activity* table

Well, that report is fine as far as *Activity* table reports go, but we could spruce it up a bit more.

Adding a Page Header and Footer

I think the report needs a meaningful title at the top of each page, plus a page number in the bottom-right corner. Let's return to the RDLC report designer and add them. Once there, right-click on the background of the report (not the body, which has the grid marks on it), as shown in Figure 20-8.

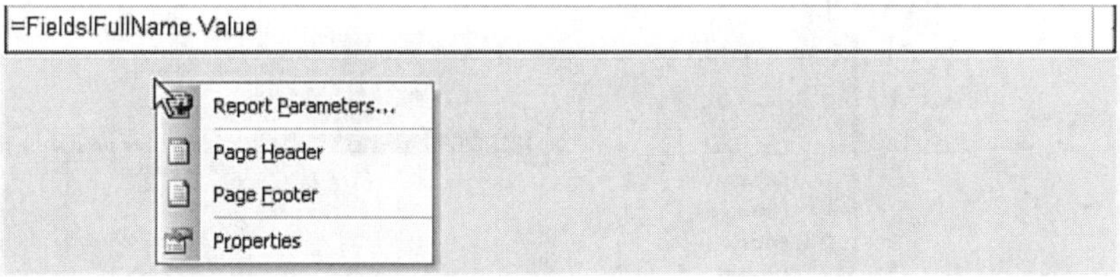

=Fields!FullName.Value

Report Parameters...

Page Header

Page Footer

Properties

Figure 20-8 Adding page headers and footers

From this menu, select **Page Header**; then bring up the menu again and select **Page Footer**. Each new band appears on the report surface.

Whether it's static, unchanging text, or text that's dynamically generated from the data source, the *TextBox* control is the control of choice for showing text content. Add a *TextBox* control from the Toolbox to both the header and footer sections. Click inside the header's text box, and type the following:

```
="The Activity Table Report"
```

You can use the *Properties* panel to adjust the look of this control, including its display font.

In the footer text box, add this text:

```
="Page " & Globals!PageNumber
```

The *Globals* pseudo-object includes a few members that you can use in the report. How did I know to use `Globals!PageNumber`? I built the expression visually using the *Expression Editor*. To access it, right-click on the *TextBox* control, and select **Expression** from the shortcut menu. The editor, shown in Figure 20-9, lets you build up an expression using lists of functions and field names. The actual functions just happen to be— hooray—Visual Basic functions.

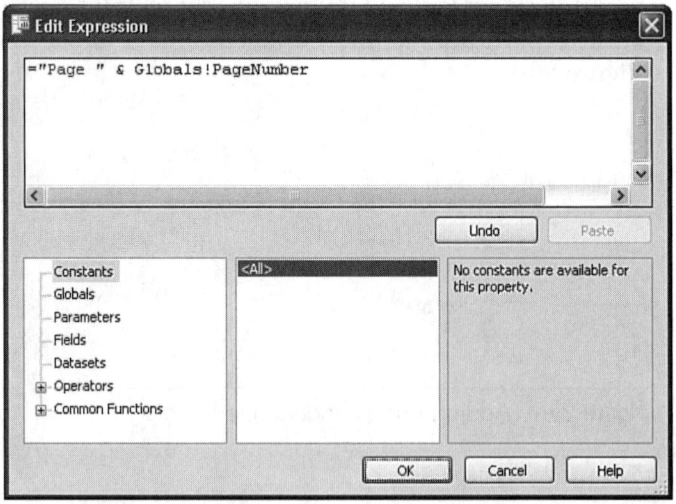

Figure 20-9 The Expression Editor

Support for Grouping and Sorting

Grouping of data is common in printed reports. To add grouping to our report, we need to embed our existing *List* control (the detail record) within another *List* control (the group), and set various properties on the group *List* control to determine the method of data grouping.

Let's try it. Add another *List* control (called *list2*) to the report body, and give it twice the height as the existing *List* control (called *list1*). Then, drag *list1* (the detail record) into *list2* (the new group), placing it toward the bottom. Your report should look like Figure 20-10.

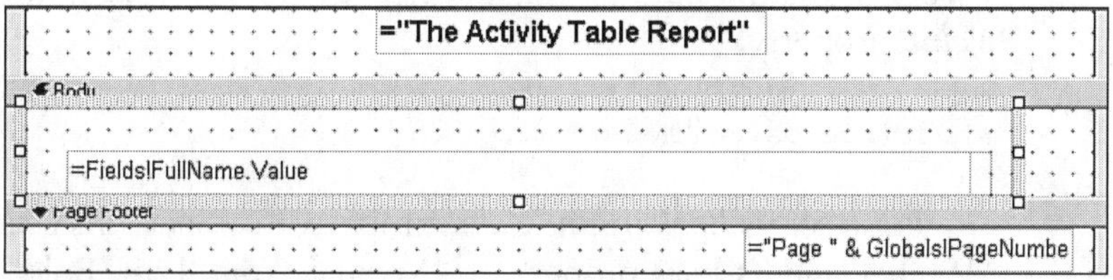

Figure 20-10 A grouping list added to the report

To configure the group, right-click on it and select **Properties** from the shortcut menu. The *List Properties* form appears. On its *General* tab, click the **Edit details group** button, which sets the grouping. On the *Grouping and Sorting Properties* form that appears, enter the following text into the first row of the **Group on** field.

```
=Left(Fields!FullName.Value, 1)
```

This expression tells the *list2* control to group its detail results by the first character of the first name field.

On this same form, add the following text to the **Document map label** field.

```
="Letter: " & Left(Fields!FullName.Value, 1)
```

The document map enables a clickable hyperlink list into the different groups of the report. When we run the report a little later, we'll see this map just to the left of the report display surface.

The records in the *Activity* table are ordered for the convenience of the programmer (me). But the report user probably wants to see them sorted in some reasonable fashion. Click on the *Sorting* tab, and add the following text to the **Sort on** field, in the **Expression** column.

```
=Fields!FullName.Value
```

As expected, this will sort the data by the *FullName* field. Click the **OK** buttons all the way out, and return to the report surface.

We still need to add something that will make each group stand out. Add a *TextBox* control to the *list2* grouping control. Put it in the upper-left corner of that parent control, and type the following text into it (or into its *Value* property).

```
=Left(Fields!FullName.Value, 1)
```

I also set its *BackgroundColor* property to "Black," its *Color* property to "White," and its *Font* property to "Normal, Arial, 12pt, Bold" just for looks.

Running the report gives the results in Figure 20-11. Notice the document map along the left-edge of the window, and the grouped single-letter titles before each grouped section.

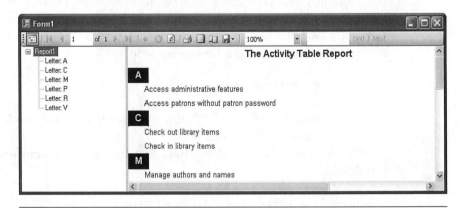

Figure 20-11 The full report, with grouping and sorting enabled

Enhanced Style Formatting

Probably the coolest feature of RDLC reports is that many of the properties for items placed on the report surface can include conditional expressions. This means that you can conditionally alter, say, the visual properties of a *TextBox* control based on the value of a field in the current record.

In the project section of this chapter, we'll write a report that uses due dates for items currently checked out. If the item is past due, I want to show the due date in red. Normally, a *TextBox* control's *Color* property (which controls font color) is "Black." To have that field respond to overdue items, I will replace "Black" with the following expression.

```
=IIf(Fields!DueDate.Value < Today, "Red", "Black")
```

Using Custom Data

Although it is very common to generate reports from databases, you can actually use data from virtually any source. When using the *ReportViewer* control, any data source that implements the *IEnumerable* interface is good enough. That includes all collections and arrays. The report isn't that picky, as long as the data is formatted as it expects. For the report we just made, we can ditch the actual data, and supply our own fake data. This intercepting and substituting data is like something out of a spy thriller. But there are a few rules we must follow to make it work.

- When we dragged the *Activity.FullName* field from the data source to the report surface, the report (actually, the *list1* control) got this funny idea that all data had to come from a data source named "LibraryDataSet_Activity." Any data source we use in place of the real one must keep this name.
- The fake data source must include the *FullName* field, because that is what the report fields expect.

Those rules aren't so bad. So here's what we need to do: Create a fake data source, intercept the report just before it tries to get the data from the Library database, and insert our own data instead.

For a fake data source, we'll need a class that includes at least the *FullName* field.

```
Public Class FakeActivityRecord
    Private StoredID As Long
    Private StoredFullName As String

    Public Sub New(ByVal whatID As Long, _
        ByVal whatFullName As String)
        StoredID = whatID
        StoredFullName = whatFullName
    End Sub

    Public Property ID() As Long
        Get
            Return StoredID
        End Get
        Set(ByVal value As Long)
            StoredID = value
        End Set
    End Property

    Public Property FullName() As String
        Get
            Return StoredFullName
        End Get
        Set(ByVal value As String)
            StoredFullName = value
        End Set
    End Property
End Class
```

The exposed fields must be properties, and not just public fields; the report viewer doesn't recognize standard member fields.

If you look at the source code for *Form1*, you'll find that the following code was added to the *Form_Load* event handler when we linked the report viewer with the RDLC report.

```
Me.ActivityTableAdapter.Fill(Me.LibraryDataSet.Activity)
Me.ReportViewer1.RefreshReport()
```

It's that first line that loads the data from the Library database's *Activity* table and links it to the report. We need to replace that line with code that cuts off the real data at the pass.

```vb
' ----- Create a fake table of fake records.
Dim fakeSource As New Collections.Generic.List( _
    Of FakeActivityRecord)

' ----- Add each of the fake records.
fakeSource.Add(New FakeActivityRecord(1, "Do some work"))
fakeSource.Add(New FakeActivityRecord(2, "Take a nap"))
fakeSource.Add(New FakeActivityRecord(3, "Write a program"))

' ----- The report was already bound to the true
'       data source. Delete it.
Me.ReportViewer1.LocalReport.DataSources.Clear()

' ----- Build a new data source. Remember, it must have
'       the same name.
Dim fakeReportSource As New _
    Microsoft.Reporting.WinForms.ReportDataSource
fakeReportSource.Name = "LibraryDataSet_Activity"
fakeReportSource.Value = fakeSource

' ----- Connect the data source to the report, and we're done.
Me.ReportViewer1.LocalReport.DataSources.Add(fakeReportSource)
Me.ReportViewer1.RefreshReport()
```

Figure 20-12 shows the report with the fake data on display.

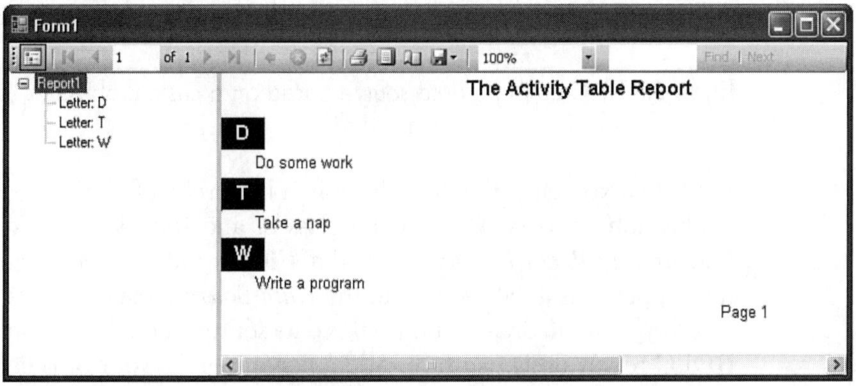

Figure 20-12 This fake data will not self-destruct in five seconds.

Supplying Custom Data Sources

Substituting data at the last second is fine and all, but what if you want to design a report that doesn't depend on a database at all? You can do that, too, by supplying a fully custom data source. RDLC reports require some sort of data source schema at design time; you just can't supply fully custom data on the fly when running the report. But you can supply a custom schema based on a class in your application.

For the class, we'll stick with the *FakeActivityRecord* we created in the previous section. Then we will design a data source from this class. Select the **Data ➤ Add New Data Source** menu command. When the *Data Source Configuration Wizard* has appeared in the past, you have always selected *Database* as the source for the data. This time, select *Object*, as shown in Figure 20-13.

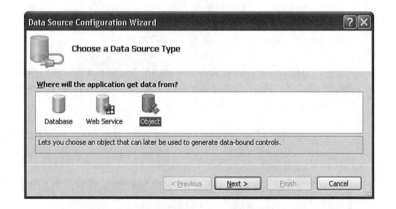

Figure 20-13 Creating a data source based on a custom object

When you click the **Next** button, a hierarchy of all the classes in your application appears. Expand the classes, and then locate and select the *FakeActivityRecord* class. Click the **Finish** button. *FakeActivityRecord* now appears as a data source in the *Data Sources* panel.

Now you can drag-and-drop this data source's *FullName* field onto a new RDLC report design surface. Add a new report to your project, and follow the same steps we used previously to design the first report. This time, use the *FakeActivityRecord* data source instead of the *LibraryDataSet* source.

To test this new report, I removed the original *Form1* from the project and added a brand new *Form1*. I also added a *ReportViewer* control to its surface and docked it, but I did not link it to the RDLC report. This keeps things a lot cleaner, as there are no binding source controls and whatnot to worry about. Then I added this code to the form's *Load* event handler.

```
' ----- Link to the RDLC report design.
Me.ReportViewer1.LocalReport.ReportEmbeddedResource = _
   "SimpleReport.Report2.rdlc"

' ----- Create a fake table of fake records.
Dim fakeSource As New Collections.Generic.List( _
   Of FakeActivityRecord)

' ----- Add each of the fake records.
fakeSource.Add(New FakeActivityRecord(1, "Breakfast"))
fakeSource.Add(New FakeActivityRecord(2, "Lunch"))
fakeSource.Add(New FakeActivityRecord(3, "Dinner"))

' ----- Build a new data source. Remember, it must have
'       the same name.
Dim fakeReportSource As New _
   Microsoft.Reporting.WinForms.ReportDataSource
fakeReportSource.Name = "SimpleReport_FakeActivityRecord"
fakeReportSource.Value = fakeSource

' ----- Connect the data source to the report, and we're done.
Me.ReportViewer1.LocalReport.DataSources.Add(fakeReportSource)
Me.ReportViewer1.RefreshReport()
```

It's pretty similar to the previous custom code, although the data source name is now "SimpleReport_FakeActivityRecord," the name this new report expects (which I found out by running the report and reading the error message).

I've saved a copy of both custom reports in the installation directory for the book's source code samples. Look in the subdirectory named *SimpleReport*.

Summary

Although this chapter included many pretty pictures and a lot of instructions, we scratched only the surface of the features available in the reporting controls included with .NET. I think I bruised my brain when I tried to study up on every available feature, but perhaps your brain is better

20. REPORTING

prepared for the task. Still, if you don't find it exactly to your liking, you can use one of the other reporting features I listed at the start of the chapter, or even opt for a third-party solution.

Reports are an important part of the business developer's daily life. Finding the right reporting tool and getting comfortable with its features is not only a good suggestion, it's a necessity in the world of report-hungry software users.

Project

When we last left the Technical Resource Kit document for the Library Project, it listed five built-in reports:

- Report #1: Items Checked Out Report
- Report #2: Items Overdue Report
- Report #3: Items Missing Report
- Report #4: Fines Owed by Patrons Report
- Report #5: Library Database Statistics Report

We'll add these five reports to the project in this chapter. Before we write any code, we need to figure out how we're going to get the data. Because the data will come from the Library database, we just need to craft the SQL statement for each report that will link to the designed report.

The fifth report, "statistics," will report things such as the number of items, the number of patrons, and other similar statistical values from the Library database. Because this data can't really come from a single SQL statement, we'll extract the data from the database and build a custom data source that feeds into the report.

Crafting the SQL Statements

The first report, "items checked out," lists the patron name and item title for every item currently checked out by the user. It involves the *Patron* table (to get the patron name), the *PatronCopy* table (the check-out event), the *ItemCopy* table (the actual item checked out), and the *NamedItem* table (where the item title appears). We'll also include the *CodeMediaType* table, which tells us if the item is a book, a CD, or some other media type.

Microsoft SQL Server Management Studio Express includes a visual *Query Designer* that we can use to design the query. Figure 20-14 shows the five needed tables as linked together by the designer.

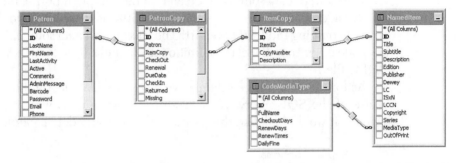

Figure 20-14 The five tables in the checked-out items query

Whether you use the query designer or build the SQL statement by hand, you eventually come up with something similar to the following, which we'll use within the Library application.

```
/* ----- Report #1: Items checked out report. */
SELECT PA.LastName + ', ' + PA.FirstName AS PatronName,
    PA.Barcode AS PatronBarcode,
    PC.DueDate, IC.CopyNumber, IC.Barcode AS ItemBarcode,
    NI.Title, CMT.FullName AS MediaName
FROM Patron AS PA
    INNER JOIN PatronCopy AS PC ON PA.ID = PC.Patron
    INNER JOIN ItemCopy AS IC ON PC.ItemCopy = IC.ID
    INNER JOIN NamedItem AS NI ON IC.ItemID = NI.ID
    INNER JOIN CodeMediaType AS CMT ON NI.MediaType = CMT.ID
WHERE PC.Returned = 0
    AND PC.Missing = 0
    AND IC.Missing = 0
ORDER BY NI.Title, IC.CopyNumber, PA.LastName, PA.FirstName
```

This query links up all of the tables, and then requests every record that has not been returned (PC.Returned = 0). It ignores any item marked as missing (PC.Missing = 0 AND IC.Missing = 0). This query will eventually drive the report. But for now, keep in mind that

RDLC reports don't actually need a real SQL statement or database table for the report schema. We can also build a compatible schema by hand using a class. This turns out to be a lot cleaner, because we won't have a lot of data-set-related files strewn throughout the project source code. (The *LibraryDataSet* data source we created in the sample report earlier in this chapter added four source files and nearly 50K of source code to the project, not counting the RDLC report! The class-based data source didn't add any code other than the class definition itself, and a little bit of XML in the RDLC file.)

As for the data source schema, we can extrapolate it from the SELECT clause of the SQL query. If we were to design a class with a matching schema, it would look like this (without the property detail code).

```
Class Report1Schema
    Public Property PatronName As String
    Public Property PatronBarcode As String
    Public Property DueDate As Date
    Public Property CopyNumber As Integer
    Public Property ItemBarcode As String
    Public Property Title As String
    Public Property MediaName As String
End Class
```

The next two reports are for "overdue items" and "missing items." For me, the schema for report #1 is exactly what I want to see in these other two reports, so let's just use the same SQL statement. All we need to do is change the WHERE clause. For the overdue items report, use this WHERE clause.

```
WHERE PC.Returned = 0
    AND PC.Missing = 0
    AND IC.Missing = 0
    AND PC.DueDate < GETDATE()
```

The missing items report will use this WHERE clause.

```
WHERE PC.Missing = 1
    OR IC.Missing = 1
```

The fourth report displays the amount of fines still owed by patrons, so it will require a different schema. Here's its SQL statement, which uses some aggregate grouping features.

```
/* ----- Report #4: Fines owed by patron. */
SELECT PA.LastName + ', ' + PA.FirstName AS PatronName,
    PA.Barcode AS PatronBarcode,
    SUM(PC.Fine - PC.Paid) AS FinesDue
FROM Patron AS PA
    INNER JOIN PatronCopy AS PC ON PA.ID = PC.Patron
GROUP BY PA.LastName + ', ' + PA.FirstName, PA.Barcode
HAVING SUM(PC.Fine - PC.Paid) > 0
ORDER BY PatronName
```

Here's the schema that goes with report number 4.

```
Class Report4Schema
    Public Property PatronName As String
    Public Property PatronBarcode As String
    Public Property FinesDue As Decimal
End Class
```

For the final report, we'll just use a schema with two string values: a statistic name, and its related value. Here's its schema.

```
Class Report5Schema
    Public Property EntryName As String
    Public Property EntryValue As String
End Class
```

Well, that's enough preparation. Let's start coding.

Project Access Load the "Chapter 20 (Before) Code" project, either through the New Project templates, or by accessing the project directly from the installation directory. To see the code in its final form, load "Chapter 20 (After) Code" instead.

---

20. REPORTING

Adding Report Schemas

The *ReportSchemas.vb* file, already added to the project, includes the three schemas used for the five built-in reports. Just to remind us of the members, here are the public property definitions included in each class, minus the *Get* and *Set* accessors, and minus the private class members.

```
Public Class ReportSchemaPatronItems
    ' ----- Used for the following reports:
    '          Report #1: Items checked out report
    '          Report #2: Items overdue report
    '          Report #3: Items missing report
    Public Property PatronName() As String
    Public Property PatronBarcode() As String
    Public Property DueDate() As Date
    Public Property CopyNumber() As Integer
    Public Property ItemBarcode() As String
    Public Property Title() As String
    Public Property MediaName() As String
End Class

Public Class ReportSchemaPatronFines
    ' ----- Used for the following reports:
    '          Report #4: Fines owed by patron
    Public Property PatronName() As String
    Public Property PatronBarcode() As String
    Public Property FinesDue() As Decimal
End Class

Public Class ReportSchemaStatistics
    ' ----- Used for the following reports:
    '          Report #5: Library database statistics report
    Public Property EntryName() As String
    Public Property EntryValue() As String
End Class
```

Once the schema classes are in the project, you will need to build the project before those classes can be used in RDLC reports as data sources. In the Library Project, build the project now with the **Build ➤ Build Library** menu command. All three schemas should then appear as sources in the *Data Sources* panel (see Figure 20-15). If the *Data Sources* panel is closed, open it using the **Data ➤ Show Data Sources** menu command.

Figure 20-15 The three data source schemas

Adding Reports

Because we already jointly created an RDLC report earlier in the chapter, I went ahead and added the five built-in reports for you.

- **ReportCheckedOut.rdlc.** This file implements report #1, the "items checked out" report. It uses the *ReportSchemaPatronItems* class schema, and includes three columns in the main data list: patron name/barcode, item name/barcode/details, and due date. For the item name field, I wanted to present additional information when available. The item name, copy number, and media type are required values, but item barcode is optional. Here's the format I desired.

```
Item Name (#CopyNumber, MediaType, Barcode)
```

To get this result, I had to concatenate the various source fields together, and use a conditional function (IIf) to optionally include the barcode and its comma.

```
=Fields!Title.Value & " (#" &
➥ CStr(Fields!CopyNumber.Value) & ", " &
➥ Fields!MediaName.Value &
➥ IIf(IsNothing(Fields!ItemBarcode.Value), "",
➥ ", " & Fields!ItemBarcode.Value) & ")"
```

20. REPORTING

As mentioned earlier, the due date field has an expression in its *Color* property that turns the text red when the item is overdue.

- **ReportOverdue.rdlc.** This report shows a list of all overdue items in the system. Because everything will be overdue, I set the due date field to always use red for its font color. Other than that and the title, the report is basically identical to the checked-out items report.

- **ReportMissing.rdlc.** This report shows a list of all items marked as missing. Even though the schema includes a due date field, I don't use it in this report. The rest of the report is basically identical to the checked-out items report.

- **ReportPatronFines.rdlc.** This report lists all patrons that still owe fines, and the amount of the fine due. It uses the *ReportSchemaPatronFines* class schema. The field that displays the fine has a "C" in its *Format* property. This formatting code forces the decimal value to display as currency using the culture settings on the local system. This *Format* property uses the same codes recognized by the *String.Format* method.

- **ReportStatistics.rdlc.** Report #5 displays record counts from some of the tables in the Library database. This is the only report that uses the *ReportSchemaStatistics* class schema. The report itself just displays two strings per record: a name and a value. It depends on the calling code to format those fields properly.

Adding a Report Viewer

It's time to add a *ReportViewer* control. Because a single *ReportViewer* control can display any type of RDLC report, we'll just add a single form to handle all five built-in reports.

Add a new form named *ReportBuiltinViewer.vb* to the project. Set its *Text* property to "Library Report," and its *WindowState* property to *Maximized*. Also, load the project's icon (*Book.ico*) into the *Icon* property. You'll find a copy of this file in the project installation directory. If you want, you can size the form to some reasonable starting point for a report (I used "680, 400"), but each report will start out maximized when used.

Add a *ReportViewer* control named *ReportContent* to the form, and set its *Dock* property to *Fill*. Set both the *ShowBackButton* and *ShowDocumentMapButton* properties to *False*.

The code we will add to this form is a variation of code we wrote earlier in this chapter. The code that starts each report will pass to this form the name of the report RDLC file, the name of the data schema used, and the actual data. Because these reports will be modeless (you can keep them open while still using other parts of the Library program), we can't let the calling code wait around for the user to close the report before we discard the report data. We'll let the report dispose of the data itself. To do this, we need to keep a reference to that data. Add the following statement to the *ReportBuiltinViewer* form class.

Insert Snippet Insert Chapter 20, Snippet Item 1.

```
Private StoreDataTable As Object
```

Remember, reports can use a variety of data source formats, including true database connections, arrays, and collections. Reports #1 through #4 will use a *System.Data.DataTable* instance, while report #5 will pass a generic *List* collection.

The best time to dispose of the data is when the report is closing. Add the following event handler to the form, which confirms that the data supports the disposal process before calling the *Dispose* method.

Insert Snippet Insert Chapter 20, Snippet Item 2.

```
Private Sub ReportBuiltinViewer_FormClosing( _
    ByVal sender As Object, ByVal e As _
    System.Windows.Forms.FormClosingEventArgs) _
    Handles Me.FormClosing
  ' ----- Get rid of the data.
  If (TypeOf StoreDataTable Is IDisposable) Then
    CType(StoreDataTable, IDisposable).Dispose()
  End If
End Sub
```

The code that opens this display form will pass in the essential report values through a public method named *StartReport*. Add its code now.

Insert Snippet Insert Chapter 20, Snippet Item 3.

```
Public Sub StartReport(ByVal whichReport As String, _
    ByVal whichDataSchema As String, _
    ByVal whichData As Object)
    ' ----- Run one of the built-in reports. whichReport is
    '         the name of the RDLC report file, in the format
    '         "Library.xxx.rdlc." whichDataSchema provides the
    '         name of the schema to use, in the format
    '         "Library_xxx." whichDataSet is the actual data
    '         to link to the report, which must match the schema.
    Dim customDataSource As New _
        Microsoft.Reporting.WinForms.ReportDataSource

    ' ----- Connect the viewer, the report, and the data.
    ReportContent.LocalReport.ReportEmbeddedResource = _
        whichReport
    customDataSource.Name = whichDataSchema
    customDataSource.Value = whichData
    ReportContent.LocalReport.DataSources.Add( _
        customDataSource)

    ' ----- Display the report.
    StoreDataTable = whichData
    Me.Show()
End Sub
```

This code tells the viewer which report to use as an embedded resource, and then attaches the data as a custom data source. "Local" in these property names indicates a local (client) report instead of a "server" report that runs within SQL Server.

When we were playing with the reports before, we saw that the default display mode was the "fill-the-entire-screen-with-page-content" mode. Personally, I like to see those fake page boundaries. The *ReportViewer* control doesn't include a property that lets us change this default view (why not?), but we can still adjust the initial display style through methods on the control. When we added the report viewer to the form, Visual Studio also added the following statement to the form's *Load* event handler.

```
ReportContent.RefreshReport()
```

Add the following code just before that statement.

Insert Snippet Insert Chapter 20, Snippet Item 4.

```
' ----- Generate and display the report.
ReportContent.SetDisplayMode( _
   Microsoft.Reporting.WinForms.DisplayMode.PrintLayout)
ReportContent.ZoomMode = _
   Microsoft.Reporting.WinForms.ZoomMode.Percent
ReportContent.ZoomPercent = 100
```

Adding Built-In Reports

I forget how long ago we added the *ReportSelect.vb* form that drives reporting, but it is already there in the project. In case you forgot what it looked like (I did), Figure 20-16 gives us a refresher.

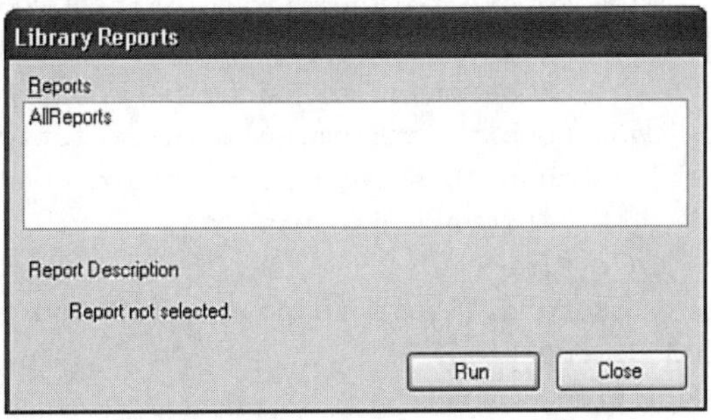

Figure 20-16 The report selection form

We previously added support for our five built-in reports in this form's code. In a tribute to the never-ending reality of forgetting to finish all of the code, we need to add some code that we overlooked earlier. If you use an XML report configuration file to populate the report list, and you provide a description for each report in the XML, each entry displays that description in the lower-half of the report selection form. But if you don't use a configuration file, and just depend on the form to add the five built-in reports by default (which it does), the form won't display associated descriptions, because we forgot to add them. Add a function to the *ReportSelect* class that returns a short description for each of the five reports.

Insert Snippet Insert Chapter 20, Snippet Item 5.

```
Private Function GetBuiltinReportDescription( _
      ByVal whichReport As ReportItemEnum) As String
   ' ----- Return a predefined description for the
   '         built-in reports.
   Select Case whichReport
      Case ReportItemEnum.BuiltInCheckedOut
         Return "Displays all items currently checked " & _
            "out, sorted by name."
      Case ReportItemEnum.BuiltInOverdue
         Return "Displays all overdue items, sorted by name."
      Case ReportItemEnum.BuiltInMissing
         Return "Displays all missing items, sorted by name."
      Case ReportItemEnum.BuiltInFinesOwed
         Return "Displays all unpaid fines owed by " & _
            "patrons, sorted by patron name."
      Case ReportItemEnum.BuiltInStatistics
         Return "Displays some record counts from the " & _
            "Library database."
      Case Else
         Return "There is no description for this report."
   End Select
End Function
```

We'll call this code from two places. The first is in the *LoadReportGroup* method. This code loads the XML report configuration file. If that file includes one of the built-in reports, but doesn't supply a description with it, we'll supply the description ourselves. About halfway through that code, you'll find these lines.

```
' ----- So, what type of entry is it?
If (scanNode.Attributes("type").Value = "built-in") Then
```

About five lines below this is the following statement.

```
reportEntry.ItemType = CType(CInt( _
    reportEntry.ReportPath), ReportItemEnum)
```

Add the following code just after that statement.

Insert Snippet Insert Chapter 20, Snippet Item 6.

```
If (reportEntry.Description = "") Then _
    reportEntry.Description = _
    GetBuiltinReportDescription(reportEntry.ItemType)
```

The second need for the built-in descriptions appears in the *RefreshReportList* method. This method makes the call to *LoadReportGroup* to retrieve the XML configuration. But if after that the report list is still empty, *RefreshReportList* adds the five default reports, which each require a description. Near the end of the method, within a *For...Next* loop, you'll find this closing statement.

```
' ----- Add the report entry to the list.
AllReports.Items.Add(reportEntry)
```

Add the following code just before that statement.

Insert Snippet Insert Chapter 20, Snippet Item 7.

```
reportEntry.Description = GetBuiltinReportDescription( _
    reportEntry.ItemType)
```

Okay, that's it for the fix-up code. Now back to writing the actual reports. The code to start each of the five reports already exists in the *ReportSelect* form's *ActRun_Click* event handler. Most of that code includes a *Select Case* statement that acts as a switchboard for the selected report. Here's the part that calls the five built-in reports.

```
Case ReportItemEnum.BuiltInCheckedOut
    ' ----- Items Checked Out
    ' TODO: Write BasicReportCheckedOut()
Case ReportItemEnum.BuiltInOverdue
    ' ----- Items Overdue
    ' TODO: Write BasicReportOverdue()
Case ReportItemEnum.BuiltInMissing
    ' ----- Items Missing
    ' TODO: Write BasicReportMissing()
Case ReportItemEnum.BuiltInFinesOwed
    ' ----- Fines Owed by Patrons
    ' TODO: Write BasicReportFines()
Case ReportItemEnum.BuiltInStatistics
    ' ----- Library Database Statistics
    ' TODO: Write BasicReportStatistics()
```

Clearly, this code isn't accomplishing much. Change each of the TODO lines, removing the ' TODO: Write portion of the statement. So in the line that says:

```
' TODO: Write BasicReportCheckedOut()
```

change the code to:

```
BasicReportCheckedOut()
```

Do that for each of the five TODO lines, and let me know when you're done.

Exposing these five method calls means that we have to write those methods, darn it. These methods will retrieve the data for the report, and send that data to the report viewer, along with the name of the RDLC file. They're actually quite short and simple, considering the beautiful reports you will get out of them. Let's start by adding the *BasicReportCheckedOut* method to the *ReportSelect* class.

Insert Snippet Insert Chapter 20, Snippet Item 8.

```
Private Sub BasicReportCheckedOut()
    ' ----- Run built-in report #1: Items checked out report.
    Dim sqlText As String
    Dim reportData As Data.DataTable
    Dim reportForm As ReportBuiltinViewer

    On Error GoTo ErrorHandler

    ' ----- Retrieve the data as a dataset.
    sqlText = "SELECT PA.LastName + ', ' + " & _
        "PA.FirstName AS PatronName, " & _
        "PA.Barcode AS PatronBarcode, " & _
        "PC.DueDate, IC.CopyNumber, " & _
        "IC.Barcode AS ItemBarcode, " & _
        "NI.Title, CMT.FullName AS MediaName " & _
        "FROM Patron AS PA " & _
        "INNER JOIN PatronCopy AS PC ON PA.ID = PC.Patron " & _
        "INNER JOIN ItemCopy AS IC ON PC.ItemCopy = IC.ID " & _
        "INNER JOIN NamedItem AS NI ON IC.ItemID = NI.ID " & _
        "INNER JOIN CodeMediaType AS CMT ON " & _
        "NI.MediaType = CMT.ID " & _
        "WHERE PC.Returned = 0 " & _
        "AND PC.Missing = 0 " & _
        "AND IC.Missing = 0 " & _
        "ORDER BY NI.Title, IC.CopyNumber, " & _
        "PA.LastName, PA.FirstName"
    reportData = CreateDataTable(sqlText)

    ' ----- Check for no data.
    If (reportData.Rows.Count = 0) Then
        reportData.Dispose()
        MsgBox("No items are checked out.", MsgBoxStyle.OkOnly _
            Or MsgBoxStyle.Exclamation, ProgramTitle)
        Return
    End If

    ' ----- Send the data to the report.
    reportForm = New ReportBuiltinViewer
    reportForm.StartReport("Library.ReportCheckedOut.rdlc", _
        "Library_ReportSchemaPatronItems", reportData)
    Return
```

```
ErrorHandler:
   GeneralError("ReportSelect.BasicReportCheckedOut", _
      Err.GetException())
   Return
End Sub
```

The code retrieves the report-specific records from the database, and makes sure that at least one record was included. (We could have added the SQL statement to the Library database as either a Stored Procedure or a View, and called that instead. For the purposes of this tutorial, it was simpler to store the statement directly in code.) It then calls the report viewer, passing the name of the RDLC file, the schema name (in the format *ProjectName_ClassName*), and the data table.

Next, add the *BasicReportOverdue* and *BasicReportMissing* methods. I won't show the code here since, except for the name of the RDLC file and the WHERE clause in the SQL statement, they are identical to *BasicReportCheckedOut*.

Insert Snippet Insert Chapter 20, Snippet Item 9.

Add in the *BasicReportFines* method, which handles built-in report #4.

Insert Snippet Insert Chapter 20, Snippet Item 10.

It's also quite similar to the *BasicReportCheckedOut* method, but it uses the SQL statement we designed earlier for patron fine retrieval. It also uses a different schema and report name.

```
reportForm.StartReport("Library.ReportPatronFines.rdlc", _
   "Library_ReportSchemaPatronFines", reportData)
```

The last method to add to *ReportSelect.vb* is *BasicReportStatistics*, which handles built-in report #5. It's a little different from the other four because it gathers data from six different tables, one at a time. In each case, it retrieves a count of the number of records in a database table. The results are then stored in a generic collection (*System.Collections.Generic.List*), where each list entry is an instance of *ReportSchemaStatistics*, the class we used for the fifth report's data schema. What a coincidence!

Here's the code for *BasicReportStatistics* for you to add now to the *ReportSelect* form class.

Insert Snippet Insert Chapter 20, Snippet Item 11.

```
Private Sub BasicReportStatistics()
    ' ----- Run built-in report #5: Library database
    '       statistics report.
    Dim sqlText As String
    Dim reportData As Collections.Generic.List( _
        Of ReportSchemaStatistics)
    Dim oneEntry As ReportSchemaStatistics
    Dim reportForm As ReportBuiltinViewer
    Dim resultValue As Integer
    Dim counter As Integer
    Const tableSets As String = "Author,Publisher," & _
        "Subject,NamedItem,ItemCopy,Patron"
    Const tableTitles As String = "Authors,Publishers," & _
        "Subject Headings,Items,Item Copies,Patrons"

    On Error GoTo ErrorHandler

    ' ----- Build the report data. It's all counts from
    '       different tables.
    reportData = New Collections.Generic.List( _
        Of ReportSchemaStatistics)
    For counter = 1 To CountSubStr(tableSets, ",") + 1
        ' ----- Process one table.
        sqlText = "SELECT COUNT(*) FROM " & _
            GetSubStr(tableSets, ",", counter)
        resultValue = DBGetInteger(ExecuteSQLReturn(sqlText))

        ' ----- Add it to the report data.
        oneEntry = New ReportSchemaStatistics
        oneEntry.EntryName = _
            GetSubStr(tableTitles, ",", counter)
        oneEntry.EntryValue = CStr(resultValue)
        reportData.Add(oneEntry)
    Next counter

    ' ----- Send the data to the report.
    reportForm = New ReportBuiltinViewer
    reportForm.StartReport("Library.ReportStatistics.rdlc", _
        "Library_ReportSchemaStatistics", reportData)
    Return
```

```
ErrorHandler:
   GeneralError("ReportSelect.BasicReportStatistics", _
      Err.GetException())
   Return
End Sub
```

Because we really need to get the same information (COUNT(*)) for each of the six tables involved, I just implemented the code as a loop, and built the SQL statement for each one as I passed through the loop. A friendly table name and the record count are then stored in the generic list, which is eventually sent to the report.

You can now run the application and use the five built-in reports. You must log in as a librarian or administrator, and then access the *Print Reports* panel on the main form.

Believe it or not, we're almost finished with the application. The only big thing left to do is to process past-due patron items to see if fines are required. We'll add this code in the next chapter, and also take a look at licensing.

CHAPTER 21

LICENSING YOUR APPLICATION

Proper .NET content licensing can mean the difference between marketplace dominance and financial bankruptcy. And I'm just talking about trying to understand the license agreement that comes with Visual Studio. You still have to figure out a licensing method for your own application before you send it to your customers.

Licensing and license agreements are an essential means of protecting the intellectual property you've worked so hard to develop. How does licensing work? The key is found in the roots of the word itself: "license" comes from "li-" (to tell a lie) and "-cense" (from "cents" as in "pennies"). Together, these roots mean "to tell lies about small units of currency." The confusion brought about in trying to figure out what this means keeps the bad guys confused and occupied long enough so that they don't steal your application.

If this method doesn't work, there are software solutions, some of which we examine in this chapter. Part of the discussion focuses on designing a licensing system that we will add to the Library Project. The .NET Framework does include classes for component licensing, but they are primarily used for designers of controls used by other programmers within the Visual Studio IDE, and not for end-user applications. We will not be covering these licensing features in this chapter. If you're curious about such features, start by reading about the *License Compiler* (lc.exe) in the Visual Studio online help.

Software Licensing Options

Back in the early days of software, licensing wasn't an issue: If you could get to the computer, it was because you were authorized. All user interaction with the system was through the programmers and technicians. If some user wanted to steal something, it would be in the form of 20 tons of steel, wires, and vacuum tubes. Fun? Yes. Easy? No.

Today, it's a different story. Most users are non-technical, and some are unethical. So now we have licensing agreements and teams of lawyers to back it all up. But we also have software, software that can delicately enforce some of the rules. For a particular piece of software, there is still the question of, "How much licensing enforcement code do I add to my application?" The amount of software control you include will fall somewhere in the "freedom-security" continuum shown in Figure 21-1.

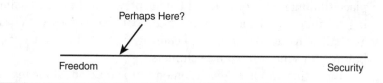

Figure 21-1 The licensing enforcement continuum: where are you on it?

If you go for the Freedom end of the spectrum (convenient for users and hackers), you will have to go on the trustworthiness of your users, and any armed guards you have dispatched to their offices, to keep the program in compliance. At the Security end of the scale (secure for programmers and highly paid law firms), the software implements practices and policies that ensure only licensed users of the application ever use or install it; no armed guards needed.

The rest of this section discusses some possible options you could choose within the Freedom-Security range.

License Agreement Only

The license-agreement-only method clearly opts for freedom over security. When you supply the user with software, it comes with a carefully crafted license agreement that lays out the terms of use for both the user and the software supplier. It generally gives the user certain rights as to installation, use, and distribution of the software.

When you write an application for use only within a specific organization or by a small group of users whom you will have regular contact with, the license-agreement-only method may be just what you need. In fact, I would bet that the majority of Visual Basic applications are in this vein. Microsoft has announced over the years that the vast majority of Visual

Basic programmers target their applications for use in a specific business organization, tied to a specific custom database. Such systems often require very little in the way of license enforcement, because the application is useless when carried outside the building where it was meant to reside.

Even if your software achieves widespread distribution, this licensing scheme may still be the way to go. Many shareware applications, including a major operating system that rhymes with "Plinux," use the Free Software Foundation's *GNU General Public License* (*http://www.fsf.org/licensing/ licenses/gpl.html*) as their primary licensing and distribution policy.

Generated General License Key

If you need a bit more control over the distribution, installation, and use of an application, you can impose a *generated general license key*—basically a password that allows the application to be installed or used. Such keys are often entered at the start of the installation process, with the user prompted for a specific key. Without the key, it's goodbye installation.

The software vendor will need a way to generate a good set of unique installation keys. There are a few options.

- Just generate a sequential serial number, and mix into it a product ID and version number. The great thing about such a key is that it is easy to generate. The installation program doesn't need to perform any complex verification logic on the key. It only needs to ensure that the general format is correct. One of the products I used to develop online help documentation for my older Visual Basic 6.0 applications used such a license key. In a way, it's not much more secure than using just a license agreement, because anyone who knows the general format can make up their own key.
- Use a hashed or scrambled key, based on some original serial number or formula that can be verified by the installation program. A well-crafted hashing algorithm can generate a wide range of keys, but make it difficult for others who don't know the formula to generate their own fake keys. Although I am not privy to Microsoft's internal processes, this appears to be the method they use for their 25-character "CD Keys," including the one supplied with Visual Studio. Although it is difficult for keys to be invented out of whole cloth, the public nature of the keys makes them subject to sharing. For some of its products, Microsoft combines a CD key with an online or phone-based registration process to enhance security.

- Supply a hashed or encrypted key based on a serial number that is (secretly) supplied with the installation program or distribution media. When the user enters the key, it is unencrypted or otherwise prepared, and then compared with the serial number. Only if it matches will the software installation complete properly.

Generated Custom License Key

A custom-generated license key is similar to a general generated key, but uses personal information supplied by the user as part of the generation process. Such a key is more interactive, and requires that the end user specifically communicate with the software vendor (or an application on its web site) to complete the installation process.

During the purchase or installation process, the user makes specific information (such as the owner's name and the date of purchase) available to the software vendor. The vendor then uses public-private key encryption (asymmetric cryptography) to either fully encrypt or digitally sign the relevant information. The encrypted signature is then returned to the end user for installation. The installation process uses the public portion of the key pair to ensure that the signature is valid.

We will use this license key method in the Library Project, so I'll have more to say about it a little later.

License Key with Hardware Identity or Lock

For paranoid software vendors, or for those who have a legitimate need to keep a tight rein on their installation base, there are solutions that involve regular access to hardware or services to confirm that previously installed software is legal and valid. One popular method uses a "dongle," typically a USB port-based device that the software must have access to each time it runs. The software vendor supplies a dongle with the licensed software, and may encode it with date-based or use-based limits.

With the prevalence of the Internet, software vendors also have the option of real-time verification over the Web. Each time the program runs, it could access a known vendor site, and use XML Web Services or a similar method to engage in a usage verification process. Such a system allows for ongoing monitoring of the software by vendors who may have a business or governmental reason to limit use of the software.

For one of my customer projects, I must access a third-party web site on a monthly basis and download proprietary data for use with that vendor's software. The vendor requires that I always access their web site from a specific machine with a specific IP address. It will refuse to supply the data if I attempt to connect from any other machine. If I have a real need to use a fresh IP address (if, for example, I change Internet Service Providers), I must submit paperwork to the vendor informing them of the new IP address. It seems pesky, and it is an irritation. But the data they supply is unique and valuable, and they feel they have a business need to protect that investment. Because my customer requires the data, I have no choice but to comply with the monthly verification procedures.

Controlled Access

The highest level of security requires a blatant distrust of the user, although there may be good reason for this. For highly sensitive applications, the software vendor may make their product available to only a limited number of customers, and then only on a lease basis. As part of the lease agreement, the customer agrees to have a trained staff member of the software vendor on-site, running and maintaining the application for the customer. At the very least, the vendor will require that one of its employees be immediately available to the customer whenever the application is used.

In a world of off-the-shelf software applications, it seems unconscionable that such a system could exist. But in high-risk situations, security concerns are raised to such a level that neither party is willing to fully assume the risks of installing and using the application apart from the other.

Although I was tempted to use this system for the Library Project, I think we'll stick with our original plan of employing a custom-generated license key.

License Agreements

A *license agreement* is a document wherein the party of the first part hereby and does amicably render to the party of the second part certain rights, *quid pro quos*, treasury bonds, and other benefits; in exchange, the party of the second part will do the same for the party of the first part without respect for any other party or festival.

Let's try that again. A license agreement tells a user, "go ahead, install and use the software, but you have to follow these rules." Although they are often written in legalese, they can also appear in a real language, such as English. They also range in granted rights, from "you can use this, but when you're finished, you must destroy all copies" to "use it, and feel free to pass a copy of the program and its source code to your friends and relations."

The Library software provided with this book comes with a license agreement. (I've included it in Appendix B, "Software License Agreement.") When you installed the sample code, you agreed to the terms of the license agreement, including the part about supporting my family financially well into my retirement years. But enough about me; let's talk about license agreements you may want to use for your applications.

If you're developing a DVD catalog program for your cousin Fred, you can probably skip the license agreement part. But any software you craft in a business capacity for use outside of your own company should include some sort of agreement between you (or your company) and the user of the software. This agreement could be defined as part of the contract that established the software development project (this is typical for software consulting), or you could include the agreement as a component of the software (common for off-the-shelf programs).

Whichever method you choose, it is important that you state it in written form, because it can save you grief down the road. I once had a customer who insisted that I fork over a copy of the source code for an application I wrote for them, so that they could enhance it and sell the new version to other businesses (the nerve!). Fortunately, we had a written contract that stated the rules of engagement. They were entitled to a copy of the source code for archive purposes, but they could not use it or derive products from it without written consent from me. This granted a level of safety for them while still providing the means for me to provide the best support possible for their organization. Fortunately, it all came to a happy conclusion, and because that Visual Basic 3.0 code doesn't even run anymore, it's a moot point.

A license agreement usually exists to protect the rights of the software vendor, but it would be useless if it didn't also grant meaningful rights to the user—and some of the rights can be rather generous. Did you know that the standard consumer licensing agreement for Microsoft Office allows you to install the product on two different systems using a single licensed copy of the program? It's not a complete install-fest. Both computers must belong to the same person, and one must be a desktop while the other is a portable device (a laptop). But it's still a meaningful benefit to the typical user.

The legal department at Addison-Wesley wants to remind you that Tim Patrick does not have a sufficient understanding of the law, and cannot advise you on the contents of any licensing agreement you may want to craft for your projects.

Obfuscation

I hinted a little about the obfuscation features in Visual Studio 2005 in Chapters 1, "Introducing .NET," and 5, ".NET Assemblies," but it's high time we actually took a look at the features. Visual Studio includes a stripped-down version of *Dotfuscator* from a company named *PreEmptive Solutions* (not a part of Microsoft—yet). To access the program, use the **Tools ➤ Dotfuscator Community Edition** menu command in Visual Studio. The main interface appears in Figure 21-2.

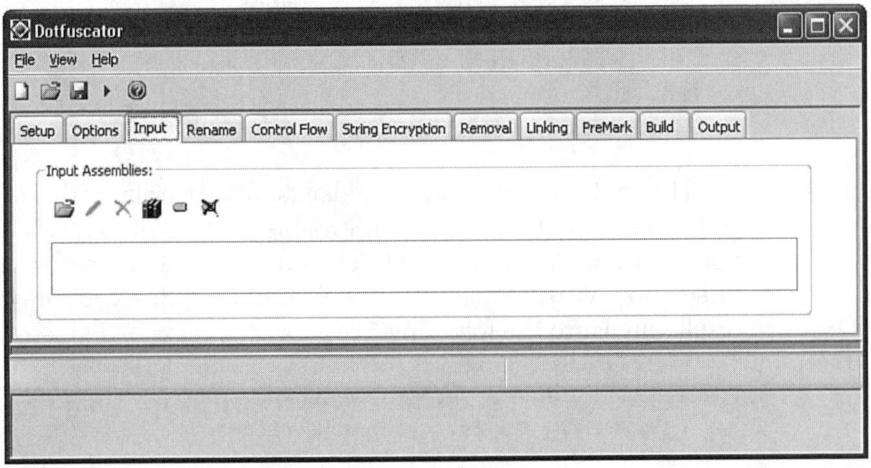

Figure 21-2 It's time to obfuscate!

Note As of this writing, *Dotfuscator Community Edition* is not included with Visual Basic 2005 Express Edition.

Even though this is the basic version of the product, you can see that it has a gazillion options. If you want to dive into its enhanced features for your project, that's fantastic. I'll just cover the basic usage here.

Let's recall quickly why you would want to obfuscate your code, or even use the word "obfuscate" in mixed company. Here's some code from the Library project.

```
Public Function CenterText(ByVal origText As String, _
    ByVal textWidth As Integer) As String
   ' ----- Center a piece of text in a field width.
   '        If the text is too wide, truncate it.
   Dim resultText As String

   resultText = Trim(origText)
   If (Len(resultText) >= textWidth) Then
      ' ----- Truncate as needed.
      Return Trim(Left(origText, textWidth))
   Else
      ' ----- Start with extra spaces.
      Return Space((textWidth - Len(origText)) \ 2) & _
         resultText
   End If
End Function
```

This code is quite easy to understand, especially with the comments and the meaningful method and variable names. Although .NET obfuscation works at the MSIL level, let's pretend that the obfuscator worked directly on Visual Basic code. Obfuscation of this code might produce results similar to the following.

```
Public Function A(ByVal AA As String, _
    ByVal AAA As Integer) As String
   Dim AAAA As String
   AAAA = Trim(AA)
   If (Len(AAAA) >= AAA) Then
      Return Trim(Left(AA, AAA))
```

```
    Else
        Return Space((AAA - Len(AA)) \ 2) & AAAA
    End If
End Function
```

In such a simple routine, we could still figure out the logic, but with more effort than in the original version. Naturally, true obfuscation goes much further than this, scrambling the readability of the code at the IL level, and confounding code readers and hackers alike.

To obfuscate an assembly:

1. Build your project in Visual Studio using the **Build ➤ Build [Project Name]** menu command.

2. Start *Dotfuscator* using the **Tools ➤ Dotfuscator Community Edition** menu command in Visual Studio.

3. When prompted for a project type, select **Create New Project**, and click the **OK** button.

4. On the **Input** tab of the Dotfuscator application window, click the **Browse and add assembly to list** toolbar button. This is the left-most button—the one that looks like a file folder with a small arrow above it—on the panel shown earlier in Figure 21-2.

5. When prompted for an assembly file, browse for your compiled application, and click the **OK** button. The assembly to use will be in the *bin\Release* subdirectory within your project's source code directory.

6. Select the **File ➤ Build** menu command to generate the obfuscated assembly. You will be prompted to save the *Dotfuscator* project file (an XML file) before the build begins. Save this file to a new directory. When the build occurs, it will save the output assembly in a *Dotfuscated* subdirectory in the same directory that contains the XML project file.

7. The build completes, and a summary appears as shown in Figure 21-3. Your obfuscated file is ready to use. The process also generates a *Map.xml* file that documents all the name changes made to types and members within your application. It would be a bad thing to distribute this file with the assembly. It is for your debugging use only.

Figure 21-3 Summary of the obfuscation, with some advertising thrown in

To prove that the obfuscation took place, use the *IL Disassembler* tool that comes with Visual Studio to examine each assembly. (On my system, this program is accessed via **Start ➤ [All] Programs ➤ Microsoft .NET Framework SDK v2.0 ➤ Tools ➤ MSIL Disassembler**.) Figure 21-4 shows the global variables included in the Library Project's *General.vb* file. The obfuscated version of these same variables appears in Figure 21-5.

Figure 21-4 Global variables before obfuscation

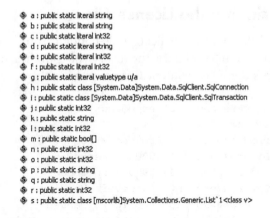

a : public static literal string
b : public static literal string
c : public static literal int32
d : public static literal string
e : public static literal int32
f : public static literal int32
g : public static literal valuetype u/a
h : public static class [System.Data]System.Data.SqlClient.SqlConnection
i : public static class [System.Data]System.Data.SqlClient.SqlTransaction
j : public static int32
k : public static string
l : public static int32
m : public static bool[]
n : public static int32
o : public static int32
p : public static string
q : public static string
r : public static int32
s : public static class [mscorlib]System.Collections.Generic.List`1<class v>

Figure 21-5 Global variables after obfuscation

I will not be performing obfuscation on the Library Project through this book's tutorial sections. Feel free to try it out on your own.

The Library Licensing System

The tools and procedures we will use to design the Library Project's licensing system can be built from features already discussed in previous chapters.

- The license file contains XML content. (Chapter 13, "XML")
- The license appears as a separate file in the same directory as the Library.exe assembly. The Library software reads content from the license file. (See Chapter 15, "Files and Directories.")
- The license will include a digital signature, which is based on public-private key encryption. (See Chapter 11, "Security.")

Each time the Library application starts up, it attempts to read the license file. If the file doesn't exist, or if it contains invalid data or an invalid signature, the program downgrades its available features, disabling those features that are considered licensed.

21. LICENSING YOUR APPLICATION

Designing the License File

The Library Project's license file contains some basic ownership and rights information related to the user who purchased rights to the software. Here's the XML content I've come up with.

```
<?xml version="1.0" encoding="utf-8"?>
<License>
  <Product>Library Project</Product>
  <LicenseDate>1/1/2000</LicenseDate>
  <ExpireDate>12/31/2999</ExpireDate>
  <CoveredVersion>1.*</CoveredVersion>
  <Licensee>John Q. Public</Licensee>
  <SerialNumber>LIB-123456789</SerialNumber>
</License>
```

That seems sufficient. The process that builds the digital signature also stores an encrypted signature within the XML content.

Generating the License File

In the "Project" section of this chapter, we'll build a new application that exists solely to generate license files for the Library application. It will have three primary components.

1. Generate and manage the public and private keys used in the signature process.
2. Prompt the user for the license date, expiration date, covered version, licensee name, and serial number for a single license. These are the values that appear in the license file's XML content.
3. Output the XML license file and digitally sign it using the private key.

Installing the License File

The "Project" portion of this chapter will show you how to generate a generic license file. This XML file will be distributed and installed with the Library application using the setup program that we will build in Chapter 24, "Deployment." The file will be named *LibraryLicense.lic* (by default), and will always appear in the same directory as the *Library.exe* application file.

If I were developing a real application for paying customers, and I had a web site that supported XML Web Services (which I'll talk about in Chapter 22, "Web Development"), here is one design for installing the license file that I might use.

1. Run the Setup program to install the application on the user's workstation.
2. During installation, the Setup program prompts the user for the license details that will ultimately appear in the XML license file.
3. The Setup program contacts an XML Web Service on my vendor web site, and passes the user-supplied values to that registration service.
4. The registration service returns a digitally signed XML file that contains the licensing content.
5. The Setup program installs this file along with the application.
6. If for any reason the licensing cannot complete successfully during Setup, the main application contains identical licensing code, and can communicate with the registration service itself.

Using the License File

Whenever the Library application runs, it reads in the XML license file, and performs many checks to ensure that the license is valid for the current application installation. If the license is invalid for any reason, the application blocks access to the enhanced administrative features included in the Library system.

Summary

Because you will often spend dozens or hundreds of hours designing and developing a quality Visual Basic application, it is important to use appropriate licensing and obfuscation technology to protect your hard work. Licensing is another one of those common programming tasks that didn't make it into the .NET Framework as an easy-to-use class—unless you are building and distributing design-time controls. For the rest of us, it's make-it-up-as-you-go time. Fortunately, .NET has great support tools, so adding licensing support isn't too difficult.

21. LICENSING YOUR APPLICATION

Project

In this chapter's project code, we'll follow two of the four licensing steps discussed in the "Library Licensing System" section of this chapter: *generating the license file* and *using the license file*. The design we created previously is good enough for our needs, although we still need to record it in the project's technical documentation. We won't formally install the license file until we create the Setup program in Chapter 24.

Update Technical Documentation

Because we'll be adding a new external file that will be processed by the Library Project, we need to document its structure in the project's Technical Resource Kit. Let's add the following new section to that document.

Report Configuration File

The Library Project reads a customer-specific license file generated by the Library License Generation support application. That program generates a digitally signed XML license file that includes licensee information. Here is a sample of the license file content.

```
<?xml version="1.0"?>
<License>
  <Product>Library Project</Product>
  <LicenseDate>1/1/2000</LicenseDate>
  <ExpireDate>12/31/2999</ExpireDate>
  <CoveredVersion>1.*</CoveredVersion>
  <Licensee>John Q. Public</Licensee>
  <SerialNumber>LIB-123456789</SerialNumber>
  <Signature>
    Digital signature appears here (not shown)
  </Signature>
</License>
```

The `<LicenseDate>` and `<ExpireDate>` tags indicate the first and last valid dates of the license. `<Licensee>` indicates the name of the license owner. `<SerialNumber>` includes the vendor-defined serial number associated with this license. The `<CoveredVersion>` tag contains data similar to the assembly version number included in .NET applications. It has up to four dot-delimited parts:

```
<major>.<minor>.<build>.<revision>
```

Each component can include a number from 0 to 9999, or the "*" character, which indicates all valid values for that position.

The `<Signature>` section contains the generated digital signature. Its format is dependent on the XML Cryptography tools in .NET that generate this section. Always use the Library License Generation support application to build license files, to ensure a proper digital signature.

That support application generates a public and private key pair for use in digital signing. The public portion of this key (as an XML file) must be added as a resource named *LicensePublicKey* to the Library application. The private portion must be kept private. For consistency, the same key-pair should be used throughout the lifetime of the Library Project's availability.

We will also store the location of the license file as an application setting in the main program. We need to record that setting with the other application settings already added to the *User Settings* section of the Resource Kit.

LicenseFileLocation—The path to the Library License file on this workstation. If not supplied, the program will look for a file named *LibraryLicense.lic* in the same folder as the application.

Library License Helper Application

Generating license files and digital signatures by hand using Notepad would be . . . well, let's not even think about it. Instead, we'll depend on a custom application to create the files and signatures for us. I've already developed that custom tool for you. You'll find it in the installation directory for this book's code, in the *LibraryLicensing* subdirectory.

This support application includes two main forms. The first (*KeyLocationForm.vb*, shown in Figure 21-6) locates or creates the public-private key files used in the digital signature process.

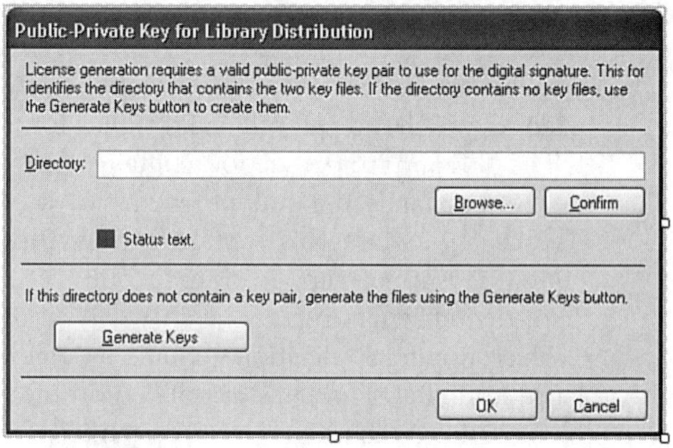

Figure 21-6 Support form for digital signatures

Most of the form's code helps locate and verify the folder that will contain the two key files (one private, one public). Some of the code in the *ActGenerate_Click* event handler creates the actual files.

```
Dim twoPartKey As RSA
Dim publicFile As String
Dim privateFile As String

' ----- Generate the keys.
twoPartKey = New RSACryptoServiceProvider
twoPartKey = RSA.Create()

' ----- Save the public key.
My.Computer.FileSystem.WriteAllText(publicFile, _
   twoPartKey.ToXmlString(False), False)

' ----- Save the private key.
My.Computer.FileSystem.WriteAllText(privateFile, _
   twoPartKey.ToXmlString(True), False)
```

That's really simple! The *System.Security.Cryptography.RSA* class and the related *RSACryptoServiceProvider* class do all the work. All you have to do is call the *RSA.Create* method, and then generate the relevant XML keys using the *ToXmlString* method, passing an argument of *False* for the public key, and *True* for the private key. If you want to look at some sample keys, open the *LicenseFiles* subdirectory in this book's source installation directory. You'll find two files, one for the public key and one for the private key. I'd print one of them here, but it all just looks like random characters.

The other support form is *MainForm.vb*, which generates the actual end-user license file, and appears in Figure 21-7.

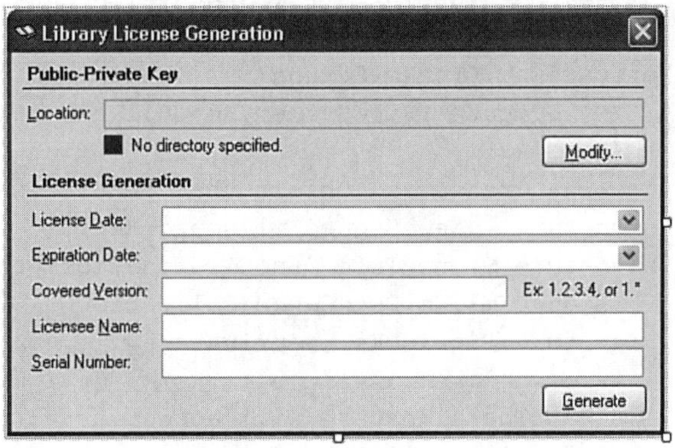

Figure 21-7 Support form for license file generation

As with the first form, most of this form's code simply ensures that the public and private key files are intact, and that the user entered valid data before generation. The *ActGenerate_Click* event handler is where the real fun is. First, we need some XML content, which we build in the *BuildXmlLicenseContent* method. It creates the content element by element, using the methods we learned about in Chapter 13. For instance, here's the part of the code that adds the serial number.

```
dataElement = result.CreateElement("SerialNumber")
dataElement.InnerText = Trim(SerialNumber.Text)
rootElement.AppendChild(dataElement)
```

21. LICENSING YOUR APPLICATION

Then comes the digital signature, via the *SignXmlLicenseContent* function, most of which appears here.

```
Private Function SignXmlLicenseContent( _
      ByVal sourceXML As XmlDocument) As Boolean
   ' ----- Add a digital signature to an XML document.
   Dim privateKeyFile As String
   Dim privateKey As RSA
   Dim signature As SignedXml
   Dim referenceMethod As Reference

   ' ----- Load in the private key.
   privateKeyFile = My.Computer.FileSystem.CombinePath( _
      KeyLocation.Text, PrivateKeyFilename)
   privateKey = RSA.Create()
   privateKey.FromXmlString( _
      My.Computer.FileSystem.ReadAllText(privateKeyFile))

   ' ----- Create the object that generates the signature.
   signature = New SignedXml(sourceXML)
   signature.SignedInfo.CanonicalizationMethod = _
      SignedXml.XmlDsigCanonicalizationUrl
   signature.SigningKey = privateKey

   ' ----- The signature will appear as a <reference>
   '       element in the XML.
   referenceMethod = New Reference("")
   referenceMethod.AddTransform(New _
      XmlDsigEnvelopedSignatureTransform(False))
   signature.AddReference(referenceMethod)

   ' ----- Add the signature to the XML content.
   signature.ComputeSignature()
   sourceXML.DocumentElement.AppendChild(signature.GetXml())

   ' ----- Finished.
   Return True
End Function
```

Digital signing occurs via the *SignedXml* class (in the *System.Security.Cryptography.Xml* namespace). This class uses a few different signing methods; the one I chose (*XmlDsigCanonicalizationUrl*) is used for typical XML and ignores embedded comments.

This signature appears as tags and values in the XML output, added through the *AppendChild* statement near the end of the routine. Because we don't want the signature itself to be considered when we later scan the XML file for valid content, the *SignedXml* class adds the signature as a <reference> tag. This occurs in code by adding a *Reference* object that is programmed for that purpose. It's added through the *signature.AddReference* method call.

Once we have the signature in the XML content, we write it all out to a file specified by the user via the standard *XmlDocument.Save* method (in the *ActGenerate_Click* event handler).

```
licenseXML.Save(LicenseSaveLocation.FileName)
```

Here's a sample XML license file that includes a digital signature. This is the one that I have included in the *LicenseFiles* directory in the book's source installation directory (with some lines wrapped to fit this page).

```
<?xml version="1.0"?>
<License>
  <Product>Library Project</Product>
  <LicenseDate>1/1/2000</LicenseDate>
  <ExpireDate>12/31/2999</ExpireDate>
  <CoveredVersion>1.*</CoveredVersion>
  <Licensee>John Q. Public</Licensee>
  <SerialNumber>LIB-123456789</SerialNumber>
  <Signature xmlns="http://www.w3.org/2000/09/xmldsig#">
    <SignedInfo>
      <CanonicalizationMethod Algorithm=
        "http://www.w3.org/TR/2001/REC-xml-c14n-20010315" />
      <SignatureMethod Algorithm=
        "http://www.w3.org/2000/09/xmldsig#rsa-sha1" />
      <Reference URI="">
        <Transforms>
          <Transform Algorithm="http://www.w3.org/2000/09/
            xmldsig#enveloped-signature" />
        </Transforms>
        <DigestMethod Algorithm="http://www.w3.org/2000/09/
          xmldsig#sha1" />
        <DigestValue>Dn6JYIBI/qQudmvSiMvuOvnVBGU=
          </DigestValue>
      </Reference>
    </SignedInfo>
```

```
    <SignatureValue>NULghI4WbzDLroIcf2u9aoybfSjXPJRN5
        0UMrCPYa5bup+c7RJnqTM+SzP4jmfJWPPs7pOvDC/fbdNY
        VMaoyXW0jL3Lk8du3X4JXpW3xp9Nxq31y/Ld8E+RkoiPO6
        KRGDI+RRZ8MAQda8WS+L2fMyenRAjo+fR9KL3sQ/hOfQX8=
    </SignatureValue>
  </Signature>
</License>
```

The digital signature appears as the scrambled content within the <SignatureValue> tag. Now, if anyone tries to modify any of the license values, the license will no longer match the signature, and the entire license will become invalid.

Instead of using a digital signature, we could have just encrypted the entire licensing file with the private key, and later used the public key to decrypt it and examine its contents. But I like the digital signature better, because it allows anyone to open up the license file and check the parameters of the license itself while still preventing any changes.

Adding the License to the Library Program

Let's return to the Library application already in progress.

Project Access Load the "Chapter 21 (Before) Code" project, either through the New Project templates, or by accessing the project directly from the installation directory. To see the code in its final form, load "Chapter 21 (After) Code" instead.

The program will adjust its behavior depending on whether it is licensed or not. But to make that determination, it needs to ensure that the contents of the licensing file are valid and haven't been tampered with. To do this, it needs a way to unscramble the signature, and compare it with the rest of the license to make sure it matches. We built the signature using the private key; we must unscramble it using the public key.

We could store the public key in its own file outside of the program, but then it might get lost (just like my real keys). Instead, we'll store the public key as an application resource, found externally in the source code's *Resources* folder. I've already added the resource to your copy of the program, and named it *LicensePublicKey*. With this key embedded in the application, *any regeneration of the public and private keys will require modification of this resource*. In code, we refer to the XML content of the public key using its resource name.

```
My.Resources.LicensePublicKey
```

Some of the security features use classes found in the *System.Security.Cryptography.Xml* namespace. This is not one of the namespaces included by default in new Visual Basic applications, so we'll have to add it ourselves. Open the project properties window, and select the *References* tab. Just below the list of *References*, click the **Add** button, and then select *System.Security* from the *.NET* tab of the *Add Reference* window that appears.

Because the project properties window is still open, click over to the *Settings* tab. Add a new *String* setting and use "LicenseFileLocation" for its name. We'll use this setting to store the path to the license file. Save and close the project properties window.

Our general licensing needs throughout the application are pretty simple. We only need to know the current status of the licensing file, and have access to a few of the licensing values so that we can display a short message about the license. We may need to do this in various parts of the program, so let's add some useful generic code to the *General.vb* module. Open that module now.

Right at the top of that file, the code already includes a reference to the *System.Security.Cryptography* namespace, because we include code that encrypts user passwords. But this doesn't cover the standard or secure XML stuff. So add two new *Imports* statements as well.

Insert Snippet Insert Chapter 21, Snippet Item 1.

```
Imports System.Xml
Imports System.Security.Cryptography.Xml
```

We'll use an enumeration to indicate the status of the license. Add it now to the *General* module.

Insert Snippet Insert Chapter 21, Snippet Item 2.

```
Public Enum LicenseStatus
    ValidLicense
    MissingLicenseFile
    CorruptLicenseFile
    InvalidSignature
    NotYetLicensed
    LicenseExpired
    VersionMismatch
End Enum
```

Let's also add a simple structure that communicates the values extracted from the license file. Add this code to the *General* module.

Insert Snippet Insert Chapter 21, Snippet Item 3.

```
Public Structure LicenseFileDetail
    Public Status As LicenseStatus
    Public Licensee As String
    Public LicenseDate As Date
    Public ExpireDate As Date
    Public CoveredVersion As String
    Public SerialNumber As String
End Structure
```

By default, the license file appears in the same directory as the application, using the name *LibraryLicense.lic*. Add a global constant to the *General* module that identifies this default name.

Insert Snippet Insert Chapter 21, Snippet Item 4.

```
Public Const DefaultLicenseFile _
    As String = "LibraryLicense.lic"
```

All we need now is some code to fill in the *LicenseFileDetail* structure.
Add the new *ExamineLicense* function to the *General* module.

Insert Snippet Insert Chapter 21, Snippet Item 5.

```vb
Public Function ExamineLicense() As LicenseFileDetail
    ' ----- Examine the application's license file, and
    '       report back what's inside.
    Dim result As New LicenseFileDetail
    Dim usePath As String
    Dim licenseContent As XmlDocument
    Dim publicKey As RSA
    Dim signedDocument As SignedXml
    Dim matchingNodes As XmlNodeList
    Dim versionParts() As String
    Dim counter As Integer
    Dim comparePart As String

    ' ----- See if the license file exists.
    result.Status = LicenseStatus.MissingLicenseFile
    usePath = My.Settings.LicenseFileLocation
    If (usePath = "") Then usePath = _
        My.Computer.FileSystem.CombinePath( _
        My.Application.Info.DirectoryPath, DefaultLicenseFile)
    If (My.Computer.FileSystem.FileExists(usePath) = False) _
        Then Return result

    ' ----- Try to read in the file.
    result.Status = LicenseStatus.CorruptLicenseFile
    Try
        licenseContent = New XmlDocument()
        licenseContent.Load(usePath)
    Catch ex As Exception
        ' ----- Silent error.
        Return result
    End Try

    ' ----- Prepare the public key resource for use.
    publicKey = RSA.Create()
    publicKey.FromXmlString(My.Resources.LicensePublicKey)
```

```
' ----- Confirm the digital signature.
Try
    signedDocument = New SignedXml(licenseContent)
    matchingNodes = licenseContent.GetElementsByTagName( _
        "Signature")
    signedDocument.LoadXml(CType(matchingNodes(0), _
        XmlElement))
Catch ex As Exception
    ' ----- Still a corrupted document.
    Return result
End Try
If (signedDocument.CheckSignature(publicKey) = False) Then
    result.Status = LicenseStatus.InvalidSignature
    Return result
End If

' ----- The license file is valid. Extract its members.
Try
    ' ----- Get the licensee name.
    matchingNodes = licenseContent.GetElementsByTagName( _
        "Licensee")
    result.Licensee = matchingNodes(0).InnerText

    ' ----- Get the license date.
    matchingNodes = licenseContent.GetElementsByTagName( _
        "LicenseDate")
    result.LicenseDate = CDate(matchingNodes(0).InnerText)

    ' ----- Get the expiration date.
    matchingNodes = licenseContent.GetElementsByTagName( _
        "ExpireDate")
    result.ExpireDate = CDate(matchingNodes(0).InnerText)

    ' ----- Get the version number.
    matchingNodes = licenseContent.GetElementsByTagName( _
        "CoveredVersion")
    result.CoveredVersion = matchingNodes(0).InnerText

    ' ----- Get the serial number.
    matchingNodes = licenseContent.GetElementsByTagName( _
        "SerialNumber")
    result.SerialNumber = matchingNodes(0).InnerText
Catch ex As Exception
```

```
        ' ----- Still a corrupted document.
        Return result
    End Try


    ' ----- Check for out-of-range dates.
    If (result.LicenseDate > Today) Then
        result.Status = LicenseStatus.NotYetLicensed
        Return result
    End If
    If (result.ExpireDate < Today) Then
        result.Status = LicenseStatus.LicenseExpired
        Return result
    End If


    ' ----- Check the version.
    versionParts = Split(result.CoveredVersion, ".")
    For counter = 0 To UBound(versionParts)
        If (IsNumeric(versionParts(counter)) = True) Then
            ' ----- The version format is
            '       major.minor.build.revision.
            Select Case counter
                Case 0 : comparePart = _
                    CStr(My.Application.Info.Version.Major)
                Case 1 : comparePart = _
                    CStr(My.Application.Info.Version.Minor)
                Case 2 : comparePart = _
                    CStr(My.Application.Info.Version.Build)
                Case 3 : comparePart = _
                    CStr(My.Application.Info.Version.Revision)
                Case Else
                    ' ----- Corrupt verison number.
                    Return result
            End Select
            If (Val(comparePart) <> _
                    Val(versionParts(counter))) Then
                result.Status = LicenseStatus.VersionMismatch
                Return result
            End If
        End If
    Next counter


    ' ----- Everything seems to be in order.
    result.Status = LicenseStatus.ValidLicense
    Return result
End Function
```

That's a lot of code, but most of it just loads and extracts values from the XML license file. The signature-checking part is relatively short.

```
publicKey = RSA.Create()
publicKey.FromXmlString(My.Resources.LicensePublicKey)
signedDocument = New SignedXml(licenseContent)
matchingNodes = licenseContent.GetElementsByTagName( _
    "Signature")
signedDocument.LoadXml(CType(matchingNodes(0), XmlElement))
If (signedDocument.CheckSignature(publicKey) = False) Then
    ' ----- Invalid
End If
```

The *SignedXml* object—which we also used to generate the original license file—needs to know exactly which of the XML tags in its content represents the digital signature. You would think that having an element named <Signature> would be a big tip-off, but perhaps not. Anyway, once you've assigned that node using the *SignedXml.LoadXml* method, you call the *CheckSignature* method, passing it the public key. If it returns *True*, you're good. I mean, not in a moral sense; the code doesn't know anything about you. But the signature is good.

Display License on the About Form

When we added the *About* form to the project a few hundred pages ago, we included a *Label* control named *LabelLicensed*. It currently always displays "Unlicensed," but now we have the tools to display a proper license, if available. Open the source code for the *About.vb* form, and add the following code to the start of the *AboutProgram_Load* event handler.

Insert Snippet Insert Chapter 21, Snippet Item 6.

```
' ----- Prepare the form.
Dim licenseDetails As LicenseFileDetail

' ----- Display the licensee.
licenseDetails = ExamineLicense()
If (licenseDetails.Status = LicenseStatus.ValidLicense) Then
    LabelLicensed.Text = _
        "Licensed to " & licenseDetails.Licensee & vbCrLf & _
        "Serial number " & licenseDetails.SerialNumber
End If
```

Figure 21-8 shows the *About* form in use with details displayed from the license file.

Figure 21-8 Displaying a valid license

Just for fun, I changed the version number in my license file from "1.*" to "2.*" without updating the digital signature. Sure enough, when I displayed the *About* form again, it displayed "Unlicensed," because the check of the signature failed. How did I test the code this early? I copied the *LibraryLicense.lic* file from the book's installed *LicenseFiles* subdirectory, and placed that copy in the *bin\Debug* subdirectory of the project's source code. Later on, you'll be able to put the file anywhere you want and browse for it, but we're getting ahead of ourselves.

Enforcing the License

At some point, a missing or invalid license should have a negative impact on the use of the application. When that happens, we should give the user a chance to correct the problem by locating a valid license file. We'll do this through the new *LocateLicense.vb* form. I've already added the form to your project. It appears in Figure 21-9.

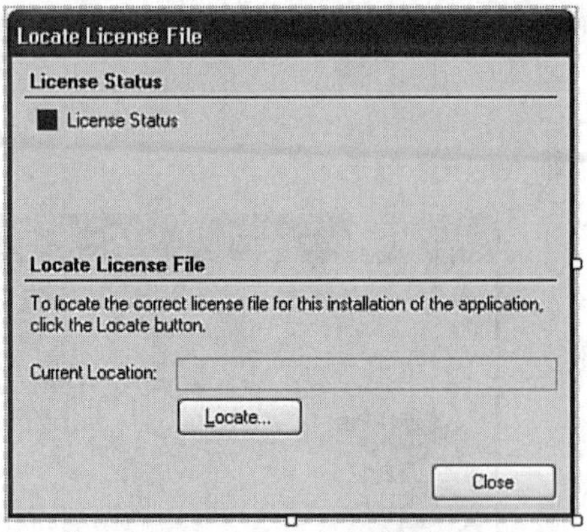

Figure 21-9 The gentle way to enforce a product license

This form starts up with a call to its public *ChangeLicense* function, which returns *True* if the user changes the license. Most of this form's code manages the display, presenting detailed reasons why a license is valid or invalid using the results of the *ExamineLicense* function. If for any reason the license is invalid, a click on the *Locate* button lets the user browse for a better version.

```
Private Sub ActLocate_Click(ByVal sender As System.Object, _
     ByVal e As System.EventArgs) Handles ActLocate.Click
   ' ----- Prompt the user for a new license file.
   If (LocateLicenseDialog.ShowDialog() <> _
     Windows.Forms.DialogResult.OK) Then Return

   ' ----- Store the new path.
   My.Settings.LicenseFileLocation = _
     LocateLicenseDialog.FileName
   LocationModified = True

   ' ----- Update the display.
   DisplayLicenseStatus()
   LicensePath.Text = My.Settings.LicenseFileLocation
End Sub
```

The *LocationModified* form-level variable gets sent back to the caller as a trigger to refresh the status of the license.

For the Library Project in particular, I didn't see a point in enforcing the license on startup, because it's not the patrons' fault that the library stole this important work of software. Instead, I delay the verification process until an administrator or librarian tries to access the enhanced features of the application. Then, if the license check fails, the user should be able to browse the disk for a valid license file.

I think the best place to add the license check is just after the administrator successfully supplies a password. If we checked before that point, it would give ordinary patrons the ability to browse the disk, which is probably a no-no, because anyone and their uncle can walk up and use a patron workstation. Open the source code for the *ChangeUser.vb* form, locate the *ActOK_Click* event handler, and locate the "Successful login" comment.

```
' ----- Successful login.
LoggedInUserID = CInt(dbInfo!ID)
LoggedInUserName = CStr(dbInfo!LoginID)
...
```

Just **before** this block of code, add the following license-checking code.

Insert Snippet Insert Chapter 21, Snippet Item 7.

```
' ----- Don't allow the login if the program is unlicensed.
Do While (ExamineLicense().Status <> _
    LicenseStatus.ValidLicense)
  ' ----- Ask the user what to do.
  If (MsgBox("This application is not properly licensed " & _
      "for administrative use. If you have access to " & _
      "a valid license file, you can verify it now. " & _
      "Would you like to locate a valid license file " & _
      "at this time?", MsgBoxStyle.YesNo Or _
      MsgBoxStyle.Question, ProgramTitle) <> _
      MsgBoxResult.Yes) Then
    dbInfo.Close()
    dbInfo = Nothing
    Return
  End If

  ' ----- Prompt for an updated license.
  Call LocateLicense.ChangeLicense()
  LocateLicense = Nothing
Loop
```

This code gives the user an unlimited number of chances to locate a valid license file. Once the license is validated, the code moves forward and enables administrative access.

Daily Item Processing

The last major set of code to be added to the Library Project isn't related to licensing, but it's important nonetheless: the processing of fines for overdue items. We'll add a common method that will perform the processing, and then call it where needed throughout the application.

Add the new *DailyProcessByPatronCopy* method to the *General* module.

Insert Snippet Insert Chapter 21, Snippet Item 8.

```
Public Sub DailyProcessByPatronCopy( _
     ByVal patronCopyID As Integer, ByVal untilDate As Date)
   ' ----- This routine does the most basic work of
   '       processing overdue fines. All other daily
   '       processing routines eventually call this routine.
   Dim sqlText As String
   Dim dbInfo As SqlClient.SqlDataReader
   Dim daysToFine As Integer
   Dim lastProcess As Date
   Dim fineSoFar As Decimal

   On Error GoTo ErrorHandler

   ' ----- Get all of the basic values needed to process
   '       this entry.
   sqlText = "SELECT PC.DueDate, PC.ProcessDate, " & _
      "PC.Fine, CMT.DailyFine FROM PatronCopy AS PC " & _
      "INNER JOIN ItemCopy AS IC ON PC.ItemCopy = IC.ID " & _
      "INNER JOIN NamedItem AS NI ON IC.ItemID = NI.ID " & _
      "INNER JOIN CodeMediaType AS CMT ON " & _
      "NI.MediaType = CMT.ID " & _
      "WHERE PC.ID = " & patronCopyID & _
      " AND PC.DueDate <= " & DBDate(Today) & _
      " AND PC.Returned = 0 AND PC.Missing = 0 " & _
      "AND IC.Missing = 0"
```

```
dbInfo = CreateReader(sqlText)
If (dbInfo.Read = False) Then
   ' ----- Missing the patron copy record. Oh well.
   '        It was probably because this item was not
   '        yet overdue, or it was missing, or something
   '        valid like that where fines should not increase.
   dbInfo.Close()
   dbInfo = Nothing
   Return
End If

' ----- If we have already processed this record for today,
'        don't do it again.
If (IsDBNull(dbInfo!ProcessDate) = False) Then
   If (CDate(dbInfo!ProcessDate) >= untilDate) Then
      dbInfo.Close()
      dbInfo = Nothing
      Return
   End If
   lastProcess = CDate(dbInfo!ProcessDate)
Else
   lastProcess = CDate(dbInfo!DueDate)
End If

' ----- Fines are due on this record. Figure out how much.
daysToFine = CInt(DateDiff(DateInterval.Day, _
   CDate(dbInfo!DueDate), untilDate) - _
   DateDiff(DateInterval.Day, CDate(dbInfo!DueDate), _
   lastProcess) - FineGraceDays)
If (daysToFine < 0) Then daysToFine = 0
fineSoFar = 0@
If (IsDBNull(dbInfo!Fine) = False) Then _
   fineSoFar = CDec(dbInfo!Fine)
fineSoFar += CDec(dbInfo!DailyFine) * CDec(daysToFine)
dbInfo.Close()
dbInfo = Nothing

' ----- Update the record with the lastest fine and
'        processing information.
sqlText = "UPDATE PatronCopy SET " & _
   "ProcessDate = " & DBDate(untilDate) & _
   ", Fine = " & Format(fineSoFar, "0.00") & _
   " WHERE ID = " & patronCopyID
```

```
   ExecuteSQL(sqlText)
   Return

ErrorHandler:
   GeneralError("DailyProcessByPatronCopy", Err.GetException())
   Resume Next
End Sub
```

This code examines a *PatronCopy* record—the record that marks the checking-out of a single item by a patron—to see if it is overdue, and if so, what penalty needs to be added to the record. Each record includes a *ProcessDate* field. We don't want to charge the patron twice on the same day for a single overdue item (no, we don't), so we use the *ProcessDate* to confirm which days are uncharged.

There are a few places throughout the application where we want to call this processing routine without bothering the user. The first appears in the *PatronRecord* form, the form that displays the fines a patron still owes. Just before showing that list, we should refresh each item checked out by the patron to make sure we display the most up-to-date fine information. Open that form's source code, locate the *PatronRecord_Load* event handler, and add the following code, just before the call to *RefreshPatronFines(–1)* that appears halfway through the routine.

Insert Snippet   Insert Chapter 21, Snippet Item 9.

```
' ----- Make sure that each item is up-to-date.
For counter = 0 To ItemsOut.Items.Count - 1
   newEntry = CType(ItemsOut.Items(counter), PatronDetailItem)
   DailyProcessByPatronCopy(newEntry.DetailID, Today)
Next counter
```

The overdue status for an item must also be refreshed just before it is checked in. Open the source code for the *MainForm* form and locate the *ActDoCheckIn_Click* event handler. About halfway through its code, you'll find a comment that starts with, "Handle missing items." Just before that comment, insert the following code.

Insert Snippet   Insert Chapter 21, Snippet Item 10.

```
' ----- Bring the status of the item up to date.
DailyProcessByPatronCopy(patronCopyID, CheckInDate.Value)
```

Check-out needs to refresh the patron's fines as well, just before letting the patron know if there are, in fact, any fines due. Move to the *MainForm.ActCheckOutPatron_Click* event handler, and add the following declarations to the top of the routine.

Insert Snippet Insert Chapter 21, Snippet Item 11.

```
Dim dbTable As Data.DataTable
Dim dbRow As Data.DataRow
```

In this same method, find a comment that starts with "Show the patron if there are any fines due." As usual, it's about halfway through the routine. Insert the following code just before that comment.

Insert Snippet Insert Chapter 21, Snippet Item 12.

```
' ----- Bring the patron record up to date.
sqlText = "SELECT ID FROM PatronCopy WHERE Returned = 0 " & _
    "AND Missing = 0 AND DueDate < " & DBDate(Today) & _
    " AND (ProcessDate IS NULL OR ProcessDate < " & _
    DBDate(Today) & ") AND Patron = " & patronID
dbTable = CreateDataTable(sqlText)
For Each dbRow In dbTable.Rows
    DailyProcessByPatronCopy(CInt(dbRow!ID), Today)
Next dbRow
dbTable.Dispose()
dbTable = Nothing
```

In addition to automatic fine processing, the Library Project also allows an administrator or librarian to perform daily processing of all patron items at will. This occurs through the *Daily Processing* panel on the main form (see Figure 21-10).

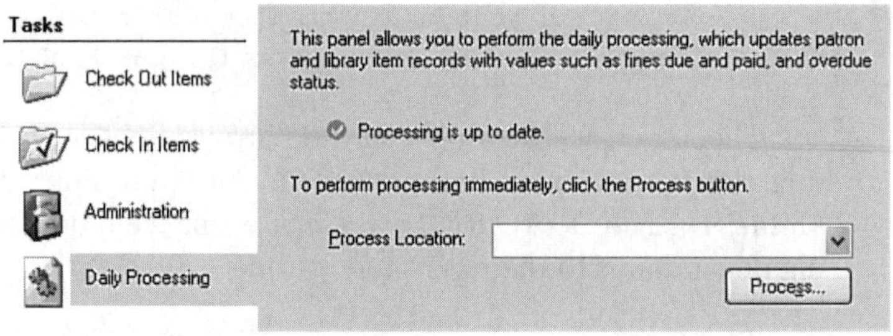

Figure 21-10 Daily administrative processing

Currently, the panel doesn't do much of anything, so let's change that. The first task is to update the status label that appears at the top of the panel. Add a new method named *RefreshProcessLocation* to the *MainForm* form's class.

Insert Snippet Insert Chapter 21, Snippet Item 13.

I won't show its code here, but it basically checks the *CodeLocation.LastProcessing* database field for either all locations, or for the user-selected location, and updates the status display accordingly.

The user selects a location for processing with the *ProcessLocation* drop-down list, but we haven't yet added any code to populate that list. Find the *TaskProcess* method in the main form's source code, and add these declarations to the top of its code.

Insert Snippet Insert Chapter 21, Snippet Item 14.

```
Dim sqlText As String
Dim dbInfo As SqlClient.SqlDataReader

On Error GoTo ErrorHandler
```

Then add the following statements to the end of the method.

```
' ----- Refresh the list of locations.
ProcessLocation.Items.Clear()
ProcessLocation.Items.Add(New ListItemData( _
   "<All Locations>", -1))
ProcessLocation.SelectedIndex = 0
sqlText = "SELECT ID, FullName FROM CodeLocation " & _
   "ORDER BY FullName"
dbInfo = CreateReader(sqlText)
Do While dbInfo.Read
   ProcessLocation.Items.Add(New ListItemData( _
      CStr(dbInfo!FullName), CInt(dbInfo!ID)))
Loop
dbInfo.Close()
dbInfo = Nothing
RefreshProcessLocation()
Return

ErrorHandler:
   GeneralError("MainForm.TaskProcess", Err.GetException())
   Resume Next
```

Each time the user selects a different location from the list, we need to update the status display. Add the following code to the *ProcessLocation_SelectedIndexChanged* event handler.

```
' ----- Update the status based on the current location.
RefreshProcessLocation()
```

Daily processing occurs when the user clicks on the **Process** button. Add the following code to the *ActDoProcess_Click* event handler.

Insert Snippet Insert Chapter 21, Snippet Item 17.

```
' ----- Process all of the checked-out books.
Dim sqlText As String
Dim dbTable As Data.DataTable
Dim dbRow As Data.DataRow
Dim locationID As Integer

On Error GoTo ErrorHandler
Me.Cursor = Cursors.WaitCursor

' ----- Get the list of all items that likely need processing.
sqlText = "SELECT PC.ID FROM PatronCopy AS PC " & _
    "INNER JOIN ItemCopy AS IC ON PC.ItemCopy = IC.ID "& _
    "WHERE PC.Returned = 0 AND PC.Missing = 0 " & _
    "AND IC.Missing = 0 AND PC.DueDate < " & DBDate(Today) & _
    " AND (PC.ProcessDate IS NULL OR PC.ProcessDate < " & _
    DBDate(Today) & ")"
If (ProcessLocation.SelectedIndex <> -1) Then
    locationID = CInt(CType(ProcessLocation.SelectedItem, _
        ListItemData))
    If (locationID <> -1) Then sqlText &= _
        " AND IC.Location = " & locationID
Else
    locationID = -1
End If
dbTable = CreateDataTable(sqlText)
For Each dbRow In dbTable.Rows
    DailyProcessByPatronCopy(CInt(dbRow!ID), Today)
Next dbRow
dbTable.Dispose()
dbTable = Nothing
Me.Cursor = Cursors.Default
MsgBox("Processing complete.", MsgBoxStyle.OkOnly Or _
    MsgBoxStyle.Information, ProgramTitle)
```

```
' ----- Update the processing date.
sqlText = "UPDATE CodeLocation SET LastProcessing = " & _
   DBDate(Today)
If (locationID <> -1) Then sqlText &= _
   " WHERE ID = " & locationID
ExecuteSQL(sqlText)

' ----- Update the status display.
ProcessStatus.Text = "       Processing is up to date."
ProcessStatus.ImageIndex = StatusImageGood
Return

ErrorHandler:
   GeneralError("MainForm.ActDoProcess_Click", Err.GetException())
   Resume Next
```

To try out the code, run it, locate a valid license file, and test out the different administrative features.

This marks the end of primary coding for the Library Project. Congratulations! But there's still plenty to do, as you can tell by the presence of four more chapters. Now would **not** be the time to close the book and call it a day. But it would be good time to learn about ASP.NET, the topic of the next chapter.

CHAPTER 22

WEB DEVELOPMENT

When Sir Tim Berners-Lee (knighted in 2004!) invented the World Wide Web in 1989, it really wasn't a big deal. As the primary designer of HTTP and HTML, he certainly was no slouch. But most of the technologies that went into structuring and transporting web pages had been around for years, even decades. SGML (the basis of HTML) and hyper-linking systems had been around since the 1960s, and Internet-based transmission of data between clients and servers was already common among university campuses and some businesses. Still, here we are in the twenty-first century, and the World Wide Web is the focus of so much computer technology that it makes my head spin. Thank you, Mr. B-L.

Microsoft promotes .NET as *the* system for developing web pages and related software. And it really is a great system. As we get into the code, you'll find that about 90 percent of what you do to write Web applications in Visual Studio is identical to what you do when writing desktop applications. It's easy to do, and kind of fun, so you'll probably want to write some programs using it. And that's what we'll do in this chapter. But first, let's briefly review what happens in the world of client-server World Wide Web communications.

How the Internet Works

Before .NET, developing applications for "the Web" was cumbersome and boring. And with good reason: The World Wide Web was not designed as a programming or logic-processing platform. It was originally all about sending specially formatted text files from one computer to another. No programming languages to learn. No custom logic. Just plain text, and maybe a binary graphic image or two.

Early web browsers were really just glorified file-copy programs. When you started up the *Mosaic* browser (pretty much all there was back then) and requested a Web page from another computer, here is what would happen.

- The web browser determines the IP address of the remote system.
- The web browser contacts the remote system via TCP/IP port number 80.
- The remote system accepts the connection.
- The web browser says, "Hey, I'm looking for a file named *index.html*. Could you send it to me?"
- The remote system says, "I have it," and immediately sends it.
- The remote system closes the connection.

Much of this process is hidden from view, but you can actually see it happen. If you're interested, open the Windows command prompt, and type the following command.

```
telnet www.google.com 80
```

This runs the *telnet* program, a terminal emulation program that lets you connect to remote systems through a text interface. Telnet usually connects to TCP/IP port 23, but you can specify any port you want, as we did here with the default WWW port of 80.

Your screen may go blank, or it may just sit there, looking dead. If you're lucky, you'll see a "connected" message, but perhaps not. And that's okay. Your system is connected to Google's web server. Type the following command.

```
GET / HTTP/1.0
```

Don't miss the spaces surrounded the first slash. Follow this command with two light taps on the Enter key. This command asks the remote system to send the default web page at the top of that server's Web hierarchy. And because you asked, it will.

```
HTTP/1.0 200 OK
Cache-Control: private
Content-Type: text/html
Set-Cookie: PREF=ID=f2a86cd6479fb5ec:TM=1147737754:
➡ LM=1147737754:S=Wpw0SS-C3B-eTJJu; expires=Sun,
➡ 17-Jan-2038 19:14:07 GMT; path=/; domain=.google.com
```

```
Server: GWS/2.1
Date: Tue, 16 May 2006 00:02:34 GMT
Connection: Close

<html><head>
    ...rest of HTML web page content here...
</body></html>

Connection to host lost.
```

Of course, you do not normally see all this. The web browser carries on this dialog for you, and nicely formats the response as a web page. This is actually all there is to the World Wide Web. You have just experienced the major features involved: the transfer of basic data through a TCP/IP port. So where does programming come in?

Programming the Internet

Static pages were good for a while, but then the Internet became humdrum. Finally someone had a bright idea: "We have a program running on our web server that is responding to clients, and feeding them requested pages. What if we could enhance that program so that, for certain pages, it would call a program or script that would generate the HTML content on-the-fly, and have that content returned to the client?" So they changed the server process. Now, when the client asked for a web page ending with the extension *.cgi*, the web server process ran a separate script that generated the content. The system also provided a means for some client-supplied content to make its way to the script, making possible customization and personalization features.

From there it was a short step to a generic solution. On the Microsoft platform, *Internet Information Server* supported add-ins that could be called based on the file extension of the requested file. This led to *Active Server Pages* (ASP), a solution that allowed developers to embed server-side script (often using "VBScript," a variation of Visual Basic) right in the HTML content, and have it adjust the content before it was sent to the client.

Someone else said, "If we can write scripts on the server side, couldn't we also include a 'client-side script' right in the HTML content that a smart web browser could process?" Before long, client-side and server-side developers were battling it out in the streets, but the battle didn't get very far because all the programmers were exhausted. The cause? Programming in script! Whether it's embedding script in HTML (the client side) or generating HTML from script (the server side), script programming is cumbersome, slow, high in "bad" cholesterol, and almost impossible to debug interactively.

Some web script programmers hadn't used a language compiler for years, and were on the verge of lapsing into fatal script-induced comas. You could compile some server-side logic into a DLL and use it to process web pages, but it was far from easy, and these DLLs were still often linked into the HTML content via short scripts.

Then came .NET, and its support for compiled server-side application development. Script programmers breathed a collective sigh of relief from their hospital beds; they could now use the full power of Visual Studio and .NET languages to build HTML content. And this new system, "ASP.NET," was designed so that you could craft entire web applications without even looking at a single HTML tag. The design goal: to make web development nearly identical to desktop application development. And Microsoft largely succeeded. It didn't solve the client scripting problem (maybe soon!), but some of the new server-side features included in ASP.NET greatly reduced the need for custom client-side scripts.

The pages you build in ASP.NET are called "Web Forms," and because they are so closely tied together, I sometimes use ASP.NET and Web Forms interchangeably. But they aren't exactly the same thing: ASP.NET includes Web Forms.

ASP.NET Features

ASP.NET includes many new advances in web development technology. Here are just a few of the more famous ones.

- **Compiled code.** All of the code you write for ASP.NET applications is fully compiled into standard .NET DLL assemblies. When the client makes a request for a file with an *.aspx* extension, *Internet Information Server* locates this file (which contains HTML or combined HTML/ASP.NET content) and the associated compiled DLL, and uses them together to process the page content. You can pre-compile the DLL before deployment, or you can let ASP.NET compile it on the fly the first time the *.aspx* file gets called.

- **.NET support.** ASP.NET applications can access the full .NET Framework Class Libraries (except those that specifically target desktop development). Any of the cool features and classes you have in desktop .NET applications are right there in web applications as well.

- **Object-based.** HTML tags, such as the `<textarea>` tag, are really just text strings within a larger HTML text file. Pre-.NET server-side scripting was an exercise in string concatenation, building up a larger file from smaller content strings. ASP.NET treats all web-page elements as true objects, complete with properties and events. And some of these objects implement complex client-side controls, backed up by hundreds of lines of client-side script that you get for free.

- **Deployment simplicity.** Managing server-side scripts and custom DLLs before .NET was not very fun. Certain types of changes required a full shutdown of *Internet Information Server*, or at least of the portion that controlled the application being changed. ASP.NET lets you make changes on a production system without impacting active users. If you replace a compiled DLL, ASP.NET will start using it immediately, but still keep the older version around until all existing clients have detached from it.

- **Browser independence.** The web-page objects that you use in ASP.NET take responsibility for generating their own HTML and client-side script content. Many of them take the client's browser type and version into account, enhancing or reducing features automatically when needed. As an ASP.NET developer, you don't even have to know which browser is being used.

- **Extensibility.** If you want to enhance a web-page element, you can derive from its class and add the new enhanced features, just as you do with any other .NET class.

Of course, there are more great features than the few I listed here. But you're probably ready to see ASP.NET in action. Let's get started.

Trying Out ASP.NET

Let's build a very simple ASP.NET application, and examine it and its parts to discover what it's all about.

News, but Not Bad News If you are using *Visual Basic 2005 Express Edition*, you will not be able to fully follow these instructions directly because that product does not include any ASP.NET or web development features. Instead, you need to download *Visual Web Developer 2005 Express Edition* from the Microsoft MSDN web site (msdn.microsoft.com). Its user interface, though streamlined, offers much of the same functionality as the full Visual Studio product. The tutorial included here was written using *Visual Studio 2005 Professional Edition*.

Start Visual Studio and select the **File ➤ New Web Site** menu command. The *New Web Site* form appears. Unlike desktop applications, you must immediately tell Visual Studio where you are going to store the files. We'll choose a location on the local file system, but this form also lets you work on a remote web site via FTP or HTTP. Choose the "ASP.NET Web Site" template, enter a directory path where you want to store the files, and click the **OK** button.

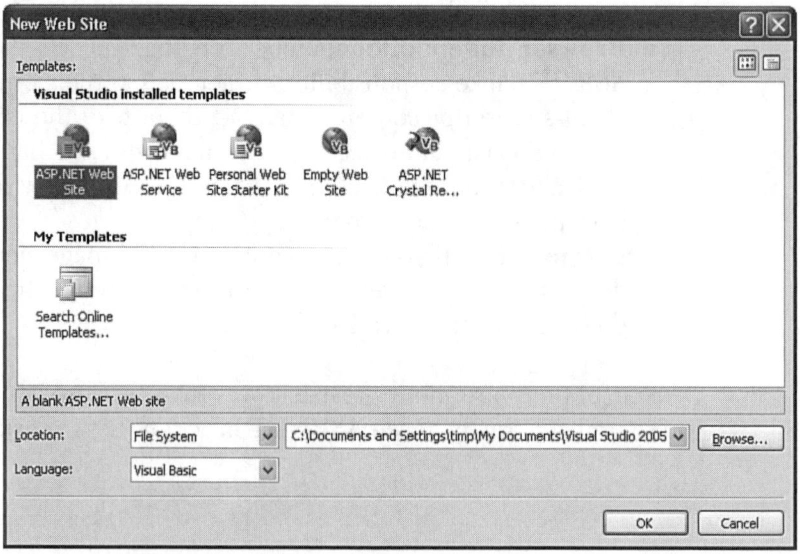

Figure 22-1 Creating a new ASP.NET application

Figure 22-2 shows Visual Studio ready to start your new web application (the toolbars displayed are per my preferences).

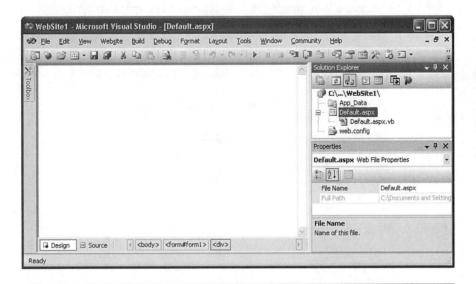

Figure 22-2 A blank form is sometimes a good sign.

The *Solution Explorer* panel already shows three files and a folder included in the project. If you browse to the project's directory—the default location is *My Documents\Visual Studio 2005\WebSites\WebSite1*—you'll see these same files. The *web.config* file is an XML file that contains application-specific settings; it's related to the *app.config* file used in desktop applications. *Default.aspx* is the web page itself, which will contain a mixture of HTML and special ASP.NET tags and directives. The related *Default.aspx.vb* file contains the Visual Basic "code behind" source code that will eventually be compiled to a DLL. The DLL gets stored in the *App_Data* directory when the site first loads.

Visual Studio also creates another folder at *My Documents\Visual Studio 2005\WebSite1*. This folder contains the solution files normally created with any Visual Studio project. They're put out of the way so that they don't get included with the deployed web site.

The blank area you see in Visual Studio is a web page, just waiting for text and control content. If you want proof, click the **Source** section button in the bottom-left corner of the display, or use the **View ➤ Markup** menu command. The window changes to HTML source code.

```
<%@ Page Language="VB" AutoEventWireup="false"
➥ CodeFile="Default.aspx.vb" Inherits="_Default" %>

<!DOCTYPE html PUBLIC "-//W3C//DTD XHTML 1.0 Transitional//EN"
➥ "http://www.w3.org/TR/xhtml1/DTD/xhtml1-transitional.dtd">

<html xmlns="http://www.w3.org/1999/xhtml" >
<head runat="server">
   <title>Untitled Page</title>
</head>
<body>
   <form id="form1" runat="server">
   <div>

   </div>
   </form>
</body>
</html>
```

Well, *most* of it is HTML. There's a line at the top that starts with `<%@` that doesn't look like real HTML—and it's not. This is an ASP.NET *page directive*. It includes properties that help guide ASP.NET in the processing of the page. Borrowing a standard from its ASP predecessor, ASP.NET uses the `<%...%>` bracket pair to mark ASP.NET-specific commands and code. That's enough of HTML. Who wanted to see it anyway? Click the **Design** section button, or use the **View ➤ Designer** menu command to return to the blank page.

Let's create an application that multiplies two user-supplied numbers together and displays the product. For such a simple feature, we could just write some JavaScript and include it as a client-side script, but we're trying to avoid doing stuff like that. Type the following into the web page.

```
To multiply two values together, enter them in the
➥ text fields, and click the Multiply button.
```

I made the word "Multiply" bold by using the Control-B key sequence, just as I would do in a word processor. Press Enter twice. By default, the web page lays out all elements like a word-processing document, a method called *flow layout mode*. You can also use *absolute positioning* of individual elements to place them at a specific location on the page.

There's another way to organize elements on the page: through an HTML table. Let's add one now. Use the **Layout ➤ Insert Table** menu command. When the *Insert Table* dialog appears, specify a custom table that is three rows by two columns. Then click **OK**. The table should immediately appear in the body of the web page.

Type "Operand 1:" in the upper-left cell, and type "Operand 2:" in the cell just below it. Your page should look like Figure 22-3.

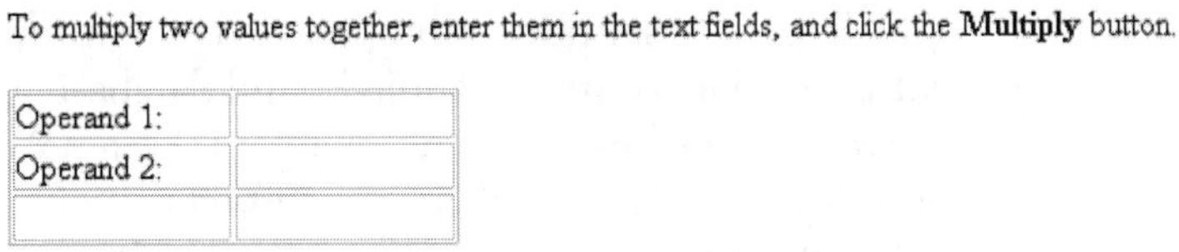

To multiply two values together, enter them in the text fields, and click the **Multiply** button.

Operand 1:	
Operand 2:	

Figure 22-3 Just getting started on this application

It's not much to look at, but it will get better. So far, we haven't done much more than we could do in Notepad. But now we're ready to add some controls. If you open the Toolbox, you'll see controls that look a lot like those found in a Windows Forms application (see Figure 22-4).

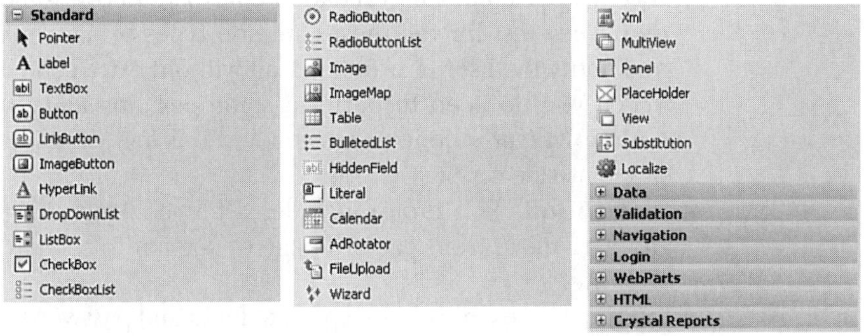

Standard		
Pointer	RadioButton	Xml
A Label	RadioButtonList	MultiView
TextBox	Image	Panel
Button	ImageMap	PlaceHolder
LinkButton	Table	View
ImageButton	BulletedList	Substitution
A HyperLink	HiddenField	Localize
DropDownList	Literal	Data
ListBox	Calendar	Validation
CheckBox	AdRotator	Navigation
CheckBoxList	FileUpload	Login
	Wizard	WebParts
		HTML
		Crystal Reports

Figure 22-4 Some of the Web Forms Toolbox

The controls are grouped by functionality.

- **Standard.** You will generally use the controls in this section to build the user interface of your web page. Many of these controls represent standard windows controls, with direct parallels in the Windows Forms world. For instance, the *ListBox* entry implements a standard Windows *ListBox* control within the web page. To you, the programmer, these controls look like standard .NET control classes, with properties, methods, and events. To the end user, they look like standard web-page controls, delivered using ordinary HTML. Some of these controls are composite controls, single controls built from multiple HTML controls working together, possibly with client-side scripting doing some of the work.
- **Data.** The data controls handle bound database interactions. As you may remember from previous chapters, I am not a big fan of bound controls in standard applications. But when you are communicating static data through a web page, they actually turn out to be a great timesaver. Some of these controls perform the data binding, while others perform the actual data presentation. You'll also find the *ReportViewer* control, the web version of the report technology we discussed in Chapter 20, "Reporting." It displays reports using the same RDLC files you built for your desktop application.
- **Validation.** Users are a lot of fun, especially when they enter wacky data into your quality software. Verifying the data they enter is hard enough in desktop applications, but it's even more cumbersome when the client system only talks to the application host a few dozen seconds per hour. The validation controls remove some of the burden. They test for the most common types of data entry mistakes, and notify the user of problems, all without extra code on your part. When you do need to perform some custom validation logic, the *CustomValidator* control lets you add this logic as an event handler or client-side script.
- **Navigation.** This group includes a few controls designed to help the user move from page to page or section to section within your web site.
- **Login.** These controls encapsulate login and password management features so that the user can create a new user account, provide an authenticated password, or perform other security-related actions.

- **WebParts.** WebParts are control containers that the user rearranges using drag-and-drop within the web page. This reorganization of the display allows the user to personalize the display to fulfill the selfish wants that cloud his or her mind. You can record the state of the WebParts for redisplay the next time the user returns to the site or page.
- **HTML.** These are the standard HTML controls, such as `<textarea>`, that web page developers have been using for years. Visual Studio does provide some *IntelliSense* and property validation for you, but using these controls is identical to typing the matching HTML tag directly into the page markup.
- **Crystal Reports.** Crystal Reports includes both a desktop and a web-based set of reporting tools. The controls in this section specifically target ASP.NET applications.

Let's add a few controls from the *Standard* section of the Toolbox to the web page. In the bottom-left cell of the table we added earlier, add a *Button* control, give it the name *ActMultiple*, and set its *Text* property to "Multiply."

Add two *TextBox* controls to the top two cells in the right-hand table column. Name one of them *FirstOperand*, and name the other one *SecondOperand*.

Add a *Label* control to the bottom-right corner cell of the table. Name it *Product*, and set its *Text* property to *0* (that is, zero).

Did you notice how setting each property for these controls was no different from what you did in the main Library application? Simple! By now, your web page should look like the one in Figure 22-5.

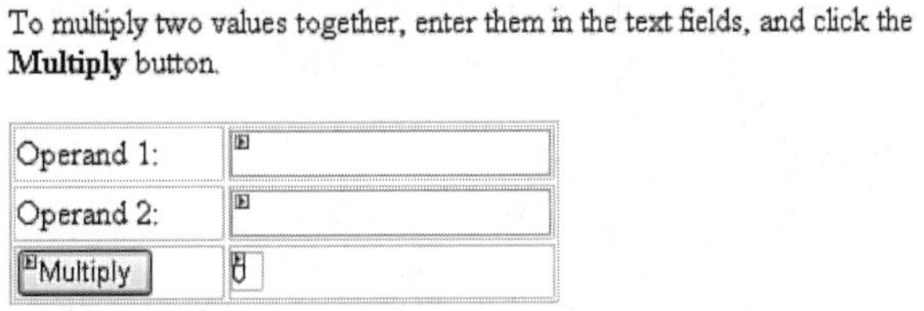

To multiply two values together, enter them in the text fields, and click the **Multiply** button.

Operand 1:	▣
Operand 2:	▣
▣Multiply	▯

Figure 22-5 The completed user interface

Return briefly to the HTML markup for this page by clicking on the **Source** section button at the bottom of the page. If you're familiar with HTML, you'll notice the `<table>` tag for the table we added. But you'll also find something unfamiliar within the first table row.

```
<table>
  <tr>
    <td style="width: 100px">
      Operand 1:</td>
    <td style="width: 100px">
      <asp:TextBox ID="FirstOperand"
        runat="server"></asp:TextBox></td>
  </tr>
```

It's that `<asp:TextBox>` tag. It looks something like other HTML tags, but there are no HTML tags that start with "asp." This is a special ASP.NET tag that represents a Web Forms control class. These controls, and the `runat="server"` attributes strewn throughout the markup, are what make ASP.NET pages what they are. As ASP.NET processes the *.aspx* page, it strips out these custom control tags, and calls on the related controls to generate their own browser-neutral HTML.

The user interface is done; let's add the logic. We want the program to multiply the two operands together when we click on the **Multiply** button. Return to the web page design, and double-click on the **Multiply** button. It jumps to the code template for a button's *Click* event, just as you expected it to do.

```
Partial Class _Default
    Inherits System.Web.UI.Page

    Protected Sub ActMultiply_Click(ByVal sender As Object, _
        ByVal e As System.EventArgs) Handles ActMultiply.Click

    End Sub
End Class
```

The design goal of ASP.NET was to have code that was as close to desktop application code as possible, and this is it. Add the following logic to the event handler.

```
' ----- Multiply the two numbers.
Product.Text = Val(FirstOperand.Text) * _
   Val(SecondOperand.Text)
If (Val(Product.Text) < 0) Then
    Product.ForeColor = Drawing.Color.Red
Else
    Product.ForeColor = Drawing.Color.Black
End If
```

As you were typing, did you notice all of the *IntelliSense* responding to your every keystroke? I couldn't tell that this was a web-based application, and that's great.

Press the F5 key to start the application. You'll be prompted to turn on debugging, which you want to do. This will modify the application's *web.config* file to support debugging. Later, you'll want to disable that feature so that your users won't be able to debug the application. If you open the *web.config* file, you'll see this line:

```
<compilation debug="true" strict="false" explicit="true"/>
```

Just change the *debug* attribute to "false" to turn off debugging.

ASP.NET is a server application; it requires a living, breathing web server before pages can be processed. You may or may not have *Internet Information Server* installed on your system, but that's OK. Visual Studio 2005 includes its own "ASP.NET Development Server" that exists just so you can test your ASP.NET applications. Figure 22-6 shows it popping up in the system tray.

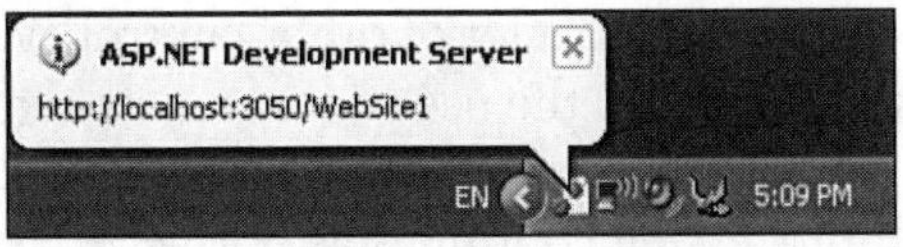

Figure 22-6 Your built-in web server endeavors to give good service.

Figure 22-7 shows the application running in my default web browser, Internet Explorer. (Dear web browser companies, for information on product placement in this page, contact me directly.)

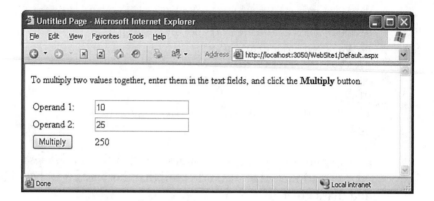

Figure 22-7 Wow, a whole web application in less than ten lines of code

More About Events

So far, our application looks just like a desktop application; the form displayed our initial drag-and-drop and property settings, and it responded to a button click by returning to the processing computer for the logic. But let's be honest. There's no way that a web application can ever be truly as responsive to events as a desktop application. What happens when the Internet connection goes down or it is just plain slow? How do you handle things like *TextChanged* events in text fields? You can't have the web page go back to the web server every time the user types a key.

The ASP.NET *TextBox* control has a *TextChanged* event, but it does not trigger for each keystroke. In fact, it doesn't trigger at all (by default) until something (like a button click) causes the page to go back to the server. And there are a lot of other control events that work like this. They are all saved up until the user does something to bring the whole page back to the web server for processing. At that time, these delayed events finally fire, and processing continues as normal.

So there are really two types of events: regular and premium. I mean postback and non-postback. **Postback events** are those that cause the web page to immediately return to the server for processing. **Non-postback events** delay their event handlers until something else causes a return to the server. Most events are one or the other, but some can be changed. The *CheckBox* control has a *CheckedChanged* that fires (in a non-postback way) when the user alters the state of the checkbox. However, if you set the control's *AutoPostBack* property to *True*, the page will immediately return to the server anytime the user clicks the checkbox.

Besides control events, the entire page has a few events. The most significant is the *Page_Load* event. This is analogous to the Windows Forms's *Form_Load* event; it's a great place to configure initial control properties, fill in drop-down lists, etc. I'm going to add the following code to my page's *Load* event.

```
Protected Sub Page_Load(ByVal sender As Object, _
     ByVal e As System.EventArgs) Handles Me.Load
   ' ----- Initialize the data.
   Product.Text = "No Data"
End Sub
```

Now the *Product* label will display "No Data" the first time the page appears. The thing about the *Load* event handler is that it **runs every single time the web page is displayed**. Because this test application keeps using the same page over and over again for its results, the *Load* event handler will run afresh each time. For this test program, it's not really a big deal; the code in the *ActMultiply_Click* event handler overrides its initial "No Data" value. But in other applications, you might not want to keep reinitializing the data. Fortunately, the *Load* event will let you know if this is the first time through or not through a page-level member called *IsPostBack*.

```
' ----- Initialize the data, but only the first time.
If (Me.IsPostBack = False) Then Product.Text = "No Data"
```

State and View State

Wait a minute. If I am reloading the page from scratch every time with the need to initialize values in the *Page_Load* event handler, how is it that the two text boxes kept the user-entered values when the page reloaded? We didn't add any code to save and restore those values during initialization.

Here's the story. Although the *Page_Load* event does give you the opportunity to initialize the page every time the page loads, for most fields the page will remember what was in each field. Remember, ASP.NET is designed so that you think it is running just like a Windows Forms application. You would never be happy if the fields on your Windows Form kept clearing out every time the user clicked a button. You wouldn't be happy if they cleared out in a Web Forms application either.

Because web pages are disconnected from the web server most of the time, each web page needs some way to retain the **state**—the current property and data settings—of each control between page loads. The Web Forms system does this through a feature called **View State**. Here's how it works: Each ASP.NET web page includes a hidden static field that includes an encrypted and compressed version of all important state information for the controls. When the user makes changes to each control and triggers some event that returns the page to the web server, it returns with both the embedded View State (built up from the previous construction of the page) and all the current settings for every control. Using this combined information, ASP.NET is able to reconstruct the true client-visible state of every control, and communicate that correctly to you in your server-side event handler code.

When you run an ASP.NET application, use the **View ➤ Source** menu command in Internet Explorer or your favorite browser of the month, and you'll see something like the following:

```
<input type="hidden" name="__VIEWSTATE" id="__VIEWSTATE"
➥ value="/wEPDwUKMTEyMTc3MTQwNg9kFgICAw9kFgICBw8P
➥ FgIeBFRleHQFB05vIERhdGFkGQME+xLedutk85TvXy9OJd
➥ kQF02YA==" />
```

That's the View State. Don't ask me how it works; I won't tell you (because I don't know). But it's not important to know how it works. It's only important that ASP.NET knows how it works so it can keep your application working like the Windows Forms system it truly isn't.

As you add additional controls to your page, the View State will increase in size. Because all of the web page's content must be transported repeatedly over the Internet, a larger View State results in longer transmission times. It is possible to turn off view state for specific controls using their *EnableViewState* property. If you don't need a control's value retained from page use to page use, it's a good idea to turn it off.

Data Validation

Because this sample code uses the Visual Basic *Val* function to preprocess the user-supplied data, it almost always works without error. Any data considered invalid is simply converted to zero. Another option would be to chastise the user for invalid entry before processing occurs, to *validate* the supplied values. The five validators in the *Validation* section of the Web Forms Toolbox help you do just that.

- **RequiredFieldValidator.** Confirms that the user supplied any value at all in a control.
- **RangeValidator.** Complains if a control's value does not fall between two values.
- **RegularExpressionValidator.** Lets you compare a control's value against a regular expression pattern. For instance, you could compare the user's entry of a serial number to a pattern to ensure that it included two letters followed by five digits.
- **CompareValidator.** Involves two controls, comparing the value between them. The control also doubles as a data type validator, confirming that a single field contains the proper type of data, such as a date value or an integer.
- **CustomValidator.** Lets you perform any type of validation you want through code you supply.

All of these controls perform server-side validation, and they optionally do their data check using client-side scripts (the default). Having the client-side check reduces the need to go back to the web server just to ensure a required field has data. Having the server-side check ensures that the data is valid even if the client has disabled scripting support.

The validators display their own error messages, so you place them on the page where you want the error message to appear. You can also have multiple validators display their collective issues in a single location by using a *ValidationSummary* control.

Let's add some validation to the two input fields in the multiplication sample. We want to ensure that the data is supplied, and that both values are valid integers. To do this, we must add both a *RequiredFieldValidator* and a *CompareValidator* for each field. Right-click in the bottom-right cell of the table, just after the *Product* label, and choose **Insert ➤ Column to the Right** from the shortcut menu that pops up. In the new upper-right column, add a *RequiredFieldValidator* control. Set the following properties:

- Set *ControlToValidate* to "FirstOperand."
- Set *Display* to "Dynamic." This lets the size of the validator shrink to nothing when there is no error to display.
- Set *ErrorMessage* to "Missing."

Just to the right of that validator, in the same table cell, add a *CompareValidators*, and set these properties:

- Set *ControlToValidate* to "FirstOperand."
- Set *ErrorMessage* to "Must be an integer."
- Set *Operator* to "DataTypeCheck."
- Set *Type* to "Integer."

Add a similar pair of validators to the second table row, using "SecondOperand" for the *ControlToValidate*. Your web page should look like Figure 22-8.

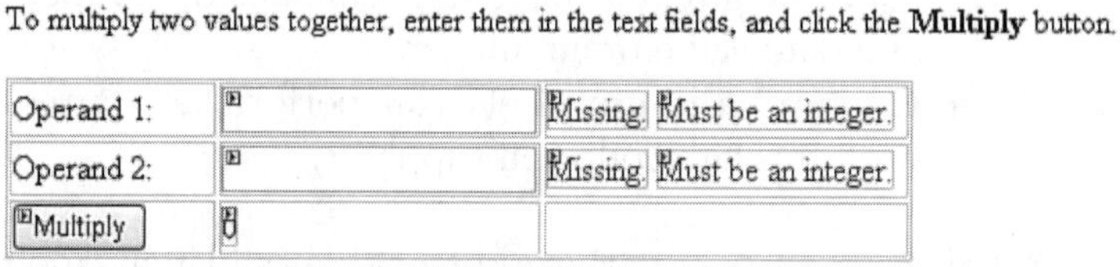

To multiply two values together, enter them in the text fields, and click the **Multiply** button.

Operand 1:	▣		Missing. Must be an integer.
Operand 2:	▣		Missing. Must be an integer.
▣Multiply	▣		

Figure 22-8 Bulking up on the validation support

Run the program and just try to enter faulty data in the input cells. The page will complain immediately when you click the **Multiply** button.

That's all the multiplying we'll do for now. I've saved a copy of the project for you in the *WebSite1* subdirectory in the main directory where you installed this book's sample code.

Database Integration

Connecting ASP.NET pages to a database, especially if you use some of the wizard-style features of Visual Studio, is extremely easy. That's because many of the controls included with ASP.NET are specifically designed to display and interact with data from tabular data sources. We'll try out a quick wizard example here, and do a lot more database integration in this chapter's "Project" section.

In Chapter 20, the first of the five built-in reports we created for the Library system displayed a list of all checked-out items. We designed an RDLC report for it, and because ASP.NET includes an RDLC Report Viewer control, we could reuse that for a Web-based report. But instead we'll display the report using one of the Web Forms controls, *GridView*. Here's the query that retrieves the checked-out items.

```
SELECT PA.LastName + ', ' + PA.FirstName AS PatronName,
    PA.Barcode AS PatronBarcode,
    PC.DueDate, IC.CopyNumber, IC.Barcode AS ItemBarcode,
    NI.Title, CMT.FullName AS MediaName
FROM Patron AS PA
    INNER JOIN PatronCopy AS PC ON PA.ID = PC.Patron
    INNER JOIN ItemCopy AS IC ON PC.ItemCopy = IC.ID
    INNER JOIN NamedItem AS NI ON IC.ItemID = NI.ID
    INNER JOIN CodeMediaType AS CMT ON NI.MediaType = CMT.ID
WHERE PC.Returned = 0
    AND PC.Missing = 0
    AND IC.Missing = 0
ORDER BY NI.Title, IC.CopyNumber, PA.LastName, PA.FirstName
```

That should look familiar. Create a new ASP.NET web site through Visual Studio. Type the following line at the top of the content page.

```
ACME Library Checked Out Items
```

Feel free to embellish it to make it look nicer. I added <h1> tags around it in the markup to make it stand out. Below that title line, add a new *GridView* control to the page. I found it in the *Data* section of my Visual Studio Toolbox. The control's smart tag opens and shows a panel of GridView Tasks, as shown in Figure 22-9.

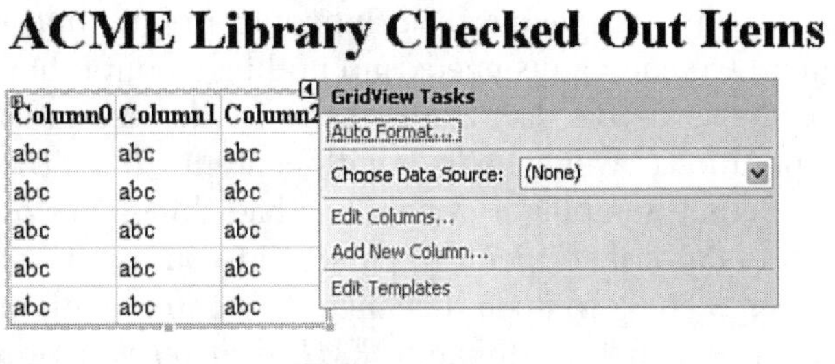

Figure 22-9 A short list of tasks for the GridView control

If you want to click on the "Auto Format" task and change the look of the grid, you can, but the important task for now is "Choose Data Source." Select "<Add New Source>" from the list. Our old friend the *Data Source Configuration Wizard* appears again, although with some changes specific to ASP.NET. Select "Database" for the data source type and click the **OK** button. When prompted for the connection, you should already have a Library database connection in the list. Select it (or create a new connection) and click **Next**.

You'll be asked to save the connection string in the application configuration file. If you do, it will add an entry to the <connectionStrings> section of the *web.config* file created for the ASP.NET application. If you like to play power games with your system administrator, leave the field unchecked. But if you want an easy way to modify the connection information later, you had better leave the field as it is, giving the entry a reasonable name. Then click **Next**.

The wizard prompts you for table and field details. Select **Specify a custom SQL statement or stored procedure**, click **Next**, and type in the checked-out-item query. Click **Next** again. The wizard gives you one last chance to test the query before you click the **Finish** button.

Now here's the simple part. Visual Studio connects to the database, reads the schema, and creates columns in the grid perfectly designed for the query. Your application is complete. Press F5 to run it.

We're going to stop there for now and pick this up in the "Project" section.

XML Web Services

Have you ever wanted to extract one piece of data from a web site for use in your Visual Basic application? No? Well let me tell you: It's called "screen scraping," and it's a pain in the neck. Most web sites with valuable content are designed by selfish people, programmers who think only about their own company's needs and nothing about other developers who need to pilfer essential data from—I mean, who need to add value to their own applications by enhancing it with content from a trusted third party.

Screen scraping is generally a bad thing. Not only is the HTML content ludicrously difficult to parse, but you never know when the web site owner is going to up and change the content without the courtesy of contacting you first. Fortunately, *XML Web Services* provides a solution to this problem. If a site has content or processes that need to be used by external applications, it can include a Web Service on the site that makes screen scraping unnecessary. XML Web Services implement the Web-based equivalent of function calls, complete with parameters and return values, all of which can be accessed remotely. They are based on published standards such as SOAP (Simple Object Access Protocol) that use plaintext and XML to simulate the function call between two systems.

There are a lot of technologies involved in making XML Web Services possible, but you don't really need to know them. Instead, you will build a standard Visual Basic method, mark it for use as a Web Service, and make it available on your web site.

Web services appear as *.asmx* files on your web site. In Visual Studio, you can either create a new web site and select "ASP.NET Web Service" as the project type, or add a "Web Service" item to an existing web site project. When you do, Visual Studio adds the necessary files to your project. The first is the actual *.asmx* file. It's a smart interface conduit between the web site and the actual web service code. Here's what I found in my *WebService.asmx* file.

```
<%@ WebService Language="VB" CodeBehind=
➥ "~/App_Code/WebService.vb" Class="WebService" %>
```

This directive refers the caller to the *WebService* class in the associated *WebService.vb* source code file. That file is much more interesting.

```
Imports System.Web
Imports System.Web.Services
Imports System.Web.Services.Protocols

<WebService(Namespace:="http://tempuri.org/")> _
<WebServiceBinding(ConformsTo:=WsiProfiles.BasicProfile1_1)> _
<Global.Microsoft.VisualBasic.CompilerServices. _
DesignerGenerated()> _
Public Class WebService
    Inherits System.Web.Services.WebService

    <WebMethod()> _
    Public Function HelloWorld() As String
        Return "Hello World"
    End Function
End Class
```

This code decorates the class and its methods with several attributes that mark those methods as Web Services. Remember that an attribute adds metadata to an assembly so that the compiler or some other program will do something special with the marked items. In this case, the <WebMethod> attribute tells ASP.NET to treat the *HelloWorld* function as a Web Service. ASP.NET responds by connecting all of the plumbing code that makes Web Services possible.

I'm going to replace the *HelloWorld* function with another one that at least pretends to do some real work.

```
<WebMethod()> _
Public Function NumberToText(ByVal sourceNumber _
     As Integer) As String
   Select Case sourceNumber
      Case 0 : Return "Zero"
      Case 1 : Return "One"
      Case 2 : Return "Two"
      Case 3 : Return "Three"
      Case 4 : Return "Four"
      Case 5 : Return "Five"
      Case 6 : Return "Six"
      Case 7 : Return "Seven"
      Case 8 : Return "Eight"
      Case 9 : Return "Nine"
      Case Else : Return "Out of range"
   End Select
End Function
```

The first attribute in the file refers to *http://tempuri.org*. You need to replace this with a namespace that is unique to your organization so that Web Services with the same name from different vendors don't conflict. Normally you put a URL for a web page that may or may not exist (it doesn't matter). As long as it's unique to your organization, you can put whatever you want. You can also change the name of the class if you wish, although you'll need to update the related *.asmx* file appropriately.

If you run this application in Visual Studio, your web browser opens with the page shown in Figure 22-10.

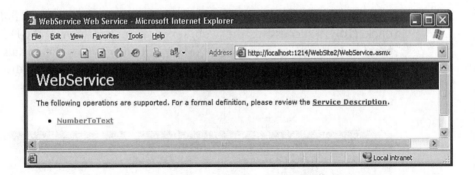

Figure 22-10 A web service running in your web browser

Web services are methods, and a web browser isn't a typical medium for running subroutines and functions, so the page in Figure 22-10 appears instead. Besides, the web service expects specially formatted XML content to run properly. If you click on the *NumberToText* link on the web page, it brings up a page from which you can test the service.

Web services are generally consumed by standard application code. Because I have this web service running on my system using my test ASP.NET web server, I'll write a desktop application to call the *NumberToText* method. Start a separate instance of Visual Studio and create a new Windows Forms project. Select the **Project ➤ Add Web Reference** menu command. The *Add Web Reference* form appears, a tool you use to locate local and remote web services. If you click on the **Web services on the local machine** link to find your custom web service, nothing will happen. Actually it will fail, because the test web server is not advertising the service. But you can specifically request the service if you know its address. To determine this, double-click on the ASP.NET Development Web Server icon in the system tray. The *Root URL* field will provide the base of the address. On my system at this particular moment, it says "http://localhost:1214/WebSite2," although it will change port numbers if I restart the service. Add to this the name of the *.asmx* file for your service, plus "?WSDL" as a query string.

```
http://localhost:1214/WebSite2/WebService.asmx?WSDL
```

Enter this address in the *Add Web Reference* form's **URL** field, and click **Go**. If successful, the web server responds with a WSDL (Web Service Description Language) XML file that provides the details of the web service. These details appear in the dialog as shown in Figure 22-11. Click the **Add Reference** button.

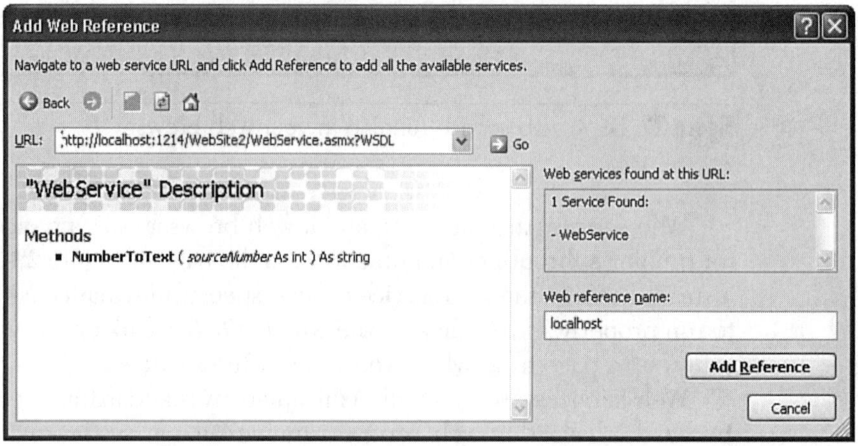

Figure 22-11 A recognized web service

Visual Studio automatically adds the reference to the *My.WebServices* object. To test out the service, I added a *TextBox* control and a *Button* control to *Form1*, and added the following code.

```
Private Sub Button1_Click(ByVal sender As System.Object, _
    ByVal e As System.EventArgs) Handles Button1.Click
    MsgBox(My.WebServices.WebService.NumberToText( _
    CInt(Val(TextBox1.Text))))
End Sub
```

Running the program, typing in a number from zero to nine, and then clicking the button correctly calls the web service and returns the English version of the number. And it would have worked just as well if the *NumberToText* service were running on a web server at one of the research facilities at the South Pole.

Summary

I really used to hate writing ASP applications. It was a pain to embed VBScript within HTML content. Although ASP.NET still supports a variation of this method, it's much better to use the code behind features of Web Forms. This makes web development only slightly more difficult than desktop application. XML Web Services also make interactions between web-based code and desktop code as easy as developing a class with methods.

When Microsoft first came out with the .NET Framework, their marketing department really went full strength on the web development aspects of Visual Studio. I was dubious. And although I am still mainly a desktop application developer, I no longer lose up to a week of sleep when I contemplate the building of Internet applications.

Project

For this chapter's project, I built a simple multi-page web site that (1) lets the user look up items in the Library database; and (2) duplicates the Library Statistics report created in Chapter 20, but without the RDLC component. I went ahead and included the completed project in your installed source code directory, in the *LibraryWebSite* subdirectory. You can open it by locating its directory with the **File ➤ Open Web Site** menu command in Visual Studio.

As shown in Figure 22-12, the project includes 11 files and two subdirectories.

Figure 22-12 The Library web site project files

Here's a quick rundown of each file and subdirectory.

- **App_Code.** The directory for all project code that is not code-behind for an actual ASP.NET web page. All of your general modules and classes for a project appear here.
- **General.vb.** A code module with six methods that I stole almost verbatim from the main Library Project's *General.vb* file. I made just a few changes, mostly to deal with not having the *LibraryDB* global variable sitting around with its connection information.
- **BoundSchemas.vb.** When we started the checked-out-item report earlier in this chapter, we bound a *GridView* control to a database query. The *GridView* control, like most of the Web Forms controls, can also bind to any class that supports the *IList* interface, including the generic collection classes. The classes in this file will be used for instances within a generic collection in two of the web pages.
- **App_Data.** This directory normally contains data needed by the application. It was created automatically by Visual Studio. I don't use it in this project.
- **Default.aspx** and **Default.aspx.vb.** This is the entry point of the Library web site. The client browser requests the *Default.aspx* web page to start the library experience. The page includes a link to the statistics report, plus fields that let you look up library items by title or author.
- **SearchResults.aspx** and **SearchResults.aspx.vb.** Searches performed from the *Default.aspx* page end up here, with queries processed in code and then bound to a grid.
- **SearchDetail.aspx** and **SearchDetail.aspx.vb.** Each search result includes a link to this page. It provides additional detail for an item, in the same format used in the main Library project's *ItemLookup.vb* file.
- **Statistics.aspx** and **Statistics.aspx.vb.** This page displays the Library Statistics report as a bound web page.
- **Web.config.** Every ASP.NET project includes a *web.config* file used to specify project-specific settings in the development and production environments.

Configuring the Database

The *web.config* file contains a place for database connection strings. I've added an entry within it for the Library database.

```
<connectionStrings>
    <add name="LibraryConnection" connectionString=
    ➥ "Data Source=MYSERVER\SQLEXPRESS;
    ➥ Initial Catalog=Library;Integrated Security=True" />
</connectionStrings>
```

Modify the "MYSERVER\SQLEXPRESS" portion to the name of your SQL Server database instance, and modify the other parts of the connection string as needed. All four of the web pages use the Library database, and they all access the connection string from this entry, via the *ConfigurationManager* object.

```
Public LibraryDB As System.Data.SqlClient.SqlConnection
```

...and later...

```
LibraryDB = New SqlClient.SqlConnection( _
    ConfigurationManager.ConnectionStrings( _
    "LibraryConnection").ConnectionString)
LibraryDB.Open()
```

...and later still...

```
LibraryDB.Close()
```

The Default Page

The *Default.aspx* page is the starting point for the Library web application, and appears in Figure 22-13.

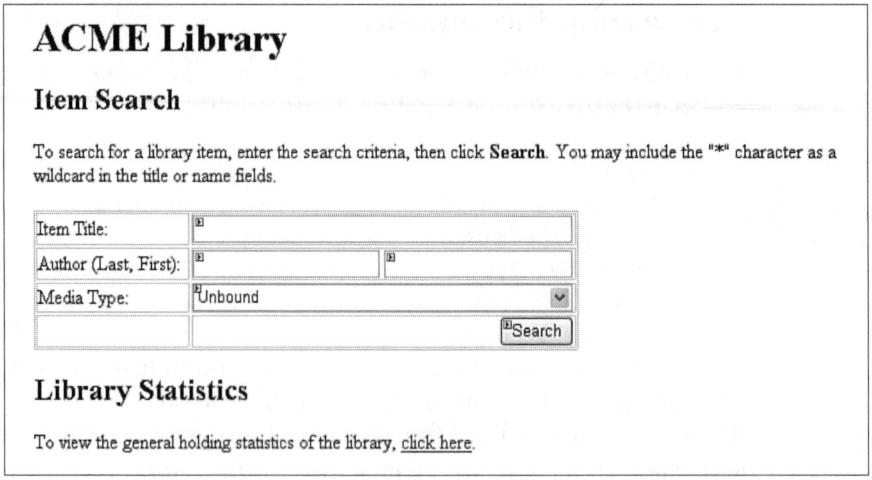

ACME Library

Item Search

To search for a library item, enter the search criteria, then click **Search**. You may include the "*" character as a wildcard in the title or name fields.

Item Title:	
Author (Last, First):	
Media Type:	Unbound
	Search

Library Statistics

To view the general holding statistics of the library, click here.

Figure 22-13 The Library web site's default page

Its code is not much to talk about. It simply fills in the *Media Type* drop-down list with the available types from the database.

```
sqlText = "SELECT ID, FullName FROM CodeMediaType " & _
    "ORDER BY FullName"
dbInfo = CreateReader(sqlText, LibraryDB)
Do While dbInfo.Read
    SearchMediaType.Items.Add(New WebControls.ListItem( _
        CStr(dbInfo!FullName), CStr(dbInfo!ID)))
Loop
dbInfo.Close()
```

The page itself is a little more interesting. When we built the sample ASP.NET web application earlier, each click on the **Multiply** button sent the page back *to itself*. It was a one-page application. Most web applications would be useless with only a single page, so button clicks and links need to jump elsewhere in the project. The report link at the bottom of this page is a standard hyperlink to *Statistics.aspx*, another page within the application. In the search portion of the page, the **Search** button (*ActSearch*) also jumps to another project page, *SearchResults.aspx*. It does this through its

PostBackUrl property, which is set to "~/SearchResults.aspx." The new page will have indirect access to all of the field selections on this starting page.

Search Results

The *SearchResults.aspx* page displays any matching results from the *Default.aspx* item search section. As shown in Figure 22-14, it includes a *GridView* control for the listing of results, plus a *Label* control that shows a count of the matches.

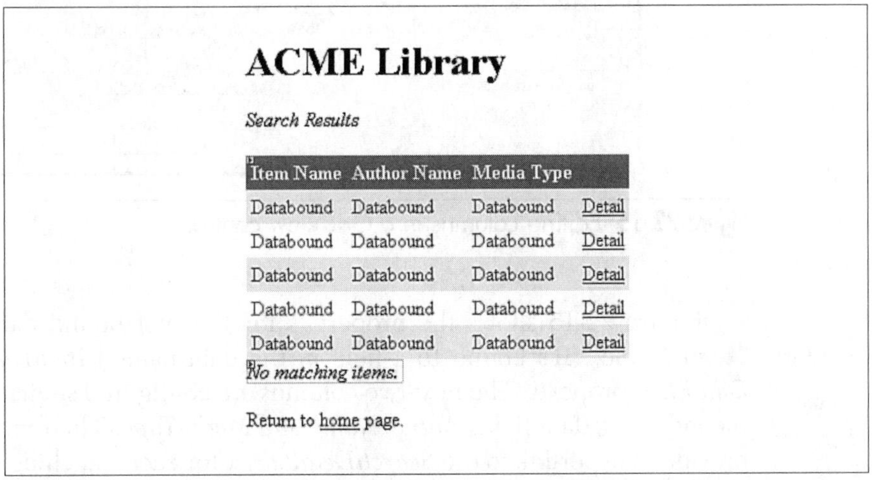

ACME Library

Search Results

Item Name	Author Name	Media Type	
Databound	Databound	Databound	Detail
Databound	Databound	Databound	Detail
Databound	Databound	Databound	Detail
Databound	Databound	Databound	Detail
Databound	Databound	Databound	Detail

No matching items.

Return to <u>home</u> page.

Figure 22-14 The Library web site's search results page

Unlike the *GridView* populated earlier, this one does not connect directly to a database query. Instead, I hand-build instances of the *BoundSchemaSearchResults* class (from *BoundSchemas.vb*), collect them into a generic *List*, and bind them to the fields in the *GridView*. Actually, binding in this way is a snap. Each column I configured in the *GridView* control looks for a property in the incoming records that matches a specific field name. These columns are defined through the *Column Editor* (see Figure 22-15), accessed via the control's *Columns* property.

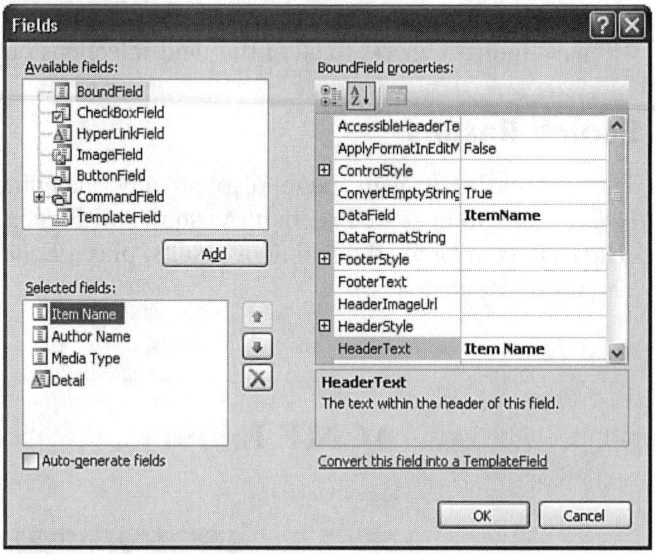

Figure 22-15 Editing columns in a GridView control

Figure 22-15 shows the properties for the first bound data column, "Item Name." It's bound to a field in the data named *ItemData* via the *DataField* property. The next two columns are configured similarly, but use the incoming data fields *AuthorName* and *MediaType*. The fourth column provides a hyperlink to the *SearchDetail.aspx* for each matching record. To build this column, I added it as a *HyperLinkField* column instead of a *BoundField* column. I set its *Text* property to "Detail," which will appear on every record. Clicking on the link will pass the ID of the matching item (I set the *DataNavigateUrlFields* to *ID*) to the target page via a query string. The *DataNavigateUrlFormatString* property contains a string that will be sent to the *String.Format* method, along with the fields listed in *DataNavigateUrlFields*. Here is the format string.

```
SearchDetail.aspx?ID={0}
```

The "{0}" part gets replaced with the value of each record's *ID* field.

This page's *Load* event handler is triggered by a call from the **Search** button on the *Default.aspx* page. When a Web Forms page called itself, it can directly examine the values in its controls. But the controls on the

Default.aspx page don't exist here in the *SearchResults.aspx* page. Fortunately, the previous page's controls are sent as data to the new page. You can access them through the *PreviousPage* object. The following code extracts the values from each of the search fields.

```
' ----- Get the title search text.
sourceTextBox = CType(PreviousPage.FindControl( _
    "SearchTitle"), TextBox)
If (sourceTextBox IsNot Nothing) Then _
    useTitle = Trim(sourceTextBox.Text)


' ----- Get the last name search text.
sourceTextBox = CType(PreviousPage.FindControl( _
    "SearchLastName"), TextBox)
If (sourceTextBox IsNot Nothing) Then _
    useLastName = Trim(sourceTextBox.Text)


' ----- Get the first name search text.
sourceTextBox = CType(PreviousPage.FindControl( _
    "SearchFirstName"), TextBox)
If (sourceTextBox IsNot Nothing) Then _
    useFirstName = Trim(sourceTextBox.Text)


' ----- Get the media type value.
sourceMediaType = CType(PreviousPage.FindControl( _
    "SearchMediaType"), DropDownList)
If (sourceMediaType IsNot Nothing) Then _
    useMediaType = sourceMediaType.SelectedValue
```

Amazingly, the previous page didn't just send its fields as string values. Instead, they retained their existence as true objects. Using the *CType* function to convert them to *TextBox* and *DropDownList* controls was enough to access their control properties.

I use the user-supplied values to build a SQL statement and query the database for results. If there are any, the resulting data is massaged into a list of objects.

```
Dim oneEntry As BoundSchemaSearchResults
Dim reportData As Collections.Generic.List( _
    Of BoundSchemaSearchResults)
```

```
Do While dbInfo.Read
   ' ----- Add it to the report data.
   oneEntry = New BoundSchemaSearchResults
   oneEntry.ID = CInt(dbInfo!ID)
   oneEntry.ItemName = CStr(dbInfo!Title)
   If (IsDBNull(dbInfo!LastName) = True) Then _
      useLastName = "" Else _
      useLastName = CStr(dbInfo!LastName)
   If (IsDBNull(dbInfo!FirstName) = True) Then _
      useFirstName = "" Else _
      useFirstName = CStr(dbInfo!FirstName)
   If (useFirstName <> "") Then
      If (useLastName <> "") Then useLastName &= ", "
      useLastName &= useFirstName
   End If
   oneEntry.AuthorName = useLastName
   oneEntry.MediaType = CStr(dbInfo!MediaName)

   reportData.Add(oneEntry)
Loop
```

The results are bound to the grid, and a count is displayed to the user.

```
ResultsGrid.DataSource = reportData
ResultsGrid.DataBind()
MatchCount.Text = reportData.Count & " matching items."
```

You must call the *GridView* control's *DataBind* method or you won't see any results.

Search Detail

When the user clicks on one of the **Detail** links in the search results, it sends the ID of the selected *NamedItem* record to the *SearchDetail.aspx* page as a query string. The page itself, which I won't show here, includes many *Label* controls that attempt to mimic the output on the detail panel of the *ItemLookup.vb* form in the main Library application. I even use almost the same Cascading Style Sheet instructions in this page that I use in the application.

When the page's *Load* event handler fires, it first examines the query string to extract the supplied *NamedItem* ID. A missing ID results in a return to the main search form.

```
itemID = Val(Page.Request.QueryString("ID"))
If (itemID <= 0) Then
    Response.Redirect("Default.aspx")
    Return
End If
```

Most of the formatting code for this page comes from the *ItemLookup.vb* file in the main application. It queries the database for details of the specified *NamedItem* record, and updates each label using these values. The only thing that is interesting—besides the fact that this seems all too easy for web-page development—is the creation of the table of item copies near the bottom of the page. In the *ItemLookup.vb* version of the code, I hand-crafted an HTML `<table>` set, and filled in its columns with the status of each available copy of the named library item. I thought it was a shame to ignore all of that great code, so I just copied it nearly unchanged into the code for *SearchDetail.aspx.vb*. So far, I haven't had to do anything with HTML itself, except when I wanted to add `<h1>` tags around the page titles. But because I had written the HTML-generating code, and because ASP.NET applications target HTML, I thought I could use it.

And I can. One of the Web Forms controls is *Literal*, a control that exists only so you can set its *Text* property to properly formatted HTML content. After building up the table structure in a *StringBuilder* object named *copyTable*, I assign that HTML content to the *Literal* control.

```
' ----- Add the table to the output.
PutTableHere.Text = copyTable.ToString()
```

Statistics Report

The *Statistics.aspx* page displays the same summary information included in one of the reports from Chapter 20. In the original Statistics report, I displayed record counts from six different tables, and presented them as a list in an RDLC report format. In this web page, I do those same six queries, build a generic list of the results, and bind that list to—surprise—a *GridView* control, which is quickly becoming our favorite. Here's the code for the page in its entirety.

```
Imports System.Data

Partial Class Statistics
    Inherits System.Web.UI.Page

    Public LibraryDB As System.Data.SqlClient.SqlConnection

    Protected Sub Page_Load(ByVal sender As Object, _
            ByVal e As System.EventArgs) Handles Me.Load
        ' ----- Prepare the data for the report.
        Dim sqlText As String
        Dim reportData As Collections.Generic.List( _
            Of BoundSchemaStatistics)
        Dim oneEntry As BoundSchemaStatistics
        Dim resultValue As Integer
        Dim counter As Integer
        Dim tableSets() As String = {"Author", "Publisher", _
            "Subject", "NamedItem", "ItemCopy", "Patron"}
        Dim tableTitles() As String = {"Authors", "Publishers", _
            "Subject Headings", "Items", "Item Copies", "Patrons"}

        ' ----- Connect to the database.
        LibraryDB = New SqlClient.SqlConnection( _
            ConfigurationManager.ConnectionStrings( _
            "LibraryConnection").ConnectionString)
        LibraryDB.Open()

        ' ----- Build the report data. It's all counts from
        '       different tables.
        reportData = New Collections.Generic.List( _
            Of BoundSchemaStatistics)
        For counter = 0 To UBound(tableSets)
            ' ----- Process one table.
            sqlText = "SELECT COUNT(*) FROM " & _
                tableSets(counter)
            resultValue = CInt(ExecuteSQLReturn(sqlText, _
                LibraryDB))
```

```
            ' ----- Add it to the report data.
            oneEntry = New BoundSchemaStatistics
            oneEntry.EntryName = tableTitles(counter)
            oneEntry.EntryValue = CStr(resultValue)
            reportData.Add(oneEntry)
        Next counter

        ' ----- Finished with the connection.
        LibraryDB.Close()

        StatisticsGrid.DataSource = reportData
        StatisticsGrid.DataBind()
    End Sub
End Class
```

I only included a minimum set of features in this web site, and don't start cracking jokes about my web page design skills. If I were planning to deploy this web site, I would certainly enable some links on the *SearchDetail.aspx* page so that the user could click to search for other items by the same author, publisher, series, and so on. I would also add patron-specific features that would let them check their current checked-out items and any fines due. Another great feature to add would be online help content that told the patron or administrator how to use the system. And that just happens to be the topic for the next chapter. Lucky you.

ADDING ONLINE HELP

If there's one thing I've learned in nearly 25 years of programming, it's that users often need some help to run software on their systems. Programmers need help too, but getting back to computers: It's rare that you find a technically conversant user. If you write applications that target businesses and departments within organizations (that's what I do), you find that the users are very skilled at their job, but not necessarily skilled at using a computer. That's why it is imperative that you make your programs as straightforward to use as possible.

You should also add online help to your applications. These ready documents act as the first wave of support for your user's software needs. Of course, they seldom read it, and so you (or your technical support staff) will actually become the first wave of support. But it's somewhat refreshing to be able to say, "Did you check the online help, which covers this issue in detail?"

In this chapter, we'll discuss the online help options available to you in Visual Basic, and focus in on HTML Help 1.x, Microsoft's standard Windows XP help system.

Windows Online Help Options

Online help has been a part of Windows since its initial release, back in the days when applications and operating systems still shipped with printed manuals and never required more than two floppy disks. I really miss those days. That sense of touch; the cold, smooth pages in my hands. I remember the first Windows software I ever purchased, a newly released "Personal Information Manager." It had everything I needed, including a 400-page user's guide and reference manual. Sheer delight.

Those days are gone, replaced by online help systems and HTML readme files. Now you buy books like this one to bring back that included-user's-guide feeling. But you can do a lot with online help, especially these days with the ability to include dynamic, active content in online help pages.

WinHelp

The original Windows help system was *WinHelp*. It included simple formatted help pages with hyperlinks to other pages. A separate "contents" file added table-of-contents support; you had to ship the ".cnt" contents file with the ".hlp" file as a set. These basic help files were (and in many ways, still are) good enough for most users' needs, and they are still supported by all releases of Microsoft Windows.

To build a WinHelp file, you needed to craft your pages as RTF (Rich Text Format) files, a document format supported by Microsoft Word and most other word processors. It was great for writing the main content of your help files because it was just word-processing content. Unfortunately, preparing the different elements that supported the help-specific features, like hyperlinks, was a little more involved. It required that special codes and symbols be precisely formatted—some as hidden text, and some as footnotes. This system worked, but it was not always pleasant, especially when you accidentally erased a piece of hidden text that you didn't even know was there.

Some third-party companies sold tools that made WinHelp development a little easier, either by generating the RTF content for you, or by interfacing with Microsoft Word. And to get to the advanced features supported by WinHelp, you really did need to defer to one of these off-the-shelf products, a pattern that would continue into future help systems.

HTML Help

RTF documents are so 1980s. When the Internet started sweeping the world with its ability to generate beautifully formatted pages through the common HTML tag-based language, Microsoft decided to upgrade its help system to one that used standard HTML documents: *HTML Help*. As its name implies, HTML Help is truly HTML-based. Anything that generates HTML can generate HTML Help content: third-party web-page designer tools, word processors, your own custom applications, and even Notepad. As usual, some vendors designed tools specifically targeting the HTML Help system.

HTML Help is better than WinHelp, due to its dependence on HTML and other related technologies. Each page of your online help file is a separate HTML page/file. Hyperlinks to other help pages are standard HTML hyperlinks. And HTML Help employs most of the features used in any web page, including Cascading Style Sheets and Java scripting.

Compiled HTML Help files have a ".chm" extension, and a single file includes primary content, the table of contents, and a predefined index of terms. We will use HTML Help technology to add online help content to the Library Project. I'll skip the details of the system until a little later in the chapter.

Microsoft Help 2

Most applications sold as of this writing use HTML Help, but not all. One big exception is Visual Studio itself. Its help system, *Microsoft Help 2*, combines HTML and XML content into a set of collections that work together as one. If you've installed the full version of SQL Server on a system with Visual Studio, they together share a common help interface. You can even search for pages in both collections at the same time.

Microsoft makes a "Help Integration Kit" available for developers who wish to merge their own content into the Microsoft Help 2 system. This is most useful for vendors who develop third-party controls and tools that integrate with .NET or SQL Server.

Assistance Platform

Windows Vista will use a new help system called *Assistance Platform*. The initial Vista release will use the new system for all operating system online help. Unfortunately, Microsoft will not have a development platform available for Assistance Platform until after Vista comes out. If you want to develop applications for Windows Vista, and have them ready in time for the Vista release, you will need to use HTML Help for the online help content. Microsoft will release a help support system once Vista is out so that third parties (that's you) can develop Assistance Platform content.

Other Methods

Not every application uses these Microsoft-defined help systems. Some applications include no online help at all because they are designed by bad people. No, I'm just kidding. There may be instances where online help adds no value to a program. But it's usually best to include some sort of written assistance.

Stand-alone HTML pages are just one step down from HTML Help files, and are a viable alternative for simple applications, or those hosted on a web site. You can use other standard formats, such as word processing or text documents, if you just don't have the resources to generate true online help files. And of course there are books, which will get my attention.

Visual Studio includes a feature that lets you generate documentation from the XML comments added to each member of your class. (I don't discuss this in this book; see the Visual Studio online help—aren't you glad it's there—for additional information on "XML Comments.") Don't even consider using this for your own user documentation needs unless you are developing class-based components for use by other developers.

Designing HTML Help

HTML Help files are built up from multiple source files.

- Content files, especially standard HTML files, communicate core information to the user, either through static text and graphics, or through advanced web page-style behaviors and scripts normally available in web pages.
- The Help Contents file uses ".hhc" for its file extension. Using standard HTML `<ul>` and `<li>` tags, the file specifies the hierarchical table of contents used by the help file.
- The Help Keywords file uses an ".hhk" file extension, and documents the index used to access help pages from specific predefined keywords.
- The Help Project file, using an ".hhp" file extension, defines an entire help project and its target *.chm* file. This INI-style text file identifies all the other files that will be compiled into the target help file. It also defines a few file-wide options.

The primary content files can be built by hand using any standard HTML tool you wish, as long as the output format matches what is expected by the HTML Help Compiler (supplied by Microsoft). For the content files, it generally doesn't matter what tool you use, because standard HTML is sufficient. Any hyperlinks that you include in the content to other help pages in the same directory will become standard help links in the compiled help file.

The non-content files require a very precise format; they are all based on HTML, except the Help Project file, which is an INI file. You will either need to design these files by hand using the expected format, or use a tool that can generate these files for you in the right format.

Microsoft provides a free tool that helps you create the non-content files, and joins together the content files with them for final compilation. You can download *HTML Help Workshop* directly from Microsoft's web site. Go to the Microsoft Download Center:

```
http://www.microsoft.com/downloads
```

and search for "HTML Help Workshop." You will receive a few results, but the first one in the list (when sorted by popularity) should be the one you need. Figure 23-1 shows the main page of the HTML Help Workshop application with an active project file open.

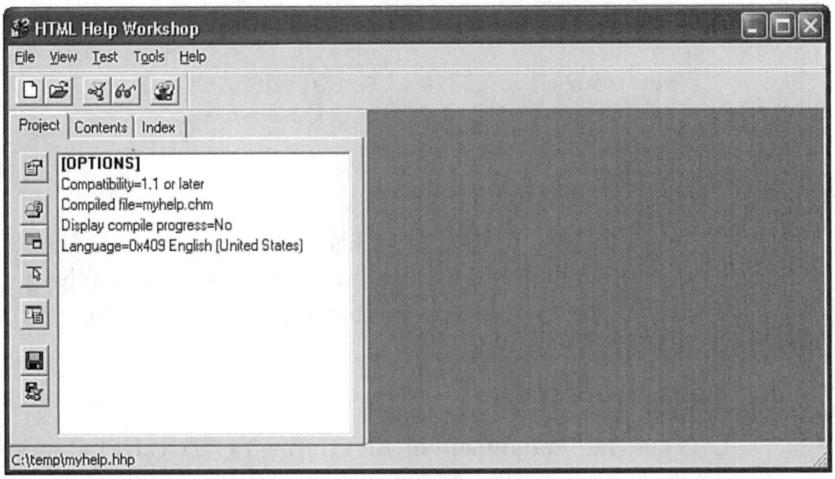

Figure 23-1 Giving help to those who really need it

In the rest of this section, we'll use HTML Help Workshop to build a simple HTML Help file that contains two pages: a welcome page, and a "more information" page. You can find this sample help project in the *HTMLHelpSample* subdirectory of the book's installation directory.

Content Files

Our mini-project includes two content files: *welcome.htm* and *moreinfo.htm*. Ever the technology maven, I crafted them in Notepad. Here's the content for *welcome.htm*.

```
<html>
  <head><title>Welcome to My Help</title></head>
  <body>
    Welcome to My Help. For more information,
    <a href="moreinfo.htm">click here</a>.
  </body>
</html>
```

The *moreinfo.htm* file is a lot like it.

```
<html>
  <head><title>My Help Additional Info</title></head>
  <body>
    Not much more to say. For a greeting,
    <a href="welcome.htm">click here</a>.
  </body>
</html>
```

You can add graphics files (like JPEG and GIF files) and link them in as you normally would in a web page. Be sure to store the graphic files in the same directory (or subdirectory) as the main file for easy access.

Help Project File

Let's generate the remaining files through HTML Help Workshop. Start it up, and use the **File ➤ New** menu command to create a new project. Using the *New Project* wizard, identify the location and name of your new ".hhp" file. I'll create a file named *Simple.hhp* in the same folder as the two content files. The wizard prompts you for files already created. Check the **HTML files** field, as shown in Figure 23-2.

Figure 23-2 Locate the files now, or you can do it later.

Add the two HTML files in the next step, and complete the wizard. The project file is created with references to your two files.

The project is pretty empty; it doesn't even have a window title defined for the compiled help file. You can set the title and other general settings through the project options, accessed through the top-most button in the Toolbar that runs on the left side of the main window. You can also double-click on the *[OPTIONS]* item in the project details list. When the option window appears, enter "Simple Help" in the **Title** field, then click **OK**.

Here is what the project file contains at this point.

```
[OPTIONS]
Compatibility=1.1 or later
Compiled file=Simple.chm
Default topic=welcome.htm
Display compile progress=No
Language=0x409 English (United States)
Title=Simple Help

[FILES]
welcome.htm
moreinfo.htm

[INFOTYPES]
```

23. ADDING ONLINE HELP

The file will change as we add the other two non-content files, but not by much.

Compiling the file right now (using the **File ➤ Compile** menu command) and running it displays a very simple help window, as shown in Figure 23-3.

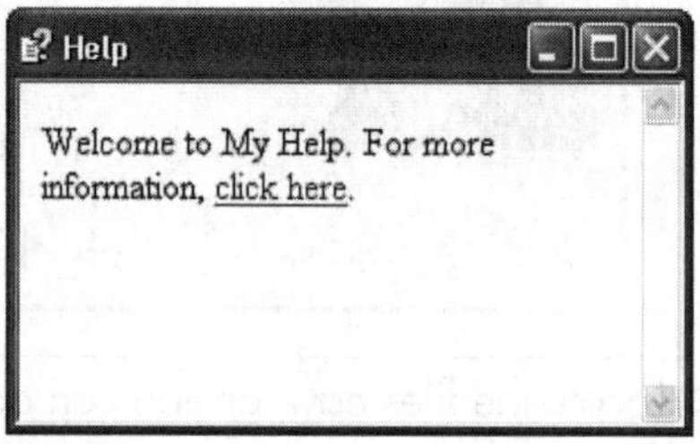

Figure 23-3 A little help, very little

Help Contents File

A table of contents will help the user peruse this massive online help experience. To add a contents file, click on the *Contents* tab on the left side of the main form, and respond to the prompt that you wish to create a new file, naming it *Simple.hhc*. The form changes to display a table-of-contents editor. Another way to create the contents file is by using the **File ➤ New** menu command, and choosing "Table of Contents" from the *New* selection form. This is more indirect, as it doesn't immediately connect the contents file with the project.

Use the new Toolbar buttons running down the left side of the window to add and modify contents entries. First, use the top button (**Contents properties**) to edit the options for the table of contents. On the *Table of Contents Properties* form, uncheck the **Use folders instead of books** field, and click **OK**.

The next two buttons—the book button (**insert a heading**) and the page/question mark button (**insert a page**)—are the main buttons used to add new entries to the contents. I clicked the **insert a page** button to get to the *Table of Contents Entry* form shown in Figure 23-4.

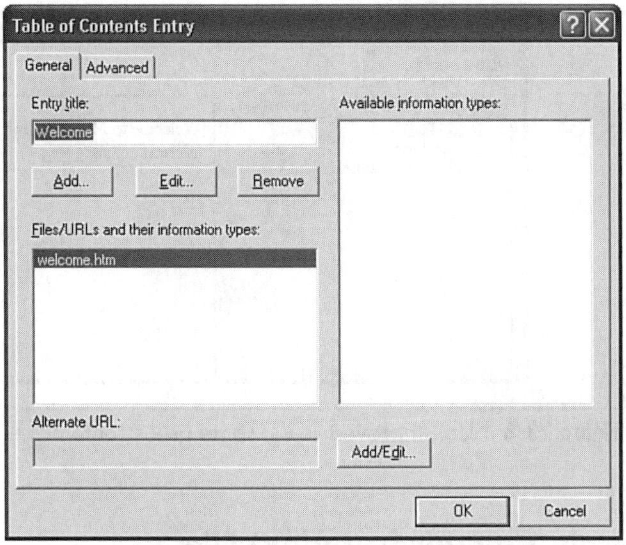

Figure 23-4 Adding a help page

As shown in the figure, I set the entry title (Welcome), and selected the "Welcome to My Help" (*welcome.htm*) file through the **Add** button. I did the same for the *moreinfo.htm* file, giving it a title of "More Information." I also added a heading entry using the **insert a heading** Toolbar button on the main form, naming it "Other Pages." I used the arrow Toolbar buttons to move the *moreinfo.htm* entry into this heading section. Then I took a well-deserved break and looked at my completed table of contents in Figure 23-5.

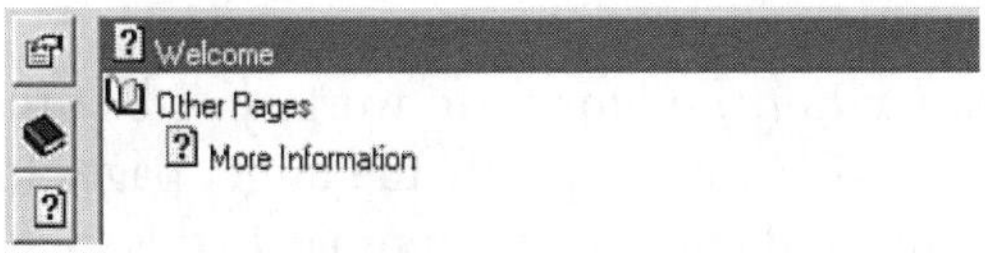

Figure 23-5 The full table of contents

If you compile and run the file, it now includes the table of contents in a separate panel, plus a Toolbar (see Figure 23-6).

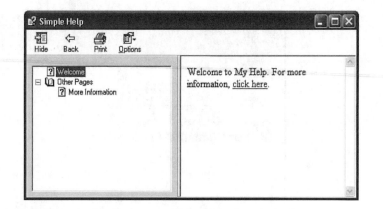

Figure 23-6 New improved TOC; same great content

Help Keywords (Index) File

An index file lets the user access specific pages by searching for a concept or subject from a list. There is a many-to-many relationship between these keywords and the help pages: one keyword can lead to one or more pages, and a single page can be the target of multiple keywords.

Create an index by clicking on the *Index* tab on the left half of the main form, and respond to the prompt that you want to create a new index file, calling it *Simple.hhk*. As with the *Contents* editor, the *Index* editor includes a small vertical toolbar. Use the second button in the toolbar, the one with the key image, to create new keyword entries. I will add three keywords:

- "basic," linking to *welcome.htm*
- "advanced," linking to *moreinfo.htm*
- "everything," linking to both pages

The *Index Entry* editor form works just like the *Table of Contents Entry* form, allowing you to specify the target pages for each keyword.

Saving and compiling the project adds index features to the compiled help file.

Formatting Help Windows

On my system, running the compiled help file displayed the content in a little window in the upper-right corner of the screen. But my help content is important; I want it to appear much closer to the middle of the screen, and in a larger window. Fortunately, you can control the windows used to display the content. Return to the *Project* tab and click on the third toolbar button down on the left side of the window. This button, **Add/modify window definitions**, lets you define one or more windows to use for distinct help pages in your file. When prompted, add a *New Window Type* named *SimpleWindow*.

The *Window Types* dialog that appears has many options for getting just the window you want, although you're probably being too picky if you need more than, say, 243 different window types. The *Position* tab is a lot of fun. It includes an **Autosizer** button that lets you drag a window to the desired size. Adjust the size to something reasonable, add a **Title bar text** of "Simple Help" back on the *General* tab, and click **OK**. Because this is the only defined window, it becomes the default, and will be used for the main help display the next time you compile and run the file.

Accessing HTML Help

Visual Studio provides two primary methods of integrating online help into desktop applications. The first uses the *HelpProvider* control, found in the *Components* section of the Visual Studio Toolbox. The second uses the *Help.ShowHelp* method of the Windows forms package. Both methods let you display specific pages or portions of a compiled HTML Help file.

HelpProvider Control

The *HelpProvider* control can be added to a form to enable access to online help. It provides two primary online help experiences: (1) standard access to compiled HTML Help files; and (2) popup help. Both methods put the focus on individual controls of a form, and on the specific help features to be tied to each control.

Accessing HTML Help Files

To use the *HelpProvider* control with compiled HTML Help files, set the control's *HelpNamespace* property to the location of a valid help file. Then adjust the properties of other controls on the form to refer to specific features within the help file. The *HelpProvider* control impacts other controls by adding several additional properties to each. Figure 23-7 shows the four additional properties (*HelpKeyword*, *HelpNavigator*, *HelpString*, and *ShowHelp*) automatically added to a *Button* control.

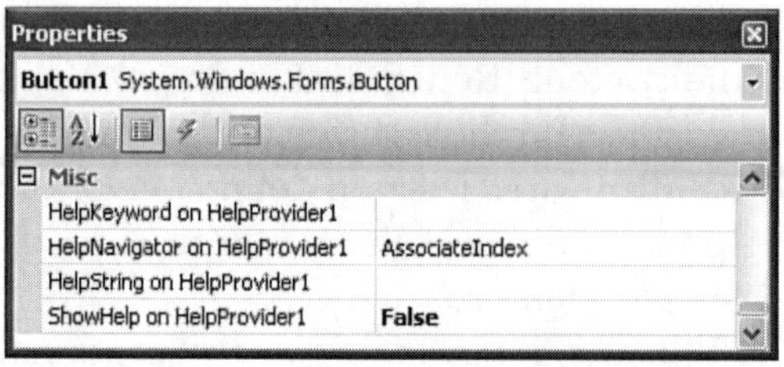

Properties

Button1 System.Windows.Forms.Button

⊟ Misc	
HelpKeyword on HelpProvider1	
HelpNavigator on HelpProvider1	AssociateIndex
HelpString on HelpProvider1	
ShowHelp on HelpProvider1	**False**

Figure 23-7 Adding help support to individual controls

The *HelpNavigator* property added to each control defines what features of the help file to access when the user presses the F1 key while that control has the focus. To access a specific page within the help file (such as *welcome.htm*), set the target control's *HelpNavigator* property to "Topic" and set the related *HelpKeyword* property to the file name of the page ("welcome.htm").

The *HelpNavigator* property for a control can be set to access non-page sections of the online help file as well. The value "TableOfContents" displays the file's contents outline; "Index" jumps to the keyword index. There are a few other choices as well.

Showing Popup Help

The *HelpProvider* control also enables "popup" help on individual controls. This help variation causes a small tool tip window to appear just above a control, displaying a short message that provides usage information for that control, as shown in Figure 23-8.

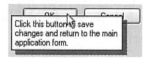

Click this button to save
changes and return to the main
application form.

Figure 23-8 Popup help on a button control

Popup help works when you enable the "Popup Button" in the form's title bar. To set popup help for a control, follow these steps.

1. Add a *HelpProvider* control to the form, but don't bother setting its *HelpNamespace* property to a file.
2. Set the form's *HelpButton* property to *True*.
3. Set the form's *MaximizeBox* and *MinimizeBox* properties to *False*.
4. Set the *HelpString on HelpProvider1* property to some informational text on each control that will display its own popup help.

The user displays popup help by first clicking on the question-mark "help" button in the form's title bar, and then clicking on a control.

ShowHelp Method

The *System.Windows.Forms.Help.ShowHelp* method displays specific portions of a compiled HTML Help file based on the arguments passed to the method. It's quite similar to the file-based help portion of the *HelpProvider* control, but in method form. To display a specific page within a help file, use this syntax.

```
Windows.Forms.Help.ShowHelp(Me, "Simple.chm", _
    HelpNavigator.Topic, "moreinfo.htm")
```

The first argument is a reference to the form calling the method.

A common way of using this method is to monitor the form for the F1 key, and call *ShowHelp* from the form's *KeyDown* event handler.

```
Private Sub Form1_KeyDown(ByVal sender As Object, _
    ByVal e As System.Windows.Forms.KeyEventArgs) _
    Handles Me.KeyDown
    ' ----- Call online help.
    If (e.KeyCode = Keys.F1) Then
        Windows.Forms.Help.ShowHelp(Me, "Simple.chm", _
            HelpNavigator.Topic, "moreinfo.htm")
    End If
End Sub
```

You must set the form's *KeyPreview* property to *True* to trigger the form-level *KeyDown* event. Otherwise, all keys go to the active control and bypass the form-level events.

The *ShowHelp* method offers a lot more control over the user's online help experience because you (and not the *HelpProvider* control) determine exactly when to access the help file.

Summary

If it is your plan to stand over the shoulder of each user and give running verbal instructions while they sit before your software, then by all means skip the writing of any online help or other user documentation. But if you plan on having a life, make it easier by including usage support right in the application. These are not the bad old days where you had to provide your own method of online help display, or dig through the Windows API library to find the function that linked to the help file. This is .NET! It has all the help features you need built right in.

Crafting compiled HTML files is not too difficult with the HTML Help Workshop tool. But if you will work on any sizeable help file, or if you want to add enhanced features consistently, you should think about plunking down a few hundred dollars on a third-party help development tool.

Project

Once you have access to an online help file, you have access to every page of it. That's usually a good thing, because users are curious. (I mean, they are inquisitive, and not merely objects of curiosity.) But in the case of the Library Project, that curiosity could lead to topics that are really no business of ordinary patrons. Most of the features in the Library application are for administrative use only. To keep things as calm as possible, the Library Project includes two online help files.

- **LibraryBasic.chm.** A patron-focused help file that describes only the parts of the program the patron can access.
- **LibraryAdmin.chm.** A file targeting administrators and librarians that fully describes the features of the application.

This chapter's project section builds both of these online help files, and integrates them into the Library application.

Building the Help Files

I've written the content for both online help files for you. You'll find it all in the *Online Help* subdirectory in the primary install directory for this book, with distinct directory branches for *Basic* and *Admin* files. Figures 23-9 and Figure 23-10 list the files found in each directory.

LibraryBasic.chm   ItemLookup.htm   MainForm_Library.htm   PatronRecord.htm
LibraryBasic.hhp   LocateDatabase.htm   MainForm_Out.htm   Welcome.htm
ChangeUser.htm   LocateLicense.htm   MainForm_Patron.htm   LibraryBasic.hhk
CheckLookup_Out.htm   MainForm_Basic.htm   PatronAccess.htm   LibraryBasic.hhc
Copyright.htm   MainForm_Help.htm   PatronPassword.htm

Figure 23-9 The files for patron-level online help

LibraryAdmin.chm   ChangeUser.htm   KeywordAdd.htm   PatronAccess.htm
BarcodeToolBarcode.gif   CheckLookup_In.htm   ListEditRecords.htm   PatronLimit.htm
BarcodeToolDelete.gif   CheckLookup_Out.htm   LocateDatabase.htm   PatronPassword.htm
BarcodeToolDown.gif   CodeAuthorType.htm   LocateLicense.htm   PatronPayment.htm
BarcodeToolLine.gif   CodeCopyStatus.htm   MainForm_Admin.htm   PatronRecord.htm
BarcodeToolNumber.gif   CodeLocation.htm   MainForm_Basic.htm   Publisher.htm
BarcodeToolRect.gif   CodeMediaType.htm   MainForm_Daily.htm   PublisherAddLocate.htm
BarcodeToolText.gif   CodePatronGroup.htm   MainForm_Help.htm   PublisherLimit.htm
BarcodeToolUp.gif   CodeSeries.htm   MainForm_In.htm   ReportSelect.htm
LibraryAdmin.hhp   Copyright.htm   MainForm_Library.htm   SeriesAddLocate.htm
Author.htm   GroupName.htm   MainForm_Out.htm   SubjectAdd.htm
AuthorAddLocate.htm   Holiday.htm   MainForm_Patron.htm   SystemValue.htm
AuthorLimit.htm   ItemAuthorEdit.htm   MainForm_Print.htm   UserName.htm
BarcodeLabel.htm   ItemCopy.htm   Maintenance.htm   Welcome.htm
BarcodePage.htm   ItemLimit.htm   NamedItem.htm   LibraryAdmin.hhk
BarcodePrint.htm   ItemLookup.htm   Patron.htm   LibraryAdmin.hhc

Figure 23-10 The files for administrator-level online help

Most of the HTML files have a one-to-one link with specific forms in the application. For instance, the *ItemLookup.htm* file contains the online help content for the *ItemLookup.vb* form in the application. And this help page shows up in both the basic and administrative versions of the file. When the user presses F1 from the Item Lookup form, the application tries to show the online help page "ItemLookup.htm." If the user is a standard patron, it accesses this page in the *LibraryBasic.chm* file; administrative users access the same page name, but from the *LibraryAdmin.chm* file instead.

Each help source folder contains *.hhp*, *.hhc*, and *.hhk* files that define the project, the contents, and the index details respectively. The administrative version also includes a few GIF graphic files.

I've already compiled each file and placed a copy of the *.chm* file in these directories.

Add Help Support to the Application

To keep things simple and somewhat centralized, we'll employ the *ShowHelp* method described earlier to display online help for each form in the application. Because of the busy-work nature of the changes involved in this chapter's project code, I've already made all of the updates to the project. Most of the changes involve making the exact same change to every form in the project, all of which I'll describe next.

Project Access Load the "Chapter 23 (After) Code" project, either through the New Project templates, or by accessing the project directly from the installation directory. This chapter does not include a "Before" variation of the project code.

The *Maintenance.vb* form already provides a way for the administrator to specify the locations of each online help file. It updates two settings through the *My.Settings* object.

```
My.Settings.HelpFile = Trim(RecordBasicHelp.Text)
My.Settings.HelpFileAdmin = Trim(RecordAdminHelp.Text)
```

Those settings also get stored in two global variables.

```
MainHelpFile = RecordBasicHelp.Text
MainAdminHelpFile = RecordAdminHelp.Text
```

That means that we only need to call *ShowHelp* from each form and access one of the two files whenever the user presses F1.

But what if the administrator never uses the *Maintenance.vb* form to configure the locations of the help files? Because the help files will probably be installed in the same folder as the *Library.exe* program file, we should look there automatically. The *InitializeSystem* method in *General.vb* already sets the two global variables to the values stored in the settings.

```
' ----- Locate the online help files.
MainHelpFile = My.Settings.HelpFile & ""
MainAdminHelpFile = My.Settings.HelpFileAdmin & ""
```

Just in case these settings don't exist, let's add code, just after these lines, that provides default access to the files.

```
If (MainHelpFile = "") Then MainHelpFile = _
   My.Computer.FileSystem.CombinePath( _
   My.Application.Info.DirectoryPath, "LibraryBasic.chm")
If (MainAdminHelpFile = "") Then MainAdminHelpFile = _
   My.Computer.FileSystem.CombinePath( _
   My.Application.Info.DirectoryPath, "LibraryAdmin.chm")
```

Because we need to continuously adapt to the current user state of the application (whether the user is a patron or an administrator), a centralized routine that displays help from the correct file seems best. Here's the code for *OnlineHelp*, a new method in the *General.vb* file.

```
Public Sub OnlineHelp(ByVal whichForm As _
      System.Windows.Forms.Form, _
      ByVal contextName As String)
   ' ----- Show the online help. Differentiate between the
   '       basic and the administrative online help usage.
   Dim fileToUse As String

   ' ----- Which file to use.
   If (LoggedInUserID = -1) Then
      fileToUse = MainHelpFile
   Else
      fileToUse = MainAdminHelpFile
   End If
   If (fileToUse = "") Then
      MsgBox("Online help is not properly configured.", _
         MsgBoxStyle.OkOnly Or MsgBoxStyle.Exclamation, _
         ProgramTitle)
      Return
   End If

   ' ----- Show the online help.
   Try
      Help.ShowHelp(whichForm, fileToUse, _
         HelpNavigator.Topic, contextName)
```

```
Catch
    MsgBox("An error occurred while trying to access " & _
        "the online help file.", MsgBoxStyle.OkOnly Or _
        MsgBoxStyle.Exclamation, ProgramTitle)
End Try
End Sub
```

The biggest task in this chapter involves going to each form in the project and making these two changes.

- Set the form's *KeyPreview* property to *True*.
- Add a call to *OnlineHelp* from the form's *KeyDown* event handler.

Here's the code added to the *ChangeUser.vb* form.

```
Private Sub ChangeUser_KeyDown(ByVal sender As Object, _
    ByVal e As System.Windows.Forms.KeyEventArgs) _
    Handles Me.KeyDown
    ' ----- F1 shows online help.
    If (e.KeyCode = Keys.F1) Then _
        OnlineHelp(Me, "ChangeUser.htm")
End Sub
```

A few of the forms process online help requests a little differently from the others. *About.vb* doesn't include its own online help page. Instead, it displays *Welcome.htm*. *Splash.vb* doesn't show any online help because the user isn't really supposed to interact with it. *ReportBuiltInViewer.vb*, the form that shows each of the five built-in reports, displays help for a related form via *ReportSelect.htm*. *CheckLookup.vb* form has two associated online help pages: one for check-out and one for check-in of items. Its *KeyDown* event handler chooses the right page based on the current mode of the form.

```
If (e.KeyCode = Keys.F1) Then
    If (CheckInMode = True) Then
        OnlineHelp(Me, "CheckLookup_In.htm")
    Else
        OnlineHelp(Me, "CheckLookup_Out.htm")
    End If
End If
```

The *Main.vb* form is even more diverse, choosing from among nine distinct online help pages when in administrative mode. Each panel on the main form is like a whole separate form, so I added an online help page for each panel. Code in the form's *KeyDown* event handler shows the right page based on the currently displayed panel.

```
If (PanelLibraryItem.Visible = True) Then
    OnlineHelp(Me, "MainForm_Library.htm")
ElseIf (PanelPatronRecord.Visible = True) Then
    OnlineHelp(Me, "MainForm_Patron.htm")
ElseIf (PanelHelp.Visible = True) Then
    OnlineHelp(Me, "MainForm_Help.htm")
ElseIf (PanelCheckOut.Visible = True) Then
    OnlineHelp(Me, "MainForm_Out.htm")
ElseIf (PanelCheckIn.Visible = True) Then
    OnlineHelp(Me, "MainForm_In.htm")
ElseIf (PanelAdmin.Visible = True) Then
    OnlineHelp(Me, "MainForm_Admin.htm")
ElseIf (PanelProcess.Visible = True) Then
    OnlineHelp(Me, "MainForm_Daily.htm")
ElseIf (PanelReports.Visible = True) Then
    OnlineHelp(Me, "MainForm_Print.htm")
Else
    OnlineHelp(Me, "MainForm_Basic.htm")
End If
```

The *Help* panel on the main form includes buttons designed to jump to the table of contents and index of the current online help file. I added event handlers for these buttons. The code for both *MainForm.ActHelpContents_Click* and *MainForm.ActHelpIndex_Click* is just like the code in the generic *OnlineHelp* routine, except for the final call to *ShowHelp*.

```
Private Sub ActHelpContents_Click(ByVal sender As Object, _
    ByVal e As System.EventArgs) _
    Handles ActHelpContents.Click
    ' ----- Show the online help table of contents.
    ...
    Help.ShowHelp(Me, fileToUse, _
    HelpNavigator.TableOfContents)
    ...
End Sub
```

```
Private Sub ActHelpIndex_Click(ByVal sender As Object, _
      ByVal e As System.EventArgs) _
      Handles ActHelpIndex.Click
   ' ----- Show the online help index.
   ...
   Help.ShowHelp(Me, fileToUse, HelpNavigator.Index)
   ...
End Sub
```

Once the online help (*.chm*) files are in place, and once the application is properly configured to locate those files on the workstation, the user can access help from any form by pressing the F1 key. Figure 23-11 shows help accessed from the *Library Items* panel of the main form.

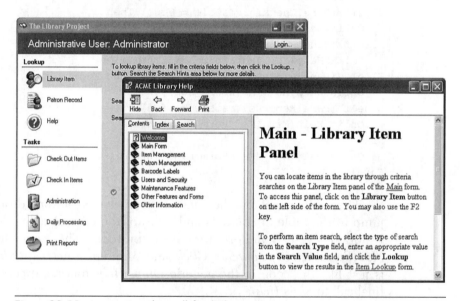

Figure 23-11 Answering the call for help

Speaking of correctly configuring the *.chm* files, we still have to figure out how to get the entire application—including the online help files—onto the client workstation, and at a cost that will put food on the table. We'll look at these deployment issues in the next chapter.

DEPLOYMENT

Although Aesop lived thousands of years ago, he has much to tell us about software development. His story of the boy who cried wolf is a perfect example. It concerns a young shepherd boy who tricks the nearby villagers repeatedly by shouting, "Wolf!" when no such danger exists. The trick was good for a few laughs, but then the boy found out the consequences of his actions: He couldn't get any villagers to buy his sheep, and he had to eat them all by himself. Yuck! If only the boy had learned how to properly deploy his flock into the hands of the villagers instead of making up wolf-based lies, he would never have come to such a tragic end.

So Aesop clearly shows us how important deployment is. And Microsoft took this lesson to heart by including several different options right in Visual Studio that let you install your compiled applications and supporting files onto a target workstation. We'll look at these methods in this chapter, and use one of the methods to build a Setup program for the Library Project.

What's Involved in Deployment?

In the days before Microsoft Windows, deployment wasn't so difficult. Many programs were nothing more than an MS-DOS executable file, with perhaps one or two supporting data and help files. That was it. Once you copied those files into some folder on the client workstation and updated the PATH environment variable, you were done.

Microsoft Windows applications (and large and complex MS-DOS programs) were not as easy to install. They often had these DLL file things hanging off of them—files that had to be put in the proper places. And sometimes you didn't know what that proper place was, because a third-party vendor may have supplied the DLL without sufficient documentation. Then there were the help files, the configuration files, supporting data files, user-specific and workstation-specific changes to the system registry, shortcuts on the desktop and in the *Start* menu, uninstall settings and programs, two sets of forms (in triplicate) to the Library of Congress, online help files, the readme and license agreement files for the distribution CD, special fonts that may be required for the program, and on and on and on.

I don't think I even included half the files you need to deploy a full-bodied Windows application, but you can already see how involved it is. Fortunately, Visual Studio will share the burden with you in exchange for some simple configuration on your part.

The deployment features in Visual Studio provide you with the basic features you need to distribute standard desktop and web-based applications. If your deployment needs are complex, you can also purchase a third-party setup and deployment tool that includes advanced features such as scripting support.

Deployment Methods within Visual Studio

With the early releases of Visual Basic, if you wanted to install your custom software using a setup program, you either had to write it yourself or use a purchased tool. Deployment tools did eventually appear in Visual Basic, especially the infamous "Package and Deployment Wizard." This canned setup program was written in Visual Basic, and you could enhance it to meet your own custom deployment needs. But it wasn't easy. And the rest of the world was already adopting the new "Windows Installer" platform for standardized deployment via ".msi" files. The Package and Deployment Wizard used the older ".cab" file format. Even for someone like me who actually enjoyed programming, the need to write effective installation programs sometimes made life ugly.

When Visual Basic .NET 2002 came out, life became beautiful again. Visual Studio included tools that let you target the Windows Installer technology, just like the big boys used. Sure, it was a stripped-down version that only let you release the simplest of applications, but third-party vendors have to have some fun.

These days, Visual Studio includes several deployment methods, a tribute to the different types of applications, the different types of users, and the different types of secure environments that a programmer may need to target. Read through each of the available methods to see which one best meets the needs of your program. I've already made my selection for the

Library Project, which I'll reveal in a public ceremony about halfway through this chapter.

Direct ASP.NET Deployment

ASP.NET applications are clearly different from desktop applications. One big difference is that, for the final user, ASP.NET applications don't really have any deployment. You just browse to the right web site and you're using the application. But there is still deployment needed for the hosting web server.

If your web server has Microsoft FrontPage Extensions installed, you can install a compiled ASP.NET application right from the comfort and safety of your development environment. I just glossed over it back in Chapter 22, "Web Development," but Visual Studio presents you with the option to put a web application on a real live web site when you first try to create the ASP.NET application. In the *New Web Site* form, you can select an HTTP URL as the development location, as shown in Figure 24-1.

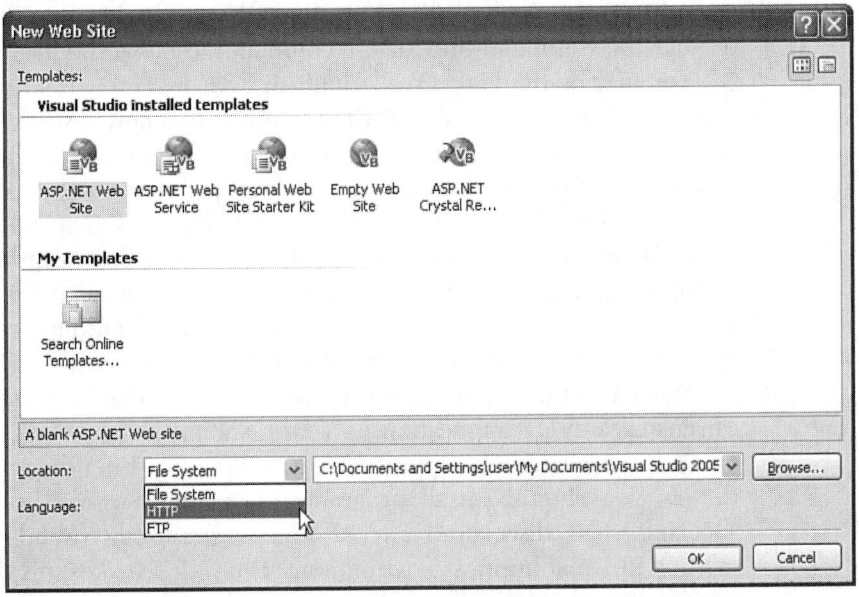

Figure 24-1 Getting an early start on that web site

Because you will be interactively developing your web site, you might not want to use this method on a production server. Instead, you can develop locally in a directory or on a development web server, and then later *publish* the site to the production server. This is just as easy as setting the HTTP location from the start. With the web site open in Visual Studio, select the **Build ➤ Publish Web Site** menu command, and specify the URL of the new web site. No separate setup program is required.

ASP.NET is careful about how it handles the files in your application. It will not publish your source code. It will copy your *web.config* file to the server (it's a required file), which may contain your database connection string. But a properly configured ASP.NET web server will keep this file from prying eyes.

XCopy Deployment

Compiled .NET assemblies contain a manifest that fully describes the assembly and its needs. This means that you can copy any assembly to another system that has the correct version of the .NET Framework installed, and as long as the other files the assembly needs are copied as well, the program will run. This is called "XCopy deployment" because you can use the command-line *XCopy* command to move the files.

You may be thinking, "Well, duh! An EXE assembly is a real Windows program. Of course it will run when I copy it to a new system." Well that's true. But it wasn't true for older Visual Basic applications. The ActiveX controls used by COM-based Visual Basic applications had to be registered in the Windows Registry before they could be accessed at runtime. Older Visual Basic programs also required that the Visual Basic runtime libraries be installed. The .NET Framework must also be installed for .NET programs, but because the Framework is managed automatically by the Windows Update system, this is not as big of a headache.

What I've taken too many sentences to say is that in most cases, you can install a .NET application on a workstation just by copying the program, and maybe a few support files, to a directory. I'm not saying that this is how you should install programs. Actually, I would be shocked—shocked!—if I discovered any of my programming friends using this method in a real business environment. But .NET makes this deployment option available to you if you don't want to be my friend anymore.

If you do use XCopy deployment, you probably won't have any issues with security or administrative limitations that may be imposed on the workstation. Chances are, if you're installing software using the *XCopy* command, or by dragging-and-dropping files, it's probably because you are friends with the owner of the workstation, and it's really none of my business who you want to have as your friends.

Windows Installer Deployment

Windows Installer is the official installation system provided by Microsoft. It serves as the base system for standard Visual Studio-generated installation packages, and also provides the underpinnings for most popular third-party installation tools.

Before Windows Installer, each installation package vendor pretty much did things as they saw fit. But this meant that installed products sometimes clobbered each other, because one software package didn't necessarily look out for files installed by another tool. Repairing such damage was difficult for the user, who usually didn't even know which files were installed or updated.

Microsoft sought to change that with Windows Installer. One of the key features of the system is its database of updated and installed files. It also supports a full uninstall/restore and rollback capability, so that any failure can be fully undone, restoring the system to its previous state. Other features include support for patching, rebooting, custom enhancements, some limited user interface and prompt design, the ability to repair or "heal" a previously installed but damaged program, and install-on-demand, which keeps features or full applications on the installation media until the user tries to use that feature.

Windows Installer version 3.x is the latest version for Windows XP and other parallel Windows systems. (You can still get version 2.x for some older Windows systems, like Windows 98.) Windows Vista will introduce version 4.x of the installer technology.

The heart of the Windows Installer system is the MSI file (with an *.msi* file extension), the single file that contains all the files and instructions needed to install, update, and uninstall a software product. Visual Studio can create Setup projects based on the MSI standard, although you can't use some of the more advanced features of Windows Installer through Visual Studio. Still, if your needs are simple—and most business-level software written in Visual Basic has simple installation needs—Visual Studio is probably all you need.

Building a setup project is just as easy as creating regular Visual Studio development projects. But first, I need something to set up. For the discussion in this section, I've created a desktop application. Well, not a very good one. I simply created a new *WindowsApplication1* project with its default *Form1*, and saved it to my *C:\temp* folder. All it does when you run it is display *Form1*.

To create an MSI installation file for a Visual Basic project, open that project in Visual Studio, and use the **File ➤ Add ➤ New Project** menu command to add a setup project to the entire solution that contains your original project. Figure 24-2 shows the *Add New Project* dialog. Select the **Setup and Deployment** project type, and then the **Setup Wizard** template to create a setup program for the active project. Set the **Name** and **Location** fields according to your needs, and then click **OK**.

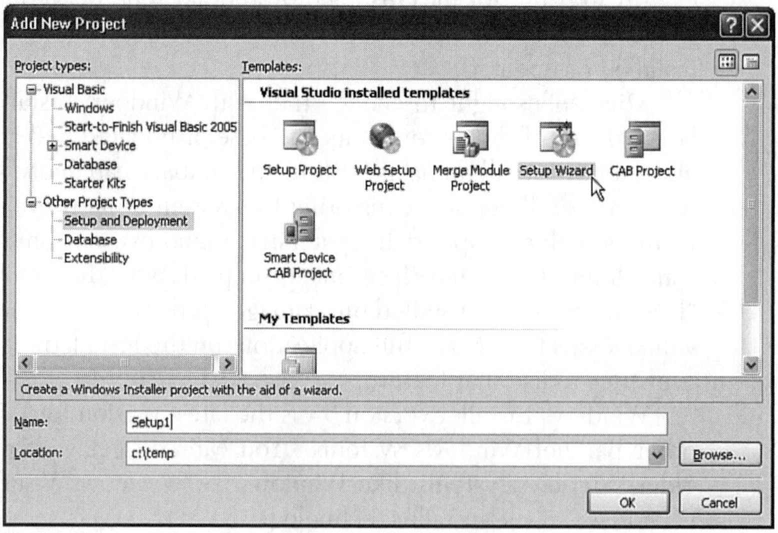

Figure 24-2 Adding a setup project to your solution

The *Setup Wizard* appears, leading you through five steps to peace, harmony, and a working MSI file.

Step 1

The first wizard step just says "Welcome," so click **Next** and get on with the real work.

Step 2

Step 2 asks you for the type of setup project to generate. Personally, I think it could have figured this out from the content of the already loaded projects, but if the wizard did everything, why would the world need programmers like us? There are four choices, shown in Figure 24-3.

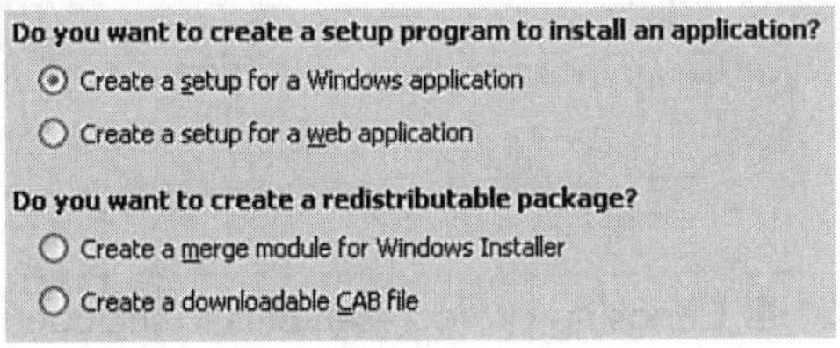

Do you want to create a setup program to install an application?
- ◉ Create a setup for a Windows application
- ○ Create a setup for a web application

Do you want to create a redistributable package?
- ○ Create a merge module for Windows Installer
- ○ Create a downloadable CAB file

Figure 24-3 Choosing the type of setup program

The first two choices create full setup files for either desktop or web-based applications. (The web-based setup would be delivered to a web site administrator for installation on the server.) *Merge modules* let you create a portion of an installation that can later be merged into a full MSI file. This is a good choice if you are designing a library that will be used for multiple applications, but it's useless on its own. The CAB file option creates an archive of files that can be installed using slightly older file distribution technology. It's also the distribution system used for handheld devices. Because I'm targeting a desktop application, I'll choose **Create a setup for a Windows application** and click **Next**.

Step 3

While you can create a setup program that simply installs miscellaneous files scavenged from your hard disk, you usually build a setup project based on the files or compiled output of other projects. The third wizard step prompts you to include elements from the other projects found in the active Visual Studio solution. I've chosen to include the compiled EXE file from my desktop project, as shown in Figure 24-4.

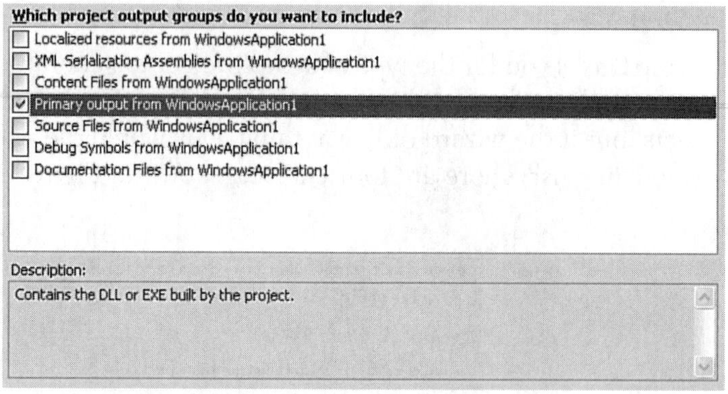

Which project output groups do you want to include?
- [ ] Localized resources from WindowsApplication1
- [ ] XML Serialization Assemblies from WindowsApplication1
- [ ] Content Files from WindowsApplication1
- [x] Primary output from WindowsApplication1
- [ ] Source Files from WindowsApplication1
- [ ] Debug Symbols from WindowsApplication1
- [ ] Documentation Files from WindowsApplication1

Description:
Contains the DLL or EXE built by the project.

Figure 24-4 Choosing project elements to include in the setup

I generally don't want to include my source code in the Setup project, so I'll leave that element unchecked. But the "Content Files" item may be useful. If my project had a compiled online help file (with a *.chm* file extension), I could have added it as a standard content file to the main project via the **Project ➤ Add Existing Item** menu command. That file would be classified as Content, and could move into this Setup project through the "Content Files" selection. But there are other ways to include online help in the installation, which we'll see in the next step. For now, I'll stick with the "Primary output" selection, and click the **Next** button.

Step 4

In this step, you can add any additional non-project-specific files you want to the setup project (see Figure 24-5). "Readme" files, online help content, license agreements, pictures of your kids, and pretty much anything else can be included here. I've got nothing more to add. Click **Next**.

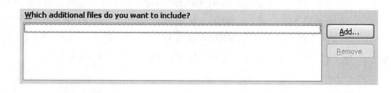

Which additional files do you want to include?

| | Add... |
| | Remove |

Figure 24-5 Add those other files that have always wanted a chance at Setup project stardom

Step 5

The final step displays a summary of the choices you made (see Figure 24-6). Well, that wizard was pretty easy. We had to do work in only three of the five steps. Click **Finish** to complete the wizard.

> Summary:
>
> Project type: Create a setup for a Windows application
>
> Project groups to include:
>   Primary output from WindowsApplication1
>
> Additional files: (none)
>
> Project Directory: c:\temp\Setup1\Setup1.vdproj

Figure 24-6 Confirming our choices for the setup project

After the Wizard

Once the wizard completes, the primary interface for Visual Studio setup project design appears in the development window. Figure 24-7 shows Visual Studio displaying the newly generated setup project for *WindowsApplication1*, another project that also appears in the *Solution Explorer* panel.

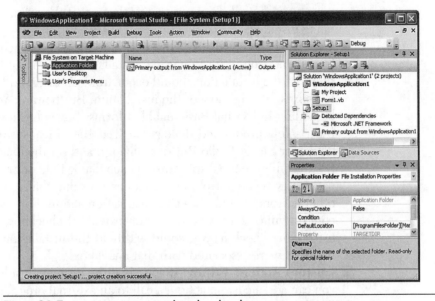

Figure 24-7 A setup project within the development environment

The main window in Figure 24-7 is one of several "editors" that let you customize the setup project. You can access each editor through the **View ➤ Editors** menu command, or by using the toolbar buttons in the *Solution Explorer* panel.

- **File System Editor.** That's the editor you already saw in Figure 24-7. It presents a standard folder/item view of portions of the target system's file system. Through this hierarchy, you place files (the EXE output from your main project, help files, configuration files, shortcuts to any of these files, etc.) into special folders (Application Folder, User Desktop, Program Files, Fonts, the Start Menu folder, and others). If you don't see a folder you want in the *File System on Target Machine* panel, use the **Action ➤ Add Special Folder** menu command to include it in the list. Besides the standard special folders, the **Add Special Folder** menu includes a **Custom Folder** option that lets you create a specific folder anywhere on the target system.

- **Registry Editor.** This editor displays a truncated hierarchy of the registry hives. Any keys or values added here will be created in the user's registry during installation.

- **File Types Editor.** This editor lets you define associations between a file extension (such as ".txt") and specific programs or actions. Any custom action, such as Open or Print, can be linked to any command text you wish, including commands that target the primary assembly being installed.

- **User Interface Editor.** The default setup project includes a few forms that prompt for things like installation location and confirmation that the installation should occur. You can insert additional dialog boxes into the flow of the installation. But beware: You will not be adding full Visual Basic-enabled forms. Instead, you will choose from a few predefined dialogs (such as the "License Agreement" dialog, or the "4 Radio Buttons" dialog), and set the dialog properties to configure the display text of each dialog field or prompt. Each user entry field/control includes a named value that you use in the other editors to limit a specific installation action. For instance, you could monitor the value of a user-prompted checkbox, and if the user didn't check it, you could withhold the installation of certain files that were associated with that checkbox.

- **Custom Actions Editor.** If you need the ultimate level of control, you can add a custom action, a call to an external program or script, that runs at a certain point in the install (or uninstall) process.

■ **Launch Conditions Editor.** If the target workstation must be in a certain state before you can successfully install the project, this editor lets you define the limiting conditions. By default, the installer adds the .NET Framework as an installation condition; the Framework must be installed before the project can be installed. You can look for specific files or registry keys that must be present before installation begins. For instance, you might want to confirm that the target database drivers are on the system before you install a database-dependent application.

Generating the MSI File

Once you've set up your project through the various editors, you output the final MSI file by building the solution (via the **Build ➤ Build Solution** menu command). The MSI file appears in the location specified in the setup project's properties (**Project ➤ Properties**). This file contains all the instructions and content required to fully install the application on the target workstation.

ClickOnce Deployment

Visual Studio 2005 includes a new deployment method called *ClickOnce*. It is designed to provide the ultimate in setup deployment ease for desktop (Windows Forms) applications. It still involves a wizard, darn it, but for basic installations, that's all there is to it. Once your application is "published" through ClickOnce, the user can install it directly from a web site or other stored location.

This sounds like a standard MSI installation, but it is different in several ways:

■ ClickOnce deployments can be installed even if the current user does not have local administrative privileges. Many software installs affect key files in the *Windows* and *Windows\System32* folders, or in other important but restricted folders. If you are a developer, it's likely that you never experience this problem because you are the administrator on your own workstation. But in IT department-managed organizations with many users, there is a benefit in reducing the privilege level of individual users. One negative side effect of this is that an administrator must be present to install any software. But that's not the case with ClickOnce. Is your entire IT department out to lunch? (I mean that literally.) No problem. Any

ClickOnce-published application can be installed by any user. The software is installed in a "sandbox" that protects the system and other applications from the ClickOnce-installed program's villainous intents.

■ A ClickOnce-deployed application can trigger its own automatic software updates. If configured in this way, the program will check the original deployment location for a new version each time it runs. If there is a new version, it will be installed automatically without the user having to do a thing.

■ ClickOnce applications are designed for ease of installation. With an MSI-deployed application, you need to download the MSI file and process it through the Windows Installer system. Although you also have to download a ClickOnce deployment, it happens more or less transparently. A ClickOnce-published application can be configured so that it looks like an extension of a web page: Click a link, and the program immediately runs, displaying its main form to the user. (There may be some delay as the program is downloaded over the Internet.)

That sounds great. But it's not all peaches and cream. Because ClickOnce-enabled applications (by default) run in their own sandbox, they are limited in their access to some local resources. Also, to fully support all of the automatic-updating features, you must add additional code to your application that performs the actual update. (The *My.Application.Deployment* property provides access to these features.)

To deploy your project via ClickOnce, use the **Build ➤ Publish** menu command in Visual Studio. After asking you some very basic questions about where the user will obtain the deployment file (from a web site, a network folder, or a CD/DVD), Visual Studio generates the installation file and makes it immediately available for use.

Of course, that method only gives you the most basic installation options. It makes the primary EXE or DLL of your project (and its dependencies) available for installation on the target workstation, but that's about it. If you want more control over the publishing process and the components it will include, use the *Publish* tab of your project's properties, as shown in Figure 24-8.

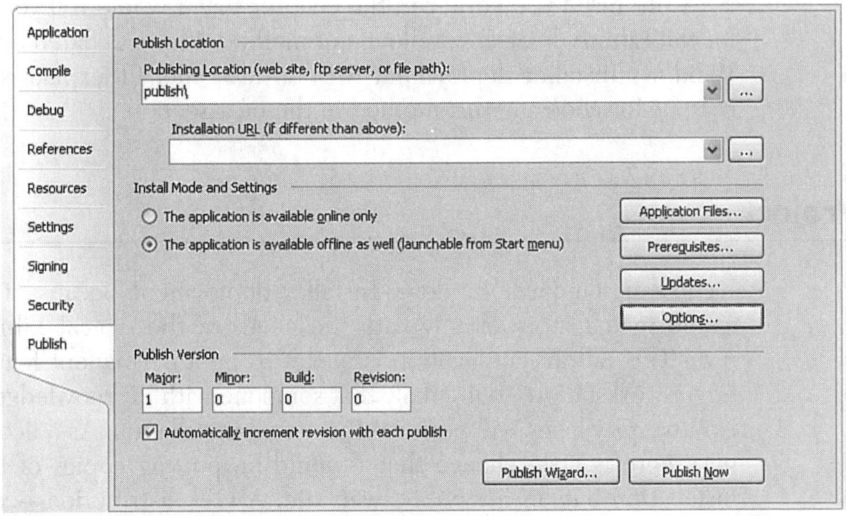

Figure 24-8 The world of publishing just a mouse click away

This panel includes fields that let you set the version number for the published installation package. If you modify this version number and republish the application, the custom deployment code you added to the application can detect the new version and initiate an update from the distribution location.

Summary

It's really nice that Visual Studio provides a few different deployment methods for your custom applications. Visual Basic and the larger Visual Studio environment were designed as general-purpose programming systems that allow you to solve almost any development problem facing you or your users. But that doesn't mean that every single feature in the system is applicable to all environments. By having a few different deployment options available, Visual Studio is even more general-purpose that before, and I think that's just great. Sure you have to take five minutes and decide between MSI and ClickOnce. But in most projects, the needs of the users will push you in one direction or the other.

I promised you earlier in the chapter that I would tell you my choice for the Library Project's deployment method. I have decided on a standard Windows Installer deployment with an MSI file. I'll explain some of my reasons for choosing this method in the next section.

Project

I chose a standard Windows Installer deployment because I thought it would match more closely with the needs of the typical Library system user. The Library application is meant to be a permanent feature on the target workstation, so it's likely that someone with IT knowledge or administrative privileges will perform the actual installation. As a licensed product, there is little chance that I would be putting copies of the Library installation out on my public web site. A CD distribution—common for MSI installations—is the expected medium. Also, because it's a quality piece of software from a trusted vendor (that's me), there isn't a need for a protective sandbox. Still, the application does include several files, including two online help files, so an *XCopy* installation would be a burden. All in all, a standard MSI installation is the best deployment plan.

Planning the Deployment

The Setup Wizard automatically adds my project assembly to the MSI file, but I am sure there are other files needed to properly deploy the Library Project. A quick look through the previous chapters reveals the following list of file requirements:

- **The .NET Framework 2.0.** This must be installed on the target system to run the Library application. The Setup program will need to automatically install the Framework if it isn't already on the target system. (If you are a .NET release junkie, you probably already know that the .NET Framework 3.0 is the same as version 2.0, but with the features formally known as *WinFX* also included. So you can have the MSI file require version 3.0 if you want.)
- **Library.exe.** This is the primary assembly. The install would be useless without it.
- **LibraryBasic.chm** and **LibraryAdmin.chm.** These online help files will be installed in the same folder as the primary application.

- **The barcode font.** If you have obtained distribution rights for a barcode font, your Setup program can copy it directly to the target system's *Fonts* folder.
- **LibraryLicense.lic.** Ah, the license file. Remember, this hand-generated file needs to be custom-crafted for each customer purchasing the Library application. Compiling it directly into the Setup program seems extreme, because I would have to regenerate Setup for each customer. Instead, I will put the file on the distribution media (the CD), and have the user locate it when running the Library program.
- **ACME Library Resource Kit.pdf.** This administrator-level file shouldn't be installed by default on a workstation. It will remain on the distribution CD instead.
- **Database Creation Script.sql.** If I was developing a full end-user application, I would build a separate setup system for the server portion, focusing mainly on the database setup. Because this book is designed as an introduction only, I will just copy the database build script to the distribution CD, and assume that a qualified Information Technology representative or database administrator will take charge of this installation step.
- **The Library web site.** As with the database creation script, I am just going to copy the web site files to the CD and let the administrator figure things out.
- **Readme.htm.** The CD should include an informational file right at the root that will tell the user how to use the files on the CD. I haven't written this file yet, but I will before the chapter ends.

The generated Setup file will include only the first four items in that list (three if you are excluding the font), and the first two are added automatically by the Setup Wizard. This won't be too difficult.

Building the Setup Project

Earlier in the chapter, we added a new Setup project to an existing project, combining them into a single solution. It is possible to build a Setup project that appears alone within Visual Studio. In such projects, you need to browse for the target assembly (*release\Library.exe*) to include it in the Setup output. However, the Setup Wizard doesn't do much for you if you go that route. So for the Library project, let's add a new Setup project to a Library project already loaded into Visual Studio.

Project Access Load the "Chapter 23 (After) Code" project, either through the New Project templates, or by accessing the project directly from the installation directory. Then save the project to a folder where you want to build the complete Setup solution. I have also included a "Chapter 24" folder in the installation directory, but not as a project template. This folder already contains a linked Setup project. If you want to view this finished solution, open the *Library.sln* file in the "Chapter 24" folder.

The first few steps parallel those we performed earlier in the chapter. Once you have the Library project loaded and saved to its target folder, add a new Setup project using the **File ➤ Add ➤ New Project** menu command. Select "Setup Wizard" as the template, enter "LibrarySetup" for the **Name**, and use the just-saved Library project's folder as the **Location**. Apply the following settings within the wizard.

- In Step 2, select **Create a setup for a Windows application**.
- In Step 3, select "Primary output from Library" from the list.
- In Step 4, locate and add the *LibraryBasic.chm* and *LibraryAdmin.chm* files. In this book's installation directory, you can find them in the subdirectory named *Online Help*.

Complete the wizard and use the **File ➤ Save All** menu command. When prompted to save the solution file (*Library.sln*), just store it in the Library project directory, which should already be selected.

As before, the Setup project opens to the *File System Editor*. Before making any changes within the editor, let's set some Setup-wide properties. Click on "LibrarySetup" in the *Solution Explorer* panel, and modify the following properties in the *Properties* panel.

- Set the *Author* property to "Tim Patrick" or your own name.
- Set the *Manufacturer* property to "ACME."
- Set the *ManufacturerURL* property to "http://www.timaki.com" or any web site you wish to use.
- Set the *ProductName* property to "ACME Library."
- Set the *Title* property to "ACME Library Setup."

Because the *File System Editor* is open, let's make a few changes there. When we added the *Library.exe* assembly through the wizard, it figured out all of the required dependencies. Not only do the main program and help file items appear in the "Application Folder" section, but three additional DLLs appear, all used to run the library reports (see Figure 24-9).

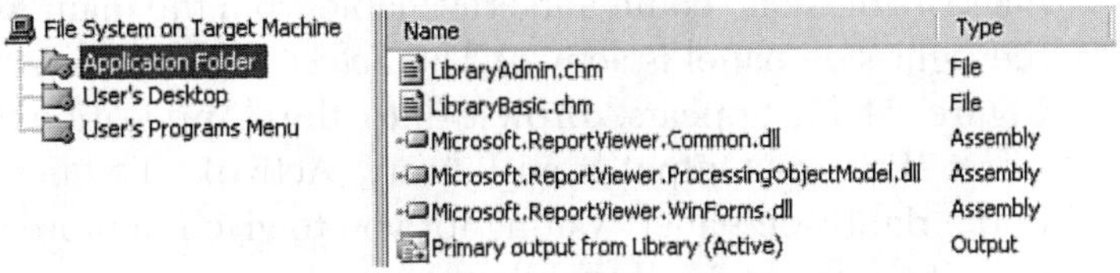

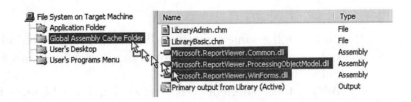

Figure 24-9 A lot more files than we bargained for

Because these three DLLs are supplied by Microsoft as part of .NET, it doesn't make much sense to store them in my own application's installation directory. They should go in the Global Assembly Cache, the special system folder that maintains shared .NET assemblies. The Global Assembly Cache isn't one of the folder choices displayed in the editor, but it can be. Make sure that the left-hand panel of the *File System Editor* is selected (the one with "File System on Target Machine"), and then use the **Action ➤ Add Special Folder ➤ Global Assembly Cache Folder** menu command. A new folder, "Global Assembly Cache Folder," appears in the left-side panel. Select the "Application Folder" item again, and then drag the three DLL items into the new Global Assembly Cache Folder item, as shown in Figure 24-10.

Figure 24-10 Make the three DLL files someone else's responsibility

Let's add two shortcuts to the user's system during installation: one on the desktop and one in the *Start* menu's *Programs* section. Both shortcuts point to the main *Library.exe* assembly. The Setup wizard anticipated our needs to adding the "User's Desktop" and "User's Program Menu" folders to the *File System Editor*. All we have to do is add a shortcut to each folder.

Let's start with the desktop. Select the "User's Desktop" folder, and then right-click in the right-side panel (where the files would appear). From the context menu, choose the **Create New Shortcut** menu command. (This same command is available from the main **Action** menu when the right-side panel is active.) The *Select Item in Project* dialog, shown in Figure 24-11, appears. Browse into the "Application Folder" item and select "Primary Output from Library (Active)." The new shortcut appears in the right-side panel, waiting for you to give it a more meaningful name. Give it the name "ACME Library."

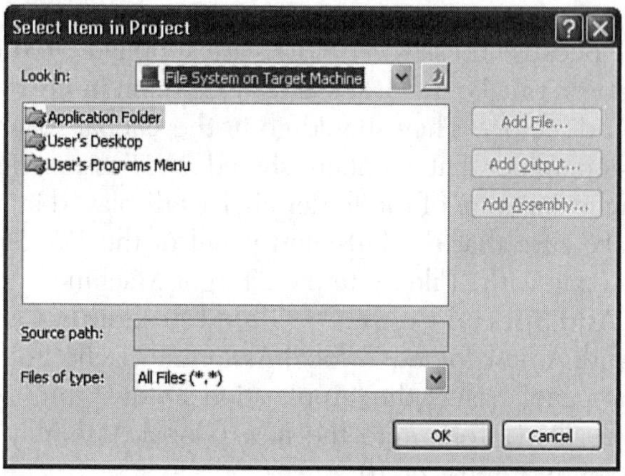

Figure 24-11 Adding a new shortcut to a target file system folder

To create the same shortcut in the *Start* menu, follow all the steps in the previous paragraph, but start from the "User's Programs Menu" folder instead of the "User's Desktop" folder.

Adding those shortcuts was a good idea, but whenever I install new software, I always immediately delete any shortcut that was added to the desktop. Adding an icon to the *Start* menu's *Programs* folder makes sense, but I like keeping a nice, clean desktop. Laugh if you want, but keeping that desktop free from clutter is what helps make me a world-famous author and developer.

What we need is a way to alter the behavior of the Setup program so that it doesn't create the desktop icon if the user doesn't want one. The Setup project provides a way to do this. First, we need to add a prompt where the user indicates a desktop-icon preference, and then we need to act on that preference. The first step involves altering the user interface of the Setup program. Such changes occur through the *User Interface Editor*. Display this editor with the **View ➤ Editor ➤ User Interface** menu command. The *User Interface Editor* appears in Figure 24-12.

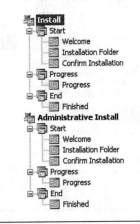

Figure 24-12 The user interface editor displays each dialog and each prompt.

The User Interface is divided into two main installation types: "Install" and "Administrative Install." The administrative branch is only used when an administrator wants to store the setup image on a shared network folder. It doesn't allow the type of changes we want to make. So let's focus on the standard "Install" branch, which manages standard user installations on a client workstation. Both branches include step-by-step prompts that appear to the user during the setup process. Custom data collection prompts can only be added to the "Start" entry in the "Install" main branch.

During actual setup, the user interface prompts the user in a wizard-like fashion. During the initial "Start" phase, the Setup program collects the user's desires for the remainder of the process. Once this section completes, installation proceeds until it completes or fails. What we want to do is insert a new step in the wizard process, displaying a checkbox to the user that asks whether the desktop icon should appear or not. Additional data collection fields like these are added through new "dialogs." And there just happens to be a dialog that includes a customizable checkbox. In the "Install" branch, right-click on the "Start" item, and select **Add Dialog** from the context menu. The *Add Dialog* window, shown in Figure 24-13, displays the available dialogs. Select the "Checkboxes (A)" item from the list and click **OK**.

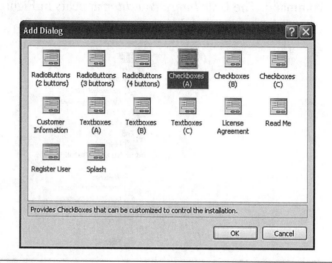

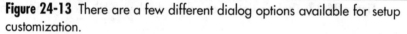

Figure 24-13 There are a few different dialog options available for setup customization.

The new "Checkboxes (A)" item appears in the "Install/Start" section. Use the mouse to drag it up until it appears between the "Welcome" and "Installation Folders" dialogs. The Checkboxes dialog lets you display up to four checkbox selections with custom captions. Make sure it is selected in the dialog outline, and then use the *Properties* panel to set this new dialog's properties:

- Set the *BannerText* property to "Installation Options." This text appears near the top of the dialog window, displaying a large main title.
- Set the *BodyText* property to "Select the options you wish to use for this installation."
- Set the *Checkbox1Label* property to "Add an icon for ACME Library to the desktop." This defines the custom text for the first checkbox control.
- Set the *Checkbox1Property* property to "LIBRARY_DESKTOP_LINK." This gives the checkbox a name that we can use later to alter the install process.

- Set the *Checkbox1Value* property to "Checked." This defaults the installation to include the desktop icon.
- Set the *Checkbox2Visible*, *Checkbox3Visible*, and *Checkbox4Visible* properties to "False," hiding the other three unused checkboxes.

During the setup process, the user sees the new dialog prompt in Figure 24-14. It includes the banner text, the body text, and the single checkbox as configured in the custom dialog's properties.

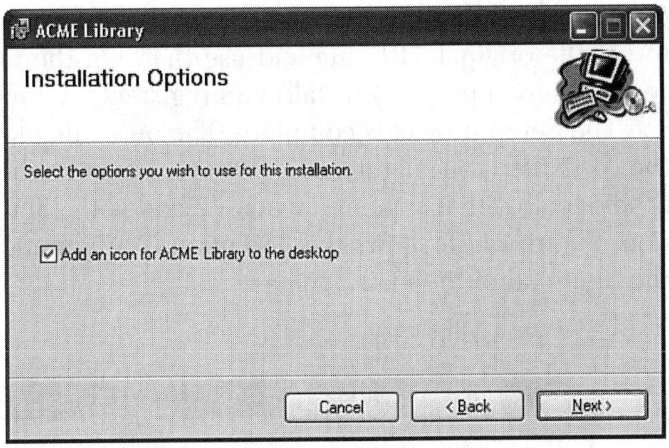

Figure 24-14 The sparse but useful checkbox dialog in action

Now it's time to use that checkbox setting. Close the *User Interface Editor* and return to the *File System Editor*. Select the "User's Desktop" folder in the left-side panel; then go to the *Properties* panel. One of the few listed properties is *Condition*, which lets you define a Boolean condition that, when true, installs the associated files on the user's desktop. However, if the condition is false, no associated files will be placed on the user's desktop during installation. Set this property to the following text.

```
LIBRARY_DESKTOP_LINK
```

This is the name we gave to the first checkbox back in the dialog design. During installation, the setup program checks the user's selection, and alters the desktop update as requested.

One thing I won't be adding to my version of the Setup program is the barcode font. Sadly, I have not acquired a license to distribute a third-party font to you or anyone else reading this book. The good news is that I just saved you $10 on the cost of the book. The bad news is that I will have to tell you how to add the font, but not actually do it.

Actually, you can probably already guess how to do it. The "Fonts" folder is one of the special folders available in the *File System Editor*. When the left-side panel is active, use the **Action ➤ Add Special Folder ➤ Fonts Folder** menu command. Then add the original font file (a TrueType ".ttf" file) to the "Fonts" folder section. You won't be able to add this font directly from your *Windows\Fonts* folder. Instead, you will need to get the original ".ttf" file and use that. On the target workstation, the setup program properly installs and registers the font for use in Windows.

The Setup project is complete. The only thing left to do is to generate the MSI file. You might have noticed a new control in the main Visual Studio toolbar that appeared when we added the Setup project to the solution. Figure 24-15 shows this "Solution Configurations" drop-down list at the right end of the main toolbar.

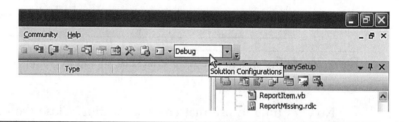

Figure 24-15 The Solution Configurations selector in the toolbar

This control is part of the Configuration Management system built into Visual Studio. It lets you set up different compilation and release scenarios for internal and public use. By default, Visual Studio always creates a "Debug" and "Release" configuration for you. The Debug configuration includes the necessary files and components that enable full debugging of your application. These extras are, of course, missing from the Release configuration. Normally, you use the Release configuration when building your Setup project because you don't want your customer poking around in the debuggable source code. Now would be a great time to choose "Release" from this tool.

It's time to build the MSI file. Right-click on the "LibrarySetup" root in the *Solution Explorer* panel, and select **Build** from the context menu. In just a few seconds, your MSI file will be baked and ready to eat. You'll find it in the Setup project's *Release* subdirectory. This directory also includes a *Setup.exe* file that acts as a bootstrapper. Any workstation with the Windows Installer system present will work with just the plain MSI file, but providing a *Setup.exe* file may add a level of comfort to novice users.

The Distribution Media

I hate it when users come over to my office and try to copy the MSI file directly from my hard drive. I find that providing the file on a CD tends to improve the vendor-customer relationship. So let's build a CD for client use.

The distribution CD contains all of the content needed by the library IT staff to support the application. It contains distinct directories for each type of content. Here's what I am planning to put in the root of the CD.

- **Readme.htm.** An HTML file that displays information about the contents of the CD.
- **Database.** A directory containing the database creation script, *Database Creation Script.sql*.
- **License.** A directory containing the specific user's license file, *LibraryLicense.lic*.
- **Setup.** A directory containing the main MSI file, *LibrarySetup.msi*.
- *Technical*. A directory containing the technical support documentation, *ACME Library Resource Kit.pdf*.
- **Web.** A directory containing the full source code for the Library web site that we created in Chapter 22. The administrator can use this as the basis for an expanded Library web site.

I've put all these directories and their files in the book's installation directory, in a subdirectory named *Library CD Contents*.

The *Readme.htm* file contains the following administrator-friendly content.

ACME Library 1.0

Welcome to the ACME Library system. This product was developed as part of the *Start-to-Finish Visual Basic 2005* book project, written by Tim Patrick. When installed and configured properly, the application should give you years of library management value.

This installation CD includes the following folders:

- **Database**—The *Database Creation Script.sql* file contains a SQL Server script that you can use to build a new ACME Library database.
- **License**—The *LibraryLicense.lic* file contains the license for your site. Once you have installed the Library application on a workstation, copy the license file to that workstation. Using the Library application, log in as an administrator. You will be prompted for the license file path at that time.
- **Setup**—The *LibrarySetup.msi* file performs a standard client installation of the Library product.
- **Technical**—The *ACME Library Resource Kit.pdf* file contains technical information about the ACME Library system, its configuration files, and its database.
- **Web**—This directory contains a sample ASP.NET web-based application that you can modify to allow patrons to interact with the ACME Library database through a web browser.

This CD and its contents are Copyright © 2006 by Tim Patrick.

I want this file to appear automatically when the user inserts the CD into the workstation drive. This requires one additional file named "autorun.inf" at the root of the CD. This simple INI-style file supports the

Auto Run feature used by Windows CDs. Here is the content of the file that will display the *Readme.htm* file automatically.

```
[Autorun]
Open=explorer.exe Readme.htm
```

Copying all of these directories and files to a CD and adding a pretty label should result in a happy librarian.

We're quickly approaching the end of the book. Only one chapter remains. Turn the page to find out what exciting content you'll find there.

Project Complete

You've done it! You've completed the Library Project and met with acclaim from users and fellow programmers alike. And you've also accomplished something that few thought was possible: You slogged through all 25 chapters of this book. You're probably anxious to get on with your life as a highly-paid software consultant, working just six months per year as the programmer who other programmers call when systems fail. Well, I won't keep you too long. But there are a few more issues to discuss concerning the Library Project and programming in general.

The Library Project

The Library Project is filled with features that target small library-style organizations. But it may not meet the needs of everyone. And that's okay. The users know your address and phone number; you'll hear from them. When they call, you can tell them that the software wasn't designed for everyone; no software can be. All software, even general-purpose applications such as Visual Studio, can never meet the needs of every person or organization. What is important is that the features included in the project meet the needs of the intended audience. That audience may be the card-catalog-using public, or it may just be a small library with one part-time staff member.

Still, there is always room for improvement. Because the Library Project's real target audience was you—the student of Visual Basic and .NET—it did not have all the features that most libraries would require. Looking quickly back through the source code, I came up with at least the following changes that could be made to the project to bring a lot more value to library administrators and users.

- **Error logging.** The application includes rudimentary error detection and handling features, but they could definitely be improved. The logging feature used in the application's *GeneralError* method (which includes a call to *My.Application.Log.WriteException*) sends the written content to any registered log listener. We just used the default listeners, but we could have added listeners to centrally collect error reports and details in a database or file for later analysis.

- **Error handling.** When an error does occur, most of the Library code simply reports the error and moves on. Some methods ignore errors completely. In general, the code could do a better job of processing error results. Some errors are more fatal than others, and specific errors should include additional options that the user can access to better recover from the fault.

- **Multi-threading.** We did not discuss or take advantage of any of the threading features included in the .NET Framework. Processor-intensive activities tend to kill the responsiveness of the user interface, but there are ways of mitigating the impact. In the Library Project, two specific areas would benefit from the use of background worker threads, by either using the features of the *System.Threading* namespace directly, or by using the *BackgroundWorker* control: (1) searching for library items through the *ItemLookup* form; and (2) processing overdue and fine data for a single day at all locations through the *MainForm.ActDoProcess_Click* event handler.

- **User interface and presentation.** Although I included some cute graphics on the main Library Project form and the *Splash* form, I didn't do much beyond that. Mostly it was an issue of time and effort, but I also have very little talent for the graphic arts. The program could use an update in its general look and presentation. And with the new graphics features built into Windows Vista, you could enable some really amazing effects with little programming effort.

- **User interface consistency.** Although I tried to be careful, there are probably labels, controls, and error messages that use two different names for the same thing. Perhaps I used the word "book" or "DVD" when I should have used the more general term "item."

Although tracking down such inconsistencies is a lot of work, it increases the level of professionalism in your application. It also makes the task of foreign-language translation easier when localizing the program.

■ **Testing new databases.** The *LocateDatabase.vb* form builds a connection string from the fields supplied by the user, but it does not test the connection to see if it works. Providing an option to test the entered values could reduce long-term errors. An even better option would be to let the user search for the database, similar to the way that SQL Server itself sniffs out and presents located servers and databases.

■ **Numeric title searches.** The check-out and check-in features let you locate an item either by name or by barcode. If you enter a number, the program assumes that you have entered a barcode and retrieves the matching item. But there are some book titles that are numeric. For instance, David McCullough's book *1776* would cause the program some difficulty if each copy did not include its own barcode. An enhancement to the program would provide the user additional disambiguation options when a numeric entry matched both a barcode and a title.

■ **Enhanced item searches.** Although I have much reason to be impressed by my item lookup code, the program could do so much more. When you use the card catalog systems at larger libraries, the lookup features include "proximity searches" that return results that are alphabetically close to the search terms provided by the user. SQL Server also has a "full text search" option that could be used to broaden the item lookups.

■ **Reserves and holds.** I started to add a "reserves" feature to the Library Project, so that patrons could add their names to a waiting list for checked-out library items, and have those items placed aside by the library staff when they were returned by the previous patron. Although this would be a cool and useful feature for a library, it didn't add any pedagogic value to the book, so I left it out. But I still hear the software sniffling and crying once in a while when it thinks of the feature that might have been. This would be a great enhancement for "version 2."

- **Incomplete item history.** On the *PatronRecord.vb* form, the *Fines* list shows a patron's previously checked-out library items only if those items had once been overdue and had incurred fines. Items that were returned on time cannot be displayed in the list using the current form logic. A satisfying change would add a "Show all returned items" checkbox that would include these checked-in items. This would allow a librarian to charge for things such as damage on items that were otherwise free of fines.

- **Return of missing items.** If an item is marked as missing, the library staff may charge the patron for the loss of the book. If the patron later returns that item, the librarian can process a reimbursement to the patron. But the program could make this task easier by automatically marking the item as eligible for such a refund. This would require a new status field on the *PatronCopy* database table to track this status.

- **Barcode design interaction.** The *BarcodeLabel.vb* form is, I think, pretty amazing with its graphic preview of the barcode. But the preview is unidirectional only; the user is not able to select a display element by clicking on that element in the preview. Instead, it is necessary to click on the related item in the *DisplayItems* list. Enhancing the program to detect clicks on the preview and translate those clicks into item selections would make the program much more like other applications that support basic drawing features.

- **Database setup features.** Although we built the setup program for the main Library application, we skimped on the server side, providing only the database creation scripts as text files on the installation media. A more professional system would provide a separate installation program that could build and configure a new database from an existing SQL Server installation.

- **Support for library standards.** Just as the software development world has standard formats and protocols, such as XML, library systems also share common standards. Two accepted standards are MARC (Machine-Readable Cataloging, a standard card catalog data format) and the Z39.50 interface (a communications protocol used for inter-computer searches and data retrieval). Incorporating these standards into a small library system may be overkill, but they would bring a much higher level of automation and convenience to the library staff.

- **Bug fixes.** I probably left a few bugs in the application. No, wait. I think I put them in there on purpose to test you, to see if you were learning and growing in your programming skills. Did you find them?

These are just some of the improvements that I thought of off the top of my head. If I had gone all the way down to my shoulders, I could have come up with even more. If your software will target the general population of users, you will probably release updates on a regular schedule, such as annually, and charge appropriately for the improved features. If you wrote the application for one specific customer, the updates may be more frequent, even weekly or daily in some cases. Whatever the audience size, your opportunities to improve and enhance the software will be regularly and ongoing.

Visual Basic Flexibility

I started using Visual Basic back when version 2.0 of the product was still in vogue. As a result, I picked up some pre-.NET coding habits that have been hard to break, even with my full-time focus on .NET code. I've reached a level of comfort in my Visual Basic coding, and that comfort shows in my .NET coding style.

As I mentioned in earlier chapters, many of the features that previously existed in Visual Basic before .NET were moved out of the language and into Framework classes. The most noticeable of these were the mathematics features now found in the *System.Math* class. But there were other non-math Visual Basic language keywords that also became class methods. Many of these appear in the *Microsoft.VisualBasic* namespace, including methods such as *Left*, *Trim*, and *MsgBox*.

When I wrote the Library Project code, I freely used some features found in the *Microsoft.VisualBasic* namespace. Although I don't have a problem with this practice, you may encounter other Visual Basic developers who don't agree with how I've written the code. They point out that most, and possibly all, of the features in *Microsoft.VisualBasic* have Framework Class Library equivalents, and these should be used for reasons of compatibility with other .NET languages and systems.

A key example is the *MsgBox* function. I've used it throughout the Library source code. The keyword *MsgBox* has always been a part of the Visual Basic language, but beyond its continued existence in *Microsoft.VisualBasic*, it is not a part of the Framework classes. Instead of *MsgBox*, other programmers (including C# programmers) use the *System.Windows.Forms.MessageBox.Show* method. It does offer more options than *MsgBox*, and it displays a message box that is every bit as beautiful as the Visual Basic version. But for me, my fingers have gotten used to typing the short six-character *MsgBox* keyword. (*MessageBox.Show* has 15 characters!) Also, the arguments passed to *MessageBox.Show* are slightly rearranged from those used in *MsgBox*. Using both of them in a single program could result in some confusion.

Supporters of *MessageBox.Show* emphasize that if you ever needed to convert Visual Basic code to C#, the presence of *MsgBox* would slow down the conversion. Although I understand this and other concerns, I have not yet been fully convinced that there is any problem using *MsgBox*. Any conversion tool that existed to change Visual Basic code into C# would certainly know how to handle *MsgBox*.

As another example, consider the older *Exit Sub* statement. It still exists in Visual Basic for .NET, but the new *Return* keyword performs the same job of immediately exiting from the current method. (*Return* had a different meaning in Visual Basic before .NET, but now it only exits methods.) You can use either *Exit Sub* or *Return* in your code; they are identical in functionality. There are programmers who consider the older *Exit Sub* statement to be—well—older.

But unlike my reticence to leave my favored *MsgBox* method, I have wholeheartedly embraced the new *Return* statement. If it was just an issue of *Exit Sub* versus *Return*, I might not have made the switch. But there is the related issue of *Exit Function* versus *Return*. I was never happy with the way that pre-.NET Visual Basic functions obtained their return values through an assignment statement to the name of the function. I was ready to make the switch to the newer *Return* statement. I did so for clarity; keeping the return value as close as possible to the statement that triggers the return to the calling code is a good thing. Before .NET, you might assign the return value, and then not leave the function for dozens of lines. Combining the assignment and the return in a single statement makes sense to me. From there, it was a short trip to replacing *Exit Sub* with *Return*. You will not find (I hope) a single *Exit Sub* statement in the Library Project. My transformation in this area is complete.

Why do I bring all this up? I do it to encourage you to make flexibility your friend when it comes to the different coding variations that exist in

Visual Basic. If two different ways of developing a block of code seem to be morally equivalent, and you can make the logic clear no matter which method you pick, then choose and enjoy the coding style that you are most comfortable with. Some programmers may tell you to do it one way or another, and that's okay. (If you are part of a development team, the entire team should agree on a common style.) Remember that Visual Basic is a "general purpose" programming language, and it has a certain amount of flexibility built into the language and related features. Experiment with the variations, and find patterns that you enjoy and that increase your effectiveness as a developer.

The Programming Mindset

As you enter deeper into the world of software development, you will quickly discover that the application-building process is about much more than syntax, statements, and logic. It is also about who you are as a programmer. The way you think about software, and the care with which you approach the task of programming, have a direct impact on the quality of the code you write. This is certainly true in other areas of life. If you are a portrait painter, but you don't take your strokes seriously, or if you are sloppy in your use of paints and brushes, it will show in the low quality of your work.

In one of my previous books, *The Visual Basic .NET Style Guide* (Upper Saddle River, NJ: Prentice Hall Professional Technical Reference, 2002), I wrote about three traits that provide a strong basis for the programming life, as follows:

- **Discipline.** The act of self-training with a goal of increasing order, focus, and quality in your projects and work ethic.
- **Planning.** The careful analysis and implementation of procedures and standards that scream out for quality.
- **Ethics.** The inner character drive that shows itself through public and private honesty in attitudes and actions.

If you are deficient in any of these three areas of your programming life, your applications and code will also be deficient by a similar factor. I have tried to sprinkle some humor and fun throughout the pages of this book. But on this point, I make no jokes. You need these three elements in your work life.

If you are serious about a career in software development, take the time to ask yourself questions that focus on these three aspects. Do I employ regular discipline on the way that I craft my software? Do I create reasonable and reliable plans, and then stick to them during a project? Do I exhibit ethical standards in the way I communicate with my customers, my employer, my coworkers, and even myself? If you are not able to answer these questions to your satisfaction, find resources that can help you overcome the lapses. It will make your programming work so much easier, and it will positively impact the other areas of your life as well.

Summary

Now you've really reached the end of the book. You can read through the appendices and the index if you're still hungry for more. But a better solution would be to find out if I've come out with the next edition of the book and buy it. Ha!

I thank you for taking the time to read through *Start-to-Finish Visual Basic 2005*. It was written so that you might expand your understanding and expertise of a very practical and very enjoyable subject: Visual Basic. And "enjoyable" is the key word. Nobody has to be a computer programmer, no matter what historians say. You should take on the role of a Visual Basic developer only if you truly take pleasure in helping other people become more productive through specialized or general software. If, even after reading this book, you find coding to be a bore and sheer drudgery, I recommend the food services industry as an alternative.

For those of you still excited about Visual Basic programming, have as much fun with it as possible. Microsoft is constantly updating the language and its Visual Studio shell so that you can really enjoy yourself as you program. Why do you think they put in all of those animation features? Take time to go beyond the mundane in your code and in your user interfaces. Challenge yourself by trying out new features within the language and in the Framework. And above all, smile each time you successfully complete a project. Your author, and your users, will thank you.

INSTALLING THE SOFTWARE

You are holding more than just a book. You are holding an idea. No wait, that's what you get when you hold a philosophy book. In this case, what you also get is software—free software. And it's all found on the publisher's web site for this book:

http://www.awprofessional.com/titles/0321398009

When you download and run the setup program provided on the web site, the following items are added to your system.

- A directory structure with all chapter-specific source code and documentation.
- A "vsi" file that installs a set of Visual Studio Project templates. Each template creates a new project based on "before" or "after" source code images for most chapters in the book. Once installed, you will have the option of accessing chapter-specific projects using the **File ➤ New Project** menu command in Visual Studio.
- A directory of "code snippets" that let you follow along with the action in each chapter's "Project" section, all without the need to retype every line of code printed in the book.

The installation requires approximately 50Mb of disk space. This appendix discusses the download and installation procedures.

Download the Software

To obtain the software for the book, browse to the book's web site:

http://www.awprofessional.com/titles/0321398009

Locate the Source Code link on this page and click it. When prompted, save the download file to your system using the standard file download features of your browser. You can save the file, named *Start-to-Finish Visual Basic 2005.exe*, to a temporary area of your system. Once you complete installation, this file will no longer be needed, unless you wish to retain it as a backup.

Install the Software

Double-click or run the downloaded *Start-to-Finish Visual Basic 2005.exe* file. When prompted, indicate the target directory to use for the installation of all project files. Once the files are extracted, a readme file appears describing the remaining installation steps.

Install Project Templates

One of the files installed in the target directory is named *Start-to-Finish Visual Basic 2005 Templates.vsi*. Double-click or open this file to install the project templates for the book. The *Visual Studio Content Installer* window appears, as shown in Figure A-1.

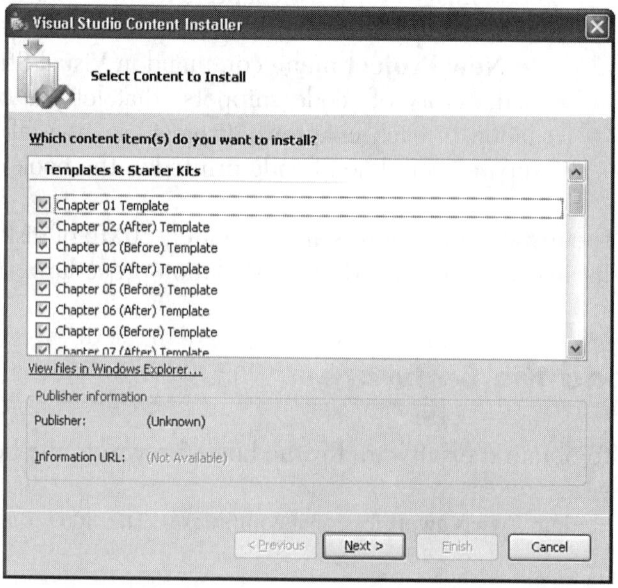

Figure A-1 The Visual Studio Content Installer

To complete the installation, click the **Next** button, followed by a click on the **Finish** button. The next time you run Visual Studio, all of the installed project templates will appear when you use the **File ➤ New Project** menu command.

Install Code Snippets

Code snippets are installed from within the Visual Studio application. Start Visual Studio, and run the **Tools ➤ Code Snippets Manager** menu command. The *Code Snippets Manager* window appears, as shown in Figure A-2.

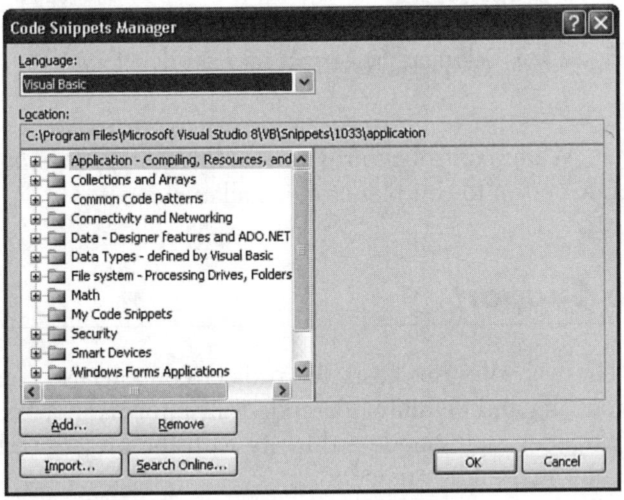

FIGURE A-2 The Code Snippets Manager

Click the **Add** button and browse to the directory where you extracted this book's downloaded content. Browse within the *Code Snippets* directory, select the *Start-to-Finish Visual Basic 2005* subdirectory, and click the **Open** button, as demonstrated in Figure A-3.

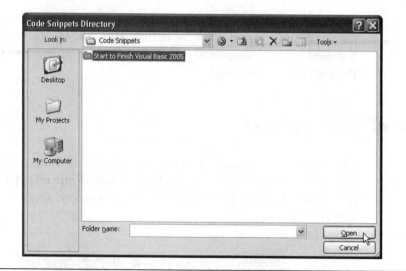

Figure A-3 Selecting the correct snippets directory

When control returns to the *Code Snippets Manager* form, click the **OK** button to complete the installation.

Barcode Support

The web site that hosts the project content also contains information on locating and obtaining barcode font information. You may use one of the barcodes mentioned on this site with the project code, or you may obtain your own valid barcode font.

SOFTWARE LICENSE AGREEMENT

When you download and install the software provided with this book, you agree to the terms of the software license agreement.

Terms of Use

The source code and software components provided with *Start-to-Finish Visual Basic 2005* (collectively known as the "software") are designed for use with that book, and are available only to those who obtain and use the book. As such, the software is covered by the copyright and licensing of the book itself. However, there are a few additional terms and conditions that should make the software even more useful to your development and learning activities.

- **Using the software with the book.** You may install and use the software in conjunction with your reading of the text. If you use multiple workstations in your tutorial endeavors, feel free to install the software on each of those systems.
- **Distributing the supplied software.** You may not package, distribute, sell, or otherwise make available to others the partial or complete applications provided with the book. Claiming that this work is your own, and attempting to distribute or sell it as such, is wrong and an all-around bad idea.
- **Using portions of the software in your projects.** You may use portions of this software in your own applications and development projects. If you include significant portions of the software in your derived work, please give credit where credit is due, and make it known that your application employs the useful content provided with *Start-to-Finish Visual Basic 2005*.

- **Acknowledgments.** The software was developed by Tim Patrick, author of *Start-to-Finish Visual Basic 2005*. Tim Patrick and Addison-Wesley/Pearson Education gladly make this software available to you for your education and enjoyment.
- **Warranty.** No warranty is provided with the software. Although every attempt has been made to keep the software safe and benign when installed on any target system, such safety is not guaranteed. Tim Patrick and Addison-Wesley/Pearson Education shall not be liable for any harm or damage that comes to your system or to any data stored on your system as a result of installing this software.
- **Other terms and conditions.** There may be additional terms and conditions instituted on the download web site where you obtained this software. Please read those carefully as they contain important information concerning downloads accessed from the web site.
- **Enjoy.** I hope that these terms and conditions didn't scare you off. The software exists to help you learn and to advance in your understanding of Visual Basic software development concepts. I think you'll find the software to be quite useful in your training, so download and enjoy.

INDEX

BOOKS ONLINE
ENABLED

THIS BOOK IS SAFARI ENABLED

INCLUDES FREE 45-DAY ACCESS TO THE ONLINE EDITION

The Safari® Enabled icon on the cover of your favorite technology book means the book is available through Safari Bookshelf. When you buy this book, you get free access to the online edition for 45 days.

Safari Bookshelf is an electronic reference library that lets you easily search thousands of technical books, find code samples, download chapters, and access technical information whenever and wherever you need it.

TO GAIN 45-DAY SAFARI ENABLED ACCESS TO THIS BOOK:

- Go to **http://www.awprofessional.com/safarienabled**

- Complete the brief registration form

- Enter the coupon code found in the front of this book on the "Copyright" page

Addison
Wesley